Demonology and Devil-lore

Volumes I and II - Complete

By Moncure Daniel Conway

Published by Pantianos Classics

ISBN-13: 978-1543106183

First published in 1879

Contents

Preface

Three Friars, says a legend, hid themselves near the Witch Sabbath orgies that they might count the devils; but the Chief of these, discovering the friars, said—'Reverend Brothers, our army is such that if all the Alps, their rocks and glaciers, were equally divided among us, none would have a pound's weight.' This was in one Alpine valley. Any one who has caught but a glimpse of the world's Walpurgis Night, as revealed in Mythology and Folklore, must agree that this courteous devil did not overstate the case. Any attempt to catalogue the evil spectres which have haunted mankind were like trying to count the shadows cast upon the earth by the rising sun. This conviction has grown upon the author of this work at every step in his studies of the subject.

In 1859 I contributed, as one of the American 'Tracts for the Times,' a pamphlet entitled 'The Natural History of the Devil.' Probably the chief value of that essay was to myself, and this in that its preparation had revealed to me how pregnant with interest and importance was the subject selected. Subsequent researches in the same direction, after I had come to reside in Europe, revealed how slight had been my conception of the vastness of the domain upon which that early venture was made. In 1872, while preparing a series of lectures for the Royal Institution on Demonology, it appeared to me that the best I could do was to print those lectures with some notes and additions; but after they were delivered there still remained with me unused the greater part of materials collected in many countries, and the phantasmal creatures which I had evoked would not permit me to rest from my labours until I had dealt with them more thoroughly.

The fable of Thor's attempt to drink up a small spring, and his failure because it was fed by the ocean, seems aimed at such efforts as mine. But there is another aspect of the case which has yielded me more encouragement. These phantom hosts, however unmanageable as to number, when closely examined, present comparatively few types; they coalesce by hundreds; from being at first overwhelmed by their multiplicity, the classifier finds himself at length beating bushes to start a new variety. Around some single form—the physiognomy, it may be, of Hunger or Disease, of Lust or Cruelty—ignorant imagination has broken up nature into innumerable bits which, like mirrors of various surface, reflect the same in endless sizes and distortions; but they vanish if that central fact be withdrawn.

In trying to conquer, as it were, these imaginary monsters, they have sometimes swarmed and gibbered around me in a mad comedy which travestied their tragic sway over those who believed in their reality. Gargoyles extended their grin over the finest architecture, cornices coiled to serpents, the very words of speakers started out of their conventional sense into images that tripped my attention. Only as what I believed right solutions were given to their problems were my sphinxes laid; but through this psychological experience it appeared that when one was so laid his or her legion disappeared also. Long ago such phantasms ceased to haunt my nerves, because I discovered their unreality; I am now venturing to believe that their mythologic forms cease to haunt my studies, because I have found out their reality.

Why slay the slain? Such may be the question that will arise in the minds of many who see this book. A Scotch song says, 'The Devil is dead, and buried at Kirkcaldy;' if so, he did not die until he had created a world in his image. The natural world is overlaid by an unnatural religion, breeding bitterness around simplest thoughts, obstructions to science, estrangements not more reasonable than if they resulted from varying notions of lunar figures,—all derived from the Devil-bequeathed dogma that certain beliefs and disbeliefs are of infernal instigation. Dogmas moulded in a fossil demonology make the foundation of institutions which divert wealth, learning, enterprise, to fictitious ends. It has not, therefore, been mere intellectual curiosity which has kept me working at this subject these many years, but an increasing conviction that the sequelæ of such superstitions are exercising a still formidable influence. When Father Delaporte lately published his book on the Devil, his Bishop wrote—'Reverend Father, if every one busied himself with the Devil as you do, the kingdom of God would gain by it.' Identifying the kingdom here spoken of as that of Truth, it has been with a certain concurrence in the Bishop's sentiment that I have busied myself with the work now given to the public.

Volume I

Part I - Demonolatry

Chapter I - Dualism

Origin of Deism—Evolution from the far to the near—Illustrations from witchcraft—The primitive Pantheism—The dawn of Dualism.

A college in the State of Ohio has adopted for its motto the words 'Orient thyself.' This significant admonition to Western youth represents one condition of attaining truth in the science of mythology. Through neglect of it the glowing personifications and metaphors of the East have too generally migrated to the West only to find it a Medusa turning them to stone. Our prosaic literalism changes their ideals to idols. The time has come when we must learn rather to see ourselves in them: out of an age and civilisation where we live in habitual recognition of natural forces we may transport ourselves to a period and region where no sophisticated eye looks upon nature. The sun is a chariot drawn by shining steeds and driven by a refulgent deity; the stars ascend and move by arbitrary power or command; the tree is the bower of a spirit; the fountain leaps from the urn of a naiad. In such gay costumes did the laws of nature hold their carnival until Science struck the hour for unmasking. The costumes and masks have with us become materials for studying the history of the human mind, but to know them we must translate our senses back into that phase of our own early existence, so far as is consistent with carrying our culture with us.

Without conceding too much to Solar mythology, it may be pronounced tolerably clear that the earliest emotion of worship was born out of the wonder with which man looked up to the heavens above him. The splendours of the morning and evening; the azure vault, painted with frescoes of cloud or blackened by the storm; the night, crowned with constellations: these awakened imagination, inspired awe, kindled admiration, and at length adoration, in the being who had reached intervals in which his eye was lifted above the earth. Amid the rapture of Vedic hymns to these sublimities we meet sharp questionings whether there be any such gods as the priests say, and suspicion is sometimes cast on sacrifices. The forms that peopled the celestial spaces may have been those of ancestors, kings, and great men, but anterior to all forms was the poetic enthusiasm which built heavenly mansions for them; and the crude cosmogonies of primitive science were probably caught up by this spirit, and consecrated as slowly as scientific generalisations now are. Our modern ideas of evolution might suggest the reverse of this—that human worship began with things low and gradually ascended to high objects; that from rude ages, in which adoration was directed to stock and stone, tree and reptile, the human mind climbed by degrees to the contemplation and reverence of celestial grandeurs. But the accord of this view with our ideas of evolution is apparent only. The real progress seems here to have been from the far to the near, from the great to the small. It is, indeed, probably inexact to speak of the worship of stock and stone, weed and wort, insect and reptile, as primitive. There are many indications that such things were by no race considered intrinsically sacred, nor were they really worshipped until the origin of their sanctity was lost; and even now, ages after their oracular or symbolical character has been forgotten, the superstitions that have survived in connection with such insignificant objects point to an original association with the phenomena of the heavens. No religions could, at first glance, seem wider apart than the worship of the serpent and that of the glorious sun; yet many ancient temples are covered with symbols combining sun and snake, and no form is more familiar in Egypt than the solar serpent standing erect upon its tail, with rays around its head.

Nor is this high relationship of the adored reptile found only in regions where it might have been raised up by ethnical combinations as the mere survival of a savage symbol. William Craft, an African who resided for some time in the kingdom of Dahomey, informed me of the following incident which he had witnessed there. The sacred serpents are kept in a grand house, which they sometimes leave to crawl in their neighbouring grounds. One day a negro from some distant region encountered one of these animals and killed it. The people learning that one of their gods had been slain, seized the stranger, and having surrounded him with a circle of brushwood, set it on fire. The poor wretch broke through the circle of fire and ran, pursued by the crowd, who struck him with heavy sticks. Smarting from the flames and blows, he rushed into a river; but no sooner had he entered there than the pursuit ceased, and he was told that, having gone through fire and water, he was purified, and might emerge with safety. Thus, even in that distant and savage region, serpent-worship was associated with fire-worship and river-worship, which have a wide representation in both Aryan and Semitic symbolism. To this day the orthodox Israelites set beside their dead, before burial, the lighted candle and a basin of pure water. These have been associated in rabbinical mythology with the angels Michael (genius of Water) and Gabriel (genius of Fire); but they refer both to the phenomenal glories and the purifying effects of the two elements as reverenced by the Africans in one direction and the Parsees in another.

Not less significant are the facts which were attested at the witch-trials. It was shown that for their pretended divinations they used plants—as rue and vervain—well known in the ancient Northern religions, and often recognised as examples of tree-worship; but it also appeared that around the cauldron a mock zodiacal circle was drawn, and that every herb employed was alleged to have derived its potency from having been gathered at a certain hour of the night or day, a particular quarter of the moon, or from some spot where sun or moon did or did not shine upon it. Ancient planet-worship is, indeed, still reflected in the habit of village herbalists, who gather their simples at certain phases of the moon, or at certain of those holy periods of the year which conform more or less to the pre-christian festivals.

These are a few out of many indications that the small and senseless things which have become almost or quite fetishes were by no means such at first, but were mystically connected with the heavenly elements and splendours, like the animal forms in the zodiac. In one of the earliest hymns of the Rig-Veda it is said—'This earth belongs to Varuna (Οὐρανός) the king, and the wide sky: he is contained also in this drop of water.' As the sky was seen reflected in the shining curve of a dew-drop, even so in the shape or colour of a leaf or flower, the transformation of a chrysalis, or the burial and resurrection of a scarabæus' egg, some sign could be detected making it answer in place of the typical image which could not yet be painted or carved.

The necessities of expression would, of course, operate to invest the primitive conceptions and interpretations of celestial phenomena with those pictorial images drawn from earthly objects of which the early languages are chiefly composed. In many cases that are met in the most ancient hymns, the designations of exalted objects are so little descriptive of them, that we may refer them to a period anterior to the formation of that refined and complex symbolism by which primitive religions have acquired a representation in definite characters. The Vedic comparisons of the various colours of the dawn to horses, or the rain-clouds to cows, denotes a much less mature development of thought than the fine observation implied in the connection of the forked lightning with the forked serpent-tongue and forked mistletoe, or symbolisation of the universe in the concentric folds of an onion. It is the presence of these more mystical and complex ideas in religions which indicate a progress of the human mind from the large and obvious to the more delicate and occult, and the growth of the higher vision which can see small things in their large relationships. Although the exaltation in the Vedas of Varuna as king of heaven, and as contained also in a drop of water, is in one verse, we may well recognise an immense distance in time between the two ideas there embodied. The first represents that primitive pantheism which is the counterpart of ignorance. An unclassified outward universe is the reflection of a mind without form and void: it is while all within is as yet undiscriminating wonder that the religious vesture of nature will be this undefined pantheism. The fruit of the tree of the knowledge of good and evil has not yet been tasted. In some of the earlier hymns of the Rig-Veda, the Maruts, the storm-deities, are praised along with Indra, the sun; Yama, king of Death, is equally adored with the goddess of Dawn. 'No real foe of yours is known in heaven, nor in earth.' 'The storms are thy allies.' Such is the high optimism of sentences found even in sacred books which elsewhere mask the dawn of the Dualism which ultimately superseded the harmony of the elemental Powers. 'I create light and I create darkness, I create good and I create evil.' 'Look unto Yezdan, who causeth the shadow to fall.' But it is easy to see what must be the result when this happy family of sun-god and storm-god and fire-god, and their innumerable co-ordinate divinities, shall be divided by discord. When each shall have become associated with some earthly object or fact, he or she will appear as friend or foe, and their connection with the sources of human pleasure and pain will be reflected in collisions and wars in the heavens. The rebel clouds will be transformed to Titans and Dragons. The adored Maruts will be no longer storm-heroes with unsheathed swords of lightning, marching as the retinue of Indra, but fire-breathing monsters—Vritras and Ahis,—and the morning and evening shadows from faithful watch-dogs become the treacherous hell-hounds, like Orthros and Cerberus. The vehement antagonisms between animals and men and of tribe against tribe, will be expressed in the conception of struggles among gods, who will thus be classified as good or evil deities.

This was precisely what did occur. The primitive pantheism was broken up: in its place the later ages beheld the universe as the arena of a tremendous conflict between good and evil Powers, who severally, in the process of time, marshalled each and everything, from a world to a worm, under their flaming banners.

Chapter II - The Genesis of Demons

Their good names euphemistic—Their mixed character—Illustrations: Beelzebub, Loki—Demon-germs—The knowledge of good and evil—Distinction between Demon and Devil.

The first pantheon of each race was built of intellectual speculations. In a moral sense, each form in it might be described as more or less demonic; and, indeed, it may almost be affirmed that religion, considered as a service rendered to superhuman beings, began with the propitiation of demons, albeit they might be called gods. Man found that in the earth good things came with difficulty, while thorns and weeds sprang up everywhere. The evil powers seemed to be the strongest. The best deity had a touch of the demon in him. The sun is the most beneficent, yet he bears the sunstroke along with the sunbeam, and withers the blooms he calls forth. The splendour, the might, the majesty, the menace, the grandeur and wrath of the heavens and the elements were blended in these personifications, and reflected in the trembling adoration paid to them. The flattering names given to these powers by their worshippers must be interpreted by the costly sacrifices with which men sought to propitiate them. No sacrifice would have been offered originally to a purely benevolent power. The Furies were called the Eumenides, 'the well-meaning,' and there arises a temptation to regard the name as preserving the primitive meaning of the Sanskrit original of Erinyes, namely, Saranyu, which signifies the morning light stealing over the sky. But the descriptions of the Erinyes by the Greek poets—especially of Æschylus, who pictures them as black, serpent-locked, with eyes dropping blood, and calls them hounds—show that Saranyu as morning light, and thus the revealer of deeds of darkness, had gradually been degraded into a personification of the Curse. And yet, while recognising the name Eumenides as euphemistic, we may admire none the less the growth of that rationalism which ultimately found in the epithet a suggestion of the soul of good in things evil, and almost restored the beneficent sense of Saranyu. 'I have settled in this place,' says Athene in the 'Eumenides' of Æschylus, 'these mighty deities, hard to be appeased; they have obtained by lot to administer all things concerning men. But he who has not found them gentle knows not whence come the ills of life.' But before the dread Erinyes of Homer's age had become the 'venerable goddesses' (σεμναὶ θεαὶ) of popular phrase in Athens, or the Eumenides of the later poet's high insight, piercing their Gorgon form as portrayed by himself, they had passed through all the phases of human terror. Cowering generations had tried to soothe the remorseless avengers by complimentary phrases. The worship of the serpent, originating in the same fear, similarly raised that animal into the region where poets could invest it with many profound and beautiful significances. But these more distinctly terrible deities are found in the shadowy border-land of mythology, from which we may look back into ages when the fear in which worship is born had not yet been separated into its elements of awe and admiration, nor the heaven of supreme forces divided into ranks of benevolent and malevolent beings; and, on the other hand, we may look forward to the ages in which the moral consciousness of man begins to form the distinctions between good and evil, right and wrong, which changes cosmogony into religion, and impresses every deity of the mind's creation to do his or her part in reflecting the physical and moral struggles of mankind.

Fig. 1.—Beelzebub (Calmet).

The intermediate processes by which the good and evil were detached, and advanced to separate personification, cannot always be traced, but the indications of their work are in most cases sufficiently clear. The relationship, for instance, between Baal and Baal-zebub cannot be doubted. The one represents the Sun in his glory as quickener of Nature and painter of its beauty, the other the insect-breeding power of the Sun. Baal-zebub is the Fly-god. Only at a comparatively recent period did the deity of the Philistines, whose oracle was consulted by Ahaziah (2 Kings i.), suffer under the reputation of being 'the Prince of Devils,' his name being changed by a mere pun to Beelzebul (dung-god). It is not impossible that the modern Egyptian mother's hesitation to disturb flies settling on her sleeping child, and the sanctity attributed to various insects, originated in the awe felt for him. The title Fly-god is paralleled by the reverent epithet ἀπόμυιος, applied to Zeus as worshipped at Elis,1 the Myiagrus deus of the Romans,2 and the Myiodes mentioned by Pliny.3 Our picture is probably from a protecting charm, and evidently by the god's believers. There is a story of a peasant woman in a French church who was found kneeling before a marble group, and was warned by a priest that she was worshipping the wrong figure—namely, Beelzebub. 'Never mind,' she replied, 'it is well enough to have friends on both sides.' The story, though now only ben trovato, would represent the actual state of mind in many a Babylonian invoking the protection of the Fly-god against formidable swarms of his venomous subjects.

Not less clear is the illustration supplied by Scandinavian mythology. In Sæmund's Edda the evil-minded Loki says:—

Odin! dost thou remember
When we in early days
Blended our blood together?

The two became detached very slowly; for their separation implied the crumbling away of a great religion, and its distribution into new forms; and a religion requires, relatively, as long to decay as it does to grow, as we who live under a crumbling religion have good reason to know. Protap Chunder Mozoomdar, of the Brahmo-Somaj, in an address in London, said, 'The Indian Pantheon has many millions of deities, and no space is left for the Devil.' He might have added that these deities have distributed between them all the work that the Devil could perform if he were admitted. His remark recalled to me the Eddaic story of Loki's entrance into the assembly of gods in the halls of Oegir. Loki—destined in a later age to be identified with Satan—is angrily received by the deities, but he goes round and mentions incidents in the life of each one which show them to be little if any better than himself. The gods and goddesses, unable to reply, confirm the cynic's criticisms in theologic fashion by tying him up with a serpent for cord.

The late Theodore Parker is said to have replied to a Calvinist who sought to convert him—'The difference between us is simple: your god is my devil.' There can be little question that the Hebrews, from whom the Calvinist inherited his deity, had no devil in their mythology, because the jealous and vindictive Jehovah was quite equal to any work of that kind,—as the hardening of Pharaoh's heart, bringing plagues upon the land, or deceiving a prophet and then destroying him for his false prophecies.4 The same accommodating relation of the primitive deities to all natural phenomena will account for the absence of distinct representatives of evil of the most primitive religions.

The earliest exceptions to this primeval harmony of the gods, implying moral chaos in man, were trifling enough: the occasional monster seems worthy of mention only to display the valour of the god who slew him. But such were demon-germs, born out of the structural action of the human mind so soon as it began to form some philosophy concerning a universe upon which it had at first looked with simple wonder, and destined to an evolution of vast import when the work of moralising upon them should follow.

Let us take our stand beside our barbarian, but no longer savage, ancestor in the far past. We have watched the rosy morning as it waxed to a blazing noon: then swiftly the sun is blotted out, the tempest rages, it is a sudden night lit only by the forked lightning that strikes tree, house, man, with angry thunder-peal. From an instructed age man can look upon the storm blackening the sky not as an enemy of the sun, but one of its own superlative effects; but some thousands of years ago, when we were all living in Eastern barbarism, we could not conceive that a luminary whose very business it was to give light, could be a party to his own obscuration. We then looked with pity upon the ignorance of our ancestors, who had sung hymns to the storm-dragons, hoping to flatter them into quietness; and we came by irresistible logic to that Dualism which long divided the visible, and still divides the moral, universe into two hostile camps.

This is the mother-principle out of which demons (in the ordinary sense of the term) proceeded. At first few, as distinguished from the host of deities by exceptional harmfulness, they were multiplied with man's growth in the classification of his world. Their principle of existence is capable of indefinite expansion, until it shall include all the realms of darkness, fear, and pain. In the names of demons, and in the fables concerning them, the struggles of man in his ages of weakness with peril, want, and death, are recorded more fully than in any inscriptions on stone. Dualism is a creed which all superficial appearances attest. Side by side the desert and the fruitful land, the sunshine and the frost, sorrow and joy, life and death, sit weaving around every life its vesture of bright and sombre threads, and Science alone can detect how each of these casts the shuttle to the other. Enemies to each other they will appear in every realm which knowledge has not mastered. There is a refrain, gathered from many ages, in William Blake's apostrophe to the tiger:—

Tiger! tiger! burning bright
In the forests of the night;
What immortal hand or eye
Framed thy fearful symmetry?
In what distant deeps or skies
Burned that fire within thine eyes?
On what wings dared he aspire?
What the hand dared seize the fire?
When the stars threw down their spears
And water heaven with their tears,
Did he smile his work to see?
Did he who made the lamb make thee?

That which one of the devoutest men of genius whom England has produced thus asked was silently answered in India by the serpent-worshipper kneeling with his tongue held in his hand; in Egypt, by Osiris seated on a throne of chequer.5 It is necessary to distinguish clearly between the Demon and the Devil, though, for some purposes, they must be mentioned together. The world was haunted with demons for many ages before there was any embodiment of their spirit in any central form, much less any conception of a Principle of Evil in the universe. The early demons had no moral character, not any more than the man-eating tiger. There is no outburst of moral indignation mingling with the shout of victory when Indra slays Vritra, and Apollo's face is serene when his dart pierces the Python. It required a much higher development of the moral sentiment to give rise to the conception of a devil. Only that intensest light could cast so black a shadow athwart the world as the belief in a purely malignant spirit. To such a conception—love of evil for its own sake— the word Devil is limited in this work; Demon is applied to beings whose harmfulness is not gratuitous, but incidental to their own satisfactions.

Deity and Demon are from words once interchangeable, and the latter has simply suffered degradation by the conventional use of it to designate the less beneficent powers and qualities, which originally inhered in every deity, after they were detached from these and separately personified. Every bright god had his shadow, so to say; and under the influence of Dualism this shadow attained a distinct existence and personality in the popular imagination. The principle having once been established, that what seemed beneficent and what seemed the reverse must be ascribed to different powers, it is obvious that the evolution of demons must be continuous, and their distribution co-extensive with the ills that flesh is heir to.

Notes

1 Pausan. v. 14, 2.
2 Solin. Polyhistor, i.
3 Pliny, xxix. 6, 34, init.
4 Ezekiel xiv. 9.
5 As in the Bembine Tablet in the Bodleian Library.

Chapter III - Degradation

The degradation of deities-Indicated in names-Legends of their fall--Incidental signs of the divine origin of demons and devils.

The atmospheric conditions having been prepared in the human mind for the production of demons, the particular shapes or names they would assume would be determined by a variety of circumstances, ethnical, climatic, political, or even accidental. They would, indeed, be rarely accidental; but Professor Max Müller, in his notes to the Rig-Veda, has called attention to a remarkable instance in which the formation of an imposing mythological figure of this kind had its name determined by what, in all probability, was an accident. There appears in the earliest Vedic hymns the name of Aditi, as the holy Mother of many gods, and thrice there is mentioned the female name Diti. But there is reason to believe that Diti is a mere reflex of Aditi, the a being dropped originally by a reciter's license. The later reciters, however, regarding every letter in so sacred a book, or even the omission of a letter, as of eternal significance, Diti—this decapitated Aditi—was evolved into a separate and powerful being, and, every niche of beneficence being occupied by its god or goddess, the new form was at once relegated to the newly-defined realm of evil, where she remained as the mother of the enemies of the gods, the Daityas. Unhappily this accident followed the ancient tendency by which the Furies and Vices have, with scandalous constancy, been described in the feminine gender.

The close resemblance between these two names of Hindu mythology, severally representing the best and the worst, may be thus accidental, and only serve to show how the demon-forming tendency, after it began, was able to press even the most trivial incidents into its service. But generally the names of demons, and for whole races of demons, report far more than this; and in no inquiry more than that before us is it necessary to remember that names are things. The philological facts supply a remarkable confirmation of the statements already made as to the original identity of demon and deity. The word 'demon' itself, as we have said, originally bore a good instead of an evil meaning. The Sanskrit deva, 'the shining one,' Zend daêva, correspond with the Greek θεος, Latin deus, Anglo-Saxon Tiw; and remain in 'deity,' 'deuce' (probably; it exists in Armorican, teuz, a phantom), 'devel' (the gipsy name for God), and Persian dīv, demon. The Demon of Socrates represents the personification of a being still good, but no doubt on the path of decline from pure divinity. Plato declares that good men when they die become 'demons,' and he says 'demons are reporters and carriers between gods and men.' Our familiar word bogey, a sort of nickname for an evil spirit, comes from the Slavonic word for God—bog. Appearing here in the West as bogey (Welsh bwg, a goblin), this word bog began, probably, as the 'Baga' of cuneiform inscriptions, a name of the Supreme Being, or possibly the Hindu 'Bhaga,' Lord of Life. In the 'Bishop's Bible' the passage occurs, 'Thou shalt not be afraid of any bugs by night:' the word has been altered to 'terror.' When we come to the particular names of demons, we find many of them bearing traces of the splendours from which they have declined. 'Siva,' the Hindu god of destruction, has a meaning ('auspicious') derived from Svī, 'thrive'—thus related ideally to Pluto, 'wealth'—and, indeed, in later ages, appears to have gained the greatest elevation. In a story of the Persian poem Masnavi, Ahriman is mentioned with Bahman as a fire-fiend, of which class are the Magian demons and the Jinns generally; which, the sanctity of fire being considered, is an evidence of their high origin. Avicenna says that the genii are ethereal animals. Lucifer— light-bearing—is the fallen angel of the morning star. Loki—the nearest to an evil power of the Scandinavian personifications—is the German leucht, or light. Azazel—a word inaccurately rendered 'scape-goat' in the Bible— appears to have been originally a deity, as the Israelites were originally required to offer up one goat to Jehovah and another to Azazel, a name which appears to signify the 'strength of God.' Gesenius and Ewald regard Azazel as a demon belonging to the pre-Mosaic religion, but it can hardly be doubted that the four arch-demons mentioned by the Rabbins— Samaël, Azazel, Asaël, and Maccathiel—are personifications of the elements as energies of the deity. Samaël would appear to mean the 'left hand of God;' Azazel, his strength; Asaël, his reproductive force; and Maccathiel, his retributive power, but the origin of these names is doubtful..

Although Azazel is now one of the Mussulman names for a devil, it would appear to be nearly related to Al Uzza of the Koran, one of the goddesses of whom the significant tradition exists, that once when Mohammed had read, from the Sura called 'The Star,' the question, 'What think ye of Allat, Al Uzza, and Manah, that other third goddess?' he himself added, 'These are the most high and beauteous damsels, whose intercession is to be hoped for,' the response being afterwards attributed to a suggestion of Satan.1 Belial is merely a word for godlessness; it has become personified through the misunderstanding of the phrase in the Old Testament by the translators of the Septuagint, and thus passed into christian use, as in 2 Cor. vi. 15, 'What concord hath Christ with Belial?' The word is not used as a proper name in the Old Testament, and the late creation of a demon out of it may be set down to accident.

Even where the names of demons and devils bear no such traces of their degradation from the state of deities, there are apt to be characteristics attributed to them, or myths connected with them, which point in the direction indicated. Such is the case with Satan, of whom much must be said hereafter, whose Hebrew name signifies the adversary, but who, in the Book of Job, appears among the sons of God. The name given to the devil in the Koran—Eblis—is almost certainly diabolos Arabicised; and while this Greek word is found in Pindar2 (5th century B.C.), meaning a slanderer, the fables in the Koran concerning Eblis describe him as a fallen angel of the highest rank.

One of the most striking indications of the fall of demons from heaven is the wide-spread belief that they are lame. Mr. Tylor has pointed out the curious persistence of this idea in various ethnical lines of development.3 Hephaistos was lamed by his fall when hurled by Zeus from Olympos; and it is not a little singular that in the English travesty of limping Vulcan, represented in Wayland the Smith,4 there should appear the suggestion, remarked by Mr. Cox, of the name 'Vala' (coverer), one of the designations of the dragon destroyed by Indra. 'In Sir Walter Scott's romance,' says Mr. Cox, 'Wayland is a mere impostor, who avails himself of a popular superstition to keep up an air of mystery about himself and his work, but the character to which he makes pretence belongs to the genuine Teutonic legend.'5 The Persian demon Aeshma—the Asmodeus of the Book of Tobit—appears with the same characteristic of lameness in the 'Diable Boiteux' of Le Sage. The christian devil's clubbed or cloven foot is notorious.

Even the horns popularly attributed to the devil may possibly have originated with the aureole which indicates the glory of his 'first estate.' Satan is depicted in various relics of early art wearing the aureole, as in a miniature of the tenth century (from Bible No. 6, Bib. Roy.), given by M. Didron.6 The same author has shown that Pan and the Satyrs, who had so much to do with the shaping of our horned and hoofed devil, originally got their horns from the same high source as Moses in the old Bibles,7 and in the great statue of him at Rome by Michel Angelo.

It is through this mythologic history that the most powerful demons have been associated in the popular imagination with stars, planets,—Ketu in India, Saturn and Mercury the 'Infortunes,'—comets, and other celestial phenomena. The examples of this are so numerous that it is impossible to deal with them here, where I can only hope to offer a few illustrations of the principles affirmed; and in this case it is of less importance for the English reader, because of the interesting volume in which the subject has been specially dealt with.8 Incidentally, too, the astrological demons and devils must recur from time to time in the process of our inquiry. But it will probably be within the knowledge of some of my readers that the dread of comets and of meteoric showers yet lingers in many parts of Christendom, and that fear of unlucky stars has not passed away with astrologers. There is a Scottish legend told by Hugh Miller of an avenging meteoric demon. A shipmaster who had moored his vessel near Morial's Den, amused himself by watching the lights of the scattered farmhouses. After all the rest had gone out one light lingered for some time. When that light too had disappeared, the shipmaster beheld a large meteor, which, with a hissing noise, moved towards the cottage. A dog howled, an owl whooped; but when the fire-ball had almost reached the roof, a cock crew from within the cottage, and the meteor rose again. Thrice this was repeated, the meteor at the third cock-crow ascending among the stars. On the following day the shipmaster went on shore, purchased the cock, and took it away with him. Returned from his voyage, he looked for the cottage, and found nothing but a few blackened stones. Nearly sixty years ago a human skeleton was found near the spot, doubled up as if the body had been huddled into a hole: this revived the legend, and probably added some of those traits which make it a true bit of mosaic in the mythology of Astræa.9

The fabled 'fall of Lucifer' really signifies a process similar to that which has been noticed in the case of Saranyu. The morning star, like the morning light, as revealer of the deeds of darkness, becomes an avenger, and by evolution an instigator of the evil it originally disclosed and punished. It may be remarked also that though we have inherited the phrase 'Demons of Darkness,' it was an ancient rabbinical belief that the demons went abroad in darkness not only because it facilitated their attacks on man, but because being of luminous forms, they could recognise each other better with a background of darkness.

Notes

1 See Sale's Koran, p. 281.
2 Pindar, Fragm., 270.
3 Tylor's 'Early Hist. of Mankind,' p. 358; 'Prim. Cult.,' vol. ii. p. 230.
4 The Gascons of Labourd call the devil 'Seigneur Voland,' and some revere him as a patron.
5 'Myth. of the Aryan Nations,' vol. ii. p. 327.
6 'Christian Iconography,' Bohn, p. 158.
7 'Videbant faciem egredientis Moysis esse cornutam.'—Vulg. Exod. xxxiv. 35.
8 'Myths and Marvels of Astronomy.' By R. A. Proctor. Chatto & Windus, 1878.
9 'Scenes and Legends,' etc., p. 73.

Chapter IV - The Abgott

The ex-god—Deities demonised by conquest—Theological animosity—Illustration from the Avesta—Devil-worship an arrested Deism—Sheik Adi—Why demons were painted ugly—Survivals of their beauty.

The phenomena of the transformation of deities into demons meet the student of Demonology at every step. We shall have to consider many examples of a kind similar to those which have been mentioned in the preceding chapter; but it is necessary to present at this stage of our inquiry a sufficient number of examples to establish the fact that in every country forces have been at work to degrade the primitive gods into types of evil, as preliminary to a consideration of the nature of those forces.

We find the history of the phenomena suggested in the German word for idol, Abgott—ex-god. Then we have 'pagan,' villager, and 'heathen,' of the heath, denoting those who stood by their old gods after others had transferred their faith to the new. These words bring us to consider the influence upon religious conceptions of the struggles which have occurred between races and nations, and consequently between their religions. It must be borne in mind that by the time any tribes had gathered to the consistency of a nation, one of the strongest forces of its coherence would be its priesthood. So soon as it became a general belief that there were in the universe good and evil Powers, there must arise a popular demand for the means of obtaining their favour; and this demand has never failed to obtain a supply of priesthoods claiming to bind or influence the præternatural beings. These priesthoods represent the strongest motives and fears of a people, and they were gradually intrenched in great institutions involving powerful interests. Every invasion or collision or mingling of races thus brought their respective religions into contact and rivalry; and as no priesthood has been known to consent peaceably to its own downfall and the degradation of its own deities, we need not wonder that there have been perpetual wars for religious ascendency. It is not unusual to hear sects among ourselves accusing each other of idolatry. In earlier times the rule was for each religion to denounce its opponent's gods as devils. Gregory the Great wrote to his missionary in Britain, the Abbot Mellitus, second Bishop of Canterbury, that 'whereas the people were accustomed to sacrifice many oxen in honour of demons, let them celebrate a religious and solemn festival, and not slay the animals to the devil (diabolo), but to be eaten by themselves to the glory of God.' Thus the devotion of meats to those deities of our ancestors which the Pope pronounces demons, which took place chiefly at Yule-tide, has survived in our more comfortable Christmas banquets. This was the fate of all the deities which Christianity undertook to suppress. But it had been the habit of religions for many ages before. They never denied the actual existence of the deities they were engaged in suppressing. That would have been too great an outrage upon popular beliefs, and might have caused a reaction; and, besides, each new religion had an interest of its own in preserving the basis of belief in these invisible beings. Disbelief in the very existence of the old gods might be followed by a sceptical spirit that might endanger the new. So the propagandists maintained the existence of native gods, but called them devils. Sometimes wars or intercourse between tribes led to their fusion; the battle between opposing religions was drawn, in which case there would be a compromise by which several deities of different origin might continue together in the same race and receive equal homage. The differing degrees of importance ascribed to the separate persons of the Hindu triad in various localities of India, suggest it as quite probable that Brahma, Vishnu, and Siva signalled in their union the political unity of certain districts in that country.1 The blending of the names of Confucius and Buddha, in many Chinese and Japanese temples, may show us an analogous process now going on, and, indeed, the various ethnical ideas combined in the christian Trinity render the fact stated one of easy interpretation. But the religious difficulty was sometimes not susceptible of compromise. The most powerful priesthood carried the day, and they used every ingenuity to degrade the gods of their opponents. Agathodemons were turned into kakodemons. The serpent, worshipped in many lands, might be adopted as the support of sleeping Vishnu in India, might be associated with the rainbow ('the heavenly serpent') in Persia, but elsewhere was cursed as the very genius of evil.

The operation of this force in the degradation of deities, is particularly revealed in the Sacred Books of Persia. In that country the great religions of the East would appear to have contended against each other with especial fury, and their struggles were probably instrumental in causing one or more of the early migrations into Western Europe. The great celestial war between Ormuzd and Ahriman—Light and Darkness—corresponded with a violent theological conflict, one result of which is that the word deva, meaning 'deity' to Brahmans, means 'devil' to Parsees. The following extract from the Zend-Avesta will serve as an example of the spirit in which the war was waged:—

'All your devas are only manifold children of the Evil Mind—and the great one who worships the Saoma of lies and deceits; besides the treacherous acts for which you are notorious throughout the seven regions of the earth.

'You have invented all the evil which men speak and do, which is indeed pleasant to the Devas, but is devoid of all goodness, and therefore perishes before the insight of the truth of the wise.

'Thus you defraud men of their good minds and of their immortality by your evil minds—as well through those of the Devas as that of the Evil Spirit—through evil deeds and evil words, whereby the power of liars grows.'2

That is to say—Ours is the true god: your god is a devil.

The Zoroastrian conversion of deva (deus) into devil does not alone represent the work of this odium theologicum. In the early hymns of India the appellation asuras is given to the gods. Asura means a spirit. But in the process of time asura, like dæmon, came to have a sinister meaning: the gods were called suras, the demons asuras, and these were said to contend together. But in Persia the asuras—demonised in India—retained their divinity, and gave the name ahura to the supreme deity, Ormuzd (Ahura-mazda). On the other hand, as Mr. Muir supposes, Varenya, applied to evil spirits of darkness in the Zendavesta, is cognate with Varuna (Heaven); and the Vedic Indra, king of the gods—the Sun—is named in the Zoroastrian religion as one of the chief councillors of that Prince of Darkness.

But in every country conquered by a new religion, there will always be found some, as we have seen, who will hold on to the old deity under all his changed fortunes. These will be called 'bigots,' but still they will adhere to the ancient belief and practise the old rites. Sometimes even after they have had to yield to the popular terminology, and call the old god a devil, they will find some reason for continuing the transmitted forms. It is probable that to this cause was originally due the religions which have been developed into what is now termed Devil-worship. The distinct and avowed worship of the evil Power in preference to the good is a rather startling phenomenon when presented baldly; as, for example, in a prayer of the Madagascans to Nyang, author of evil, quoted by Dr. Réville:—'O Zamhor! to thee we offer no prayers. The good god needs no asking. But we must pray to Nyang. Nyang must be appeased. O Nyang, bad and strong spirit, let not the thunder roar over our heads! Tell the sea to keep within its bounds! Spare, O Nyang, the ripening fruit, and dry not up the blossoming rice! Let not our women bring forth children on the accursed days. Thou reignest, and this thou knowest, over the wicked; and great is their number, O Nyang. Torment not, then, any longer the good folk!'3

14

This is natural, and suggestive of the criminal under sentence of death, who, when asked if he was not afraid to meet his God, replied, 'Not in the least; it's that other party I'm afraid of.' Yet it is hardly doubtful that the worship of Nyang began in an era when he was by no means considered morally baser than Zamhor. How the theory of Dualism, when attained, might produce the phenomenon called Devil-worship, is illustrated in the case of the Yezedis, now so notorious for that species of religion. Their theory is usually supposed to be entirely represented by the expression uttered by one of them, 'Will not Satan, then, reward the poor Izedis, who alone have never spoken ill of him, and have suffered so much for him?'4 But these words are significant, no doubt, of the underlying fact: they 'have never spoken ill of' the Satan they worship. The Mussulman calls the Yezedi a Satan-worshipper only as the early Zoroastrian held the worshipper of a deva to be the same. The chief object of worship among the Yezedis is the figure of the bird Taous, a half-mythical peacock. Professor King of Cambridge traces the Taous of this Assyrian sect to the "sacred bird called a phœnix," whose picture, as seen by Herodotus (ii. 73) in Egypt, is described by him as 'very like an eagle in outline and in size, but with plumage partly gold-coloured, partly crimson,' and which was said to return to Heliopolis every five hundred years, there to burn itself on the altar of the Sun, that another might rise from its ashes.5 Now the name Yezedis is simply Izeds, genii; and we are thus pointed to Arabia, where we find the belief in genii is strongest, and also associated with the mythical bird Rokh of its folklore. There we find Mohammed rebuking the popular belief in a certain bird called Hamâh, which was said to take form from the blood near the brain of a dead person and fly away, to return, however, at the end of every hundred years to visit that person's sepulchre. But this is by no means Devil-worship, nor can we find any trace of that in the most sacred scripture of the Yezedis, the 'Eulogy of Sheikh Adi.' This Sheikh inherited from his father, Moosafir, the sanctity of an incarnation of the divine essence, of which he (Adi) speaks as 'the All-merciful.'

By his light he hath lighted the lamp of the morning.
I am he that placed Adam in my Paradise.
I am he that made Nimrod a hot burning fire.
I am he that guided Ahmet mine elect,
I gifted him with my way and guidance.
Mine are all existences together,
They are my gift and under my direction.
I am he that possesseth all majesty,
And beneficence and charity are from my grace,
I am he that entereth the heart in my zeal;
And I shine through the power of my awfulness and majesty.
I am he to whom the lion of the desert came:
I rebuked him and he became like stone.
I am he to whom the serpent came,
And by my will I made him like dust.
I am he that shook the rock and made it tremble,
*And sweet water flowed therefrom from every side.*6

The reverence shown in these sacred sentences for Hebrew names and traditions—as of Adam in Paradise, Marah, and the smitten rock—and for Ahmet (Mohammed), appears to have had its only requital in the odious designation of the worshippers of Taous as Devil-worshippers, a label which the Yezedis perhaps accepted as the Wesleyans and Friends accepted such names as 'Methodist' and 'Quaker.'
Mohammed has expiated the many deities he degraded to devils by being himself turned to an idol (mawmet), a term of contempt all the more popular for its resemblance to 'mummery.' Despite his denunciations of idolatry, it is certain that this earlier religion represented by the Yezedis has never been entirely suppressed even among his own followers. In Dr. Leitner's interesting collection there is a lamp, which he obtained from a mosque, made in the shape of a peacock, and this is but one of many similar relics of primitive or alien symbolism found among the Mussulman tribes.

Fig. 2.—Handle of Hindu Chalice.

The evolution of demons and devils out of deities was made real to the popular imagination in every country where the new religion found art existing, and by alliance with it was enabled to shape the ideas of the people. The theoretical degradation of deities of previously fair association could only be completed where they were presented to the eye in repulsive forms. It will readily occur to every one that a rationally conceived demon or devil would not be repulsive. If it were a demon that man wished to represent, mere euphemism would prevent its being rendered odious. The main characteristic of a demon—that which distinguishes it from a devil—is, as we have seen, that it has a real and human-like motive for whatever evil it causes. If it afflict or consume man, it is not from mere malignancy, but because impelled by the pangs of hunger, lust, or other suffering, like the famished wolf or shark. And if sacrifices of food were offered to satisfy its need, equally we might expect that no unnecessary insult would be offered in the attempt to portray it. But if it were a devil—a being actuated by simple malevolence—one of its essential functions, temptation, would be destroyed by hideousness. For the work of seduction we might expect a devil to wear the form of an angel of light, but by no means to approach his intended victim in any horrible shape, such as would repel every mortal. The great representations of evil, whether imagined by the speculative or the religious sense, have never been, originally, ugly. The gods might be described as falling swiftly like lightning out of heaven, but in the popular imagination they retained for a long time much of their splendour. The very ingenuity with which they were afterwards invested with ugliness in religious art, attests that there were certain popular sentiments about them which had to be distinctly reversed. It was because they were thought beautiful that they must be painted ugly; it was because they were—even among converts to the new religion— still secretly believed to be kind and helpful, that there was employed such elaboration of hideous designs to deform them. The pictorial representations of demons and devils will come under a more detailed examination hereafter: it is for the present sufficient to point out that the traditional blackness or ugliness of demons and devils, as now thought of, by no means militates against the fact that they were once the popular deities. The contrast, for instance, between the horrible physiognomy given to Satan in ordinary christian art, and the theological representation of him as the Tempter, is obvious. Had the design of Art been to represent the theological theory, Satan would have been portrayed in a fascinating form. But the design was not that; it was to arouse horror and antipathy for the native deities to which the ignorant clung tenaciously. It was to train children to think of the still secretly-worshipped idols as frightful and bestial beings. It is important, therefore, that we should guard against confusing the speculative or moral attempts of mankind to personify pain and evil with the ugly and brutal demons and devils of artificial superstition, oftenest pictured on church walls. Sometimes they are set to support water-spouts, often the brackets that hold their foes, the saints. It is a very ancient device. Our figure 2 is from the handle of a chalice in possession of Sir James Hooker, meant probably to hold the holy water of Ganges. These are not genuine demons or devils, but carefully caricatured deities. Who that looks upon the grinning bestial forms carved about the roof of any old church—as those on Melrose Abbey and York Cathedral7—which, there is reason to believe, represent the primitive deities driven from the interior by potency of holy water, and chained to the uncongenial service of supporting the roof-gutter—can see in these gargoyles (Fr. gargouille, dragon), anything but carved imprecations? Was it to such ugly beings, guardians of their streams, hills, and forests, that our ancestors consecrated the holly and mistletoe, or with such that they associated their flowers, fruits, and homes? They were caricatures inspired by missionaries, made to repel and disgust, as the images of saints beside them were carved in beauty to attract. If the pagans had been the artists, the good looks would have been on the other side. And indeed there was an art of which those pagans were the unconscious possessors, through which the true characters of the imaginary beings they adored have been transmitted to us. In the fables of their folklore we find the Fairies that represent the spirit of the gods and goddesses to which they are easily traceable. That goddess who in christian times was pictured as a hag riding on a broom-stick was Frigga, the Earth-mother, associated with the first sacred affections clustering around the hearth; or Freya, whose very name was consecrated in frau, woman and wife. The mantle of Bertha did not cover more tenderness when it fell to the shoulders of Mary. The German child's name for the pre-christian Madonna was Mother Rose: distaff in hand, she watched over the industrious at their household work: she hovered near the cottage, perhaps to find there some weeping Cinderella and give her beauty for ashes.

Notes

1 *'Any Orientalist will appreciate the wonderful hotchpot of Hindu and Arabic language and religion in the following details, noted down among rude tribes of the Malay Peninsula. We hear of Jin Bumi, the earth-god (Arabic jin = demon, Sanskrit bhümi = earth); incense is burnt to Jewajewa (Sanskrit dewa = god), who intercedes with Pirman, the supreme invisible deity above the sky (Brahma?); the Moslem Allah Táala, with his wife Nabi Mahamad (Prophet Mohammed), appear in the Hinduised characters of creator and destroyer of all things; and while the spirits worshipped in stones are called by the Hindu term of 'dewa' or deity, Moslem conversion has so far influenced the mind of the stone-worshipper that he will give to his sacred boulder the name of Prophet Mohammed.'—Tylor's 'Primitive Culture,' vol. ii. p. 230.*
2 *Yaçna, 32.*
3 *'The Devil,' etc., from the French of the Rev. A. Réville, p. 5.*
4 *Tylor's 'Primitive Culture,' vol. ii. p. 299.*
5 *'The Gnostics,' etc., by C. W. King, M.A., p. 153.*
6 *Those who wish to examine this matter further will do well to refer to Badger, 'Nestorians and their Rituals,' in which the whole of the 'Eulogy' is translated; and to Layard, 'Ninevah and Babylon,' in which there is a translation of the same by Hormuzd Rassam, the King of Abyssinia's late prisoner.*
7 *The significance of the gargoyles on the churches built on the foundations of pagan temples may be especially observed at York, where the forms of various animals well known to Indo-Germanic mythology appear. They are probably copies of earlier designs, surviving from the days when the plan of Gregory for the conversion of temples prevailed. 'The temples of the idols in that nation,' wrote the Pope, A.C. 601, 'ought not to be destroyed; but let the idols that are in them be destroyed; let holy water be made and sprinkled in the said temples, let altars be erected and relics placed. For if those temples are well built, it is requisite that they be converted from the worship of devils to the service of the true God.'—Bede, Eccl. Hist. ch. 30.*

Chapter V - Classification

The obstructions of man—The twelve chief classes—Modifications of particular forms for various functions—Theological demons.

The statements made concerning the fair names of the chief demons and devils which have haunted the imagination of mankind, heighten the contrast between their celestial origin and the functions attributed to them in their degraded forms. The theory of Dualism, representing a necessary stage in the mental development of every race, called for a supply of demons, and the supply came from the innumerable dethroned, outlawed, and fallen deities and angels which had followed the subjugation of races and their religions. But though their celestial origin might linger around them in some slight legend or characteristic as well as in their names, the evil phenomenon to which each was attached as an explanation assigned the real form and work with which he or she was associated in popular superstition. We therefore find in the demons in which men have believed a complete catalogue of the obstacles with which they have had to contend in the long struggle for existence. In the devils we discover equally the history of the moral and religious struggles through which priesthoods and churches have had to pass. And the relative extent of this or that particular class of demons or devils, and the intensity of belief in any class as shown in the number of survivals from it, will be found to reflect pretty faithfully the degree to which the special evil represented by it afflicted primitive man, as attested by other branches of pre-historic investigation.

As to function, the demons we shall have to consider are those representing—1. Hunger; 2. Excessive Heat; 3. Excessive Cold; 4. Destructive elements and physical convulsions; 5. Destructive animals; 6. Human enemies; 7. The Barrenness of the Earth, as rock and desert; 8. Obstacles, as the river or mountain; 9. Illusion, seductive, invisible, and mysterious agents, causing delusions; 10. Darkness (especially when unusual), Dreams, Nightmare; 11. Disease; 12. Death.

These classes are selected, in obedience to necessary limitations, as representing the twelve chief labours of man which have given shape to the majority of his haunting demons, as distinguished from his devils. Of course all classifications of this character must be understood as made for convenience, and the divisions are not to be too sharply taken. What Plotinus said of the gods, that each contained all the rest, is equally true of both demons and devils. The demons of Hunger are closely related to the demons of Fire: Agni devoured his parents (two sticks consumed by the flame they produce); and from them we pass easily to elemental demons, like the lightning, or demons of fever. And similarly we find a relationship between other destructive forces. Nevertheless, the distinctions drawn are not fanciful, but exist in clear and unmistakable beliefs as to the special dispositions and employments of demons; and as we are not engaged in dealing with natural phenomena, but with superstitions concerning them, the only necessity of this classification is that it shall not be arbitrary, but shall really simplify the immense mass of facts which the student of Demonology has to encounter.

But there are several points which require especial attention as preliminary to a consideration of these various classes of demons.

First, it is to be borne in mind that a single demonic form will often appear in various functions, and that these must not be confused. The serpent may represent the lightning, or the coil of the whirlwind, or fatal venom; the earthquake may represent a swallowing Hunger-demon, or the rage of a chained giant. The separate functions must not be lost sight of because sometimes traceable to a single form, nor their practical character suffer disguise through their fair euphemistic or mythological names.

Secondly, the same form appears repeatedly in a diabolic as well as a demonic function, and here a clear distinction must be maintained in the reader's mind. The distinction already taken between a demon and a devil is not arbitrary: the word demon is related to deity; the word devil, though sometimes connected with the Sanskrit deva, has really no relation to it, but has a bad sense as 'calumniator:' but even if there were no such etymological identity and difference, it would be necessary to distinguish such widely separate offices as those representing the afflictive forces of nature where attributed to humanly appreciable motives on the one hand, and evils ascribed to pure malignancy or a principle of evil on the other. The Devil may, indeed, represent a further evolution in the line on which the Demon has appeared; Ahriman the Bad in conflict with Ormuzd the Good may be a spiritualisation of the conflict between Light and Darkness, Sun and Cloud, as represented in the Vedic Indra and Vritra; but the two phases represent different classes of ideas, indeed different worlds, and the apprehension of both requires that they shall be carefully distinguished even when associated with the same forms and names.

Thirdly, there is an important class of demons which the reader may expect to find fully treated of in the part of my work more particularly devoted to Demonology, which must be deferred, or further traced in that portion relating to the Devil; they are forms which in their original conception were largely beneficent, and have become of evil repute mainly through the anathema of theology. The chequer-board on which Osiris sat had its development in hosts of primitive shapes of light opposing shapes of darkness. The evil of some of these is ideal; others are morally amphibious: Teraphim, Lares, genii, were ancestors of the guardian angels and patron saints of the present day; they were oftenest in the shapes of dogs and cats and aged human ancestors, supposed to keep watch and ward about the house, like the friendly Domovoi respected in Russia; the evil disposition and harmfulness ascribed to them are partly natural but partly also theological, and due to the difficulty of superseding them with patron saints and angels. The degradation of beneficent beings, already described in relation to large demonic and diabolic forms, must be understood as constantly acting in the smallest details of household superstition, with what strange reaction and momentous result will appear when we come to consider the phenomena of Witchcraft.

Finally, it must be remarked that the nature of our inquiry renders the consideration of the origin of myths—whether 'solar' or other—of secondary importance. Such origin it will be necessary to point out and discuss incidentally, but our main point will always be the forms in which the myths have become incarnate, and their modifications in various places and times, these being the result of those actual experiences with which Demonology is chiefly concerned. A myth, as many able writers have pointed out, is, in its origin, an explanation by the uncivilised mind of some natural phenomenon—not an allegory, not an esoteric conceit. For this reason it possesses fluidity, and takes on manifold shapes. The apparent sleep of the sun in winter may be represented in a vast range of myths, from the Seven Sleepers to the Man in the Moon of our nursery rhyme; but the variations all have relation to facts and circumstances. Comparative Mythology is mainly concerned with the one thread running through them, and binding them all to the original myth; the task of Demonology is rather to discover the agencies which have given their several shapes. If it be shown that Orthros and Cerberus were primarily the morning and evening twilight or howling winds, either interpretation is here secondary to their personification as dogs. Demonology would ask, Why dogs? why not bulls? Its answer in each case detaches from the anterior myth its mode, and shows this as the determining force of further myths.

Part II - The Demon

Chapter I - Hunger

Hunger-demons—Kephn—Miru—Kagura—Ráhu the Hindu sun-devourer—The earth monster at Pelsall—A Franconian custom—Sheitan as moon-devourer—Hindu offerings to the dead—Ghoul—Goblin—Vampyres—Leanness of demons—Old Scotch custom.—The origin of sacrifices.

In every part of the earth man's first struggle was for his daily food. With only a rude implement of stone or bone he had to get fish from the sea, bird from the air, beast from the forest. For ages, with such poor equipment, he had to wring a precarious livelihood from nature. He saw, too, every living form around him similarly trying to satisfy its hunger. There seemed to be a Spirit of Hunger abroad. And, at the same time, there was such a resistance to man's satisfaction of his need—the bird and fish so hard to get, the stingy earth so ready to give him a stone when he asked for bread—that he came to the conclusion that there must be invisible voracious beings who wanted all good things for themselves. So the ancient world was haunted by a vast brood of Hunger-demons. There is an African tribe, the Karens, whose representation of the Devil (Kephn) is a huge stomach floating through the air; and this repulsive image may be regarded as the type of nearly half the demons which have haunted the human imagination. This, too, is the terrible Miru, with her daughters and slave, haunting the South Sea Islander. 'The esoteric doctrine of the priests was, that souls leave the body ere breath has quite gone, and travel to the edge of a cliff facing the setting sun (Rā). A large wave now approaches the base of the cliff, and a gigantic bua tree, covered with fragrant blossoms, springs up from Avaiki (nether world) to receive on its far-reaching branches human spirits, who are mysteriously impelled to cluster on its limbs. When at length the mystic tree is covered with human spirits, it goes down with its living freight to the nether world. Akaanga, the slave of fearful Miru, mistress of the invisible world, infallibly catches all these unhappy spirits in his net and laves them to and fro in a lake. In these waters the captive ghosts exhaust themselves by wriggling about like fishes, in the vain hope of escape. The net is pulled up, and the half-drowned spirits enter into the presence of dread Miru, who is ugliness personified. The secret of Miru's power over her intended victims is the 'kava' root (Piper mythisticum). A bowl of this drink is prepared for each visitor to the shades by her four lovely daughters. Stupefied with the draught, the unresisting victims are borne off to a mighty oven and cooked. Miru, her peerless daughters, her dance-loving son, and the attendants, subsist exclusively on human spirits decoyed to the nether world and then cooked. The drinking-cups of Miru are the skulls of her victims. She is called in song 'Miru-the-ruddy,' because her cheeks ever glow with the heat of the oven where her captives are cooked. As the surest way to Miru's oven is to die a natural death, one need not marvel that the Rev. Mr. Gill, who made these statements before the Anthropological Institute in London (February 8, 1876), had heard 'many anecdotes of aged warriors, scarcely able to hold a spear, insisting on being led to the field of battle in the hope of gaining the house of the brave.' As the South Sea paradise seems to consist in an eternal war-dance, or, in one island, in an eternal chewing of sugar-cane, it is not unlikely that the aged seek violent death chiefly to avoid the oven. We have here a remarkable illustration of the distinguishing characteristic of the demon. Fearful as Miru is, it may be noted that there is not one gratuitous element of cruelty in her procedure. On the contrary, she even provides her victims with an anæsthetic draught. Her prey is simply netted, washed, and cooked, as for man are his animal inferiors. In one of the islands (Aitutaki), Miru is believed to resort to a device which is certainly terrible—namely, the contrivance that each soul entering the nether world shall drink a bowl of living centipedes; but this is simply with the one end in view of appeasing her own pangs of hunger, for the object and effect of the draught is to cause the souls to drown themselves, it being apparently only after entire death that they can be cooked and devoured by Miru and her household. Fortunately for the islanders, Miru is limited in her tortures to a transmundane sphere, and room is left for many a slip between her dreadful cup and the human lip. The floating stomach Kephn is, however, not other-worldly. We see, however, a softened form of him in some other tribes. The Greenlanders, Finns, Laps, conceived the idea that there is a large paunch-demon which people could invoke to go and suck the cows or consume the herds of their enemies; and the Icelanders have a superstition that some people can construct such a demon out of bones and skins, and send him forth to transmute the milk or flesh of cattle into a supply of flesh and blood. A form of this kind is represented in the Japanese

Kagura (figure 3), the favourite mask of January dancers and drum-beaters seeking money. The Kagura is in precise contrast with the Pretas (Siam), which, though twelve miles in height, are too thin to be seen, their mouths being so small as to render it impossible to satisfy their fearful hunger.

The pot-bellies given to demons in Travancore and other districts of India, and the blood-sacrifices by which the natives propitiate them—concerning which a missionary naively remarks, that even these heathen recognise, though in corrupted form, 'the great truth that without shedding of blood there is no remission of sins'1—refer to the Hunger-demon. They are the brood of Kali, girt round with human skulls.

Fig. 3—A Swallower.

The expedition which went out to India to observe the last solar eclipse was incidentally the means of calling attention to a remarkable survival of the Hunger-demon in connection with astronomic phenomena. While the English observers were arranging their apparatus, the natives prepared a pile of brushwood, and, so soon as the eclipse began, they set fire to this pile and began to shout and yell as they danced around it. Not less significant were the popular observances generally. There was a semi-holiday in honour of the eclipse. The ghauts were crowded with pious worshippers. No Hindu, it is thought, ought to do any work whatever during an eclipse, and there was a general tendency to prolong the holiday a little beyond the exact time when the shadow disappears, and indeed to prolong it throughout the day. All earthenware vessels used for cooking were broken, and all cooked food in the houses at the time of the eclipse was thrown out. It is regarded as a time of peculiar blessings if taken in the right way, and of dread consequences to persons inclined to heterodoxy or neglect of the proper observances. Between nine and ten in the evening two shocks of an earthquake occurred, the latter a rather unpleasant one, shaking the tables and doors in an uncomfortable fashion for several seconds. To the natives it was no surprise—they believe firmly in the connection of eclipses and earthquakes.2

Especially notable is the breaking of their culinary utensils by the Hindus during an eclipse. In Copenhagen there is a collection of the votive weapons of ancient Norsemen, every one broken as it was offered up to the god of their victory in token of good faith, lest they should be suspected of any intention to use again what they had given away. For the same reason the cup was offered—broken—with the libation. The Northman felt himself in the presence of the Jötunn (giants), whose name Grimm identifies as the Eaters. For the Hindu of to-day the ceremonies appropriate at an eclipse, however important, have probably as little rational meaning as the occasional Belfire that lights up certain dark corners of Europe has for those who build it. But the traditional observances have come up from the childhood of the world, when the eclipse represented a demon devouring the sun, who was to have his attention called by outcries and prayers to the fact that if it was fire he needed there was plenty on earth; and if food, he might have all in their houses, provided he would consent to satisfy his appetite with articles of food less important than the luminaries of heaven.

Such is the shape now taken in India of the ancient myth of the eclipse. When at the churning of the ocean to find the nectar of immortality, a demon with dragon-tail was tasting that nectar, the sun and moon told on him, but not until his head had become immortal; and it is this head of Ráhu which seeks now to devour the informers—the Sun and Moon.3 Mythologically, too, this Ráhu has been divided; for we shall hereafter trace the dragon-tail of him to the garden of Eden and in the christian devil, whereas in India he has been improved from a vindictive to a merely voracious demon.

The fires kindled by the Hindus to frighten Ráhu on his latest appearance might have defeated the purpose of the expedition by the smoke it was sending up, had not two officers leaped upon the fire and scattered its fuel; but just about the time when these courageous gentlemen were trampling out the fires of superstition whose smoke would obscure the vision of science, an event occurred in England which must be traced to the same ancient belief—the belief, namely, that when anything is apparently swallowed up, as the sun and moon by an eclipse, or a village by earthquake or flood, it is the work of a hungry dragon, earthworm, or other monster. The Pelsall mine was flooded, and a large number of miners drowned. When the accident became known in the village, the women went out with the families of the unfortunate men, and sat beside the mouth of the flooded pit, at the bottom of which the dead bodies yet remained. These women then yelled down the pit with voices very different from ordinary lamentation. They also refused unanimously to taste food of any kind, saying, when pressed to do so, that so long as they could refrain from eating, their husbands might still be spared to them. When, finally, one poor woman, driven by the pangs of hunger, was observed to eat a crust of bread, the cries ceased, and the women, renouncing all hope, proceeded in silent procession to their homes in Pelsall.

The Hindu people casting their food out of the window during an eclipse, the Pelsall wives refusing to eat when the mine is flooded, are acting by force of immemorial tradition, and so are doing unconsciously what the African woman does consciously when she surrounds the bed of her sick husband with rice and meat, and beseeches the demon to devour them instead of the man. To the same class of notions belong the old custom of trying to discover the body of one drowned by means of a loaf of bread with a candle stuck in it, which it was said would pause above the body, and the body might be made to appear by firing a gun over it—that is, the demon holding it would be frightened off. A variant, too, is the Persian custom of protecting a woman in parturition by spreading a table, with a lamp at each corner, with seven kinds of fruits and seven different aromatic seeds upon it.

In 1769, when Pennant made his 'Scottish Tour,' he found fully observed in the Highlands the ceremony of making the Beltane Cake on the first of May, and dedicating its distributed fragments to birds and beasts of prey, with invocation to the dread being of whom they were the supposed agents to spare the herds. Demons especially love milk: the Lambton Worm required nine cows' milk daily; and Jerome mentions a diabolical baby which exhausted six nurses.

The Devil nominally inherits, among the peasantry of Christendom, the attributes of the demons which preceded him; but it must be understood that in every case where mere voracity is ascribed to the Devil, a primitive demon is meant, and of this fact the superstitious peasant is dimly conscious. In Franconia, when a baker is about to put dough biscuits into an oven to be baked, he will first throw half-a-dozen of them into the fire, saying, 'There, poor devil! those are for you.' If pressed for an explanation, he will admit his fear that but for this offering his biscuits are in danger of coming out burnt; but that the 'poor devil' is not bad-hearted, only driven by his hunger to make mischief. The being he fears is, therefore, clearly not the Devil at all—whose distinction is a love of wickedness for its own sake—but the half-starved gobbling ghosts of whom, in Christian countries, 'Devil' has become the generic name. Of their sacrifices, Grace before meat is a remnant. In Moslem countries, however, 'Sheitan' combines the demonic and the malignant voracities. During the late lunar eclipse, the inhabitants of Pera and Constantinople fired guns over their houses to drive 'Sheitan' (Satan) away from the moon, for, whoever the foe, the Turk trusts in gunpowder. But superstitions representing Satan as a devourer are becoming rare. In the church of Nôtre Dame at Hal, Belgium, the lectern shows a dragon attempting to swallow the Bible, which is supported on the back of an eagle.

There is another and much more formidable form in which the Hunger-demon appears in Demonology. The fondness for blood, so characteristic of supreme gods, was distributed as a special thirst through a large class of demons. In the legend of Ishtar descending to Hades4 to seek some beloved one, she threatens if the door be not opened—

I will raise the dead to be devourers of the living!
Upon the living shall the dead prey!

This menace shows that the Chaldæan and Babylonian belief in the vampyre, called Akhkharu in Assyrian, was fully developed at a very early date. Although the Hunger-demon was very fully developed in India, it does not appear to have been at any time so cannibalistic, possibly because the natives were not great flesh-eaters. In some cases, indeed, we meet with the vampyre superstition; as in the story of Vikram and the Vampyre, and in the Tamil drama of Harichándra, where the frenzied Sandramáti says to the king, 'I belong to the race of elves, and I have killed thy child in order that I might feed on its delicate flesh.' Such expressions are rare enough to warrant suspicion of their being importations. The Vetala's appetite is chiefly for corpses. The poor hungry demons of India—such as the Bhút, a dismal, ravenous ghost, dreaded at the moon-wane of the month Katik (Oct.-Nov.)—was not supposed to devour man, but only man's food. The Hindu demons of this class may be explained by reference to the sráddha, or oblation to ancestors, concerning which we read directions in the Manu Code. 'The ancestors of men are satisfied a whole month with tila, rice, etc.; two months with fish, etc. The Manes say, Oh, may that man be born in our line who may give us milky food, with honey and pure butter, both on the thirteenth of the moon and when the shadow of an elephant falls to the east!' The bloodthirsty demons of India have pretty generally been caught up like Kali into a higher symbolism, and their voracity systematised and satisfied in sacrificial commutations. The popular belief in the southern part of that country is indicated by Professor Monier Williams, in a letter written from Southern India, wherein he remarks that the devils alone require propitiation. It is generally a simple procedure, performed by offerings of food or other articles supposed to be acceptable to disembodied beings. For example, when a certain European, once a terror to the district in which he lived, died in the South of India, the natives were in the constant habit of depositing brandy and cigars on his tomb to propitiate his spirit, supposed to roam about the neighbourhood in a restless manner, and with evil proclivities. The very same was done to secure the good offices of the philanthropic spirit of a great European sportsman, who, when he was alive, delivered his district from the ravages of tigers. Indeed all evil spirits are thought to be opposed by good ones, who, if duly propitiated, make it their business to guard the inhabitants of particular places from demonic intruders. Each district, and even every village, has its guardian genius, often called its Mother.5

Such ideas as these are represented in Europe in some varieties of the Kobold and the Goblin (Gk. κόβαλος). Though the goblin must, according to folk-philosophy, be fed with nice food, it is not a deadly being; on the contrary, it is said the Gobelin tapestry derives its name because the secret of its colours was gained from these ghosts. Though St. Taurin expelled one from Evreux, he found it so polite that he would not send it to hell, and it still haunts the credulous there and at Caen, without being thought very formidable.

The demon that 'lurks in graveyards' is universal, and may have suggested cremation. In the East it is represented mainly by such forms as the repulsive ghoul, which preys on dead bodies; but it has been developed in some strange way to the

Slavonic phantom called Vampyre, whose peculiar fearfulness is that it represents the form in which any deceased person may reappear, not ghoul-like to batten on the dead, but to suck the blood of the living. This is perhaps the most formidable survival of demonic superstition now existing in the world.

A people who still have in their dictionary such a word as 'miscreant' (misbeliever) can hardly wonder that the priests of the Eastern Church fostered the popular belief that heretics at death changed into drinkers of the blood of the living. The Slavonic vampyres have declined in England and America to be the 'Ogres,' who 'smell the blood of an Englishman,' but are rarely supposed to enjoy it; but it exposes the real ugliness of the pious superstitions sometimes deemed pretty, that, in proportion to the intensity of belief in supernaturalism, the people live in terror of the demons that go about seeking whom they may devour. In Russia the watcher beside a corpse is armed with holy charms against attack from it at midnight. A vampyre may be the soul of any outcast from the Church, or one over whose corpse, before burial, a cat has leaped or a bird flown. It may be discovered in a graveyard by leading a black colt through; the animal will refuse to tread on the vampyre's grave, and the body is taken out and a stake driven through it, always by a single blow. A related class of demons are the 'heart-devourers.' They touch their victim with an aspen or other magical twig; the heart falls out, and is, perhaps, replaced by some baser one. Mr. Ralston mentions a Mazovian story in which a hero awakes with the heart of a hare, and remains a coward ever after;6 and in another case a quiet peasant received a cock's heart and was always crowing. The Werewolf, in some respects closely related to the vampyre, also pursues his ravages among the priest-ridden peasantry of the South and East.

In Germany, though the more horrible forms of the superstition are rare, the 'Nachzehrer' is much dreaded. Even in various Protestant regions it is thought safest that a cross should be set beside every grave to impede any demonic propensities that may take possession of the person interred; and where food is not still buried with the corpse to assuage any pangs of hunger that may arise, a few grains of corn or rice are scattered upon it in reminiscence of the old custom. In Diesdorf it is believed that if money is not placed in the dead person's mouth at burial, or his name not cut from his shirt, he is likely to become a Nachzehrer, and that the ghost will come forth in the form of a pig. It is considered a sure preventative of such a result to break the neck of the dead body. On one occasion, it is there related, several persons of one family having died, the suspected corpse was exhumed, and found to have eaten up its own grave-clothes. Dr. Dyer, an eminent physician of Chicago, Illinois, told me (1875) that a case occurred in that city within his personal knowledge, where the body of a woman who had died of consumption was taken out of the grave and the lungs burned, under a belief that she was drawing after her into the grave some of her surviving relatives. In 1874, according to the Providence Journal, in the village of Peacedale, Rhode Island, U.S., Mr. William Rose dug up the body of his own daughter, and burned her heart, under the belief that she was wasting away the lives of other members of his family.

The characteristics of modern 'Spiritualism' appear to indicate that the superstitious have outgrown this ancient fear of ghostly malevolence where surrounded by civilisation. It is very rare in the ancient world or in barbarous regions to find any invocations for the return of the spirits of the dead. Mr. Tylor has quoted a beautiful dirge used by the Ho tribe of India, beginning—

We never scolded you, never wronged you;
Come to us back!

But generally funereal customs are very significant of the fear that spirits may return, and their dirges more in the vein of the Bodo of North-East India: 'Take and eat: heretofore you have eaten and drunk with us, you can do so no more: you were one of us, you can be so no longer: we come no more to you, come you not to us.' 'Even,' says Mr. Tylor, 'in the lowest culture we find flesh holding its own against spirit, and at higher stages the householder rids himself with little scruple of an unwelcome inmate. The Greenlanders would carry the dead out by the window, not by the door, while an old woman, waving a firebrand behind, cried 'Piklerrukpok!' i.e., 'There is nothing more to be had here!' the Hottentots removed the dead from the hut by an opening broken out on purpose, to prevent him from finding the way back; the Siamese, with the same intention, break an opening through the house wall to carry the coffin through, and then hurry it at full speed thrice round the house; the Siberian Chuwashes fling a red-hot stone after the corpse is carried out, for an obstacle to bar the soul from coming back; so Brandenburg peasants pour out a pail of water at the door after the coffin to prevent the ghost from walking; and Pomeranian mourners returning from the churchyard leave behind the straw from the hearse, that the wandering soul may rest there, and not come back so far as home.'7

It may be remarked, in this connection, that in nearly all the pictures of demons and devils, they are represented as very lean. The exceptions will be found generally in certain Southern and tropical demons which represent cloud or storm—Typhon, for instance—and present a swollen or bloated appearance. No Northern devil is fat. Shakespeare ascribes to Cæsar a suspicion of leanness—

Yond' Cassius hath a lean and hungry look:
He thinks too much: such men are dangerous.

When Antony defends Cassius, Cæsar only replies, 'Would he were fatter!' This mistrust of leanness is a reflection from all the Hunger-demons; it interprets the old sayings that a devil, however fair in front, may be detected by hollowness of the back, and that he is usually so thin as to cast no shadow.8

Fig. 4.—St. Anthony's Lean Persecutor (Salvator Rosa).

Illustrations of the Hunger-demon and its survivals might be greatly multiplied, were it necessary. It need only, however, be mentioned that it is to this early and most universal conception of præternatural danger that the idea of sacrifice as well as of fasting must be ascribed. It is, indeed, too obvious to require extended demonstration that the notion of offering fruits and meat to an invisible being could only have originated in the belief that such being was hungry, however much the spiritualisation of such offerings may have attended their continuance among enlightened peoples. In the evolution of purer deities, Fire—'the devouring element'—was substituted for a coarser method of accepting sacrifices, and it became a sign of baser beings—such as the Assyrian Akhkharu, and the later Lamia—to consume dead bodies with their teeth; and this fire was the spiritual element in the idolatries whose objects were visible. But the original accent of sacrifice never left it. The Levitical Law says: 'The two kidneys, and the fat that is upon them, which is by the flanks, and the caul above the liver, with the kidneys, it shall he take away. And the priest shall burn them upon the altar: it is the food of the offering made by fire for a sweet savour: all the fat is the Lord's. It shall be a perpetual statute for your generations throughout all your dwellings, that ye eat neither fat nor blood.'9 We find the Hunger-demon shown as well in the wrath of Jehovah against the sons of Eli for eating the choice parts of the meats offered on his altar, as in that offering of tender infants to Moloch which his priests denounced, or in Saturn devouring his children, whom Aryan faith dethroned; and they all reappear as phantoms thinly veiled above the spotless Lamb offered up on Calvary, the sacrificed Macaria ('Blessed'), the pierced heart of Mary. The beautiful boy Menœceus must be sacrificed to save Thebes; the gods will not have aged and tough Creon, though a king, in his place. Iphigenia, though herself saved from the refined palate of Artemis, through the huntress's fondness for kid's blood, becomes the priestess of human sacrifices. The human offering deemed half-divine could alone at last satisfy the Deity, gathered in his side this sheaf of sacrificial knives, whetted in many lands and ages, and in his self-sacrifice the Hunger-demon himself was made the victim. Theologians have been glad to rescue the First Person of their Trinity from association with the bloodthirsty demons of barbarous ages by describing the sacrifice of Jesus as God himself becoming the victim of an eternal law. But, whatever may be said of this complex device, it is sufficient evidence that man's primitive demon which personified his hunger has ended with being consumed on his own altar. For though fasting is a survival of the same savage notion that man may secure benefits from invisible beings by leaving them the food, it is a practice which survives rather through the desire of imitating ascetic saints than because of any understood principle. The strange yet natural consummation adds depth of meaning to the legend of Odin being himself sacrificed in his disguise on the Holy Tree at Upsala, where human victims were hung as offerings to him; and to his rune in the Havamal—

23

I know that I hung
On a wind-rocked tree
Nine whole nights,
With a spear wounded,
And to Odin offered
Myself to myself.

Notes

1 *'The Land of Charity,' by Rev. Samuel Mateer, p. 214.*
2 *London 'Times' Calcutta correspondence.*
3 *The Persian poet Sádi uses the phrase, 'The whale swallowed Jonah,' as a familiar expression for sunset; which is in curious coincidence with a Mimac (Nova Scotian) myth that the holy hero Glooscap was carried to the happy Sunset Land in a whale. The story of Jonah has indeed had interesting variants, one of them being that legend of Oannes, the fish-god, emerging from the Red Sea to teach Babylonians the arts (a saga of Dagon); but the phrase in the Book of Jonah—'the belly of Hell'—had a prosaic significance for the christian mind, and, in connection with speculations concerning Behemoth and Leviathan, gave us the mediæval Mouth of Hell.*
4 *Tablet K 162 in the British Museum. See 'Records of the Past,' i. 141.*
5 *London 'Times,' July 11, 1877.*
6 *'Songs of the Russian People,' p. 409.*
7 *'Primitive Culture.'*
8 *Cæsarius D'Heisterbach, Miracul. iii.*
9 *Lev. iii. 15.*

Chapter II - Heat

Demons of Fire—Agni—Asmodeus—Prometheus—Feast of fire—Moloch—Tophet—Genii of the lamp—Bel-fires—Hallowe'en—Negro superstitions—Chinese fire-god—Volcanic and incendiary demons—Mangaian fire-demon—Demons' fear of water.

Fire was of old the element of fiends. No doubt this was in part due to the fact that it also was a devouring element.
Sacrifices were burnt; the demon visibly consumed them. But the great flame-demons represent chiefly the destructive and painful action of intense heat. They originate in regions of burning desert, of sunstroke, and drouth.
Agni, the Hindu god of fire, was adored in Vedic hymns as the twin of Indra.
'Thy appearance is fair to behold, thou bright-faced Agni, when like gold thou shinest at hand; thy brightness comes like the lightning of heaven; thou showest splendour like the splendour of the bright sun.
'Adorable and excellent Agni, emit the moving and graceful smoke.
'The flames of Agni are luminous, powerful, fearful, and not to be trusted.
'I extol the greatness of that showerer of rain, whom men celebrate as the slayer of Vritra: the Agni, Vaiswanara, slew the stealer of the waters.'
The slaying of Vritra, the monster, being the chief exploit of Indra, Agni could only share in it as being the flame that darted with Indra's weapon, the disc (of the sun).
'Thou (Agni) art laid hold off with difficulty, like the young of tortuously twining snakes, thou who art a consumer of many forests as a beast is of fodder.'
Petrifaction awaits all these glowing metaphors of early time. Verbal inspiration will make Agni a literally tortuous serpent and consuming fire. His smoke, called Kali (black), is now the name of Siva's terrible bride.
Much is said in Vedic hymns of the method of producing the sacred flame symbolising Agni; namely, the rubbing together of two sticks. 'He it is whom the two sticks have engendered, like a new-born babe.' It is a curious coincidence that a similar phrase should describe 'the devil on two sticks,' who has come by way of Persia into European romance.
Asmodeus was a lame demon, and his 'two sticks' as 'Diable Boiteux' are crutches; but his lameness may be referable to the attenuated extremities suggested by spires of flame—'tortuously twining snakes,'—rather than to the rabbinical myth that he broke his leg on his way to meet Solomon. Benfey identified Asmodeus as Zend Aêshma-daêva, demon of lust. His goat-feet and fire-coal eyes are described by Le Sage, and the demon says he was lamed by falling from the air, like Vulcan, when contending with Pillardoc. It is not difficult to imagine how flame engendered by the rubbing of sticks might have attained personification as sensual passion, especially among Zoroastrians, who would detach from the

adorable Fire all associations of evil. It would harmonise well with the Persian tendency to diabolise Indian gods, that they should note the lustful character occasionally ascribed to Agni in the Vedas. 'Him alone, the ever-youthful Agni, men groom like a horse in the evening and at dawn; they bed him as a stranger in his couch; the light of Agni, the worshipped male, is lighted.' Agni was the Indian 'Brulefer' or love-charmer, and patron of marriage; the fire-god Hephaistos was the husband of Aphrodite; the day of the Norse thunder-and-lightning god Thor (Thursday), is in Scandinavian regions considered the luckiest for marriages.

The process of obtaining fire by friction is represented by a nobler class of myths than that referred to. In the Mahábhárata the gods and demons together churn the ocean for the nectar of immortality; and they use for their churning-stick the mountain Manthara. This word appears in pramantha, which means a fire-drill, and from it comes the great name of Prometheus, who stole fire from heaven, and conferred on mankind a boon which rendered them so powerful that the jealousy and wrath of Zeus were excited. This fable is generally read in its highly rationalised and mystical form, and on this account belongs to another part of our general subject; but it may be remarked here that the Titan so terribly tortured by Zeus could hardly have been regarded, originally, as the friend of man. At the time when Zeus was a god genuinely worshipped—when he first stood forth as the supplanter of the malign devourer Saturn—it could have been no friend of man who was seen chained on the rock for ever to be the vulture's prey. It was fire in some destructive form which must have been then associated with Prometheus, and not that power by which later myths represented his animating with a divine spark the man of clay. The Hindu myth of churning the ocean for the immortal draught, even if it be proved that the ocean is heaven and the draught lightning, does not help us much. The traditional association of Prometheus with the Arts might almost lead one to imagine that the early use of fire by some primitive inventor had brought upon him the wrath of his mates, and that Zeus' thunderbolts represented some early 'strike' against machinery.

It is not quite certain that it may not have been through some euphemistic process that Fire-worship arose in Persia. Not only does fire occupy a prominent place in the tortures inflicted by Ahriman in the primitive Parsee Inferno, but it was one of the weapons by which he attempted to destroy the heavenly child Zoroaster. The evil magicians kindled a fire in the desert and threw the child on it; but his mother, Dogdo, found him sleeping tranquilly on the flames, which were as a pleasant bath, and his face shining like Zohore and Moschteri (Jupiter and Mercury).1 The Zoroastrians also held that the earth would ultimately be destroyed by fire; its metals and minerals, ignited by a comet, would form streams which all souls would have to pass through: they would be pleasant to the righteous, but terrible to the sinful,—who, however, would come through, purified, into paradise, the last to arrive being Ahriman himself.

The combustible nature of many minerals under the surface of the earth,—which was all the realm of Hades (invisible),—would assist the notion of a fiery abode for the infernal gods. Our phrase 'plutonic rock' would then have a very prosaic sense. Pliny says that in his time sulphur was used to keep off evil spirits, and it is not impossible that it first came to be used as a medicine by this route.2

Fire-festivals still exist in India, where the ancient raiment of Agni has been divided up and distributed among many deities. At the popular annual festival in honour of Dharma Rajah, called the Feast of Fire, the devotees walk barefoot over a glowing fire extending forty feet. It lasts eighteen days, during which time those that make a vow to keep it must fast, abstain from women, lie on the bare ground, and walk on a brisk fire. The eighteenth day they assemble on the sound of instruments, their heads crowned with flowers, their bodies daubed with saffron, and follow the figures of Dharma Rajah and Draupadi his wife in procession. When they come to the fire, they stir it to animate its activity, and take a little of the ashes, with which they rub their foreheads; and when the gods have been carried three times round it they walk over a hot fire, about forty feet. Some carry their children in their arms, and others lances, sabres, and standards. After the ceremony the people press to collect the ashes to rub their foreheads with, and obtain from devotees the flowers with which they were adorned, and which they carefully preserve.3

The passion of Agni reappears in Draupadi purified by fire for her five husbands, and especially her union with Dharma Rajah, son of Yama, is celebrated in this unorthodox passion-feast. It has been so much the fashion for travellers to look upon all 'idolatry' with biblical eyes, that we cannot feel certain with Sonnerat that there was anything more significant in the carrying of children by the devotees, than the supposition that what was good for the parent was equally beneficial to the child. But the identification of Moloch with an Aryan deity is not important; the Indian Feast of Fire and the rites of Moloch are derived by a very simple mental process from the most obvious aspects of the Sun as the quickening and the consuming power in nature. The child offered to Moloch was offered to the god by whom he was generated, and as the most precious of all the fruits of the earth for which his genial aid was implored and his destructive intensity deprecated. Moloch, a word that means 'king,' was a name almost synonymous with human sacrifice. It was in all probability at first only a local (Ammonite) personification growing out of an ancient shrine of Baal. The Midianite Baal accompanied the Israelites into the wilderness, and that worship was never thoroughly eradicated. In the Egyptian Confession of Faith, which the initiated took even into their graves inscribed upon a scroll, the name of God is not mentioned, but is expressed only by the words Nuk pu Nuk, 'I am he who I am.'4 The flames of the burning bush, from which these same words came to Moses, were kindled from Baal, the Sun; and we need not wonder that while the more enlightened chiefs of Israel preserved the higher ideas and symbols of the countries they abandoned, the ignorant would still cling to Apis (the Golden Calf), to Ashtaroth, and to Moloch. Amos (v. 26), and after him Stephen the martyr (Acts vii. 43), reproach the Hebrews with having carried into the wilderness the tabernacle of their god Moloch. And though the passing of children through the fire to Moloch was, by the Mosaic Law, made a capital crime, the superstition and the corresponding practice retained such strength that we find Solomon building a temple to Moloch on the Mount of Olives (1 Kings xi. 7), and, long after, Manasseh making his son pass through the fire in honour of the same god.

It is certain from the denunciations of the prophets5 that the destruction of children in these flames was actual. From Jeremiah xix. 6, as well as other sources, we know that the burnings took place in the Valley of Tophet or Hinnom (Gehenna). The idol Moloch was of brass, and its throne of brass; its head was that of a calf, and wore a royal crown; its stomach was a furnace, and when the children were placed in its arms they were consumed by the fierce heat,—their cries being drowned by the beating of drums; from which, toph meaning a 'drum,' the place was also called Tophet. In the fierce war waged against alien superstitions by Josiah, he defiled Gehenna, filling it with ordure and dead men's bones to make it odious, 'that no man might make his son or his daughter to pass through the fire to Moloch' (2 Kings xxiii. 10), and a perpetual fire was kept there to consume the filth of Jerusalem.

From this horrible Gehenna, with its perpetual fire, its loathsome worm, its cruelties, has been derived the picture of a never-ending Hell prepared for the majority of human beings by One who, while they live on earth, sends the rain and sunshine alike on the evil and the good. Wo Chang, a Chinaman in London, has written to a journal6 his surprise that our religious teachers should be seized with such concern for the victims of Turkish atrocities in Bulgaria, while they are so calm in view of the millions burning, and destined to burn endlessly, in the flames of hell. Our Oriental brothers will learn a great deal from our missionaries; among other things, that the theological god of Christendom is still Moloch.

The Ammonites, of whom Moloch was the special demon, appear to have gradually blended with the Arabians. These received from many sources their mongrel superstitions, but among them were always prominent the planet-gods and fire-gods, whom their growing monotheism (to use the word still in a loose sense) transformed to powerful angels and genii. The genii of Arabia are slaves of the lamp; they are evoked by burning tufts of hair; they ascend as clouds of smoke. Though, as subordinate agents of the Fire-fiend, they may be consumed by flames, yet those who so fight them are apt to suffer a like fate, as in the case of the Lady of Beauty in the Arabian Nights' Entertainments. Many stories of this kind preceded the declarations of the Old Testament, that Jehovah breathes fire and brimstone, his breath kindling Tophet; and also the passages of the Koran, and of the New Testament describing Satan as a fiery fiend.

Various superstitions connecting infernal powers with fire survive among the Jews of some remote districts of Europe. The Passover is kept a week by the Jewish inhabitants in the villages on the Vosges mountains and on the banks of the Rhine. The time of omer is the interval between the Passover and Pentecost, the seven weeks elapsing from the departure from Egypt and the giving of the law, marked in former days by the offering of an omer of barley daily at the temple. It is considered a fearful time, during which every Jew is particularly exposed to the evil influence of evil spirits. There is something dangerous and fatal in the air; every one should be on the watch, and not tempt the schedim (demons) in any way. Have a strict eye upon your cattle, say the Jews, for the sorceress will get into your stables, mount your cows and goats, bring diseases upon them, and turn their milk sour. In the latter case, try to lay your hand upon the suspected person; shut her up in a room with a basin of sour milk, and beat the milk with a hazel-wand, pronouncing God's name three times. Whilst you are doing this, the sorceress will make great lamentation, for the blows are falling upon her. Only stop when you see blue flames dancing on the surface of the milk, for then the charm is broken. If at nightfall a beggar comes to ask for a little charcoal to light his fire, be very careful not to give it, and do not let him go without drawing him three times by his coat-tail; and without losing time, throw some large handfuls of salt on the fire. In all of which we may trace traditions of parched wildernesses and fiery serpents, as well as of Abraham's long warfare with the Fire-worshippers, until, according to the tradition, he was thrown into the flames he refused to worship.

It is probable that in all the popular superstitions which now connect devils and future punishments with fire are blended both the apotheosis and the degradation of demons. The first and most universal of deities being the Sun, whose earthly representative is fire, the student of Comparative Mythology has to pick his way very carefully in tracing by any ethnological path the innumerable superstitions of European folklore in which Fire-worship is apparently reflected. The collection of facts and records contained in a work so accessible to all who care to pursue the subject as that of Brand and his editors,7 renders it unnecessary that I should go into the curious facts to any great extent here. The uniformity of the traditions by which the midsummer fires of Northern Europe have been called Baal-fires or Bel-fires warrant the belief that they are actually descended from the ancient rites of Baal, even apart from the notorious fact that they have so generally been accompanied by the superstition that it is a benefit to children to leap over or be passed through such fires. That this practice still survives in out-of-the way places of the British Empire appears from such communications as the following (from the Times), which are occasionally addressed to the London journals:—'Lerwick (Shetland), July 7, 1871.—Sir,—It may interest some of your readers to know that last night (being St. John's Eve, old style) I observed, within a mile or so of this town, seven bonfires blazing, in accordance with the immemorial custom of celebrating the Midsummer solstice. These fires were kindled on various heights around the ancient hamlet of Sound, and the children leaped over them, and 'passed through the fire to Moloch,' just as their ancestors would have done a thousand years ago on the same heights, and their still remoter progenitors in Eastern lands many thousand years ago. This persistent adherence to mystic rites in this scientific epoch seems to me worth taking note of.—A. J.'

To this may be added the following recent extract from a Scotch journal:—

'Hallowe'en was celebrated at Balmoral Castle with unusual ceremony, in the presence of her Majesty, the Princess Beatrice, the ladies and gentlemen of the royal household, and a large gathering of the tenantry. The leading features of the celebration were a torchlight procession, the lighting of large bonfires, and the burning in effigy of witches and warlocks. Upwards of 150 torch-bearers assembled at the castle as dark set in, and separated into two parties, one band proceeding to Invergelder, and the other remaining at Balmoral. The torches were lighted at a quarter before six o'clock, and shortly after the Queen and Princess Beatrice drove to Invergelder, followed by the Balmoral party of torchbearers. The two parties then united and returned in procession to the front of Balmoral Castle, where refreshments were served to all, and dancing was engaged in round a huge bonfire. Suddenly there appeared from the rear of the Castle a grotesque apparition representing a witch with a train of followers dressed like sprites, who danced and gesticulated in all fashions. Then followed a warlock of demoniac shape, who was succeeded by another warlock drawing a car, on which was seated the figure of a witch, surrounded by other figures in the garb of demons. The unearthly visitors having marched several times round the burning pile, the principal figure was taken from the car and tossed into the flames amid the burning of blue lights and a display of crackers and fireworks. The health of her Majesty the Queen was then pledged, and drunk with Highland honours by the assembled hundreds. Dancing was then resumed, and was carried on till a late hour at night.'

The Sixth Council of Constantinople (an. 680), by its sixty-fifth canon, forbids these fires in the following terms:—'Those bonefires that are kindled by certain people before their shops and houses, over which also they use ridiculously to leap, by a certain ancient custom, we command them from henceforth to cease. Whoever, therefore, shall do any such thing, if he be a clergyman, let him be deposed; if he be a layman, let him be excommunicated. For in the Fourth Book of the Kings it is thus written: And Manasseh built an altar to all the host of heaven, in the two courts of the Lord's house, and made his children to pass through the fire.' There is a charming naïveté in this denunciation. It is no longer doubtful that this 'bonefire' over which people leaped came from the same source as that Gehenna from which the Church derived the orthodox theory of hell, as we have already seen. When Shakespeare speaks (Macbeth) of 'the primrose way to the everlasting bonfire,'[8] he is, with his wonted felicity, assigning the flames of hell and the fires of Moloch and Baal their right archæological relation.

In my boyhood I have often leaped over a bonfire in a part of the State of Virginia mainly settled by Scotch families, with whom probably the custom migrated thither. In the superstitions of the negroes of that and other Southern States fire plays a large part, but it is hardly possible now to determine whether they have drifted there from Africa or England. Sometimes there are queer coincidences between their notions and some of the early legends of Britain. Thus, the tradition of the shepherd guided by a distant fire to the entrance of King Arthur's subterranean hall, where a flame fed by no fuel coming through the floor reveals the slumbering monarch and his court, resembles somewhat stories I have heard from negroes of their being led by distant fires to lucky—others say unlucky—or at any rate enchanted spots. A negro belonging to my father told me that once, as he was walking on a country road, he saw a great fire in the distance; he supposed it must be a house on fire, and hastened towards it, meantime much puzzled, since he knew of no house in that direction. As he went on his way he turned into a small wood near which the fire seemed to be, but when he emerged, all he found was a single fire-coal burning in the path. There were no other traces whatever of fire, but just then a large dog leaped past him with a loud bark and disappeared.

In a letter on 'Voudouism in Virginia,' which appeared in the New York Tribune, dated Richmond, September 17, 1875, occurs an account of a class of superstitions generally kept close from the whites, as I have always believed because of their purely African origin. As will be seen, fire represents an important element in the superstitious practices.

'If an ignorant negro is smitten with a disease which he cannot comprehend, he often imagines himself the victim of witchcraft, and having no faith in 'white folks' physic' for such ailments, must apply to one of these quacks. A physician residing near this city was invited by such a one to witness his mode of procedure with a dropsical patient for whom the physician in question had occasionally charitably prescribed. Curiosity led him to attend the seance, having previously informed the quack that since the case was in such hands he relinquished all connection with it. On the coverlet of the bed on which the sick man lay was spread a quantity of bones, feathers, and other trash. The charlatan went through with a series of so-called conjurations, burned feathers, hair, and tiny fragments of wood in a charcoal furnace, and mumbled gibberish past the physician's comprehension. He then proceeded to rip open the pillows and bolsters, and took from them some queer conglomerations of feathers. These he said had caused all the trouble. Sprinkling a whitish powder over them, he burnt them in his furnace. A black offensive smoke was produced, and he announced triumphantly that the evil influence was destroyed and that the patient would surely get well. He died not many days later, believing, in common with all his friends and relatives, that the conjurations of the 'trick doctor' had failed to save him only because resorted to too late.'

The following account of a spell from which his wife was rescued, was given me by a negro in Virginia:—

'The wizard,' to quote the exact words of my informant, 'threw a stick on a chest; the stick bounded like a trapball three times; then he opened the chest, took out something looking like dust or clay, and put it into a cup with water over a fire; then he poured it over a board (after chopping it three times), which he then put up beneath the shingles of the house. Returning to the chest he took a piece of old chain, near the length of my hand, took a hoe and buried the chain near the sill of the door of my wife's house where she would pass; then he went away. I saw my wife coming and called to her not to pass, and to go for a hoe and dig up the place. She did this, and I took up the chain, which burned the ends of all my fingers clean off. The same night the conjuror came back: my wife took two half dollars and a quarter in silver and threw them on the ground before him. The man seemed as if he was shocked, and then offered her his hand, which she refused to take, as I had bid her not to let him touch her. He left and never came to the house again. The spell was broken.'

I am convinced that this is a pure Voudou procedure, and it is interesting in several regards. The introduction of the chain may have been the result of the excitement of the time, for it was during the war when negroes were breaking their chains. The fire and water show how wide-spread in Africa is that double ordeal which, as we have seen, is well known in the kingdom of Dahomey.9 But the mingling of 'something like dust' with the water held in a cup over the fire, is strongly suggestive of the Jewish method of preparing holy water, 'the water of separation.' 'For an unclean person they shall take of the dust of the burnt heifer of purification for sin, and running water shall be put thereto in a vessel.'10 The fiery element of the mixture was in this case imported with the ashes of the red heifer. As for this sacrifice of the red heifer itself11 it was plainly the propitiation of a fiery demon. In Egypt red hair and red animals of all kinds were considered infernal, and all the details of this sacrifice show that the colour of this selected heifer was typical. The heifer was not a usual sacrifice: a red one was obviously by its colour marked for the genii of fire—the terrible Seven—and not to be denied them. Its blood was sprinkled seven times before the tabernacle, and the rest was utterly consumed—including the hide, which is particularly mentioned—and the ashes taken to make the 'water of separation.' Calmet notes, in this connection, that the Apis of India was red-coloured.

The following interesting story of the Chinese Fire-god was supplied to Mr. Dennys12 by Mr. Playfair of H.M. Consulate, to whom it was related in Peking:—

'The temples of the God of Fire are numerous in Peking, as is natural in a city built for the most part of very combustible materials. The idols representing the god are, with one exception, decked with red beards, typifying by their colour the element under his control. The exceptional god has a white beard, and 'thereby hangs a tale.'

'A hundred years ago the Chinese imperial revenue was in much better case than it is now. At that time they had not yet come into collision with Western Powers, and the word 'indemnity' had not, so far, found a place in their vocabulary; internal rebellions were checked as soon as they broke out, and, in one word, Kien Lung was in less embarrassed circumstances than Kwang Hsu; he had more money to spend, and did lay out a good deal in the way of palaces. His favourite building, and one on which no expense had been spared, was the 'Hall of Contemplation.' This hall was of very large dimensions; the rafters and the pillars which supported the roof were of a size such as no trees in China furnish now-a-days. They were not improbably originally sent as an offering by the tributary monarch of some tropical country, such as Burmah or Siam. Two men could barely join hands round the pillars; they were cased in lustrous jet-black lacquer, which, while adding to the beauty of their appearance, was also supposed to make them less liable to combustion. Indeed, every care was taken that no fire should approach the building; no lighted lamp was allowed in the precincts, and to have smoked a pipe inside those walls would have been punished with death. The floor of the hall was of different-coloured marbles, in a mosaic of flowers and mystic Chinese characters, always kept polished like a mirror. The sides of the room were lined with rare books and precious manuscripts. It was, in short, the finest palace in the imperial city, and it was the pride of Kien Lung.

'Alas for the vanity of human wishes! In spite of every precaution, one night a fire broke out, and the Hall of Contemplation was in danger. The Chinese of a century ago were not without fire-engines, and though miserably inefficient as compared with those of our London fire brigade, they were better than nothing, and a hundred of them were soon working round the burning building. The Emperor himself came out to superintend their efforts and encourage them to renewed exertions. But the hall was doomed; a more than earthly power was directing the flames, and mortal efforts were of no avail. For on one of the burning rafters Kien Lung saw the figure of a little old man, with a long white beard, standing in a triumphant attitude. 'It is the God of Fire,' said the Emperor, 'we can do nothing;' so the building was allowed to blaze in peace. Next day Kien Lung appointed a commission to go the round of the Peking temples in order to discover in which of them there was a Fire-god with a white beard, that he might worship him, and appease the offended deity. The search was fruitless; all the Fire-gods had red beards. But the commission had done its work badly; being highly respectable mandarins of genteel families, they had confined their search to such temples as were in good repair and of creditable exterior. Outside the north gate of the imperial city was one old, dilapidated, disreputable shrine which they had overlooked. It had been crumbling away for years, and even the dread figure of the God of Fire, which sat above the altar, had not escaped desecration. 'Time had thinned his flowing locks,' and the beard had fallen away altogether. One day some water-carriers who frequented the locality thought, either in charity or by way of a joke, that the face would look the better for a new beard. So they unravelled some cord, and with the frayed-out hemp adorned the beardless chin. An official passing the temple one day peeped in out of curiosity, and saw the hempen beard. 'Just the thing the Emperor was inquiring about,' said he to himself, and he took the news to the palace without delay. Next day there was a state visit to the dilapidated temple, and Kien Lung made obeisance and vowed a vow. 'O Fire-god,' said he, 'thou hast been wroth with me in that I have built me palaces, and left thy shrine unhonoured and in ruins. Here do I vow to build thee a temple surpassed by none other of the Fire-gods in Peking; but I shall expect thee in future not to meddle with my palaces.'

'The Emperor was as good as his word. The new temple is on the site of the old one, and the Fire-god has a flowing beard of fine white hair.'

In the San Francisco Bulletin, I recently read a description of the celebration by the Chinese in that city of their Feast for the Dead, in which there are some significant features. The chief attention was paid, says the reporter, to a figure 'representing what answers in their theology to our devil, and whom they evidently think it necessary to propitiate before proceeding with their worship over individual graves.' This figure is on the west side of their temple; before and around it candles and joss-sticks were kept burning. On the east side was the better-looking figure, to which they paid comparatively little attention.

It was of course but natural that the demons of fire should gradually be dispelled from that element in its normal aspects, as its uses became more important through human invention, and its evil possibilities were mastered. Such demons became gradually located in the region of especially dangerous fires, as volcanoes and boiling springs. The Titan whom the ancients believed struggling beneath Ætna remained there as the Devil in the christian age. St. Agatha is said to have prevented his vomiting fire for a century by her prayers. St. Philip ascended the same mountain, and with book and candle pronounced a prayer of exorcism, at which three devils came out like fiery flying stones, crying, 'Woe is us! we are still hunted by Peter through Philip the Elder!' The volcanoes originated the belief that hell is at the earth's centre, and their busy Vulcans of classic ages have been easily transformed into sulphurous lords of the christian Hell. Such is the mediæval Haborym, demon of arson, with his three heads—man, cat, and serpent—who rides through the air mounted on a serpent, and bears in his hand a flaming torch. The astrologers assigned him command of twenty-six legions of demons in hell, and the superstitious often saw him laughing on the roofs of burning houses.13 But still more dignified is Raum, who commands thirty legions, and who destroys villages; hence, also, concerned in the destructions of war, he became the demon who awards dignities; and although this made his usual form of apparition on the right bank of the Rhine that of the Odinistic raven, on the left bank he may be detected in the little red man who was reported as the familiar of Napoleon I. during his career.

Among Mr. Gill's South Pacific myths is one of a Prometheus, Maui, who by assistance of a red pigeon gets from the subterranean fire-demon the secret of producing fire (by rubbing sticks), the demon (Mauike) being then consumed with his realm, and fire being brought to the upper world to remain the friend of man. In Vedic legend, when the world was enveloped in darkness, the gods prayed to Agni, who suddenly burst out as Tvashtri—pure fire, the Vedic Vulcan—to the dismay of the universe. In Eddaic sagas, Loki was deemed the most voracious of beings until defeated in an eating match with Logi (devouring fire).

Survivals of belief in the fiery nature of demons are very numerous. Thus it is a very common belief that the Devil cannot touch or cross water, and may therefore be escaped by leaping a stream. This has sometimes been supposed to have something to do with the purifying character of water; but there are many instances in Christian folklore where the Devil is shown quite independent of even holy water if it is not sprinkled on him or does not wet his feet. Thus in the Norfolk legend concerning St. Godric, the Devil is said to have thrown the vessel with its holy water at the saint's head out of anger at his singing a canticle which the Virgin taught him. But when the Devil attacked him in various ferocious animal shapes, St. Godric escaped by running into the Wear, where he sometimes stood all night in water up to his neck.

The Kobolds get the red jackets they are said to wear from their fiery nature. Originally the lar familiaris of Germany, the Kobold became of many varieties; but in one line he has been developed from the house-spirit, whose good or evil temper was recognised in the comforts or dangers of fire, to a special Stone-demon. The hell-dog in Faust's room takes refuge from the spell of 'Solomon's Key' behind the stone, and is there transformed to human shape. The German maidens read many pretty oracles in the behaviour of the fire, and the like in that of its fellow Wahrsager the house-dog. It is indeed a widespread notion that imps and witches lurk about the fireside, obviously in cat and dog, and ride through the air on implements that usually stand about the fire,—shovel, tongs, or broom. In Paris it was formerly the custom to throw twenty-four cats into the fire on St. John's night, the animals being, according to M. De Plancy, emblems of the devil. So was replaced the holocaust of human witches, until at last civilisation rang out its curfew for all such fires as that.

Notes

1 Du Perron, 'Vie de Zoroastre.'
2 The principle similia similibus curantur is a very ancient one; but though it may have originated in a euphemistic or propitiatory aim, the homoeopathist may claim that it could hardly have lived unless it had been found to have some practical advantages.

3 Sonnerat's 'Travels,' ii. 38.
4 Deutsch, 'Literary Remains,' p. 178.
5 Isa. lvii. 5; Ezek. xvi. 20; Jer. xix. 5.
6 The 'Jewish World.'
7 'Observations on Popular Antiquities,' etc., by John Brand. With the additions of Sir Henry Ellis. An entirely new and revised edition. Chatto & Windus, 1877. See especially the chapter on 'Summer Solstice,' p. 165.
8 'Pyra, a bonefire, wherein men's bodyes were burned.'—Cooper's Thesaurus. Probably from Fr. bon; Wedgewood gives Dan. baun, beacon.
9 See Chapter i. Compare Numbers xxxi. 23.
10 Numbers xix. 17.
11 Ibid. xix. 2, seq.
12 'Folklore of China,' p. 121.
13 In Russia the pigeon, from being anciently consecrated to the thunder god, has become emblem of the Holy Ghost, or celestial fire, and as such the foe of earthly fire. Pigeons are trusted as insurers against fire, and the flight of one through a house is regarded as a kindly warning of conflagration.

Chapter III - Cold

Descent of Ishtar into Hades—Bardism—Baldur—Hercules—Christ—Survivals of the Frost Giant in Slavonic and other countries—The Clavie—The Frozen Hell—The Northern abode of demons—North side of churches.

Even across immemorial generations it is impossible to read without emotion the legend of the Descent of Ishtar into Hades.1 Through seven gates the goddess of Love passes in search of her beloved, and at each some of her ornaments and clothing are removed by the dread guardian. Ishtar enters naked into the presence of the Queen of Death. But gods, men, and herds languish in her absence, and the wonder-working Hea, the Saviour, so charms the Infernal Queen, that she bids the Judge of her realm, Annunak, absolve Ishtar from his golden throne.

'He poured out for Ishtar the waters of life and let her go.
Then the first gate let her forth, and restored to her the first garment of her body.
The second gate let her forth, and restored to her the diamonds of her hands and feet.
The third gate let her forth, and restored to her the central girdle of her waist.
The fourth gate let her forth, and restored to her the small lovely gems of her forehead.
The fifth gate let her forth, and restored to her the precious stones of her head.
The sixth gate let her forth, and restored to her the earrings of her ears.
The seventh gate let her forth, and restored to her the great crown on her head.'

This old miracle-play of Nature—the return of summer flower by flower—is deciphered from an ancient Assyrian tablet in a town within only a few hours of another, where a circle of worshippers repeat the same at every solstice! Myfyr Morganwg, the Arch-Druid, adores still Hea by name as his Saviour, and at the winter solstice assembles his brethren to celebrate his coming to bruise the head of the Serpent of Hades (Annwn, nearly the same as in the tablet), that seedtime and harvest shall not fail.2

Is this a survival? No doubt; but there is no cult in the world which, if 'scratched,' as the proverb says, will not reveal beneath it the same conception. However it may be spiritualised, every 'plan of salvation' is cast in the mould of Winter conquered by the Sun, the Descent of Love to the Under World, the delivery of the imprisoned germs of Life.

It is very instructive to compare with the myth of Ishtar that of Hermödr, seeking the release of Baldur the Beautiful from Helheim.

The deadly powers of Winter are represented in the Eddaic account of the death of Baldur, soft summer Light, the Norse Baal. His blind brother Hödr is Darkness; the demon who directed his arrow is Loki, subterranean fire; the arrow itself is of mistletoe, which, fostered by Winter, owes no duty to Baldur; and the realm to which he is borne is that of Hel, the frozen zone. Hermödr, having arrived, assured Hel that the gods were in despair for the loss of Baldur. The Queen replied that it should now be tried whether Baldur was so beloved. 'If, therefore, all things in the world, both living and lifeless, weep for him, he shall return to the Æsir.' In the end all wept but the old hag Thokk (Darkness), who from her cavern sang—

Thokk will wail

With dry eyes
Baldur's bale-fire.
Nought quick or dead
For Carl's son care I.
Let Hel hold her own.

So Baldur remained in Helheim. The myth very closely resembles that of Ishtar's Descent. In similar accent the messenger of the Southern gods weeps and lacerates himself as he relates the grief of the upper world, and all men and animals 'since the time that mother Ishtar descended into Hades.' But in the latter the messenger is successful, in the North he is unsuccessful. In the corresponding myths of warm and sunny climes the effort at release is more or less successful, in proportion to the extent of winter. In Adonis released from Hades for four months every year, and another four if he chose to abandon Persephone for Aphrodite, we have a reflection of a variable year. That, and the similar myth of Persephone, varied in the time specified for their passing in the upper and under worlds, probably in accordance with the climatic averages of the regions in which they were told. But in the tropics it was easy to believe the release complete, as in the myth of Ishtar. In Mangaian myths the hero, Maui, escapes from a nether world of fire, aided by a red pigeon. When this contest between Winter's Death and Spring's Life became humanised, it was as Hercules vanquishing Death and completely releasing Alcestis. When it became spiritualised it was as Christ conquering Death and Hell, and releasing the spirits from prison. The wintry desolation had to be artificially imitated in a forty days' fast and Lent, closing with a thrust from the spear (the mistletoe arrow) amid darkness (blind Hödr). But the myth of a swift resurrection had to be artificially preserved in the far North. The legend of a full triumph over Death and Hell could never have originated among our Norse ancestors. Their only story resembling it, that of Iduna, related how her recovery from the Giants brought back health to the gods, not men. But it was from the South that men had to hear tidings of a rescue for the earth and man.

We cannot realise now what glad tidings were they which told this new gospel to peoples sitting in regions of ice and gloom, after it had been imposed on them against their reluctant fears. In manifold forms the old combat was renewed in their festivals, and peoples who had long been prostrate and helpless before the terrible powers of nature were never weary of the Southern fables of heroic triumphs over them, long interpreted in the simple physical sense.

The great Demon of the Northern World is still Winter, and the hereditary hatred of him is such that he is still cursed, scourged, killed, and buried or drowned under various names and disguises. In every Slavonic country, says Mr. Ralston, there are to be found, about carnival time, traces of ancient rites, intended to typify the death of Winter and the birth of Spring or Summer. In Poland a puppet made of hemp or straw is flung into a pond or swamp with the words, 'The Devil take thee!' Then the participators in the deed scamper home, and if one of them stumbles and falls it is believed he will die within the year. In Upper Lausatia a similar figure is fastened on a pole to be pelted, then taken to the village boundary and thrown across it or cast into the water, its bearers returning with green boughs. Sometimes the figure is shrouded in white, representing snow, and bears in its hands a broom (the sweeping storm) and a sickle (the fatal reaper). In Russia the 'Straw Mujik' is burned, and also in Bulgaria; in the latter the bonfire is accompanied by the firing of guns, and by dances and songs to Lado, goddess of Spring. This reminiscence of Leto, on whose account Apollo slew the Python, is rendered yet more striking by the week of archery which accompanies it, recalling the sunbeam darts of the god. In Spain and Italy the demon puppet is scourged under the name of Judas, as indeed is the case in the annual Good Friday performance of Portuguese sailors in the London Docks. Mr. Tylor found in Mexico a similar custom, the Judas being a regular horned and hoofed devil. In Scotland the pre-christian accessories of a corresponding custom are more pronounced both in the time selected (the last day of the year, old style) and the place. 'The Clavie,' as the custom of burning the puppet of Winter is mysteriously called, occurred on January 12 of this year (1878) at Burghead, a fishing village near Forres, where stands an old Roman altar locally named the 'Douro.' A tar-barrel was set on fire and carried by a fisherman round the town, while the people shouted and hallooed. (If the man who carries the barrel falls it is an evil omen.) The lighted barrel, having gone round the town, was carried to the top of the hill and placed on the Douro. More fuel was added. The sparks as they fly upwards are supposed to be witches and evil spirits leaving the town; the people therefore shout at and curse them as they disappear in vacancy. When the burning tar-barrel falls in pieces, the fishwomen rush in and endeavour to get a lighted bit of wood from its remains; with this light the fire on the cottage hearth is at once kindled, and it is considered lucky to keep this flame alive all the rest of the year. The charcoal of the Clavie is collected and put in bits up the chimney to prevent the witches and evil spirits coming into the house. The Douro is covered with a thick layer of tar from the fires that are annually lighted upon it. Close to it is a very ancient Roman well. It is an instance of the irony of etymology that the word 'Hell' means a place of fireless darkness. Nor is the fact that the name of the Scandinavian demoness Hel, phonetically corresponding with Kali, 'the Black One' (Goth. Halja), whose abode was an icy hole, has her name preserved as a place of fiery torment, without significance. In regions where cold was known to an uncomfortable extent as well as heat, we usually find it represented in the ideas of future punishment. The realm called Hades, meaning just the same as Hell, suggests cold. Tertullian and Jerome say that Christ's own phrases 'outer darkness' and the 'gnashing (chattering) of teeth' suggest a place of extreme cold alternating with the excessive heat. Traces of similar speculations are found with the Rabbins. Thus Rabbi Joseph says Gehenna had both water and fire. Noah saw the angel of death approaching and hid from him twelve months. Why twelve? Because (explains Rabbi Jehuda) such is the trial of sinners,—six in water, six in fire. Dante (following Virgil) has frigid as well as burning hells; and the idea was refined by some scholiasts to a statement which would seem to make the alternations of future punishment amount to a severe ague and fever. Milton (Paradise Lost, ii.) has blended the rabbinical notions with those of Virgil (Æn. vi.) in his terrible picture of the frozen continent, where

The parching air
Burns frore, and cold performs th' effect of fire:
Thither by harpy-footed Furies haled
At certain revolutions all the damn'd
Are brought; and feel by turns the bitter change
Of fierce extremes, extremes by change more fierce,
From beds of raging fire to starve in ice
Their soft etherial warmth, and there to pine
Immovable, infix'd, and frozen round.

With which may be compared Shakespeare's lines in 'Measure for Measure'—

The de-lighted spirit
To bathe in fiery floods, or to reside
In thrilling region of thick-ribbed ice.

In Thibet hell is believed to have sixteen circles, eight burning, eight frozen, which M. Delepierre attributes to the rapid changes of their climate between the extremes of heat and cold.3 Plutarch, relating the vision of Thespesius in Hades, speaks of the frozen region there. Denys le Chartreux (De Pœnis Inferni) says the severest of infernal torments is freezing. In the 'Kalendar of Shepherds' (1506) a legend runs:—'Lazarus sayde, 'I sawe a flode of frosone yce in the whiche envyous men and women were plonged unto the navyll, and then sodynly came a colde wynde ryght great that blewe and dyd depe downe all the envyous into the colde water that nothynge was seen of them.' Such, too, is Persian Ardá Viráf's vision.

The Demon of Cold has a habitat, naturally, in every Northern region. He is the Ke-mung of China, who—man-shaped, dragon-headed—haunts the Chang river, and causes rain-storms.4 In Greenland it is Erleursortok, who suffers perpetual agues, and leaps on souls at death to satisfy his hunger. The Chenoos (demons) of the Mimacs of Nova Scotia present certain features of the race-demons, but are fearfully cold. The Chenoo weapon is a dragon's horn, his yell is fatal to the hearer, his heart is a block of ice. This heart must be destroyed if the demon is to be slain, but it can only be done by melting in the fire: the chief precaution required is that one is not drowned in the flood so caused. The icy demon survived long in Scotland. Sir James Melville, in his 'Memoirs,' says 'the spirit or devil that helped the Scottish witches to raise a storm in the sea of Norway was cold as ice and his body hard as iron; his face was terrible, his nose like the beak of an eagle, great burning eyes, his hands and legs hairy, with claws on his nails like a griffin.' Dr. Fian was burnt for raising this demon to oppose James I. on his stormy passage from Denmark.

This type of demon haunted people's minds in Scandinavia, where, though traditions of a flame demon (Loki) and the end of the world by fire were imported, the popular belief seems to have been mainly occupied with Frost giants, and the formidable Oegir, god of the bleak sea east winds, preserved in our word awe (Anglo-Saxon ege), and more directly in the name of our familiar demon, the Ogre, so often slain in the child's Gladsheim. Loki (fire) was, indeed, speedily relegated by the Æsir (gods) to a hidden subterranean realm, where his existence could only be known by the earthquakes, geysers, and Hecla eruptions which he occasioned. Yet he was to come forth at Ragnarök, the Twilight of the Gods. We can see a singular blending of tropical and frigid zones—the one traditional, the other native—in the Prose Edda. Thus:— 'What will remain,' said Gangler, 'after heaven and earth and the whole universe shall be consumed, and after all the gods and the homes of Valhalla and all mankind shall have perished?' 'There will be many abodes,' replied Thridi, 'some good, some bad. The best place of all to be in will be Gimil, in heaven; and all who delight in quaffing good drink will find a great store in the hall called Brimir, which is also in heaven in the region Okolni. There is also a fair hall of ruddy gold, (for) Sindri, which stands on the mountains of Nida. In those halls righteous and well-minded men shall abide. In Ná-strönd there is a vast and direful structure with doors that face the north. It is formed entirely of the backs of serpents, wattled together like wicker-work. But the serpents' heads are turned towards the inside of the hall, and continually vomit forth floods of venom, in which wade all those who commit murder or who forswear themselves. As it is said in the Völuspá:—

She saw a hall
Far from the sun
In Náströnd standing,
Northward the doors look,
And venom-drops
Fall in through loopholes.
Formed is that hall
Of wreathed serpents.
There saw she wade
Through heavy streams
Men forsworn
And murderers.

These names for the heavenly regions and their occupants indicate sunshine and fire. Gimil means fire (gímr): Brimir (brími, flame), the giant, and Sindri (cinder), the dwarf, jeweller of the gods, are raised to halls of gold. Nothing is said of a garden, or walking therein 'in the cool of the day.' On the other hand, Ná-strönd means Strand of the Dead, in that region whose 'doors face the north, far from the sun,' we behold an inferno of extreme cold. Christianity has not availed to give the Icelanders any demonic name suggestive of fire. They speak of 'Skratti' (the roarer, perhaps our Old Scratch), and 'Kolski' (the coal black one), but promise nothing so luminous and comfortable as fire or fire-fiend to the evil-doer.
In the great Epic of the Nibelungen Lied we have probably the shape in which the Northman's dream of Paradise finally cohered,—a Rose-garden in the South, guarded by a huge Worm (water-snake, or glittering glacial sea intervening), whose glowing charms, with Beauty (Chriemhild) for their queen, could be won only by a brave dragon-slaying Siegfried. In passing by the pretty lakeside home of Richard Wagner, on my way to witness the Ammergau version of another dragon-binding and paradise-regaining legend, I noted that the old name of the (Starnberg) lake was Wurmsee, from the dragon that once haunted it, while from the composer's window might be seen its 'Isle of Roses,' which the dragon guarded. Since then the myth of many forms has had its musical apotheosis at Bayreuth under his wand.
England, partly perhaps on account of its harsh climate, once had the reputation of being the chief abode of demons. A demoness leaving her lover on the Continent says, 'My mother is calling me in England.'5 But England assigned them still higher latitudes; in christianising Ireland, Iona, and other islands far north, it was preliminary to expel the demons. 'The Clavie,' the 'Deis-iuil' of Lewis and other Hebrides islands—fire carried round cattle to defend them from demons, and around mothers not yet churched, to keep the babes from being 'changed'—show that the expulsion still goes on, though in such regions Norse and christian notions have become so jumbled that it is 'fighting the devil with fire.' So in the Havamal men are warned to invoke 'fire for distempers;' and Gudrun sings—

Raise, ye Jarls, an oaken pile;
Let it under heaven the lightest be.
May it burn a breast full of woes!
The fire round my heart its sorrows melt.

The last line is in contrast with the Hindu saying, 'the flame of her husband's pyre cools the widow's breast.'
The characters of the Northern Heaven and Hell survive in the English custom of burying the dead on the southern side of a church. How widely this usage prevailed in Brand's time may be seen by reference to his chapter on churchyards. The north side of the graveyard was set apart for unbaptized infants and executed criminals, and it was permitted the people to dance or play tennis in that part. Dr. Lee says that in the churchyard at Morwenstow the southern portion only contains graves, the north part being untenanted; as the Cornish believe (following old traditions) that the north is the region of demons. In some parishes of Cornwall when a baptism occurs the north door of the nave opposite the font is thrown open, so that the devil cast out may retire to his own region, the north.6 This accords with the saying in Martin's 'Month's Mind'—ab aquilone omne malum.
Indeed, it is not improbable that the fact noted by White, in his 'History of Selborne,' that 'the usual approach to most country churches is by the south,' indicated a belief that the sacred edifice should turn its back on the region of demons. It is a singular instance of survival which has brought about the fact that people who listen devoutly to sermons describing the fiery character of Satan and his abode should surround the very churches in which those sermons are heard with evidences of their lingering faith that the devil belongs to the region of ice, and that their dead must be buried in the direction of the happy abodes of Brimir and Sindri,—Fire and Cinders!
M. François Lenormant has written an extremely instructive chapter in comparison of the Accadian and the Finnish mythologies. He there shows that they are as one and the same tree, adapted to antagonistic climates.7 With similar triad, runes, charms, and even names in some cases, their regard for the fire worshipped by both varies in a way that seems at

first glance somewhat anomalous. The Accadians in their fire-worship exhausted the resources of praise in ascription of glory and power to the flames; the Finns in their cold home celebrated the fire festival at the winter solstice, uttered invocations over the fire, and the mother of the family, with her domestic libation, said: 'Always rise so high, O my flame, but burn not larger nor more ardent!' This diminution of enthusiasm in the Northern fire-worshipper, as compared with the Southern, may only be the result of euphemism in the latter; or perhaps while the formidable character of the fire-god among the primitive Assyrians is indicated in the utter prostration before him characteristic of their litanies and invocations, in the case of the Finns the perpetual presence of the more potent cold led to the less excessive adoration. These ventured to recognise the faults of fire.

The true nature of this anomaly becomes visible when we consider that the great demon, dreaded by the two countries drawing their cult from a common source, represented the excess of the power most dreaded. The demon in each case was a wind; among the Finns the north wind, among the Accadians the south-west (the most fiery) wind. The Finnish demon was Hiisi, speeding on his pale horse through the air, with a terrible train of monster dogs, cats, furies, scattering pain, disease, and death.[8] The Accadian demon, of which the bronze image is in the Louvre, is the body of a dog, erect on eagle's feet, its arms pointed with lion's paws; it has the tail of a scorpion and the head of a skeleton, half stripped of flesh, preserving the eyes, and mounted with the horns of a goat. It has four outspread wings. On the back of this ingeniously horrible image is an inscription in the Accadian language, apprising us that it is the demon of the south-west wind, made to be placed at the door or window, to avert its hostile action.

As we observe such figures as these on the one hand, and on the other the fair beings imagined to be antagonistic to them; as we note in runes and incantations how intensely the ancients felt themselves to be surrounded by these good and evil powers, and, reading nature so, learned to see in the seasons successively conquering and conquered by each other, and alternation of longer days and longer nights, the changing fortunes of a never-ending battle; we may better realise the meaning of solstitial festivals, the customs that gathered around Yuletide and New Year, and the manifold survivals from them which annually masquerade in Christian costume and names. To our sun-worshipping ancestor the new year meant the first faint advantage of the warmer time over winter, as nearly as he could fix it. The hovering of day between superiority of light and darkness is now named after doubting Thomas. At Yuletide the dawning victory of the sun is seen as a holy infant in a manger amid beasts of the stall. The old nature-worship has bequeathed to christian belief a close-fitting mantle. But the old idea of a war between the wintry and the warm powers still haunts the period of the New Year; and the twelve days and nights, once believed to be the period of a fiercely-contested battle between good and evil demons, are still regarded by many as a period for especial watchfulness and prayer. New Year's Eve, in the north of England still 'Hogmanay,'—probably O. N. höku-nött, midwinter-night, when the sacrifices of Thor were prepared,— formerly had many observances which reflected the belief that good and evil ghosts were contending for every man and woman: the air was believed to be swarming with them, and watch must be kept to see that the protecting fire did not go out in any household; that no strange man, woman, or animal approached,—possibly a demon in disguise. Sacred plants were set in doors and windows to prevent the entrance of any malevolent being from the multitudes filling the air. John Wesley, whose noble heart was allied with a mind strangely open to stories of hobgoblins, led the way of churches and sects back into this ancient atmosphere. Nevertheless, the rationalism of the age has influenced St. Wesley's Feast— Watchnight. It can hardly recognise its brother in the Boar's Head Banquet of Queen's College, Oxford, which celebrated victory over tusky winter, the decapitated demon whose bristles were once icicles fallen beneath the sylvan spirits of holly and rosemary. Yet what the Watchnight really signifies in the antiquarian sense is just that old culminating combat between the powers of fire and frost, once believed to determine human fates. In White Russia, on New Year's Day, when the annual elemental battle has been decided, the killed and wounded on one hand, and the fortunate on the other, are told by carrying from house to house the rich and the poor Kolyadas. These are two children, one dressed in fine attire, and crowned with a wreath of full ears of grain, the other ragged, and wearing a wreath of threshed straw. These having been closely covered, each householder is called in, and chooses one. If his choice chances upon the 'poor Kolyada,' the attending chorus chant a mournful strain, in which he is warned to expect a bad harvest, poverty, and perhaps death; if he selects the 'rich Kolyada,' a cheerful song is sung promising him harvest, health, and wealth.

The natives of certain districts of Dardistan assign political and social significance to their Feast of Fire, which is celebrated in the month preceding winter, at new moon, just after their meat provision for the season is laid in to dry. Their legend is, that it was then their national hero slew their ancient tyrant and introduced good government. This legend, related elsewhere, is of a tyrant slain through the discovery that his heart was made of snow. He was slain by the warmth of torches. In the celebrations all the men of the villages go forth with torches, which they swing round their heads, and throw in the direction of Ghilgit, where the snow-hearted tyrant so long held his castle. When the husbands return home from their torch-throwing a little drama is rehearsed. The wives refuse them entrance till they have entreated, recounting the benefits they have brought them; after admission the husband affects sulkiness, and must be brought round with caresses to join in the banquet. The wife leads him forward with this song:—'Thou hast made me glad, thou favourite of the Rajah! Thou hast rejoiced me, oh bold horseman! I am pleased with thee who so well usest the gun and sword! Thou hast delighted me, oh thou invested with a mantle of honours! Oh great happiness, I will buy it by giving pleasure's price! Oh thou nourishment to us, heap of corn, store of ghee—delighted will I buy it all by giving pleasure's price!'

Notes

1 Tablet K 162 in Brit. Mus. Tr. by H. F. Talbot in 'Records of the Past.'
2 The Western Mail, March 12, 1874, contains a remarkable letter by the Arch-Druid, in which he maintains that 'Jesus' is a derivation from Hea or Hu, Light, and the Christian system a corruption of Bardism.
3 'L'Enfer,' p. 5.
4 Dennys' 'Folklore of China,' p. 98.
5 Procopius, 'De Bello Gothico,' iv. 20.
6 'Memorials of the Rev. R. S. Hawkes'.
7 'La Magie chez les Chaldéens,' iii.
8 Lönnrot, 'Abhandlung über die Magische Medicin der Finnen.'

Chapter IV - Elements

A Scottish Munasa—Rudra—Siva's lightning eye—The flaming sword—Limping demons—Demons of the storm—Helios, Elias, Perun—Thor arrows—The Bob-tailed Dragon—Whirlwind—Japanese thunder god—Christian survivals—Jinni—Inundations—Noah—Nik, Nicholas, Old Nick—Nixies—Hydras—Demons of the Danube—Tides—Survivals in Russia and England.

During some recent years curious advertisements have appeared in a journal of Edinburgh, calling for pious persons to occupy certain hours of the night with holy exercises. It would appear that they refer to a band of prayerful persons who provide that there shall be an unbroken round of prayers during every moment of the day and night. Their theory is, that it is the usual cessation of christian prayers at night which causes so many disasters. The devils being then less restrained, raise storms and all elemental perils. The praying circle, which hopes to bind these demons by an uninterrupted chain of prayers, originated, as I am informed, in the pious enthusiasm of a lady whose kindly solicitude in some pre-existent sister was no doubt personified in the Hindu Munasa, who, while all gods slept, sat in the shape of a serpent on a branch of Euphorbia to preserve mankind from the venom of snakes. It is to be feared, however, that it is hardly the wisdom of the serpent which is on prayerful watch at Edinburgh, but rather a vigilance of that perilous kind which was exercised by 'Meggie o' the Shore,' anno 1785, as related by Hugh Miller.1 On a boisterous night, when two young girls had taken refuge in her cottage, they all heard about midnight cries of distress mingling with the roar of the sea, 'Raise the window curtain and look out,' said Meggie. The terrified girls did so, and said, 'There is a bright light in the middle of the Bay of Udall. It hangs over the water about the height of a ship's mast, and we can see something below it like a boat riding at anchor, with the white sea raging around her.' 'Now drop the curtain,' said Meggie; 'I am no stranger, my lasses, to sights and noises like these—sights and noises of another world; but I have been taught that God is nearer to me than any spirit can be; and so have learned not to be afraid.' Afterwards it is not wonderful that a Cromarty yawl was discovered to have foundered, and all on board to have been drowned; though Meggie's neighbours seemed to have preserved the legend after her faith, and made the scene described a premonition of what actually occurred. It was in a region where mariners when becalmed invoke the wind by whistling; and both the whistling and the praying, though their prospects in the future may be slender, have had a long career in the past.

In the 'Rig-Veda' there is a remarkable hymn to Rudra (the Roarer), which may be properly quoted here:—

1. Sire of the storm gods, let thy favour extend to us; shut us not out from the sight of the sun; may our hero be successful in the onslaught. O Rudra, may we wax mighty in our offspring.
2. Through the assuaging remedies conferred by thee, O Rudra, may we reach a hundred winters; drive away far from us hatred, distress, and all-pervading diseases.
3. Thou, O Rudra, art the most excellent of beings in glory, the strongest of the strong, O wielder of the bolt; bear us safely through evil to the further shore; ward off all the assaults of sin.
4. May we not provoke thee to anger, O Rudra, by our adorations, neither through faultiness in praises, nor through wantonness in invocations; lift up our heroes by thy remedies; thou art, I hear, the chief physician among physicians.
5. May I propitiate with hymns this Rudra who is worshipped with invocations and oblations; may the tender-hearted, easily-entreated, tawny-haired, beautiful-chinned god not deliver us up to the plotter of evil [literally, to the mind meditating 'I kill'].

6. The bounteous giver, escorted by the storm-gods, hath gladdened me, his suppliant, with most invigorating food; as one distressed by heat seeketh the shade, may I, free from harm, find shelter in the good-will of Rudra.

7. Where, O Rudra, is that gracious hand of thine, which is healing and comforting? Do thou, removing the evil which cometh from the gods, O bounteous giver, have mercy upon me.

8. To the tawny, the fair-complexioned dispenser of bounties, I send forth a great and beautiful song of praise; adore the radiant god with prostrations; we hymn the illustrious name of Rudra.

9. Sturdy-limbed, many-shaped, fierce, tawny, he hath decked himself with brilliant ornaments of gold; truly strength is inseparable from Rudra, the sovereign of this vast world.

10. Worthy of worship, thou bearest the arrows and the bow; worthy of worship, thou wearest a resplendent necklace of many forms; worthy of worship, thou rulest over this immense universe; there is none, O Rudra, mightier than thou.

11. Celebrate the renowned and ever-youthful god who is seated on a chariot, who is, like a wild beast, terrible, fierce, and destructive; have mercy upon the singer, O Rudra, when thou art praised; may thy hosts strike down another than us.

12. As a boy saluteth his father who approacheth and speaketh to him, so, O Rudra, I greet thee, the giver of much, the lord of the good; grant us remedies when thou art praised.

13. Your remedies, O storm-gods, which are pure and helping, O bounteous givers, which are joy-conferring, which our father Manu chose, these and the blessing and succour of Rudra I crave.

14. May the dart of Rudra be turned aside from us, may the great malevolence of the flaming-god be averted; unbend thy strong bow from those who are liberal with their wealth; O generous god, have mercy upon our offspring and our posterity (i.e., our children and children's children).

15. Thus, O tawny Rudra, wise giver of gifts, listen to our cry, give heed to us here, that thou mayest not be angry with us, O god, nor slay us; may we, rich in heroic sons, utter great praise at the sacrifice.2

In other hymns the malevolent character of Rudra is made still more prominent:—

7. Slay not our strong man nor our little child, neither him who is growing nor him who is grown, neither our father nor our mother; hurt not, O Rudra, our dear selves.

8. Harm us not in our children and children's children, nor in our men, nor in our kine, nor in our horses. Smite not our heroes in thy wrath; we wait upon thee perpetually with offerings.3

In this hymn (verse 1) Rudra is described as 'having braided hair;' and in the 'Yajur-veda' and the 'Atharva-veda' other attributes of Siva are ascribed to him, such as the epithet nîla-grîva, or blue-necked. In the 'Rig-veda' Siva occurs frequently as an epithet, and means auspicious. It was used as a euphemistic epithet to appease Rudra, the lord of tempests; and finally, the epithet developed into a distinct god.

The parentage of Siva is further indicated in the legends that his glance destroyed the head of the youthful deity Ganesa, who now wears the elephant head, with which it was replaced; and that the gods persuaded him to keep his eyes perpetually winking (like sheet-lightning), lest his concentrated look (the thunderbolt) should reduce the universe to ashes. With the latter legend the gaze of the evil eye in India might naturally be associated, though in the majority of countries this was rather associated with the malign influences ascribed to certain planets, especially Saturn; the charms against the evil eye being marked over with zodiacal signs. The very myth of Siva's eye survives in the Russian demon Magarko ('Winker') and the Servian Vii, whose glance is said to have power to reduce men, and even cities, to ashes.

The terrible Rudra is represented in a vast number of beliefs, some of them perhaps survivals; in the rough sea and east-wind demon Oegir of the northern world, and Typhon in the south; and in Luther's faith that 'devils do house in the dense black clouds, and send storms, hail, thunder and lightning, and poison the air with their infernal stench,' a doctrine which Burton, the Anatomist of Melancholy, too, maintained against the meteorologists of his time.

Among the ancient Aryans lightning seems to have been the supreme type of divine destructiveness. Rudra's dart, Siva's eye, reappear with the Singhalese prince of demons Wessamonny, described as wielding a golden sword, which, when he is angry, flies out of his hand, to which it spontaneously returns, after cutting off a thousand heads.4 A wonderful spear was borne by Odin, and was possibly the original Excalibur. The four-faced Sviatevit of Russia, whose mantle has fallen to St. George, whose statue was found at Zbrucz in 1851, bore a horn of wine (rain) and a sword (lightning).

In Greece similar swords were wielded by Zeus, and also by the god of war. Through Zeus and Ares, the original wielders of the lightning—Indra and Siva—became types of many gods and semi-divine heroes. The evil eye of Siva glared from the forehead of the Cyclopes, forgers of thunderbolts; and the saving disc of Indra flashed in the swords and arrows of famous dragon-slayers—Perseus, Pegasus, Hercules, and St. George. The same sword defended the Tree of Life in Eden, and was borne in the hand of Death on the Pale Horse (a white horse was sacrificed to Sviatevit in Russia within christian times). And, finally, we have the wonderful sword which obeys the command 'Heads off!' delighting all nurseries by the service it does to the King of the Golden Mountain.

'I beheld Satan as lightning falling out of heaven.' To the Greeks this falling of rebellious deities out of heaven accounted, as we have seen explained, for their lameness. But a universal phenomenon can alone account for the many demons with crooked or crippled legs (like 'Diable Boiteux')5 all around the world. The Namaquas of South Africa have a 'deity' whose occupation it is to cause pain and death; his name is Tsui'knap, that is 'wounded knee.'6 Livingstone says of the Bakwains, another people of South Africa, 'It is curious that in all their pretended dreams or visions of their god he has always a crooked leg, like the Egyptian Thau.'7 In Mainas, South America, they believe in a treacherous demon, Uchuella-chaqui, or Lame-foot, who in dark forests puts on a friendly shape to lure Indians to destruction; but the huntsmen say they can never be deceived if they examine this demon's foot-track, because of the unequal size of the two feet.8 The native Australians believed in a demon named Biam; he is black and deformed in his lower extremities; they attributed to him many of their songs and dances, but also a sort of small-pox to which they were liable.9 We have no evidence that these superstitions migrated from a common centre; and there can be little doubt that many of these crooked legs are traceable to the crooked lightning.10 At the same time this is by no means inconsistent with what has been already said of the fall of Titans and angels from heaven as often accounting for their lameness in popular myths. But in such details it is hard to reach certainty, since so many of the facts bear a suspicious resemblance to each other. A wild boar with 'distorted legs' attacked St. Godric, and the temptation is strong to generalise on the story, but the legs probably mean only to certify that it was the devil.

Dr. Schliemann has unearthed among his other treasures the remarkable fact that a temple of Helios (the sun) once stood near the site of the present Church of Elias, at Mycenæ, which has from time immemorial been the place to which people repair to pray for rain.11 When the storm-breeding Sun was succeeded by the Prophet whose prayer evoked the cloud, even the name of the latter did not need to be changed. The discovery is the more interesting because it has always been a part of the christian folklore of that region that, when a storm with lightning occurs, it is 'Elias in his chariot of fire.' A similar phrase is used in some part of every Aryan country, with variation of the name: it is Woden, or King Waldemar, or the Grand Veneur, or sometimes God, who is said to be going forth in his chariot.

These storm-demons in their chariots have their forerunner in Vata or Vayu, the subject of one of the most beautiful Vedic hymns. 'I celebrate the glory of Vata's chariot; its noise comes rending and resounding. Touching the sky he moves onward, making all things ruddy; and he comes propelling the dust of the earth.

'Soul of the gods, source of the universe, this deity moves as he lists. His sounds have been heard, but his form is not seen; this Vata let us worship with an oblation.'12

This last verse, as Mr. Muir has pointed out, bears a startling resemblance to the passage in John, 'The Wind bloweth where it listeth, and thou canst not tell whence it cometh or whither it goeth; so is every one that is born of the Wind.'13 But an equally striking development of the Vedic idea is represented in the Siamese legend of Buddha, and in this case the Vedic Wind-god Vayu reappears by name for the Angels of Tempests, or Loka Phayu. The first portent which preceded the descent of Buddha from the Tushita heavens was 'when the Angels of the Tempest, clothed in red garments, and with streaming hair, travel among the abodes of mankind crying, 'Attend all ye who are near to death; repent and be not heedless! The end of the world approaches, but one hundred thousand years more and it will be destroyed. Exert yourselves, then, exert yourselves to acquire merit. Above all things be charitable; abstain from doing evil; meditate with love to all beings, and listen to the teachings of holiness. For we are all in the mouth of the king of death. Strive then earnestly for meritorious fruits, and seek that which is good.'14

Not less remarkable is the Targum of Jonathan Ben Uzziel to 1 Kings xix., where around Elias on the mountain gather 'a host of angels of the wind, cleaving the mountain and breaking the rocks before the Lord;' and after these, 'angels of commotion,' and next 'of fire,' and, finally, 'voices singing in silence' preceded the descent of Jehovah. It can hardly be wondered that a prophet of whom this story was told, and that of the storm evoked from a small cloud, should be caught up into that chariot of the Vedic Vayu which has rolled on through all the ages of mythology.

Mythologic streams seem to keep their channels almost as steadfastly as rivers, but as even these change at last or blend, so do the old traditions. Thus we find that while Thor and Odin remain as separate in survivals as Vayu and Parjanya in India, in Russia Elias has inherited not the mantle of the wind-god or storm-breeding sun, but of the Slavonic Thunderer Perun. There is little doubt that this is Parjanya, described in the 'Rig-Veda' as 'the thunderer, the showerer, the bountiful,'15 who 'strikes down trees' and 'the wicked.' 'The people of Novgorod,' says Herberstein, 'formerly offered their chief worship and adoration to a certain idol named Perun. When subsequently they received baptism they removed it from its place, and threw it into the river Volchov; and the story goes that it swam against the stream, and that near the bridge a voice was heard saying, 'This for you, O inhabitants of Novgorod, in memory of me;' and at the same time a certain rope was thrown upon the bridge. Even now it happens from time to time on certain days of the year that this voice of Perun may be heard, and on these occasions the citizens run together and lash each other with ropes, and such a tumult arises therefrom that all the efforts of the governor can scarcely assuage it.'16 The statue of Perun in Kief, says Mr. Ralston, had a trunk of wood, while the head was of silver, with moustaches of gold, and among its weapons was a mace. Afanasief states that in White-Russian traditions Perun is tall and well-shaped, with black hair and a long golden beard. This beard relates him to Barbarossa, and, perhaps, though distantly, with the wood-demon Barbatos, the Wild

Archer, who divined by the songs of birds.17 Perun also has a bow which is 'sometimes identified with the rainbow, an idea which is known also to the Finns. From it, according to the White Russians, are shot burning arrows, which set on fire all things that they touch. In many parts of Russia (as well as of Germany) it is supposed that these bolts sink deep into the soil, but that at the end of three or seven years they return to the surface in the shape of longish stones of a black or dark grey colour—probably belemnites, or masses of fused sand—which are called thunderbolts, and considered as excellent preservations against lightning and conflagrations. The Finns call them Ukonkiwi—the stone of thunder-god Ukko, and in Courland their name is Perkuhnsteine, which explains itself. In some cases the flaming dart of Perun became, in the imagination of the people, a golden key. With it he unlocked the earth, and brought to light its concealed treasures, its restrained waters, its captive founts of light. With it also he locked away in safety fugitives who wished to be put out of the power of malignant conjurors, and performed various other good offices. Appeals to him to exercise these functions still exist in the spells used by the peasants, but his name has given way to that of some christian personage. In one of them, for instance, the Archangel Michael is called upon to secure the invoker behind an iron door fastened by twenty-seven locks, the keys of which are given to the angels to be carried to heaven. In another, John the Baptist is represented as standing upon a stone in the Holy Sea [i.e., in heaven], resting upon an iron crook or staff, and is called upon to stay the flow of blood from a wound, locking the invoker's veins 'with his heavenly key.' In this case the myth has passed into a rite. In order to stay a violent bleeding from the nose, a locked padlock is brought, and the blood is allowed to drop through its aperture, or the sufferer grasps a key in each hand, either plan being expected to prove efficacious. As far as the key is concerned, the belief seems to be still maintained among ourselves.'18

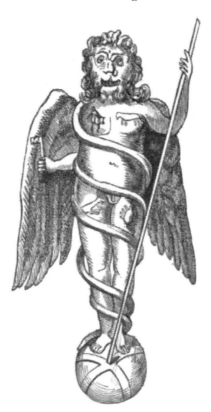

Fig. 5.

The Key has a holy sense in various religions, and consequently an infernal key is its natural counterpart. The Vedic hymns, which say so much about the shutting and opening, imprisoning and releasing, of heavenly rains and earthly fruits by demons and deities, interpret many phenomena of nature, and the same ideas have arisen in many lands. We cannot be certain, therefore, that Calmet is right in assigning an Indian origin to the subjoined Figure 5, an ancient Persian medal. The signs of the zodiac on its body show it to be one of those celestial demons believed able to bind the beneficent or loose the formidable powers of nature. The Key is of especial import in Hebrew faith. It was the high-priest Eliakim's symbol of office, as being also prefect in the king's house. 'The key of the house of David will I lay upon his shoulder: he shall open and none shall shut; he shall shut and none shall open.'19 The Rabbins had a saying that God reserves to himself four keys, which he will intrust not even to the angels: the key of rain, the key of the grave, the key of fruitfulness, and the key of barrenness. It was the sign of one set above angels when Christ was seen with the keys of Hell and Death, or when he delivered the keys of heaven to Peter,20—still thrust down the backs of protestant children to cure nose-bleed.

The ubiquitous superstition which attributes the flint arrows of pre-historic races to gods, shot by them as lightning, and, as some said, from a rainbow, is too childlike a theory to call for elaborate treatment. We need not, ethnographically, connect our 'Thor arrows' and 'Elf shots' with the stones hurled at mortals by the Thunder-Duke (Lui-tsz) of China. The ancient Parthians, who used to reply to the thunderstorm by shooting arrows at it, and the Turks, who attack an eclipse with guns, fairly represent the infancy of the human race, though perhaps with more than its average pluck. Dr. Macgowan relates, concerning the Lei-chau (Thunder District) of China, various myths which resemble those which surround the world. After thunderstorms, black stones, it is believed, may be found which emit light and peculiar sounds on being struck. In a temple consecrated to the Thunder Duke the people annually place a drum for that stormy demon to beat. The drum was formerly left on a mountain-top with a little boy as a sacrifice.[21] Mr. Dennys[22] speaks of the belief in the same country that violent winds and typhoons are caused by the passage through the air of the 'Bob-tailed Dragon,' and also of the rain-god Yü-Shüh. A storm-god connected with the 'Eagre,' or bore of the river Tsien-tang, presents a coincidence of name with the Scandinavian Oegir, which would be hardly noticeable were it not for the very close resemblance between the folklore concerning the 'Bob-tailed Dragon' and the storm-dragons of several Aryan races. Generally, in both China and Japan the Dragon is regarded with a veneration equal to the horror with which the serpent is visited. Of this phenomenon and its analogies in Britain I shall have an explanation to submit when we come to consider Dragon-myths more particularly. To this general rule the 'Bob-tailed Dragon' of China is a partial exception. His fidelity as a friend led to the ill return of an attack by which his tail was amputated, and ever since his soured temper has shown itself in raising storms. When a violent tempest arises the Cantonese say, 'The Bob-tailed Dragon is passing,' in the same proverbial way as the Aryan peasantries attribute the same phenomenon to their storm-gods.

The notion is widely prevalent in some districts of France that all whirlwinds, however slight, are caused by wizards or witches, who are in them, careering through the air; and it is stated by the Melusine that in the department of the Orne storms are attributed to the clergy, who are supposed to be circling in them. The same excellent journal states that some years ago, in that department, a parishioner who saw his crops threatened by a hail-storm fired into the cloud. The next day he heard that the parish priest had broken his leg by a fall for which he could not account.

The following examples are given by Kuhn. Near Stangenhagen is a treasure hid in a mountain which Lord von Thümen tried to seek, but was caught up with his horse by a whirlwind and deposited at home again. The Devil is believed to be seated at the centre of every whirlwind. At Biesenthal it is said a noble lady became the Wind's bride. She was in her time a famous rider and huntress, who rode recklessly over farmers' fields and gardens; now she is herself hunted by snakes and dragons, and may be heard howling in every storm.

I suspect that the bristling hair so frequently portrayed in the Japanese Oni, Devils, refers to their frequent residence at the centre of a gale of wind. Their demon of the storm is generally pictured throned upon a flower of flames, his upraised and extended fingers emitting the most terrific lightnings, which fall upon his victims and envelop them in flames. Sometimes, however, the Japanese artists poke fun at their thunder-god, and show him sprawling on the ground from the recoil of his own lightnings. The following extract from The Christian Herald (London, April 12, 1877) will show how far the dread of this Japanese Oni extends: 'A pious father writes, 'A few days ago there was a severe thunderstorm, which seemed to gather very heavily in the direction where my son lived; and I had a feeling that I must go and pray that he might be protected, and not be killed by the lightning. The impression seemed to say, 'There is no time to be lost.' I obeyed, and went and knelt down and prayed that the Lord would spare his life. I believe he heard my prayer. My son called on me afterwards, and, speaking of the shower, said, 'The lightning came downwards and struck the very hoe in my hands, and numbed me.' I said, 'Perhaps you would have been killed if some one had not been praying for you.' Since then he has been converted, and, I trust, will be saved in God's everlasting kingdom.''

Such paragraphs may now strike even many christians as 'survivals.' But it is not so very long since some eminent clergymen looked upon Benjamin Franklin as the heaven-defying Ajax of Christendom, because he undertook to show people how they might divert the lightnings from their habitations. In those days Franklin personally visited a church at Streatham, whose steeple had been struck by lightning, and, after observing the region, gave an opinion that if the steeple were again erected without a lightning-rod, it would again be struck. The audacious man who 'snatched sceptres from tyrants and lightnings from heaven,' as the proverb ran, was not listened to: the steeple was rebuilt, and again demolished by lightning.

The supreme god of the Quichuas (American), Viracocha ('sea foam'), rises out of Lake Titicaca, and journeys with lightnings for all opposers, to disappear in the Western Ocean. The Quichua is mentally brother of the Arab camel-driver. 'The sea,' it is said in the 'Arabian Nights,'—'the sea became troubled before them, and there arose from it a black pillar, ascending towards the sky, and approaching the meadow,' and 'behold it was a Jinn[23] of gigantic stature.' The Jinn is sometimes helpful as it is formidable; it repays the fisherman who unseals it from the casket fished up from the sea, as fruitfulness comes out of the cloud no larger than a man's hand evoked by Elijah. The perilous Jinn described in the above extract is the waterspout. Waterspouts are attributed in China to the battles of dragons in the air, and the same country recognises a demon of high tides. The newest goddess in China is a canonised protectress against the shipwrecking storm-demons of the coast, an exaltation recently proclaimed by the Government of the empire in obedience, as the edict stated, to the belief prevailing among sailors. In this the Chinese are a long way behind the mariners and fishermen of the French coast, who have for centuries, by a pious philology, connected 'Maria' with 'La Marée' and 'La Mer;' and whenever they have been saved from storms, bring their votive offerings to sea-side shrines of the Star of the Sea.

The old Jewish theology, in its eagerness to claim for Jehovah the absolutism which would make him 'Lord of lords,' instituted his responsibility for many doubtful performances, the burthen of which is now escaped by the device of saying that he 'permitted' them. In this way the Elohim who brought on the Deluge have been identified with Jehovah. None the less must we see in the biblical account of the Flood the action of tempestuous water-demons. What power a christian would recognise in such an event were it related in the sacred books of another religion may be seen in the vision of the Apocalypse—'The Serpent cast out of his mouth a flood of water after the woman, that he might cause her to be carried away with the flood; and the earth helped the woman and opened its mouth and swallowed up the flood.' This Demon of Inundation meets the explorer of Egyptian and Accadian inscriptions at every turn. The terrible Seven, whom even the God of Fire cannot control, 'break down the banks of the Abyss of Waters.'24 The God of the Tigris, Tourtak (Tartak of the Bible), is 'the great destroyer.'25 Leviathan 'maketh the deep to boil like a pot:' 'when he raises up himself the mighty are afraid; by reason of breakings they purify themselves.'26

In the Astronomical Tablets, which Professor Sayce dates about B.C. 1600, we have the continual association of eclipse and flood: 'On the fifteenth day an eclipse takes place. The king dies; and rains in the heaven, floods in the channels are.' 'In the month of Elul (August), the fourteenth day, an eclipse takes place.... Northward ... its shadow is seen; and to the King of Mullias a crown is given. To the king the crown is an omen; and over the king the eclipse passes. Rains in heaven, floods in the channels flow. A famine is in the country. Men their sons for silver sell.' 'After a year the Air-god inundates.'27

In the Chaldæo-Babylonian cosmogony the three zones of the universe were ruled over by a Triad as follows: the Heaven by Anu; the surface of the earth, including the atmosphere, by Bel; the under-world by Nouah.28 This same Nouah is the Assyrian Hea or Saviour; and it is Noah of the Bible. The name means a rest or residence,—the place where man may dwell. When Tiamat the Dragon, or the Leviathan, opens 'the fountains of the great deep,' and Anu 'the windows of Heaven,' it is Hea or Noah who saves the life of man. M. François Lenormant has shown this to be the probable sense of one of the most ancient Accadian fragments in the British Museum. In it allusion is made to 'the serpent of seven heads ... that beats the sea.'29 Hea, however, appears to be more clearly indicated in a fragment which Professor Sayce appends to this:—

Below in the abyss the forceful multitudes may they sacrifice.
The overwhelming fear of Anu in the midst of Heaven encircles his path.
The spirits of earth, the mighty gods, withstand him not.
The king like a lightning-flash opened.
Adar, the striker of the fortresses of the rebel band, opened.
Like the streams in the circle of heaven I besprinkled the seed of men.
His marching in the fealty of Bel to the temple I directed,
(He is) the hero of the gods, the protector of mankind, far (and) near....
O my lord, life of Nebo (breathe thy inspiration), incline thine ear.
O Adar, hero, crown of light, (breathe) thy inspiration, (incline) thine ear.
The overwhelming fear of thee may the sea know....
Thy setting (is) the herald of his rest from marching,
In thy marching Merodach (is) at rest30....
Thy father on his throne thou dost not smite.
Bel on his throne thou dost not smite.
The spirits of earth on their throne may he consume.
May thy father into the hands of thy valour cause (them) to go forth.
May Bel into the hands of thy valour cause (them) to go forth.
(The king, the proclaimed) of Anu, the firstborn of the gods.
He that stands before Bel, the heart of the life of the House of the Beloved.31
The hero of the mountain (for those that) die in multitudes.... the one god, he will not urge.32

In this primitive fragment we find the hero of the mountain (Noah), invoking both Bel and Nebo, aerial and infernal Intelligences, and Adar the Chaldæan Hercules, for their 'inspiration'—that breath which, in the biblical story, goes forth in the form of the Dove ('the herald of his rest' in the Accadian fragment), and in the 'wind' by which the waters were assuaged (in the fragment 'the spirits of the earth' which are given into the hand of the violent 'hero of the mountain,' whom alone the gods 'will not urge').

The Hydra may be taken as a type of the destructive water-demon in a double sense, for its heads remain in many mythical forms. The Syrian Dagon and Atergatis, fish-deities, have bequeathed but their element to our Undines of romance. Some nymphs have so long been detached from aqueous associations as to have made their names puzzling, and their place in demonology more so. To the Nixy (νήχω) of Germany, now merely mischievous like the British Pixy, many philologists trace the common phrase for the Devil,—'Old Nick.' I believe, however, that this phrase owes its popularity to St. Nicholas rather than to the Norse water-god whose place he was assigned after the christian accession. This saintly Poseidon, who, from being the patron of fishermen, gradually became associated with that demon whom, Sir Walter Scott said, 'the British sailor feared when he feared nothing else,' was also of old the patron of pirates; and robbers were called 'St. Nicholas' clerks.'33 In Norway and the Netherlands the ancient belief in the demon Nikke was strong; he was a kind of Wild Huntsman of the Sea, and has left many legends, of which 'The Flying Dutchman' is one. But my belief is that, through his legendary relation to boys, St. Nicholas gave the name Old Nick its modern moral accent. Because of his reputation for having restored to life three murdered children St. Nicholas was made their patron, and on his day, December 6, it was the old custom to consecrate a Boy-Bishop, who held office until the 28th of the month. By this means he became the moral appendage of the old Wodan god of the Germanic races, who was believed in winter time to find shelter in and shower benefits from evergreens, especially firs, on his favourite children who happened to wander beneath them. 'Bartel,' 'Klaubauf,' or whatever he might be called, was reduced to be the servant of St. Nicholas, whose name is now jumbled into 'Santaclaus.' According to the old custom he appeared attended by his Knecht Klaubauf—personated by those who knew all about the children—bringing a sort of doomsday. The gifts having been bestowed on the good children, St. Nicholas then ordered Klaubauf to put the naughty ones into his pannier and carry them off for punishment. The terror and shrieks thus caused have created vast misery among children, and in Munich and some other places the authorities have very properly made such tragedies illegal. But for many centuries it was the custom of nurses and mothers to threaten refractory children with being carried off at the end of the year by Nicholas; and in this way each year closed, in the young apprehension, with a Judgment Day, a Weighing of Souls, and a Devil or Old Nick as agent of retribution.

Nick has long since lost his aquatic character, and we find his name in the Far West (America) turning up as 'The Nick of the Woods,'—the wild legend of a settler who, following a vow of vengeance for his wrongs, used to kill the red men while they slept, and was supposed to be a demon. The Japanese have a water-dragon—Kappa—of a retributive and moral kind, whose office it is to swallow bad boys who go to swim in disobedience to their parents' commands, or at improper times and places. It is not improbable that such dangers to the young originated some of the water-demons,—probably such as are thought of as diminutive and mischievous,—e.g., Nixies. The Nixa was for a long time on the Baltic coast the female 'Old Nick,' and much feared by fishermen. Her malign disposition is represented in the Kelpie of Scotland,—a water-horse, believed to carry away the unwary by sudden floods to devour them. In Germany there was a river-goddess whose temple stood at Magdeburg, whence its name. A legend exists of her having appeared in the market there in christian costume, but she was detected by a continual dripping of water from the corner of her apron. In Germany the Nixies generally played the part of the naiads of ancient times.34 In Russia similar beings, called Rusalkas, are much more formidable.

In many regions of Christendom it is related that these demons, relatives of the Swan-maidens, considered in another chapter, have been converted into friendly or even pious creatures, and baptized into saintly names. Sometimes there are legends which reveal this transition. Thus it is related that in the year 1440, the dikes of Holland being broken down by a violent tempest, the sea overflowed the meadows; and some maidens of the town of Edam, in West Friesland, going in a boat to milk their cows, espied a mermaid embarrassed in the mud, the waters being very shallow. They took it into their boat and brought it to Edam, and dressed it in women's apparel, and taught it to spin. It ate as they did, but could not be brought to speak. It was carried to Haarlem, where it lived for some years, though showing an inclination to water. Parival, who tells the story, relates that they had conveyed to it some notions of the existence of a deity, and it made its reverences devoutly whenever it passed a crucifix.

Another creature of the same species was in the year 1531 caught in the Baltic, and sent as a present to Sigismund, King of Poland. It was seen by all the persons about the court, but only lived three days.

Fig. 6.—Hercules and the Hydra (Louvre).

The Hydra—the torrent which, cut off in one direction, makes many headways in others—has its survivals in the many diabolical names assigned to boiling springs and to torrents that become dangerously swollen. In California the boiling springs called 'Devil's Tea-kettle' and 'Devil's Mush-pot' repeat the 'Devil's Punch-bowls' of Europe, and the innumerable Devil's Dikes and Ditches. St. Gerard's Hill, near Pesth, on which the saint suffered martyrdom, is believed to be crowded with devils whenever an inundation threatens the city; they indulge in fiendish laughter, and play with the telescopes of the observatory, so that they who look through them afterwards see only devils' and witches' dances!35 At Buda, across the river from Pesth, is the famous 'Devil's Ditch,' which the inhabitants use as a sewer while it is dry, making it a Gehenna to poison them with stenches, but which often becomes a devastating torrent when thaw comes on the Blocksberg. In 1874 the inhabitants vaulted it over to keep away the normal stench, but the Hydra-head so lopped off grew again, and in July 1875 swallowed up a hundred people.36

The once perilous Strudel and Wirbel of the Danube are haunted by diabolical legends. From Dr. William Beattie's admirable work on 'The Danube' I quote the following passages:—'After descending the Greinerschwall, or rapids of Grein above mentioned, the river rolls on for a considerable space, in a deep and almost tranquil volume, which, by contrast with the approaching turmoil, gives increased effect to its wild, stormy, and romantic features. At first a hollow, subdued roar, like that of distant thunder, strikes the ear and rouses the traveller's attention. This increases every second, and the stir and activity which now prevail among the hands on board show that additional force, vigilance, and caution are to be employed in the use of the helm and oars. The water is now changed in its colour—chafed into foam, and agitated like a seething cauldron. In front, and in the centre of the channel, rises an abrupt, isolated, and colossal rock, fringed with wood, and crested with a mouldering tower, on the summit of which is planted a lofty cross, to which in the moment of danger the ancient boatmen were wont to address their prayers for deliverance. The first sight of this used to create no little excitement and apprehension on board; the master ordered strict silence to be observed, the steersman grasped the helm with a firmer hand, the passengers moved aside, so as to leave free space for the boatmen, while the women and children were hurried into the cabin, there to await, with feelings of no little anxiety, the result of the enterprise. Every boatman, with his head uncovered, muttered a prayer to his patron saint; and away dashed the barge through the tumbling breakers, that seemed as if hurrying it on to inevitable destruction. All these preparations, joined by the wildness of the adjacent scenery, the terrific aspect of the rocks, and the tempestuous state of the water, were sufficient to produce a powerful sensation on the minds even of those who had been all their lives familiar with dangers; while the shadowy phantoms with which superstition had peopled it threw a deeper gloom over the whole scene.'

Concerning the whirlpool called Wirbel, and the surrounding ruins, the same author writes: 'Each of these mouldering fortresses was the subject of some miraculous tradition, which circulated at every hearth. The sombre and mysterious aspect of the place, its wild scenery, and the frequent accidents which occurred in the passage, invested it with awe and terror; but above all, the superstitions of the time, a belief in the marvellous, and the credulity of the boatmen, made the navigation of the Strudel and the Wirbel a theme of the wildest romance. At night, sounds that were heard far above the roar of the Danube issued from every ruin. Magical lights flashed through their loopholes and casements, festivals were held in the long-deserted halls, maskers glided from room to room, the waltzers maddened to the strains of an infernal orchestra, armed sentinels paraded the battlements, while at intervals the clash of arms, the neighing of steeds, and the shrieks of unearthly combatants smote fitfully on the boatmen's ear. But the tower on which these scenes were most fearfully enacted was that on the Longstone, commonly called the 'Devil's Tower,' as it well deserved to be—for here, in close communion with his master, resided the 'Black Monk,' whose office it was to exhibit false lights and landmarks along the gulf, so as to decoy the vessels into the whirlpool, or dash them against the rocks. He was considerably annoyed in his quarters, however, on the arrival of the great Soliman in these regions; for to repel the turbaned host, or at least to check their triumphant progress to the Upper Danube, the inhabitants were summoned to join the national standard, and each to defend his own hearth. Fortifications were suddenly thrown up, even churches and other religious edifices were placed in a state of military defence; women and children, the aged and the sick, as already mentioned in our notice of Schaumburg, were lodged in fortresses, and thus secured from the violence of the approaching Moslem. Among the other points at which the greatest efforts were made to check the enemy, the passage of the Strudel and Wirbel was rendered as impregnable as the time and circumstances of the case would allow. To supply materials for the work, patriotism for a time got the better of superstition, and the said Devil's Tower was demolished and converted into a strong breastwork. Thus forcibly dislodged, the Black Monk is said to have pronounced a malediction on the intruders, and to have chosen a new haunt among the recesses of the Harz mountains.'

When the glaciers send down their torrents and flood the Rhone, it is the immemorial belief that the Devil may be sometimes seen swimming in it, with a sword in one hand and a golden globe in the other. Since it is contrary to all orthodox folklore that the Devil should be so friendly with water, the name must be regarded as a modern substitute for the earlier Rhone demon. We probably get closer to the original form of the superstition in the Swiss Oberland, which interprets the noises of the Furka Glacier, which feeds the Rhone, as the groans of wicked souls condemned for ever to labour there in directing the river's course; their mistress being a demoness who sometimes appears just before the floods, floating on a raft, and ordering the river to rise.

There is a tidal demonolatry also. The author of 'Rambles in Northumberland' gives a tradition concerning the river Wansbeck: 'This river discharges itself into the sea at a place called Cambois, about nine miles to the eastward, and the tide flows to within five miles of Morpeth. Tradition reports that Michael Scott, whose fame as a wizard is not confined to Scotland, would have brought the tide to the town had not the courage of the person failed upon whom the execution of this project depended. This agent of Michael, after his principal had performed certain spells, was to run from the neighbourhood of Cambois to Morpeth without looking behind, and the tide would follow him. After having advanced a certain distance he became alarmed at the roaring of the waters behind him, and forgetting the injunction, gave a glance over his shoulder to see if the danger was imminent, when the advancing tide immediately stopped, and the burgesses of Morpeth thus lost the chance of having the Wansbeck navigable between their town and the sea. It is also said that Michael intended to confer a similar favour on the inhabitants of Durham, by making the Wear navigable to their city; but his good intentions, which were to be carried into effect in the same manner, were also frustrated by the cowardice of the person who had to guide the tide.'

The gentle and just king Æolus, who taught his islanders navigation, in his mythologic transfiguration had to share the wayward dispositions of the winds he was said to rule; but though he wrecked the Trojan fleet and many a ship, his old human heart remained to be trusted on the appearance of Halcyon. His unhappy daughter of that name cast herself into the sea after the shipwreck of her husband (Cèyx), and the two were changed into birds. It was believed that for seven days before and seven after the shortest day of the year, when the halcyon is breeding, Æolus restrains his winds, and the sea is calm. The accent of this fable has been transmitted to some variants of the folklore of swans. In Russia the Tsar Morskoi or Water Demon's beautiful daughters (swans) may naturally be supposed to influence the tides which the fair bathers of our time are reduced to obey. In various regions the tides are believed to have some relation to swans, and to respect them. I have met with a notion of this kind in England. On the day of Livingstone's funeral there was an extraordinary tide in the Thames, which had been predicted and provided for. The crowds which had gathered at the Abbey on that occasion repaired after the funeral to Westminster Bridge to observe the tide, and among them was a venerable disbeliever in science, who announced to a group that there would be no high tide, 'because the swans were nesting.' This sceptic was speedily put to confusion by the result, and perhaps one superstition the less remained in the circle that seemed to regard him as an oracle.

The Russian peasantry live in much fear of the Rusalkas and Vodyanuie, water-spirits who, of course, have for their chief the surly Neptune Tsar Morskoi. In deprecation of this tribe, the peasant is careful not to bathe without a cross round the neck, nor to ford a stream on horseback without signing a cross on the water with a scythe or knife. In the Ukrain these water-demons are supposed to be the transformed souls of Pharaoh and his host when they were drowned, and they are increased by people who drown themselves. In Bohemia fishermen are known sometimes to refuse aid to one drowning, for fear the Vodyany will be offended and prevent the fish, over which he holds rule, from entering their nets. The wrath of such beings is indicated by the upheavals of water and foam; and they are supposed especially mischievous in the spring, when torrents and floods are pouring from melted snow. Those undefined monsters which Beowulf slew, Grendel and his mother, are interpreted by Simrock as personifications of the untamed sea and stormy floods invading the low flat shores, whose devastations so filled Faust with horror (II. iv.), and in combating which his own hitherto desolating powers found their task.

The Sea sweeps on in thousand quarters flowing,
Itself unfruitful, barrenness bestowing;
It breaks, and swells, and rolls, and overwhelms
The desert stretch of desolated realms....
Let that high joy be mine for evermore,
To shut the lordly Ocean from the shore,
The watery waste to limit and to bar,
And push it back upon itself afar!

In such brave work Faust had many forerunners, whose art and courage have their monument in the fairer fables of all these elemental powers in which fear saw demons. Pavana, in India, messenger of the gods, rides upon the winds, and in his forty-nine forms, corresponding with the points of the Hindu compass, guards the earth. Solomon, too, journeyed on a magic carpet woven of the winds, which still serves the purposes of the Wise. From the churned ocean rose Lakshmí (after the solar origin was lost to the myth), Hindu goddess of prosperity; and from the sea-foam rose Aphrodite, Beauty. These fair forms had their true worshipper in the Northman, who left on mastered wind and wave his song as Emerson found it—

The gale that wrecked you on the sand,
It helped my rowers to row;
The storm is my best galley hand,
And drives me where I go.

Notes

1 'Scenes and Legends of the North of Scotland.' Nimmo, 1876.
2 'Rig-Veda,' ii. 33. Tr. by Professor Evans of Michigan.
3 'Rig-Veda,' i. 114.
4 'Jour. Ceylon R. A. Soc.,' 1865–66.
5 Welcker, 'Griechische Götterlehre,' vol. i. p. 661.
6 Moffat, p. 257.
7 Livingstone, p. 124.
8 Pöppig, 'Reise in Chile,' vol. ii. p. 358.
9 Eyre, vol. ii. p. 362.
10 Tylor, 'Early Hist.,' p. 359.
11 So confirming the conjecture of Wachsmuth, in 'Das alte Griechenland im neuen,' p. 23. Elias might also easily be associated with the name Æolus.
12 'Rig-Veda,' x. (Muir).
13 John iii. 8.
14 'The Wheel of the Law,' by Henry Alabaster, Trübner & Co.
15 'Rig-Veda,' v. 83 (Wilson).
16 'Major's Tr.,' ii. 26.
17 Wierus' 'Pseudomonarchia Dæmon.'
18 'Songs of the Russian People,' by W. R. S. Ralston, M.A.
19 Isa. xxii. 22. It is remarkable that (according to Callimachus) Ceres bore a key on her shoulder. She kept the granary of the earth.
20 Rev. i. 18.; Matt. xvi. 19.
21 'Journal N. C. B. R. A. S.,' 1853.
22 'Folklore of China,' p. 124. The drum held by the imp in Fig. 3 shows his relation to the thunder-god. In Japan the thunder-god is represented as having five drums strung together. The wind-god has a large bag of compressed air between his shoulders; and he has steel claws, representing the keen and piercing wind. The Tartars in Siberia believe that a potent demon may be evoked by beating a drum; their sorcerers provide a tame bear, who starts upon the scene, and from whom they pretend to get answers to questions. In Nova Scotian superstition we find demons charmed by drums into quietude. In India the temple-drum preserved such

solemn associations even for the new theistic sect, the Brahmo-Somaj, that it is said to be still beaten as accompaniment to the organ sent to their chief church by their English friends.

23 Although the Koran and other authorities, as already stated, have associated the Jinn with etherial fire, Arabic folklore is nearer the meaning of the word in assigning the name to all demons. The learned Arabic lexicographer of Beirut, P. Bustani, says 'The Jinn is the opposite of mankind, or it is whatever is veiled from the sense, whether angel or devil.'

24 'Cuneiform Ins.,' iv. 15.

25 Ib. ii. 27.

26 Job xli.

27 'Records of the Past,' i.

28 Lenormant, 'La Magie.'

29 'Records of the Past,' iii. 129.

30 The god of the Euphrates.

31 The Assyrian has 'of the high places.'

32 'Records of the Past,' iii. 129, 130.

33 'Henry IV.,' Part 1st, Act 2. 'Heart of Mid-Lothian,' xxv. An interesting paper on this subject by Mr. Alexander Wilder appeared in The Evolution, New York, December 16, 1877.

34 De Plancy.

35 An individual by this means saw his wife among the witches, so detecting her unhallowed nature, which gave rise to a saying there that husbands must not be star-gazing on St. Gerard's Eve.

36 London 'Times,' July 8, 1875.

Chapter V - Animals

Animal demons distinguished—Trivial sources of Mythology—Hedgehog—Fox—Transmigrations in Japan—Horses bewitched—Rats—Lions—Cats—The Dog—Goethe's horror of dogs—Superstitions of the Parsees, people of Travancore, and American Negroes, Red Indians, etc.—Cynocephaloi—The Wolf—Traditions of the Nez Perces—Fenris—Fables—The Boar—The Bear—Serpent—Every animal power to harm demonised—Horns.

The animal demons—those whose evil repute is the result of something in their nature which may be inimical to man—should be distinguished from the forms which have been diabolised by association with mythological personages or ideas. The lion, tiger, and wolf are examples of the one class; the stag, horse, owl, and raven of the other. But there are circumstances which render it very difficult to observe this distinction. The line has to be drawn, if at all, between the measureless forces of degradation on the one side, discovering some evil in animals which, but for their bad associations, would not have been much thought of; and of euphemism on the other, transforming harmful beasts to benignant agents by dwelling upon some minor characteristic.

There are a few obviously dangerous animals, such as the serpent, where it is easy to pick our way; we can recognise the fear that flatters it to an agathodemon and the diminished fear that pronounces it accurst.1 But what shall be said of the Goat? Was there really anything in its smell or in its flesh when first eaten, its butting, or injury to plants, which originally classed it among the unclean animals? or was it merely demonised because of its uncanny and shaggy appearance? What explanation can be given of the evil repute of our household friend the Cat? Is it derived by inheritance from its fierce ancestors of the jungle? Was it first suggested by its horrible human-like sleep-murdering caterwaulings at night? or has it simply suffered from a theological curse on the cats said to draw the chariots of the goddesses of Beauty? The demonic Dog is, if anything, a still more complex subject. The student of mythology and folklore speedily becomes familiar with the trivial sources from which vast streams of superstition often issue. The cock's challenge to the all-detecting sun no doubt originated his ominous career from the Code of Manu to the cock-headed devils frescoed in the cathedrals of Russia. The fleshy, forked roots of a soporific plant issued in that vast Mandrake Mythology which has been the subject of many volumes, without being even yet fully explored. The Italians have a saying that 'One knavery of the hedgehog is worth more than many of the fox;' yet the nocturnal and hibernating habits and general quaintness of the humble hedgehog, rather than his furtive propensity to prey on eggs and chickens, must have raised him to the honours of demonhood. In various popular fables this little animal proves more than a match for the wolf and the serpent. It was in the form of a hedgehog that the Devil is said to have made the attempt to let in the sea through the Brighton Downs, which was prevented by a light being brought, though the seriousness of the scheme is still attested in the Devil's Dyke. There is an ancient tradition that when the Devil had smuggled himself into Noah's Ark, he tried to sink it by boring a hole; but this scheme was defeated, and the human race saved, by the hedgehog stuffing himself into the hole. In the Brighton story the Devil would appear to have remembered his former failure in drowning people, and to have appropriated the form which defeated him.

Fig. 7.—Japanese Demon.

The Fox, as incarnation of cunning, holds in the primitive belief of the Japanese almost the same position as the Serpent in the nations that have worshipped, until bold enough to curse it. In many of the early pictures of Japanese demons one may generally detect amid their human, wolfish, or other characters some traits of the kitsune (fox). He is always the soul of the three-eyed demon of Japan (fig. 7). He is the sagacious 'Vizier,' as the Persian Desatir calls him, and is practically the Japanese scape-goat. If a fox has appeared in any neighbourhood, the next trouble is attributed to his visit; and on such occasions the sufferers and their friends repair to some ancient gnarled tree in which the fox is theoretically resident and propitiate him, just as would be done to a serpent in other regions. In Japan the fox is not regarded as always harmful, but generally so. He is not to be killed on any account. Being thus spared through superstition, the foxes increase sufficiently to supply abundant material for the continuance of its demonic character. 'Take us the foxes, the little foxes that spoil the vines,'2 is an admonition reversed in Japan. The correspondence between the cunning respected in this animal and that of the serpent, reverenced elsewhere, is confirmed by Mr. Fitz Cunliffe Owen, who observed, as he informs me, that the Japanese will not kill even the poisonous snakes which crawl freely amid the decaying Buddhist temples of Nikko, one of the most sacred places in Japan, where once as many as eight thousand monastic Buddhists were harboured. It is the red fox that abounds in Japan, and its human-like cry at night near human habitations is such as might easily encourage these superstitions. But, furthermore, mythology supplies many illustrations of a creditable tendency among rude tribes to mark out for special veneration or fear any force in nature finer than mere strength. Emerson says, 'Foxes are so cunning because they are not strong.' In our Japanese demon, whose three eyes alone connect it with the præternatural vision ascribed by that race to the fox, the harelip is very pronounced. That little animal, the Hare, is associated with a large mythology, perhaps because out of its weakness proceeds its main forces of survival—timidity, vigilance, and swiftness. The superstition concerning the hare is found in Africa. The same animal is the much-venerated good genius of the Calmucs, who call him Sákya-muni (Buddha), and say that on earth he submitted himself to be eaten by a starving man, for which gracious deed he was raised to dominion over the moon, where they profess to see him. The legend is probably traceable back to the Sanskrit word sasin, moon, which means literally 'the hare-marked.' Sasa means 'hare.' Pausanias relates the story of the moon-goddess instructing exiles to build their city where they shall see a hare take refuge in a myrtle-grove.3 In the demonic fauna of Japan another cunning animal figures—the Weasel. The name of this demon is 'the sickle weasel,' and it also seems to occupy the position of a scape-goat. In the language of a Japanese report, 'When a person's clogs slip from under his feet, and he falls and cuts his face on the gravel, or when a person, who is out at night when he ought to have been at home, presents himself to his family with a freshly-scarred face, the wound is referred to the agency of the malignant invisible weasel and his sharp sickle.' In an aboriginal legend of America, also, two sister demons commonly take the form of weasels.

The popular feeling which underlay much of the animal-worship in ancient times was probably that which is reflected in the Japanese notions of to-day, as told in the subjoined sketch from an amusing book.

'One of these visitors was an old man, who himself was at the time a victim of a popular superstition that the departed revisit the scenes of their life in this world in shapes of different animals. We noticed that he was not in his usual spirits, and pressed him to unburden his mind to us. He said he had lost his little son Chiosin, but that was not so much the cause of his grief as the absurd way in which his wife, backed up by a whole conclave of old women who had taken up their abode in his house to comfort her, was going on. 'What do they all do?' we asked sympathetically. 'Why,' he replied, 'every beastly animal that comes to my house, there is a cry amongst them all, 'Chiosin, Chiosin has come back!' and the whole house swarms with cats and dogs and bats—for they say they are not quite sure which is Chiosin, and that they had better be kind to the lot than run the chance of treating him badly; the consequence is, all these brutes are fed on my rice and meat, and now I am driven out of doors and called an unnatural parent because I killed a mosquito which bit me!'4

The strange and inexplicable behaviour of animals in cases of fear, panic, or pain has been generally attributed by ignorant races to their possession by demons. Of this nature is the story of the devil entering the herd of swine and carrying them into the sea, related in the New Testament. It is said that even yet in some parts of Scotland the milkmaid carries a switch of the magical rowan to expel the demon that sometimes enters the cow. Professor Monier Williams writes from Southern India—'When my fellow-travellers and myself were nearly dashed to pieces over a precipice the other day by some restive horses on a ghat near Poona, we were told that the road at this particular point was haunted by devils who often caused similar accidents, and we were given to understand that we should have done well to conciliate Ganesa, son of the god Siva, and all his troops of evil spirits, before starting.' The same writer also tells us that the guardian spirits or 'mothers' who haunt most regions of the Peninsula are believed to ride about on horses, and if they are angry, scatter blight and disease. Hence the traveller just arrived from Europe is startled and puzzled by apparitions of rudely-formed terra-cotta horses, often as large as life, placed by the peasantry round shrines in the middle of fields as acceptable propitiatory offerings, or in the fulfilment of vows in periods of sickness.5

This was the belief of the Corinthians in the Taraxippos, or shade of Glaucus, who, having been torn in pieces by the horses with which he had been racing, and which he had fed on human flesh to make more spirited, remained to haunt the Isthmus and frighten horses during the races.

There is a modern legend in the Far West (America) of a horse called 'The White Devil,' which, in revenge for some harm to its comrades, slew men by biting and trampling them, and was itself slain after defying many attempts at its capture; but among the many ancient legends of demon-horses there are few which suggest anything about that animal hostile to man. His occasional evil character is simply derived from his association with man, and is therefore postponed. For a similar reason the Goat also must be dealt with hereafter, and as a symbolical animal. A few myths are met with which relate to its unpleasant characteristics. In South Guinea the odour of goats is accounted for by the Saga that their ancestor having had the presumption to ask a goddess for her aromatic ointment, she angrily rubbed him with ointment of a reverse kind. It has also been said that it was regarded as a demon by the worshippers of Bacchus, because it cropped the vines; and that it thus originated the Trageluphoi, or goat-stag monsters mentioned by Plato,6 and gave us also the word tragedy.7 But such traits of the Goat can have very little to do with its important relations to Mythology and Demonology.

To the list of animals demonised by association must also be added the Stag. No doubt the anxious mothers, wives, or sweethearts of rash young huntsmen utilised the old fables of beautiful hinds which in the deep forests changed to demons and devoured their pursuers,8 for admonition; but the fact that such stags had to transform themselves for evil work is a sufficient certificate of character to prevent their being included among the animal demons proper, that is, such as have in whole or part supplied in their disposition to harm man the basis of a demonic representation.

It will not be deemed wonderful that Rats bear a venerable rank in Demonology. The shudder which some nervous persons feel at sight of even a harmless mouse is a survival from the time when it was believed that in this form unshriven souls or unbaptized children haunted their former homes; and probably it would be difficult to estimate the number of ghost-stories which have originated in their nocturnal scamperings. Many legends report the departure of unhallowed souls from human mouths in the shape of a Mouse. During the earlier Napoleonic wars mice were used in Southern Germany as diviners, by being set with inked feet on the map of Europe to show where the fatal Frenchmen would march. They gained this sanctity by a series of associations with force stretching back to the Hindu fable of a mouse delivering the elephant and the lion by gnawing the cords that bound them. The battle of the Frogs and Mice is ascribed to Homer. Mice are said to have foretold the first civil war in Rome by gnawing the gold in the temple. Rats appear in various legends as avengers. The uncles of King Popelus II., murdered by him and his wife and thrown into a lake, reappear as rats and gnaw the king and queen to death. The same fate overtakes Miskilaus of Poland, through the transformed widows and orphans he had wronged. Mouse Tower, standing in the middle of the Rhine, is the haunted monument of cruel Archbishop Hatto, of Mainz, who (anno 970) bade the famine-stricken people repair to his barn, wherein he shut them fast and burned them. But next morning an army of rats, having eaten all the corn in his granaries, darkened the roads to the palace. The prelate sought refuge from them in the Tower, but they swam after, gnawed through the walls and devoured him.9

St. Gertrude, wearing the funereal mantle of Holda, commands an army of mice. In this respect she succeeds to the Pied Piper of Hamelin, who also leads off children; and my ingenious friend Mr. John Fiske suggests that this may be the reason why Irish servant-maids often show such frantic terror at sight of a mouse.10 The care of children is often intrusted to them, and the appearance of mice prognosticated of old the appearance of the præternatural rat-catcher and psychopomp. Pliny says that in his time it was considered fortunate to meet a white rat. The people of Bassorah always bow to these revered animals when seen, no doubt to propitiate them.

The Lion is a symbol of majesty and of the sun in his glory (reached in the zodiacal Leo), though here and there his original demonic character appears,—as in the combats of Indra, Samson, and Herakles with terrible lions. Euphemism, in one sense, fulfils the conditions of Samson's riddle—Sweetness coming out of the Strong—and has brought honey out of the Lion. His cruel character has subtly fallen to Sirius the Dog-star, to whom are ascribed the drought and malaria of 'dog-days' (when the sun is in Leo); but the primitive fact is intimated in several fables like that of Aristæus, who, born after his mother had been rescued from the Lybian lion, was worshipped in Ceos as a saviour from both droughts and lions. The Lion couching at the feet of beautiful Doorga in India, reappears drawing the chariot of Aphrodite, and typifies the potency of beauty rather than, as Emerson interprets, that beauty depends on strength. The chariot of the Norse Venus, Freyja, was drawn by Cats, diminished forms of her Southern sister's steeds. It was partly by these routes the Cat came to play the sometimes beneficent rôle in Russian, and to some extent in German, French, and English folklore,—e.g., Puss in Boots, Whittington and his Cat, and Madame D'Aulnoy's La Chatte Blanche. The demonic characteristics of the destructive cats have been inherited by the black,—or, as in Macbeth, the brindled,—cat. In Germany the approach of a cat to a sick-bed announces death; to dream of one is an evil omen. In Hungary it is said every black cat becomes a witch at the age of seven. It is the witch's favourite riding-horse, but may sometimes be saved from such servitude by incision of the sign of the cross. A scratch from a black cat is thought to be the beginning of a fatal spell.

De Gubernatis[11] has a very curious speculation concerning the origin of our familiar fable the Kilkenny Cats, which he traces to the German superstition which dreads the combat between cats as presaging death to one who witnesses it; and this belief he finds reflected in the Tuscan child's 'game of souls,' in which the devil and angel are supposed to contend for the soul. The author thinks this may be one outcome of the contest between Night and Twilight in Mythology; but, if the connection can be traced, it would probably prove to be derived from the struggle between the two angels of Death, one variation of which is associated with the legend of the strife for the body of Moses. The Book of Enoch says that Gabriel was sent, before the Flood, to excite the man-devouring giants to destroy one another. In an ancient Persian picture in my possession, animal monsters are shown devouring each other, while their proffered victim, like Daniel, is unharmed. The idea is a natural one, and hardly requires comparative tracing.

Dr. Dennys tells us that in China there exists precisely the same superstition as in Scotland as to the evil omen of a cat (or dog) passing over a corpse. Brand and Pennant both mention this, the latter stating that the cat or dog that has so done is killed without mercy. This fact would seem to show that the fear is for the living, lest the soul of the deceased should enter the animal and become one of the innumerable werewolf or vampyre class of demons. But the origin of the superstition is no doubt told in the Slavonic belief that if a cat leap over a corpse the deceased person will become a vampyre.

In Russia the cat enjoys a somewhat better reputation than it does in most other countries. Several peasants in the neighbourhood of Moscow assured me that while they would never be willing to remain in a church where a dog had entered, they would esteem it a good sign if a cat came to church. One aged woman near Moscow told me that when the Devil once tried to creep into Paradise he took the form of a mouse: the Dog and Cat were on guard at the gates, and the Dog allowed the evil one to pass, but the Cat pounced on him, and so defeated another treacherous attempt against human felicity.

The Cat superstition has always been strong in Great Britain. It is, indeed, in one sense true, as old Howell wrote (1647)—'We need not cross the sea for examples of this kind, we have too many (God wot) at home: King James a great while was loath to believe there were witches; but that which happened to my Lord Francis of Rutland's children convinced him, who were bewitched by an old woman that was a servant of Belvoir Castle, but, being displeased, she contracted with the Devil, who conversed with her in the form of a Cat, whom she called Rutterkin, to make away those children out of mere malignity and thirst of revenge.' It is to be feared that many a poor woman has been burned as a witch against whom her cherished cat was the chief witness. It would be a curious psychological study to trace how far the superstition owns a survival in even scientific minds,—as in Buffon's vituperation of the cat, and in the astonishing story, told by Mr. Wood, of a cat which saw a ghost (anno 1877)!

The Dog, so long the faithful friend of man, and even, possibly, because of the degree to which he has caught his master's manners, has a large demonic history. In the Semitic stories there are many that indicate the path by which 'dog' became the Mussulman synonym of infidel; and the one dog Katmir who in Arabic legend was admitted to Paradise for his faithful watching three hundred and nine years before the cave of the Seven Sleepers,[12] must have drifted among the Moslems from India as the Ephesian Sleepers did from the christian world. In the beautiful episode of the 'Mahábhárata,' Yudhisthira having journeyed to the door of heaven, refuses to enter into that happy abode unless his faithful dog is admitted also. He is told by Indra, 'My heaven hath no place for dogs; they steal away our offerings on earth;' and again, 'If a dog but behold a sacrifice, men esteem it unholy and void.' This difficulty was solved by the Dog—Yama in disguise— revealing himself and praising his friend's fidelity. It is tolerably clear that it is to his connection with Yama, god of Death, and under the evolution of that dualism which divided the universe into upper and nether, that the Dog was degraded among our Aryan ancestors; at the same time his sometimes wolfish disposition and some other natural characters supplied the basis of his demonic character. He was at once a dangerous and a corruptible guard.

Fig. 8.—Cerberus (Calmet).

In the early Vedic Mythology it is the abode of the gods that is guarded by the two dogs, identified by solar mythologists as the morning and evening twilight: a later phase shows them in the service of Yama, and they reappear in the guardian of the Greek Hades, Cerberus, and Orthros. The first of these has been traced to the Vedic Sarvara, the latter to the monster Vritra. 'Orthros' is the phonetical equivalent of Vritra. The bitch Sarama, mother of the two Vedic dogs, proved a treacherous guard, and was slain by Indra. Hence the Russian peasant comes fairly by another version of how the Dog, while on guard, admitted the Devil into heaven on being thrown a bone. But the two watch-dogs of the Hindu myth do not seem to bear an evil character. In a funeral hymn of the 'Rig-Veda' (x. 14), addressed to Yama, King of Death, we read:—'By an auspicious path do thou hasten past the two four-eyed brindled dogs, the offspring of Sarama; then approach the beautiful Pitris who rejoice together with Yama. Intrust him, O Yama, to thy two watch-dogs, four-eyed, road-guarding, and man-observing. The two brown messengers of Yama, broad of nostril and insatiable, wander about among men; may they give us again to-day the auspicious breath of life that we may see the sun!'

And now thousands of years after this was said we find the Dog still regarded as the seer of ghosts, and watcher at the gates of death, of whose opening his howl forewarns. The howling of a dog on the night of December 9, 1871, at Sandringham, where the Prince of Wales lay ill, was thought important enough for newspapers to report to a shuddering country. I read lately of a dog in a German village which was supposed to have announced so many deaths that he became an object of general terror, and was put to death. In that country belief in the demonic character of the dog seems to have been strong enough to transmit an influence even to the powerful brain of Goethe.

In Goethe's poem, it was when Faust was walking with the student Wagner that the black Dog appeared, rushing around them in spiral curves—spreading, as Faust said, 'a magic coil as a snare around them;'13 that after this dog had followed Faust into his study, it assumed a monstrous shape, until changed to a mist, from which Mephistopheles steps forth—'the kernel of the brute'—in guise of a travelling scholar. This is in notable coincidence with the archaic symbolism of the Dog as the most frequent form of the 'Lares' (fig. 9), or household genii, originally because of its vigilance. The form here presented is nearly identical with the Cynocephalus, whom the learned author of 'Mankind: their Origin and Destiny,' identifies as the Adamic being set as a watch and instructor in Eden (Gen. xvi. 15), an example of which, holding pen and tablet (as described by Horapollo), is given in that work from Philæ. Chrysippus says that these were afterwards represented as young men clothed with dog-skins. Remnants of the tutelary character of the dog are scattered through German folklore: he is regarded as oracle, ghost-seer, and gifted with second sight; in Bohemia he is sometimes made to lick an infant's face that it may see well.

Fig. 9.—Canine Lar (Herculaneum).

The passage in 'Faust' has been traced to Goethe's antipathy to dogs, as expressed in his conversation with Falk at the time of Wieland's death. 'Annihilation is utterly out of the question; but the possibility of being caught on the way by some more powerful and yet baser monas, and subordinated to it; this is unquestionably a very serious consideration; and I, for my part, have never been able entirely to divest myself of the fear of it, in the way of a mere observation of nature.' At this moment, says Falk, a dog was heard repeatedly barking in the street. Goethe, sprang hastily to the window and called to it: 'Take what form you will, vile larva, you shall not subjugate me!' After some pause, he resumed with the remark: 'This rabble of creation is extremely offensive. It is a perfect pack of monades with which we are thrown together in this planetary nook; their company will do us little honour with the inhabitants of other planets, if they happen to hear anything about them.'

In visiting the house where Goethe once resided in Weimar, I was startled to find as the chief ornament of the hall a large bronze dog, of full size, and very dark, looking proudly forth, as if he possessed the Goethean monas after all. However, it is not probable that the poet's real dislike of dogs arose solely from that speculation about monades. It is more probable that in observing the old wall-picture in Auerbach's cellar, wherein a dog stands beside Mephistopheles, Goethe was led to consider carefully the causes of that intimacy. Unfortunately, and notwithstanding the fables and the sentiment which invest that animal, there are some very repulsive things about him, such as his tendency to madness and the infliction on man of a frightful death. The Greek Mania's 'fleet hounds' (Bacchæ 977) have spread terrors far and wide.

Those who carefully peruse the account given by Mr. Lewes of the quarrel between Karl August and Goethe, on account of the opposition of the latter to the introduction of a performing dog on the Weimar stage—an incident which led to his resignation of his position of intendant of the theatre—may detect this aversion mingling with his disgust as an artist; and it may be also suspected that it was not the mere noise which caused the tortures he described himself as having once endured at Göttingen from the barking of dogs.

It is, however, not improbable that in the wild notion of Goethe, joined with his cynophobia, we find a survival of the belief of the Parsees of Surat, who venerate the Dog above all other animals, and who, when one is dying, place a dog's muzzle near his mouth, and make it bark twice, so that it may catch the departing soul, and bear it to the waiting angel. The devil-worshippers of Travancore to this day declare that the evil power approaches them in the form of a Dog, as Mephistopheles approached Faust. But before the superstition reached Goethe's poem it had undergone many modifications; and especially its keen scent had influenced the Norse imagination to ascribe to it præternatural wisdom. Thus we read in the Saga of Hakon the Good, that when Eystein the Bad had conquered Drontheim, he offered the people choice of his slave Thorer or his dog Sauer to be their king. They chose the Dog. 'Now the dog was by witchcraft gifted with three men's wisdom; and when he barked he spoke one word and barked two.' This Dog wore a collar of gold, and sat on a throne, but, for all his wisdom and power, seems to have been a dog still; for when some wolves invaded the cattle, he attacked and was torn to pieces by them.

Among the negroes of the Southern States in America I have found the belief that the most frequent form of a diabolical apparition is that of a large Dog with fiery eyes, which may be among them an original superstition attributable to their horror of the bloodhound, by which, in some regions, they were pursued when attempting to escape. Among the whites of the same region I have never been able to find any instance of the same belief, though belief in the presage of the howling dog is frequent; and it is possible that this is a survival from some region in Africa, where the Dog has an evil name of the same kind as the scape-goat. Among some tribes in Fazogl there is an annual carnival at which every one does as he likes. The king is then seated in the open air, a dog tied to the leg of his chair, and the animal is then stoned to death.

Mark Twain[14] records the folklore of a village of Missouri, where we find lads quaking with fear at the howling of a 'stray dog' in the night, but indifferent to the howling of a dog they recognise, which may be a form of the common English belief that it is unlucky to be followed by a 'strange' dog. From the same book it appears also that the dog will always have his head in the direction of the person whose doom is signified: the lads are entirely relieved when they find the howling animal has his back turned to them.

It is remarkable that these fragments of European superstition should meet in the Far West a plentiful crop of their like which has sprung up among the aborigines, as the following extract from Mr. Brinton's work, 'Myths of the New World,' will show: 'Dogs were supposed to stand in some peculiar relation to the moon, probably because they howl at it and run at night, uncanny practices which have cost them dear in reputation. The custom prevailed among tribes so widely asunder as Peruvians, Tupis, Creeks, Iroquois, Algonquins, and Greenland Eskimos to thrash the curs most soundly during an eclipse. The Creeks explained this by saying that the big Dog was swallowing the sun, and that by whipping the little ones they could make him desist. What the big Dog was they were not prepared to say. We know. It was the night goddess, represented by the Dog, who was thus shrouding the world at mid-day. In a better sense, they represented the more agreeable characteristics of the lunar goddess. Xochiquetzal, most fecund of Aztec divinities, patroness of love, of sexual pleasure, and of child-birth, was likewise called Itzcuinan, which, literally translated, is 'bitch-mother.' This strange and to us so repugnant title for a goddess was not without parallel elsewhere. When in his wars the Inca Pachacutec carried his arms into the province of Huanca, he found its inhabitants had installed in their temples the figure of a Dog as their highest deity.... This canine canonisation explains why in some parts of Peru a priest was called, by way of honour, allco, Dog!... Many tribes on the Pacific coast united in the adoration of a wild species, the coyote, the Canis latrans of naturalists.' Of the Dog-demon Chantico the legend of the Nahuas was, 'that he made a sacrifice to the gods without observing a preparatory fast, for which he was punished by being changed into a Dog. He then invoked the god of death to deliver him, which attempt to evade a just punishment so enraged the divinities that they immersed the world in water.'

The common phrase 'hell-hounds' has come to us by various routes. Diana being degraded to Hecate, the dogs of Hades, Orthros and Cerberus, multiplied into a pack of hounds for her chase, were degraded with her into infernal howlers and hunters. A like degradation of Odin's hunt took place at a later date. The Wild Huntsman, being a diabolical character, is considered elsewhere. Concerning the Dog, it may be further said here, that there are probably various characteristics of that animal reflected in his demonic character. His liability to become rabid, and to afflict human beings with hydrophobia, appears to have had some part in it. Spinoza alludes to the custom in his time of destroying persons suffering from this canine rabies by suffocation; and his English biographer and editor, Dr. Willis, tells me that in his boyhood in Scotland he always heard this spoken of as the old custom. That such treatment could have prevailed can hardly be ascribed to anything but a belief in the demonic character of the rabid dog, cognate with the unconscious superstition which still causes rural magistrates to order a dog which has bitten any one to be slain. The notion is, that if the dog goes mad thereafter, the man will also. Of course it would be rational to preserve the dog's life carefully, in order that, if it continues healthy, the bitten may feel reassured, as he cannot be if it be dead.

But the degradation of the dog had a cause even in his fidelity as a watch. For this, as we have just seen, made him a common form among Lares or domestic demons. The teraphim also were often in this shape. Christianity had therefore a special reason for ascribing an infernal character to these little idols, which interfered with the popular dependence on the saints. It will thus be seen that there were many causes operating to create that formidable class of demons which were called in the Middle Ages Cynocephaloi. The ancient holy pictures of Russia especially abound in these dog-headed devils; in the sixteenth century they were frequently represented rending souls in hell; and sometimes the dragon of the Apocalypse is represented with seven horrible canine heads.

M. Toussenel, in his transcendental interpretations, has identified the Wolf as the bandit and outlaw.15 The proverbial mediæval phrase for an outlaw—one who wears a teste lœve, caput lupinum, wulfesheofod, which the ingenious author perhaps remembered—is of good antiquity. The wolf is called robber in the 'Rig-Veda,' and he is there also demonised, since we find him fleeing before a devotee. (In the Zend 'Vendidad' the souls of the pious fear to meet the wolf on the way to heaven.) The god Pushan is invoked against the evil wolf, the malignant spirit.16 Cardano says that to dream of a wolf announces a robber. There is in the wolf, at the same time, that always attractive love of liberty which, in the well-known fable, makes him prefer leanness to the comfort of the collar-wearing dog, which makes him among demonic animals sometimes the same as the mighty huntsmen Nimrod and shaggy Esau among humanised demons. One is not surprised to find occasionally good stories about the wolf. Thus the Nez Perces tribe in America trace the origin of the human race to a wolf. They say that originally, when there were nothing but animals, there was a huge monster which devoured them whole and alive. This monster swallowed a wolf, who, when he entered its belly, found the animals therein snarling at and biting one another as they had done on the earth outside. The wolf exhorted them that their common sufferings should teach them friendliness, and finally he induced them to a system of co-operation by which they made their way out through the side of the monster, which instantly perished. The animals so released were at once transformed to men, how and why the advocates of co-operation will readily understand, and founded the Nez Perces Indians. The myths of Asia and Europe are unhappily antipodal to this in spirit and form, telling of human beings transformed to wolves. In the Norse Mythology, however, there stands a demon wolf whose story bears a touch of feeling, though perhaps it was originally the mere expression for physical law. This is the wolf Fenris, which, from being at first the pet of the gods and lapdog of the goddesses, became so huge and formidable that Asgard itself was endangered. All the skill and power of the gods could not forge chains which might chain him; he snapped them like straws and toppled over the mountains to which he was fastened. But the little Elves working underground made that chain so fine that none could see or feel it,— fashioned it out of the beards of women, the breath of fish, noise of the cat's footfall, spittle of birds, sinews of bears, roots of stones,—by which are meant things non-existent. This held him. Fenris is chained till the final destruction, when he shall break loose and devour Odin. The fine chain that binds ferocity,—is it the love that can tame all creatures? Is it the sunbeam that defines to the strongest creature its habitat?

The two monsters formed when Ráhu was cloven in twain, in Hindu Mythology, reappear in Eddaic fable as the wolves Sköll and Hati, who pursue the sun and moon. As it is said in the Völuspá:—

Eastward in the Iron-wood
The old one sitteth,
And there bringeth forth
Fenrir's fell kindred.
Of these one, the mightiest,
The moon's devourer,
In form most fiend-like,
And filled with the life-blood
Of the dead and the dying,
Reddens with ruddy gore
The seats of the high gods.

Euphemism attending propitiation of such monsters may partly explain the many good things told of wolves in popular legend. The stories of the she-wolf nourishing children, as Romulus and Remus, are found in many lands. They must, indeed, have had some prestige, to have been so largely adopted in saintly tradition. Like the bears that Elisha called to devour the children, the wolves do not lose their natural ferocity by becoming pious. They devour heretics and sacrilegious people. One guarded the head of St. Edmund the Martyr of England; another escorted St. Oddo, Abbot of Cluny, as his ancestors did the priests of Cluny. The skin of the wolf appears in folklore as a charm against hydrophobia; its teeth are best for cutting children's gums, and its bite, if survived, is an assurance against any future wound or pain.

Fig. 10.—The Wolf as Confessor (probably Dutch).

The tragedy which is so foolishly sprung upon the nerves of children, Little Red Riding-Hood, shows the wolf as a crafty animal. There are many legends of a like character which have made it a favourite figure in which to represent pious impostors. In our figure 10, the wolf appears as the 'dangerous confessor;' it was intended, as Mr. Wright thought, for Mary of Modena, Queen of James II., and Father Petre. At the top of the original are the words 'Converte Angliam' and beneath, 'It is a foolish sheep that makes the wolf her confessor.' The craft of the wolf is represented in a partly political partly social turn given by an American fabulist to one of Æsop's fables. The wolf having accused the lamb he means to devour of fouling the stream, and receiving answer that the lamb was drinking farther down the current, alters the charge and says, 'You opposed my candidature at the caucus two years ago.' 'I was not then born,' replies the lamb. The wolf then says, 'Any one hearing my accusations would testify that I am insane and not responsible for my actions,' and thereupon devours the lamb with full faith in a jury of his countrymen. M. Toussenel says the wolf is a terrible strategist, albeit the less observant have found little in his character to warrant this attribute of craft, his physiognomy and habits showing him a rather transparent highwayman. It is probable that the fables of this character have derived that trait from his association with demons and devils supposed to take on his shape.

In a beautiful hymn to the Earth in the 'Atharva Veda' it is said, 'The Earth, which endureth the burden of the oppressor, beareth up the abode of the lofty and of the lowly, suffereth the hog, and giveth entrance to the wild boar.' Boar-hounds in Brittany and some other regions are still kept at Government expense. There are many indications of this kind that in early times men had to defend themselves vigorously against the ravages of the wild boar, and, as De Gubernatis remarks,17 its character is generally demoniacal. The contests of Hercules with the Erymanthian, and of Meleager with the Calydonian, Boar, are enough to show that it was through its dangerous character that he became sacred to the gods of war, Mars and Odin. But it is also to be remembered that the third incarnation of Vishnu was as a Wild Boar; and as the fearless exterminator of snakes the pig merited this association with the Preserver. Provided with a thick coat of fat, no venom can harm him unless it be on the lip. It may be this ability to defy the snake-ordeal which, after its uncleanliness had excepted the hog from human voracity in some regions, assigned it a diabolical character. In rabbinical fable the hog and rat were created by Noah to clear the Ark of filth; but the rats becoming a nuisance, he evoked a cat from the lion's nose.

It is clear that our Asiatic and Norse ancestors never had such a ferocious beast to encounter as the Grisly Bear (Ursus horribilis) of America, else the appearances of this animal in Demonology could never have been so respectable. The comparatively timid Asiatic Bear (U. labiatus), the small and almost harmless Thibetan species (U. Thibetanus), would appear to have preponderated over the fiercer but rarer Bears of the North in giving us the Indo-Germanic fables, in which this animal is, on the whole, a favourite. Emerson finds in the fondness of the English for their national legend of 'Beauty and the Beast' a sign of the Englishman's own nature. 'He is a bear with a soft place in his heart; he says No, and helps you.' The old legend found place in the heart of a particularly representative American also—Theodore Parker, who loved to call his dearest friend 'Bear,' and who, on arriving in Europe, went to Berne to see his favourites, from which its name is derived. The fondness of the Bear for honey—whence its Russian name, medv-jed, 'honey-eater'—had probably something to do with its dainty taste for roses and its admiration for female beauty, as told in many myths. In his comparative treatment of the mythology of the Bear, De Gubernatis18 mentions the transformation of King Trisankus into a bear, and connects this with the constellation of the Great Bear; but it may with equal probability be related to the many fables of princes who remain under the form of a bear until the spell is broken by the kiss of some maiden. It is worthy of note that in the Russian legends the Bear is by no means so amiable as in those of our Western folklore. In one, the Bear-prince lurking in his fountain holds by the beard the king who, while hunting, tries to quench his thirst, and releases him only after a promise to deliver up whatever he has at home without his knowledge; the twins, Ivan and Maria, born during his absence, are thus doomed—are concealed, but discovered by the bear, who carries them away. They are saved by help of the bull. When escaping the bear Ivan throws down a comb, which becomes a tangled forest, which, however, the bear penetrates; but the spread-out towel which becomes a lake of fire sends the bear back.19 It is thus the ferocious Arctic Bear which gives the story its sombre character. Such also is the Russian tale of the Bear with iron hairs, which devastates the kingdom, devouring the inhabitants until Ivan and Helena alone remain; after the two in various ways try to escape, their success is secured by the Bull, which, more kindly than Elisha, blinds the Bear with his horns.20 (The Bear retires in winter.) In Norwegian story the Bear becomes milder,—a beautiful youth by night, whose wife loses him because she wishes to see him by lamplight: her place is taken by a long-nosed princess, until, by aid of the golden apple and the rose, she recovers her husband. In the Pentameron,21 Pretiosa, to escape the persecutions of her father, goes into the forest disguised as a she-bear; she nurses and cures the prince, who is enamoured of her, and at his kiss becomes a beautiful maid. The Bear thus has a twofold development in folklore. He used to be killed (13th century) at the end of the Carnival in Rome, as the Devil.22 The Siberians, if they have killed a bear, hang his skin on a tree and apologise humbly to it, declaring that they did not forge the metal that pierced it, and they meant the arrow for a bird; from which it is plain that they rely more on its stupidity than its good heart. In Canada, when the hunters kill a bear, one of them approaches it and places between his teeth the stem of his pipe, breathes in the bowl, and thus, filling with smoke the animal's mouth, conjures its soul not to be offended at his death. As the bear's ghost makes no reply, the huntsman, in order to know if his prayer is granted, cuts the thread under the bear's tongue, and keeps it until the end of the hunt, when a large fire is kindled, and all the band solemnly throw in it what threads of this kind they have; if these sparkle and vanish, as is natural, it is a sign that the bears are appeased.23 In Greenland the great demon, at once feared and invoked, especially by fishermen, is Torngarsuk, a huge Bear with a human arm. He is invisible to all except his priests, the Anguekkoks, who are the only physicians of that people.

The extreme point of demonic power has always been held by the Serpent. So much, however, will have to be said of the destructiveness and other characteristics of this animal when we come to consider at length its unique position in Mythology, that I content myself here with a pictorial representation of the Singhalese Demon of Serpents. If any one find himself shuddering at sight of a snake, even in a country where they are few and comparatively harmless, perhaps this figure (11) may suggest the final cause of the shudder.

Fig. 11.—Singhalese Demon of Serpents.

In conclusion, it may be said that not only every animal ferocity, but every force which can be exerted injuriously, has had its demonic representations. Every claw, fang, sting, hoof, horn, has been as certain to be catalogued and labelled in demonology as in physical science. It is remarkable also how superstition rationalises. Thus the horn in the animal world, though sometimes dangerous to man, was more dangerous to animals, which, as foes of the horned animals, were foes to man's interests. The early herdsman knew the value of the horn as a defence against dog and wolf, besides its other utilities. Consequently, although it was necessary that the horn-principle, so to say, in nature must be regarded as one of its retractile and cruel features, man never demonised the animals whose butt was most dangerous, but for such purpose transferred the horns to the head of some nondescript creature. The horn has thus become a natural weapon of man-demons. The same evolution has taken place in America; for, although among its aboriginal legends we may meet with an occasional demon-buffalo, such are rare and of apocryphal antiquity. The accompanying American figure (12) is from a photograph sent me by the President of Vanderbilt University, Tennessee, who found it in an old mound (Red Indian) in the State of Georgia. It is probably as ancient as any example of a human head with horns in the world; and as it could not have been influenced by European notions, it supplies striking evidence that the demonisation of the forces and dangers of nature belongs to the structural action of the human mind.

Fig. 12.—American Indian Demon.

Notes

1 This Protean type of both demon and devil must accompany us so continually through this volume that but little need be said of it in this chapter.
2 Canticles ii. 15.
3 De Gubernatis, II. viii.
4 'Our Life in Japan' (Jephson and Elmhirst, 9th Regiment), Chapman & Hall, 1869.
5 London 'Times,' June 11, 1877.
6 Rep. 488.
7 Literally, goat-song. More probably it has an astrological sense.
8 E.g., the demon Huorco in the 'Pentamerone.'
9 See De Gubernatis' 'Zoological Mythology,' which contains further curious details on this subject.
10 'Myths and Myth-makers.' Boston: Osgood & Co.
11 'Zoological Mythology,' p. 64.
12 Koran, xviii.
13
Wagner. Behold him stop—upon his belly crawl....
The clever scholar of the students, he!
14 'The Adventures of Tom Sawyer.' London: Chatto & Windus.
15 'Spirit of the Beasts of France,' ch. i.
16 'Rigv.' i. 105, 18, 42, 2; 'Vendidad,' xix. 108. Quoted by De Gubernatis ('Zoolog. Mythology,' ii. 142), to whose invaluable work I am largely indebted in this chapter.
17 'Zoolog. Myth.,' ii. 7. Trübner & Co.
18 'Zoolog. Myth.,' ii. 108 seq.

19 *Afanasief, v. 28.*
20 *Ibid., v. 27.*
21 *ii. 6 (De Gubernatis, ii. 117).*
22 *Rather the devil of lust than of cruelty, according to Du Cange: "Occidunt ursum, occiditur diabolus, id est, temptator nostræ carnis."*
23 *De Plancy (Dict. Inf.), who also relates an amusing legend of the bear who came to a German choir, as seen by a sleepy chorister as he awoke; the naïve narrator of which adds, that this was the devil sent to hold the singers to their duty! The Lives of the Saints abound with legends of pious bears, such as that commemorated along with St. Sergius in Troitska Lavra, near Moscow; and that which St. Gallus was ungracious enough to banish from Switzerland after it had brought him firewood in proof of its conversion.*

Chapter VI - Enemies

Aryas, Dasyus, Nagas—Yakkhos—Lycians—Ethiopians—Hirpini—Polites—Sosipolis—Were-wolves—Goths and Scythians—Giants and Dwarfs—Berserkers—Britons—Iceland—Mimacs—Gog and Magog.

We paint the Devil black, says George Herbert. On the other hand the negro paints him white, with reason enough. The name of the Devil at Mozambique is Muzungu Maya, or Wicked White Man. Of this demon they make little images of extreme hideousness, which are kept by people on the coast, and occasionally displayed, in the belief that if the White Devil is lurking near them he will vanish out of sheer disgust with a glimpse of his own ugliness. The hereditary horror of the kidnapper displayed in this droll superstition may possibly have been assisted by the familiarity with all things infernal represented in the language of the white sailors visiting the coast. Captain Basil Hall, on visiting Mozambique about fifty years ago, found that the native dignitaries had appropriated the titles of English noblemen, and a dumpy little Duke of Devonshire met him with his whole vocabulary of English,—'How do you do, sir. Very glad see you. Damn your eyes. Johanna man like English very much. God damn. That very good? Eh? Devilish hot, sir. What news? Hope your ship stay too long while very. Damn my eye. Very fine day.'

In most parts of India Siva also is painted white, which would indicate that there too was found reason to associate diabolism with the white face. It is said the Thugs spared Englishmen because their white faces suggested relationship to Siva. In some of the ancient Indian books the monster whom Indra slew, Vritra, is called Dasyu (enemy), a name which in the Vedas designates the Aborigines as contrasted with the Aryans of the North. 'In the old Sanskrit, in the hymns of the Veda, ârya occurs frequently as a national name and as a name of honour, comprising the worshippers of the gods of the Brahmans, as opposed to their enemies, who are called in the Veda Dasyus. Thus one of the gods, Indra, who in some respects answers to the Greek Zeus, is invoked in the following words (Rigveda, i. 57, 8):—'Know thou the Aryas, O Indra, and those who are Dasyus; punish the lawless, and deliver them unto thy servant! Be thou the mighty helper of the worshippers, and I will praise all these thy deeds at the festivals.'[1]

Naglok (snakeland) was at an early period a Hindu name for hell. But the Nagas were not real snakes,—in that case they might have fared better,—but an aboriginal tribe in Ceylon, believed by the Hindus to be of serpent origin,—'naga' being an epithet for 'native.'[2] The Singhalese, on the other hand, have adapted the popular name for demons in India, 'Rakshasa,' in their Rakseyo, a tribe of invisible cannibals without supernatural powers (except invisibility), who no doubt merely embody the traditions of some early race. The dreaded powers were from another tribe designated Yakkhos (demons), and believed to have the power of rendering themselves invisible. Buddha's victories over these demonic beings are related in the 'Mahawanso.' 'It was known (by inspiration) by the vanquishers that in Lanka, filled by yakkhos, ... would be the place where his religion would be glorified. In like manner, knowing that in the centre of Lanka, on the delightful bank of a river, ... in the agreeable Mahanaga garden, ... there was a great assembly of the principal yakkhos, ... the deity of happy advent, approaching that great congregation, ... immediately over their heads hovering in the air, ... struck terror into them by rains, tempests, and darkness. The yakkhos, overwhelmed with awe, supplicated of the vanquisher to be released from their terror.... The consoling vanquisher thus replied: 'I will release ye yakkhos from this your terror and affliction: give ye unto me here by unanimous consent a place for me to alight on.' All these yakkhos replied: 'Lord, we confer on thee the whole of Lanka, grant thou comfort to us.' The vanquisher thereupon dispelling their terror and cold shivering, and spreading his carpet of skin on the spot bestowed on him, he there seated himself. He then caused the aforesaid carpet, refulgent with a fringe of flames, to extend itself on all sides: they, scorched by the flames, (receding) stood around on the shores (of the island) terrified. The Saviour then caused the delightful isle of Giri to approach for them. As soon as they transferred themselves thereto (to escape the conflagration), he restored it to its former position.'[3]

This legend, which reminds one irresistibly of the expulsion of reptiles by saints from Ireland, and other Western regions, is the more interesting if it be considered that these Yakkhos are the Sanskrit Yakshas, attendants on Kuvera, the god of wealth, employed in the care of his garden and treasures. They are regarded as generally inoffensive. The transfer by English authorities of the Tasmanians from their native island to another, with the result of their extermination, may suggest the possible origin of the story of Giri.

Buddha's dealings with the serpent-men or nagas is related as follows in the same volume:—

'The vanquisher (i.e., of the five deadly sins), ... in the fifth year of his buddhahood, while residing at the garden of (the prince) Jeto, observing that, on account of a disputed claim for a gem-set throne between the naga Mahodaro and a similar Chalodaro, a maternal uncle and nephew, a conflict was at hand, ... taking with him his sacred dish and robes, out of compassion to the nagas, visited Nagadipo.... These mountain nagas were, moreover, gifted with supernatural powers.... The Saviour and dispeller of the darkness of sin, poising himself in the air over the centre of the assembly, caused a terrifying darkness to these nagas. Attending to the prayer of the dismayed nagas, he again called forth the light of day. They, overjoyed at having seen the deity of felicitous advent, bowed down at the feet of the divine teacher. To them the vanquisher preached a sermon of reconciliation. Both parties rejoicing thereat, made an offering of the gem-throne to the divine sage. The divine teacher, alighting on the earth, seated himself on the throne, and was served by the naga kings with celestial food and beverage. The lord of the universe procured for eighty kotis of nagas, dwelling on land and in the waters, the salvation of the faith and the state of piety.'

At every step in the conversion of the native Singhalese,—the demons and serpent-men,—Buddha and his apostles are represented as being attended by the devas,—the deities of India,—who are spoken of as if glad to become menials of the new religion. But we find Zoroaster using this term in a demonic sense, and describing alien worshippers as children of the Devas (a Semite would say, Sons of Belial). And in the conventional Persian pictures of the Last Judgment (moslem), the archfiend has the Hindu complexion. A similar phenomenon may be observed in various regions. In the mediæval frescoes of Moscow, representing infernal tortures, it is not very difficult to pick out devils representing the physical characteristics of most of the races with which the Muscovite has struggled in early times. There are also black Ethiopians among them, which may be a result of devils being considered the brood of Tchernibog, god of Darkness; but may also, not impossibly, have come of such apocryphal narratives as that ascribed to St. Augustine. 'I was already Bishop of Hippo when I went into Ethiopia with some servants of Christ, there to preach the gospel. In this country we saw many men and women without heads, who had two great eyes in their breasts; and in countries still more southerly we saw a people who had but one eye in their foreheads.'4

In considering animal demons, the primitive demonisation of the Wolf has been discussed. But it is mainly as a transformation of man and a type of savage foes that this animal has been a prominent figure in Mythology.

Professor Max Müller has made it tolerably clear that Bellerophon means Slayer of the Hairy; and that Belleros is the transliteration of Sanskrit varvara, a term applied to the dark Aborigines by their Aryan invaders, equivalent to barbarians.5 This points us for the origin of the title rather to Bellerophon's conquest of the Lycians, or Wolf-men, than to his victory over the Chimæra. The story of Lycaon and his sons—barbarians defying the gods and devouring human flesh—turned into wolves by Zeus, connects itself with the Lycians (hairy, wolfish barbarians), whom Bellerophon conquered.

It was not always, however, the deity that conquered in such encounters. In the myth of Soracte, the Wolf is seen able to hold his own against the gods. Soranus, worshipped on Mount Soracte, was at Rome the god of Light, and is identified with Apollo by Virgil.6 A legend states that he became associated with the infernal gods, though called Diespiter, because of the sulphurous exhalations from the side of Mount Soracte. It is said that once when some shepherds were performing a sacrifice, some wolves seized the flesh; the shepherds, following them, were killed by the poisonous vapours of the mountain to which the wolves retreated. An oracle gave out that this was a punishment for their pursuing the sacred animals; and a general pestilence also having followed, it was declared that it could only cease if the people were all changed to wolves and lived by prey. Hence the Hirpini, from the Sabine 'hirpus,' a wolf. The story is a variant of that of the Hirpinian Samnites, who were said to have received their name from their ancestors having followed a sacred wolf when seeking their new home. The Wolf ceremonies were, like the Roman Lupercalia, for purposes of purification. The worshippers ran naked through blazing fires. The annual festival, which Strabo describes as occurring in the grove of Feronia, goddess of Nature, became at last a sort of fair. Its history, however, is very significant of the formidable character of the Hirpini, or Wolf-tribe, which could alone have given rise to such euphemistic celebrations of the wolf.

It is interesting to note that in some regions this wolf of superstition was domesticated into a dog. Pierius says there was a temple of Vulcan in Mount Ætna, in whose grove were dogs that fawned on the pious, but rent the polluted worshippers. It will be seen by the left form of Fig. 13 that the wolf had a diminution, in pictorial representation similar to that which the canine Lares underwent (p. 135). This picture is referred by John Beaumont7 to Cartarius' work on 'The Images of the Gods of the Ancients;' the form wearing a wolf's skin and head is that of the demon Polites, who infested Temesa in Italy, according to a story related by Pausanias. Ulysses, in his wanderings, having come to this town, one of his companions was stoned to death for having ravished a virgin; after which his ghost appeared in form of this demon, which had to be appeased, by the direction of the oracle of Apollo, by the annual sacrifice to him of the most beautiful virgin in the place. Euthymus, enamoured of a virgin about to be so offered, gave battle to this demon, and, having expelled him from the country, married the virgin. However, since the infernal powers cannot be deprived of their rights without substitution, this saviour of Temesa disappeared in the river Cæcinus.

Fig. 13.—Italian and Roman Genii.

The form on the right in Fig. 13 represents the genius of the city of Rome, and is found on some of Hadrian's coins; he holds the cornucopia and the sacrificial dish. The child and the serpent in the same picture represent the origin of the demonic character attributed to the Eleans by the Arcadians. This child-and-serpent symbol, which bears resemblance to certain variants of Bel and the Dragon, no doubt was brought to Elea, or Velia in Italy, by the Phocæans, when they abandoned their Ionian homes rather than submit to Cyrus, and founded that town, B.C. 544. The two forms were jointly worshipped with annual sacrifices in the temple of Lucina, under the name Sosipolis. The legend of this title is related by Pausanias. When the Arcadians invaded the Eleans, a woman came to the Elean commander with an infant at her breast, and said that she had been admonished in a dream to place her child in front of the army. This was done; as the Arcadians approached the child was changed to a serpent, and, astounded at the prodigy, they fled without giving battle. The child was represented by the Eleans decorated with stars, and holding the cornucopia; by the Arcadians, no doubt, in a less celestial way. It is not uncommon in Mythology to find the most dangerous demons represented under some guise of weakness, as, for instance, among the South Africans, some of whom recently informed English officers that the Galeikas were led against them by a terrible sorcerer in the form of a hare. The most fearful traditional demon ever slain by hero in Japan was Shuden Dozi—the Child-faced Drinker. In Ceylon the apparition of a demon is said to be frequently under the form of a woman with a child in her arms.

Many animal demons are mere fables for the ferocity of human tribes. The Were-wolf superstition, which exists still in Russia, where the transformed monster is called volkodlák (volk, a wolf, and dlak, hair), might even have originated in the costume of Norse barbarians and huntsmen. The belief was always more or less rationalised, resembling that held by Verstegan three hundred years ago, and which may be regarded as prevalent among both the English and Flemish people of his day. 'These Were-wolves,' he says, 'are certain sorcerers, who, having anointed their bodies with an ointment they make by the instinct of the devil, and putting on a certain enchanted girdle, do not only unto the view of others seem as wolves, but to their own thinking have both the nature and shape of wolves so long as they wear the said girdle; and they do dispose themselves as very wolves, in worrying and killing, and waste of human creatures.' During the Franco-German war of 1870–71, a family of ladies on the German side of the Rhine, sitting up all night in apprehension, related to me such stories of the 'Turcos' that I have since found no difficulty in understanding the belief in weird and præternatural wolves which once filled Europe with horror. The facility with which the old Lycian wolf-girdle, so to say, was caught up and worn in so many countries where race-wars were chronic for many ages, renders it nearly certain that this superstition (Lycanthropy), however it may have originated, was continued through the custom of ascribing demonic characteristics to hostile and fierce races. It has been, indeed, a general opinion that the theoretical belief originated in the Pythagorean doctrine of metempsychosis. Thus Shakspere:—

Thou almost makest me waver in my faith,
To hold opinion with Pythagoras,
That souls of animals infuse themselves
Into the trunks of men: thy currish spirit

Governed a wolf, who, hanged for human slaughter,
Even from the gallows did his fell soul fleet,
And whilst thou layest in thy unhallowed dam
Infused itself in thee; for thy desires
Are wolfish, bloody, starved, and ravenous.

But the superstition is much older than Pythagoras, who, no doubt, tried to turn it into a moral theory of retributions,—as indeed did Plato in his story of the Vision of Er the Armenian.

Professor Weber and others have adduced evidence indicating that although belief in the transformation of men into beasts was not developed in the Vedic age of India, the matrix of it was there. But of our main fact—the association of demonic characters with certain tribes—India has presented many examples. In the mountains of Travancore there are tribes which are still generally believed to be on terms of especial familiarity with the devils of that region; and the dwellers on the plains relate that on these mountains gigantic demons, sixteen or seventeen feet high, may sometimes be seen hurling firebrands at each other.

Professor Monier Williams contributes an interesting note concerning this general phase of South-Indian demonology. 'Furthermore, it must not be forgotten that although a belief in devils and homage to bhutas, or spirits, of all kinds is common all over India, yet what is called devil-worship is far more systematically practised in the South of India and Ceylon than in the North. And the reason may be that as the invading Aryans advanced towards Southern India, they found portions of it peopled by wild aboriginal savages, whose behaviour and aspect appeared to them to resemble that of devils. The Aryan mind, therefore, naturally pictured to itself the regions of the South as the chief resort and stronghold of the demon race, and the dread of demonical agency became more deeply rooted in Southern India than in the North. Curiously enough, too, it is commonly believed in Southern India that every wicked man contributes by his death to swell the ever-increasing ranks of devil legions. His evil passions do not die with him; they are intensified, concentrated, and perpetuated in the form of a malignant and mischievous spirit.'8

It is obvious that this principle may be extended from individuals to entire tribes. The Cimmerians were regarded as dwelling in a land allied with hell. In the legend of the Alhambra, as told by Washington Irving, the astrologer warns the Moorish king that the beautiful damsel is no doubt one of those Gothic sorceresses of whom they have heard so much. Although, as we have seen, England was regarded on the Continent as an island of demons because of its northern latitude, probably some of its tribes were of a character dangerous enough to prolong the superstition. The nightmare elves were believed to come from England, and to hurry away through the keyholes at daybreak, saying 'The bells are calling in England.'9 Visigoth probably left us our word bigot; and 'Goths and Vandals' sometimes designate English roughs, as 'Turks' those of Constantinople. Herodotus says the Scythians of the Black Sea regarded the Neurians as wizards, who transformed themselves into wolves for a few days annually; but the Scythians themselves are said by Herodotus to have sprung from a monster, half-woman half-serpent; and possibly the association of the Scotch with the Scythians by the Germans, who called them both Scutten, had something to do with the uncanny character ascribed to the British Isles. Sir Walter Raleigh described the Red Men of America as gigantic monsters. 'Red Devils' is still the pioneer's epithet for them in the Far West. The hairy Dukes of Esau were connected with the goat, and demonised as Edom; and Ishmael was not believed much better by the more peaceful Semitic tribes. Such notions are akin to those which many now have of the Thugs and Bashi-Bazouks, and are too uniform and natural to tax much the ingenuity of Comparative Mythology.

Underlying many of the legends of giants and dwarfs may be found a similar demonologic formation. A principle of natural selection would explain the existence of tribes, which, though of small stature, are able to hold their own against the larger and more powerful by their superior cunning. That such equalisation of apparently unequal forces has been known in pre-historic ages may be gathered from many fables. Before Bali, the monarch already mentioned, whose power alarmed the gods themselves, Vishnu appeared as a dwarf, asking only so much land as he could measure with three steps; the apparently ridiculous request granted, the god strode over the whole earth with two steps and brought his third on the head of Bali. In Scandinavian fable we have the young giantess coming to her mother with the plough and ploughman in her apron, which she had picked up in the field. To her child's inquiry, 'What sort of beetle is this I found wriggling in the sand?' the giantess replies, 'Go put it back in the place where thou hast found it. We must be gone out of this land, for these little people will dwell in it.'

The Sagas contain many stories which, while written in glorification of the 'giant' race, relate the destruction of their chiefs by the magical powers of the dwarfs. I must limit myself to a few notes on the Ynglinga Saga. 'In Swithiod,' we are told, 'are many great domains, and many wonderful races of men, and many kinds of languages. There are giants, and there are dwarfs, and there are also blue men. There are wild beasts, and dreadfully large dragons.' We learn that in Asaland was a great chief, Odin, who went out to conquer Vanaland. The Vanalanders are declared to have magic arts,— such as are ascribed to Finns and Lapps to this day by the more ignorant of their neighbours. But that the people of Asaland learned their magic charms. 'Odin was the cleverest of them all, and from him all the others learned their magic arts.' 'Odin could make his enemies in battle blind, or deaf, or terror-struck, and their weapons so blunt that they could no more cut than a willow twig; on the other hand, his men rushed forward without armour, were as mad as dogs or wolves, bit their shields, and were as strong as bears or wild bulls, and killed people at a blow, and neither fire nor iron told upon them. These were called Berserkers.' (From ber, bear, and serkr, sark or coat; the word being probably, as Maurer says, a survival of an earlier belief in the transformation of men into bears.) But the successors of Odin did not preserve his occult power. Svegdir, for instance, saw a large stone and a dwarf at the door entering in it. The dwarf called him to come in and he should see Odin. 'Swedger ran into the stone, which instantly closed behind him, and Swedger never came back.' The witchcraft of the Finn people is said to have led Vanlandi (Svegdir's son) to his death by Mara (night-mare). Vanlandi's son too, Visbur, fell a victim to sorcery. Such legends as these, and many others which may be found in Sturleson's Heimskringla, have influenced our popular stories whose interest turns on the skill with which some little Jack or Thumbling overcomes his adversary by superior cunning.

Superstitions concerning dwarf-powers are especially rife in Northumberland, where they used to be called Duergar, and they were thought to abound on the hills between Rothbury and Elsdon. They mislead with torches. One story relates that a traveller, beguiled at night into a hut where a dwarf prepared a comfortable fire for him, found himself when daylight returned sitting upon the edge of a deep rugged precipice, where the slightest movement had caused him to be dashed to pieces.10 The Northumbrian stories generally, however, do not bear the emphasis of having grown out of aboriginal conditions, or even of having been borrowed for such. The legends of Scotland, and of the South-West of England, appear to me much more suggestive of original struggles between large races and small. They are recalled by the superstitions which still linger in Norway concerning the Lapps, who are said to carry on unholy dealings with gnomes.

In the last century the 'Brownie' was commonly spoken of in Scotland as appearing in shape of 'a tall man,' and the name seems to refer to the brown complexion of that bogey, and its long brown hair, hardly Scottish.11 It is generally the case that Second Sight, which once attained the dignity of being called 'Deuteroscopia,' sees a doomed man or woman shrink to the size of a dwarf. The 'tall man' is not far off in such cases. 'In some age of the world more remote than even that of Alypos,' says Hugh Miller, 'the whole of Britain was peopled by giants—a fact amply supported by early English historians and the traditions of the North of Scotland. Diocletian, king of Syria, say the historians, had thirty-three daughters, who, like the daughters of Danaus, killed their husbands on their wedding night. The king, their father, in abhorrence of the crime, crowded them all into a ship, which he abandoned to the mercy of the waves, and which was drifted by tides and winds till it arrived on the coast of Britain, then an uninhabited island. There they lived solitary, subsisting on roots and berries, the natural produce of the soil, until an order of demons, becoming enamoured of them, took them for their wives; and a tribe of giants, who must be regarded as the true aborigines of the country, if indeed the demons have not a prior claim, were the fruit of these marriages. Less fortunate, however, than even their prototypes the Cyclops, the whole tribe was extirpated a few ages after by Brutus the parricide, who, with a valour to which mere bulk could offer no effectual resistance, overthrew Gog-Magog and Termagol, and a whole host of others with names equally terrible. Tradition is less explicit than the historians in what relates to the origin and extinction of the race, but its narratives of their prowess are more minute. There is a large and ponderous stone in the parish of Edderston which a giantess of the tribe is said to have flung from the point of a spindle across the Dornoch Firth; and another, within a few miles of Dingwall, still larger and more ponderous, which was thrown by a person of the same family, and which still bears the marks of a gigantic finger and thumb.'12

Perhaps we may find the mythological descendants of these Titans, and also of the Druids, in the so-called 'Great Men' once dreaded by Highlanders. The natives of South Uist believed that a valley, called Glenslyte, situated between two mountains on the east side of the island, was haunted by these Great Men, and that if any one entered the valley without formally resigning themselves to the conduct of those beings, they would infallibly become mad. Martin, having remonstrated with the people against this superstition, was told of a woman's having come out of the valley a lunatic because she had not uttered the spell of three sentences. They also told him of voices heard in the air. The Brownie ('a tall man with very long brown hair'), who has cow's milk poured out for him on a hill in the same region, probably of this giant tribe, might easily have been demonised at the time when the Druids were giving St. Columba so much trouble, and trying to retain their influence over the people by professing supernatural powers.13

The man of the smaller stature, making up for his inferiority by invention, perhaps first forged the sword, the coat of mail, and the shield, and so confronted the giant with success. The god with the Hammer might thus supersede the god of the Flint Spear. Magic art seemed to have rendered invulnerable the man from whom the arrow rebounded.

It would appear from King Olaf Tryggvason's Saga that nine hundred years ago the Icelanders and the Danes reciprocally regarded each other as giants and dwarfs. The Icelanders indited lampoons against the Danes which allude to their diminutive size:—

The gallant Harald in the field
Between his legs lets drop his shield,

Into a pony he was changed, etc.

On the other hand, the Danes had by no means a contemptuousidea of their Icelandic enemies, as the following narrative from Heimskringla proves. 'King Harald told a warlock to hie to Iceland in some altered shape, and to try what he could learn there to tell him: and he set out in the shape of a whale. And when he came near to the land he went to the west side of Iceland, north around the land, when he saw all the mountains and hills full of land-serpents, some great, some small. When he came to Vapnafiord he went in towards the land, intending to go on shore; but a huge dragon rushed down the dale against him, with a train of serpents, paddocks, and toads, that blew poison towards him. Then he turned to go westward around the land as far as Eyafiord, and he went into the fiord. Then a bird flew against him, which was so great that its wings stretched over the mountains on either side of the fiord, and many birds, great and small, with it. Then he swam further west, and then south into Breidafiord. When he came into the fiord a large grey bull ran against him, wading into the sea, and bellowing fearfully, and he was followed by a crowd of land-serpents. From thence he went round by Reikaness and wanted to land at Vikarsted, but there came down a hill-giant against him with an iron staff in his hands. He was a head higher than the mountains, and many other giants followed him.' The most seductive Hesperian gardens of the South and East do not appear to have been so thoroughly guarded or defended as Iceland, and one can hardly call it cowardice when (after the wizard-whale brought back the log of its voyage) it is recorded: 'Then the Danish king turned about with his fleet and sailed back to Denmark.'

It is a sufficiently curious fact that the Mimacs, aborigines of Nova Scotia,14 were found with a whale-story, already referred to (p. 46), so much like this. They also have the legend of an ancient warrior named Booin, who possessed the præternatural powers especially ascribed to Odin, those of raising storms, causing excessive cold, increasing or diminishing his size, and assuming any shape. Besides the fearful race of gigantic ice-demons dreaded by this tribe, as elsewhere stated (p. 84), they dread also a yellow-horned dragon called Cheepichealm, (whose form the great Booin sometimes assumes). They make offerings to the new moon. They believe in pixies, calling them Wigguladum-moochkik, 'very little people.' They anciently believed in two great spirits, good and evil, both called Manitoos; since their contact with christians only the evil one has been so called.

The entire motif of the Mimac Demonology is, to my mind, that of early conflicts with some formidable races. It is to be hoped that travellers will pay more attention to this unique race before it has ceased to exist. The Chinese theory of genii is almost exactly that of the Mimacs. The Chinese genii are now small as a moth, now fill the world; can assume any form; they command demons; they never die, but, at the end of some centuries, ride to heaven on a dragon's back.15 Ordinarily the Chinese genii use the yellow heron as an aerial courser. The Mimacs believe in a large præternatural water-bird, Culloo, which devours ordinary people, but bears on its back those who can tame it by magic.

Mr. Mayers, in his 'Chinese Reader's Manual,' suggests that the designation of Formosa as 'Isles of the Genii' (San Shén Shan) by the Chinese, has some reference to their early attempts at colonisation in Japan. Su Fuh, a necromancer, who lived B.C. 219, is said to have announced their discovery, and at the head of a troop of young men and maidens, voyaged with an expedition towards them, but, when within sight of the magic islands, were driven back by contrary winds.

Gog and Magog stand in London Guildhall, though much diminished in stature, to suit the English muscles that had to bear them in processions, monuments of the præternatural size attributed to the enemies which the Aryan race encountered in its great westward migrations. Even to-day, when the progress of civilisation is harassed by untamed Scythian hordes, how strangely fall upon our ears the ancient legends and prophecies concerning them!

Thus saith the Lord Jehovah:
Behold I am against thee, O Gog,
Prince of Rosh, of Meshech, and of Tubul:
And I will turn thee back, and leave but the sixth part of thee;
And I will cause thee to come up from the north parts,
And will bring thee upon the mountains of Israel:
And I will smite thy bow out of thy left hand,
And will cause thine arrows to fall from thy right hand.
Thou shalt fall upon the mountains of Israel,
*Thou and all thy bands.*16

In the Koran it is related of Dhulkarnein:—'He journeyed from south to north until he came between the two mountains, beneath which he found a people who could scarce understand what was said. And they said, O Dhulkarnein, verily Gog and Magog waste the land; shall we, therefore, pay thee tribute, on condition that thou build a rampart between us and them? He answered, The power wherewith my Lord hath strengthened me is better than your tribute; but assist me strenuously and I will set a strong wall between you and them.... Wherefore when this wall was finished, Gog and Magog could not scale it, neither could they dig through it. And Dhulkarnein said, This is a mercy from my Lord; but when the prediction of my Lord shall come to be fulfilled, he will reduce the wall to dust.'

The terror inspired by these barbarians is reflected in the prophecies of their certain irruption from their supernaturally-built fastnesses; as in Ezekiel:—

Thou shalt ascend and come like a storm,
Thou shalt be like a cloud to cover the land,
Thou and all thy bands,
And many people with thee;

and in the Koran, 'Gog and Magog shall have a passage open for them, and they shall hasten from every high hill;' and in the Apocalypse, 'Satan shall be loosed out of his prison, and shall go out to deceive the nations which are in the four quarters of the earth, Gog and Magog, to gather them in battle: the number of whom is as the sand of the sea.' Five centuries ago Sir John Maundeville was telling in England the legend he had heard in the East. 'In that same regioun ben the mountaynes of Caspye, that men clepen Uber in the contree. Betwene the mountaynes the Jews of 10 lynages ben enclosed, that men clepen Gothe and Magothe: and they mowe not gon out on no syde. There weren enclosed 22 kynges, with hire peple, that dwelleden betwene the mountayns of Sythe. There King Alisandre chacede hem betwene the mountaynes, and there he thought for to enclose hem thorghe work of his men. But when he saughe that he might not doon it, ne bringe it to an ende, he preyed to God of Nature, that he wolde performe that that he had begoune. And all were it so, that he was a Payneme, and not worthi to ben herd, zit God of his grace closed the mountaynes to gydre: so that thei dwellen there, all fast ylokked and enclosed with highe mountaynes all aboute, saf only on o syde; and on that syde is the See of Caspye.'

Notes

1 Max Müller, 'Science of Language,' i. 275.
2 The term is now used very vaguely. Mr. Talboys Wheeler, speaking of the 'Scythic Nagas' (Hist. of India, i. 147), says: 'In process of time these Nagas became identified with serpents, and the result has been a strange confusion between serpents and human beings.' In the 'Padma Purana' we read of 'serpent-like men.' (See my 'Sacred Anthology,' p. 263.)
3 'Mahawanso' (Turnour), pp. 3, 6.
4 Ser. xxxiii. Hardly consistent with De Civ. Dei, xvi. 8.
5 'Chips,' ii.
6 'Sancti custos Soractis Apollo.'—Æn. xi. 785.
7 'Treatise of Spirits,' by John Beaumont, Gent., London, 1705.
8 London 'Times,' June 11, 1877.
9 Wuttke, 'Volksaberglaube,' 402. Pliny (iv. 16) says: 'Albion insula sic dicta ab albis rupibus quas mare alluit.' This etymon of Albion from the white cliffs is very questionable; but, since Alb and Elf are generally related, it might have suggested the notion about English demons. Heine identifies the 'White Island,' or Pluto's realm of Continental folklore, as England.
10 Richardson's 'Borderer's Fable-Book,' vi. 97.
11 Martin, Appendix to Report on 'Ossian,' p. 310.
12 'Scenes and Legends,' p. 13.
13 Dr. James Browne's 'History of the Highlands,' p. 113.
14 'North American Review,' January 1871.
15 Dennys, p. 81 et seq.
16 Ezekiel xxxix.

Chapter VII - Barrenness

Indian famine and Sun-spots—Sun-worship—Demon of the Desert—The Sphinx—Egyptian plagues described by Lepsius: Locusts, Hurricane, Flood, Mice, Flies—The Sheikh's ride—Abaddon—Set—Typhon—The Cain wind—Seth—Mirage—The Desert Eden—Azazel—Tawiscara and the Wild Rose.

In their adoration of rain-giving Indra as also a solar majesty, the ancient Hindus seem to have been fully aware of his inconsistent habits. 'Thy inebriety is most intense,' exclaims the eulogist, and soothingly adds, 'Thou desirest that both thy inebriety and thy beneficence should be the means of destroying enemies and distributing riches.'[1] Against famine is invoked the thunderbolt of Indra, and it is likened to the terrible Tvashtri, in whose fearful shape (pure fire) Agni once appeared to the terror of gods and men.2 This Tvashtri was not an evil being himself, but, as we have seen, an artificer for the gods similar to Vulcan; he was, however, father of a three-headed monster who has been identified with Vritra. Though these early worshippers recognised that their chief trouble was connected with 'glaring heat' (which Tvashtri seems to mean in the passage just referred to), Indra's celebrants beheld him superseding his father Dyaus, and reigning in the day's splendour as well as in the cloud's bounty. This monopolist of parts in their theogony anticipated Jupiter Pluvius. Vedic mythology is pervaded with stories of the demons that arrested the rain and stole the cloud-cows of Indra—shutting them away in caves,—and the god is endlessly praised for dealing death to such. He slays Vritra, the 'rain-arresting,' and Dribhika, Bala, Urana, Arbuda, 'devouring Swasna,' 'unabsorbable Súshna,' Pipru, Namuchi, Rudhikrá, Varchin and his hundred thousand descendants;3 the deadly strangling serpent Ahi, especial type of Drouth as it dries up rivers; and through all these combats with the alleged authors of the recurring Barrenness and Famine, as most of these monsters were, the seat of the evil was the Sun-god's adorable self!

Almost pathetic does the long and vast history appear just now, when competent men of science are giving us good reason to believe that right knowledge of the sun, and the relation of its spots to the rainfall, might have covered India with ways and means which would have adapted the entire realm to its environment, and wrested from Indra his hostile thunderbolt—the sunstroke of famine. The Hindus have covered their lands with temples raised to propitiate and deprecate the demons, and to invoke the deities against such sources of drouth and famine. Had they concluded that famine was the result of inexactly quartered sun-dials, the land would have been covered with perfect sun-dials; but the famine would have been more destructive, because of the increasing withdrawal of mind and energy from the true cause, and its implied answer. Even so were conflagrations in London attributed to inexact city clocks; the clocks would become perfect, the conflagrations more numerous, through misdirection of vigilance. But how much wiser are we of Christendom than the Hindus? They have adapted their country perfectly for propitiation of famine-demons that do not exist, at a cost which would long ago have rendered them secure from the famine-forces that do exist. We have similarly covered Christendom with a complete system of securities against hells and devils and wrathful deities that do not exist, while around our churches, chapels, cathedrals, are the actually-existent seething hells of pauperism, shame, and crime. 'Nothing can advance art in any district of this accursed machine-and-devil-driven England until she changes her mind in many things.' So wrote John Ruskin recently. Of course, so long as the machine toils and earns wealth and other power which still goes to support and further social and ecclesiastical forms, constituted with reference to salvation from a devil or demons no longer believed in, the phrase 'machine-and-devil-driven' is true. Until the invention and enterprise of the nation are administered in the interest of right ideas, we may still sigh, like John Sterling, for 'a dozen men to stand up for ideas as Cobden and his friends do for machinery.' But it still remains as true that all the machinery and wealth of England devoted to man might make its every home happy, and educate every inhabitant, as that every idolatrous temple in India might be commuted into a shield against famine.

Our astronomers and economists have enabled us to see clearly how the case is with the country whose temples offer no obstruction to christian vision. The facts point to the conclusion that the sun-spots reach their maximum and minimum of intensity at intervals of eleven years, and that their high activity is attended with frequent fluctuations of the magnetic needle, and increased rainfall. In 1811, and since then, famines in India have, with one exception, followed years of minimum sun-spots.4 These facts are sufficiently well attested to warrant the belief that English science and skill will be able to realise in India the provision which Joseph is said to have made for the seven lean years of which Pharaoh dreamed.

Until that happy era shall arrive, the poor Hindus will only go on alternately adoring and propitiating the sun, as its benign or its cruel influences shall fall upon them. The artist Turner said, 'The sun is God.' The superb effects of light in Turner's pictures could hardly have come from any but a sun-worshipper dwelling amid fogs. Unfamiliarity often breeds reverence. There are few countries in which the sun, when it does shine, is so likely to be greeted with enthusiasm, and observed in all its variations of splendour, as one in which its appearance is rare. Yet the superstition inherited from regions where the sun is equally a desolation was strong enough to blot out its glory in the mind of a writer famous in his time, Tobias Swinden, M.A., who wrote a work to prove the sun to be the abode of the damned.5 The speculation may now appear only curious, but, probably, it is no more curious than a hundred years from now will seem to all the vulgar notion of future fiery torments for mankind, the scriptural necessity of which led the fanciful rector to his grotesque conclusion. These two extremes—the Sun-worship of Turner, the Sun-horror of Swinden,—survivals in England, represent the two antagonistic aspects of the sun, which were of overwhelming import to those who dwelt beneath its greatest potency. His ill-humour, or his hunger and thirst, in any year transformed the earth to a desert, and dealt death to thousands.

In countries where drouth, barrenness, and consequent famine were occasional, as in India, it would be an inevitable result that they would represent the varying moods of a powerful will, and in such regions we naturally find the most extensive appliances for propitiation. The preponderant number of fat years would tell powerfully on the popular imagination in favour of priestly intercession, and the advantage of sacrifices to the great Hunger-demon who sometimes consumed the seeds of the earth. But in countries where barrenness was an ever-present, visible, unvarying fact, the

Demon of the Desert would represent Necessity, a power not to be coaxed or changed. People dwelling in distant lands might invent theoretical myths to account for the desert. It might be an accident resulting from the Sun-god having given up his chariot one day to an inexperienced driver who came too close to the earth. But to those who lived beside the desert it could only seem an infernal realm, quite irrecoverable. The ancient civilisation of Egypt, so full of grandeur, might, in good part, have been due to the lesson taught them by the desert, that they could not change the conditions around them by any entreaties, but must make the best of what was left. If such, indeed, was the force that built the ancient civilisation whose monuments remain so magnificent in their ruins, its decay might be equally accounted for when that primitive faith passed into a theological phase. For as Necessity is the mother of invention, Fate is fatal to the same. Belief in facts, and laws fixed in the organic nature of things, stimulates man to study them and constitute his life with reference to them; but belief that things are fixed by the arbitrary decree of an individual power is the final sentence of enterprise. Fate might thus steadily bring to ruin the grandest achievements of Necessity.

Had we only the true history of the Sphinx—the Binder—we might find it a landmark between the rise and decline of Egyptian civilisation. When the great Limitation surrounding the powers of man was first personified with that mystical grandeur, it would stand in the desert not as the riddle but its solution. No such monument was ever raised by Doubt. But once personified and outwardly shaped, the external Binder must bind thought as well; nay, will throttle thought if it cannot pierce through the stone and discover the meaning of it. 'How true is that old fable of the Sphinx who sat by the wayside propounding her riddle to the passengers, which if they could not answer she destroyed them! Such a Sphinx is this Life of ours to all men and societies of men. Nature, like the Sphinx, is of womanly celestial loveliness and tenderness; the face and bosom of a goddess, but ending in claws and the body of a lioness. There is in her a celestial beauty,—which means celestial order, pliancy to wisdom; but there is also a darkness, a ferocity, fatality, which are infernal. She is a goddess, but one not yet disimprisoned; one still half-imprisoned,—the articulate, lovely still encased in the inarticulate, chaotic. How true! And does she not propound her riddles to us? Of each man she asks daily, in mild voice, yet with a terrible significance, 'Knowest thou the meaning of this Day? What thou canst do To-day, wisely attempt to do.' Nature, Universe, Destiny, Existence, howsoever we name this grand unnameable Fact, in the midst of which we live and struggle, is as a heavenly bride and conquest to the wise and brave, to them who can discern her behests and do them; a destroying fiend to them who cannot. Answer her riddle, it is well with thee. Answer it not, pass on regarding it not, it will answer itself; the solution for thee is a thing of teeth and claws; Nature to thee is a dumb lioness, deaf to thy pleadings, fiercely devouring. Thou art not now her victorious bridegroom; thou art her mangled victim, scattered on the precipices, as a slave found treacherous, recreant, ought to be, and must.'6

On the verge of the Desert, Prime Minister to the Necropolis at whose gateway it stands, the Sphinx reposes amid the silence of science and the centuries. Who built it? None can answer, so far as the human artist, or the king under whom he worked, is concerned. But the ideas and natural forces which built the Sphinx surround even now the archæologist who tries to discover its history and chronology. As fittest appendage to Carlyle's interpretation, let us read some passages from Lepsius.

'The Oedipus for this king of the Sphinxes is yet wanting. Whoever would drain the immeasurable sand-flood which buries the tombs themselves, and lay open the base of the Sphinx, the ancient temple-path, and the surrounding hills, could easily decide it. But with the enigmas of history there are joined many riddles and wonders of nature, which I must not leave quite unnoticed. The newest of all, at least, I must describe.

'I had descended with Abeken into a mummy-pit, to open some newly discovered sarcophagi, and was not a little astonished, upon descending, to find myself in a regular snow-drift of locusts, which, almost darkening the heavens, flew over our heads from the south-west from the desert in hundreds of thousands to the valley. I took it for a single flight, and called my companions from the tombs, where they were busy, that they might see this Egyptian wonder ere it was over. But the flight continued; indeed the work-people said it had begun an hour before. Then we first observed that the whole region, near and far, was covered with locusts. I sent an attendant into the desert to discover the breadth of the flock. He ran for the distance of a quarter of an hour, then returned and told us that, as far as he could see, there was no end to them. I rode home in the midst of the locust shower. At the edge of the fruitful plain they fell down in showers; and so it went on the whole day until the evening, and so the next day from morning till evening, and the third; in short to the sixth day, indeed in weaker flights much longer. Yesterday it did seem that a storm of rain in the desert had knocked down and destroyed the last of them. The Arabs are now lighting great smoke-fires in the fields, and clattering and making loud noises all day long to preserve their crops from the unexpected invasion. It will, however, do little good. Like a new animated vegetation, these millions of winged spoilers cover even the neighbouring sand-hills, so that scarcely anything is to be seen of the ground; and when they rise from one place they immediately fall down somewhere in the neighbourhood; they are tired with their long journey, and seem to have lost all fear of their natural enemies, men, animals, smoke, and noise, in their furious wish to fill their stomachs, and in the feeding of their immense number. The most wonderful thing, in my estimation, is their flight over the naked wilderness, and the instinct which has guided them from some oasis over the inhospitable desert to the fat soil of the Nile vale. Fourteen years ago, it seems, this Egyptian plague last visited Egypt with the same force. The popular idea is that they are sent by the comet which we have observed

63

for twelve days in the South-west, and which, as it is now no longer obscured by the rays of the moon, stretches forth its stately tail across the heavens in the hours of the night. The Zodiacal light, too, so seldom seen in the north, has lately been visible for several nights in succession.'

Other plagues of Egypt are described by Lepsius:—

'Suddenly the storm grew to a tremendous hurricane, such as I have never seen in Europe, and hail fell upon us in such masses as almost to turn day into night.... Our tents lie in a valley, whither the plateau of the pyramids inclines, and are sheltered from the worst winds from the north and west. Presently I saw a dashing mountain flood hurrying down upon our prostrate and sand-covered tents, like a giant serpent upon its certain prey. The principal stream rolled on to the great tent; another arm threatened mine without reaching it. But everything that had been washed from our tents by the shower was torn away by the two streams, which joined behind the tents, and carried into a pool behind the Sphinx, where a great lake immediately formed, which fortunately had no outlet. Just picture this scene to yourself! Our tents, dashed down by the storm and heavy rain, lying between two mountain torrents, thrusting themselves in several places to the depth of six feet in the sand, and depositing our books, drawings, sketches, shirts, and instruments—yes, even our levers and iron crow-bars; in short, everything they could seize, in the dark foaming mud-ocean. Besides this, ourselves wet to the skin, without hats, fastening up the weightier things, rushing after the lighter ones, wading into the lake to the waist to fish out what the sand had not yet swallowed; and all this was the work of a quarter of an hour, at the end of which the sun shone radiantly again, and announced the end of this flood by a bright and glorious rainbow.

'Now comes the plague of mice, with which we were not formerly acquainted; in my tent they grow, play, and whistle, as if they had been at home here all their lives, and quite regardless of my presence. At night they have already run across my bed and face, and yesterday I started terrified from my slumbers, as I suddenly felt the sharp tooth of such a daring guest at my foot.

'Above me a canopy of gauze is spread, in order to keep off the flies, these most shameless of the plagues of Egypt, during the day, and the mosquitos at night.... Scorpions and serpents have not bitten us yet, but there are very malicious wasps, which have often stung us.

'The dale (in the Desert) was wild and monotonous, nothing but sandstone rock, the surfaces of which were burned as black as coals, but turned into burning golden yellow at every crack, and every ravine, whence a number of sand-rivulets, like fire-streams from black dross, ran and filled the valleys. No tree, no tuft of grass had we yet seen, also no animals, except a few vultures and crows feeding on the carcase of the latest fallen camel.... Over a wild and broken path, and cutting stones, we came deeper and deeper into the gorge. The first wide basins were empty, we therefore left the camels and donkeys behind, climbed up the smooth granite wall, and thus proceeded amidst these grand rocks from one basin to another; they were all empty. Behind there, in the farthest ravine, the guide said there must be water, for it was never empty; but there proved to be not a single drop. We were obliged to return dry.... We saw the most beautiful mirages very early in the day; they most minutely resemble seas and lakes, in which mountains, rocks, and everything in their vicinity, are reflected as in the clearest water. They form a remarkable contrast with the staring dry desert, and have probably deceived many a poor wanderer, as the legend goes. If one be not aware that no water is there, it is quite impossible to distinguish the appearance from the reality. A few days ago I felt quite sure that I perceived an overflowing of the Nile, or a branch near El Mechêref, and rode towards it, but only found Bahr Sheitan, Satan's water, as the Arabs call it.'7

Amid such scenery the Sphinx arose. Egypt was able to recognise the problem of blended barrenness and beauty—alternation of Nature's flowing breast and leonine claw—but could she return the right answer? The primitive Egyptian answer may, indeed, as I have guessed, be the great monuments of her civilisation, but her historic solution has been another world. This world a desert, with here and there a momentary oasis, where man may dance and feast a little, stimulated by the corpse borne round the banquet, ere he passes to paradise. So thought they and were deceived; from generation to generation have they been destroyed, even unto this day. How destroyed, Lepsius may again be our witness.

'The Sheîkh of the Saadîch-derwishes rides to the chief Sheîkh of all the derwishes of Egypt, El Bekri. On the way thither, a great number of these holy folk, and others, too, who fancy themselves not a whit behind-hand in piety, throw themselves flat on the ground, with their faces downward, and so that the feet of one lie close to the head of the next; over this living carpet the sheîkh rides on his horse, which is led on each side by an attendant, in order to compel the animal to the unnatural march. Each body receives two treads of the horse; most of them jump up again without hurt, but whoever suffers serious, or as it occasionally happens, mortal injury, has the additional ignominy to bear of not having pronounced, or not being able to pronounce, the proper prayers and magical charms that alone could save him.'

'What a fearful barbarous worship' (the Sikr, in which the derwishes dance until exhausted, howling 'No God but Allah') 'which the astounded multitude, great and small, gentle and simple, gaze upon seriously, and with stupid respect, and in which it not unfrequently takes a part! The invoked deity is manifestly much less an object of reverence than the fanatic saints who invoke him; for mad, idiotic, or other psychologically-diseased persons are very generally looked upon as holy by the Mohammedans, and treated with great respect. It is the demoniacal, incomprehensibly-acting, and therefore fearfully-observed, power of nature that the natural man always reveres when he perceives it, because he is sensible of

64

some connection between it and his intellectual power, without being able to command it; first in the mighty elements, then in the wondrous but obscure law-governed instincts of animals, and at last in the yet more overpowering ecstatical or generally abnormal mental condition of his own race.'

The right answer to the enigma of the Sphinx is Man. But this creature prostrating himself under the Sheîkh's horse, or under the invisible Sheîkh called Allah, and ascribing sanctity to the half-witted, is not Man at all. Those hard-worked slaves who escaped into the wilderness, and set up for worship an anthropomorphic Supreme Will, and sought their promised milk and honey in this world alone, carried with them the only force that could rightly answer the Sphinx. Their Allah or Elohim they heard say,—'Why howlest thou to me? Go forward.' Somewhat more significant than his usual jests was that cartoon of Punch which represented the Sphinx with relaxed face smiling recognition on the most eminent of contemporary Israelites returning to the land of his race's ancient bondage, to buy the Suez Canal. The Suez Canal half answers the Sphinx; when man has subdued the Great Desert to a sea, the solution will be complete, and the Sphinx may cast herself into it.

Far and wide through the Southern world have swarmed the locusts described by Lepsius, and with them have migrated many superstitions. The writer of this well remembers the visit of the so-called 'Seventeen-year locusts,' to the region of Virginia where he was born, and across many years can hear the terrible never-ceasing roar coming up from the woods, uttering, as all agreed, the ominous word 'Pharaoh.' On each wing every eye could see the letter W, signifying War. With that modern bit of ancient Egypt in my memory, I find the old Locust-mythology sufficiently impressive.

By an old tradition the Egyptians, as described by Lepsius, connected the locusts with the comet. In the Apocalypse (ix.) a falling star is the token of the descent of the Locust-demon to unlock the pit that his swarms may issue forth for their work of destruction. Their king Abaddon, in Greek Apollyon,—Destroyer,—has had an evolution from being the angel of the two (rabbinical) divisions of Hades to the successive Chiefs of Saracenic hordes. It is interesting to compare the graphic description of a locust-storm in Joel, with its adaptation to an army of human destroyers in the Apocalypse. And again the curious description of these hosts of Abaddon in the latter book, partly repeat the strange notions of the Bedouins concerning the locust,—one of whom, says Niebuhr, 'compared the head of the locust to that of the horse; its breast to that of a lion; its feet to those of a camel; its body to that of the serpent; its tail to that of the scorpion; its horns (antennæ) to the locks of hair of a virgin.' The present generation has little reason to deny the appropriateness of the biblical descriptions of Scythian hordes as locusts. 'The land is as the garden of Eden before them, and behind them a desolate wilderness.'

The ancient seeming contest between apparent Good and Evil in Egypt, was represented in the wars of Ra and Set. It is said (Gen. iv. 26), 'And to Seth, to him also was born a son; and he called his name Enos; then began men to call upon the name of the Lord.' Aquila reads this—'Then Seth began to be called by the name of the Lord.' Mr. Baring-Gould remarks on this that Seth was at first regarded by the Egyptians as the deity of light and civilisation, but that they afterwards identified as Typhon, because he was the chief god of the Hyksos or shepherd kings; and in their hatred of these oppressors the name of Seth was everywhere obliterated from their monuments, and he was represented as an ass, or with an ass's head.8 But the earliest date assigned to the Hyksos dominion in Egypt, B.C. 2000, coincides with that of the Egyptian planisphere in Kircher,9 where Seth is found identified with Sirius, or the dog-headed Mercury, in Capricorn. This is the Sothiac Period, or Cycle of the Dog-star. He was thus associated with the goat and the winter solstice, to which (B.C. 2000) Capricorn was adjacent. That Seth or Set became the name for the demon of disorder and violence among the Egyptians is, indeed, probably due to his being a chief god, among some tribes Baal himself, among the Asiatics, before the time of the Hyksos. It was already an old story to put their neighbours' Light for their own Darkness. The Ass's ears they gave him referred not to his stupidity, but to his hearing everything, as in the case of the Ass of Apuleius, and the ass Nicon of Plutarch, or, indeed, the many examples of the same kind which preceeded the appearance of this much misunderstood animal as the steed of Christ's triumphal entry into Jerusalem. In Egyptian symbolism those long ears were as much dreaded as devils' horns. From the eyes of Ra all beneficent things, from the eyes of Set all noxious things, were produced. Amen-Ra, as the former was called, slew the son of Set, the great serpent Naka, which in one hymn is perhaps tauntingly said to have 'saved his feet.' Amen-Ra becomes Horus and Set becomes Typhon. The Typhonian myth is very complex, and includes the conflict between the Nile and all its enemies—the crocodiles that lurk in it, the sea that swallows it, the drouth that dries it, the burning heat that brings malaria from it, the floods that render it destructive— and Set was through it evolved to a point where he became identified with Saturn, Sheitan, or Satan. Plutarch, identifying Set with Typho, says that those powers of the universal Soul, which are subject to the influences of passions, and in the material system whatever is noxious, as bad air, irregular seasons, eclipses of the sun and moon, are ascribed to Typho. The name Set, according to him, means 'violent' and 'hostile;' and he was described as 'double-headed,' 'he who has two countenances,' and 'the Lord of the World.' Not the least significant fact, in a moral sense, is that Set or Typho is represented as the brother of Osiris whom he slew.

Without here going into the question of relationship between Typhaon and Typhoeus, we may feel tolerably certain that the fire-breathing hurricane-monster Typhaon of Homer, and the hundred-headed, fierce-eyed roarer Typhoeus—son of Tartarus, father of Winds and Harpies—represent the same ferocities of Nature. No fitter place was ever assigned him than the African desert, and the story of the gods and goddesses fleeing before Typhon into Egypt, and there transforming themselves into animals, from terror, is a transparent tribute to the dominion over the wilderness of sand exercised by the typhoon in its many moods. The vulture-harpy tearing the dead is his child. He is many-headed; now hot, stifling, tainted; now tempestuous; here sciroc, there hurricane, and often tornado. It may be indeed that as at once coiled in the whirlwind and blistering, he is the fiery serpent to appease whom Moses lifted the brasen serpent for the worship of Israel. I have often seen snakes hung up by negroes in Virginia, to bring rain in time of drouth. Typhon, as may easily be seen by the accompanying figure (14), is a hungry and thirsty demon. His tongue is lolling out with thirst.10 His later

Fig. 14.—Typhon (Wilkinson).

connection with the underworld is shown in various myths, one of which seems to suggest a popular belief that Typhon is not pleased with the mummies withheld from him, and that he can enjoy his human viands only through burials of the dead. In Egypt, after the Coptic Easter Monday—called Shemmen-Nesseem (smelling the zephyr)—come the fifty-days' hot wind, called Khamseen or Cain wind. After slaying Abel, Cain wandered amid such a wind, tortured with fever and thirst. Then he saw two birds fight in the air; one having killed the other scratched a hole in the desert sand and buried it. Cain then did the like by his brother's body, when a zephyr sprang up and cooled his fever. But still, say the Alexandrians, the fifty-days' hot Cain wind return annually.

In pictures of the mirage, or in cloud-shapes faintly illumined by the afterglow, the dwellers beside the plains of sand saw, as in phantasmagoria, the gorgeous palaces, the air-castles, and mysterious cities, which make the romance of the desert. Unwilling to believe that such realms of barrenness had ever been created by any good god, they beheld in dreams, which answer to nature's own mirage-dreaming, visions of dynasties passed away, of magnificent palaces and monarchs on whose pomp and heaven-defying pride the fatal sand-storm had fallen, and buried their glories in the dust for ever. The desert became the emblem of immeasurable all-devouring Time. In many of these legends there are intimations of a belief that Eden itself lay where now all is unbroken desert. In the beautiful legend in the Midrash of Solomon's voyage on the Wind, the monarch alighted near a lofty palace of gold, 'and the scent there was like the scent of the garden of Eden.' The dust had so surrounded this palace that Solomon and his companions only learned that there had been an entrance from an eagle in it thirteen centuries old, which had heard from its father the tradition of an entrance on the western side. The obedient Wind having cleared away the sand, a door was found on whose lock was written, 'Be it known to you, ye sons of men, that we dwelt in this palace in prosperity and delight many years. When the famine came upon us we ground pearls in the mill instead of wheat, but it profited us nothing.' Amid marvellous splendours, from chamber to chamber garnished with ruby, topaz, emerald, Solomon passed to a mansion on whose three gates were written admonitions of the transitory nature of all things but—Death. 'Let not fortune deceive thee.' 'The world is given from one to another.' On the third gate was written, 'Take provision for thy journey, and make ready food for thyself while it is yet day; for thou shalt not be left on the earth, and thou knowest not the day of thy Death.' This gate Solomon opened and saw within a life-like image seated: as the monarch approached, this image cried with a loud voice, 'Come hither, ye children of Satan; see! King Solomon is come to destroy you.' Then fire and smoke issued from the nostrils of the image; and there were loud and bitter cries, with earthquake and thunder. But Solomon uttered against them the Ineffable Name, and all the images fell on their faces, and the sons of Satan fled and cast themselves into the sea, that they might not fall into the hands of Solomon. The king then took from the neck of the image a silver tablet, with an inscription which he could not read, until the Almighty sent a youth to assist him. It said:—'I, Sheddad, son of Ad, reigned over a thousand thousand provinces, and rode on a thousand thousand horses; a thousand thousand kings were subject to me, and a thousand thousand warriors I slew. Yet in the hour that the Angel of Death came against me, I could not withstand him. Whoso shall read this writing let him not trouble himself greatly about this world, for the end of all men is to die, and nothing remains to man but a good name.'11

Azazel—'of doubtful meaning'—is the biblical name of the Demon of the Desert (Lev. xvi.). 'Aaron shall cast lots upon the two goats: one lot for Jehovah, and the other for Azazel. And Aaron shall bring the goat upon which the lot for Jehovah fell, and offer him for a sin-offering: But the goat, on which the lot for Azazel fell, shall be presented alive before Jehovah, to make an atonement with him, to let him go to Azazel in the wilderness.... And Aaron shall lay both his hands upon the head of the live goat, and confess over him all the iniquities of the children of Israel, and all their transgressions in all their sins, putting them upon the head of the goat, and send him away by the hand of a fit man into the desert. And the goat shall bear upon him all their iniquities unto a land not inhabited; and he shall let go the goat in the desert.' Of the moral elements here involved much will have to be said hereafter. This demon ultimately turned to a devil; and persisting through both forms is the familiar principle that it is 'well enough to have friends on both sides' so plainly at work in the levitical custom; but it is particularly interesting to observe that the same animal should be used as offerings to the antagonistic deities. In Egyptian Mythology we find that the goat had precisely this two-fold consecration. It was sacred to Chem, the Egyptian Pan, god of orchards and of all fruitful lands; and it became also sacred to Mendes, the 'Destroyer,' or 'Avenging Power' of Ra. It will thus be seen that the same principle which from the sun detached the fructifying from the desert-making power, and made Typhon and Osiris hostile brothers, prevailed to send the same animal to Azazel in the Desert and Jehovah of the milk and honey land. Originally the goat was supreme. The Samaritan Pentateuch, according to Aben Ezra (Preface to Esther), opens, 'In the beginning Ashima created the heaven and the earth.' In the Hebrew culture-myth of Cain and Abel, also brothers, there may be represented, as Goldziher supposes, the victory of the agriculturist over the nomad or shepherd; but there is also traceable in it the supremacy of the Goat, Mendez or Azima. 'Abel brought the firstling of the goats.'

Very striking is the American (Iroquois) myth of the conflict between Joskeha and Tawiscara,—the White One and the Dark One. They were twins, born of a virgin who died in giving them life. Their grandmother was the moon (Ataensic, she who bathes). These brothers fought, Joskeha using as weapon the horns of a stag, Tawiscara the wild-rose. The latter fled sorely wounded, and the blood gushing from him turned to flint-stones. The victor, who used the stag-horns (the same weapon that Frey uses against Beli, in the Prose Edda, and denoting perhaps a primitive bone-age art), destroyed a monster frog which swallowed all the waters, and guided the torrents into smooth streams and lakes. He stocked the woods with game, invented fire, watched and watered crops, and without him, says the old missionary Brebeuf, 'they think they could not boil a pot.' The use by the desert-demon Tawiscara of a wild rose as his weapon is a beautiful touch in this myth. So much loveliness grew even amid the hard flints. One is reminded of the closing scene in the second part of Goethe's Faust. There, when Faust has realised the perfect hour to which he can say, 'Stay, thou art fair!' by causing by his labour a wilderness to blossom as a rose, he lies down in happy death; and when the demons come for his soul, angels pelt them with roses, which sting them like flames. Not wild roses were these, such as gave the Dark One such poor succour. The defence of Faust is the roses he has evoked from briars.

Notes

1 'Rig-Veda,' iv. 175, 5 (Wilson).
2 Ibid., i. 133, 6.
3 'Rig-Veda,' vi. 14.
4 'The Nineteenth Century,' November 1877. Article: 'Sun-Spots and Famines,' by Norman Lockyer and W. W. Hunter.
5 'An Inquiry into the Nature and Place of Hell,' by Tobias Swinden, M.A., late Rector of Cuxton-in-Kent. 1727.
6 Carlyle, 'Past and Present,' i. 2.
7 'Discoveries in Egypt,' etc. (Bentley.) 1852.
8 'Legends of Old Testament Characters,' i. p. 83.
9 Œdip., 1. II. ii. See 'Mankind: their Origin and Destiny,' p. 699.
10 Compare Kali, Fig. 18.
11 Soc. of Heb. Literature's Publications. 2d Series. 'Legends from the Midrash,' by Thomas Chenery (Trübner & Co.). The same legend is referred to in the story of the Astrologer in Washington Irving's 'Alhambra.'

Chapter VIII - Obstacles

Mephistopheles on Crags—Emerson on Monadnoc—Ruskin on Alpine peasants—Holy and Unholy Mountains—The Devil's Pulpit—Montagnards—Tarns—Tenjo—T'ai-shan—Apocatequil—Tyrolese Legends—Rock Ordeal—Scylla and Charybdis—Scottish Giants—Pontifex—Devil's Bridges—Le géant Yéous.

Related to the demons of Barrenness, and to the hostile human demons, but still possessing characteristics of their own, are the demons supposed to haunt gorges, mountain ranges, ridges of rocks, streams which cannot be forded and are yet unbridged, rocks that wreck the raft or boat. Each and every obstruction that stood in the way of man's plough, or of his first frail ship, or his migration, has been assigned its demon. The reader of Goethe's page has only to turn to the opening lines of Walpurgisnacht in Faust to behold the real pandemonium of the Northern man, as in Milton he may find that of the dweller amid fiery deserts and volcanoes. That labyrinth of vales, crossed with wild crag and furious torrent, is the natural scenery to surround the orgies of the phantoms which flit from the uncultured brain to uncultured nature. Elsewhere in Goethe's great poem, Mephistopheles pits against the philosophers the popular theory of the rugged remnants of chaos in nature, and the obstacles before which man is powerless.

Faust. For me this mountain mass rests nobly dumb;
I ask not whence it is, nor why 'tis come?

Herself when Nature in herself did found
This globe of earth, she then did purely round;
The summit and abyss her pleasure made,
Mountain to mountain, rock to rock she laid;
The hillocks down she neatly fashion'd then,
To valleys soften'd them with gentle train.
Then all grew green and bloom'd, and in her joy
She needs no foolish spoutings to employ.
Mephistopheles. So say ye! It seems clear as noon to ye,
Yet he knows who was there the contrary.
I was hard by below, when seething flame
Swelled the abyss, and streaming fire forth came;
When Moloch's hammer forging rock to rock,
Far flew the fragment-cliffs beneath the shock:
Of masses strange and huge the land was full;
Who clears away such piles of hurl'd misrule?
Philosophers the reason cannot see;
There lies the rock, and they must let it be.
We have reflected till ashamed we've grown;
The common folk can thus conceive alone,
And in conception no disturbance know,
Their wisdom ripen'd has long while ago:
A miracle it is, they Satan honour show.
My wanderer on faith's crutches hobbles on
*Towards the devil's bridge and devil's stone.*1

The great American poet made his pilgrimage to the mountain so beautiful in the distance, thinking to find there the men of equal elevation. Did not Milton describe Freedom as 'a mountain nymph?'

To myself I oft recount
The tale of many a famous mount,—
Wales, Scotland, Uri, Hungary's dells;
Roys, and Scanderbergs, and Tells.
Here Nature shall condense her powers,
Her music, and her meteors,
And lifting man to the blue deep
Where stars their perfect courses keep,
Like wise preceptor, lure his eye.
To sound the science of the sky.

But instead of finding there the man using those crags as a fastness to fight pollution of the mind, he

searched the region round
And in low hut my monarch found:
He was no eagle, and no earl;—
Alas! my foundling was a churl,
With heart of cat and eyes of bug,
*Dull victim of his pipe and mug.*2

Ruskin has the same gloomy report to make of the mountaineers of Europe. 'The wild goats that leap along those rocks have as much passion of joy in all that fair work of God as the men that toil among them. Perhaps more.' 'Is it not strange to reflect that hardly an evening passes in London or Paris but one of those cottages is painted for the better amusement of the fair and idle, and shaded with pasteboard pines by the scene-shifter; and that good and kind people,—poetically minded,—delight themselves in imagining the happy life led by peasants who dwell by Alpine fountains, and kneel to crosses upon peaks of rock? that nightly we lay down our gold to fashion forth simulacra of peasants, in gay ribbons and white bodices, singing sweet songs and bowing gracefully to the picturesque crosses; and all the while the veritable peasants are kneeling, songlessly, to veritable crosses in another temper than the kind and fair audiences dream of, and assuredly with another kind of answer than is got out of the opera catastrophe.'3

The writer remembers well the emphasis with which a poor woman at whose cottage he asked the path to the Natural Bridge in Virginia said, 'I don't know why so many people come to these rocks; for my part, give me a level country.' Many ages lay between that aged crone and Emerson or Ruskin, and they were ages of heavy war with the fortresses of nature. The fabled ordeals of water and fire through which the human race passed were associated with Ararat and Sinai, because to migrating or farming man the mountain was always an ordeal, irrespective even of its torrents or its occasional lava-streams. A terrible vista is opened by the cry of Lot, 'I cannot escape to the mountain lest some evil take me!' Not even the fire consuming Sodom in the plains could nerve him to dare cope with the demons of the steep places. As time went on, devotees proved to the awe-stricken peasantries their sanctity and authority by combating those mountain demons, and erecting their altars in the 'high places.' So many summits became sacred. But this very sanctity was the means of bringing on successive demoniac hordes to haunt them; for every new religion saw in those altars in 'high places' not victories over demons, but demon-shrines. And thus mountains became the very battlefields between rival deities, each demon to his or her rival; and the conflict lasts from the cursing of the 'high places' by the priests of Israel4 to the Devil's Pulpits of the Alps and Apennines. Among the beautiful frescoes at Baden is that of the Angel's and the Devil's Pulpit, by Götzenberger. Near Gernsbach, appropriately at the point where the cultivable valley meets the unconquerable crests of rock, stand the two pulpits from which Satan and an Angel contended, when the first Christian missionaries had failed to convert the rude foresters. When, by the Angel's eloquence, all were won from the Devil's side except a few witches and usurers, the fiend tore up great masses of rock and built the 'Devil's Mill' on the mountain-top; and he was hurled down by the Almighty on the rocks near 'Lord's Meadow,' where the marks of his claws may still be seen, and where, by a diminishing number of undiminished ears, his groans are still heard when a storm rages through the valley.

Such conflicts as these have been in some degree associated with every mountain of holy or unholy fame. Each was in its time a prosaic Hill Difficulty, with lions by no means chained, to affright the hearts of Mistrust and Timorous, till Dervish or Christian impressed there his holy footprint, visible from Adam's Peak to Olivet, or built there his convents, discernible from Meru and Olympus to Pontyprydd and St. Catharine's Hill. By necessary truces the demons and deities repair gradually to their respective summits,—Seir and Sinai hold each their own. But the Holy Hills have never equalled the number of Dark Mountains5 dreaded by man. These obstructive demons made the mountains Moul-ge and Nin-ge, names for the King and Queen of the Accadian Hell; they made the Finnish Mount Kippumaki the abode of all Pests. They have identified their name (Elf) with the Alps, given nearly every tarn an evil fame, and indeed created a special class of demons, 'Montagnards,' much dreaded by mediæval miners, whose faces they sometimes twisted so that they must look backward physically, as they were much in the habit of doing mentally, for ever afterward. Gervais of Tilbury, in his Chronicle, declares that on the top of Mount Canigon in France, which has a very inaccessible summit, there is a black lake of unknown depth, at whose bottom the demons have a palace, and that if any one drops a stone into that water, the wrath of the mountain demons is shown in sudden and frightful tempests. From a like tarn in Cornwall, as Cornish Folklore claims, on an accessible but very tedious hill, came up the hand which received the brand Escalibore when its master could wield it no more,—as told in the Morte D'Arthur, with, however, clear reference to the sea.

I cannot forbear enlivening my page with the following sketch of a visit of English officers to the realm of Ten-jo, the long-nosed Mountain-demon of Japan, which is very suggestive of the mental atmosphere amid which such spectres exist. The mountains and forests of Japan are, say these writers, inhabited as thickly by good and evil spirits as the Hartz and Black Forest, and chief among them, in horrible sanctity, is O-yama,—the word echoes the Hindu Yama, Japanese Amma, kings of Hades,—whose demon is Ten-jo. 'Abdul and Mulney once started, on three days' leave, with the intention of climbing to the summit—not of Ten-jo's nose, but of the mountain; their principal reason for so doing being simply that they were told by every one that they had better not. They first tried the ascent on the most accessible side, but fierce two-sworded yakomins jealously guarded it; and they were obliged to make the attempt on the other, which was almost inaccessible, and was Ten-jo's region. The villagers at the base of the mountain begged them to give up the project; and one old man, a species of patriarch, reasoned with them. 'What are you going to do when you get to the top?' he asked. Our two friends were forced to admit that their course, then, would be very similar to that of the king of France and his men—come down again.

The old man laughed pityingly, and said, 'Well, go if you like; but, take my word for it, Ten-jo will do you an injury.' They asked who Ten-jo was.

'Why Ten-jo,' said the old man, 'is an evil spirit, with a long nose, who will dislocate your limbs if you persist in going up the mountain on this side.'

'How do you know he has got a long nose?' they asked, 'Have you ever seen him?'

'Because all evil spirits have long noses'—here Mulney hung his head,—'and,' continued the old man, not noticing how dreadfully personal he was becoming to one of the party, 'Ten-jo has the longest of the lot. Did you ever know a man with a long nose who was good?'

'Come on,' said Mulney hurriedly to Abdul, 'or the old fool will make me out an evil spirit.'

'Syonara,' said the old man as they walked away, 'but look out for Ten-jo!'

After climbing hard for some hours, and not meeting a single human being,—not even the wood-cutter could be tempted by the fine timber to encroach on Ten-jo's precincts,—they reached the top, and enjoyed a magnificent view. After a rest they started on their descent, the worst part of which they had accomplished, when, as they were walking quietly along a good path, Abdul's ankle turned under him, and he went down as if he had been shot, with his leg broken in two places. With difficulty Mulney managed to get him to the village they had started from, and the news ran like wild-fire that Ten-jo had broken the leg of one of the adventurous tojins.

'I told you how it would be,' exclaimed the old man, 'but you would go. Ah, Ten-jo is a dreadful fellow!'

All the villagers, clustering round, took up the cry, and shook their heads. Ten-jo's reputation had increased wonderfully by this accident. Poor Abdul was on his back for eleven weeks, and numbers of Japanese—for he was a general favourite amongst them—went to see him, and to express their regret and horror at Ten-jo's behaviour.6

It is obvious that to a demon dwelling in a high mountain a long nose would be variously useful to poke into the affairs of people dwelling in the plains, and also to enjoy the scent of their sacrifices offered at a respectful distance. That feature of the face which Napoleon I. regarded as of martial importance, and which is prominent in the warriors marked on the Mycenæ pottery, has generally been a physiognomical characteristic of European ogres, who are blood-smellers. That the significance of Ten-jo's long nose is this, appears probable when we compare him with the Calmuck demon Erlik, whose long nose is for smelling out the dying. The Cossacks believed that the protector of the earth was a many-headed elephant. The snouted demon (figure 15) is from a picture of Christ delivering Adam and Eve from hell, by Lucas Van Leyden, 1521.

Fig. 15.—Snouted Demon.

The Chinese Mountains also have their demons. The demon of the mountain T'ai-shan, in Shantung, is believed to regulate the punishments of men in this world and the next. Four other demon princes rule over the principal mountain chains of the Empire. Mr. Dennys remarks that mountainous localities are so regularly the homes of fairies in Chinese superstition that some connection between the fact and the relation of 'Elf' to 'Alp' in Europe is suggested.7 But this coincidence is by no means so remarkable as the appearance among these Chinese mountain sprites of the magical 'Sesame,' so familiar to us in Arabian legend. The celebrated mountain Ku'en Lun (usually identified with the Hindoo Kush) is said to be peopled with fairies, who cultivate upon its terraces the 'fields of sesamum and gardens of coriander seeds,' which are eaten as ordinary food by those who possess the gift of longevity.

In the superstitions of the American Aborigines we find gigantic demons who with their hands piled up mountain-chains as their castles, from whose peak-towers they hurled stones on their enemies in the plains, and slung them to the four corners of the earth.8 Such was the terrible Apocatequil, whose statue was erected on the mountains, with that of his mother on the one hand and his brother on the other. He was Prince of Evil and the chief god of the Peruvians. From Quito to Cuzco every Indian would give all he possessed to conciliate him. Five priests, two stewards, and a crowd of slaves served his image. His principal temple was surrounded by a considerable village, whose inhabitants had no other occupation than to wait on him.9

The plaudits which welcomed the first railway train that sped beneath the Alps, echoing amid their crags and gorges, struck with death the old phantasms which had so long held sway in the imagination of the Southern peasantry. The great tunnel was hewn straight through the stony hearts of giants whom Christianity had tried to slay, and, failing that, baptised and adopted. It is in the Tyrol that we find the clearest survivals of the old demons of obstruction, the mountain monarchs. Such is Jordan the Giant of Kohlhütte chasm, near Ungarkopf, whose story, along with others, is so prettily told by the Countess Von Gunther. This giant is something of a Ten-jo as to nose, for he smells 'human meat' where his pursued victims are hidden, and his snort makes things tremble as before a tempest; but he has not the intelligence ascribed to large noses, for the boys ultimately persuade him that the way to cross a stream is to tie a stone around his neck, and he is drowned. One of the giants of Albach could carry a rock weighing 10,000 pounds, and his comrades, while carrying others of 700 pounds, could leap from stone to stone across rivers, and stoop to catch the trout with their hands as they leaped. The ferocious Orco, the mountain-ghost who never ages, fulfils the tradition of his classic name by often appearing as a monstrous black dog, from whose side stones rebound, and fills the air with a bad smell (like Mephisto). His employment is hurling wayfarers down precipices. In her story of the 'Unholdenhof'—or 'monster farm' in the Stubeithal—the Countess Von Gunther describes the natural character of the mountain demons.

'It was on this self-same spot that the forester and his son took up their abode, and they became the dread and abomination of the whole surrounding country, for they practised, partly openly and partly in secret, the most manifold iniquities, so that their nature and bearing grew into something demoniacal. As quarrellers very strong, and as enemies dreadfully revengeful, they showed their diabolical nature by the most inhuman deeds, which brought down injury not only on those against whom their wrath was directed, but also upon their families for centuries. In the heights of the mountains they turned the beds of the torrents, and devastated by this means the most flourishing tracts of land; on other places the Unholde set on fire whole mountain forests, to allow free room for the avalanches to rush down and overwhelm the farms. Through certain means they cut holes and fissures in the rocks, in which, during the summer, quantities of water collected, which froze in the winter, and then in the spring the thawing ice split the rocks, which then rolled down into the valleys, destroying everything before them.... But at last Heaven's vengeance reached them. An earthquake threw the forester's house into ruins, wild torrents tore over it, and thunderbolts set all around it in a blaze; and by fire and water, with which they had sinned, father and son perished, and were condemned to everlasting torments. Up to the present day they are to be seen at nightfall on the mountain in the form of two fiery boars.'10

Some of these giants, as has been intimated, were converted. Such was the case with Heimo, who owned and devastated a vast tract of country on the river Inn, which, however, he bridged—whence Innsbruck—when he became a christian and a monk. This conversion was a terrible disappointment to the devil, who sent a huge dragon to stop the building of the monastery; but Heimo attacked the dragon, killed him, and cut out his tongue. With this tongue, a yard and a half long, in his hand, he is represented in his statue, and the tongue is still preserved in the cloister. Heimo became a monk at Wilten, lived a pious life, and on his death was buried near the monastery. The stone coffin in which the gigantic bones repose is shown there, and measures over twenty-eight feet.

Of nearly the same character as the Mountain Demons, and possessing even more features of the Demons of Barrenness, are the monsters guarding rocky passes. They are distributed through land, sea, and rivers. The famous rocks between Italy and Sicily bore the names of dangerous monsters, Scylla and Charybdis, which have now become proverbial expressions for alternative perils besetting any enterprise. According to Homer, Scylla was a kind of canine monster with six long necks, the mouths paved each with three rows of sharp teeth; while Charybdis, sitting under her fig-tree, daily swallowed the waters and vomited them up again.11 Distantly related to these fabulous monsters, probably, are many of the old notions of ordeals undergone between rocks standing close together, or sometimes through holes in rocks, of which examples are found in Great Britain. An ordeal of this kind exists at Pera, where the holy well is reached through a narrow slit. Visitors going there recently on New Year's Day were warned by the dervish in charge—'Look through it at the water if you please, but do not essay to enter unless your consciences are completely free from sin, for as sure as you try to pass through with a taint upon your soul, you will be gripped by the rock and held there for ever.'12 The 'Bocca della Verità'—a great stone face like a huge millstone—stands in the portico of the church S. Maria in Cosmedin at Rome, and its legend is that a suspected person was required to place his hand through the open mouth; if he swore falsely it would bite off the hand—the explanation now given being that a swordsman was concealed behind to make good the judicial shrewdness of the stone in case the oath were displeasing to the authorities.

The myth of Scylla, which relates that she was a beautiful maiden, beloved by Glaucus, whom Circe through jealousy transformed to a monster by throwing magic herbs into the well where she was wont to bathe, is recalled by various European legends. In Thuringia, on the road to Oberhof, stands the Red Stone, with its rosebush, and a stream issuing from beneath it, where a beautiful maid is imprisoned. Every seven years she may be seen bathing in the stream. On one occasion a peasant passing by heard a sneeze in the rock, and called out, 'God help thee!' The sneeze and the benediction were repeated, until at the seventh time the man cried, 'Oh, thou cursed witch, deceive not honest people!' As he then walked off, a wailing voice came out of the stone, 'Oh, hadst thou but only wished the last time that God would help me. He would have helped me, and thou wouldst have delivered me; now I must tarry till the Day of Judgment!' The voice once cried out to a wedding procession passing by the stone, 'To-day wed, next year dead;' and the bride having died a year after, wedding processions dread the spot.

The legends of giants and giantesses, so numerous in Great Britain, are equally associated with rocky mountain-passes, or the boulders they were supposed to have tossed thence when sportively stoning each other. They are the Tor of the South and Ben of the North. The hills of Ross-shire in Scotland are mythological monuments of Cailliachmore, great woman, who, while carrying a pannier filled with earth and stones on her back, paused for a moment on a level spot, now the site of Ben-Vaishard, when the bottom of the pannier gave way, forming the hills. The recurrence of the names Gog and

Magog in Scotland suggests that in mountainous regions the demons were especially derived from the hordes of robbers and savages, among whom, in their uncultivable hills, the ploughshare could never conquer the spear and club. Richard Doyle enriched the first Exhibition of the Grosvenor Gallery in London, 1877, with many beautiful pictures inspired by European Folklore. They were a pretty garniture for the cemetery of dead religions. The witch once seen on her broom departing from the high crags of Cuhillan, cheered by her faithful dwarf, is no longer unlovely as in the days when she was burned by proxy in some poor human hag; obedient to art—a more potent wand than her own—she reascends to the clouds from which she was borne, and is hardly distinguishable from them. Slowly man came to learn with the poet—

It was the mountain streams that fed
*The fair green plain's amenities.*13

Then the giants became fairies, and not a few of these wore at last the mantles of saints. A similar process has been undergone by another subject, which finds its pretty epitaph in the artist's treatment. We saw in two pictures the Dame Blanche of Normandy, lurking in the ravine beside a stream under the dusk, awaiting yon rustic wood-cutter who is presently horizontal in the air in that mad dance, after which he will be found exhausted. As her mountain-sister is faintly shaped out of the clouds that cap Cuhillan, this one is an imaginative outgrowth of the twilight shadows, the silvery glintings of moving clouds mirrored in pools, and her tresses are long luxuriant grasses. She is of a sisterhood which passes by hardly perceptible gradations into others, elsewhere described—the creations of Illusion and Night. She is not altogether one of these, however, but a type of more direct danger—the peril of fords, torrents, thickets, marshes, and treacherous pools, which may seem shallow, but are deep.

The water-demons have been already described in their obvious aspects, but it is necessary to mention here the simple obstructive river-demons haunting fords and burns, and hating bridges. Many tragedies, and many personifications of the forces which caused them, preceded the sanctity of the title Pontifex. The torrent that roared across man's path seemed the vomit of a demon: the sacred power was he who could bridge it. In one of the most beautiful celebrations of Indra it is said: 'He tranquillised this great river so that it might be crossed; he conveyed across it in safety the sages who had been unable to pass over it, and who, having crossed, proceeded to realise the wealth they sought; in the exhilaration of the soma, Indra has done these deeds.'14 In Ceylon, the demon Tota still casts malignant spells about fords and ferries. Many are the legends of the opposition offered by demons to bridge-building, and of the sacrifices which had to be made to them before such works could be accomplished. A few specimens must suffice us. Mr. Dennys relates a very interesting one of the 'Loh-family bridge' at Shanghai. Difficulty having been found in laying the foundations, the builder vowed to Heaven two thousand children if the stones could be placed properly. The goddess addressed said she would not require their lives, but that the number named would be attacked by small-pox, which took place, and half the number died. A Chinese author says, 'If bridges are not placed in proper positions, such as the laws of geomancy indicate, they may endanger the lives of thousands, by bringing about a visitation of small-pox or sore eyes.' At Hang-Chow a tea-merchant cast himself into the river Tsien-tang as a sacrifice to the Spirit of the dikes, which were constantly being washed away. The 'Devil's Bridges,' to which Mephistopheles alludes so proudly, are frequent in Germany, and most of them, whether natural or artificial, have diabolical associations. The oldest structures often have legends in which are reflected the conditions exacted by evil powers, of those who spanned the fords in which men had often been drowned. Of this class is the Montafon Bridge in the Tyrol, and another is the bridge at Ratisbon. The legend of the latter is a fair specimen of those which generally haunt these ancient structures. Its architect was apprentice to a master who was building the cathedral, and laid a wager that he would bridge the Danube before the other laid the coping-stone of the sacred edifice. But the work of bridging the river was hard, and after repeated failures the apprentice began to swear, and wished the devil had charge of the business! Whereupon he of the cloven foot appeared in guise of a friar, and agreed to build the fifteen arches—for a consideration. The fee was to be the first three that crossed the bridge. The cunning apprentice contrived that these three should not be human, but a dog, a cock, and a hen. The devil, in wrath at the fraud, tore the animals to pieces and disappeared; a procession of monks passed over the bridge and made it safe; and thereon are carved figures of the three animals. In most of the stories it is a goat which is sent over and mangled, that poor animal having preserved its character as scape-goat in a great deal of the Folklore of Christendom. The Danube was of old regarded as under the special guardianship of the Prince of Darkness, who used to make great efforts to obstruct the Crusaders voyaging down it to rescue the Holy Land from pagans. On one occasion, near the confluence of the Vilz and Danube, he began hurling huge rocks into the river-bed from the cliffs; the holy warriors resisted successfully by signing the cross and singing an anthem, but the huge stone first thrown caused a whirl and swell in that part of the river, which were very dangerous until it was removed by engineers.

It is obvious, especially to the English, who have so long found a defensive advantage in the silver streak of sea that separates them from the Continent, that an obstacle, whether of mountain-range or sea, would, at a certain point in the formation of a nation, become as valuable as at another it might be obstructive. Euphemism is credited with having given the friendly name 'Euxine' to the rough 'Axine' Sea,—'terrible to foreigners.' But this is not so certain. Many a tribe has found the Black Sea a protection and a friend. In the case of mountains, their protective advantages would account at once for Milton's celebration of Freedom as a mountain nymph, and for the stupidity of the people that dwell amid them, so often remarked; the very means of their independence would also be the cause of their insulation and barbarity. It is for those who go to and fro that knowledge is increased. The curious and inquiring are most apt to migrate; the enterprising will not submit to be shut away behind rocks and mountains; by their departure there would be instituted, behind the barriers of rock and hill, a survival of the stupidest. These might ultimately come to worship their chains and cover their craggy prison-walls with convents and crosses. The demons of aliens would be their gods. The climbing Hannibals would be their devils. It might have been expected, after the passages quoted from Mr. Ruskin concerning the bovine condition of Alpine peasantries, that he would salute the tunnel through Mont Cenis. The peasantries who would see in the sub-alpine engine a demon are extinct. Admiration of the genii of obstruction, and horror of the demons that vanquished them, are discoverable only in folk-tales distant enough to be pretty, such as the interesting Serbian story of 'Satan's jugglings and God's might,' in which fairies hiding in successively opened nuts vainly try to oppose with fire and flood a she-demon pursuing a prince and his bride, to whose aid at last comes a flash of lightning which strikes the fiend dead.

One of the beautiful 'Contes d'une Grand'mère,' by George Sand, Le géant Yéous, has in it the sense of many fables born of man's struggle with obstructive nature. With her wonted felicity she places the scene of this true human drama near the mountain Yéous, in the Pyrenees, whose name is a far-off echo of Zeus. The summit bore an enormous rock which, seen from a distance, appeared somewhat like a statue. The peasant Miquelon, who had his little farm at the mountain's base, whenever he passed made the sign of the cross and taught his little son Miquel to do the same, telling him that the great form was that of a pagan god, an enemy of the human race. An avalanche fell upon the home and garden of Miquelon; the poor man himself was disabled for life, his house and farm turned in a moment into a wild mass of stones. Miquel looked up to the summit of Yéous; the giant had disappeared; henceforth it was the mighty form of an organic monster which the boy saw stretched over what had once been their happy home and smiling acres. The family went about begging, Miquelon repeating his strange appeal, 'Le géant s'est couché sur moi.' But when at last the old man dies, the son resolves to fulfil the silent dream of his life; he will encounter the giant Yéous still in possession of his paternal acres. With eyes of the young world this boy sees starting up here and there amid the vast debris, the head of the demon he wishes to crush. He hurls stones hither and thither where some fearful feature or limb appears. He is filled with rage; his dreams are filled with attacks on the giant, in which the colossal head tumbles only to reappear on the shoulders; every broken limb has the self-repairing power. There is no progress. But as the boy grows, and the contest grows, and need comes, there gathers in Miquel a desire to clear the ground. When he begins to think, it is no longer the passion to avenge his father on the stony giant which possesses him, but to recover their lost garden. Thus, indeed, the giant himself could alone be conquered. The huge rocks are split by gunpowder, some fragments are made into fences, others into a comfortable mansion for Miquel's mother and sisters. When the garden smiles again, and all are happy the demon form is no longer discoverable.15

This little tale interprets with fine insight the demonology of barrenness and obstruction. The boy's wrath against the unconscious cause of his troubles is the rage often observed in children who retaliate upon the table or chair on which they have been bruised, and it repeats embryologically the rage of the world's boyhood inspired by ascription of personal motives to inanimate obstructions. Possibly such wrath might have added something to the force with which man entered upon his combat with nature; but George Sand's tale reminds us that whatever was gained in force was lost in its misdirection. Success came in the proportion that fury was replaced by the youth's growing recognition that he was dealing with facts that could not be raged out of existence. It is crowned when he makes friends with the unconquerable remnant of the giant, and sees that he is not altogether evil.

It is at this stage that the higher Art, conversant with Beauty, enters to relieve man of many moral wounds received in the struggle. Clothed with moss and clematis, Yéous appears not so hideous after all. Further invested by the genius of a Turner, he would be beautiful. Yéous is a fair giant after all, only he needed finish. He is a type of nature.

The boyhood of the world has not passed away with Miquel. We find a fictitious dualism cherished by the lovers of nature in their belief or feeling that nature exerts upon man some spiritual influence. Ruskin has said that in looking from the Campanile at Venice to the circle of snow which crowns the Adriatic, and then to the buildings which contain the works of Titian and Tintoret, he has felt unable to answer the question of his own heart, By which of these—the nature or the manhood—has God given mightier evidence of Himself? So nature may teach the already taught. While Ruskin looks from the Campanile, the peasant is fighting the mountain and calling its rocky grandeurs by the devil's name; before the pictures he kneels. Untaught by art and science, the mind can derive no elevation from nature, can find no sympathy in it. It is a false notion that there is any compensation for the ignorant, denied access to art-galleries, in ability to pass their Sundays amid natural scenery. Health that may bring them, but mentally they are still inside the prison-walls from which look the stony eyes of Fates and Furies. Natural sublimities cannot refine minds crude as themselves; they must pass through thought before they can feed thought; it is nature transfigured in art that changes the snow-clad mountain from a heartless giant to a saviour in snow-pure raiment.

1 Faust, ii. Act 4 (Hayward's Translation).

2 'Emerson's Poems. Monadnoc.'

3 'Modern Painters,' Part V. 19.

4 Bel's mountain, 'House of the Beloved,' is called 'high place' in Assyrian, and would be included in these curses ('Records of the Past,' iii. 129).

5 Jer. xiii. 16.

6 'Our Life in Japan.' By Jephson and Elmhirst.

7 Another derivation of Elf (Alf) is to connect it with Sanskrit Alpa = little; so that the Elves are the Little Folk. Professor Buslaef of Moscow suggests connection with the Greek Alphito, a spectre. See pp. 160n. and 223.

8 Brinton, p. 85.

9 Ibid., p. 166.

10 'Tales and Legends of the Tyrol.' (Chapman and Hall, 1874.)

11 Od. xii. 73; 235, etc.

12 London Daily Telegraph Correspondence.

13 John Sterling.

14 'Rig-Veda,' ii. 15, 5. Wilson. 1854.

15 'Du monstre qui m'avait tant ennuyé, il n'était plus question; il était pour jamais réduit au silence. Il n'avait plus forme de géant. Déjà en partie couvert de verdure, de mousse et de clématites qui avaient grimpé sur la partie où j'avais cessé de passer, il n'était plus laid; bientôt on ne le verrait plus du tout. Je me sentais si heureux que je voulus lui pardonner, et, me tournant vers lui:—A present, lui dis-je, tu dormiras tous tes jours et toutes tes nuits sans que je te dérange. Le mauvais esprit qui était en toi est vaincu, je lui défends de revenir. Je t'en ai délivré en te forçant à devenir utile à quelque chose; que la foudre t'épargne et que la neige te soit légère! Il me sembla passer, le long de l'escarpement, comme un grand soupir de résignation qui se perdit dans les hauteurs. Ce fut la dernière fois que je l'entendais, et je ne l'ai jamais revu autre qu'il n'est maintenant.'

Chapter IX - Illusion

Maya—Natural Treacheries—Misleaders—Glamour—Lorelei—Chinese Mermaid—Transformations—Swan Maidens—Pigeon Maidens—The Seal-skin—Nudity—Teufelsee—Gohlitsee—Japanese Siren—Dropping Cave—Venusberg—Godiva—Will-o'-Wisp—Holy Fräulein—The Forsaken Merman—The Water-Man—Sea Phantom—Sunken Treasures—Suicide.

Most beautiful of all the goddesses of India is Maya, Illusion. In Hindu iconography she is portrayed in drapery of beautiful colours, with decoration of richest gems and broidery of flowers. From above her crown falls a veil which, curving above her knees, returns on the other side, making, as it were, also an apron in which are held fair animal forms—prototypes of the creation over which she has dominion. The youthful yet serious beauty of her face and head is surrounded with a semi-aureole, fringed with soft lightning, striated with luminous sparks; and these are background for a cruciform nimbus made of three clusters of rays. Maya presses her full breasts, from which flow fountains of milk which fall in graceful streams to mingle with the sea on which she stands.

So to our Aryan ancestors appeared the spirit that paints the universe, flushing with tints so strangely impartial fruits forbidden and unforbidden for man and beast. Mankind are slandered by the priest's creed, Populus vult decipi; they are justly vindicated in Plato's aphorism, 'Unwillingly is the soul deprived of truth;' but still they are deceived. Large numbers are truly described by Swedenborg, who found hells whose occupants believed themselves in heaven and sang praises therefor. Such praises we may hear in the loud laughter proceeding from dens where paradise has been gained by the cheap charm of a glass of gin or a prostitute's caress. Serpent finds its ideal in serpent. In heaven, says Swedenborg, we shall see things as they are. But it is the adage of those who have lost their paradise, and eat still the dry dust of reality not raised by science; the general world has not felt that divine curse, or it has been wiped away so that the most sensual fool may rejoice in feeling himself God's darling, and pities the paganism of Plato. Man and beast are certain that they do see things as they are. Maya's milk is tinctured from the poppies of her robe; untold millions of misgivings have been put to sleep by her tender bounty; the waters that sustain her are those of Lethe.

But beneath every illusive heaven Nature stretches also an illusive hell. The poppies lose their force at last, and under the scourge of necessity man wakes to find all his paradise of roses turned to briars. Maya's breast-fountains pass deeper than the surface—from one flows soft Lethe, the other issues at last in Phlegethon. Fear is even a more potent painter than Hope, and out of the manifold menaces of Nature can at last overlay the fairest illusions. It is a pathetic fact, that so soon as man begins to think his first theory infers a will at work wherever he sees no cause; his second, to suppose that it will harm him!

Harriet Martineau's account of her childish terror caused by seeing some prismatic colours dancing on the wall of a vacant room she was entering—'imps' that had no worse origin than a tremulous candelabrum, but which haunted her nerves through life—is an experience which may be traced in the haunted childhood of every nation. There are other phenomena besides these prismatic colours, which have had an evil name in popular superstition, despite their beauty. Strange it might seem to a Buddhist that yon exquisite tree with its blood-red buds should be called the Judas-tree, as to us that the graceful swan which might be the natural emblem of purity should be associated with witchcraft! But the student of mythology will at every moment be impressed by the fact that myths oftener represent a primitive science than mere fancies and conceits. The sinuous neck of the swan, its passionate jealousy, and the uncanny whistle, or else dumbness, found where, from so snowy an outside, melody might have been looked for, may have made this animal the type of a double nature. The treacherous brilliants of the serpent, or honey protected by stings, or the bright blossoms of poisons, would have trained the instinct which apprehends evil under the apparition of beauty. This, as we shall have occasion to see, has had a controlling influence upon the ethical constitution of our nature. But it is at present necessary to observe that the primitive science generally reversed the induction of our later philosophy; for where an evil or pain was discovered in anything, it concluded that such was its raison d'être, and its attractive qualities were simply a demon's treacherous bait. However, here are the first stimulants to self-control in the lessons that taught distrust of appearances.

Because many a pilgrim perished through a confidence in the lake-pictures of the mirage which led to carelessness about economising his skin of water, the mirage gained its present name—Bahr Sheitan, or Devil's Water. The 'Will o' wisp,' which appeared to promise the night-wanderer warmth or guidance, but led him into a bog, had its excellent directions as to the place to avoid perverted by an unhappy misunderstanding into a wilful falsehood, and has been branded ignis fatuus. Most of the mimicries in nature gradually became as suspicious to the primitive observer as aliases to a magistrate. The thing that seemed to be fire, or water, but was not; the insect or animal which took its hue or form from some other, from the leaf-spotted or stem-striped cats to that innocent insect whose vegetal disguise has gained for it the familiar name of 'Devil's Walking-stick;' the humanlike hiss, laugh, or cry of animals; the vibratory sound or movement which so often is felt as if near when it really is far; the sand which seems hard but sinks; the sward which proves a bog;—all these have their representation in the demonology of delusion. The Coroados of Brazil says that the Evil One 'sometimes transforms (himself) into a swamp, etc., leads him astray, vexes him, brings him into danger, and even kills him.'1 It is like an echo of Burton's account. 'Terrestrial devils are those lares, genii, faunes, satyrs, wood-nymphs, foliots, fairies, Robin Good-fellows, trulli, etc., which, as they are most conversant with men, so they do them most harm. These are they that dance on heaths and greens, as Lavater thinks with Trithemius, and, as Olaus Magnus adds, leave that green circle which we commonly find in plain fields. They are sometimes seen by old women and children. Hieron. Pauli, in his description of the city of Bercino, Spain, relates how they have been familiarly seen near that town, about fountains and hills. 'Sometimes,' saith Trithemius, 'they lead simple people into the recesses of mountains and show them wonderful sights,' etc. Giraldus Cambrensis gives an instance of a monk of Wales that was so deluded. Paracelsus reckons up many places in Germany where they do usually walk about in little coats, some two feet long.2 Real dangers beset the woods and mountain passes, the swamp and quicksand; in such forms did they haunt the untamed jungles of imagination!

Over that sea on which Maya stands extends the silvery wand of Glamour. It descended to the immortal Old Man of the Sea, favourite of the nymphs, oracle of the coasts, patron of fishermen, friend of Proteus, who could see through all the sea's depths and assume all shapes. How many witcheries could proceed from the many-tinted sea to affect the eyes and enable them to see Triton with his wreathed horn, and mermaids combing their hair, and marine monsters, and Aphrodite poised on the white foam! Glaucoma it may be to the physicians; but Glaucus it is in the scheme of Maya, who has never left land or sea without her witness. Beside the Polar Sea a Samoyed sailor, asked by Castrén 'where is Num' (i.e., Jumala, his god), pointed to the dark distant sea, and said, He is there.

To the ancients there were two seas,—the azure above, and that beneath. The imaginative child in its development passes all those dreamy coasts; sees in clouds mountains of snow on the horizon, and in the sunset luminous seas laving golden isles. When as yet to the young world the shining sun was Berchta, the white fleecy clouds were her swans. When she descended to the sea, as a thousand stories related, it was to repeat the course of the sun for all tribes looking on a westward sea. No one who has read that charming little book, 'The Gods in Exile,'3 will wonder at the happy instinct of learning shown in Heine's little poem, 'Sonnenuntergang,'4 wherein we see shining solar Beauty compelled to become the spinning housewife, or reluctant spouse of Poseidon:—

A lovely dame whom the old ocean-god
For convenience once had married;
And in the day-time she wanders gaily
Through the high heaven, purple-arrayed,
And all in diamonds gleaming,
And all beloved, and all amazing

To every worldly being,
And every worldly being rejoicing
With warmth and splendour from her glances.
Alas! at evening, sad and unwilling,
Back must she bend her slow steps
To the dripping house, to the barren embrace
Of grisly old age.

This of course is Heinesque, and has no relation to any legend of Bertha, but is a fair specimen of mythology in the making, and is quite in the spirit of many of the myths that have flitted around sunset on the sea. Whatever the explanation of their descent, the Shining One and her fleecy retinue were transformed. When to sea or lake came Berchta (or Perchta), it was as Bertha of the Large Foot (i.e., webbed), or of the Long Nose (beak), and her troop were Swan-maidens. Their celestial character was changed with that of their mistress. They became familiars of sorcerers and sorceresses. To 'wear yellow slippers' became the designation of a witch.

How did these fleecy white cloud-phantoms become demonised? What connection is there between them and the enticing Lorelei and the dangerous Rhine-daughters watching over golden treasures, once, perhaps, metaphors of moonlight ripples? They who have listened to the wild laughter of these in Wagner's opera, Das Rheingold, and their weird 'Heiayaheia!' can hardly fail to suspect that they became associated with the real human nymphs whom the summer sun still finds freely sporting in the bright streams of Russia, Hungary, Austria, and East Germany, naked and not ashamed. Many a warning voice against these careless Phrynes, who may have left tattered raiment on the shore to be transfigured in the silvery waves, must have gone forth from priests and anxious mothers. Nor would there be wanting traditions enough to impress such warnings. Few regions have been without such stories as those which the traveller Hiouen-Thsang (7th century) found in Buddhist chronicles of the Rakshasis of Ceylon. 'They waylay the merchants who land in the isle, and, changing themselves to women of great beauty, come before them with fragrant flowers and music; attracting them with kind words to the town of Iron, they offer them a feast, and give themselves up to pleasure with them; then shut them in an iron prison, and eat them one after the other.'

There is a strong accent of human nature in the usual plot of the Swan-maiden legend, her garments stolen while she bathes, and her willingness to pay wondrous prices for them—since they are her feathers and her swanhood, without which she must remain for ever captive of the thief. The stories are told in regions so widely sundered, and their minor details are so different, that we may at any rate be certain that they are not all traceable solely to fleecy clouds. Sometimes the garments of the demoness—and these beings are always feminine—are not feathery, as in the German stories, but seal-skins, or of nondescript red tissue. Thus, the Envoy Li Ting-yuan (1801) records a Chinese legend of a man named Ming-ling-tzu, a poor and worthy farmer without family, who, on going to draw water from a spring near his house, saw a woman bathing in it. She had hung her clothes on a pine tree, and, in punishment for her 'shameless ways' and for her fouling the well, he carried off the dress. The clothing was unlike the familiar Lewchewan in style, and 'of a ruddy sunset colour.' The woman, having finished her bath, cried out in great anger, 'What thief has been here in broad day? Bring back my clothes, quick.' She then perceived Ming-ling-tzu, and threw herself on the ground before him. He began to scold her, and asked why she came and fouled his water; to which she replied that both the pine tree and the well were made by the Creator for the use of all. The farmer entered into conversation with her, and pointed out that fate evidently intended her to be his wife, as he absolutely refused to give up her clothes, while without them she could not get away. The result was that they were married. She lived with him for ten years, and bore him a son and a daughter. At the end of that time her fate was fulfilled: she ascended a tree during the absence of her husband, and having bidden his children farewell, glided off on a cloud and disappeared.5

In South Africa a parallel myth, in its demonological aspect, bears no trace of a cloud origin. In this case a Hottentot, travelling with a Bushwoman and her child, met a troop of wild horses. They were all hungry; and the woman, taking off a petticoat made of human skin, was instantly changed into a lioness. She struck down a horse, and lapped its blood; then, at the request of the Hottentot, who in his terror had climbed a tree, she resumed her petticoat and womanhood, and the friends, after a meal of horseflesh, resumed their journey.6 Among the Minussinian Tartars these demons partake of the nature of the Greek Harpies; they are bloodthirsty vampyre-demons who drink the blood of men slain in battle, darken the air in their flight, and house themselves in one great black fiend.7 As we go East the portrait of the Swan-maiden becomes less dark, and she is not associated with the sea or the under-world. Such is one among the Malays, related by Mr. Tylor. In the island of Celebes it is said that seven nymphs came down from the sky to bathe, and were seen by Kasimbaha, who at first thought them white doves, but in the bath perceived they were women. He stole the robe of one of them, Utahagi, and as she could not fly without it, she became his wife and bare him a son. She was called Utahagi because of a single magic white hair she had; this her husband pulled out, when immediately a storm arose, and she flew to heaven. The child was in great grief, and the husband cast about how he should follow her up into the sky.

76

The Swan-maiden appears somewhat in the character of a Nemesis in a Siberian myth told by Mr. Baring-Gould. A certain Samoyed who had stolen a Swan-maiden's robe, refused to return it unless she secured for him the heart of seven demon robbers, one of whom had killed the Samoyed's mother. The robbers were in the habit of hanging up their hearts on pegs in their tent. The Swan-maiden procured them. The Samoyed smashed six of the hearts; made the seventh robber resuscitate his mother, whose soul, kept in a purse, had only to be shaken over the old woman's grave for that feat to be accomplished, and the Swan-maiden got back her plumage and flew away rejoicing.8

In Slavonic Folklore the Swan-maiden is generally of a dangerous character, and if a swan is killed they are careful not to show it to children for fear they will die. When they appear as ducks, geese, and other water-fowl, they are apt to be more mischievous than when they come as pigeons; and it is deemed perilous to kill a pigeon, as among sailors it was once held to kill an albatross. Afanasief relates a legend which shows that, even when associated with the water-king, the Tsar Morskoi or Slavonic Neptune, the pigeon preserves its beneficent character. A king out hunting lies down to drink from a lake (as in the story related on p. 146), when Tsar Morskoi seizes him by the beard, and will not release him until he agrees to give him his infant son. The infant prince, deserted on the edge of the fatal lake, by advice of a sorceress hides in some bushes, whence he presently sees twelve pigeons arrive, which, having thrown off their feathers, disport themselves in the lake. At length a thirteenth, more beautiful than the rest, arrives, and her sorochka (shift) Ivan seizes. To recover it she agrees to be his wife, and, having told him he will find her beneath the waters, resumes her pigeon-shape and flies away. Beneath the lake he finds a beautiful realm, and though the Tsar Morskoi treats him roughly and imposes heavy tasks on him, the pigeon-maiden (Vassilissa) assists him, and they dwell together happily.9

In Norse Mythology the vesture of the uncanny maid is oftenest a seal-skin, and a vein of pathos enters the legends. Of the many legends of this kind, still believed in Sweden and Norway, one has been pleasantly versified by Miss Eliza Keary. A fisherman having found a pretty white seal-skin, took it home with him. At night there was a wailing at his door; the maid enters, becomes his wife, and bears him three children. But after seven years she finds the skin, and with it ran to the shore. The eldest child tells the story to the father on his return home.

Then we three, Daddy,
Ran after, crying, 'Take us to the sea!
Wait for us, Mammy, we are coming too!
Here's Alice, Willie can't keep up with you!
Mammy, stop—just for a minute or two!'
At last we came to where the hill
Slopes straight down to the beach,
And there we stood all breathless, still
Fast clinging each to each.
We saw her sitting upon a stone,
Putting the little seal-skin on.
O Mammy! Mammy!
She never said goodbye, Daddy,
She didn't kiss us three;
She just put the little seal-skin on
And slipt into the sea!

Some of the legends of this character are nearly as realistic as Mr. Swinburne's 'Morality' of David and Bathsheba. To imagine the scarcity of wives in regions to which the primitive Aryan race migrated, we have only to remember the ben trovato story of Californians holding a ball in honour of a bonnet, in the days before women had followed them in migration. To steal Bathsheba's clothes, and so capture her, might at one period have been sufficiently common in Europe to require all the terrors contained in the armoury of tradition concerning the demonesses that might so be taken in, and might so tempt men to take them in. In the end they might disappear, carrying off treasures in the most prosaic fashion, or perhaps they might bring to one's doors a small Trojan war. It is probable that the sentiment of modesty, so far as it is represented in the shame of nudity, was the result of prudential agencies. Though the dread of nudity has become in some regions a superstition in the female mind strong enough to have its martyrs—as was seen at the sinking of the Northfleet and the burning hotel in St. Louis—it is one that has been fostered by men in distrust of their own animalism. In barbarous regions, where civilisation introduces clothes, the women are generally the last to adopt them; and though Mr. Herbert Spencer attributes this to female conservatism, it appears more probable that it is because the men are the first to lose their innocence and the women last to receive anything expensive. It is noticeable how generally the Swan-maidens are said in the myths to be captured by violence or stratagem. At the same time the most unconscious temptress might be the means of breaking up homes and misleading workmen, and thus become invested with all the wild legends told of the illusory phenomena of nature in popular mythology.

It is marvellous to observe how all the insinuations of the bane were followed by equal dexterities in the antedote. The fair tempters might disguise their intent in an appeal to the wayfarer's humanity; and, behold, there were a thousand well-attested narratives ready for the lips of wife and mother showing the demoness appealing for succour to be fatalest of all!

There is a stone on the Müggelsberger, in Altmark, which is said to cover a treasure; this stone is sometimes called 'Devil's Altar,' and sometimes it is said a fire is seen there which disappears when approached. It lies on the verge of Teufelsee,—a lake dark and small, and believed to be fathomless. Where the stone lies a castle once stood which sank into the ground with its fair princess. But from the underground castle there is a subterranean avenue to a neighbouring hill, and from this hill of an evening sometimes comes an old woman, bent over her staff. Next day there will be seen a most beautiful lady combing her long golden hair. To all who pass she makes her entreaties that they will set her free, her pathetic appeals being backed by offer of a jewelled casket which she holds. The only means of liberating her is, she announces, that some one shall bear her on his shoulders three times round Teufelsee church without looking back. The experiment has several times been made. One villager at his first round saw a large hay-waggon drawn past him by four mice, and following it with his eyes received blows on the ears. Another saw a waggon drawn by four coal-black fire-breathing horses coming straight against him, started back, and all disappeared with the cry 'Lost again for ever!' A third tried and almost got through. He was found senseless, and on recovering related that when he took the princess on his shoulders she was light as a feather, but she grew heavier and heavier as he bore her round. Snakes, toads, and all horrible animals with fiery eyes surrounded him; dwarfs hurled blocks of wood and stones at him; yet he did not look back, and had nearly completed the third round, when he saw his village burst into flames; then he looked behind—a blow felled him—and he seems to have only lived long enough to tell this story. The youth of Köpernick are warned to steel their hearts against any fair maid combing her hair near Teufelsee. But the folklore of the same neighbourhood admits that it is by no means so dangerous for dames to listen to appeals of this kind. In the Gohlitzsee, for example, a midwife was induced to plunge in response to a call for aid; having aided a little Merwoman in travail, she was given an apronful of dust, which appeared odd until on shore it proved to be many thalers.

In countries where the popular imagination, instead of being scientific, is trained to be religiously retrospective, it relapses at the slightest touch into the infantine speculations of the human race. Not long ago, standing at a shop-window in Ostend where a 'Japanese Siren' was on view, the clever imposture interested me less than the comments of the passing and pausing observers. The most frequent wonders seriously expressed were, whether she sang, or combed her hair, or was under a doom, or had a soul to be saved. Every question related to Circe, Ulysses and the Sirens, and other conceptions of antiquity. The Japanese artists rightly concluded they could float their Siren in any intellectual waters where Jonah in his whale could pass, or a fish appear with its penny. Nay, even in their primitive form the Sirens find their kith and kin still haunting all the coasts of northern Europe. A type of the Irish and Scottish Siren may be found in the very complete legend of one seen by John Reid, shipmaster of Cromarty. With long flowing yellow hair she sat half on a rock, half in water, nude and beautiful, half woman half fish, and John managed to catch and hold her tight till she had promised to fulfil three wishes; then, released, she sprang into the sea. The wishes were all fulfilled, and to one of them (though John would never reveal it) the good-luck of the Reids was for a century after ascribed.10

The scene of this legend is the 'Dropping Cave,' and significantly near the Lover's Leap. One of John's wishes included the success of his courtship. These Caves run parallel with that of Venusberg, where the minstrel Tannhäuser is tempted by Venus and her nymphs. Heine finishes off his description of this Frau Venus by saying he fancied he met her one day in the Place Bréda. 'What do you take this lady to be?' asked he of Balzac, who was with him. 'She is a mistress,' replied Balzac. 'A duchess rather,' returned Heine. But the friends found on further explanation that they were both quite right. Venus' doves, soiled for a time, were spiritualised at last and made white, while the snowy swan grew darker. An old German word for swan, elbiz, originally denoting its whiteness (albus), furthered its connection with all 'elfish' beings—elf being from the same word, meaning white; but, as in Goethe's 'Erl König,' often disguising a dark character. The Swan and the Pigeon meet (with some modifications) as symbols of the Good and Evil powers in the legend of Lohengrin. The witch transforms the boy into a Swan, which, however, draws to save his sister, falsely accused of his murder, the Knight of the Sangreal, who, when the mystery of his holy name is inquired into by his too curious bride, is borne away by white doves. These legends all bear in them, however faintly, the accent of the early conflict of religion with the wild passions of mankind. Their religious bearings bring us to inquiries which must be considered at a later phase of our work. But apart from purely moral considerations, it is evident that there must have been practical dangers surrounding the early social chaos amid which the first immigrants in Europe found themselves.

Although the legend of Lady Godiva includes elements of another origin, it is probable that in the fate of Peeping Tom there is a distant reflection of the punishment sometimes said to overtake those who gazed too curiously upon the Swan-maiden without her feathers. The devotion of the nude lady of Coventry would not be out of keeping with one class of these mermaiden myths. There is a superstition, now particularly strong in Iceland, that all fairies are children of Eve, whom she hid away on an occasion when the Lord came to visit her, because they were not washed and presentable. So he condemned them to be for ever invisible. This superstition seems to be related to an old debate whether these præternatural beings are the children of Adam and Eve or not. A Scotch story bears against that conclusion. A beautiful nymph, with a slight robe of green, came from the sea and approached a fisherman while he was reading his Bible. She asked him if it contained any promise of mercy for her. He replied that it contained an offer of salvation to 'all the children of Adam;' whereupon with a loud shriek she dashed into the sea again. Euphemism would co-operate with natural compassion in saying a good word for 'the good little people,' whether hiding in earth or sea. In Altmark, 'Will-o'-wisps' are believed to be the souls of unbaptized children—sometimes of lunatics—unable to rest in their graves; they are called 'Light-men,' and it is said that though they may sometimes mislead they often guide rightly, especially if a small coin be thrown them,—this being also an African plan of breaking a sorcerer's spell. Christianity long after its advent in Germany had to contend seriously with customs and beliefs found in some lakeside villages where the fishermen regarded themselves as in friendly relations with the præternatural guardians of the waters, and unto this day speak of their presiding sea-maiden as a Holy Fräulein. They hear her bells chiming up from the depths in holy seasons to mingle with those whose sounds are wafted from church towers; and it seems to have required many fables, told by prints of fishermen found sitting lifeless on their boats while listening to them, to gradually transfer reverence to the new christian fairy.

It may be they heard some such melody as that which has found its finest expression in Mr. Matthew Arnold's 'Forsaken Merman:'—

Children dear, was it yesterday
(Call yet once) that she went away?
Once she sate with you and me,
On a red gold throne in the heart of the sea,
And the youngest sate on her knee.
She comb'd its bright hair, and she tended it well,
When down swung the sound of the far-off bell.
She sigh'd, she look'd up through the clear green sea;
She said: 'I must go, for my kinsfolk pray
In the little grey church on the shore to-day.
'Twill be Easter-time in the world—ah me!
And I lose my poor soul, Merman, here with thee.'
I said, 'Go up, dear heart, through the waves,
Say thy prayer, and come back to the kind sea-caves.'
She smil'd, she went up through the surf in the bay.
Children dear, was it yesterday?

Perhaps we should find the antecedents of this Merman's lost Margaret, whom he called back in vain, in the Danish ballad of 'The Merman and the Marstig's Daughter,' who, in Goethe's version, sought the winsome May in church, thither riding as a gay knight on

horse of the water clear,
The saddle and bridle of sea-sand were.
They went from the church with the bridal train,
They danced in glee, and they danced full fain;
They danced them down to the salt-sea strand,
And they left them standing there, hand in hand.
'Now wait thee, love, with my steed so free,
And the bonniest bark I'll bring for thee.'
And when they passed to the white, white sand,
The ships came sailing on to the land;
But when they were out in the midst of the sound,
Down went they all in the deep profound!
Long, long on the shore, when the winds were high,
They heard from the waters the maiden's cry.
I rede ye, damsels, as best I can—
Tread not the dance with the Water-Man!

According to other legends, however, the realm under-sea was not a place for weeping. Child-eyes beheld all that the Erl-king promised, in Goethe's ballad—

Wilt thou go, bonny boy? wilt thou go with me?
My daughters shall wait on thee daintily;
My daughters around thee in dance shall sweep,
And rock thee and kiss thee, and sing thee to sleep!

Or perhaps child-eyes, lingering in the burning glow of manhood's passion, might see in the peaceful sea some picture of lost love like that so sweetly described in Heine's 'Sea Phantom:'—

But I still leaned o'er the side of the vessel,
Gazing with sad-dreaming glances
Down at the water, clear as a mirror,
Looking yet deeper and deeper,—
Till far in the sea's abysses,
At first like dim wavering vapours,
Then slowly—slowly—deeper in colour,
Domes of churches and towers seemed rising,
And then, as clear as day, a city grand....
Infinite longing, wondrous sorrow,
Steal through my heart,—
My heart as yet scarce healed;
It seems as though its wounds, forgotten,
By loving lips again were kissed,
And once again were bleeding
Drops of burning crimson,
Which long and slowly trickle down
Upon an ancient house below there
In the deep, deep sea-town,
On an ancient, high-roofed, curious house,
Where, lone and melancholy,
Below by the window a maiden sits,
Her head on her arm reclined,—
Like a poor and uncared-for child;
And I know thee, thou poor and long-sorrowing child!
... I meanwhile, my spirit all grief,
Over the whole broad world have sought thee,
And ever have sought thee,
Thou dearly beloved,
Thou long, long lost one,
Thou finally found one,—
At last I have found thee, and now am gazing
Upon thy sweet face,
With earnest, faithful glances,
Still sweetly smiling;
And never will I again on earth leave thee.
I am coming adown to thee,
And with longing, wide-reaching embraces,
Love, I leap down to thy heart!

The temptations of fishermen to secure objects seen at the bottom of transparent lakes, sometimes appearing like boxes or lumps of gold, and even more reflections of objects in the upper world or air, must have been sources of danger; there are many tales of their being so beguiled to destruction. These things were believed treasures of the little folk who live under water, and would not part with them except on payment. In Blumenthal lake, 'tis said, there is an iron-bound yellow coffer which fishermen often have tried to raise, but their cords are cut as it nears the surface. At the bottom of the same lake valuable clothing is seen, and a woman who once tried to secure it was so nearly drowned that it is thought safer to leave it. The legends of sunken towns (as in Lake Paarsteinchen and Lough Neagh), and bells (whose chimes may be heard on certain sacred days), are probably variants of this class of delusions. They are often said to have been sunk by some final vindictive stroke of a magician or witch resolved to destroy the city no longer trusting them. Landslides, engulfing seaside homes, might originate legends like that of King Gradlon's daughter Dahut, whom the Breton peasant sees in rough weather on rocks around Poul-Dahut, where she unlocked the sluice-gates on the city Is in obedience to her fiend-lover.

If it be remembered that less than fifty years ago Dr. Belon[11] thought it desirable to anatomise gold fishes, and prove in various ways that it is a fallacy to suppose they feed on pure gold (as many a peasant near Lyons declares of the laurets sold daily in the market), it will hardly be thought wonderful that perilous visions of precious things were seen by early fishermen in pellucid depths, and that these should at last be regarded as seductive arts of Lorelei, who have given many lakes and rivers the reputation of requiring one or more annual victims.

Possibly it was through accumulation of many dreams about beautiful realms beneath the sea or above the clouds that suicide became among the Norse folk so common. It was a proverb that the worst end was to die in bed, and to die by suicide was to be like Egil, and Omund, and King Hake, like nearly all the heroes who so passed to Valhalla. The Northman had no doubt concerning the paradise to which he was going, and did not wish to reach it enfeebled by age. But the time would come when the earth and human affection must assert their claims, and the watery tribes be pictured as cruel devourers of the living. Even so would the wood-nymphs and mountain-nymphs be degraded, and fearful legends of those lost and wandering in dark forests be repeated to shuddering childhood. The actual dangers would mask themselves in the endless disguises of illusion, the wold and wave be peopled with cruel and treacherous seducers. Thus suicide might gradually lose its charms, and a dismal underworld of heartless gnomes replace the grottoes and fairies.

We may close this chapter with a Scottish legend relating to the 'Shi'ichs,' or Men of Peace, in which there is a strange intimation of a human mind dreaming that it dreams, and so far on its way to waking. A woman was carried away by these shadowy beings in order that she might suckle her child which they had previously stolen. During her retention she once observed the Shi'ichs anointing their eyes from a caldron, and seizing an opportunity, she managed to anoint one of her own eyes with the ointment. With that one eye she now saw the secret abode and all in it 'as they really were.' The deceptive splendour had vanished. The gaudy ornaments of a fairy grot had become the naked walls of a gloomy cavern. When this woman had returned to live among human beings again, her anointed eye saw much that others saw not; among other things she once saw a 'man of peace,' invisible to others, and asked him about her child. Astonished at being recognised, he demanded how she had been able to discover him; and when she had confessed, he spit in her eye and extinguished it for ever.

Notes

1 Von Spix and Von Martin's 'Travels in Brazil,' p. 243.
2 'Anatomy of Melancholy.' Fifteenth Edition, p. 124.
3 'Les Dieux en Exile.' Heinrich Heine. Revue des Deux Mondes, April, 1853.
4 'Book of Songs.' Translated by Charles E. Leland. New York: Henry Holt & Co. 1874.
5 Dennys.
6 Bleek, 'Hottentot Fables,' p. 58.
7 Baring-Gould, 'Curious Myths,' etc.
8 Ibid., ii. 299.
9 'Shaski,' vi. 48.
10 Hugh Miller, 'Scenes and Legends,' p. 293.
11 'The Mirror,' April 7, 1832.

Chapter X - Darkness

Shadows—Night Deities—Kobolds—Walpurgisnacht—Night as Abettor of Evil-doers—Nightmare—Dreams—Invisible Foes—Jacob and his Phantom—Nott—The Prince of Darkness—The Brood of Midnight—Second-Sight—Spectres of Souter Fell—The Moonshine Vampyre—Glamour—Glam and Grettir—A Story of Dartmoor.

From the little night which clings to man even by day—his own shadow—to the world's great shade of darkness, innumerable are the coverts from which have emerged the black procession of phantoms which have haunted the slumbers of the world, and betrayed the enterprise of man.

How strange to the first man seemed that shadow walking beside him, from the time when he saw it as a ghost tracking its steps and giving him his name for a ghost, on to the period in which it seemed the emanation of an occult power, as to them who brought their sick into the streets to be healed by the passing shadow of Peter; and still on to the day when Beaumont wrote—

Our acts our angels are, or good or ill,
Our fatal shadows that walk by us still;

or that in which Goethe found therein the mystical symbol of the inward arrest of our moral development, and said 'No man can jump off of his shadow.' And then from the culture of Europe we pass to the Feejee-Islanders, and find them believing that every man has two spirits. One is his shadow, which goes to Hades; the other is his image as reflected in water, and it is supposed to stay near the place where the man dies.1 But, like the giants of the Brocken, these demons of the Shadow are trembled at long after they are known to be the tremblers themselves mirrored on air. Have we not priests in England still fostering the belief that the baptized child goes attended by a white spirit, the unbaptized by a dark one? Why then need we apologise for the Fijians?

But little need be said here of demons of the Dark, for they are closely related to the phantasms of Delusion, of Winter, and others already described. Yet have they distinctive characters. As many as were the sunbeams were the shadows; every goddess of the Dawn (Ushas) cast her shadow; every Day was swallowed up by Night. This is the cavern where hide the treacherous Panis (fog) in Vedic mythology, they who steal and hide Indra's cows; this is the realm of Hades (the invisible); this is the cavern of the hag Thökk (dark) in Scandinavian mythology,—she who alone of all in the universe refused to weep for Baldur when he was shut up in Helheim, where he had been sent by the dart of his blind brother Hödr (darkness). In the cavern of Night sleep the Seven Sleepers of Ephesus, and Barbarossa, and all slumbering phantoms whose genius is the night-winged raven. Thorr, the Norse Hercules, once tried to lift a cat—as it seemed to him—from the ground; but it was the great mid-earth serpent which encircles the whole earth. Impossible feat as it was for Thorr—who got only one paw of the seeming cat off the ground—in that glassless and gasless era, invention has accomplished much in that direction; but the black Cat is still domiciled securely among idols of the mental cave.

There is an Anglo-Saxon word, cof-godas (lit. cove-gods), employed as the equivalent of the Latin lares (the Penates, too, are interpreted as cof-godu, cofa signifying the inner recess of a house, penetrale). The word in German corresponding to this cofa, is koben; and from this Hildebrand conjectures kob-old to be derived. The latter part of the word he supposes to be walt (one who 'presides over,' e.g., Walter); so that the original form would be kob-walt.2 Here, then, in the recesses of the household, among the least enlightened of its members—the menials, who still often neutralise the efforts of rational people to dispel the delusions of their children—the discredited deities and demons of the past found refuge, and through a little baptismal change of names are familiars of millions unto this day. In the words of the ancient Hebrew, 'they lay in their own houses prisoners of darkness, fettered with the bonds of a long night.' 'No power of the fire might give them light, neither could the bright flames of the stars lighten that horrible night.'3 Well is it added, 'Fear is nothing else but a betraying of the succours which reason offereth,' a truth which finds ample illustration in the Kobolds. These imaginary beings were naturally associated with the dark recesses of mines. There they gave the name to our metal Cobalt. The value of Cobalt was not understood until the 17th century, and the metal was first obtained by the Swedish chemist Brandt in 1733. The miners had believed that the silver was stolen away by Kobolds, and these 'worthless' ores left in its place. Nickel had the like history, and is named after Old Nick. So long did those Beauties slumber in the cavern of Ignorance till Science kissed them with its sunbeam, and led them forth to decorate the world!

How passed this (mental) cave-dweller even amid the upper splendours and vastnesses of his unlit world? A Faust guided by his Mephistopheles only amid interminable Hartz labyrinths.

How sadly rises, incomplete and ruddy,
The moon's lone disk, with its belated glow,
And lights so dimly, that, as one advances,
At every step one strikes a rock or tree!
Let us then use a Jack-o'-lantern's glances:
I see one yonder, burning merrily.
Ho, there! my friend! I'll levy thine attendance:
Why waste so vainly thy resplendence?
Be kind enough to light us up the steep!
Tell me, if we still are standing,
Or if further we're ascending?
All is turning, whirling, blending,
Trees and rocks with grinning faces,
Wandering lights that spin in mazes,
*Still increasing and expanding.*4

It could only have been at a comparatively late period of social development that Sancho's benediction on the inventor of sleep could have found general response. The Red Indian found its helplessness fatal when the 'Nick of the Woods' was abroad; the Scotch sailor found in it a demon's opiate when the 'Nigg of the Sea' was gathering his storms above the sleeping watchman. It was among the problems of Job, the coöperation of darkness with evil-doers.

The eye of the adulterer waiteth for the twilight;
He saith, No eye will see me,
And putteth a mask upon his face.
In the dark men break into houses;
In the day-time they shut themselves up;
They are strangers to the light.
The morning to them is the shadow of death;
They are familiar with the dark terrors of midnight.

Besides this fact that the night befriends and masks every treacherous foe, it is also to be remembered that man is weakest at night. Not only is he weaker than by day in the veil drawn over his senses, but physiologically also. When the body is wearied out by the toils or combats of the day, and the mind haunted by dreams of danger, there are present all the terrors which Byron portrays around the restless pillow of Sardanapalus. The war-horse of the day becomes a night-mare in the darkness. In the Heimskringla it is recorded: 'Vanland, Svegdir's son, succeeded his father and ruled over the Upsal domain. He was a great warrior, and went far around in different lands. Once he took up his winter abode in Finland with Snio the Old, and got his daughter Drisa in marriage; but in spring he set out leaving Drisa behind, and although he had promised to return within three years he did not come back for ten. Then Drisa sent a message to the witch Hulda; and sent Visbur, her son by Vanland, to Sweden. Drisa bribed the witch-wife Hulda, either that she should bewitch Vanland to return to Finland or kill him. When this witch-work was going on Vanland was at Upsal, and a great desire came over him to go to Finland, but his friends and counsellors advised him against it, and said the witchcraft of the Fin people showed itself in this desire of his to go there. He then became very drowsy, and laid himself down to sleep; but when he had slept but a little while he cried out, saying, 'Mara was treading on him.' His men hastened to help him; but when they took hold of his head she trod on his legs, and when they laid hold of his legs she pressed upon his head; and it was his death.'5

This witch is, no doubt, Hildur, a Walkyr of the Edda, leading heroes to Walhalla. Indeed, in Westphalia, nightmare is called Walriderske. It is a curious fact that 'Mara' should be preserved in the French word for nightmare, Cauche-mar, 'cauche' being from Latin calcare, to tread. Through Teutonic folklore this Night-demon of many names, having floated from England in a sieve paddled with cow-ribs, rides to the distress of an increasingly unheroic part of the population. Nearly always still the 'Mahrt' is said to be a pretty woman,—sometimes, indeed, a sweetheart is involuntarily transformed to one,—every rustic settlement abounding with tales of how the demoness has been captured by stopping the keyhole, calling the ridden sleeper by his baptismal name, and making the sign of the cross; by such process the wicked beauty appears in human form, and is apt to marry the sleeper, with usually evil results. The fondness of cats for getting on the breasts of sleepers, or near their breath, for warmth, has made that animal a common form of the 'Mahrt.' Sometimes it is a black fly with red ring around its neck. This demoness is believed to suffer more pain than it inflicts, and vainly endeavours to destroy herself.

In savage and nomadic times sound sleep being an element of danger, the security which required men to sleep on their arms demanded also that they should sleep as it were with one eye open. Thus there might have arisen both the intense vividness which demons acquired by blending subjective and objective impressions, and the curious inability, so frequent among barbarians and not unknown among the men civilised, to distinguish dream from fact. The habit of day-dreaming seems, indeed, more general than is usually supposed. Dreams haunt all the region of our intellectual twilight,—the borderland of mystery, where rise the sources of the occult and the mystical which environ our lives. The daily terrors of barbarous life avail to haunt the nerves of civilised people, now many generations after they have passed away, with special and irrational shudders at certain objects or noises: how then must they have haunted the dreams of humanity when, like the daughter of Nathan the Wise, rescued from flames, it passed the intervals of strife

With nerves unstrung through fear,
And fire and flame in all she sees or fancies;
Her soul awake in sleep, asleep when wide awake?

Among the sources of demoniac beliefs few indeed are more prolific than Dreams. 'The witchcraft of sleep,' says Emerson, 'divides with truth the empire of our lives. This soft enchantress visits two children lying locked in each other's arms, and carries them asunder by wide spans of land and sea, wide intervals of time. 'Tis superfluous to think of the dreams of multitudes; the astonishment remains that one should dream; that we should resign so quietly this deifying reason and become the theatre of delusions, shows, wherein time, space, persons, cities, animals, should dance before us in merry and mad confusion, a delicate creation outdoing the prime and flower of actual nature, antic comedy alternating with horrid spectres. Or we seem busied for hours and days in peregrinations over seas and lands, in earnest dialogues, strenuous actions for nothings and absurdities, cheated by spectral jokes, and waking suddenly with ghostly laughter, to be rebuked by the cold lonely silent midnight, and to rake with confusion in memory among the gibbering nonsense to find the motive of this contemptible cachinnation.'6

It has always been the worst of periods of religious excitement that they shape the dreams of old and young, and find there a fearful and distorted, but vivid and realistic, embodiment of their feverish experiences. In the days of witchcraft thousands visited the Witches' Sabbaths, as they believed and danced in the Walpurgis orgies, borne (by hereditary orthodox canon) on their own brooms up their own chimneys; and to-day, by the same morbid imaginations, the victims are able to see themselves or others elongated, levitated, floating through the air. If people only knew how few are ever really wide-awake, these spiritual nightmares would soon reach their termination. The natural terrors before which helpless man once cowered, have been prolonged past all his real victories over his demons by a succession of such nightmares, so that the vulgar religion might be portrayed somewhat as Richard Wagner described his first tragedy, in which, having killed off forty-two of his characters, he had to bring them back as ghosts to carry on the fifth act!

The perils of darkness, as ambush of foes human and animal, concealer of pitfalls, misguider of footsteps, misdirector of aims, were more real than men can well imagine in an age of gaslight plus the policeman. The myth of Joshua commanding the sun to stand still; the cry of Ajax when darkness fell on the combat, 'Grant me but to see!' refer us to the region from which come all childish shudders at going into the dark. The limit of human courage is reached where its foe is beyond the reach of its force. Fighting in the dark may even be suicidal. A German fable of blindfold zeal—the awakened sleeper demolishing his furniture and knocking out his own teeth in the attempt to punish cats—has its tragical illustrations also. But none of these actual dangers have been of more real evil to man than the demonisation of them. This rendered his very skill a blunder, his energy weakness. If it was bad to retreat in the dusk from an innocent bush into an unrecognised well, it was worse to meet the ghost with rune or crucifix and find it an assassin. When man fights with his shadow, he instantly makes it the demon he fears; ghoul-like it preys upon his paralysed strength, vampyre-like it sucks his blood, and he is consigned disarmed to the evil that is no shadow. The Scottish Sinclair marching through Norway, in the 16th century, owes his monument at Wiblungen rather to the magpie believed to precede him as a spy, with night and day upon its wings, than to his own prowess or power.

In a sense all demons, whatever their shapes, are the ancient brood of night. Mental darkness, even more moral darkness within, supply the phantasmagoria in which unknown things shape themselves as demons. Esau is already reconciled, but guilty Jacob must still wrestle with him as a phantom of Fear till daybreak. A work has already been written on 'The Night-side of Nature,' but it would require many volumes to tell the story of what monsters have been conjured out of the kind protecting darkness. How great is the darkness which man makes for himself out of the imagination which should be his light and vision! Much of the so-called 'religion' of our time is but elaborate demoniculture and artificial preservation of mental Walpurgis-nights. Nott (Night) says the Edda rides first on her horse called Hrimfaxi (frost-maned), which every morning as he ends his course bedews the earth with the foam that falls from his bit. Though the horse of Day—Skinfaxi, or Shining-mane—follows hard after her, yet the foam is by no means drunk up by his fires. Foam of the old phantasms still lingers in our mediæval liturgies, and even falls afresh where the daylight is shut out that altar-candles may burn, or for other dark seances are prepared the conditions necessary for whatsoever loves not the light.

What we call the Dark Ages were indeed spiritually a perpetual seance with lights lowered. Nay, human superstition was able to turn the very moon and stars into mere bluish night-tapers, giving just light enough to make the darkness visible in fantastic shapes fluttering around the Prince of Darkness,—or Non-existence in Chief! How much of the theosophic speculation of our time is the mere artificial conservation of that darkness? How much that still flits bat-winged from universities, will, in the future, be read with the same wonder as that with which even the more respectable bats can now read account of the midnight brood which now for the most part sleep tranquilly in such books as Burton's 'Anatomy of Melancholy'? 'There are,' he says, 'certain spirits which Miraldus calls Ambulones, that walk about midnight on great heaths and desert places, which (saith Lavater) draw men out of their way, and lead them all night by a byway, or quite bar them of their way. These have several names in several places. We commonly call them Pucks. In the deserts of Lop, in Asia, such illusions of walking spirits are often perceived, as you may read in M. Paulus, the Venetian, his travels. If one lose his company by chance, these devils will call him by his name, and counterfeit voices of his companions to seduce him. Lavater and Cicogna have a variety of examples of spirits and walking devils in this kind. Sometimes they sit by the wayside to give men falls, and make their horses stumble and start as they ride (according to the narration of that holy man Ketellus in Nubrigensis, that had an especial grace to see devils); and if a man curse and spur his horse for stumbling, they do heartily rejoice at it.'

While observing a spirited and imaginative picture by Macallum of the Siege of Jerusalem, it much interested me to observe the greater or less ease with which other visitors discovered the portents in the air which, following the narrative of Josephus, the artist had vaguely portrayed. The chariots and horsemen said to have been seen before that event were here faintly blent with indefinite outlines of clouds; and while some of the artist's friends saw them with a distinctness greater, perhaps, than that with which they impressed the eye of the artist himself, others could hardly be made to see anything except shapeless vapour, though of course they all agreed that they were there and remarkably fine. It would seem that thus, in a London studio, there were present all the mental pigments for frescoing the air and sky with those visions of aërial armies or huntsmen which have become so normal in history as to be, in a subjective sense, natural. In the year 1763, an author, styling himself Theophilus Insulanus, published at Edinburgh a book on Second-Sight, in which he related more than a hundred instances of the power he believed to exist of seeing events before they had occurred, and whilst, of course, they did not exist. It is not difficult in reading them to see that they are all substantially one and the same story, and that the sight in operation was indeed second; for man or woman, at once imaginative and illiterate, have a second and supernumerary pair of eyes inherited from the traditional superstitions and ghost stories which fill all the air they breathe from the cradle to the grave. While the mind is in this condition, that same nature whose apparitions and illusions originally evoked and fostered the glamoury, still moves on with her minglings of light and shade, cloud and mirage, giving no word of explanation. There are never wanting the shadowy forms without that cast their shuttles to the dark idols of the mental cave, together weaving subtle spells round the half-waking mind. In the year 1743 all the North of England and Scotland was in alarm on account of some spectres which were seen on the mountain of Souter Fell in Cumberland. The mountain is about half-a-mile high. On a summer evening a farmer and his servant, looking from Wilton Hall, half a mile off, saw the figures of a man and a dog pursuing some horses along the mountain-side, which is very steep; and on the following morning they repaired to the place, expecting to find dead bodies, but finding none. About one year later a troop of horsemen were seen riding along the same mountain-side by one of the same persons, the servant, who then called others who also saw the aërial troopers. After a year had elapsed the above vision was attested before a magistrate by two of those who saw it. The event occurred on the eve of the Rebellion, when horsemen were exercising, and when also the popular mind along the Border may be supposed to have been in a highly excited condition.

What was seen on this strongly-authenticated occasion? Was anything seen? None can tell. It is open to us to believe that there may have been some play of mirage. As there are purely aërial echoes, so are there aërial reflectors for the eye. On the other hand, the vision so nearly resembles the spectral processions which have passed through the mythology of the world, that we can never be sure that it was not the troop of King Arthur, emerging from Avallon to announce the approaching strife. A few fleecy, strangely-shaped clouds, chasing each other along the hillside in the evening's dusk would have amply sufficed to create the latter vision, and the danger of the time would easily have supplied all the Second-Sight required to reveal it to considerable numbers. In questions of this kind a very small circumstance—a phrase, a name, perhaps—may turn the balance of probabilities. Thus it may be noted that, in the instance just related, the vision was seen on the steep side of Souter Fell. Fell means a hill or a steep rock, as in Drachenfels. But as to Souter, although, as Mr. Robert Ferguson says, the word may originally have meant sheep,[7] it is found in Scotland used as 'shoemaker' in connection with the fabulous giants of that region. Sir Thomas Urquhart, in the seventeenth century, relates it as the tradition of the two promontories of Cromarty, called 'Soutars,' that they were the work-stools of two giants who supplied their comrades with shoes and buskins. Possessing but one set of implements, they used to fling these to each other across the opening of the firth, where the promontories are only two miles apart. In process of time the name Soutar, shoemaker, was bequeathed by the craftsmen to their stools. It is not improbable that the name gradually connected itself with other places bearing traditions connecting them with the fabulous race, and that in this way the Souter Fell, from meaning in early times much the same as Giants' Hill, preserved even in 1743–44 enough of the earlier uncanny associations to awaken the awe of Borderers in a time of rebellion. The vision may therefore have been seen by light which had journeyed all the way from the mythologic heavens of ancient India: substantially subjective—such stuff as dreams and dreamers are made of—no doubt there were outer clouds, shapes and afterglows enough, even in the absence of any fata morgana to supply canvas and pigment to the cunning artist that hides in the eye.

In an old tale, the often-slain Vampyre-bat only requests, with pathos, that his body may be laid where no sunlight, but only the moonlight, will fall on it—only that! But it is under the moonshine that it always gains new life. No demon requires absolute darkness, but half-darkness, in which to live: enough light to disclose a Somewhat, but not enough to define and reveal its nature, is just what has been required for the bat-eyes of fable and phantasy, which can make vampyre of a sparrow or giant out of a windmill.

Glamour! A marvellous history has this word of the artists and poets,—sometimes meaning the charm with which the eye invests any object; or, in Wordsworth's phrase, 'the light that never was on land or sea.' But no artist or poet ever rose to the full height of the simple term itself, which well illustrates Emerson's saying, 'Words are fossil poetry.' Professor Cowell of Cambridge says: 'Glám, or in the nominative Glámr, is also a poetical name for the Moon. It does not actually occur in the ancient literature, but it is given in the glossary in the Prose Edda in the list of the very old words for the Moon.' Vigfusson in his dictionary says, 'The word is interesting on account of its identity with Scot. Glamour, which shows that the tale of Glam was common to Scotland and Iceland, and this much older than Grettir (in the year 1014).' The Ghost or Goblin Glam seems evidently to have arisen from a personification of the delusive and treacherous effects of moonlight on the benighted traveller,

Quale per incertam lunam sub luce malignâ,
Est iter in sylvis.

Now, there is a curious old Sanskrit word, glau or gláv, which is explained in all the old native lexicons as meaning 'the moon.' It might either be taken as 'waning,' or in a casual sense 'obscuring.'

The following lines from an early mediæval poet, Bhása (seventh century), will illustrate the deceptive character of moonlight from a Hindu point of view. The strong and wild Norse imagination delights in what is terrible and gloomy: the Hindu loves to dwell on the milder and quieter aspects of human life.

'The cat laps the moonbeams in the bowl of water, thinking them to be milk: the elephant thinks that the moonbeams, threaded through the intervals of the trees, are the fibres of the lotus-stalk. The woman snatches at the moonbeams as they lie on the bed, taking them for her muslin garment: oh, how the moon, intoxicated with radiance, bewilders all the world!'

A similar passage, no doubt imitated from this, is also quoted:

'The bewildered herdsmen place the pails under the cows, thinking that the milk is flowing; the maidens also put the blue lotus blossom in their ears, thinking that it is the white; the mountaineer's wife snatches up the jujube fruit, avaricious for pearls. Whose mind is not led astray by the thickly clustering moonbeams?'8

In the Icelandic legend of the struggle between the hero Grettir, translated by Magnússen and Morris (London, 1869), the saga supplies a scenery as archæological as if the philologists had been consulted. 'Bright moonlight was there without, and the drift was broken, now drawn over the moon, now driven off from her; and even as Glam fell, a cloud was driven from the moon, and Glam glared up against her.' When the hero beheld these glaring eyes of the giant Ghost, he felt some fiendish craft in them, and could not draw his short sword, and 'lay well nigh 'twixt home and hell.' This half-light of the moon, which robs the Strong of half his power, is repeated in Glam's curse: 'Exceedingly eager hast thou sought to meet me, Grettir, but no wonder will it be deemed, though thou gettest no good hap of me; and this I must tell thee, that thou now hast got half the strength and manhood which was thy lot if thou hadst not met me: now I may not take from thee the strength which thou hast got before this; but that may I rule, that thou shalt never be mightier than now thou art ... therefore this weird I lay on thee, ever in those days to see these eyes with thine eyes, and thou wilt find it hard to be alone—and that shalt drag thee unto death.'

The Moon-demon's power is limited to the spell of illusion he can cast. Presently he is laid low; the 'short sword' of a sunbeam pales, decapitates him. But after Glam is burned to cold coals, and his ashes buried in skin of a beast 'where sheep-pastures were fewest, or the ways of men,' the spell lay upon the hero's eyes. 'Grettir said that his temper had been nowise bettered by this, that he was worse to quiet than before, and that he deemed all trouble worse than it was; but that herein he found the greatest change, in that he was become so fearsome a man in the dark, that he durst go nowhither alone after nightfall, for then he seemed to see all kinds of horrors. And that has fallen since into a proverb, that Glam lends eyes, or gives Glamsight to those who see things nowise as they are.'

In reading which one may wonder how this world would look if for a little moment one's eyes could be purged of glamour. Even at the moon's self one tries vainly to look: where Hindu and Zulu see a hare, the Arab sees coils of a serpent, and the Englishman sees a man; and the most intelligent of these several races will find it hard to see in the moon aught save what their primitive ancestors saw. And this small hint of the degree to which the wisest, like Merlin, are bound fast in an air-prison by a Vivien whose spells are spun from themselves, would carry us far could we only venture to follow it out. 'The Moon,' observed Dr. Johnson unconsciously, 'has great influence in vulgar philosophy.' How much lunar theology have we around us, so that many from the cradle to the grave get no clear sight of nature or of themselves! Very closely did Carlyle come to the fable of Glam when speaking of Coleridge's 'prophetic moonshine,' and its effect on poor John Sterling. 'If the bottled moonshine be actually substance? Ah, could one but believe in a church while finding it incredible!... The bereaved young lady has taken the veil then!... To such lengths can transcendental moonshine, cast by some morbidly radiating Coleridge into the chaos of a fermenting life, act magically there, and produce divulsions and convulsions and diseased developments.' One can almost fancy Carlyle had ringing in his memory the old Scottish ballad of the Rev. Robert Kirk, translator of the Psalms into Gaelic, who, while walking in his night-gown at Aberfoyle, was 'snatched away to the joyless Elfin bower.'

It was between the night and day
When the fairy-king has power.

The item of the night-gown might have already prepared us for the couplet; and it has perhaps even a mystical connection with the vestment of the 'black dragoon' which Sterling once saw patrolling in every parish, to whom, however, he surrendered at last.

A story is told of a man wandering on a dark night over Dartmoor, whose feet slipped over the edge of a pit. He caught the branch of a tree suspended over the terrible chasm, but unable to regain the ground, shrieked for help. None came, though he cried out till his voice was gone; and there he remained dangling in agony until the grey light revealed that his feet were only a few inches from the solid ground. Such are the chief demons that bind man till cockcrow. Such are the apprehensions that waste also the moral and intellectual strength of man, and murder his peace as he regards the necessary science of his time to be cutting some frail tenure sustaining him over a bottomless pit, instead of a release from real terror to the solid ground.

Notes

1 *'The Origin of Civilisation,' etc. By Sir John Lubbock.*
2 *Hildebrand in Grimm's 'Wörterbuch.'*
3 *Wisdom of Solomon, xvii. What this impressive chapter says of the delusions of the guilty are equally true of those of ignorance. 'They sleeping the same sleep that night ... were partly vexed with monstrous apparitions, and partly fainted, their heart failing them ... whosoever there fell down was straitly kept, shut up in a prison without iron bars.... Whether it were a whistling wind, or a melodious noise of birds among the spreading branches, or a pleasing fall of water running violently, or a terrible sound of stones cast down, or a running that could not be seen of skipping beasts, or a roaring voice of most savage wild beasts, or a rebounding echo from the hollow mountains: these things made them to swoon for fear. The whole world shined with clear light ... over them only was spread a heavy night, an image of that darkness which should afterward receive them: but yet were they to themselves more grievous than that darkness.'*
4 *Bayard Taylor's 'Faust.' Walpurgis-night.*
5 *i. 228.*
6 *North American Review. March 1877.*
7 *In his very valuable work, 'Northmen in Cumberland and Westmoreland.' Longmans. 1856.*
8 *'Journal of Philology,' vi. No. II. On the Word Glamour and the Legend of Glam, by Professor Cowell.*

Chapter XI - Disease

The Plague Phantom—Devil-dances—Destroying Angels—Ahriman in Astrology—-Saturn—Satan and Job—Set—The Fatal Seven—Yakseyo—The Singhalese Pretraya—Reeri—Maha Sohon—Morotoo—Luther on Disease-demons—Gopolu—Madan—Cattle-demon in Russia—Bihlweisen—The Plough.

A familiar fable in the East tells of one who met a fearful phantom, which in reply to his questioning answered—'I am Plague: I have come from yon city where ten thousand lie dead: one thousand were slain by me, the rest by Fear.' Perhaps even this story does not fully report the alliance between the plague and fear; for it is hardly doubtful that epidemics retain their power in the East largely because they have gained personification through fear as demons whose fatal power man can neither prevent nor cure, before which he can only cower and pray.

In the missionary school at Canterbury the young men prepare themselves to help the 'heathen' medically, and so they go forth with materia medica in one hand, and in the other an infallible revelation from heaven reporting plagues as the inflictions of Jehovah, or the destroying angel, or Satan, and the healing of disease the jealously reserved monopoly of God.[1]

The demonisation of diseases is not wonderful. To thoughtful minds not even science has dispelled the mystery which surrounds many of the ailments that afflict mankind, especially the normal diseases besetting children, hereditary complaints, and the strange liabilities to infection and contagion. A genuine, however partial, observation would suggest to primitive man some connection between the symptoms of many diseases and the mysterious universe of which he could not yet recognise himself an epitome. There were indications that certain troubles of this kind were related to the seasons, consequently to the celestial rulers of the seasons,—to the sun that smote by day, and the moon at night. Professor Monier Williams, describing the Devil-dances of Southern India, says that there seems to be an idea among them that when pestilences are rife exceptional measures must be taken to draw off the malignant spirits, supposed to cause them, by tempting them to enter into these wild dancers, and so become dissipated. He witnessed in Ceylon a dance performed by three men who personated the forms and phases of typhus fever.[2] These dances probably belong to the same class of ideas as those of the dervishes in Persia, whose manifold contortions are supposed to repeat the movements of planets. They are invocations of the souls of good stars, and propitiations of such as are evil. Belief in such stellar and planetary influences has pervaded every part of the world, and gave rise to astrological dances. 'Gebelin says that the minuet was the danse oblique of the ancient priests of Apollo, performed in their temples. The diagonal line and the two parallels described in this dance were intended to be symbolical of the zodiac, and the twelve steps of which it is composed were meant for the twelve signs and the months of the year. The dance round the Maypole and the Cotillon has the same origin. Diodorus tells us that Apollo was adored with dances, and in the island of Iona the god danced all night. The Christians of St. Thomas till a very late day celebrated their worship with dances and songs. Calmet says there were dancing-girls in the temple at Jerusalem.'3

The influence of the Moon upon tides, the sleeplessness it causes, the restlessness of the insane under its occasional light, and such treacheries of moonshine as we have already considered, have populated our uninhabited satellite with demons. Lunar legends have decorated some well-founded suspicions of moonlight. The mother draws the curtain between the moonshine and her little Endymion, though not because she sees in the waning moon a pining Selene whose kiss may waste away the beauty of youth. A mere survival is the 'bowing to the new moon:' a euphonism traceable to many myths about 'lunacy,' among them, as I think, to Delilah ('languishing'), in whose lap the solar Samson is shorn of his locks, leaving him only the blind destructive strength of the 'moonstruck.'

In the purely Semitic theories of the Jews we find diseases ascribed to the wrath of Jehovah, and their cure to his merciful mood. 'Jehovah will make thy plagues wonderful, and the plagues of thy seed; ... he will bring upon thee all the diseases of Egypt whereof thou wast afraid.'4 The emerods which smote the worshippers of Dagon were ascribed directly to the hand of Jehovah.5 In that vague degree of natural dualistic development which preceded the full Iranian influence upon the Jews, the infliction of diseases was delegated to an angel of Jehovah, as in the narratives of smiting the firstborn of Egypt, wasting the army of Sennacherib, and the pestilence sent upon Israel for David's sin. In the progress of this angel to be a demon of disease we find a phase of ambiguity, as shown in the hypochondria of Saul. 'The spirit of Jehovah departed from Saul, and an evil spirit from Jehovah troubled him.'6

All such ambiguities disappeared under the influence of Iranian dualism. In the Book of Job we find the infliction of diseases and plagues completely transferred to a powerful spirit, a fully formed opposing potentate. The 'sons of God,' who in the first chapter of Job are said to have presented themselves before Jehovah, may be identified in the thirty-eighth as the stars which shouted for joy at the creation. Satan is the wandering or malign planet which leads in the Ahrimanic side of the Persian planisphere. In the cosmographical theology of that country Ormuzd was to reign for six thousand years, and then Ahriman was to reign for a similar period. The moral associations of this speculation are discussed elsewhere; it is necessary here only to point out the bearing of the planispheric conception upon the ills that flesh is heir to. Ahriman is the 'star-serpent' of the Zendavasta. 'When the pâris rendered this world desolate, and overran the universe; when the star-serpent made a path for himself between heaven and earth,' etc.; 'when Ahriman rambles on the earth, let him who takes the form of a serpent glide on the earth; let him who takes the form of the wolf run on the earth, and let the violent north wind bring weakness.'7

The dawn of Ormuzd corresponds with April. The sun returns from winter's death by sign of the lamb (our Aries), and thenceforth every month corresponds with a thousand years of the reign of the Beneficent. September is denoted by the Virgin and Child. To the dark domain of Ahriman the prefecture of the universe passes by Libra,—the same balances which appear in the hand of Satan. The star-serpent prevails over the Virgin and Child. Then follow the months of the scorpion, the centaur, goat, etc., every month corresponding to a thousand years of the reign of Ahriman.

While this scheme corresponds in one direction with the demons of cold, and in another with the entrance and reign of moral evil in the world, beginnings of disease on earth were also ascribed to this seventh thousand of years when the Golden Age had passed. The depth of winter is reached in domicile of the goat, or of Sirius, Seth, Saturn, Satan—according to the many variants. And these, under their several names, make the great 'infortune' of astrology, wherein old Culpepper amply instructed our fathers. 'In the general, consider that Saturn is an old worn-out planet, weary, and of little estimation in this world; he causeth long and tedious sicknesses, abundance of sadness, and a Cartload of doubts and fears; his nature is cold, and dry, and melancholy. And take special notice of this, that when Saturn is Lord of an Eclipse (as he is one of the Lords of this), he governs all the rest of the planets, but none can govern him. Melancholy is made of all the humors in the body of man, but no humor of melancholy. He is envious, and keeps his anger long, and speaks but few words, but when he speaks he speaks to purpose. A man of deep cogitations; he will plot mischief when men are asleep; he hath an admirable memory, and remembers to this day how William the Bastard abused him; he cannot endure to be a slave; he is poor with the poor, fearful with the fearful; he plots mischief against the Superiours, with them that plot mischief against them; have a care of him, Kings and Magistrates of Europe; he will show you what he can do in the effects of this Eclipse; he is old, and therefore hath large experience, and will give perilous counsel; he moves but slowly, and therefore doth the more mischief; all the planets contribute their natures and strength to him, and when he sets on doing mischief he will do it to purpose; he doth not regard the company of the rest of the Planets, neither do any of the rest of the Planets regard his; he is a barren Planet, and therefore delights not in women; he brings the Pestilence; he is destructive to the fruits of the earth; he receives his light from the Sun, and yet he hates the Sun that gives it him.'8

Many ages anterior to this began in India the dread of Ketu, astronomically the ninth planet, mythologically the tail of the demon Rahu, cut in twain as already told (p. 46), supposed to be the prolific source of comets, meteors, and falling stars,

88

also of diseases. From this Ketu or dragon's tail were born the Arunah Ketavah (Red Ketus or apparitions), and Ketu has become almost another word for disease.9

Strongly influenced as were the Jews by the exact division of the duodecimal period between Good and Evil, affirmed by the Persians, they never lost sight of the ultimate supremacy of Jehovah. Though Satan had gradually become a voluntary genius of evil, he still had to receive permission to afflict, as in the case of Job, and during the lifetime of Paul appears to have been still denied that 'power of death' which is first asserted by the unknown author of the Epistle to the Hebrews.10 Satan's especial office was regarded as the infliction of disease. Paul delivers the incestuous Corinthian to Satan 'for the destruction of the flesh,' and he also attributed the sickness and death of many to their communicating unworthily.11 He also recognises his own 'thorn in the flesh' as 'an angel from Satan,' though meant for his moral advantage.12

A penitential Psalm (Assyrian) reads as follows:—

O my Lord! my sins are many, my trespasses are great; and the wrath of the gods has plagued me with disease, and with sickness and sorrow.

I fainted, but no one stretched forth his hand!
I groaned, but no one drew nigh!
I cried aloud, but no one heard!
O Lord, do not abandon thy servant!
In the waters of the great storm seize his hand!
*The sins which he has committed turn them to righteousness.*13

This Psalm would hardly be out of place in the English burial-service, which deplores death as a visitation of divine wrath. Wherever such an idea prevails, the natural outcome of it is a belief in demons of disease. In ancient Egypt—following the belief in Ra the Sun, from whose eyes all pleasing things proceeded, and Set, from whose eyes came all noxious things,—from the baleful light of Set's eyes were born the Seven Hathors, or Fates, whose names are recorded in the Book of the Dead. Mr. Fox Talbot has translated 'the Song of the Seven Spirits:'—

They are seven! they are seven!
In the depths of ocean they are seven!
In the heights of heaven they are seven!
In the ocean-stream in a palace they were born!
Male they are not: female they are not!
Wives they have not: children are not born to them!
Rule they have not: government they know not!
Prayers they hear not!
*They are seven! they are seven! twice over they are seven!*14

These demons have a way of herding together; the Assyrian tablets abundantly show that their occupation was manifested by diseases, physical and mental. One prescription runs thus:—

The god (...) shall stand by his bedside:
Those seven evil spirits he shall root out, and shall expel them from his body:
And those seven shall never return to the sick man again!

It is hardly doubtful that these were the seven said to have been cast out of Mary Magdalen; for their father Set is Shedîm (devils) of Deut. xxxii. 17, and Shaddai (God) of Gen. xvi. 1. But the fatal Seven turn to the seven fruits that charm away evil influences at parturition in Persia, also the Seven Wise Women of the same country traditionally present on holy occasions. When Ardá Viráf was sent to Paradise by a sacred narcotic to obtain intelligence of the true faith, seven fires were kept burning for seven days around him, and the seven wise women chanted hymns of the Avesta.15

The entrance of the seven evil powers into a dwelling was believed by the Assyrians to be preventible by setting in the doorway small images, such as those of the sun-god (Hea) and the moon-goddess, but especially of Marduk, corresponding to Serapis the Egyptian Esculapius. These powers were reinforced by writing holy texts over and on each side of the threshold. 'In the night time bind around the sick man's head a sentence taken from a good book.' The phylacteries of the Jews were originally worn for the same purpose. They were called Tefila, and were related to teraphim, the little idols16 used by the Jews to keep out demons—such as those of Laban, which his daughter Rachel stole.

The resemblance of teraphim to the Tarasca (connected by some with G. τέρας, a monster) of Spain may be noted,—the serpent figures carried about in Corpus Christi processions. The latter word is known in the south of France also, and gave its name to the town Tarascon. The legend is that an amphibious monster haunted the Rhone, preventing navigation and committing terrible ravages, until sixteen of the boldest inhabitants of the district resolved to encounter it. Eight lost their lives, but the others, having destroyed the monster, founded the town of Tarascon, where the 'Fête de la tarasque' is still kept up.17 Calmet, Sedley, and others, however, believe that teraphim is merely a modification of seraphim, and the Tefila, or phylacteries, of the same origin.

The phylactery was tied into a knot. Justin Martyr says that the Jewish exorcists used 'magic ties or knots.' The origin of this custom among the Jews and Babylonians may be found in the Assyrian Talismans preserved in the British Museum, of which the following has been translated by Mr. Fox Talbot:—

Hea says: Go, my son!
Take a woman's kerchief,
Bind it round thy right hand, loose it from the left hand!
Knot it with seven knots: do so twice:
Sprinkle it with bright wine:
Bind it round the head of the sick man:
Bind it round his hands and feet, like manacles and fetters.
Sit down on his bed:
Sprinkle holy water over him.
He shall hear the voice of Hea,
Darkness shall protect him!
*And Marduk, eldest son of Heaven, shall find him a happy habitation.*18

The number seven holds an equally high degree of potency in Singhalese demonolatry, which is mainly occupied with diseases. The Capuas or conjurors of that island enumerate 240,000 magic spells, of which all except one are for evil, which implies a tolerably large preponderance of the emergencies in which their countervailing efforts are required by their neighbours. That of course can be easily appreciated by those who have been taught that all human beings are included under a primal curse. The words of Micah, 'Thou wilt cast all their sins into the depths of the sea,'19 are recalled by the legend of these evil spells of Ceylon. The king of Oude came to marry one of seven princesses, all possessing præternatural powers, and questioned each as to her art. Each declared her skill in doing harm, except one who asserted her power to heal all ills which the others could inflict. The king having chosen this one as his bride, the rest were angry, and for revenge collected all the charms in the world, enclosed them in a pumpkin—the only thing that can contain spells without being reduced to ashes—and sent this infernal machine to their sister. It would consume everything for sixteen hundred miles round; but the messenger dropped it in the sea. A god picked it up and presented it to the King of Ceylon, and these, with the healing charm known to his own Queen, make the 240,000 spells known to the Capuas of that island, who have no doubt deified the rescuer of the spells on the same principle that inspires some seaside populations to worship Providence more devoutly on the Sunday after a valuable wreck in their neighbourhood.

The astrological origin of the evils ascribed to the Yakseyo (Demons) of Ceylon, and the horoscope which is a necessary preliminary to any dealing with their influences; the constant recurrence of the number seven, denoting origin with races holding the seven-planet theories of the universe; and the fact that all demons are said, on every Saturday evening, to attend an assemblage called Yaksa Sabawa (Witches' Sabbath), are facts that may well engage the attention of Comparative Mythologists.20 In Dardistan the evil spirits are called Yatsh; they dwell 'in the regions of snow,' and the overthrow of their reign over the country is celebrated at the new moon of Daykio, the month preceding winter.

The largest proportion of the Disease Demons of Ceylon are descended from its Hunger Demons. The Preta there is much the same phantom as in Siam, only they are not quite so tall.21 They range from two to four hundred feet in height, and are so numerous that a Pali Buddhist book exhorts people not to throw stones, lest they should harm one of these harmless starveling ghosts, who die many times of hunger, and revive to suffer on in expiation of their sins in a previous existence. They are harmless in one sense, but filthy; and bad smells are personified in them. The great mass of demons resemble the Pretraya, in that their king (Wessamony) has forbidden them to satisfy themselves directly upon their victims, but by inflicting diseases they are supposed to receive an imaginative satisfaction somewhat like that of eating people.

Reeri is the Demon of Blood-disease. His form is that of a man with face of a monkey; he is fiery red, rides on a red bull, and all hemorrhages and diseases of the blood are attributed to him. Reeri has eighteen different disguises or avatars. One of these recalls his earlier position as a demon of death, before Vishnu revealed to Capuas the means of binding him: he is now supposed to be present at every death-bed in the form of a delighted pigmy, one span and six inches high. On such occasions he bears a cock in one hand, a club in the other, and in his mouth a corpse. In the same country Maha

Sohon is the 'great graveyard demon.' He resides in a hill where he is supposed to surround himself with carcases. He is 122 feet high, has four hands and three eyes, and a red skin. He has the head of a bear; the legend being that while quarrelling with another giant his head was knocked off, and the god Senasura was gracious enough to tear off the head of a bear and clap it on the decapitated giant. His capua threatens him with a repetition of this catastrophe if he does not spare any threatened victim who has called in his priestly aid. Except for this timidity about his head, Maha is formidable, being chief of 30,000 demons. But curiously enough he is said to choose for his steeds the more innocent animals,—goat, deer, horse, elephant, and hog.

One of the demons most dreaded in Ceylon is the 'Foreign Demon' Morotoo, said to have come from the coast of Malabar, and from his residence in a tree disseminated diseases which could not be cured until, the queen being afflicted, one capua was found able to master him. Seven-eighths of the charms used in restraining the disease-demons of Ceylon, of which I have mentioned but a few, are in the Tamil tongue. In various parts of India are found very nearly the same systematic demonolatry and 'devil-dancing;' for example in Travancore, to whose superstitions of this character the Rev. Samuel Mateer has devoted two chapters in his work 'The Land of Charity.'

The great demon of diseases in Ceylon is entitled Maha Cola Sanni Yakseya. His father, a king, ordered his queen to be put to death in the belief that she had been faithless to him. Her body was to be cut in two pieces, one of which was to be hung upon a tree (Ukberiya), the other to be thrown at its foot to the dogs. The queen before her execution said, 'If this charge be false, may the child in my womb be born this instant a demon, and may that demon destroy the whole of this city and its unjust king.' So soon as the executioners had finished their work, the two severed parts of the queen's body reunited, a child was born who completely devoured his mother, and then repaired to the graveyard (Sohon), where for a time he fattened on corpses. Then he proceeded to inflict mortal diseases upon the city, and had nearly depopulated it when the gods Iswara and Sekkra interfered, descending to subdue him in the disguise of mendicants. Possibly the great Maha Sohon mentioned above, and the Sohon (graveyard) from which Sanni dealt out deadliness, may be best understood by the statement of the learned writer from whom these facts are quoted, that, 'excepting the Buddhist priests, and the aristocrats of the land, whose bodies were burnt in regular funeral-piles after death, the corpses of the rest of the people were neither burned nor buried, but thrown into a place called Sohona, which was an open piece of ground in the jungle, generally a hollow among the hills, at the distance of three or four miles from any inhabited place, where they were left in the open air to be decomposed or devoured by dogs and wild beasts.'[22] There would appear to be even more ground for the dread of the Great Graveyard Demon in many parts of Christendom, where, through desire to preserve corpses for a happy resurrection, they are made to steal through the water-veins of the earth, and find their resurrection as fell diseases. Iswara and Sekkra were probably two reformers who persuaded the citizens to bury the poor deep in the earth; had they been wise enough to place the dead where nature would give them speedy resurrection and life in grass and flowers, it would not have been further recorded that 'they ordered him (the demon) to abstain from eating men, but gave him Wurrun or permission to inflict disease on mankind, and to obtain offerings.' This is very much the same as the privilege given our Western funeral agencies and cemeteries also; and when the Modliar adds that Sanni 'has eighteen principal attendants,' one can hardly help thinking of the mummers, gravediggers, chaplains, all engaged unconsciously in the work of making the earth less habitable.

The first of the attendants of this formidable avenger of his mother's wrongs is named Bhoota Sanni Yakseya, Demon of Madness. The whole demonolatry and devil-dancing of that island are so insane that one is not surprised that this Bhoota had but little special development. It is amid clear senses we might naturally look for full horror of madness, and there indeed do we find it. One of the most horrible forms of the disease-demon was the personification of madness among the Greeks, as Mania.[23] In the Hercules Furens of Euripides, where Madness, 'the unwedded daughter of black Night,' and sprung of 'the blood of Cœlus,' is evoked from Tartarus for the express purpose of imbreeding in Hercules 'child-slaying disturbances of reason,' there is a suggestion of the hereditary nature of insanity. Obedient to the vindictive order of Juno, 'in her chariot hath gone forth the marble-visaged, all-mournful Madness, the Gorgon of Night, and with the hissing of hundred heads of snakes, she gives the goad to her chariot, on mischief bent.' We may plainly see that the religion which embodied such a form was itself ending in madness. Already ancient were the words μαντική (prophecy) and μανική (madness) when Plato cited their identity to prove one kind of madness the special gift of Heaven:[24] the notion lingers in Dryden's line, 'Great wits to madness sure are near allied;' and survive in regions where deference is paid to lunatics and idiots. Other diseases preserve in their names indications of similar association: e.g., Nympholepsy, St. Vitus's Dance, St. Anthony's Fire. Wesley attributes still epilepsy to 'possession.' This was in pursuance of ancient beliefs. Typhus, a name anciently given to every malady accompanied with stupor (τῦφος), seemed the breath of feverish Typhon. Max Müller connects the word quinsy with Sanskrit amh, 'to throttle,' and Ahi the throttling serpent, its medium being angina; and this again is κυνάγχη, dog-throttling, the Greek for quinsy.[25]

The genius of William Blake, steeped in Hebraism, never showed greater power than in his picture of Plague. A gigantic hideous form, pale-green, with the slime of stagnant pools, reeking with vegetable decays and gangrene, the face livid with the motley tints of pallor and putrescence, strides onward with extended arms like a sower sowing his seeds, only in this case the germs of his horrible harvest are not cast from the hands, but emanate from the fingers as being of their essence. Such, to the savage mind, was the embodiment of malaria, sultriness, rottenness, the putrid Pretraya, invisible, but smelt and felt. Such, to the ignorant imagination, is the Destroying Angel to which rationalistic artists and poets have tried to add wings and majesty; but which in the popular mind was no doubt pictured more like this form found at Ostia (fig. 16), and now passing in the Vatican for a Satan,—probably a demon of the Pontine Marshes, and of the fever that still has victims of its fatal cup (p. 291). In these fearful forms the poor savage believed with such an intensity that he was able to shape the brain of man to his phantasy; bringing about the anomaly that the great reformer, Luther, should affirm,

even while fighting superstition, that a Christian ought to know that he lives in the midst of devils, and that the devil is nearer to him than his coat or his shirt. The devils, he tells us, are all around us, and are at every moment seeking to ensnare our lives, salvation, and happiness. There are many of them in the woods, waters, deserts, and in damp muddy places, for the purpose of doing folk a mischief. They also house in the dense black clouds, and send storms, hail, thunder and lightning, and poison the air with their infernal stench. In one place, Luther tells us that the devil has more vessels and boxes full of poison, with which he kills people, than all the apothecaries in the whole world. He sends all plagues and diseases among men. We may be sure that when any one dies of the pestilence, is drowned, or drops suddenly dead, the devil does it.

Knowing nothing of Zoology, the primitive man easily falls into the belief that his cattle—the means of life—may be the subjects of sorcery. Jesus sending devils into a herd of swine may have become by artificial process a divine benefactor in the eye of Christendom, but the myth makes Him bear an exact resemblance to the dangerous sorcerer that fills the savage mind with dread. It is probable that the covetous eye denounced in the decalogue means the evil eye, which was supposed to blight an object intensely desired but not to be obtained.

Gopolu, already referred to (p. 136) as the Singhalese demon of hydrophobia, bears the general name of the 'Cattle Demon.' He is said to have been the twin of the demigod Mangara by a queen on the Coromandel coast. The mother died, and a cow suckled the twins, but afterwards they quarrelled, and Gopolu being slain was transformed into a demon. He repaired to Arangodde, and fixed his abode in a Banyan where there is a large bee-hive, whence proceed many evils. The population around this Banyan for many miles being prostrated by diseases, the demigod Mangara and Pattini (goddess of chastity) admonished the villagers to sacrifice a cow regularly, and thus they were all resuscitated. Gopolu now sends all cattle diseases. India is full of the like superstitions.

Fig. 16.—Demon found at Ostia.

The people of Travancore especially dread the demon Madan, 'he who is like a cow,' believed to strike oxen with sudden illness,—sometimes men also.

In Russia we find superstition sometimes modified by common sense. Though the peasant hopes that Zegory (St. George) will defend his cattle, he begins to see the chief foes of his cattle. As in the folk-song—

We have gone around the field,
We have called Zegory....
O thou, our brave Zegory,
Save our cattle,
In the field and beyond the field,
In the forest and beyond the forest,
Under the bright moon,
Under the red sun,
From the rapacious wolf,
From the cruel bear,
*From the cunning beast.*26

Nevertheless when a cattle plague occurs many villages relapse into a normally extinct state of mind. Thus, a few years ago, in a village near Moscow, all the women, having warned the men away, stripped themselves entirely naked and drew a plough so as to make a furrow entirely around the village. At the point of juncture in this circle they buried alive a cock, a cat, and a dog. Then they filled the air with lamentations, crying—'Cattle Plague! Cattle Plague! spare our cattle! Behold, we offer thee cock, cat, and dog!' The dog is a demonic character in Russia, while the cat is sacred; for once when the devil tried to get into Paradise in the form of a mouse, the dog allowed him to pass, but the cat pounced on him—the two animals being set on guard at the door. The offering of both seems to represent a desire to conciliate both sides. The nudity of the women may have been to represent to the hungry gods their utter poverty, and inability to give more; but it was told me in Moscow, where I happened to be staying at the time, that it would be dangerous for any man to draw near during the performance.

In Altmark27 the demons who bewitch cattle are called 'Bihlweisen,' and are believed to bury certain diabolical charms under thresholds over which the animals are to pass, causing them to wither away, the milk to cease, etc. The prevention is to wash the cattle with a lotion of sea cabbage boiled with infusion of wine. In the same province it is related that once there appeared in a harvest-field at one time fifteen, at another twelve men (apparently), the latter headless. They all laboured with scythes, but though the rustling could be heard no grain fell. When questioned they said nothing, and when the people tried to seize them they ran away, cutting fruitlessly as they ran. The priests found in this a presage of the coming cattle plague. The Russian superstition of the plough, above mentioned, is found in fragmentary survivals in Altmark. Thus, it is said that to plough around a village and then sit under the plough (placed upright), will enable any one to see the witches; and in some villages, some bit of a plough is hung up over a doorway through which cattle pass, as no devil can then approach them. The demons have a natural horror of honest work, and especially the culture of the earth. Goethe, as we have seen, notes their fear of roses: perhaps he remembered the legend of Aspasia, who, being disfigured by a tumour on the chin, was warned by a dove-maiden to dismiss her physicians and try a rose from the garland of Venus; so she recovered health and beauty.

Notes

1 2 Chron. xvi. 12; 2 Kings xx.; Mark v. 26; James v. 14; etc., etc. The Catholic Church follows the prescription by St. James of prayer and holy anointing for the sick only after medical aid—of which Asa died when he preferred it to the Lord—has failed; i.e. extreme unction. Castelar remarks that the Conclave which elected Pius IX. sat in the Quirinal rather than the Vatican, 'because, while it hoped for the inspirations of the Holy Spirit in every place, it feared that in the palace par excellence divine inspirations would not sufficiently counteract the effluvias of the fever.' The legal prosecutions of the 'Peculiar People' for obeying the New Testament command in case of sickness supply a notable example of the equal hypocrisy of the protestant age. England has distributed the Bible as a divine revelation in 150 different languages; and in London it punishes a sect for obedience to one of its plainest directions.

2 London 'Times,' June 11, 1877.

3 'Mankind: their Origin and Destiny' (Longmans, 1872), p. 91. See also Voltaire's Dictionary for an account of the sacred dances in the Catholic Churches of Spain.

4 Deut. xxviii. 60.

5 1 Sam. v. 6.

6 1 Sam. xvi. 14. In chap. xviii. 10, this evil spirit is said to have proceeded from Elohim, a difference indicating a further step in that evolution of Jehovah into a moral ruler which is fully traced in our chapter on 'Elohim and Jehovah.'

7 Boundesch, ii. pp. 158, 188. For an exhaustive treatment of the astrological theories and pictures of the planispheres, see 'Mankind: their Origin and Destiny' (Longmans, 1872).

8 'Catastrophe Magnatum: or the Fall of Monarchie. A Caveat to Magistrates, deduced from the Eclipse of the Sunne, March 29, 1652. With a probable Conjecture of the Determination of the Effects.' By Nich. Culpeper, Gent., Stud. in Astrol. and Phys. Dan. ii. 21, 22: He changeth the times and the seasons: he removeth Kings, and setteth up Kings: he giveth wisdome to the Wise, and knowledge to them that know understanding: he revealeth the deep and secret things, he knoweth what is in the darkness, and the light dwelleth with him. London: Printed for T. Vere and Nath. Brooke, in the Old Baily, and at the Angel in Cornhil, 1652.'

9 See the Dictionary of Böhtlingk and Roth.

10 Heb. ii. 14.

11 1 Cor. v. 5; xi. 30.

12 2 Cor. xii. 7.

13 'Records of the Past,' iii. p. 136. Tr. by Mr. Fox Talbot.

14 Ibid., iii. p. 143. The refrain recalls the lines of Edgar A. Poe:—
They are neither man nor woman,
They are neither brute nor human,
They are ghouls!

15 The Pahlavi Text has been prepared by Destur Jamaspji Asa, and translated by Haug and West. Trübner, 1872.

16 Cf. fig. 9.

17 Larousse's 'Dict. Universel.'

18 'Records,' etc., iii. p. 141. Marduk is the Chaldæan Hercules.

19 Micah vii. 19.

20 See the excellent article in the Journal of the Ceylon Branch of the R.A.S., by Dundris De Silva Gooneratnee Modliar (1865–66). With regard to this sanctity of the number seven it may be remarked that it has spread through the world with Christianity,—seven churches, seven gifts of the Spirit, seven sins and virtues. It is easy therefore to mistake orthodox doctrines for survivals. In the London 'Times' of June 24, 1875, there was reported an inquest at Corsham, Wiltshire, on the body of Miriam Woodham, who died under the prescriptions of William Bigwood, herbalist. It was shown that he used pills made of seven herbs. This was only shown to be a 'pagan survival' when Bigwood stated that the herbs were 'governed by the sun.'

21 *See p. 44.*

22 *'Jour. Ceylon R. A. Soc.,' 1865–66.*

23 *This demoness is not to be connected with the Italian Mania, probably of Etruscan origin, with which nurses frightened children. This Mania, from an old word manus signifying 'good,' was, from the relation of her name to Manes, supposed to be mother of the Lares, whose revisitations of the earth were generally of ill omen. According to an oracle which said heads should be offered for the sake of heads, children were sacrificed to this household fiend up to the time of Junius Brutus, who substituted poppy-heads.*

24 *Phædrus, i. 549. Cf. Ger. selig and silly.*

25 *'Lect. on Language,' i. 435.*

26 *Ralston's 'Songs of the Russian People,' p. 230.*

27 *'Sagen der Altmark.' Von A. Kuhn. Berlin, 1843.*

Chapter XII - Death

The Vendetta of Death—Teoyaomiqui—Demon of Serpents—Death on the Pale Horse—Kali—War-gods—Satan as Death—Death-beds—Thanatos—Yama—Yimi—Towers of Silence—Alcestis—Hercules, Christ, and Death—Hel—Salt—Azraël—Death and the Cobbler—Dance of Death—Death as Foe, and as Friend.

Savage races believe that no man dies except by sorcery. Therefore every death must be avenged. The Actas of the Philippines regard the 'Indians' as the cause of the deaths among them; and when one of them loses a relative, he lurks and watches until he has spied an 'Indian' and killed him.[1] It is a progress from this when primitive man advances to the belief that the fatal sorcerer is an invisible man—a demon. When this doctrine is taught in the form of a belief that death entered the world through the machinations of Satan, and was not in the original scheme of creation, it is civilised; but when it is inculcated under a set of African or other non-christian names, it is barbarian.

The following sketch, by Mr. Gideon Lang, will show the intensity of this conviction among the natives of New South Wales:—

'While at Nanima I constantly saw one of these, named Jemmy, a remarkably fine man, about twenty-eight years of age, who was the 'model Christian' of the missionaries, and who had been over and over again described in their reports as a living proof that, taken in infancy, the natives were as capable of being truly christianised as a people who had had eighteen centuries of civilisation. I confess that I strongly doubted, but still there was no disputing the apparent facts. Jemmy was not only familiar with the Bible, which he could read remarkably well, but he was even better acquainted with the more abstruse tenets of christianity; and so far as the whites could see, his behaviour was in accordance with his religious acquirements. One Sunday morning I walked down to the black fellows' camp, to have a talk with Jemmy, as usual. I found him sitting in his gunyah, overlooking a valley of the Macquarrie, whose waters glanced brightly in the sunshine of the delicious spring morning. He was sitting in a state of nudity, excepting his waistcloth, very earnestly reading the Bible, which indeed was his constant practice; and I could see that he was perusing the Sermon on the Mount. I seated myself, and waited till he concluded the chapter, when he laid down the Bible, folded his hands, and sat with his eyes fixed abstractedly on his fire. I bade him 'good morning,' which he acknowledged without looking up. I then said, 'Jemmy, what is the meaning of your spears being stuck in a circle round you?' He looked me steadily in the eyes, and said solemnly and with suppressed fierceness, 'Mother's dead!' I said that I was very sorry to hear it; 'but what had her death to do with the spears being stuck around so?' 'Bogan black-fellow killed her!' was the fierce and gloomy reply. 'Killed by a Bogan black!' I exclaimed: 'why, your mother has been dying a fortnight, and Dr. Curtis did not expect her to outlive last night, which you know as well as I do.' His only reply was a dogged repetition of the words: 'A Bogan black-fellow killed her!' I appealed to him as a Christian—to the Sermon on the Mount, that he had just been reading; but he absolutely refused to promise that he would not avenge his mother's death. In the afternoon of that day we were startled by a yell which can never be mistaken by any person who has once heard the wild war-whoop of the blacks when in battle array. On marching out we saw all the black fellows of the neighbourhood formed into a line, and following Jemmy in an imaginary attack upon an enemy. Jemmy himself disappeared that evening. On the following Wednesday morning I found him sitting complacently in his gunyah, plaiting a rope of human hair, which I at once knew to be that of his victim. Neither of us spoke; I stood for some time watching him as he worked with a look of mocking defiance of the anger he knew I felt. I pointed to a hole in the middle of his fire, and said, 'Jemmy, the proper place for your Bible is there.' He looked up with his eyes flashing as I turned away, and I never saw him again. I afterwards learned that he had gone to the district of the Bogan tribe, where the first black he met happened to be an old friend and companion of his own. This man had just made the first cut in the bark of a tree, which he was about to climb for an opossum; but on hearing footsteps he leaped down and faced round, as all blacks do, and whites also, when blacks are in question. Seeing that it was only Jemmy, however, he resumed his occupation, but had no sooner set to work than Jemmy sent a spear through his back and nailed him to the tree.2

Perhaps if Jemmy could have been cross-examined by the non-missionary mind, he might have replied with some effect to Mr. Lang's suggestion that he ought to part with his Bible. Surely he must have found in that volume a sufficient number of instances to justify his faith in the power of demons over human health and life. Might he not have pondered the command, 'thou shalt not suffer a witch to live,' and imagined that he was impaling another Manasseh, who 'used enchantments, and used witchcraft, and dealt with a familiar spirit, and with wizards (and) wrought much evil in the sight of the Lord to provoke Him to anger.'3 Those who hope that the Bible may carry light into the dark places of superstition and habitations of cruelty might, one would say, reflect upon the long contest which European science had with bibliolators in trying to relieve the popular mind from the terrors of witchcraft, whose genuineness it was (justly) declared contrary to the Scriptures to deny. There are districts in Great Britain and America, and many more on the continent of Europe, where the spells that waste and destroy are still believed in; where effigies of wax or even onions are labelled with some hated name, and stuck over with pins, and set near fires to be melted or dried up, in full belief that some subject of the charm will be consumed by disease along with the object used. Under every roof where such coarse superstitions dwell the Bible dwells beside them, and experience proves that the infallibility of all such talismans diminishes pari passu.

Fig. 17.—Teoyaomiqui.

What the savage is really trying to slay when he goes forth to avenge his relative's death on the first alien he finds may be seen in the accompanying figure (17), which represents the Mexican goddess of death—Teoyaomiqui. The image is nine feet high, and is kept in a museum in the city of Mexico. Mr. Edward B. Tylor, from whose excellent book of travels in that country the figure is copied, says of it:—'The stone known as the statue of the war-goddess is a huge block of basalt covered with sculptures. The antiquaries think that the figures on it stand for different personages, and that it is three gods—Huitzilopochtli, the god of war; Teoyaomiqui, his wife; and Mictlanteuctli, the god of hell. It has necklaces of alternate hearts and dead men's hands, with death's heads for a central ornament. At the bottom of the block is a strange sprawling figure, which one cannot see now, for it is the base which rests on the ground; but there are two shoulders projecting from the idol, which show plainly that it did not stand on the ground, but was supported aloft on the tops of two pillars. The figure carved upon the bottom represents a monster holding a skull in each hand, while others hang from his knees and elbows. His mouth is a mere oval ring, a common feature of Mexican idols, and four tusks project just above it. The new moon laid down like a bridge forms his forehead, and a star is placed on each side of it. This is thought to have been the conventional representation of Mictlanteuctli (Lord of the Land of the Dead), the god of hell, which was a place of utter and eternal darkness. Probably each victim as he was led to the altar could look up between the two pillars and see the hideous god of hell staring down upon him from above. There is little doubt that this is the famous war-idol which stood on the great teocalli of Mexico, and before which so many thousands of human beings were sacrificed. It lay undisturbed under ground in the great square, close to the very site of the teocalli, until sixty years ago. For many years after that it was kept buried, lest the sight of one of their old deities might be too exciting for the Indians, who, as I have mentioned before, had certainly not forgotten it, and secretly ornamented it with garlands of flowers while it remained above ground.'

If my reader will now turn to the (fig. 11) portrait of the Demon of Serpents, he will find a conception fundamentally similar to the Mexican demoness of death or slaughter, but one that is not shut up in a museum of antiquities; it still haunts and terrifies a vast number of the people born in Ceylon. He is the principal demon invoked in Ceylon by the malignant sorcerers in performing the 84,000 different charms that afflict evils (Hooniyan). His general title is Oddy Cumara Hooniyan Dewatawa; but he has a special name for each of his six several apparitions, the chief of these being Cali Oddisey, or demon of incurable diseases, therefore of death, and Naga Oddisey, demon of serpents—deadliest of animals. Beneath him is the Pale Horse which has had its career so long and far,—even to the White Mare on which, in some regions, Christ is believed to revisit the earth every Christmas; and also the White Mare of Yorkshire Folklore which bore its rider from Whitestone Cliff to hell. This Singhalese form also, albeit now associated by Capuas with fatal disease, was probably at first, like the Mexican, a war goddess and god combined, as is shown by the uplifted sword, and reeking hand uplifted in triumph. Equally a god of war is our 'Death on the Pale Horse,' which christian art, following the so-called Apocalypse, has made so familiar. 'I looked, and behold a pale horse: and his name that sat on him was Death, and Hell followed with him. And power was given to him over the fourth part of the earth, to kill with sword, and with hunger, and with death, and with the beasts of the earth.' This is but a travesty of the Greek Ares, the Roman Mars, or god of War. In the original Greek-form Ares was not solely the god of war, but of destruction generally. In the Œdipus Tyrannus of Sophocles we have the popular conception of him as one to whom the deadly plague is ascribed. He is named as the 'god unhonoured among gods,' and it is said:—'The city is wildly tossing, and no more can lift up her head from the waves of death; withering the ripening grain in the husks, withering the kine in their pastures; blighted are the babes through the failing labours of women; the fire-bearing god, horrid Pestilence, having darted down, ravages the city; by him the house of Cadmus is empty, and dark Hades enriched with groans and lamentations.'

Mother of the deadliest 'Calas' of Singhalese demonolatry, sister of the Scandinavian Hel in name and nature, is Kali. Although the Hindu writers repudiate the idea that there is any devil among their three hundred and thirty millions of deities, it is difficult to deny Kali that distinction. Her wild dance of delight over bodies of the slain would indicate pleasure taken in destruction for its own sake, so fulfilling the definition of a devil; but, on the other hand, there is a Deccan legend that reports her as devouring the dead, and this would make her a hunger-demon. We may give her the benefit of the doubt, and class her among the demons—or beings whose evil is not gratuitous—all the more because the mysteriously protruding tongue, as in the figure of Typhon (p. 185), probably suggests thirst. Hindu legend does, indeed, give another interpretation, and say that when she was dancing for joy at having slain a hundred-headed giant demigod, the shaking of the earth was so formidable that Siva threw himself among the slain, whom she was crushing at every step, hoping to induce her to pause; but when, unheeding, she trod upon the body of her husband, she paused and thrust out her tongue from surprise and shame. The Vedic description of Agni as an ugra (ogre), with 'tongue of flame,' may better interpret Kali's tongue. It is said Kali is pleased for a hundred years by the blood of a tiger; for a thousand by that of a man; for a hundred thousand by the blood of three men.

Fig. 18.—Kali.

How are we to understand this dance of Death, and the further legend of her tossing dead bodies into the air for amusement? Such a figure found among a people who shudder at taking life even from the lowest animals is hardly to be explained by the destructiveness of nature personified in her spouse Siva. Her looks and legends alike represent slaughter by human violence. May it not be that Kali represents some period when the abhorrence of taking life among a vegetarian people—a people, too, believing in transmigration—might have become a public danger? When Krishna appeared it was, according to the Bhágavat Gita, as charioteer inciting Arjoon to war. There must have been various periods when a peaceful people must fall victims to more savage neighbours unless they could be stimulated to enter on the work of destruction with a light heart. There may have been periods when the human Kalis of India might stimulate their husbands and sons to war with such songs as the women of Dardistan sing at the Feast of Fire (p. 91). The amour of the Greek goddess of Beauty with the god of War, leaving her lawful spouse the Smith, is full of meaning. The Assyrian Venus, Istar, appeared in a vision, with wings and halo, bearing a bow and arrow for Assurbanipal. The Thug appears to have taken some such view of Kali, regarding her as patroness of their plan for reducing population. They are said to have claimed that Kali left them one of her teeth for a pickaxe, her rib for a knife, her garment's hem for a noose, and wholesale murder for a religion. The uplifted right hand of the demoness has been interpreted as intimating a divine purpose in the havoc around her, and it is possible that some such euphemism attached to the attitude before the Thug accepted it as his own benediction from this highly decorated personage of human cruelty.

The ancient reverence for Kali has gradually passed to her mitigated form—Durgá. Around her too are visible the symbols of destruction; but she is supposed to be satisfied with pumpkin-animals, and the weapons in her ten hands are believed to be directed against the enemies of the gods, especially against the giant king Muheshu. She is mother of the beautiful boy Kartik, and of the elephant-headed inspirer of knowledge Ganesa. She is reverenced now as female energy, the bestower of beauty and fruitfulness on women.

The identity of war-gods and death-demons, in the most frightful conceptions which have haunted the human imagination, is of profound significance. These forms do not represent peaceful and natural death, not death by old age,—of which, alas, those who cowered before them knew but little,—but death amid cruelty and agony, and the cutting down of men in the vigour of life. That indeed was terrible,—even more than these rude images could describe.

But there are other details in these hideous forms. The priest has added to the horse and sword of war the adored serpent, and hideous symbols of the 'Land of the Dead.' For it is not by terror of death, but of what he can persuade men lies beyond, that the priest has reigned over mankind. When Isabel (in 'Measure for Measure') is trying to persuade her brother that the sense of death lies most in apprehension, the sentenced youth still finds death 'a fearful thing.'

Ay, but to die, and go we know not where;
To lie in cold obstruction and to rot;
This sensible warm motion to become
A kneaded clod; and the delighted spirit
To bathe in fiery floods, or to reside
In thrilling region of thick-ribbed ice;
To be imprisoned in the viewless winds,
And blown with violence round about
The pendent world; or to be worse than worst
Of these, that lawless and incertain thoughts
Imagine howling!—'tis too horrible!
The weariest and most loathed worldly life
That age, ache, penury, and imprisonment
Can lay on nature, is a paradise
To what we fear of death.

In all these apprehensions of Claudio there is no thought of annihilation. What if he had seen death as an eternal sleep? Let Hamlet answer:—

To die,—to sleep;—
No more;—and, by a sleep, to say we end
The heartache, and the thousand natural shocks
That flesh is heir to,—'tis a consummation
Devoutly to be wished.

The greater part of the human race still belong to religions which, in their origin, promised eternal repose as the supreme final bliss. Had death in itself possessed horrors for the human mind, the priest need not have conjured up beyond it those tortures that haunted Hamlet with the dreams of possible evils beyond which make even the wretched rather bear the ills they have than fly to others they know not of. It would have been sufficient sanction to promise immortality only to the pious. But as in Claudio's shuddering lines every hell is reflected—whether of ice, fire, or brutalisation—so are the same mixed with the very blood and brain of mankind, even where literally outgrown. Christianity superadded to the horrors by importing the idea that death came by human sin, and so by gradual development ascribing to Satan the power of death; thereby forming a new devil who bore in him the power to make death a punishment. How the matter stood in the mediæval belief may be seen in figure 19, copied from a Russian Bible of the (early) seventeenth century. Lazarus smiles to see the nondescript soul of Dives torn from him by a devil with a hook, while another drowns the groans with a drum. Satan squirts an infernal baptism on the departing soul, and the earnest co-operation of the archangel justifies the satisfaction of Lazarus and Abraham. This degraded belief is still found in the almost gleeful pulpit-picturings of physical agonies as especially attending the death-beds of 'infidels,'—as Voltaire and Paine,—and its fearful result is found in the degree to which priesthoods are still able to paralyse the common sense and heart of the masses by the barbaric ceremonials with which they are permitted to surround death, and the arrogant line drawn between unorthodox goats and credulous sheep by 'consecrated' ground.

Fig. 19.—Dives and Lazarus (Russian; 17th cent.).

Mr. Keary, in his interesting volume on 'The Dawn of History,'4 says that it has been suggested that the youthful winged figure on the drum of a column from the temple of Diana at Ephesus to the British Museum, may be a representation of Thanatos, Death. It would be agreeable to believe that the only important representation of Death left by Greek art is that exquisite figure, whose high tribute is that it was at first thought to be Love! The figure is somewhat like the tender Eros of preraphaelite art, and with the same look of gentle melancholy. Such a sweet and simple form of Death would be worthy of the race which, amid all the fiery or cold rivers of the underworld which had gathered about their religion, still saw running there the soft-flowing stream of forgetfulness. Let one study this Ephesian Thanatos reverently—no engraving or photograph can do it even partial justice—and then in its light read those myths of Death which seem to bear us back beyond the savagery of war and the artifices of priests to the simpler conceptions of humanity. In its serene light we may especially read both Vedic and Iranian hymns and legends of Yama.

The first man to die became the powerful Yama of the Hindus, the monarch of the dead; and he became invested with metaphors of the sun that had set.5 In a solemn and pathetic hymn of the Vedas he is said to have crossed the rapid waters, to have shown the way to many, to have first known the path on which our fathers crossed over.6 But in the splendours of sunset human hope found its prophetic pictures of a heaven beyond. The Vedic Yama is ever the friend. It is one of the most picturesque facts of mythology that, after Yama had become in India another name for Death, the same name reappeared in Persia, and in the Avesta, as a type at once of the Golden Age in the past and of paradise in the future. Such was the Iranian Yima. He was that 'flos regum' whose reign represented 'the ideal of human happiness, when there was neither illness nor death, neither heat nor cold,' and who has never died. 'According to the earlier traditions of the

Avesta,' says Spiegel, 'Jima does not die, but when evil and misery began to prevail on earth, retires to a smaller space, a kind of garden or Eden, where he continues his happy life with those who remained true to him.' Such have been the antecedents of our many beautiful myths which ascribe even an earthly immortality to the great,—to Barbarossa, Arthur, and even to the heroes of humbler races as Hiawatha and Glooscap of North American tribes,—who are or were long believed to have 'sailed into the fiery sunset,' or sought some fair island, or to slumber in a hidden grotto, until the world shall have grown up to their stature and requires their return.

In Japan the (Sintoo) god of Hell is now named Amma, and one may suspect that it is some imitation of Yama by reason of the majesty he still retains in the popular conception. He is pictured as a grave man, wearing a judicial cap, and no cruelties seem to be attributed to him personally, but only to the oni or demons of whom he is lord.

The kindly characteristics of the Hindu Yama seem in Persia to have been replaced by the bitterness of Ahriman, or Anra-mainyu, the genius of evil. Haug interprets Anra-mainyu as 'Death-darting.' The word is the counterpart of Speñta-mainyu, and means originally the 'throttling spirit;' being thus from anh, philologically the root of all evil, as we shall see when we consider its dragon brood. Professor Whitney translates the name 'Malevolent.' But, whatever may be the meaning of the word, there is little doubt that the Twins of Vedic Mythology—Yama and Yami—parted into genii of Day and Night, and were ultimately spiritualised in the Spirit of Light and Spirit of Darkness which have made the basis of all popular theology from the time of Zoroaster until this day.

Nothing can be more remarkable than the extreme difference between the ancient Hindu and the Persian view of death. As to the former it was the happy introduction to Yama, to the latter it was the visible seal of Ahriman's equality with Ormuzd. They held it in absolute horror. The Towers of Silence stand in India to-day as monuments of this darkest phase of the Parsî belief. The dead body belonged to Ahriman, and was left to be devoured by wild creatures; and although the raising of towers for the exposure of the corpse, so limiting its consumption to birds, has probably resulted from a gradual rationalism which has from time to time suggested that by such means souls of the good may wing their way to Ormuzd, yet the Parsî horror of death is strong enough to give rise to such terrible suspicions, even if they were unfounded, as those which surrounded the Tower (Khao's Dokhma) in June 1877. The strange behaviour of the corpse-bearers in leaving one tower, going to another, and afterwards (as was said) secretly repairing to the first, excited the belief that a man had been found alive in the first and was afterwards murdered. The story seems to have begun with certain young Parsîs themselves, and, whether it be true or not, they have undoubtedly interpreted rightly the ancient feeling of that sect with regard to all that had been within the kingdom of the King of Terrors. 'As sickness and death,' says Professor Whitney, 'were supposed to be the work of the malignant powers, the dead body itself was regarded with superstitious horror. It had been gotten by the demons into their own peculiar possession, and became a chief medium through which they exercised their defiling action upon the living. Everything that came into its neighbourhood was unclean, and to a certain extent exposed to the influences of the malevolent spirits, until purified by the ceremonies which the law prescribed.'7 It is to be feared this notion has crept in among the Brahmans; the Indian Mirror (May 26, 1878) states that a Chandernagore lady, thrown into the Ganges, but afterwards found to be alive, was believed to be possessed by Dano (an evil spirit), and but for interference would have found a watery grave. The Jews also were influenced by this belief, and to this day it is forbidden a Cohen, or descendant of the priesthood, to touch a dead body.

The audience at the Crystal Palace which recently witnessed the performance of Euripides' Alcestis could hardly, it is to be feared, have realised the relation of the drama to their own religion. Apollo induces the Fates to consent that Admetus shall not die provided he can find a substitute for him. The pure Alcestis steps forward and devotes herself to death to save her husband. Apollo tries to persuade Death to give back Alcestis, but Death declares her fate demanded by justice. While Alcestis is dying, Admetus bids her entreat the gods for pity; but Alcestis says it is a god who has brought on the necessity, and adds, 'Be it so!' She sees the hall of the dead, with 'the winged Pluto staring from beneath his black eyebrows.' She reminds her husband of the palace and regal sway she might have enjoyed in Thessaly had she not left it for him. Bitterly does Pheres reproach Admetus for accepting life through the vicarious suffering and death of another. Then comes Hercules; he vanquishes Death; he leads forth Alcestis from 'beneath into the light.' With her he comes into the presence of Admetus, who is still in grief. Admetus cannot recognise her; but when he recognises her with joy, Hercules warns him that it is not lawful for Alcestis to address him 'until she is unbound from her consecration to the gods beneath, and the third day come.'

It only requires a change of names to make Alcestis a Passion-play. The unappeasable Justice which is as a Fate binding the deity, though it may be satisfied vicariously; 'the last enemy, Death;' the atonement by sacrifice of a saintly human being, who from a father's palace is brought by love freely to submit to death; the son of a god (Zeus) by a human mother (Alcmene),—the god-man Herakles,—commissioned to destroy earthly evils by twelve great labours,—descending to conquer Death and deliver one of the 'spirits in prison,' the risen spirit not recognised at first, as Jesus was not by Mary; still bearing the consecration of the grave until the third day, which forbade intercourse with the living ('Touch me not, for I am not yet ascended to my Father'),—all these enable us to recognise in the theologic edifices around us the fragments of a crumbled superstition as they lay around Euripides.

From the old pictures of Christ's triumphal pilgrimage on earth parallels for the chief Labours of Herakles may be found; he is shown treading on the lion, asp, dragon, and Satan; but the myths converge in the Descent into Hades and the conquest of Death. It is remarkable that in the old pictures of Christ delivering souls from Hades he is generally represented closely followed by Eve, whose form so emerging would once have been to the greater part of Europe already familiar as that of either Alcestis, Eurydice, or Persephone. One of the earliest examples of the familiar subject, Christ conquering Death, is that in the ancient (tenth century) Missal of Worms,—that city whose very name preserves the record of the same combat under the guise of Siegfried and the Worm, or Dragon. The cross is now the sword thrust near the monster's mouth. The picture illustrates the chant of Holy Week: 'De manu Mortis liberabo eos, de Morte redimam eos. Ero Mors tua, O Mors; morsus tuus ero, inferne.' From the pierced mouth of Death are vomited flames, which remind us of his ethnical origin; but it is not likely that to the christianised pagans of Worms the picture could ever have conveyed an impression so weirdly horrible as that of their own goddess of Death, Hel. 'Her hall is called Elvidnir, realm of the cold storm: Hunger is her table; Starvation, her knife; Delay, her man; Slowness, her maid; Precipice, her threshold; Care, her bed; burning Anguish, the hangings of her apartments. One half of her body is livid, the other half the colour of human flesh.'

With the Scandinavian picture of the Abode of Death may be compared the description of the Abode of Nin-ki-gal, the Assyrian Queen of Death, from a tablet in the British Museum, translated by Mr. Fox Talbot:8—

To the House men enter—but cannot depart from:
To the Road men go—but cannot return.
The abode of darkness and famine
Where Earth is their food: their nourishment Clay:
Light is not seen; in darkness they dwell:
Ghosts, like birds, flutter their wings there;
On the door and the gate-posts the dust lies undisturbed.

The Semitic tribes, undisturbed, like the importers of their theology into the age of science, by the strata in which so many perished animal kingdoms are entombed, attributed all death, even that of animals, to the forbidden fruit. The Rabbins say that not only Adam and Eve, but the animals in Eden, partook of that fruit, and came under the power of Sammaël the Violent, and of his agent Azraël, the demon of Death. The Phœnix, having refused this food, preserved the power of renovating itself.

It is an example of the completeness and consistency with which a theory may organise its myth, that the fatal demons are generally represented as abhorring salt—the preserving agent and foe of decay. The 'Covenant of Salt' among the ancient Jews probably had this significance, and the care with which Job salted his sacrifice is considered elsewhere. Aubrey says, 'Toads (Saturnine animals) are killed by putting salt upon them. I have seen the experiment.' The devil, as heir of death-demons, appears in all European folklore as a hater of salt. A legend, told by Heine, relates that a knight, wandering in a wood in Italy, came upon a ruin, and in it a wondrous statue of the goddess of Beauty. Completely fascinated, the knight haunted the spot day after day, until one evening he was met by a servant who invited him to enter a villa which he had not before remarked. What was his surprise to be ushered into the presence of the living image of his adored statue! Amid splendour and flowers the enraptured knight is presently seated with his charmer at a banquet. Every luxury of the world is there; but there is no salt! When he hints this want a cloud passes over the face of his Beauty. Presently he asks the servant to bring the salt; the servant does so, shuddering; the knight helps himself to it. The next sip of wine he takes elicits a cry from him: it is liquid fire. Madness seizes upon him; caresses, burning kisses follow, until he falls asleep on the bosom of his goddess. But what visions! Now he sees her as a wrinkled crone, next a great bat bearing a torch as it flutters around him, and again as a frightful monster, whose head he cuts off in an agony of terror. When the knight awakes it is in his own villa. He hastens to his ruin, and to the beloved statue; he finds her fallen from the pedestal, and the beautiful head cut from the neck lying at her feet.

The Semitic Angel of Death is a figure very different from any that we have considered. He is known in theology only in the degradation which he suffered at the hands of the Rabbins, but originally was an awful but by no means evil genius. The Persians probably imported him, under the name of Asuman, for we do not find him mentioned in their earlier books, and the name has a resemblance to the Hebrew shamad, to exterminate, which would connect it with the biblical 'destroyer' Abaddon. This is rendered more probable because the Zoroastrians believed in an earlier demon, Vízaresha, who carried souls after death to the region of Deva-worshippers (India). The Chaldaic Angel of Death, Malk-ad Mousa, may have derived his name from the legend of his having approached Moses with the object of forcing his soul out of his body, but, being struck by the glory of Moses' face, and by virtue of the divine name on his rod, was compelled to retire. The legend is not so ancient as the name, and was possibly a Saga suggested by the name; it is obviously the origin of the tradition of the struggle between Michael and Satan for the body of Moses (Jude 9.). This personification had thus declined among the Jews into being evil enough to be identified with Samaël,—who, in the Book of the Assumption of

100

Moses, is named as his assailant,—and subsequently with Satan himself, named in connection with the New Testament version. It was on account of this degradation of a being described in the earlier books of the Bible as the commissioner of Jehovah that there was gradually developed among the Jews two Angels of Death, one (Samaël, or his agent Azraël) for those who died out of the land of Israel, and the other (Gabriel) for those who had the happier lot of dying in their own country.

This relegation of Samaël to the wandering Jews—who if they died abroad were not supposed to reach Paradise with facility, if at all—is significant. For Samaël is pretty certainly a conception borrowed from outlying Semitic tribes. What that conception was we find in Job xviii. 18, where he is 'the king of Terrors,' and still more in the Arabic Azraël. The legend of this typical Angel of Death is that he was promoted to his high office for special service. When Allah was about to create man he sent the angels Gabriel, Michael, and Israfil to the earth to bring clay of different colours for that purpose; but the Earth warned them that the being about to be formed would rebel against his creator and draw down a curse upon her (the Earth), and they returned without bringing the clay. Then Azraël was sent by Allah, and he executed his commission without fear; and for this he was appointed the angel to separate souls from bodies. Azraël had subordinate angels under him, and these are alluded to in the opening lines of the Sura 79 of the Koran:

By the angels who tear forth the souls of some with violence;
And by those who draw forth the souls of others with gentleness.

The souls of the righteous are drawn forth with gentleness, those of the wicked torn from them in the way shown in the Russian picture (Fig. 19), which is indeed an illustration of the same mythology.

These terrible tasks were indeed such as were only too likely to bring Azraël into the evil repute of an executioner in the course of time; but no degradation of him seems to have been developed among the Moslems. He seems to have been associated in their minds with Fate, and similar stories were told of him. Thus it is related that once when Azraël was passing by Solomon he gazed intently upon a man with whom Solomon was conversing. Solomon told his companion that it was the Angel of Death who was looking at him, and the man replied, 'He seems to want me: order the wind to carry me from hence into India;' when this was done Azraël approached Solomon and said, 'I looked earnestly at that man from wonder, for I was commanded to take his soul in India.'9

Azraël was often represented as presenting to the lips a cup of poison. It is probable that this image arose from the ancient ordeal by poison, whereby draughts, however manipulated beforehand with reference to the results, were popularly held to be divinely mingled for retributive or beneficent effects. 'Cup' thus became among Semitic tribes a symbol of Fate. The 'cup of consolation,' 'cup of wrath,' 'cup of trembling,' which we read of in the Old Testament; the 'cup of blessing,' and 'cup of devils,' spoken of by Paul, have this significance. The cup of Nestor, ornamented with the dove (Iliad, xi. 632), was probably a 'cup of blessing,' and Mr. Schliemann has found several of the same kind at Mycenæ. The symbol was repeatedly used by Christ,—'Let this cup pass from me,' 'The cup that my Father hath given me to drink shall I not drink it,' 'Are ye able to drink of the cup that I drink of,'—and the familiar association of Azraël's cup is expressed in the phrase 'taste of death.'

One of the most pleasing modifications of the belief in the Angel of Death is that found by Lepsius10 among the Mohammedan negroes of Kordofan. Osraîn (Azraël), it is said, receives the souls of the dead, and leads the good to their reward, the bad to punishment. 'He lives in a tree, el segerat mohana (the tree of fulfilling), which has as many leaves as there are inhabitants in the world. On each leaf is a name, and when a child is born a new one grows. If any one becomes ill his leaf fades, and should he be destined to die, Osraîn breaks it off. Formerly he used to come visibly to those whom he was going to carry away, and thus put them in great terror. Since the prophet's time, however, he has become invisible; for when he came to fetch Mohammed's soul he told him that it was not good that by his visible appearance he should frighten mankind. They might then easily die of terror, before praying; for he himself, although a courageous and spirited man, was somewhat perturbed at his appearance. Therefore the prophet begged God to make Osraîn invisible, which prayer was granted.' Mr. Mackenzie adds on this that, among the Moravian Jews, at new moon a branch is held in its light, and the name of a person pronounced: his face will appear between the horns of the moon, and should he be destined to die the leaves will fade.

Fig. 20.—The Knight and Death.

Mr. John Ruskin has been very severe upon the Italians for the humour with which they introduce Death as a person of their masque. 'When I was in Venice in 1850,' he says, 'the most popular piece of the comic opera was "Death and the Cobbler," in which the point of the plot was the success of a village cobbler as a physician, in consequence of the appearance of Death to him beside the bed of every patient who was not to recover; and the most applauded scene in it was one in which the physician, insolent in success, and swollen with luxury, was himself taken down into the abode of Death, and thrown into an agony of terror by being shown lives of men, under the form of wasting lamps, and his own ready to expire.' On which he expresses the opinion that 'this endurance of fearful images is partly associated with indecency, partly with general fatuity and weakness of mind.'11 But may it not rather be the healthy reaction from morbid images of terror, with which a purely natural and inevitable event has so long been invested by priests, and portrayed in such popular pictures as 'The Dance of Death?' The mocking laughter with which the skeletons beset the knight in our picture (Fig. 20), from the wall of La Chaise Dieu, Auvergne, marks the priestly terrorism, which could not fail to be vulgarised even more by the frivolous. In 1424 there was a masquerade of the Dance of Death in the Cemetery of the Innocents at Paris, attended by the Duke of Bedford and the Duke of Burgundy, just returned from battle. It may have been the last outcome in the west of Kali's dance over the slain; but it is fortunate when Fanaticism has no worse outcome than Folly. The Skeleton Death has the advantage over earlier forms of suggesting the naturalness of death. It is more scientific. The gradual discovery by the people that death is not caused by sin has largely dissipated its horrors in regions where the ignorance and impostures of priestcraft are of daily observation; and although the reaction may not be expressed with good taste, there would seem to be in it a certain vigour of nature, reasserting itself in simplicity.

In the northern world we are all too sombre in the matter. It is the ages of superstition which have moulded our brains, and too generally given to our natural love of life the unnatural counterpart of a terror of death. What has been artificially bred into us can be cultivated out of us. There are indeed deaths corresponding to the two Angels—the death that comes by lingering disease and pain, and that which comes by old age. There are indeed Azraëls in our cities who poison the food and drink of the people, and mingle death in the cup of water; and of them there should be increasing horror until the gentler angel abides with us, and death by old age becomes normal. The departure from life being a natural condition of entering upon it, it is melancholy indeed that it should be ideally confused with the pains and sorrows often attending it. It is fabled that Menippus the Cynic, travelling through Hades, knew which were the kings there by their howling louder than the rest. They howled loudest because they had parted from most pleasures on earth. But all the happy and young have more reason to lament untimely death than kings. The only tragedy of Death is the ruin of living Love. Mr. Watts, in his great picture of Love and Death (Grosvenor Gallery, 1877), revealed the real horror. Not that skeleton which has its right time and place, not the winged demon (called angel), who has no right time or place, is here, but a huge, hard, heartless form, as of man half-blocked out of marble; a terrible emblem of the remorseless force that embodies the incompleteness and ignorance of mankind—a force that steadily crushes hearts where intellects are devoting their energies to alien worlds. Poor Love has little enough science; his puny arm stretched out to resist the colossal form is weak as the prayers of agonised parents and lovers directed against never-swerving laws; he is almost exhausted; his lustrous wings are broken and torn in the struggle; the dove at his feet crouches mateless; the rose that climbed on his door is prostrate; over his shoulder the beam-like arm has set the stony hand against the door where the rose of joy must fall.

The aged when they die do but follow the treasures that have gone before. One by one the old friends have left them, the sweet ties parted, and the powers to enjoy and help become feeble. When of the garden that once bloomed around them memory alone is left, friendly is death to scatter also the leaves of that last rose where the loved ones are sleeping. This is the real office of death. Nay, even when it comes to the young and happy it is not Death but Disease that is the real enemy; in disease there is almost no compensation at all but learning its art of war; but Death is Nature's pity for helpless pain; where love and knowledge can do no more it comes as a release from sufferings which were sheer torture if prolonged. The presence of death is recognised oftenest by the cessation of pain. Superstition has done few heavier wrongs to humanity than by the mysterious terrors with which it has invested that change which, to the simpler ages, was pictured as the gentle river Lethe, flowing from the abode of sleep, from which the shades drank oblivion alike of their woes and of the joys from which they were torn.

Notes

1 Wake's 'Evolution of Morality,' i. 107.
2 'The Aborigines of Australia' (1865), p. 15.
3 2 Chron. xxxiii. 6.
4 Published by Mozley and Smith, 1878.
5 Max Müller. 'Lectures on Language,' ii. p. 562, et seq.
6 See the beautifully translated funereal hymn of the Veda in Professor Whitney's 'Oriental and Linguistic Studies,' p. 52, etc.
7 'The Avesta.' 'Oriental and Linguistic Studies,' p. 196.
8 'Records of the Past,' i. 143.
9 Sale's 'Koran' (ed. 1836). See pp. 4, 339, 475.
10 'Discoveries,' etc., p. 223.
11 'Modern Painters,' Part V. xix.

Part III - The Dragon

Chapter I - Decline of Demons

The Holy Tree of Travancore—The growth of Demons in India and their decline—The Nepaul Iconoclast—Moral Man and unmoral Nature—Man's physical and mental migrations—Heine's 'Gods in Exile'—The Goban Saor—Master Smith—A Greek caricature of the Gods—The Carpenter v. Deity and Devil—Extermination of the Werewolf—Refuges of Demons—The Giants reduced to Little People—Deities and Demons returning to nature.

Having indicated, necessarily in mere outline and by selected examples, the chief obstacles encountered by primitive man, and his apprehensions, which he personified as demons, it becomes my next task to show how and why many of these demons declined from their terrible proportions and made way for more general forms, expressing comparatively abstract conceptions of physical evil. This will involve some review of the processes through which man's necessary adaptation to his earthly environment brought him to the era of Combat with multiform obstruction.

There was, until within a few recent years, in a mountain of Travancore, India, an ancient, gigantic Tree, regarded by the natives as the residence of a powerful and dangerous deity who reigned over the mountains and the wild beasts.[1] Sacrifices were offered to this tree, sermons preached before it, and it seems to have been the ancient cathedral of the district. Its trunk was so large that four men with outstretched arms could not compass it.

This tree in its early growth may symbolise the upspringing of natural religion. Its first green leaves may be regarded as corresponding to the first crude imaginations of man as written, for instance, on leaves of the Vedas. Perceiving in nature, as we have seen, a power of contrivance like his own, a might far superior to his own, man naturally considered that all things had been created and were controlled by invisible giants; and bowing helplessly beneath them sang thus his hymns and supplications.

'This earth belongs to Varuna, the king, and the wide sky, with its ends far apart: the two seas (sky and ocean) are Varuna's loins; he is also contained in this drop of water. He who would flee far beyond the sky even he would not be rid of Varuna. His spies proceed from heaven towards this earth.'

'Through want of strength, thou ever strong and bright god, have I gone wrong: have mercy, have mercy!'

'However we break thy laws from day to day, men as we are, O god Varuna, do not deliver us to death!'

'Was it an old sin, Varuna, that thou wished to destroy the friend who always praises thee!'

'O Indra, have mercy, give me my daily bread! Raise up wealth to the worshipper, thou mighty Dawn!'

'Thou art the giver of horses, Indra, thou art the giver of cows, the giver of corn, the strong lord of wealth: the old guide of man disappointing no desires: to him we address this song. All this wealth around here is known to be thine alone: take from it conqueror, bring it hither!'

In these characteristic sentences from various hymns we behold man making his first contract with the ruling powers of nature: so much adoration and flattery on his part for so much benefit on theirs. But even in these earliest hymns there are intimations that the gods were not fulfilling their side of the engagement. 'Why is it,' pleads the worshipper, 'that you wish to destroy one who always praises you? Was it an old sin?' The simple words unconsciously report how faithfully man was performing his part of the contract. Having omitted no accent of the prayer, praise, or ritual, he supposes the continued indifference of the gods must be due to an old sin, one he has forgotten, or perhaps one committed by some ancestor.

In this state of mind the suggestion would easily take root that words alone were too cheap to be satisfactory to the gods. There must be offerings. Like earthly kings they must have their revenues. We thus advance to the phase of sacrifices. But still neither in answer to prayer, flattery, or sacrifice did the masses receive health or wealth. Poverty, famine, death, still continued their remorseless course with the silent machinery of sun, moon, and star.

But why, then, should man have gone on fulfilling his part of the contract—believing and worshipping deities, who when he begged for corn gave him famine, and when he asked for fish gave him a serpent? The priest intervened with ready explanation. And here we may consult the holy Tree of Travancore again? Why should that particular Tree—of a species common in the district and not usually very large—have grown so huge? 'Because it is holy,' said the priest. 'Because it was believed holy,' says the fact. For ages the blood and ashes of victims fed its roots and swelled its trunk; until, by an argument not confined to India, the dimensions of the superstition were assumed to prove its truth. When the people complained that all their offerings and worship did not bring any returns the priest replied, You stint the gods and they stint you. The people offered the fattest of their flocks and fruits: More yet! said the priest. They built fine altars and temples for the gods: More yet! said the priest. They built fine houses for the priests, and taxed themselves to support them. And when thus, fed by popular sacrifices and toils, the religion had grown to vast power, the priest was able to call to his side the theologian for further explanation. The theologian and the priest said—'Of course there must be good reasons why the gods do not answer all your prayers (if they did not answer some you would be utterly consumed); mere mortals must not dare to inquire into their mysteries; but that there are gods, and that they do attend to human affairs, is made perfectly plain by this magnificent array of temples, and by the care with which they have supplied all the wants of us, their particular friends, whose cheeks, as you see, hang down with fatness.'

If, after this explanation, any scepticism or rebellion arose among the less favoured, the priest might easily add—'Furthermore, we and our temples are now institutions; we are so strong and influential that it is evident that the gods have appointed us to be their representatives on earth, the dispensers of their favours. Also, of their disfavours. We are able to make up for the seeming indifference of the gods, rewarding you if you give us honour and wealth, but ruining you if you turn heretical.'

So grew the holy Tree. But strong as it was there was something stronger. Some few years ago a missionary from London went to Travancore, and desired to build a chapel near the same tree, no doubt to be in the way of its worshippers and to borrow some of the immemorial sanctity of the spot. This missionary fixed a hungry eye upon that holy timber, and reflected how much holier it would be if ending its career in the beams of a christian chapel. So one day—English authorities being conveniently near—he and his workmen began to cut down the sacred Tree. The natives gradually gathered around, and looked on with horror. While the cutting proceeded a tiger drew near, but shouts drove him off: the natives breathed freer; the demon had come and looked on, but could not protect the Tree from the Englishman. They still shuddered, however, at the sacrilege, and when at last the Holy Tree of Travancore fell, its crash was mingled with the cries and screams of its former worshippers. The victorious missionary may be pointing out in his chapel the cut-up planks which reveal the impotence of the deity so long feared by the natives; and perhaps he is telling them of the bigness of his Tree, and claiming its flourishing condition in Europe as proof of its supernatural character. Possibly he may omit to mention the blood and ashes which have fattened the root and enlarged the trunk of his Holy Tree!

That Tree in Travancore could never have been so destroyed if the primitive natural religion in which lay its deeper root had not previously withered. The gods, the natural forces, which through so many ages had not heeded man's daily martyrdoms, had now for a long time been shown quite as impotent to protect their own shrines, images, holy trees, and other interests. The priests as vainly invoked those gods to save their own country from subjugation by other nations with foreign gods, as the masses had invoked their personal aid. For a long time the gods in some parts of India have received only a formal service, coextensive with their association with a lingering order, or as part of princely establishments; but they topple down from time to time, as the masses realise their freedom to abandon them with impunity. They are at the mercy of any strong heretic who arises. The following narrative, quoted by Mr. Herbert Spencer, presents a striking example of what some Hindoos had been doing before the missionary cut down the Tree at Travancore:—

'A Nepaul king, Rum Bahâdur, whose beautiful queen, finding her lovely face had been disfigured by smallpox, poisoned herself, cursed his kingdom, her doctors, and the gods of Nepaul, vowing vengeance on all. Having ordered the doctors to be flogged, and the right ear and nose of each to be cut off, he then wreaked his vengeance on the gods of Nepaul, and after abusing them in the most gross way, he accused them of having obtained from him 12,000 goats, some hundred-weights of sweetmeats, 2000 gallons of milk, etc., under false pretences. He then ordered all the artillery, varying from three to twelve-pounders, to be brought in front of the palace. All the guns were then loaded to the muzzle, and down he marched to the headquarters of the Nepaul deities. All the guns were drawn up in front of the several deities, honouring the most sacred with the heaviest metal. When the order to fire was given, many of the chiefs and soldiers ran away panic-stricken, and others hesitated to obey the sacrilegious order; and not till several gunners had been cut down were the guns opened. Down came the gods and the goddesses from their hitherto sacred positions; and after six hours' heavy cannonading, not a vestige of the deities remained.'

However panic-stricken the Nepaulese may have been at this ferocious manifestation, it was but a storm bred out of a more general mental and moral condition. Rum Bahâdur only laid low in a few moments images of gods who, passing from the popular interest, had been successively laid to sleep on the innumerable shelves of Hindu mythology. The early Dualism was developed into Moral Man on one side, and Unmoral Nature on the other. Man had discovered that moral order in nature was represented solely by his own power: by his culture or neglect the plant or animal grew or withered, and where his control did not extend, there sprang the noxious weed or beast. So far as good gods had been imagined they were respected now only as incarnate in men. But the active powers of evil still remained, hurtful and hateful to man, and the pessimist view of nature became inevitable. To man engaged in his life-and-death struggle with nature many a beauty which now nourishes the theist's optimism was lost. The fragrant flower was a weed to the man hungry for bread, and he viewed many an idle treasure with the disappointment of Sâdi when, travelling in the desert, he found a bag in which he hoped to discover grain, but found only pearls. Fatal to every deity not anthropomorphic was the long pessimistic phase of human faith. Each became more purely a demon, and passed on the road to become a devil.

Many particular demons man conquered as he progressively carried order amid the ruggedness and wildness of his planet. Every new weapon or implement he invented punctured a thousand phantoms. Only in the realms he could not yet conquer remained the hostile forces to which he ascribed præternatural potency, because not able to pierce them and see through them. Nevertheless, the early demonic forms had to give way, for man had discovered that they were not his masters. He could cut down the Upas and root up the nightshade; he had bruised many a serpent's head and slain many a wolf. In detail innumerable enemies had been proved his inferiors in strength and intelligence. Important migrations took place: man passes, geographically, away from the region of some of his worst enemies, inhabits countries more fruitful, less malarious, his habitat exceeding that of his animal foe in range; and, still better, he passes by mental migration out of the stone age, out of other helpless ages, to the age of metal and the skill to fashion and use it. He has made the fire-fiend his friend. No longer henceforth a naked savage, with bit of stone or bone only to meet the crushing powers of the world and win its reluctant supplies!

There is a sense far profounder than its charming play of fancy in Heine's account of the 'Gods in Exile,' an essay which Mr. Pater well describes as 'full of that strange blending of sentiment which is characteristic of the traditions of the Middle Age concerning the Pagan religions.'2 Heine writes: 'Let me briefly remind the reader how the gods of the older world, at the time of the definite triumph of Christianity, that is, in the third century, fell into painful embarrassments, which greatly resembled certain tragical situations of their earlier life. They now found themselves exposed to the same troublesome necessities to which they had once before been exposed during the primitive ages, in that revolutionary epoch when the Titans broke out of the custody of Orcus, and, piling Pelion on Ossa, scaled Olympus. Unfortunate gods! They had, then, to take flight ignominiously, and hide themselves among us here on earth under all sorts of disguises. Most of them betook themselves to Egypt, where for greater security they assumed the form of animals, as is generally known. Just in the same way they had to take flight again, and seek entertainment in remote hiding-places, when those iconoclastic zealots, the black brood of monks, broke down all the temples, and pursued the gods with fire and curses. Many of these unfortunate emigrants, entirely deprived of shelter and ambrosia, had now to take to vulgar handicrafts as a means of earning their bread. In these circumstances, many, whose sacred groves had been confiscated, let themselves out for hire as wood-cutters in Germany, and had to drink beer instead of nectar. Apollo seems to have been content to take service under graziers, and as he had once kept the cows of Admetus, so he lived now as a shepherd in Lower Austria. Here, however, having become suspected, on account of his beautiful singing, he was recognised by a learned monk as one of the old pagan gods, and handed over to the spiritual tribunal. On the rack he confessed that he was the god Apollo; and before his execution he begged that he might be suffered to play once more upon the lyre and to sing a song. And he played so touchingly, and sang with such magic, and was withal so beautiful in form and feature that all the women wept, and many of them were so deeply impressed that they shortly afterwards fell sick. And some time afterwards the people wished to drag him from the grave again, that a stake might be driven through his body, in the belief that he had been a vampire, and that the sick women would by this means recover. But they found the grave empty.'

Naturally: it is hard to bury Apollo. The next time he appeared was, no doubt, as musical director in the nearest cathedral. The young singers and artists discovered by such severe lessons that it was dangerous to sing Pagan ballads too realistically; that a cowl is capable of a high degree of decoration; that Pan's pipe sounds well evolved into an organ; that Cupids look just as well if called Cherubs. It is odd that it should have required Robert Browning three centuries away to detect the real form and face beneath the vestment of the Bishop who orders his tomb at Saint Praxed's Church:—

The bas-relief in bronze ye promised me,
Those Pans and Nymphs ye wot of, and perchance
Some tripod, thyrsus, with a vase or so,
The Saviour at his sermon on the mount,
Saint Praxed in a glory, and one Pan
Ready to twitch the Nymph's last garment off,
And Moses with the tables....

So in one direction grew the hermitage to the Vatican; so Zeus regained his throne by exchanging his thunderbolts for Peter's keys, and Mars regained his steed as St. George, and Hercules as Christ wrestles with Death once more. But while these artificial restorations were going on in one direction, in another some of the gods were passing through many countries, outwitting and demolishing their former selves as lowered to demons. There are many legends which report this strange phase of development, one of the finest being that of The Goban Saor, told by Mr. Kennedy. The King of

106

Munster sent for this wonderful craftsman to build him a castle. The Goban could fashion a spear with three strokes of his hammer—St. Patrick, who found the Trinity in the shamrock, may have determined the number of strokes,—and when he wished to drive in nails high up, had only to throw his hammer at them. On his way to work for the King, Goban, accompanied by his son, passed the night at the house of a farmer, whose daughters—one dark and industrious, the other fair and idle—received from him (Goban) three bits of advice: 'Always have the head of an old woman by the hob; warm yourselves with your work in the morning; and some time before I come back take the skin of a newly-killed sheep to the market, and bring itself and the price of it home again.' As Goban, with his son, journeyed on, they found a poor man vainly trying to roof his house with three joists and mud; and by simply making one end of each joist rest on the middle of another, the other ends being on the wall, the structure was perfect. He relieved puzzled carpenters by putting up for them the pegless and nailless bridge described in Cæsar's Commentaries. Having done various great things, Goban returns to the homestead of the girls who had received his three bits of advice. The idle one had, of course, blundered at each point, and been ridiculed in the market for her proposition to bring back the sheep's skin and its price. The other, by kindly taking in an aged female relative, by working till she was warm, and by plucking and selling the wool of the sheep's skin and bringing home the latter, had obeyed the Goban's advice, and was selected as his daughter-in-law—the prince attending the wedding. Now, as to building the castle, Goban knew that the King had employed on previous castles four architects and then slain them, so that they should never build another palace equal to his. He therefore says he has left at home a necessary implement which his wife will only give to himself or one of royal blood. The King sends his son, who is kept as hostage till the husband's safe return.

This is the Master Smith of Norse fable, who has a chair from which none can rise, and who therein binds the devil; which again is the story of Hephaistos, and the chair in which he entrapped Hera until she revealed the secret of his birth. The 'devil' whom the Master Smith entraps is, in Norse mythology, simply Loki: and as Loki is a degraded Hephaistos, fire in its demonic forms, we have in all these legends the fire-fiend fought with fire.

This re-dualisation of the gods into demonic and saintly forms had a long preparation. The forces that brought it about may be seen already beginning in Hesiod's representations of the gods, in their presentation on the stage by Euripides, in a manner certain to demonise them to the vulgar, and to subject them to such laughter among scholars as still rings across the ages in the divine dialogues of Lucian. What the gods had become to the Lucians before they reached the Heines may be gathered from the accompanying caricature (Fig. 21).3 Nothing can be more curious than the encounters of the gods with their dead selves, their Manes. What unconscious ingenuity in the combinations! St. Martin on his grey steed divides with the beggar the cloud-cloak of Wodan on his black horse, treading down just such paupers in his wild hunt; as saint he now shelters those whom as storm-demon he chilled; but the identity of Junker Martin is preserved in both titles and myths, and the Martinhorns (cakes), twisted after fashion of the horns of goat or buck pursued by Wodan, are deemed potent like horse-shoes to defend house or stable from the outlawed god.4

Fig. 21.—Greek Caricature of the Gods.

The more impressive and attractive myths transferred to christian saints—as the flowers sacred to Freyja became Our Lady's-glove, or slipper, or smock—there remained to the old gods, in their own name, only the repulsive and puerile, and by this means they were doomed at once to become unmitigated knaves and fools. If Titans, Jötunn or Jinni, they were giant humbugs, whom any small Hans or Jack might outwit and behead. Our Fairy lore is full of stories which show that in the North as well as in Latin countries there had already been a long preparation for the contempt poured by Christianity upon the Norse deities. Many of the stories, as they now stand in Folktales, speak of the vanquished demon or giant as the devil, but it is perfectly easy to detach the being meant from the name so indiscriminately bestowed by christian priests upon most of the outlawed deities. In Lithuania, where survived too much reverence for some of the earlier deities to admit of their being identified with the devil, we still find them triumphed over by the wit and skill of the artisan. Such is the case in a favourite popular legend of that country in which Perkunas—the ancient Thunder-god, corresponding to Perun in Russia—is involved in disgrace along with the devil by the sagacity and skill of a carpenter. The aged god, the venerable Devil, and the young Carpenter, united for a journey. Perkun kept the beasts off with thunder and lightning, the Devil hunted up food, the Carpenter cooked. At length they built a hut and lived in it, and planted the ground with vegetables. Presently a thief invaded their garden. Perkun and the Devil successively tried to catch him, but were well thrashed; whereas the Carpenter by playing the fiddle fascinated the thief, who was a witch, a hag whose hand the fiddler managed to get into a split tree (under pretence of giving her a music lesson), holding her there till she gave up her iron waggon and the whip which she had used on his comrades. After this the three, having decided to separate, disputed as to which should have the hut; and they finally agreed that it should be the possession of him who should succeed in frightening the two others. The Devil raised a storm which frightened Perkun, and Perkun with his thunder and lightning frightened the Devil; but the Carpenter held out bravely, and, in the middle of the night, came in with the witch's waggon, and, cracking her whip, the Devil and Perkun both took flight, leaving the Carpenter in possession of the hut.5

So far as Perkun is concerned, and may be regarded as representative of the gods, the hut may be symbol of Europe, and the Carpenter type of the power which conquered all that was left of them after their fair or noble associations had been transferred to christian forms. Somewhat later, the devil was involved in a like fate, as we shall have to consider in a future chapter.

The most horrible superstitions, if tracked in their popular development, reveal with special impressiveness the progressive emancipation of man from the phantasms of ferocity which represented his primal helplessness. The universal werewolf superstition, for instance, drew its unspeakable horrors from deep and wide-spreading roots. Originating, probably, in occasional relapses to cannibalism among tribes or villages which found themselves amid circumstances as urgent as those which sometimes lead a wrecked crew to draw lots which shall die to support the rest, it would necessarily become demonised by the necessity of surrounding cannibalism with dangers worse than starvation. But it would seem that individuals are always liable, by arrest of development which usually takes the form of disease or insanity, to be dragged back to the savage condition of their race. In the course of this dark history, we note first an increasing tendency to show the means of the transformation difficult. In the Volsunga Saga it is by simply putting on a 'wolf-shirt' (wolfskin) that a man may become a wolf. Then it is said it is done by a belt made of the skin of a man who has been hung—all executed persons being sacred to Wodan (because not dying a natural death), to whom also the wolf was sacred. Then it is added, that the belt must be marked with the signs of the zodiac, and have a buckle with seven teeth. Then it is said that 'only a seventh son' is possessed of this diabolical power; or others say one whose brows meet over his nose. The means of detecting werewolves and retransforming them to human shape multiplied as those of transformation diminished in number, and such remedies reflected the advance of human skill. The werewolf could be restored by crossing his path with a knife or polished steel; by a sword laid on the ground with point towards him; by a silver ball. Human skill was too much for him. In Posen mothers had discovered that one who had bread in his or her mouth could by even such means discover werewolves; and fathers, to this hint about keeping 'the wolf from the door,' added that no one could be attacked by any such monster if he were in a cornfield. The Slav levelled a plough at him. Thus by one prescription and another, and each representing a part of man's victory over chaos, the werewolf was driven out of all but a few 'unlucky' days in the year, and especially found his last refuge in Twelfth Night. But even on that night the werewolf might be generally escaped by the simple device of not speaking of him. If a wolf had to be spoken of he was then called Vermin, and Dr. Wuttke mentions a parish priest named Wolf in East Prussia who on Twelfth Night was addressed as Mr. Vermin! The actual wolf being already out of the forests in most places by art of the builder and the architect; the phantasmal wolf driven out of fear for most of the year by man's recognition of his own superiority to this exterminated beast; even the proverbial 'ears' of the vanishing werewolf ceased to be visible when on his particular fest-night his name was not mentioned.

The last execution of a man for being an occasional werewolf was, I believe, in 1589, near Cologne, there being some evidence of cannibalism. But nine years later, in France, where the belief in the Loup-garou had been intense, a man so accused was simply shut up in a mad-house. It is an indication of the revolution which has occurred, that when next governments paid attention to werewolves it was because certain vagabonds went about professing to be able to transform themselves into wolves, in order to extort money from the more weak-minded and ignorant peasants.6 There could hardly be conceived a more significant history: the werewolf leaves where he entered. Of ignorance and weakness trying, too often in vain, 'to keep the wolf from the door,' was born this voracious phantom; with the beggar and vagabond, survivals of helplessness become inveterate, he wanders thin and crafty. He keeps out of the way of all culture, whether of field or mind. So is it indeed with all demons in decline—of which I can here only adduce a few characteristic examples. So runs the rune—

When the barley there is,
Then the devils whistle;
When the barley is threshed,
Then the devils whine;
When the barley is ground,
Then the devils roar;
When the flour is produced,
Then the devils perish.

The old Scottish custom, mentioned by Sir Walter Scott, of leaving around each cultivated field an untilled fringe, called the Gude Man's Croft, is derived from the ancient belief that unless some wild place is left to the sylvan spirits they will injure the grain and vegetables; and, no doubt, some such notion leads the farmers of Thurgau still to graft mistletoe upon their fruit-trees. Many who can smile at such customs do yet preserve in their own minds, or those of their servants or neighbours, crofts which the ploughshare of science is forbidden to touch, and where the præternatural troops still hide their shrivelled forms. But this wild girdle becomes ever narrower, and the images within it tend to blend with rustling leaf and straw, and the insects, and to be otherwise invisible, save to that second sight which is received from Glam. As in some shadow-pantomime, the deities and demons pursue each other in endless procession, dropping down as awe-inspiring Titans, vanishing as grotesque pigmies—vanishing beyond the lamp into Nothingness!

So came most of the monsters we have been describing—Animals, Volcanoes, Icebergs, Deserts, though they might be—by growing culture and mastery of nature to be called 'the little people;' and perhaps it is rather through pity than euphemism when they were so often called, as in Ireland (Duine Matha), 'the good little people.'7 At every step in time or space back of the era of mechanic arts the little fairy gains in physical proportions. The house-spirits (Domovoi) of Russia are full-sized, shaggy human-shaped beings. In Lithuania the corresponding phantoms (Kaukas) average only a foot in height. The Krosnyata, believed in by the Slavs on the Baltic coast, are similarly small; and by way of the kobolds, elves, fays, travelling westward, we find the size of such shapes diminishing, until warnings are given that the teeth must never be picked with a straw, that slender tube being a favourite residence of the elf! In Bavaria a little red chafer with seven spots (Coccinella septempunctata) is able to hold Thor with his lightnings, and in other regions is a form of the goddess of Love!8 Our English name for the tiny beetle 'Lady-bug' is derived from the latter notion; and Mr. Karl Blind has expressed the opinion that our children's rune—

Lady-bug, lady-bug, fly away home,
Thy house is on fire, thy children will roam—

is last echo of the Eddaic prophecies of the destruction of the universe by the fire-fiend Loki!9 Such reductions of the ancient gods, demons, and terrors to tiny dimensions would, of course, be only an indirect result of the general cause stated. They were driven from the great world, and sought the small world: they survived in the hut and were adapted to the nerves of the nursery. So alone can Tithonos live on: beyond the age for which he is born he shrinks to a grasshopper; and it is now by only careful listening that in the chirpings of the multitudinous immortals, of which Tithonos is type, may be distinguished the thunders and roarings of deities and demons that once made the earth to tremble.

Notes

1 The history of this tree which I use for a parable is told in the Rev. Samuel Mateer's 'Land of Charity.' London: John Snow & Co. 1871.
2 'Studies in the History of the Renaissance.' Macmillan & Co. 1873.
3 Concerning which Mr. Wright says: 'It is taken from an oxybaphon which was brought from the Continent to England, where it passed into the collection of Mr. William Hope.... The Hyperborean Apollo himself appears as a quack-doctor, on his temporary stage, covered by a sort of roof, and approached by wooden steps. On the stage lies Apollo's luggage, consisting of a bag, a bow, and his Scythian cap. Chiron (XIPΩN) is represented as labouring under the effects of age and blindness, and supporting himself by the aid of a crooked staff, as he repairs to the Delphian quack-doctor for relief. The figure of the centaur is made to ascend by the aid of a companion, both being furnished with the masks and other attributes of the comic performers. Above are the mountains, and on them the nymphs of Parnassus (NYMΦAI), who, like all the other actors in the scene, are disguised with masks, and those of a very gross character.... Even a pun is employed to heighten the drollery of the scene, for instead of ΠΥΘΙΑΣ, the Pythian, placed over the head of the burlesque Apollo, it seems evident that the artist had written ΠΕΙΘΙΑΣ, the consoler.'—'History of Caricature,' p. 18. But who is the leaf-crowned figure, without mask, on the right hand? Was it some early Offenbach, who found such representation of the gods welcome at Athens where the attempt to produce our modern Offenbach's Belle Helène recently caused a theatrical riot?
4 Wuttke. 'Volksaberglaube,' 18.

5 Schleicher, 'Litauische Märchen,' 141–145. Mr. Ralston's translation abridged.
6 Of this latter kind of hungry werewolf a specimen still occasionally revisits the glimpses of the moonshine which, for too many minds, still replaces daylight. So recently as January 17, 1878, one Kate Bedwell, a 'pedlar, was sentenced in the Marylebone Police Court, London, to three months' hard labour for obtaining various sums of money, amounting to 9s. 10d., by terrorism, from Eliza Rolf, a cook. The pedlar came to the plaintiff's place of work and asked her if she would like to have her fortune told. Eliza replied, 'No, I know it; it is hard work or starving.' The fortune-teller asked her next time if she would have her planet ruled; the other still said no; but her nerves yielded when the 'Drud' told her 'she lived under three stars, one good the others bad, and that she could disfigure her or turn her into something else.' 'Thank God, she did not!' exclaimed the poor woman in court. However, she seemed to have trusted rather in her money than in any other providence for her immunity from an unhappy transformation. But even into this rare depth of ignorance enough light had penetrated to enable Eliza to cope with her werewolf in the civilised way of haling her before a magistrate. When Fenris gets three months with hard labour, he no doubt realises that he has exceeded his mental habitat, and that the invisible cords have bound him at last.
7 Elf has, indeed, been referred by some to the Sanskrit alpa=little; but the balance of authority is in favour of the derivation given in a former chapter.
8 Mannhardt, 'Götter,' 287.
9 Freia-Holda, the Teutonic goddess of Love. 'Cornhill Magazine,' May, 1872.

Chapter II - Generalisation of Demons

The Demons' bequest to their conquerors—Nondescripts—Exaggerations of tradition—Saurian Theory of Dragons—The Dragon not primitive in Mythology—Monsters of Egyptian, Iranian, Vedic, and Jewish Mythologies—Turner's Dragon—Della Bella—The Conventional Dragon.

After all those brave victories of man over the first chaos, organic and inorganic, whose effect upon his phantasms has been indicated; after fire had slain its thousands, and iron its tens of thousands of his demons, and the rough artisan become a Nemesis with his rudder and wheel pursuing the hosts of darkness back into Night and Invisibility; still stood the grim fact of manyformed pain and evil in the world, still defying the ascending purposes of mankind. Moreover, confronting these, he is by no means so different mentally from that man he was before conquering many foes in detail, and laying their phantoms, as he was morally. More courage man had gained, and more defiance; and, intellectually, a step had been taken, if only one: he had learned that his evils are related to each other. Hunger is of many heads and forms. Its yawning throat may be seen in the brilliant sky that lasts till it is as brass, in the deluge, the earthquake, in claw and fang; and then these together do but relate the hunger-brood to Fire and Ferocity; the summer sunbeam may be venomous as a serpent, and the end of them all is Death. Some tendency to these more general conceptions of an opposing principle and power in the world seems to be represented in that phase of development at which nondescript forms arise. These were the conquered demons' bequest.

It is, of course, impossible to measure the various forces which combined to produce the complex symbolical forms of physical evil. Tradition is not always a good draughtsman, and in portraying for a distant generation in Germany a big snake killed in India might not be exact as to the number of its heads or other details. Heroes before Falstaff were liable to overstate their foes in buckram. The less measurable a thing by fact, the more immense in fancy: werewolves of especial magnitude haunted regions where there had not been actual wolves for centuries; huge serpents play a large part in the annals of Ireland, where not even the smallest have been found. But after all natural influences have been considered, one can hardly look upon the sphynx, the chimæra, or on a conventional dragon, without perceiving that he is in presence of a higher creation than a demonic bear or a giant ruffian. The fundamental difference between the two classes is that one is natural, the other præternatural. Of course a werewolf is as præternatural as a gryphon to the eye of science, but as original expressions of human imagination the former could hardly have been a more miraculous monster than the Siamese twins to intelligent people to-day. The demonic forms are generally natural, albeit caricatured or exaggerated. And this effort at a præternatural conception is, in this early form, by no means mere superstition; rather is it poetic and artistic,—a kind of crude effort at allgemeinheit, at realisation of the types of evil—the claw-principle, fang-principle in the universe, the physiognomies of venom and pain detached from forms to which they are accidental.

Some of the particular forms we have been considering are, indeed, by no means of the prosaic type. Such conceptions as Ráhu, Cerberus, and several others, are transitional between the natural and mystical conceptions; while the sphynx, however complete a combination of ideal forms, is not all demonic. In this Part III. are included those forms whose combination is not found in objective nature, but which are yet travesties of nature and genuine fauna of the human mind.

Perhaps it may be thought somewhat arbitrary that I should describe all these intermediate forms between demon and devil by the term Dragon; but I believe there is no other fabulous form which includes so many individual types of transition, or whose evolution may be so satisfactorily traced from the point where it is linked with the demon to that where it bequeathes its characters to the devil. While, however, this term is used as the best that suggests itself, it cannot be accepted as limiting our inquiry or excluding other abstract forms which ideally correspond to the dragon,—the generalised expression for an active, powerful, and intelligent enemy to mankind, a being who is antagonism organised, and able to command every weapon in nature for an antihuman purpose.

The opinion has steadily gained that the conventional dragon is the traditional form of some huge Saurian. It has been suggested that some of those extinct forms may have been contemporaneous with the earliest men, and that the traditions of conflicts with them, transmitted orally and pictorially, have resulted in preserving their forms in fable (proximately). The restorations of Saurians on their islet at the Crystal Palace show how much common sense there is in this theory. The discoveries of Professor Marsh of Yale College have proved that the general form of the dragon is startlingly prefigured in nature; and Mr. Alfred Tylor, in an able paper read before the Anthropological Society, has shown that we are very apt to be on the safe side in sticking to the theory of an 'object-origin' for most things. Concerning this theory, it may be said that the earliest descriptions, both written and pictorial, which have been discovered of the reptilian monsters around which grew the germs of our dragon-myths, are crocodiles or serpents, and not dragons of any conventional kind,—with a few doubtful exceptions. In an Egyptian papyrus there is a hieroglyphic picture of San-nu Hut-ur, 'plunger of the sea;' it is a marine, dolphin-like monster, with four feet, and a tail ending in a serpent's head.1 With wings, this might approach the dragon-form. Again, Amen-Ra slew Naka, and this serpent 'saved his feet.' Possibly the phrase is ironical, and means that the serpent saved nothing; but apart from that, the poem is too highly metaphorical—the victorious god himself being described in it as a 'beautiful bull'—for the phrase to be important. On Egyptian monuments are pictured serpents with human heads and members, and the serpent Nahab-ka is pictured on amulets with two perfect human legs and feet.2 Winged serpents are found on Egyptian monuments, but almost as frequently with the incredible number of four as with the conceivable two wings of the pterodactyl. The forms of the serpents thus portrayed with anthropomorphic legs and slight wings are, in their main shapes, of ordinary species. In the Iranian tradition of the temptation of the first man and woman, Meschia and Meschiane, by the 'two-footed serpent of lies.' And it is possible that out of this myth of the 'two-footed' serpent grew the puzzling legend of Genesis that the serpent of Eden was sentenced thereafter to crawl on his belly. The snake's lack of feet, however, might with equal probability have given rise to the explanation given in mussulman and rabbinical stories of his feet being cut off by the avenging angel. But the antiquity of the Iranian myth is doubtful; while the superior antiquity of the Hindu fable of Ráhu, to which it seems related, suggests that the two legs of the Ahriman serpent, like the four arms of serpent-tailed Ráhu, is an anthropomorphic addition. In the ancient planispheres we find the 'crooked serpent' mentioned in the Book of Job, but no dragon.

The two great monsters of Vedic mythology, Vritra and Ahi, are not so distinguishable from each other in the Vedas as in more recent fables. Vritra is very frequently called Vritra Ahi—Ahi being explained in the St. Petersburg Dictionary as 'the Serpent of the Heavens, the demon Vritra.' Ahi literally means 'serpent,' answering to the Greek ἐχι-ς, ἐχι-δνα; and when anything is added it appears to be anthropomorphic—heads, arms, eyes—as in the case of the Egyptian serpent-monsters. The Vedic demon Urana is described as having three heads, six eyes, and ninety-nine arms.

There would appear to be as little reason for ascribing to the Tannin of the Old Testament the significance of dragon, though it is generally so translated. It is used under circumstances which show it to mean whale, serpent, and various other beasts. Jeremiah (xiv. 6) compares them to wild asses snuffing the wind, and Micah (i. 8) describes their 'wailing.' The fiery serpents said to have afflicted Israel in the wilderness are called seraphim, but neither in their natural or mythological forms do they anticipate our conventional dragon beyond the fiery character that is blended with the serpent character. Nor do the descriptions of Behemoth and Leviathan comport with the dragon-form.

The serpent as an animal is a consummate development. Its feet, so far from having been amputated, as the fables say, in punishment of its sin, have been withdrawn beneath the skin as crutches used in a feebler period. It is found as a tertiary fossil. Since, therefore, the dragon form ex hypothesi is a reminiscence of the huge, now fossil, Saurians which preceded the serpent in time, the early mythologies could hardly have so regularly described great serpents instead of dragons. If the realistic theory we are discussing were true, the earliest combats—those of Indra, for

Fig. 22.—A Witch Mounted (Della Bella).

instance—ought to have been with dragons, and the serpent enemies would have multiplied as time went on; but the reverse is the case—the (alleged) extinct forms being comparatively modern in heroic legend.

Mr. John Ruskin once remarked upon Turner's picture of the Dragon guarding the Hesperides, that this conception so early as 1806, when no Saurian skeleton was within the artist's reach, presented a singular instance of the scientific imagination. As a coincidence with such extinct forms Turner's dragon is surpassed by the monster on which a witch rides in one of the engravings of Della Bella, published in 1637. In that year, on the occasion of the marriage of the grand duke Ferdinand II. in Florence, there was a masque d'Inferno, whose representations were engraved by Della Bella, of which this is one, so that it may be rather to some scenic artist than to the distinguished imitator of Callot that we owe this grotesque form, which the late Mr. Wright said 'might have been borrowed from some distant geological period.' If so, the fact would present a curious coincidence with the true history of Turner's Dragon; for after Mr. Ruskin had published his remark about the scientific imagination represented in it, an old friend of the artist declared that Turner himself had told him that he copied that dragon from a Christmas spectacle in Drury Lane theatre. But Turner had shown the truest scientific instinct in repairing to the fossil-beds of human imagination, and drawing thence the conventional form which never had existence save as the structure of cumulative tradition.

Notes

1 *'Records of the Past,' vi. 124.*
2 *See Cooper's 'Serpent-Myths of Ancient Egypt,' figs. 109 and 112. Serapis as a human-headed serpent is shown in the same essay (from Sharpe), fig. 119.*

Chapter III - The Serpent

The beauty of the Serpent—Emerson on ideal forms—Michelet's thoughts on the viper's head—Unique characters of the Serpent—The monkey's horror of Snakes—The Serpent protected by superstition—Human defencelessness against its subtle powers—Dubufe's picture of the Fall of Man.

In the accompanying picture, a medal of the ancient city of Tyre, two of the most beautiful forms of nature are brought together,—the Serpent and the Egg. Mr. D. R. Hay has shown the endless extent to which the oval arches have been reproduced in the ceramic arts of antiquity; and the same sense of symmetry which made the Greek vase a combination of Eggs prevails in the charm which the same graceful outline possesses wherever suggested,—as in curves of the swan, crescent of the moon, the elongated shell,—on which Aphrodite may well be poised, since the same contours find their consummate expression in the flowing lines attaining their repose in the perfect form of woman. The Serpent—model of the 'line of grace and beauty'—has had an even larger fascination for the eye of the artist and the poet. It is the one active form in nature which cannot be ungraceful, and to estimate the extent of its use in decoration is impossible, because all undulating and coiling lines are necessarily serpent forms. But in addition to the perfections of this form—which fulfil all the ascent of forms in Swedenborg's mystical morphology, circular, spiral, perpetual-circular, vortical, celestial—the Serpent bears on it, as it were, gems of the underworld that seem to find their counterpart in galaxies.

Fig. 23.—Serpent and Egg (Tyre).

One must conclude that Serpent-worship is mainly founded in fear. The sacrifices offered to that animal are alone sufficient to prove this. But as it is certain that the Serpent appears in symbolism and poetry in many ways which have little or no relation to its terrors, we may well doubt whether it may not have had a career in the human imagination previous to either of the results of its reign of terror,—worship and execration. It is the theory of Pestalozzi that every child is born an artist, and through its pictorial sense must be led on its first steps of education. The infant world displayed also in its selection of sacred trees and animals a profound appreciation of beauty. The myths in which the Serpent is represented as kakodemon refer rather to its natural history than to its appearance; and even when its natural history came to be observed, there was—there now is—such a wide discrepancy between its physiology and its functions, also between its intrinsic characters and their relation to man, that we can only accept its various aspects in mythology without attempting to trace their relative precedence in time.

The past may in this case be best interpreted by the present. How different now to wise and observant men are the suggestions of this exceptional form in nature!

Let us read a passage concerning it from Ralph Waldo Emerson:—

'In the old aphorism, nature is always self-similar. In the plant, the eye or germinative point opens to a leaf, then to another leaf, with a power of transforming the leaf into radicle, stamen, pistil, petal, bract, sepal, or seed. The whole art of the plant is still to repeat leaf on leaf without end, the more or less of heat, light, moisture, and food, determining the form it shall assume. In the animal, nature makes a vertebra, or a spine of vertebræ, and helps herself still by a new spine, with a limited power of modifying its form,—spine on spine, to the end of the world. A poetic anatomist, in our own day, teaches that a snake being a horizontal line, and man being an erect line, constitute a right angle; and between the lines of this mystical quadrant, all animated beings find their place: and he assumes the hair-worm, the span-worm, or the snake, as the type or prediction of the spine. Manifestly, at the end of the spine, nature puts out smaller spines, as arms; at the end of the arms, new spines, as hands; at the other end she repeats the process, as legs and feet. At the top of the column she puts out another spine, which doubles or loops itself over, as a span-worm, into a ball, and forms the skull, with extremities again: the hands being now the upper jaw, the feet the lower jaw, the fingers and toes being represented this time by upper and lower teeth. This new spine is destined to high uses. It is a new man on the shoulders of the last.'[1]

As one reads this it might be asked, How could its idealism be more profoundly pictured for the eye than in the Serpent coiled round the egg,—the seed out of which all these spines must branch out for their protean variations? What refrains of ancient themes subtly sound between the lines,—from the Serpent doomed to crawl on its belly in the dust, to the Serpent that is lifted up!

Now let us turn to the page of Jules Michelet, and read what the Serpent signified to one mood of his sympathetic nature. 'It was one of my saddest hours when, seeking in nature a refuge from thoughts of the age, I for the first time encountered the head of the viper. This occurred in a valuable museum of anatomical imitations.

The head marvellously imitated and enormously enlarged, so as to remind one of the tiger's and the jaguar's, exposed in its horrible form a something still more horrible. You seized at once the delicate, infinite, fearfully prescient precautions by which the deadly machine is so potently armed. Not only is it provided with numerous keen-edged teeth, not only are these teeth supplied with an ingenious reservoir of poison which slays immediately, but their extreme fineness which renders them liable to fracture is compensated by an advantage that perhaps no other animal possesses, namely, a magazine of supernumerary teeth, to supply at need the place of any accidentally broken. Oh, what provisions for killing! What precautions that the victim shall not escape! What love for this horrible creature! I stood by it scandalised, if I may so speak, and with a sick soul. Nature, the great mother, by whose side I had taken refuge, shocked me with a maternity so cruelly impartial. Gloomily I walked away, bearing on my heart a darker shadow than rested on the day itself, one of the sternest in winter. I had come forth like a child; I returned home like an orphan, feeling the notion of a Providence dying away within me.'[2]

Many have so gone forth and so returned; some to say, 'There is no God;' a few to say (as is reported of a living poet), 'I believe in God, but am against him;' but some also to discern in the viper's head Nature's ironclad, armed with her best science to defend the advance of form to humanity along narrow passes.

The primitive man was the child that went forth when his world was also a child, and when the Serpent was still doing its part towards making him and it a man. It was a long way from him to the dragon-slayer; but it is much that he did not merely cower; he watched and observed, and there is not one trait belonging to his deadly crawling contemporaries that he did not note and spiritualise in such science as was possible to him.

The last-discovered of the topes in India represents Serpent-worshippers gathered around their deity, holding their tongues with finger and thumb. No living form in nature could be so fitly regarded in that attitude. Not only is the Serpent normally silent, but in its action it has 'the quiet of perfect motion.' The maximum of force is shown in it, relatively to its size, along with the minimum of friction and visible effort. Footless, wingless, as a star, its swift gliding and darting is sometimes like the lightning whose forked tongue it seemed to incarnate. The least touch of its ingenious tooth is more destructive than the lion's jaw. What mystery in its longevity, in its self-subsistence, in its self-renovation! Out of the dark it comes arrayed in jewels, a crawling magazine of death in its ire, in its unknown purposes able to renew its youth, and

113

fable for man imperishable life! Wonderful also are its mimicries. It sometimes borrows colours of the earth on which it reposes, the trees on which it hangs, now seems covered with eyes, and the 'spectacled snake' appeared to have artificially added to its vision. Altogether it is unique among natural forms, and its vast history in religious speculation and mythology does credit to the observation of primitive man.

Recent experiments have shown the monkeys stand in the greatest terror of snakes. Such terror is more and more recognised as a survival in the European man. The Serpent is almost the only animal which can follow a monkey up a tree and there attack its young. Our arboreal anthropoid progenitors could best have been developed in some place naturally enclosed and fortified, as by precipices which quadrupeds could not scale, but which apes might reach by swinging and leaping from trees. But there could be no seclusion where the Serpent could not follow. I am informed by the King of Bonny that in his region of Africa the only serpent whose worship is fully maintained is the Nomboh (Leaper), a small snake, white and glistening, whose bite is fatal, and which, climbing into trees, springs thence upon its prey beneath, and can travel far by leaping from branch to branch. The first arboreal man who added a little to the natural defences of any situation might stand in tradition as a god planting a garden; but even he would not be supposed able to devise any absolute means of defence against the subtlest of all the beasts. Among the three things Solomon found too wonderful for him was 'the way of a serpent upon a rock' (Prov. xxx. 19). This comparative superiority of the Serpent to any and all devices and contrivances known to primitive men—whose proverbs must have made most of Solomon's wisdom—would necessarily have its effect upon the animal and mental nerves of our race in early times, and the Serpent would find in his sanctity a condition favourable to survival and multiplication. It is this fatal power of superstition to change fancies into realities which we find still protecting the Serpent in various countries. From being venerated as the arbiter of life and death, it might thus actually become such in large districts of country. In Dubufe's picture of the Fall of Man, the wrath of Jehovah is represented by the lightning, which has shattered the tree beneath which the offending pair are now crouching; beyond it Satan is seen in human shape raising his arm in proud defiance against the blackened sky. So would the Serpent appear. His victims were counted by many thousands where the lightning laid low one. Transmitted along the shuddering nerves of many generations came the confession of the Son of Sirach, 'There is no head above the head of a serpent.'

Notes

1 'Representative Men,' American edition of 1850, p. 108.
2 'L'Oiseau,' par Jules Michelet.

Chapter IV - The Worm

An African Serpent-drama in America—The Veiled Serpent—The Ark of the Covenant—Aaron's Rod—The Worm—An Episode on the Dii Involuti—The Serapes—The Bambino at Rome—Serpent-transformations.

On the eve of January 1, 1863,—that historic New Year's Day on which President Lincoln proclaimed freedom to American slaves,—I was present at a Watchnight held by negroes in a city of that country. In opening the meeting the preacher said,—though in words whose eloquent shortcomings I cannot reproduce:—'Brethren and sisters, the President of the United States has promised that, if the Confederates do not lay down their arms, he will free all their slaves to-morrow. They have not laid down their arms. To-morrow will be the day of liberty to the oppressed. But we all know that evil powers are around the President. While we sit here they are trying to make him break his word. But we have come together to watch, and see that he does not break his word. Brethren, the bad influences around the President to-night are stronger than any Copperheads.1 The Old Serpent is abroad to-night, with all his emissaries, in great power. His wrath is great, because he knows his hour is near. He will be in this church this evening. As midnight comes on we shall hear his rage. But, brethren and sisters, don't be alarmed. Our prayers will prevail. His head will be bruised. His back will be broken. He will go raging to hell, and God Almighty's New Year will make the United States a true land of freedom.' The sensation caused among the hundreds of negroes present by these words was profound; they were frequently interrupted by cries of 'Glory!' and there were tears of joy. But the scene and excitement which followed were indescribable. A few moments before midnight the congregation were requested to kneel, which they did, and prayer succeeded prayer with increasing fervour. Presently a loud, prolonged hiss was heard. There were cries—'He's here! he's here!' Then came a volley of hisses; they seemed to proceed from every part of the room, hisses so entirely like those of huge serpents that the strongest nerves were shaken; above them rose the preacher's prayer that had become a wild incantation, and ecstatic ejaculations became so universal that it was a marvel what voices were left to make the hisses. Finally, from a neighbouring steeple the twelve strokes of midnight sounded on the frosty air, and immediately the hisses diminished, and presently died away altogether, and the New Year that brought freedom to four millions of slaves was ushered in by the jubilant chorus of all present singing a hymn of victory.

Far had come those hisses and that song of victory, terminating the dragon-drama of America. In them was the burden of Ezekiel: 'Son of man, set thy face against Pharaoh, king of Egypt, and prophesy against him and against all Egypt, saying, Thus saith the Lord Jehovah: Behold I am against thee, Pharaoh king of Egypt, the great dragon that lieth in the midst of the rivers ... I will put a hook in thy jaws.' In them was the burden of Isaiah: 'In that day Jehovah with his sore and great and strong sword shall punish Leviathan the piercing serpent, even Leviathan that crooked serpent: he shall slay the dragon that is in the sea.' In it was the cry of Zophar: 'His meat in his bowels is turned, it is the gall of asps within him. He hath swallowed down riches, and he shall vomit them up again: God shall cast them out of his belly.' And these Hebrew utterances, again, were but the distant echoes of far earlier voices of those African slaves still seen pictured with their chains on the ruined walls of Egypt,—voices that gathered courage at last to announce the never-ending struggle of man with Oppression, as that combat between god and serpent which never had a nobler event than when the dying hiss of Slavery was heard in America, and the victorious Sun rose upon a New World of free and equal men.

The Serpent thus exalted in America to a type of oppression is very different from any snake that may this day be found worshipped as a deity by the African in his native land. The swarthy snake-worshipper in his migration took his god along with him in his chest or basket—at once ark and altar—and in that hiding-place it underwent transformations. He

Fig. 24.—Serpent and Ark (from a Greek coin).

emerged as the protean emblem of both good and evil. In a mythologic sense the serpent certainly held its tail in its mouth. No civilisation has reached the end of its typical supremacy.

Concerning the accompanying Eleusinian form (Fig. 24), Calmet says:—'The mysterious trunk, coffer, or basket, may be justly reckoned among the most remarkable and sacred instruments of worship, which formed part of the processional ceremonies in the heathen world. This was held so sacred that it was not publicly exposed to view, or publicly opened, but was reserved for the inspection of the initiated, the fully initiated only. Completely to explain this symbol would require a dissertation; and, indeed, it has been considered, more or less, by those who have written on the nature of the Ark of the testimony among the Hebrews. Declining the inquiry at present, we merely call the attention of the reader to what this mystical coffer was supposed to contain—a serpent!'

The French Benedictine who wrote this passage, though his usual candour shames the casuistry of our own time, found it necessary to conceal the Hebrew Ark: it was precisely so that the occupant of the Ark was originally concealed; and though St. John exorcised it from the Chalice its genius lingers in the Pyx, before whose Host 'lifted up' the eyes of worshippers are lowered.

The writer of the Epistle to the Hebrews (chap. ix.), describing the Tabernacle, says: 'After the second veil, the tabernacle which is called the Holiest of all; which had the golden censer, and the ark of the covenant overlaid round about with gold, wherein was the golden pot that had manna, and Aaron's rod that budded, and the tables of the covenant.' But this rod of Aaron, which, by budding, had swallowed up all rival pretensions to the tribal priesthood, was the same rod which had been changed to a serpent, and swallowed up the rod-serpents of the sorcerers in Pharaoh's presence. So soft and subtle is 'the way of a serpent upon a rock!'

This veiling of the Serpent, significant of a great deal, is characteristic even of the words used to name it. Of these I have selected one to head this chapter, because it is one of the innumerable veils which shielded this reptile's transformation from a particular external danger to a demonic type. This general description of things that wind about or turn (vermes, traced by some to the Sanskrit root hvar, 'curved'), gradually came into use to express the demon serpents. Dante and Milton call Satan a worm. No doubt among the two hundred names for the Serpent, said to be mentioned in an Arabic work, we should find parallels to this old adaptation of the word 'worm.' In countries—as Germany and England—where no large serpents are found, the popular imagination could not be impressed by merely saying that Siegfried or Lambton had slain a snake. The tortuous character of the snake was preserved, but, by that unconscious dexterity which so often appears in the making of myths, it was expanded so as to include a power of supernatural transformation. The Lambton worm comes out of the well very small, but it afterwards coils in nine huge folds around its hill. The hag-ridden daughter of the King of Northumberland, who

crept into a hole a worm
And out stept a fair ladye,
did but follow the legendary rule of the demonic serpent tribe.

Why was the Serpent slipped into the Ark or coffer and hid behind veils? To answer this will require here an episode. In the Etruscan theology and ceremonial the supreme power was lodged with certain deities that were never seen. They were called the Dii Involuti, the veiled gods. Not even the priests ever looked upon them. When any dire calamity occurred, it was said these mysterious deities had spoken their word in the council of the gods,—a word always final and fatal.

There have been fine theories on the subject, and the Etruscans have been complimented for having high transcendental views of the invisible nature of the Divine Being. But a more prosaic theory is probably true. These gods were wrapped up because they were not fit to be seen. The rude carvings of some savage tribe, they had been seen and adored at first: temples had been built for them, and their priesthood had grown powerful; but as art advanced and beautiful statues arose, these rude designs could not bear the contrast, and the only way of preserving reverence for them, and the institutions grown up around them, was to hide them out of sight altogether. Then it could be said they were so divinely beautiful that the senses would be overpowered by them.

There have been many veiled deities, and though their veils have been rationalised, they are easily pierced. The inscription on the temple of Isis at Sais was: 'I am that which has been, which is, and which shall be, and no one has yet lifted the veil that hides me.' Isis at this time had probably become a negro Madonna, like that still worshipped in Spain as holiest of images, and called by the same title, 'Our Immaculate Lady.' As the fair race and the dark mingled in Egypt, the primitive Nubian complexion and features of Isis could not inspire such reverence as more anciently, and before her also a curtain was hung. The Ark of Moses carried this veil into the wilderness, and concealed objects not attractive to look at—probably two scrawled stones, some bones said to be those of Joseph, a pot of so-called manna, and the staff said to have once been a serpent and afterwards blossomed. Fashioned by a rude tribe, the Ark was a fit thing to hide, and hidden it has been to this day. When the veil of the Temple was rent,—allegorically at the death of Christ, actually by Titus,—nothing of the kind was found; and it would seem that the Jews must long have been worshipping before a veil with emptiness behind it. Paul discovered that the veil said to have covered the face of Moses when he descended from Sinai was a myth; it meant that the people should not see to the end of what was nevertheless transient. 'Their minds were blinded; for unto this day, when Moses is read, that veil is on their heart.'

Kircher says the Seraphs of Egypt were images without any eminency of limbs, rolled as it were in swaddling clothes, partly made of stone, partly of metal, wood, or shell. Similar images, he says, were called by the Romans 'secret gods.' As an age of scepticism advanced, it was sometimes necessary that these 'involuti' should be slightly revealed, lest it should be said there was no god there at all. Such is the case with the famous bambino of Aracœli Church in Rome. This effigy, said to have been carved by a pilgrim out of a tree on the Mount of Olives, and painted by St. Luke while the pilgrim was sleeping, is now kept in its ark, and visitors are allowed to see part of its painted face. When the writer of this requested a sight of the whole form, or of the head at any rate, the exhibiting priest was astounded at the suggestion. No doubt he was right: the only wonder is that the face is not hid also, for a more ingeniously ugly thing than the flat, blackened, and rouged visage of the bambino it were difficult to conceive. But it wears a very cunning veil nevertheless. The face is set in marvellous brilliants, but these are of less effect in hiding its ugliness than the vesture of mythology around it. The adjacent walls are covered with pictures of the miracles it has performed, and which have attracted to it such faith that it is said at one time to have received more medical fees than all the physicians in Rome together. Priests have discovered that a veil over the mind is thicker than a veil on the god. Such is the popular veneration for the bambino, that, in 1849, the Republicans thought it politic to present the monks with the Pope's state coach to carry the idol about. In the end it was proved that the Pope was securely seated beside the bambino, and he presently emerged from behind his veil also. There came, then, a period when the Serpent crept behind the veil, or lid of the ark, or into a chalice,—a very small worm, but yet able to gnaw the staff of Solomon. No wisdom could be permitted to rise above fear itself, though its special sources might be here and there reduced or vanquished. The snake had taught man at last its arts of war. Man had summoned to his aid the pig, and the ibis made havoc among the reptiles; and some of that terror which is the parent of that kind of devotion passed away. When it next emerged, it was in twofold guise,—as Agathodemon and Kakodemon,— but in both forms as the familiar of some higher being. It was as the genius of Minerva, of Esculapius, of St. Euphemia. We have already seen him (Fig. 13) as the genius of the Eleans, the Sosopolis, where also we see the Serpent hurrying into his cavern, leaving the mother and child to be worshipped in the temple of Lucina. In Christian symbolism the Seraphim— 'burning (sáraf) serpents'—veiled their faces and forms beneath their huge wings, crossed in front, and so have been able to become 'the eminent,' and to join in the praises of modern communities at being delivered from just such imaginary fiery worms as themselves!

Note

1 A deadly Southern snake, coloured like the soil on which it lurks, had become the current name for politicians who, while professing loyalty to the Union, aided those who sought to overthrow it.

Chapter V - Apophis

The considerations advanced in the previous chapter enable us to dismiss with facility many of the rationalistic interpretations which have been advanced to explain the monstrous serpents of sacred books by reference to imaginary species supposed to be now extinct. Flying serpents, snakes many-headed, rain-bringing, woman-hating, etc., may be suffered to survive as the fauna of bibliolatrous imaginations. Such forms, however, are of such mythologic importance that it is necessary to watch carefully against this method of realistic interpretation, especially as there are many actual characteristics of serpents sufficiently mysterious to conspire with it. A recent instance of this literalism may here be noticed.

Mr. W. R. Cooper[1] supposes the evil serpent of Egyptian Mythology to have a real basis in 'a large and unidentified species of coluber, of great strength and hideous longitude,' which 'was, even from the earliest ages, associated as the representative of spiritual, and occasionally physical evil, and was named Hof, Rehof, or Apophis,' the 'destroyer, the enemy of the gods, and the devourer of the souls of men.' That such a creature, he adds, 'once inhabited the Libyan desert, we have the testimony of both Hanno the Carthaginian and Lucan the Roman, and if it is now no longer an inhabitant of that region, it is probably owing to the advance of civilisation having driven it farther south.'

Apart from the extreme improbability that African exploration should have brought no rumours of such a monster if it existed, it may be said concerning Mr. Cooper's theory: (1.) If, indeed, the references cited were to a reptile now unknown, we might be led by mythologic analogy to expect that it would have been revered beyond either the Asp or the Cobra. In proportion to the fear has generally been the exaltation of its objects. Primitive peoples have generally gathered courage to pour invective upon evil monsters when—either from their non-existence or rarity—there was least danger of its being practically resented as a personal affront. (2.) The regular folds of Apophis on the sarcophagus of Seti I. and elsewhere are so evidently mystical and conventional that, apparently, they refer to a serpent-form only as the guilloche on a wall may refer to sea-waves. Apophis (or Apap) would have been a decorative artist to fold himself in such order. These impossible labyrinthine coils suggest Time, as the serpent with its tail in its mouth signifies Eternity,—an evolution of the same idea. This was the interpretation given by a careful scholar, the late William Hickson,[2] to the procession of nine persons depicted on the sarcophagus mentioned as bearing a serpent, each holding a fold, all being regular enough for a frieze. 'The scene,' says this author, 'appears to relate to the Last Judgment, for Osiris is seen on his throne, passing sentence on a crowd before him; and in the same tableaux are depicted the river that divides the living from the dead, and the bridge of life. The death of the serpent may possibly be intended to symbolise the end of time.' This idea of long duration might be a general one relating to all time, or it might refer to the duration of individual life; it involved naturally the evils and agonies of life; but the fundamental conception is more simple, and also more poetic, than even these implications, and it means eternal waste and decay. One has need only to sit before a clock to see Apophis: there coil upon coil winds the ever-moving monster, whose tooth is remorseless, devouring little by little the strength and majesty of man, and reducing his grandest achievements—even his universe—to dust. Time is the undying Worm.

God having made me worm, I make you—smoke.
Though safe your nameless essence from my stroke,
Yet do I gnaw no less
Love in the heart, stars in the livid space,—
God jealous,—making vacant thus your place,—
And steal your witnesses.
Since the star flames, man would be wrong to teach
That the grave's worm cannot such glory reach;
Naught real is save me.
Within the blue, as 'neath the marble slab I lie,
I bite at once the star within the sky,
The apple on the tree.
To gnaw yon star is not more tough to me
Than hanging grapes on vines of Sicily;
I clip the rays that fall;
Eternity yields not to splendours brave.
Fly, ant, all creatures die, and nought can save

The constellations all.
The starry ship, high in the ether sea,
Must split and wreck in the end: this thing shall be:
The broad-ringed Saturn toss
To ruin: Sirius, touched by me, decay,
As the small boat from Ithaca away
*That steers to Kalymnos.*3

The natural history of Apophis, so far as he has any, is probably suggested in the following passage cited by Mr. Cooper from Wilkinson:—'Ælian relates many strange stories of the asp, and the respect paid to it by the Egyptians; but we may suppose that in his sixteen species of asps other snakes were included. He also speaks of a dragon which was sacred in the Egyptian Melite, and another kind of snake called Paries or Paruas, dedicated to Æsculapius. The serpent of Melite had priests and ministers, a table and bowl. It was kept in a tower, and fed by the priests with cakes made of flour and honey, which they placed there in a bowl. Having done this they retired. The next day, on returning to the apartment, the food was found to be eaten, and the same quantity was again put into the bowl, for it was not lawful for any one to see the sacred reptile.'4

It was in this concealment from the outward eye that the Serpent was able to assume such monstrous proportions to the eye of imagination; and, indeed, it is not beyond conjecture that this serpent of Melite, coming in conflict with Osirian worship, was degraded and demonised into that evil monster (Apophis) whom Horus slew to avenge his destruction of Osiris (for he was often identified with Typhon).

Though Horus cursed and slew this terrible demon-serpent, he reappears in all Egyptian Mythology with undiminished strength, and all evil powers were the brood of himself or Typhon, who were sometimes described as brothers and sometimes as the same beings. From the 'Ritual of the Dead' we learn that it was the high privilege and task of the heroic dead to be reconstructed and go forth to encounter and subdue the agents of Apophis, who sent out to engage them the crocodiles Seb, Hem, and Shui, and other crocodiles from north, south, east, and west; the hero having conquered these, acquires their might, and next prevails over the walking viper Ru; and so on with other demons called 'precursors of Apophis,' until their prince himself is encountered and slain, all the hero's guardian deities attending to fix a knife in each of the monster's folds. These are the Vanquishers of Time,—the immortal.

In Apophis we find the Serpent fairly developed to a principle of evil. He is an 'accuser of the sun;' the twelve gateways into Hades are surmounted by his representatives, which the Sun must pass—twelve hours of night. He is at once the 'Nachash beriach' and 'Nachash aktalon'—the 'Cross-bar serpent' and the 'Tortuous serpent'—which we meet with in Isa. xxvii. 1: 'In that day the Lord with his sore and great and strong sword shall punish leviathan the piercing serpent, even leviathan that crooked serpent.' The marginal translation in the English version is 'crossing like a bar,' instead of piercing, and the Vulgate has serpens vectis. This refers to the moral function of the serpent, as barring the way, or guarding the door. No doubt this is the 'crooked serpent' of Job xxvi. 13, for the astrological sense of it does not invalidate the terrestrial significance. Imagination could only project into the heavens what it had learned on earth. Bochart in identifying 'Nachash-beriach' as 'the flying Serpent,' is quite right: the Seraph, or winged Serpent, which barred the way to the tree of life in Eden, and in some traditions was the treacherous guard at the gate of the garden, and which bit Israel in the wilderness, was this same protean Apophis. For such tasks, and to soar into the celestial planisphere, the Serpent must needs have wings; and thus it is already far on its way to become the flying Dragon. But in one form, as the betrayer of man, it must lose its wings and crawl upon the ground for ever. The Serpent is thus not so much agathodemon and kakodemon in one form, as a principle of destructiveness which is sometimes employed by the deity to punish his enemies, as Horus employs fiery Kheti, but sometimes requires to be himself punished.

There have been doubts whether the familiar derivation of ὄφις, serpent, from ὄψ, the eye, shall continue. Some connect the Greek word with ἔχις, but Curtius maintains that the old derivation from ὄψ is correct.5 Even were this not the etymology, the popularity of it would equally suggest the fact that this reptile was of old supposed to kill with its glance; and it was also generally regarded as gifted with præternatural vision. By a similar process to that which developed avenging Furies out of the detective dawn—Erinyes from Saranyu, Satan from Lucifer6—this subtle Spy might have become also a retributive and finally a malignant power. The Furies were portrayed bearing serpents in their hands, and each of these might carry ideally the terrors of Apophis: Time also is a detective, and the guilty heard it saying, 'Your sin will find you out.'

Through many associations of this kind the Serpent became at an early period an agent of ordeal. Any one handling it with impunity was regarded as in league with it, or specially hedged about by the deity whose 'hands formed the crooked serpent.' It may have been as snake-charmers that Moses and Aaron appeared before Pharaoh and influenced his imagination; or, if the story be a myth, its existence still shows that serpent performances would then have been regarded as credentials of divine authentication. So when Paul was shipwrecked on Malta, where a viper is said to have fastened on his hand, the barbarians, having at first inferred that he was a murderer, 'whom though he hath escaped the sea, yet

Vengeance suffereth not to live,' concluded he was a god when they found him unharmed. Innumerable traditions preceded the words ascribed to Christ (Luke x. 19), 'Behold, I give unto you power to tread on serpents and scorpions, and over all the power of the enemy, and nothing shall by any means hurt you.' It is instructive to compare this sentence attributed to Christ with the notion of the barbarians concerning Paul's adventure, whatever it may have been. Paul's familiarity with the Serpent seems to them proof that he is a god. Such also is the idea represented in Isa. xi. 8, 'The sucking child shall play on the hole of the asp.' But the idea of treading on serpents marks a period more nearly corresponding to that of the infant Hercules strangling the serpents. Yet though these two conceptions—serpent-treading, and serpent-slaying—approach each other, they are very different in source and significance, both morally and historically. The word used in Luke, πατεῖν, conveys the idea of walking over something in majesty, not in hostility; it must be interpreted by the next sentence (x. 20), 'Notwithstanding, in this rejoice not, that the spirits are subject unto you (τα πνεύματα ὑποτάσσεται).' The serpent-slayer or dragon-slayer is not of Semitic origin. The awful supremacy of Jehovah held all the powers of destruction chained to his hand; and to ask man if he could draw out Leviathan with a hook was only another form of reminding him of his own inferiority to the creator and lord of Leviathan. How true the Semitic ideas running through the Bible, and especially represented in the legend of Paul in Malta, are to the barbarian nature is illustrated by an incident related in Mr. Brinton's 'Myths of the New World.' The pious founder of the Moravian Brotherhood, Count Zinzendorf, was visiting a missionary station among the Shawnees in the Wyoming Valley, America. Recent quarrels with the white people had so irritated the red men that they resolved to make him their victim. After he had retired to his hut several of the braves softly peered in. Count Zinzendorf was seated before a fire, lost in perusal of the Scriptures; and while the red men gazed they saw what he did not—a huge rattlesnake trailing across his feet to gather itself in a coil before the comfortable warmth of the fire. Immediately they forsook their murderous purpose, and retired noiselessly, convinced that this was indeed a divine man.

Notes

1 See his learned and valuable treatise, 'The Serpent Myths of Ancient Egypt.' Hardwicke, 1873.
2 'Time and Faith,' i. 204. Groombridge, 1857.
3 'The Epic of the Worm,' by Victor Hugo. Translated by Bayard Taylor from 'La Légende des Siècles.'
4 Bruce relates of the Abyssinians that a serpent is commonly kept in their houses to consult for an augury of good or evil. Butter and honey are placed before it, of which if it partake, the omen is good; if the serpent refuse to eat, some misfortune is sure to happen. This custom seems to throw a light on the passage—'Butter and honey shall he eat, that he may know to refuse the evil and choose the good' (Isa. vii. 15).—Time and Faith, i. 60.
Compare the apocryphal tale of Bel and the Dragon. Bel was a healing god of the Babylonians, and the Dragon whom he slew may have been regarded in later times as his familiar
5 'Principles of Greek Etymology,' ii. 63. English translation.
6 See pp. 8 and 20.

Chapter VI - The Serpent in India

The Kankato na—The Vedic Serpents not worshipful—Ananta and Sesha—The Healing Serpent—The guardian of treasures—Miss Buckland's theory—Primitive rationalism—Underworld plutocracy—Rain and lightning—Vritra—History of the word 'Ahi'—The Adder—Zohák—A Teutonic Laokoon.

That Serpent-worship in India was developed by euphemism seems sufficiently shown in the famous Vedic hymn called Kankato na, recited as an antidote against all venom, of which the following is a translation:—

1. Some creature of little venom; some creature of great venom; or some venomous aquatic reptile; creatures of two kinds, both destructive of life, or poisonous, unseen creatures, have anointed me with their poison.
2. The antidote coming to the bitten person destroys the unseen venomous creatures; departing it destroys them; deprived of substance it destroys them by its odour; being ground it pulverises them.
3. Blades of sara grass, of kusara, of darhba, of sairya, of munja, of virana, all the haunt of unseen venomous creatures, have together anointed me with their venom.
4. The cows had lain down in their stalls; the wild beasts had retreated to their lairs; the senses of men were at rest; when the unseen venomous creatures anointed me with their venom.
5. Or they may be discovered in the dark, as thieves in the dusk of evening; for although they be unseen yet all are seen by them; therefore, men be vigilant.

6. Heaven, serpents, is your father; Earth, your mother; Soma, your brother; Aditi, your sister; unseen, all-seeing, abide in your holes; enjoy your own good pleasure.

7. Those who move with their shoulders, those who move with their bodies, those who sting with sharp fangs, those who are virulently venomous; what do ye here, ye unseen, depart together far from us.

8. The all-seeing Sun rises in the East, the destroyer of the unseen, driving away all the unseen venomous creatures, and all evil spirits.

9. The Sun has risen on high, destroying all the many poisons; Aditya, the all-seeing, the destroyer of the unseen, rises for the good of living beings.

10. I deposit the poison in the solar orb, like a leathern bottle in the house of a vendor of spirits; verily that adorable Sun never dies; nor through his favour shall we die of the venom; for, though afar off, yet drawn by his coursers he will overtake the poison: the science of antidotes converted thee, Poison, to ambrosia.

11. That insignificant little bird has swallowed thy venom; she does not die; nor shall we die; for although afar off, yet, drawn by his coursers, the Sun will overtake the poison: the science of antidotes has converted thee, Poison, to ambrosia.

12. May the thrice-seven sparks of Agni consume the influence of the venom; they verily do not perish; nor shall we die; for although afar off, the Sun, drawn by his coursers, will overtake the poison: the science of antidotes has converted thee, Poison, to ambrosia.

13. I recite the names of ninety and nine rivers, the destroyers of poison: although afar off, the Sun, drawn by his coursers, will overtake the poison: the science of antidotes will convert thee, Poison, to ambrosia.

14. May the thrice-seven peahens, the seven-sister rivers, carry off, O Body, thy poison, as maidens with pitchers carry away water.

15. May the insignificant mungoose carry off thy venom, Poison: if not, I will crush the vile creature with a stone: so may the poison depart from my body, and go to distant regions.

16. Hastening forth at the command of Agastya, thus spake the mungoose: The venom of the scorpion is innocuous; Scorpion, thy venom is innocuous.'[1]

Though, in the sixth verse of this hymn, the serpents are said to be born of Heaven and Earth, the context does not warrant the idea that any homage to them is intended; they are associated with the evil Rakshasas, the Sun and Agni being represented as their haters and destroyers. The seven-sister rivers (streams of the sacred Ganges) supply an antidote to their venom, and certain animals, the partridge and the mungoose, are said, though insignificant, to be their superiors. The science of antidotes alluded to is that which Indra taught to Dadhyanch, who lost his head for communicating it to the Aswins. It is notable, however, that in the Vedic period there is nothing which represents the serpent as medicinal, unless by a roundabout process we connect the expression in the Rig-Veda that the wrath of the Maruts, or storm-gods, is 'as the ire of serpents,' with the fact that their chief, Rudra, is celebrated as the bestower of 'healing herbs,' and they themselves solicited for 'medicaments.' This would be stretching the sense of the hymns too far. It is quite possible, however, that at a later day, when serpent-worship was fully developed in India, what is said in the sixth verse of the hymn may have been adduced to confirm the superstition.

It seems clear, then, that at the time the Kankato na was written, the serpent was regarded with simple abhorrence. And we may remember, also, that even now, when the Indian cobra is revered as a Brahman of the highest caste, there is a reminiscence of his previous ill repute preserved in the common Hindu belief that a certain mark on his head was left there by the heel of Vishnu, Lord of Life, who trod on it when, in one of his avatars, he first stepped upon the earth. Although in the later mythology we find Vishnu, in the intervals between his avatars or incarnations, reposing on a serpent (Sesha), this might originally have signified only his lordship over it, though Sesha is also called Ananta, the Infinite. The idea of the Infinite is a late one, however, and the symbolisation of it by Sesha is consistent with a lower significance at first. In Hindu popular fables the snake appears in its simple character. Such is the fable of which so many variants are found, the most familiar in the West being that of Bethgelert, and which is the thirteenth of the 4th Hitopadesa. The Brahman having left his child alone, while he performs a rite to his ancestors, on his return finds a pet mungoose (nakula) smeared with blood. Supposing the mungoose has devoured his child, he slays it, and then discovers that the poor animal had killed a serpent which had crept upon the infant. In the Kankato na the word interpreted by Sáyana as mungoose (Viverra Mungo, or ichneumon) is not the same (nakula), but it evidently means some animal sufficiently unimportant to cast contempt upon the Serpent.

The universality of the Serpent as emblem of the healing art—found as such among the Egyptians, Greeks, Germans, Aztecs, and natives of Brazil—suggests that its longevity and power of casting its old skin, apparently renewing its youth, may have been the basis of this reputation. No doubt, also, they would have been men of scientific tendencies and of close observation who first learned the snake's susceptibilities to music, and how its poison might be drawn, or even its fangs, and who so gained reputation as partakers of its supposed powers. Through such primitive rationalism the Serpent might gain an important alliance and climb to make the asp-crown of Isis as goddess of health (the Thermuthis), to twine round the staff of Esculapius, to be emblem of Hippocrates, and ultimately survive to be the sign of the European leech, twining at last as a red stripe round the barber's pole. The primitive zoologist and snake-charmer would not only, in all likelihood, be a man cunning in the secrets of nature, but he would study to meet as far as he could the popular demand for palliatives and antidotes against snake-bites; all who escaped death after such wounds would increase his credit as a practitioner; and even were his mitigations necessarily few, his knowledge of the Serpent's habits and of its varieties might be the source of valuable precautions.

Such probable facts as these must, of course, be referred to a period long anterior to the poetic serpent-symbolism of Egypt, and the elaborate Serpent mythology of Greece and Scandinavia. How simple ideas, having once gained popular prestige, may be caught up by theologians, poets, metaphysicians, and quacks, and modified into manifold forms, requires no proof in an age when we are witnessing the rationalistic interpretations by which the cross, the sacraments, and the other plain symbols are invested with all manner of philosophical meanings. The Serpent having been adopted as the sign-post of Egyptian and Assyrian doctors—and it may have been something of that kind that was set up by Moses in the wilderness—would naturally become the symbol of life, and after that it would do duty in any capacity whatever.

An ingenious anthropologist, Mr. C. Staniland Wake,2 supposes the Serpent in India to have been there also the symbol of præternatural and occult knowledge. Possibly this may have been so to a limited extent, and in post-Vedic times, but to me the accent of Hindu serpent-mythology appears to be emphatically in the homage paid to it as the guardian of the treasures. I may mention here also the theory propounded by Miss A. W. Buckland in a paper submitted to the Anthropological Institute in London, March 10, 1874, on 'The Serpent in connection with Primitive Metallurgy.' In this learned monograph the writer maintains that a connection may be observed between the early serpent-worship and a knowledge of metals, and indeed that the Serpent was the sign of Turanian metallurgists in the same way as I have suggested that in Egypt and Assyria it was the sign of physicians. She believes that the Serpent must have played some part in the original discovery of the metals and precious stones by man, in recognition of which that animal was first assumed as a totem and thence became an emblem. She states that traditional and ornamentational evidences show that the Turanian races were the first workers in metals, and that they migrated westward, probably from India to Egypt and Chaldæa, and thence to Europe, and even to America, bearing their art and its sign; and that they fled before the Aryans, who had the further art of smelting, and that the Aryan myths of serpent-slaying record the overthrow of the Turanian serpent-worshippers.

I cannot think that Miss Buckland has made out a case for crediting nomadic Turanians with being the original metallurgists; though it is not impossible that it may have been a Scythian tribe in Southern India who gave its fame to 'the gold of Ophir,' which Max Müller has shown to have been probably an Indian region.3 But that these early jewellers may have had the Serpent as their sign or emblem is highly probable, and in explanation of it there seems little reason to resort to the hypothesis of aid having been given by the Serpent to man in his discovery of metals. Surely the jewelled decoration of the serpent would in itself have been an obvious suggestion of it as the emblem of gems. Where a reptile for some reasons associated with the snake—the toad—had not the like bright spots, the cognate superstition might arise that its jewel is concealed in its head. And, finally, when these reptiles had been connected with gems, the eye of either would easily receive added rays from manifold eye-beams of superstition.

We might also credit the primitive people with sufficient logical power to understand why they should infer that an animal so wonderfully and elaborately provided with deadliness as the Serpent should have tasks of corresponding importance. The medicine which healed man (therefore possibly gods), the treasures valued most by men (therefore by anthropomorphic deities), the fruit of immortality (which the gods might wish to monopolise),—might seem the supreme things of value, which the supreme perfection of the serpent's fang might be created to guard. This might be so in the heavens as well as in the world or the underworld. The rainbow was called the 'Celestial Serpent' in Persia, and the old notion that there is a bag of gold at the end of it is known to many an English and American child.

Whatever may have been the nature of the original suggestion, there are definite reasons why, when the Serpent was caught up to be part of combinations representing a Principle of Evil, his character as guardian of treasures should become of great importance. Wealth is the characteristic of the gods of the Hades, or unseen world beneath the surface of the earth.

In the vast Sinhalese demonology we find the highest class of demons (dewatawas) described as resident in golden palaces, glittering with gems, themselves with skins of golden hue, wearing cobras as ornaments, their king, Wessamony seated on a gem-throne and wielding a golden sword. Pluto is from the word for wealth (πλοῦτος), as also is his Latin name Dis (dives). For such are lords of all beneath the sod, or the sea's surface. Therefore, it is important to observe, they own all the seeds in the earth so long as they remain seeds. So soon as they spring to flower, grain, fruitage, they belong not to the gods of Hades but to man: an idea which originated the myth of Persephone, and seems to survive in a school of extreme vegetarians, who refuse to eat vegetables not ripened in the sun.

These considerations may enable us the better to apprehend the earlier characters of Ahi, the Throttler, and Vritra, the Coverer. As guardians of such hidden treasures as metals and drugs the Serpent might be baroneted and invoked to bestow favours; but those particular serpents which by hiding away the cloud-cows withheld the rain, or choked the rivers with drought, all to keep under-world garners fat and those of the upper world lean, were to be combated. Against them man invoked the celestial deities, reminding them that their own altars must lack offerings if they did not vanquish these thievish Binders and Concealers.

The Serpent with its jewelled raiment, its self-renovating power, and its matchless accomplishments for lurking, hiding, fatally striking, was gradually associated with undulations of rivers and sea-waves on the earth, with the Milky-way, with 'coverers' of the sky—night and cloud—above all, with the darting, crooked, fork-tongued lightning. It may have been the lightning that was the Amrita churned out of the azure sea in the myth of the 'Mahábhárata,' when the gods and demons turned the mountain with a huge serpent for cord (p. 59), meaning the descent of fire, or its discovery; but other fair and fruitful things emerged also,—the goddess of wine, the cow of plenty, the tree of heaven. The inhabitants of Burmah still have a custom of pulling at a rope to produce rain. A rain party and a drought party tug against each other, the rain party being allowed the victory, which, in the popular notion is generally followed by rain. I have often seen snakes hung up after being killed to bring rain, in the State of Virginia. For there also rain means wealth. It is there believed also that, however much it may be crushed, a snake will not die entirely until it thunders. These are distant echoes of the Vedic sentences. 'Friend Vishnu,' says Indra, 'stride vastly; sky give room for the thunderbolt to strike; let us slay Vritra and let loose the waters.' 'When, Thunderer, thou didst by thy might slay Vritra, who stopped up the streams, then thy dear steeds grew.'

Vritra, though from the same root as Varuna (the sky), means at first a coverer of the sky—cloud or darkness; hence eventually he becomes the hider, the thief, who steals and conceals the bounties of heaven—a rainless cloud, a suffocating night; and eventually Vritra coalesces with the most fearful phantasm of the Aryan mind—the serpent Ahi. The Greek word for Adder, ἔχις, is a modification of Ahi. Perhaps there exists no more wonderful example of the unconscious idealism of human nature than the history of the name of the great Throttler, as it has been traced by Professor Max Müller. The Serpent was also called ahi in Sanskrit, in Greece echis or echidna, in Latin anguis. The root is ah in Sanskrit, or amh, which means to press together, to choke, to throttle. It is a curious root this amh, and it still lives in several modern words, In Latin it appears as ango, anxi, anctum, to strangle; in angina, quinsy; in angor, suffocation. But angor meant not only quinsy or compression of the neck: it assumed a moral import, and signifies anguish or anxiety. The two adjectives angustus, narrow, and anxius, uneasy, both came from the same root. In Greek the root retained its natural and material meaning; in eggys, near, and echis, serpent, throttler. But in Sanskrit it was chosen with great truth as the proper name of sin. Evil no doubt presented itself under various aspects to the human mind, and its names are many; but none so expressive as those derived from our root amh, to throttle. Amhas in Sanskrit means sin, but it does so only because it meant originally throttling—the consciousness of sin being like the grasp of the assassin on the throat of the victim. All who have seen and contemplated the statue of Laokoon and his sons, with the serpent coiled around them from head to foot, may realise what those ancients felt and saw when they called sin amhas, or the throttler. This amhas is the same as the Greek agos, sin. In Gothic the same root has produced agis, in the sense of fear, and from the same source we have awe, in awful, i.e., fearful, and ug in ugly. The English anguish is from the French angoise, a corruption of the Latin angustitæ, a strait.4 In this wonderful history of a word, whose biography, as Max Müller in his Hibbert Lectures said of Deva, might fill a volume, may also be included our ogre, and also the German unke, which means a 'frog' or 'toad,' but originally a 'snake'—especially the little house-snake which plays a large part in Teutonic folklore, and was supposed to bring good luck.5 This euphemistic variant is, however, the only exception I can find to the baleful branches into which the root ah has grown through the world; one of its fearful fruits being the accompanying figure, copied from one of the ornamental bosses of Wells Cathedral.

The Adder demon has been universal. Herodotus relates that from a monster, half-woman, half-serpent, sprang the Scythians, and the fable has

Fig. 25.—Anguish.

often been remembered in the history of the Turks. The 'Zohák' of Firdusi is the Iranian form of Ahi. The name is the Arabicised form of the 'Azhi Daháka' of the Avesta, the 'baneful serpent' vanquished by Thraêtaono (Traitana of the Vedas), and this Iranian name again (Dásaka) is Ahi. The name reappears in the Median Astyages.6 Zohák is represented as having two serpents growing out of his shoulders, which the late Professor Wilson supposed might have been suggested by a phrase in the Kankato na (ye ansyá ye angyáh) which he translates, 'Those who move with their shoulders, those who move with their bodies,' which, however, may mean 'those produced on the shoulders, biting with them,' and 'might furnish those who seek for analogies between Iranian and Indian legends with a parallel in the story of Zohák.' The legend alluded to is a favourite one in Persia, where it is used to point a moral, as in the instruction of the learned Saib to the Prince, his pupil. Saib related to the boy the story of King Zohák, to whom a magician came, and, breathing on him, caused two serpents to come forth from the region of his breast, and told him they would bring him

122

great glory and pleasure, provided he would feed these serpents with the poorest of his subjects. This Zohák did; and he had great pleasure and wealth until his subjects revolted and shut the King up in a cavern where he became himself a prey to the two serpents. The young Prince to whom this legend was related was filled with horror, and begged Saib to tell him a pleasanter one. The teacher then related that a young Sultan placed his confidence in an artful courtier who filled his mind with false notions of greatness and happiness, and introduced into his heart Pride and Voluptuousness. To those two passions the young Sultan sacrificed the interests of his kingdom, until his subjects banished him; but his Pride and Voluptuousness remained in him, and, unable to gratify them in his exile, he died of rage and despair. The prince-pupil said, 'I like this story better than the other.' 'And yet,' said Saib, 'it is the same.'

It is curious that this old Persian fable should have survived in the witch-lore of America, and at last supplied Nathaniel Hawthorne with the theme of one of his beautiful allegorical romances,—that, namely, of the man with a snake in his bosom which ever threatened to throttle him if he did not feed it. It came to the American fabulist through many a mythical skin, so to say. One of the most beautiful it has worn is a story which is still told by mothers to their children in some districts of Germany. It relates that a little boy and girl went into the fields to gather strawberries. After they had gathered they met an aged woman, who asked for some of the fruit. The little girl emptied her basket into the old woman's lap; but the boy clutched his, and said he wanted his berries for himself. When they had passed on the old woman called them back, and presented to each a little box. The girl opened hers, and found in it two white caterpillars which speedily became butterflies, then grew to be angels with golden wings, and bore her away to Paradise. The boy opened his box, and from it issued two tiny black worms; these swiftly swelled to huge serpents, which, twining all about the boy's limbs, drew him away into the dark forest; where this Teutonic Laokoon still remains to illustrate in his helplessness the mighty power of little faults to grow into bad habits and bind the whole man.

Notes

1 'Rig-veda,' v. (Wilson).
2 In a paper on the 'Origin of Serpent-worship,' read before the Anthropological Institute in London, December 17, 1872.
3 'Science of Language,' i. 230.
4 'Lectures on Language,' i. 435.
5 Grimm's 'Mythology,' p. 650 ff. Simrock, p. 440.
6 Roth, in the 'Journal of the German Oriental Society,' vol. ii. p. 216 ff., has elucidated the whole myth.

Chapter VII - The Basilisk

The Serpent's gem—The Basilisk's eye—Basiliscus mitratus—House-snakes in Russia and Germany—King-snakes—Heraldic dragon—Henry III.—Melusina—The Laidley Worm—Victorious dragons—Pendragon—Merlin and Vortigern—Medicinal dragons.

A Dragoon once presented himself before Frederick the Great and offered the king a small pebble, which, he said, had been cut from the head of a king-snake, and would no doubt preserve the throne. Frederick probably trusted more to dragoons than dragons, but he kept the little curiosity, little knowing, perhaps, that it would be as prolific of legends as the cock's egg, to which it is popularly traceable, in cockatrices (whose name may have given rise to the cock-fables) or basilisks. It has now taken its place in German folklore that Frederick owed his greatness to a familiar kept near him in the form of a basilisk. But there are few parts of the world where similar legends might not spring up and coil round any famous reputation. An Indian newspaper, the Lawrence Gazette, having mentioned that the ex-king of Oudh is a collector of snakes, adds—'Perhaps he wishes to become possessed of the precious jewel which some serpents are said to contain, or of that species of snake by whose means, it is said, a person can fly in the air.' Dr. Dennys, in whose work on Chinese Folklore this is quoted, finds the same notion in China. In one story a foreigner repeatedly tries to purchase a butcher's bench, but the butcher refuses to sell it, suspecting there must be some hidden value in the article; for this reason he puts the bench by, and when the foreigner returns a year afterwards, learns from him that lodged in the bench was a snake, kept alive by the blood soaking through it, which held a precious gem in its mouth—quite worthless after the snake was dead. Cursing his stupidity at having put the bench out of use, the butcher cut it open and found the serpent dead, holding in its mouth something like the eye of a dried fish.

Here we have two items which may only be accidental, and yet, on the other hand, possibly possess significance. The superior knowledge about the serpent attributed to a 'foreigner' may indicate that such stories in China are traditionally alien, imported with the Buddhists; and the comparison of the dead gem to an eye may add a little to the probabilities that this magical jewel, whether in head of toad or serpent, is the reptile's eye as seen by the glamour of human eyes. The eye of the basilisk is at once its wealth-producing, its fascinating, and its paralysing talisman, though all these beliefs have their various sources and their several representations in mythology. That it was seen as a gem was due, as I think, to the jewelled skin of most serpents, which gradually made them symbols of riches; that it was believed able to fascinate may be attributed to the general principles of illusion already considered; but its paralysing power, its evil eye, connects it with a notion, found alike in Egypt and India, that the serpent kills with its eye. Among Sanskrit words for serpent are 'drig-visha' and 'drishti-visha'—literally 'having poison in the eye.'

While all serpents were lords and guardians of wealth, certain of them were crested, or had small horns, which conveyed the idea of a crowned and imperial snake, the βασιλίσκος. Naturalists have recognised this origin of the name by giving the same (Basiliscus mitratus) to a genus of Iguanidæ, remarkable for a membranous crest not only on the occiput but also along the back, which this lizard can raise and depress at pleasure. But folklore, the science of the ignorant, had established the same connection by alleging that the basilisk is hatched from the egg of a black cock,—which was the peasant's explanation of the word cockatrice. De Plancy traces one part of the belief to a disease which causes the cock to produce a small egg-like substance; but the resemblance between its comb and the crests of serpent and frog1 was the probable link between them; while the ancient eminence of the cock as the bird of dawn relegated the origin of the basilisk to a very exceptional member of the family—a black cock in its seventh year. The useful fowl would seem, however, to have suffered even so slightly mainly through a phonetic misconception. The word 'cockatrice' is 'crocodile' transformed. We have it in the Old French 'cocatrix,' which again is from the Spanish 'cocotriz,' meaning 'crocodile,'—κροκοδειλος; which Herodotus, by the way, uses to denote a kind of lizard, and whose sanctity has extended from the Nile to the Danube, where folklore declares that the skeleton of the lizard presents an image of the passion of Christ, and it must never be harmed. Thus 'cockatrice' has nothing to do with 'cock' or 'coq,' though possibly the coincidence of the sound has marred the ancient fame of the 'Bird of Dawn.' Indeed black cocks have been so generally slain on this account that they were for a long time rare, and so the basilisks had a chance of becoming extinct. There were fabulous creatures enough, however, to perpetuate the basilisk's imaginary powers, some of which will be hereafter considered. We may devote the remainder of this chapter to the consideration of a variant of dragon-mythology, which must be cleared out of our way in apprehending the Dragon. This is the agathodemonic or heraldic Dragon, which has inherited the euphemistic characters of the treasure-guarding and crowned serpent.

In Slavonic legend the king-serpent plays a large part, and innumerable stories relate the glories of some peasant child that, managing to secure a tiny gem from his crown, while the reptilian monarch was bathing, found the jewel daily surrounded with new treasures. This is the same serpent which, gathering up the myths of lightning and of comets, flies through many German legends as the red Drake, Kolbuk, Alp, or Alberflecke, dropping gold when it is red, corn if blue, and yielding vast services and powers to those who can magically master it. The harmless serpents of Germany were universally invested with agathodemonic functions, though they still bear the name that relates them to Ahi, viz., unken. Of these household-snakes Grimm and Simrock give much information. It is said that in fields and houses they approach solitary children and drink milk from the dish with them. On their heads they wear golden crowns, which they lay down before drinking, and sometimes forget when they retire. They watch over children in the cradle, and point out to their favourites where treasures are hidden. To kill them brings misfortune. If the parents surprise the snake with the child and kill it, the child wastes away. Once the snake crept into the mouth of a pregnant woman, and when the child was born the snake was found closely coiled around its neck, and could only be untwined by a milk-bath; but it never left the child's side, ate and slept with it, and never did it harm. If such serpents left a house or farm, prosperity went with them. In some regions it is said a male and female snake appear whenever the master or mistress of the house is about to die, and the legends of the Unken sometimes relapse into the original fear out of which they grew. Indeed, their vengeance is everywhere much dreaded, while their gratitude, especially for milk, is as imperishable as might be expected from their ancestor's quarrel with Indra about the stolen cows. In the Gesta Romanorum it is related that a milkmaid was regularly approached at milking-time by a large snake to which she gave milk. The maid having left her place, her successor found on the milking-stool a golden crown, on which was inscribed 'In Gratitude.' The crown was sent to the milkmaid who had gone, but from that time the snake was never seen again.2

In England serpents were mastered by the vows of a saintly Christian. The Knight Bran in the Isle of Wight is said to have picked up the cockatrice egg, to have been pursued by the serpents, which he escaped by vowing to build St. Lawrence Church in that island,—the egg having afterwards brought him endless wealth and uniform success in combat. With the manifold fables concerning the royal dragon would seem to blend traditions of the astrological, celestial, and lightning serpents. But these would coincide with a development arising from the terrestrial worms and their heroic slayers. The demonic dragon with his terrible eye might discern from afar the advent of his predestined destroyer. It might seek to devour him in infancy. As the comet might be deemed a portent of some powerful prince born on earth, so it might be a compliment to a royal family, on the birth of a prince, to report that a dragon had been seen. Nor would it be a long step from this office of the dragon as the herald of greatness to placing that monster on banners. From these banners would grow sagas of dragons encountered and slain. The devices might thus multiply. Some process of this kind would account for the entirely good reputation of the dragon in China and Japan, where it is the emblem of all national grandeur. It would also appear to underlie the proud titles of the Pythian Apollo and Bellerophon, gained from the monsters they were said to have slain. The city of Worms takes its name from the serpent instead of its slayer.3 Pendragon, in the past—and even our dragoon of the present—are names in which the horrors of the monster become transformed in the hero's fame. The dragon, says Mr. Hardwicke, was the standard of the West Saxons, and of the English previous to the Norman Conquest. It formed one of the supporters of the royal arms borne by all the Tudor monarchs, with the exception of Queen Mary, who substituted the eagle. Several of the Plantagenet kings and princes inscribed a figure of the dragon on their banners and shields. Peter Langtoffe says, at the battle of Lewis, fought in 1264, 'The king schewed forth his schild, his dragon full austere.' Another authority says the said king (Henry III.) ordered to be made 'a dragon in the manner of a banner, of a certain red silk embroidered with gold; its tongue like a flaming fire must always seem to be moving; its eyes must be made of sapphire, or of some other stone suitable for that purpose.'4

It will thus be seen that an influence has been introduced into dragon-lore which has no relation whatever to the demon itself. This will explain those variants of the legend of Melusina—the famous woman-serpent—which invest her with romance. Melusina, whose indiscreet husband glanced at her in forbidden hours, when she was in her serpent shape, was long the glory of the Chateau de Lusignan, where her cries announced the approaching death of her descendants. There is a peasant family still dwelling in Fontainebleau Forest who claim to be descended from Melusina; and possibly some instance of this kind may have dropped like a seed into the memory of the author of 'Elsie Venner' to reappear in one of the finest novels of our generation. The corresponding sentiment is found surrounding the dragon in the familiar British legend of the Laidley5 Worm. The king of Northumberland brought home a new Queen, who was also a sorceress, and being envious of the beauty of her step-daughter, changed that poor princess into the worm which devastated all Spindleton Heugh. For seven miles every green thing was blighted by its venom, and seven cows had to yield their daily supplies of milk. Meanwhile the king and his son mourned the disappearance of the princess. The young prince fitted out a ship to go and slay the dragon. The wicked Queen tries unsuccessfully to prevent the expedition. The prince leaps from his ship into the shallow sea, and wades to the rock around which the worm lay coiled. But as he drew near the monster said to him:

Oh, quit thy sword, and bend thy bow,
And give me kisses three;
If I'm not won ere the sun goes down,
Won I shall never be.
He quitted his sword and bent his bow,
He gave her kisses three;
She crept into a hole a worm,
But out stept a ladye.

In the end the prince managed to have the wicked Queen transformed into a toad, which in memory thereof, as every Northumbrian boy knows, spits fire to this day: but it is notable that the sorceress was not transformed into a dragon, as the story would probably have run if the dragon form had not already been detached from its original character, and by many noble associations been rendered an honourable though fearful shape for maidens like this princess and like Melusina.

In the same direction point the legends which show dragons as sometimes victorious over their heroic assailants. Geoffrey of Monmouth so relates of King Morvidus of Northumbria, who encountered a dragon that came from the Irish Sea, and was last seen disappearing in the monster's jaws 'like a small fish.' A more famous instance is that of Beowulf, whose Anglo-Saxon saga is summed up by Professor Morley as follows:—'Afterward the broad land came under the sway of Beowulf. He held it well for fifty winters, until in the dark night a dragon, which in a stone mound watched a hoard of gold and cups, won mastery. It was a hoard heaped up in sin, its lords were long since dead; the last earl before dying hid it in the earth-cave, and for three hundred winters the great scather held the cave, until some man, finding by chance a rich cup, took it to his lord. Then the den was searched while the worm slept; again and again when the dragon awoke there had been theft. He found not the man but wasted the whole land with fire; nightly the fiendish air-flyer made fire grow hateful to the sight of men. Then it was told to Beowulf.... He sought out the dragon's den and fought with him in awful strife. One wound the poison-worm struck in the flesh of Beowulf.' Whereof Beowulf died.

Equally significant is the legend that when King Arthur had embarked at Southampton on his expedition against Rome, about midnight he saw in a dream 'a bear flying in the air, at the noise of which all the shores trembled; also a terrible dragon, flying from the west, which enlightened the country with the brightness of its eyes. When these two met they had a dreadful fight, but the dragon with its fiery breath burned the bear which assaulted him, and threw him down scorched to the earth.' This vision was taken to augur Arthur's victory. The father of Arthur had already in a manner consecrated the symbol, being named Uther Pendragon (dragon's head). On the death of his brother Aurelius, it was told 'there appeared a star of wonderful magnitude and brightness,' darting forth a ray, at the end of which was a globe of fire, in form of a dragon, out of whose mouth issued two rays, one of which seemed to stretch out itself towards the Irish Sea, and ended in seven lesser rays.' Merlin interpreted this phenomenon to mean that Uther would be made king and conquer various regions; and after his first victory Uther had two golden dragons made, one of which he presented to Winchester Cathedral, retaining the other to attend him in his wars.

In the legend of Merlin and Vortigern we find the Dragon so completely developed into a merely warrior-like symbol that its moral character has to be determined by its colour. As in the two armies of serpents seen by Zoroaster, in Persian legends, which fought in the air, the victory of the white over the black foreshowing the triumph of Ormuzd over Ahriman, the tyranny of Vortigern is represented by a red dragon, while Aurelius and Uther are the two heads of a white dragon. Merlin, about to be buried alive, in pursuance of the astrologer's declaration to Vortigern that so only would his ever-falling wall stand firm, had revealed that the recurring disaster was caused by the struggle of these two dragons underground. When the monsters were unearthed they fought terribly, until the white one

Hent the red with all his might,
And to the ground he him cast,
And, with the fire of his blast,
Altogether brent the red,
That never of him was founden shred;
But dust upon the ground he lay.

The white dragon vanished and was seen no more; but the tyrant Vortigern fulfilled the fate of the red dragon, being burnt in his castle near Salisbury. These two dragons met again, however, as red and white roses.

Many developments corresponding to these might be cited. One indeed bears a startling resemblance to our English legends. Of King Nuat Meiamoun, whose conquest of Egypt is placed by G. Maspero about B.C. 664–654, the Ethiopian 'Stele of the Dream' relates:—'His Majesty beheld a dream in the night, two snakes, one to his right, the other to his left, (and) when His Majesty awoke ... he said: 'Explain these things to me on the moment,' and lo! they explained it to him, saying: 'Thou wilt have the Southern lands, and seize the Northern, and the two crowns will be put on thy head, (for) there is given unto thee the earth in all its width and its breadth.' These two snakes were probably suggested by the uræi of the Egyptian diadem.

Beyond the glory reflected upon a monster from his conqueror, there would be reason why the alchemist and the wizard should encourage that aspect of the dragon. The more perilous that Gorgon whose blood Esculapius used, the more costly such medicament; while, that the remedy may be advantageous, the monster must not be wholly destructive. This is so with the now destructive now preservative forces of nature, and how they may blend in the theories, and subserve the interests, of pretenders is well shown in a German work on Alchemy (1625) quoted by Mr. Hardwicke. 'There is a dragon lives in the forest, who has no want of poison; when he sees the sun or fire he spits venom, which flies about fearfully. No living animal can be cured of it; even the basilisk does not equal him. He who can properly kill this serpent has overcome all his danger. His colours increase in death; physic is produced from his poison, which he entirely consumes, and eats his own venomous tail. This must be accomplished by him, in order to produce the noblest balm. Such great virtue as we will point out herein that all the learned shall rejoice.'

It will be readily understood that these traditions and fables would combine to 'hedge about a king' by ascribing to him familiarity with a monster so formidable to common people, and even investing him with its attributes. The dragon's name, δράκων, derived from the Sanskrit word for serpent (dṛig-visha), came to mean 'the thing that sees.' While this gave rise to many legends of præternatural powers of vision gained by tasting or bathing in a dragon's blood, as in the poem of Siegfried; or from waters it guarded, as 'Eye Well,' in which Guy's dragon dipped its tail to recover from wounds; the Sanskrit sense of eye-poisoning was preserved in legends of occult and dangerous powers possessed by kings,—one of the latest being the potent evil eye popularly ascribed in Italy to the late Pius IX. But these stories are endless; the legends adduced will show the sense of all those which, if unexplained, might interfere with our clear insight into the dragon itself, whose further analysis will prove it to be wholly bad,—the concentrated terrors of nature.

Notes

1 *I have in my possession a specimen of the horned frog of America, and it is sufficiently curious.*
2 *Gesta Rom., cap. 68. Grimm's Myth., 650 ff. Simrock, p. 400.*
3 *Others derive the name from the ancient Borbetomagus.*
4 *Traditions, p. 44.*
5 *Loathely.*

Chapter VIII - The Dragon's Eye

The etymologies of the words Dragon and Ophis given in the preceding chapter, ideally the same, both refer to powers of the serpent which it does not possess in nature,—the præternatural vision and the glance that kills. The real nature of the snake is thus overlaid; we have now to deal with the creation of another world.

There are various conventionalised types of the Dragon, but through them all one feature is constant,—the idealised serpent. Its presence is the demonic or supernatural sign. The heroic dragon-slayer must not be supposed to have wrestled with mere flesh and blood, in whatever powerful form. The combat which immortalises him is waged with all the pains and terrors of earth and heaven concentrated and combined in one fearful form.

Impossible and phantasmal as was this form in nature, its mystical meaning in the human mind was terribly real. It was this Eye of anti-human nature which filled man with dismay, and conjured up the typical phantom. It was this Pain, purposed and purposing, the Agony of far-searching vision, subtlest skill, silently creeping, winged, adapted to meet his every device with a cleverer device, which gradually impressed mankind with belief in a general principle of antagonism to human happiness.

It is only as a combination that any dragon form is miraculous. Every constituent feature and factor of it is in nature, but here they are rolled together in one pandemonic expression and terror. Yet no such form loses its relations with nature: it is lightning and tempest, fever-bearing malaria and fire, venom and fang, slime and jungle, all the ferocities of the earth, air, and heavens, gathering to their fatal artistic force, and waylaying man at every step in his advance. In Turner's picture of Apollo slaying the Python there is a marvellous suggestion of the natural conceptions from which the dragon was evolved. The fearful folds of the monster, undulating with mound and rock on which he lies, at points almost blend with tangle of bushes and the jagged chaos amid which he stretches. The hard, wild, cruel aspects of inanimate nature seem here and there rankly swelling to horrible life, as yet but half-distinguishable from the stony-hearted matrix; the crag begins to coil and quiver, the jungle puts forth in claws; but above all appear the monstrous EYES, in which the forces of pain, hardship, obstacle have at last acquired purpose and direction. The god confronts them with eyes yet keener; his arrow, feathered with eyebeams, has reached its mark, straight between the monster's eyes; but there is no more anger in his face than might mar the calm strength of a gardener clearing away the stone and thicket that make the constituent parts of Python.

If we turn now to the neighbouring picture in the National Gallery by the same artist, the Hesperian Gardens and their Guard, we behold the Dragon on his high crag outlining and vitalising not only the edge of rock but also the sky it meets. His breath steams up into cloud. The heavens also have their terrors, which take on eyes and coils. On the line of the horizon were hung the pictures of the primitive art-gallery. Imagination painted them with brush dipped now in blackness of the storm, now in fires of the lightning or the sunset, but the forms were born of experience, of earthly struggle, defeat, and victory.

As I write these words, I lay aside my pen to look across a little lake amid the lonely hills of Wales to a sunset which is flooding the sky with glory. Through the almost greenish sky the wind is bearing fantastic clouds, that sometimes take the shape of chariots, in which cloud-veiled forms are seated, and now great birds with variegated plumage, all hastening as it were to some gathering-place of aerial gods. Beneath a long bar of maroon-tint stretches a sea of yellow light, on the hither side of which is set a garden of fleecy trees touched with golden fruit. Amid them plays a fountain of changing colours. On the left has stood, fast as a mountain range, a mass of dark-blue cloud with uneven peaks; suddenly a pink faint glow shines from behind that leaden mass, and next appears, sinuous with its long indented top, the mighty folds of a fiery serpent. Nay, its head is seen, its yawning lacertine jaws, its tinted crest. It is sleepless Ladon on his high barrier keeping watch and ward over the Hesperian garden.

Juno set him there, but he is the son of Ge,—the earth. The tints of heaven invest and transform, and in a sense create him; but he would never have been born mythologically had it not been that in this world stings hover near all sweetness, danger environs beauty, and, as Plato said, 'Good things come hard.' The grace and lustre of the serpent with his fatal fang preceded him, and all the perils that lurk beneath things fair and fascinating. So far there is nothing essentially moral or unmoral about him. This dragon is a shape designed by primitive meteorology and metaphysics together. Man has asked what is so, and this is the answer: he has not yet asked why it is so, whether it ought to be so, and whether it may not be otherwise. The challenge has not yet been given, the era of combat not yet arrived. The panoplied guard and ally of gods as unmoral as himself has yet to be transformed under the touch of the religious sentiment, and expelled from the heaven of nobler deities as a dragon cast down, deformed, and degraded for ever.

As thought goes on, such allies compromise their employers; the creator's work reflects the creator's character; and after many timorous ages we find the dragon-guarded deities going down with their cruel defenders. It is not without significance that in the Sanskrit dictionary the most ancient of all words for god, Asura, has for its primary meaning 'demon' or 'devil:' the gods and dragons united to churn the ocean for their own wealth, and in the end they were tarred with one brush. I have already described in the beginning of this work the degradation of deities, and need here barely recall to the reader's memory the forces which operated to that result. The bearing of that force upon the celestial or paradise-guarding Serpent is summed up in one quatrain of Omar Khayyám:—

O Thou who man of baser earth didst make,
And e'en in Paradise devised the Snake;
For all the sin wherewith the face of man
Is blackened, man's forgiveness give—and take!

The heart of humanity anticipated its logic by many ages, and, long before the daring genius of the Persian poet wrote this immortal epitaph on the divine allies of the Serpent, heroes had given battle to the whole fraternity. Nay, in their place had arisen a new race of gods, whose theoretical omnipotence was gladly surrendered in the interest of their righteousness; and there was now war in heaven; the dragon and his allies were cast down, and man was now free to fight them as enemies of the gods as well as himself. Woe henceforth to any gods suspected of taking sides with the dragon in this man's life-and-death struggle with the ferocities of nature, and with his own terrors reflected from them! The legend of Prometheus was their unconsciously-given 'notice to quit,' though it waited many centuries for its great interpreter. It is Goethe who alone has seen how pale and weak grow Jove's fireworks before the thought-thunderbolts of the artist, launched far beyond the limitations that chain him in nature. Gods are even yet going down in many lands before the sublime sentence of Prometheus:—

Curtain thy heavens, thou Jove, with clouds and mist,
And, like a boy that moweth thistles down,
Unloose thy spleen on oaks and mountain-tops;
Yet canst thou not deprive me of my earth,
Nor of my hut, the which thou didst not build,
Nor of my hearth, whose little cheerful flame
Thou enviest me!
I know not aught within the universe
More slight, more pitiful than you, ye gods!
Who nurse your majesty with scant supplies
Of offerings wrung from fear, and muttered prayers,
And needs must starve, were't not that babes and beggars
Are hope-besotted fools!
When I was yet a child, and knew not whence
My being came, nor where to turn its powers,
Up to the sun I bent my wildered eye,
As though above, within its glorious orb,
There dwelt an ear to listen to my plaint,
A heart, like mine, to pity the oppressed.
Who gave me succour
Against the Titans in their tyrannous might?
Who rescued me from death—from slavery?
Thou!—thou, my soul, burning with hallowed fire,
Thou hast thyself alone achieved it all!
Yet didst thou, in thy young simplicity,
Glow with misguided thankfulness to him
That slumbers on in idlenesse there above!
I reverence thee?
Wherefore? Hast thou ever
Lightened the sorrows of the heavy laden?
Thou ever stretch thy hand to still the tears
Of the perplexed in spirit?
Was it not
Almighty Time, and ever-during Fate—
My lords and thine—that shaped and fashioned me
Into the MAN I am?

Belike it was thy dream
That I should hate life—fly to wastes and wilds,
For that the buds of visionary thought
Did not all ripen into goodly flowers?
Here do I sit and mould
Men after mine own image—
A race that may be like unto myself,
To suffer, weep; to enjoy, and to rejoice;
And, like myself, unheeding all of thee!

The myth of Prometheus reveals the very dam of all dragons,—the mere terrorism of nature which paralysed the energies of man. Man's first combat was to be with his own quailing heart. Apollo driving back the Argives to their ships with the image of the Gorgon's head on Jove's shield is Homer's picture of the fears that unnerved heroes:—

Phœbus himself the rushing battle led;
A veil of clouds involved his radiant head:
High held before him, Jove's enormous shield
Portentous shone, and shaded all the field:
Vulcan to Jove th' immortal gift consigned,
To scatter hosts, and terrify mankind....
Deep horror seizes ev'ry Grecian breast,
Their force is humbled, and their fear confest.
So flies a herd of oxen, scattered wide,
No swain to guard them, and no day to guide,
When two fell lions from the mountain come,
And spread the carnage thro' the shady gloom....
The Grecians gaze around with wild despair,
Confused, and weary all their pow'rs with prayer.[1]

A generation whose fathers remembered the time when men educated in universities regarded Franklin with his lightning-rod as 'heaven-defying,' can readily understand the legend of Vulcan—type of the untamed force of fire—being sent to bind Prometheus, master of fire.[2] How much fear of the forces of nature, as personified by superstition, levelled against the first creative minds and hands the epithets which Franklin heard, and which still fall upon the heads of some scientific investigators! Storm, lightning, rock, ocean, vulture,—these blend together with the intelligent cruelty of Jove in the end; and behold, the Dragon! The terrors of nature, which drive cowards to their knees, raise heroes to their height. Then it is a flame of genius matched against mad thunderbolts. Whether the jealous nature-god be Jehovah forbidding sculpture, demanding an altar of unhewn stone, and refusing the fruits of Cain's garden, or Zeus jealous of the artificer's flame, they are thrown into the Opposition by the artist; and when the two next meet, he of the thunderbolt with all his mob will be the Dragon, and Prometheus will be the god, sending to its heart his arrow of light.

Fig. 26.—Swan-Dragon (French).

The dragon forms which have become familiar to us through mediæval and modern iconography are of comparatively little importance as illustrating the social or spiritual conditions out of which they grew, and

129

of which they became emblems. They long ago ceased to be descriptive, and in the rude periods or places a very few scratches were sometimes enough to indicate the dragon; such mere suggestions in the end allowing large freedom to subsequent designers in varying original types.

As to external form, the various shapes of the more primitive dragons have been largely determined by the mythologic currents amid which they have fallen, though their original basis in nature may generally be traced. In the far North, where the legends of swan-maidens, pigeon-maidens, and vampyres were paramount in the Middle Ages, we find the bird-shaped dragon very common. Sometimes the serpent-characteristics are pronounced, as in this ancient French Swan-Dragon (Fig. 26); but, again, and especially in regions where serpents are rare and comparatively innocuous, the serpent tail is often conventionalised away, as in this initial V from the Cædmon Manuscript, tenth century (Fig. 27), a fair example of the ornamental Anglo-Saxon dragon. The cuttlefish seems to have suggested the animalised form of the Hydra, which in turn helped to shape the Dragon of the Apocalypse. Yet the Hydra in pictorial representation appears to have been influenced by Assyrian ideas; for although the monster had nine heads, it is often given seven (number of the Hathors, or Fates) by the engravers, as in Fig. 6. The conflicts of Hercules with the Hydra repeated that of Bel with Tiamat ('the Deep'), and had no doubt its counterpart in that of Michael with the Dragon,—the finest representation of which, perhaps, is the great fresco by Spinello (fourteenth century) at Arezzo, a group from which is presented in Fig. 28.

Fig. 27—Anglo-Saxon Dragons (Cædmon M.S., tenth century).

Fig. 28.—From the Fresco at Arezzo.

In this case the wings represent those always attributed in Semitic mythology to the Destroying Angel. The Egyptian Dragon, of which the crocodile is the basis, at an early period entered into christian symbolism, and gradually effaced most of the pagan monsters. The crocodile and the alligator, besides being susceptible of many horrible variations in pictorial treatment, were particularly acceptable to the Christian propaganda, because of the sanctity attached to them by African tribes,—a sanctity which continues to this day in many parts of that country, where to kill one of these reptiles is believed to superinduce dangerous inundations. In Semitic traditions, also, Leviathan was generally identified as a demonic crocodile, and the feat of destroying him was calculated to impress the imaginations of all varieties of people in the Southern countries for which Christianity struggled so long. This form contributed some of its characters to the lacertine dragons which were so often painted in the Middle Ages, with what effect may be gathered from the accompanying design by Albert Durer (Fig. 29). In this loathsome creature, which seeks to prevent deliverance of 'the spirits in prison,' we may remark the sly and cruel eye: the præternatural vision of such monsters was still strong in the traditions of the sixteenth century. In looking at this lizard-guard at the mouth of hell we may realise that it has been by some principle of psychological selection that the reptilian kingdom gradually gained supremacy in these portrayals of the repulsive. If we compare with Fig. 29 the well-known form of the Chimæra (Fig. 30), most of us will be conscious of a sense of relief; for though the reptilian form is present in the latter, it is but an appendage—almost an ornament—to the lion. It is impossible to feel any loathing towards this spirited Trisomatos, and one may recognise in it a different animus from that which depicted the christian dragon. One was meant to attest the boldness of the hero who dared to assail it; the other was meant, in addition to that, to excite hatred and horror of the monster assailed. We may, therefore, find a very distinct line drawn between such forms as the Chimæra and such as the Hydra, or our conventional Dragon. The hairy inhabitants of Lycia, human or bestial, whom Bellerophon conquered,3 were not meant to be such an abstract expression of the evil principle in nature as the Dragon, and while they are generalised, the elements included are also limited. But the Dragon, with its claws, wings, scales, barbed and coiling tail, its fiery breath, forked tongue, and frequent horns, includes the organic, inorganic, the terrestrial and atmospheric, and is the combination of harmful contrivances in nature.

Fig. 29.—From Albert Durer's 'Passion.'

Nearly all of the Dragon forms, whatever their original types and their region, are represented in the conventional monster of the European stage, which meets the popular conception. This Dragon is a masterpiece of the popular imagination, and it required many generations to give it artistic shape. Every Christmas he appears in some London pantomime, with aspect similar to that which he has worn for many ages. His body is partly green, with memories of the sea and of slime, and partly brown or dark, with lingering shadow of storm-clouds. The lightning flames still in his red eyes, and flashes from his fire-breathing mouth. The thunderbolt of Jove, the spear of Wodan, are in the barbed point of his tail. His huge wings—batlike, spiked—sum up all the mythical life of extinct Harpies and Vampyres. Spine of crocodile is on his neck, tail of the serpent, and all the jagged ridges of rocks and sharp thorns of jungles bristle around him, while the ice of glaciers and brassy glitter of sunstrokes are in his scales. He is ideal of all that is hard, obstructive, perilous, loathsome, horrible in nature: every detail of him has been seen through and vanquished by man, here or there, but in selection and combination they rise again as principles, and conspire to form one great generalisation of the forms of Pain—the sum of every creature's worst.

Fig. 30.—Chimæra.

Notes

1 Pope's 'Homer,' Book xv.
2 See p. 59.
3 See p. 154.

Chapter IX - The Combat

The pre-Munchausenite world—The Colonial Dragon—Io's journey—Medusa—British Dragons—The Communal Dragon—Savage Saviours—A Mimac helper—The Brutal Dragon—Woman protected—The Saint of the Mikados.

The realm of the Unknown has now, by exploration of our planet and by science, been pretty well pressed into annexation with the Unknowable. In early periods, however, unexplored lands and seas existed only in the human imagination, and men appear to have included them within the laws of analogy as slowly as their descendants so included the planets. The monstrous forms with which superstition now peoples regions of space that cannot be visited could then dwell securely in parts of the world where their existence or non-existence could not be verified. Science had not yet shown the simplicity and unity underlying the superficial varieties of nature; and though Rudolf Raspe appeared many times, and related the adventures of his Baron Munchausen in many languages, it was only a hundred years ago that he managed to raise a laugh over them. It has taken nearly another hundred to reveal the humour of Munchausenisms that relate to invisible and future worlds.

The Dragon which now haunts the imagination of a few compulsory voyagers beyond the grave originated in speculations concerning the unseen shores of equally mythical realms, whose burning zones and frozen seas had not yet been detached from this planet to make the Inferno of another. In our section on Demonology we have considered many of these imaginary forms in detail, limiting ourselves generally to the more realistic embodiments of special obstacles. Just above that formation comes the stratum in which we find the separate features of the previous demonic fauna combining to forms which indicate the new creative power which, as we have seen, makes nature over again in its own image. Beginning thus on the physical plane, with a view of passing to the social, political, and metaphysical arenas where man has successively met his Dragons, we may first consider the combination of terrors and perils, real and imaginary, which were confronted by the early colonist. I will venture to call this the Colonial Dragon.

This form may be represented by any of those forms against which the Prometheus of Æschylus cautions Io on her way to the realm which should be called Ionia. 'When thou shalt have crossed the stream that bounds the continents to the rosy realms of the morning where the sun sets forth, ... thou shalt reach beyond the roaring sea Cisthene's Gorgonian plains, where dwell the Phorkides, ... and hard by are their three winged sisters, the Snake-haired Gorgons, by mortals abhorred, on whom none of human race can look and live.... Be on thy guard against the Gryphons, sharp-fanged hounds of Jove that

never bark, and against the cavalry host of one-eyed Arimaspians, dwelling on the gold-gushing fount, the stream of Pluto. Thou wilt reach a distant land, a dark tribe, near to the fount of the sun, where runs the river Æthiops.'1

One who has looked upon Leonardo da Vinci's Medusa at Florence—one of the finest interpretations of a mythologic subject ever painted—may comprehend what to the early explorer and colonist were the fascinations of those rumoured regions where nature was fair but girt round with terrors. The Gorgon's head alone is given, with its fearful tangle of serpent tresses; her face, even in its pain, possesses the beauty that may veil a fatal power; from her mouth is exhaled a vapour which in its outline has brought into life vampyre, newt, toad, and loathsome nondescript creatures. Here is the malaria of undrained coasts, the vermin of noxious nature. The source of these must be destroyed before man can found his city; it is the fiery poisonous breath of the Colonial Dragon.

Most of the Dragon-myths of Great Britain appear to have been importations of the Colonial monsters. Perhaps the most famous of these in all Europe was the Chimæra, which came westward upon coins, Bellerophon having become a national hero at Corinth—almost superseding the god of war himself—and his

Fig. 31.—Bellerophon and Chimæra (Corinthian).

effigy spread with many migrations. Our conventional figure of St. George is still Bellerophon, though the Dragon has been substituted for Chimæra,—a change which christian tradition and national respect for the lion rendered necessary (Fig. 31). Corresponding to this change in outward representation, the monster-myths of Great Britain have been gradually pressed into service as moral and religious lessons. The Lambton Worm illustrates the duty of attending mass and sanctity of the sabbath; the demon serpents of Ireland and Cornwall prove the potency of holy exorcism; and this process of moralisation has extended, in the case of the Boar, whose head graces the Christmas table at Queen's College, Oxford, to an illustration of the value of Aristotelian philosophy. It was with a volume of Aristotle that the monster was slain, the mythologic affinities of the legend being quaintly preserved in the item that it was thrust down the boar's throat.

But these modifications are very transparent, the British legends being mainly variants of one or two original myths which appear to have grown out of the heraldic devices imported by ancient families. These probably acquired realistic statement through the prowess and energy of chieftains, and were exaggerated by their descendants, perhaps also connected with some benefit to the community, in order to strengthen the family tenure of its estates. For this kind of duty the Colonial Dragon was the one usually imported by the family romancer or poet. The multiplication of these fables is, indeed, sufficiently curious. It looks as if there were some primitive agrarian sentiment which had to be encountered by aid of appeals to exceptional warrant. The family which could trace its title to an estate to an ancestor who rescued the whole district, was careful to preserve some memorial of the feat. On account of the interests concerned in old times we should be guarded in receiving the rationalised interpretations of such myths, which have become traditional in some localities. The barbaric achievements of knights did not lose in the ballads of minstrels any marvellous splendours, but gained many; and most of these came from the south and east. The Dragon which Guy of Warwick slew still retained traces of Chimæra; it had 'paws as a lion.' Sir William Dugdale thought that this was a romanticised version of a real combat which Guy fought with a Danish chief, A.C. 926. Similarly the Dragon of Wantley has been reduced to a fraudulent barrister.

The most characteristic of this class of legends is that of Sockburn. Soon after the Norman conquest the Conyers family received that manor by episcopal grant, the tradition being that it was because Sir John Conyers, Knight, slew a huge Worm which had devoured many people. The falchion with which this feat was achieved is still preserved, and I believe it is still the custom, when a new bishop visits that diocese, for the lord of Sockburn to present this sword. The lord of the manor meets the bishop in the middle of the river Tees, and says:—'My Lord Bishop, I here present you with the falchion wherewith the Champion Conyers slew the Worm, Dragon, or fiery flying Serpent, which destroyed man, woman, and child, in memory of which the king then reigning gave him the manor of Sockburn to hold by this tenure,—that upon the first entrance of every bishop into the country this falchion should be presented.' The bishop returns the sword and wishes the lord long enjoyment of the tenure, which has been thus held since the year 1396. The family tradition is that the Dragon was a Scotch intruder named Comyn, whom Conyers compelled to kneel before the episcopal throne. The Conyers family of Sockburn seem to have been at last overtaken by a Dragon which was too much for them: the last knight was taken from a workhouse barely in time not to die there.

In the 'Memoirs of the Somervilles' we read that one of that family acquired a parish by slaying a 'hydeous monster in forme of a worme.'2

The wode Laird of Laristone
Slew the Worme of Worme's Glen,
And wan all Linton parochine.

It was 'in lenth 3 Scots yards, and somewhat bigger than an ordinary man's leg, with a hede more proportionable to its lenth than its greatness; its forme and collour (like) to our common muir adders.'

This was a very moderate dragon compared with others, by slaying which many knights won their spurs: this, for example, which Sir Dygore killed in the fourteenth century—

———A Dragon great and grymme,
Full of fyre, and also of venymme:
With a wide throte and tuskes grete,
Uppon that knight fast gan he bete;
And as a Lionn then was his fete,
His tayle was long and ful unmete;
Between his hede and his tayle
Was xxii. fote withouten fayle;
His body was like a wine tonne,
He shone full bright ageynst the sunne;
His eyes were bright as any glasse,
His scales were hard as any brasse.

The familiar story of St. Patrick clearing the snakes out of Ireland, and the Cornish version of it, in which the exorcist is St. Petrox, presents some features which relate it to the colonist's combat with his dragon, though it is more interesting in other aspects. The Colonial Dragon includes the diseases, the wild beasts, the savages, and all manner of obstructions which environ a new country. But when these difficulties have been surmounted, the young settlement has still its foes to contend with,—war-like invaders from without, ambitious members within. We then find the Dragon taking on the form of a public enemy, and his alleged slayer is representative of the commune,—possibly in the end to transmit its more real devourer. Most of the British Dragon-myths have expanded beyond the stage in which they represent merely the struggles of immigrants with wild nature, and include the further stage where they represent the formation of the community. The growth of patriotism at length is measured by its shadow. The Colonial is transformed to the Communal Dragon. Many Dragon-myths are adaptations of the ancient symbolism to hostes communes: such are the monsters described as desolating villages and districts, until they are encountered by antagonists animated by public spirit. Such antagonists are distinguishable from the heroes that go forth to rescue the maiden in distress: their chief representative in mythology is Herakles, most of whose labours reveal the man of self-devotion redressing public wrongs, and raising the standard of humanity as well as civilisation.

The age of chivalry has its legend in the Centaurs and Cheiron. The Hippo-centaurs are mounted savages: Cheiron is the true knight, withstanding monsters in his own shape, saving Peleus from them, and giving hospitality to the Argonauts. The mounted man was dragon to the man on foot until he became the chevalier; then the demonic character passed to the strategist who had no horse. It is curious enough to find existing among the Mormons a murderous order calling themselves Danites, or Destroying Angels, after the text of Gen. xlix. 17, 'Dan shall be a serpent by the way, an adder in the path, that biteth the horse's heel that his rider shall fall backward.' The Ritter, however, so far as his Dragon was concerned, was as one winged, and every horse a Pegasus when it bore him to decide the day between the adder and its victim. It is remarkable that the Mormons should have carried from the East a cruel superstition to find even among the Red Men, who are disappearing before the western march of Saxon strength, more gentle fables.

Among the Mimacs, the aborigines of Nova Scotia, there is a legend of a young hero named Keekwajoo, who, in seeking for a wife, is befriended by a good sage named Glooscap, who warns him against a powerful magician disguised as a beaver, and two demon sisters, who will waylay him in the disguise of large weasels. The youth is admonished to beat a certain drum as his canoe passes them, and he is saved as Orpheus in passing Cerberus and Ulysses in sailing past the Syrens. The weasels, hearing the music, aspire to wed the stars, but find themselves in an indescribable nest at the top of a tall white pine.3

The chevalier encounters also the Brutal Dragon, whose victim is Woman. From immemorial time man's captive, unable to hold her own against brute force, she is at the mercy of all who are insensible to the refined and passive powers. The rock-bound Andromeda, the pursued Leto, or whatever fair maid it may be that the Dragon-slayer rescues, may have begun mythologically as emblem of the Dawn, whose swallower is the Night Cloud; but in the end she symbolises a brighter dawn,—that of civility and magnanimity among men.

It is a notable fact that far away in Japan we should find a Dragon-myth which would appear to represent, with rare beauty, the social evolution we have been considering. Their great mythological Serpent, Yamati-no-orochi, that is, the serpent of eight heads and tails, stretching over eight valleys, would pretty certainly represent a river annually overflowing its banks. One is reminded by this monster of the accounts given by Mencius of the difficulties with streams which the Chinese had to surmount before they could make the Middle States habitable. But this Colonial Dragon, in the further evolution of the country, reappears as the Brutal Dragon. The admirable legend relates that, while the rest of the world were using stone implements, there came into the possession of Sosano-o-no-Mikoto (the Prince of Sosano) a piece of iron which was wrought into a sword. That maiden-sword of the world was fleshed to save a maiden from the jaws of a monster. The prince descended from heaven to a bank of the river Hino Kawa, and the country around seemed uninhabited; but presently he saw a chopped stick floating down the stream, and concluded that there must be beings dwelling farther up; so he travelled until he came to a spot where he beheld an aged man and his wife (Asinaduti and Tenaduti), with their beautiful daughter, Himé of Inada. The three were weeping bitterly, and the prince was informed that Himé was the last of their daughters, seven of whom had been devoured by a terrible serpent. This serpent had eight heads, and the condition on which it had ceased to desolate the district was that one of these eight maidens should be brought annually to this spot to satisfy his voracity. The last had now been brought to complete the dreadful compact. The Japanese are careful to distinguish this serpent from a dragon, with them an agathodemon. It had no feet, and its heads branched by as many necks from a single body, this body being so large that it stretched over eight valleys. It was covered with trees and moss, and its belly was red as blood. The prince doubted if even with his sword he could encounter such a monster, so he resorted to stratagem; he obtained eight vast bowls, filled them with eight different kinds of wine, and, having built a fence with the same number of openings, set a bowl in each. The result may be imagined: the eight heads in passing over the bowls paused, drank deep, and were soon in a state of beastly intoxication. In this condition the heads were severed from their neck, and the maiden saved to wed the first Mikado Prince.

Notes

1 *Æsch. Prom. 790, etc.*
2 *Vol. i. p. 38.*
3 *'North American Review,' January 1871.*

Chapter X - The Dragon-slayer

Demigods—Alcestis—Herakles—The Ghilghit Fiend—Incarnate deliverer of Ghilghit—A Dardistan Madonna—The religion of Atheism—Resuscitation of Dragons—St. George and his Dragon—Emerson and Ruskin on George—Saintly allies of the Dragon.

Theology has pronounced Incarnation a mystery, but nothing is simpler. The demigod is man's appeal from the gods. It may also be, as Emerson says, that 'when the half-gods go the gods arrive,' but it is equally true that their coming signals the departure of deities which man had long invoked in vain. The great Heraklean myth presents us the ideal of godlike force united to human sympathy. Ra (the Sun) passing the twelve gates (Hours) of Hades (Night)1 is humanised in Herakles and his Twelve Labours. He is Son of Zeus by a human mother—Alcmene—and his labours for human welfare, as well as his miraculous conception, influenced Christianity. The divine Man assailing the monsters of divine creation represents human recognition of the fact that moral order in nature is co-extensive with the control of mankind.

One expression of this perception is the Alcestis of Euripides, whose significance in relation to death we have considered.[2]

'Alcestis,' as I have written in another work, 'is one of the few ancient Greek melodramas. The majority of dramas left us by the poets of Greece turn upon religious themes, and usually they are tragedies. It is evident that to them the popular religion around them was itself a tragedy. Their heroes and heroines—such as Prometheus and Macaria—were generally victims of the jealousy or caprice of the gods; and though the poets display in their dramas the irresistible power of the gods, they do so without reverence for that power, and generally show the human victims to be more honourable than the gods. But the 'Alcestis' of Euripides is not a tragedy; it ends happily, and in the rescue of one of those victims of the gods. It stands as about the first notice served on the gods that the human heart had got tired of their high-handed proceedings, and they might prepare to quit the thrones of a universe unless they could exhibit more humanity.... Knowing that neither he nor any other deity can legally resist the decree of another deity, Apollo is reduced to hope for help from man. Human justice may save when divine justice sacrifices. He prophesies to Death that although he may seize Alcestis, a man will come who will conquer him, and deliver that woman from the infernal realm.... Then Hercules comes on the scene. He has been slaying lion and dragon, and he now resolves to conquer Death and deliver Alcestis. This he does.'[3]

In this pre-christian yet christian Passion Play, the part played by the heart of woman is equally heroic with that which represents the honour of man. So in the religion which followed there was an effort to set beside the incarnate vanquisher of infernal powers the pierced heart of Mary. But among all the legends of this character it were difficult to find one more impressive than that which Dr. Leitner found in Dardistan, and one which, despite its length, will repay a careful perusal. This legend of the origin of the Ghilghit tribe and government was told by a native.

'Once upon a time there lived a race at Ghilghit whose origin is uncertain. Whether they sprung from the soil or had immigrated from a distant region is doubtful; so much is believed that they were Gayupí, i.e., spontaneous, aborigines, unknown. Over them ruled a monarch who was a descendant of the evil spirits, the Yatsh, who terrorised over the world. His name was Shiribadatt, and he resided at a castle in front of which was a course for the performance of the manly game of Polo. His tastes were capricious, and in every one of his actions his fiendish origin could be discerned. The natives bore his rule with resignation, for what could they effect against a monarch at whose command even magic aids were placed? However, the country was rendered fertile, and round the capital bloomed attractive. The heavens, or rather the virtuous Peris, at last grew tired of his tyranny, for he had crowned his iniquities by indulging in a propensity for cannibalism. This taste had been developed by an accident. One day his cook brought him some mutton broth the like of which he had never tasted. After much inquiry as to the nature of the food on which the sheep had been brought up, it was eventually traced to an old woman, its first owner. She stated that her child and the sheep were born on the same day, and losing the former, she had consoled herself by suckling the latter. This was a revelation to the tyrant. He had discovered the secret of the palatability of the broth, and was determined to have a never-ending supply of it. So he ordered that his kitchen should be regularly provided with children of a tender age, whose flesh, when converted into broth, would remind him of the exquisite dish he had once so much relished. This cruel order was carried out. The people of the country were dismayed at such a state of things, and sought slightly to improve it by sacrificing, in the first place, all orphans and children of neighbouring tribes. The tyrant, however, was insatiable, and soon was his cruelty felt by many families at Ghilghit, who were compelled to give up their children to slaughter.

'Relief came at last. At the top of the mountain Ko, which it takes a day to ascend, and which overlooks the village of Doyur, below Ghilghit, on the other side of the river, appeared three figures. They looked like men, but much more strong and handsome. In their arms they carried bows and arrows, and turning their eyes in the direction of Doyur, they perceived innumerable flocks of sheep and cattle grazing on a prairie between that village and the foot of the mountain. The three strangers were brothers, and none of them had been born at the same time. It was their intention to make Azru Shemsher, the youngest, Rajah of Ghilghit, and, in order to achieve their purpose, they hit upon the following plan. On the already noticed prairie, which is called Didingé, a sportive calf was gambolling towards and away from its mother. It was the pride of its owner, and its brilliant red colour could be seen from a distance. 'Let us see who is the best marksman,' exclaimed the eldest, and, saying this, he shot an arrow in the direction of the calf, but missed his aim. The second brother also tried to hit it, but also failed. At last, Azru Shemsher, who took a deep interest in the sport, shot his arrow, which pierced the poor animal from side to side and killed it. The brothers, whilst descending, congratulated Azru on his sportsmanship, and on arriving at the spot where the calf was lying, proceeded to cut its throat and to take out from its body the titbits, namely, the kidneys and the liver.

'They then roasted these delicacies, and invited Azru to partake of them first. He respectfully declined, on the ground of his youth, but they urged him to do so, 'in order,' they said, 'to reward you for such an excellent shot.' Scarcely had the meat touched the lips of Azru than the brothers got up, and, vanishing into the air, called out, 'Brother! you have touched impure food, which Peris never should eat, and we have made use of your ignorance of this law, because we want to make you a human being[4] who shall rule over Ghilghit; remain, therefore, at Doyur.' Azru, in deep grief at the separation, cried, 'Why remain at Doyur, unless it be to grind corn?' 'Then,' said the brothers, 'go to Ghilghit.' 'Why,' was the reply, 'go to

135

Ghilghit, unless it be to work in the gardens?' 'No, no,' was the last and consoling rejoinder; 'you will assuredly become the king of this country, and deliver it from its merciless oppressor!' No more was heard of the departing fairies, and Azru remained by himself, endeavouring to gather consolation from the great mission which had been bestowed on him. A villager met him, and, struck by his appearance, offered him shelter in his house. Next morning he went on the roof of his host's house, and calling out to him to come up, pointed to the Ko mountain, on which, he said, he plainly discerned a wild goat. The incredulous villager began to fear he had harboured a maniac, if no worse character; but Azru shot off his arrow, and, accompanied by the villager (who had assembled some friends for protection, as he was afraid his young guest might be an associate of robbers, and lead him into a trap), went in the direction of the mountain. There, to be sure, at the very spot that was pointed out, though many miles distant, was lying the wild goat, with Azru's arrow transfixing its body. The astonished peasants at once hailed him as their leader, but he exacted an oath of secrecy from them, for he had come to deliver them from their tyrant, and would keep his incognito till such time as his plans for the destruction of the monster would be matured.

'He then took leave of the hospitable people of Doyur, and went to Ghilghit. On reaching this place, which is scarcely four miles distant from Doyur, he amused himself by prowling about in the gardens adjoining the royal residence. There he met one of the female companions of Shiribadatt's daughter fetching water for the princess. This lady was remarkably handsome, and of a sweet disposition. The companion rushed back, and told the young lady to look from over the ramparts of the castle at a wonderfully handsome young man whom she had just met. The princess placed herself in a place from which she could observe any one approaching the fort. Her maid then returned, and induced Azru to come with her in the Polo ground, in front of the castle; the princess was smitten with his beauty, and at once fell in love with him. She then sent word to the young prince to come and see her. When he was admitted into her presence he for a long time denied being anything more than a common labourer. At last he confessed to being a fairy's child, and the overjoyed princess offered him her heart and hand. It may be mentioned here that the tyrant Shiribadatt had a wonderful horse, which could cross a mile at every jump, and which its rider had accustomed to jump both into and out of the fort, over its walls. So regular were the leaps which this famous animal could take that he invariably alighted at the distance of a mile from the fort, and at the same place. On that very day on which the princess had admitted young Azru into the fort King Shiribadatt was out hunting, of which he was desperately fond, and to which he used sometimes to devote a week or two at a time.

'We must now return to Azru, whom we left conversing with the princess. Azru remained silent when the lady confessed her love. Urged to declare his sentiments, he said that he would not marry her unless she bound herself to him by the most stringent oath; this she did, and they became in the sight of God as if they were wedded man and wife. He then announced that he had come to destroy her father, and asked her to kill him herself. This she refused; but as she had sworn to aid him in every way she could, he finally induced her to promise that she would ask her father where his soul was. 'Refuse food,' said Azru, 'for three or four days, and your father, who is devotedly fond of you, will ask for the reason of your strange conduct; then say, 'Father, you are often staying away from me for several days at a time, and I am getting distressed lest something should happen to you; do reassure me by letting me know where your soul is, and let me feel certain that your life is safe.' This the princess promised to do, and when her father returned refused food for several days. The anxious Shiribadatt made inquiries, to which she replied by making the already named request. The tyrant was for a few moments thrown into mute astonishment, and finally refused compliance with her preposterous demand. The love-smitten lady went on starving herself, till at last her father, fearful for his daughter's life, told her not to fret herself about him as his soul was of snow, in the snows, and that he could only perish by fire. The princess communicated this information to her lover. Azru went back to Doyur and the villages around, and assembled his faithful peasants. Them he asked to take twigs of the fir-tree, bind them together, and light them; then to proceed in a body with torches to the castle in a circle, keep close together, and surround it on every side. He then went and dug out a very deep hole, as deep as a well, in the place where Shiribadatt's horse used to alight, and covered it with green boughs. The next day he received information that the torches were ready. He at once ordered the villagers gradually to draw near the fort in the manner which he had already indicated.

King Shiribadatt was then sitting in his castle; near him his treacherous daughter, who was so soon to lose her parent. All at once he exclaimed, 'I feel very close; go out, dearest, and see what has happened.' The girl went out, and saw torches approaching from a distance; but fancying it to be something connected with the plans of her husband, she went back and said it was nothing. The torches came nearer and nearer, and the tyrant became exceedingly restless. 'Air, air,' he cried, 'I feel very ill; do see, daughter, what is the matter.' The dutiful lady went, and returned with the same answer as before. At last the torch-bearers had fairly surrounded the fort, and Shiribadatt, with a presentiment of impending danger, rushed out of the room, saying, 'that he felt he was dying.' He then ran to the stables and mounted his favourite charger, and with one blow of the whip made him jump over the wall of the castle. Faithful to its habit the noble animal alighted at the same place, but, alas! only to find itself engulfed in a treacherous pit. Before the king had time to extricate himself the villagers had run up with their torches. 'Throw them upon him,' cried Azru. With one accord all the blazing wood was thrown upon Shiribadatt, who miserably perished.'

Azru was then most enthusiastically proclaimed king, celebrated his nuptials with the fair traitor, and, as sole tribute, exacted the offering of one sheep annually, instead of the human child, from every one of the natives.

When Azru had safely ascended the throne he ordered the tyrant's place to be levelled to the ground. The willing peasants, manufacturing spades of iron, flocked to accomplish a grateful task, and sang whilst demolishing his castle:—'My nature is of a hard metal,' said Shiri and Badatt. 'Why hard? I, Koto, the son of the peasant Dem Singh, am alone hardy; with this iron spade I raze to the ground thy kingly house. Behold now, although thou art of race accursed, of Shatsho Malika, I, Dem Singh's son, am of a hard metal; for with this iron spade I level thy very palace; look out! look out!'5

An account of the Feast of Torches, instituted as a memorial of this tradition, has already been given in another connection.6 The legend, the festival, and the song just quoted constitute a noble human epic. That startling defiance of the icy-hearted god by the human-hearted peasant, that brave cry of the long cowering wretch who at last holds in his spade an iron weapon to wield against the hardness of nature, are the sublime pæan of the Dragon-slayer. Look out, ye snow-gods! Man's heart is there, and woman's heart; their courage, plus the spade, can level your palaces; their love will melt you, their arts and sciences kill you: so fatal may be torches!

All great religions were born in this grand atheism. As the worship of Herakles meant the downfall of Zeus, the worship of Christ meant the overthrow of both Jove and Jehovah. Every race adores the epoch when their fathers grew ashamed of their gods and identified them as dragons—the supreme cruelties of nature—welcoming the man who first rose from his knees and defied them. But in the end the Priests of the Dragon manage to secure a compromise, and by labelling him with the name of his slayer, manage to resuscitate and re-enthrone him. For, as we shall presently see, the Dragon never really dies.

Christianity did not fail to avail itself of the Dragon-slayer's prestige, which had preceded it in Europe and in Africa. It could not afford to offer for popular reverence saints less heroic than pagan warriors and demigods. The old Dragon-myths, especially those which made the fame of Herakles, were appropriated to invest saintly forms. St. Michael, St. Andrew, St. Margaret, and many another, were pictured subduing or treading on Dragons. Christ was shown crushing the serpent Sin, spearing the dragon Death, or even issuing from its impotent jaws, like Jason from the Dragon.7 But in this competition for the laurels of dead Dragon-slayers, and fierce hostility to dragons already slain, the real Dragon was left to revive and flourish in security, and in the end even inherited the mantle and the palm of his own former conqueror. The miscarriage of canonisation in the case of St. George is a small and merely curious thing in itself; but it is almost mystical in its coincidence with the great miscarriage which brought the cross of Christ to authorise the crucifixions of the men most like him for a thousand years.

Mr. John Ruskin has sharply challenged Ralph Waldo Emerson's penetrating touch on the effigy that decorates the escutcheons of England and Russia. 'George of Cappadocia,' says Emerson, 'born at Epiphania in Cilicia, was a low parasite, who got a lucrative contract to supply the army with bacon. A rogue and an informer, he got rich and was forced to run from justice. He saved his money, embraced Arianism, collected a library, and got promoted by a faction to the episcopal throne of Alexandria. When Julian came, A.D. 361, George was dragged to prison. The prison was burst open by the mob, and George was lynched as he deserved. And this precious knave became in good time Saint George of England, patron of chivalry, emblem of victory and civility, and the pride of the best blood of the modern world.' Whereon Emerson further remarks that 'nature trips us up when we strut.'

It is certainly rather hard for the founder of the St. George Association to be told that his patron was no Dragon-slayer at all, but the Dragon's ally. Mr. Ruskin may be right in contending that whatever may have been the facts, they who made George patron saint of England still meant their homage for a hero, or at any rate not for a rogue; but he is unsatisfactory in his argument that our St. George was another who died for his faith seventy years before the bacon-contractor. Even if the Ruskin St. George, said to have suffered under Diocletian, could be shown historical, his was a very commonplace martyrdom compared with that of a bishop torn in pieces by a 'pagan' mob. The distant christian nations would never have listened to the pagan version of the story even had it reached them. A bishop so martyred would have been the very man to give their armies a watchword. The martyr was portrayed as a Dragon-slayer only as a title might be added to the name of one knighted, or the badge of an order set upon his breast; the heraldic device grew into a variant of the common legend which suggests the origin of the mythical George. 'The magician Athanasius, successively an opponent of Christianity, a convert, and a martyr, is his chief antagonist; and the city of Alexandria appears as the Empress Alexandria, the wife of Diocletian, and herself a convert and a martyr.' This sentence from Smith's 'Dictionary of Greek and Roman Biography' tells more than Professor Ruskin's seventeenth-century authority. The Dragon is the same Athanasius whose creed sends forth its anathemas in churches dedicated to the Arian canonised for having slain him!

Though it be granted that they who made George of Cappadocia the ideal hero of England really intended their homage for a martyr and hero, it must equally be acknowledged that his halo was clearly drawn from Dragon-fire. He was a man who had taken to the sword, and by it perished; so much was known and announced in his canonisation. He was honoured as 'the Victor' among the Greeks, therefore to-day patron of Russia; as protector of Crusaders, therefore now patron of England; thus is he saint of a war waged by the strong against the weak, in interest of a church and priesthood against human freedom; therefore George was taking the side of the Dragon against Christ, restoring the priestly power he had assailed, and delivering up his brave brothers in all history to be nailed to Christianity as a cross.

Let George remain! Whether naming fashionable temples or engraved on gold coins, the fictitious Dragon-slayer will remain the right saint in the right place so long as the real Dragon-slayer is made to name every power he hated, and to consecrate every lie in whose mouth he darted his spear.

Notes

1 *'Records of the Past,' x. 79.*
2 *Page 285.*
3 *'Alcestis in England.' Printed by the South Place Society, Finsbury, London. 1877.*
4 *Eating meat was the process of incarnation.*
5 *'Results of a Tour in Dardistan, Kashmir,' etc., by Chevalier Dr. G. W. Leitner, Lahore, vol. i. part iii. Trübner & Co.*
6 *Page 91.*
7 *In the Etruscan Museum at Rome there is a fine representation of this. The old belief was that a dragon could only be attacked successfully inside.*

Chapter XI - The Dragon's Breath

Medusa—Phenomena of recurrence—The Brood of Echidna and their survival—Behemoth and Leviathan—The Mouth of Hell—The Lambton Worm—Ragnar—The Lambton Doom—The Worm's Orthodoxy—The Serpent, Superstition, and Science.

Asura has already been mentioned as the most ancient Aryan name for deity. The meaning of it is, the Breather. It has also been remarked that in the course of time the word came to signify both the good and the evil spirit. What this evil breath meant in nature is told in Leonardo da Vinci's picture of the expiring Medusa, referred to on p. 386, from whose breath noxious creatures are produced. It may have been that the artist meant only to interpret the Gorgon as a personification of the malarious vapours of nature and their organic kindred; if so, he painted better than he knew, and has suggested that fatal vitality of the evil power which raised it to its throne as a principle coeternal with good.

The phenomena of recurrence in things evil made for man the mystery of iniquity. The darkness may be dispersed, but it returns; the storm may clear away, but it gathers again; inundations, sickly seasons, dog-days, Cain-winds, they go and return; the cancer is cut out and grows again; the tyrant may be slain, tyranny survives. The serpent slipping from one skin to another coils steadily into the symbol of endlessness. In another expression it is the poisonous breath of the Dragon. It is this breath that cannot be killed; the special incarnations of it, any temporary brood of it, may be destroyed, but the principle in nature which produces them cannot be exterminated.

Dragon fables have this undertone to their brave strain. In the Rig Veda (v. 32) it is said that when Indra slew Ahi, 'another more powerful was generated.' Isaiah (xiv. 29) cries, 'Rejoice not thou, whole Palestina, because the rod of him that smote thee is broken: for out of the serpent's root shall come forth a cockatrice, and his fruit shall be a fiery flying serpent.' Herakles struggles with the giant robber, Antæus, only to find the demon's strength restored by contact with the earth. He kills one head of the Hydra only to see two grow in its place; and even when he has managed to burn away these, the central head is found to be immortal, and he can only hide it under a rock. That one is the self-multiplying principle of evil. The vast brood of Echidna in mythology expresses the brood of evil in nature. Echidna, daughter of Ge and Tartarus, Earth and Hell—phonetic reappearance of Ahi—is half-serpent, half-woman, with black eyes, fearful and bloodthirsty. She becomes the mother of fire-breathing Typhon, buried beneath the earth by Jove's lightning when he aspired to scale Olympus; of the Dragon that guarded the Hesperian garden; of the Sphinx which puzzled and devoured; of three-headed Cerberus; of the eagle that preyed on rock-bound Prometheus; of the Nemæan lion which Herakles slew; of Chimæra; and of Scylla the monster whom Homer describes sitting between two large rocks waylaying mariners on the way from Italy to Sicily,—possessing twelve feet, six long necks and mouths, each with three rows of rushing teeth. The Dragon that Cadmus slew also had terrible teeth; and it will be remembered that when these teeth were sown they sprang up as armed men. Like them, the ancient Dragon-myths were also sown, broadcast, in the mental and moral fields, cleared and ploughed by a new theology, and they sprang up as dogmas more hard and cruel than the ferocious forces of nature which gave birth to their ancestral monsters.

What the superstitious method of interpreting nature, forced as it is to personify its painful as well as its pleasant phenomena, inevitably results in, finds illustration in the two great lines of tradition—the Aryan and the Semitic—which have converged to form the christian mythology.

The Hebrew personification, Jehovah, originating in a rude period, became invested with many savage and immoral traditions; but when his worshippers had reached a higher moral culture, national sentiment had become too deeply involved with the sovereign majesty of their deity for his alleged actions to be criticised, or his absolute supremacy and omnipotence to be questioned, even to save his moral character. Thus, the Rabbins appear to have been at their wits' end to account for the existence of the two great monsters which had got into their sacred records—from an early mythology—Behemoth and Leviathan. Unwilling to admit that Jehovah had created foes to his own kingdom, or that creatures which had become foes to it were beyond his power to control, they worked out a theory that Behemoth and Leviathan were made and preserved by special order of Jehovah to execute his decrees at the Messianic Day of Judgment. They probably corresponded at an earlier period with the gryphon, or grabber, and the serpent which bit, guardians at the gate of paradise; but the need of such guards, biters, and spies by the all-powerful all-seeing Shaddai having been recognised, the monsters had to be rationalised into accord with his character as a retributive ruler. Hence Behemoth and Leviathan are represented as being fattened with the wicked, who die in order to be the food of the righteous during the unsettled times that follow the revelation of the Messiah! Behemoth is Jehovah's 'cattle on a thousand hills' (Ps. i. 10). In Pireque de Rabbi Eliezur he is described as feeding daily upon a thousand mountains on which the grass grows again every night; and the Jordan supplies him with drink, as it is said in Job (xl. 23), 'he trusteth that he can draw up Jordan into his mouth.' In the Talmud these monsters are divided into two pairs, but are said to have been made barren lest their progeny should destroy the earth. They are kept in the wilderness of Dendain, the mythical abode of the descendants of Cain, east of Eden, for the unique purpose mentioned.

But now we may remark the steady progress of these monsters to the bounds of their mythological habitat. There came a time when Behemoth and Leviathan were hardly more presentable than other personified horrors. They too must 'take the veil,'—a period in the history of mythical, corresponding to extinction in that of actual, monsters. The following passage in the Book of Enoch is believed by Professor Drummond to be a later insertion, probably from the Book of Noah, and as early as the middle of the first century:—'In that day two monsters shall be divided; a female monster named Leviathan, to dwell in the abyss of the sea, above the sources of the waters; but the male is called Behemoth, which occupies with its breast a desolate wilderness named Dendain, on the east of the garden where the elect and righteous dwell, where my grandfather (Enoch) was taken up, being the seventh from Adam, the first man whom the Lord of the spirits created. And I asked that other angel to show me the might of these monsters, how they were separated in one day, and one was set in the depth of the sea, the other on the firm land of the wilderness. And he spoke to me, 'Thou son of man, thou desirest in this to know what has been concealed.' And the other angel who went with me, and showed me what is in concealment, spake, ... 'These two monsters are prepared conformably to the greatness of God to be fed, in order that the penal judgment of God may not be in vain.'1

We may thus see that there were antecedents to the sentiment of Aquinas,—'Beati in regno cœlesti videbunt pœnas damnatorum, ut beatitudo illis magis complaceat.' Or, perhaps, one might say rather to the logic of Aquinas; for though he saw that it would be necessary for souls in bliss to be happy at vision of the damned or else deficient in bliss, it is said he could hardly be happy from thinking of the irreversible doom of Satan himself. It would appear that only the followers of the Genevan who anticipated his god's hell for Servetus managed to adapt their hearts to such logic, and glory in the endless tortures of their fellow-creatures.

An eloquent minister in New York, Octavius B. Frothingham, being requested to write out his views on the 'question' of everlasting damnation, began with the remark that he felt somewhat as a sportsman suddenly called upon to hunt the Iguanodon. Really it is Behemoth and Leviathan he was called to deal with. Leviathan transmitted from Jonah to the Middle Ages the idea of 'the belly of Hell,' and Behemoth's jaws expanded in the 'mouth of Hell' of the Miracle-plays; and their utility, as described in the Book of Enoch, perhaps originated the doctrine of souls tasting heavenly joys from the agonies of others. The dogma of Hell has followed the course of its prototype with precision. It has arrived at just that period when, as in the case of Enoch's inquiring, the investigator finds it has taken the veil. Theologians shake their heads, call it a terrible question, write about free-will and sin, but only a few, of the fatuous sort, confess belief in the old-fashioned Hell where the worm dieth not and the fire is not quenched.

Let us now take under consideration the outcome of the Aryan Dragon, which has travelled far to meet Behemoth in the west. And it is probable that we could not, with much seeking, find an example so pregnant with instruction for our present inquiry as our little Durham folk-tale of the Lambton Worm.

This Worm is said to have been slain by Sir Lambton, crusader, and ancestor of the Earls of Durham. This young Lambton was a wild fellow; he was fond of fishing in the river Wear, which runs near Durham Castle, and he had an especial taste for fishing there on Sunday mornings. He was profane, and on Sundays, when the people were all going to mass, they were often shocked by hearing the loud oaths which Lambton uttered whenever he had no rise. One Sunday morning something got hold of his hook, pulled strong, and he made sure of a good trout; what was his disappointment when instead thereof he found at the end of his line a tiny black worm. He tore it off with fierce imprecations and threw it in a well near by. However, soon after this the young man joined the crusaders and went off to the Holy Land, where he distinguished himself by slaying many Saracens.

But while he was off there things were going on badly around Durham Castle. Some peasant passing that well into which the youth had cast the tiny black worm looked into it, and beheld a creature that made him shudder,—a diabolical big snake with nine ferocious eyes. A little time only had elapsed before this creature had grown too large for the well to hold it, and it came out and crawled on, making a path of desolation, breakfasting on a village, until it came to a small hill. Around that hill it coiled with nine coils, each weighty enough to make a separate terrace. One may still see this hill with its nine terraces, and be assured of the circumstances by peasants residing near. Having taken up its headquarters on this hill, the nine-eyed monster was in the habit of sallying forth every day and satisfying his hunger by devouring the plumpest family he could find, until at length the people consulted an oracle—some say a witch, others again a priest— and were told that the monster would be satisfied if it were given each day the milk of nine cows. So nine cows were got together, and a plucky dairymaid was found to milk the cows and carry it to the dragon. If a single gill of the milk was missing the monster took a dire revenge upon the nearest village. This was the unpleasant situation which young Lambton found when he returned home from the crusades. He was now an altered man. He was no longer given to fishing and profanity. He felt keenly that by raising the demon out of the river Wear he had brought woe upon his neighbours, and he resolved to engage the Worm in single combat. But he learned that it had already been fought by several knights, and had slain them, while no wounds received by itself availed anything, since, if it were cut in twain, the pieces grew together again. The knight then consulted the oracle, witch or priest, and was told that he could prevail in the combat on certain conditions. He must provide himself with special armour, all over which must be large razor-blades. He must manage to entice the worm into the middle of the river Wear, in whose waters the combat must take place. And, finally, he must vow to slay as a sacrifice the first living thing he should meet after his victory. These conditions having been fulfilled, the knight entered the stream. The dragon, not having received his milk as usual that morning, crawled from his hill seeking whom he might devour, and seeing the knight in the river, went at him. Quickly he coiled around the armour, but its big razors cut him into many sections; and these sections could not piece themselves together again because the current of the river washed them swiftly away.

Now, observe how this dragon was pieced together mythologically. He is a storm cloud. He begins smaller than a man's hand and swells to huge dimensions; that characteristic of the howling storm was represented in the howling wolf Fenris of Norse Mythology, who was a little pet, a sort of lapdog for the gods at first, but when full grown broke the chains that tied him to mountains, and was only fettered at last by the thread finer than cobweb, which was really the sunbeam conquering winter. Then, when this worm was cut in two, the parts came together again. This feature of recurrence is especially characteristic of Hydras. In the Egyptian 'Tale of Setnau,' Ptah-nefer-ka saw the river-snake twice resume its form after he had killed it with his sword,—he succeeded the third time by placing sand between the two parts; and what returning floods taught the ancient scribe remained to characterise the dragon encountered by Guy of Warwick, which recovered from every wound by dipping its tail in the well it had guarded. The Lernean Hydra had nine heads, the Lambton Worm nine eyes and nine folds, and drank nine cows' milk. His fondness for the milk of cows connects him straightly with the dragon Vritra, whom Indra slew because he stole Indra's cows (that is, the good clouds, whose milk is gentle rain, and do no harm), and shut them up in a cavern to enjoy their milk himself. That is the oldest Dragon fable on record, and it is said in the Rig-Veda that beneath Indra's thunderbolt the monster broke up into pieces, and was washed away in a current of water. Finally, in being destroyed at last by razor blades, the dragon is connected with that slain by Ragnar, in whose armour the sun-darts of Apollo had turned to icicles. In the 'Death-Song of Ragnar Lodbrach,' preserved by Olaus Wormius, it is said that King Ella of Northumberland having captured that terror of the North (8th cent.), ordered him to be thrown into a pit of serpents. His surname, Lodbrach, or Hair Breeches, had been given because of his method of slaying a Worm which devastated Gothland, whose king had promised his daughter to the man who should slay the same. Ragnar dressed himself in hairy skins, and threw water over the hair, which, freezing, encased him in an armour of ice. The Worm, unable to bite through this, was impaled by Ragnar. Another version is that Ragnar killed two serpents which the King of Gothland had set to guard his daughter, but which had grown to such size that they terrified the country. It may be observed that the Lambton story christianises the Ragnar legend, showing that to be done in atonement for sin which in the other was done for love. The Cornish legend of St. Petrox has also taken a hint from Ragnar, and announces the rescue of christians from the serpent-pit in which the pagan hero perished. The icicles reappear on the slayer of the dragon of Wantley, represented by long spikes bristling from his armour.

The Knight Lambton, remembering his vow to slay as a sacrifice the first living thing he might meet after the combat, had arranged that a dog should be placed where it would attract his eye. But it turned out that his own father came rushing to him. As he could not kill his father, he consulted the oracle again to know what would be the penalty of non-fulfilment of his vow. It was that no representative of the family should die in his bed for nine generations. The notion is still found in that neighbourhood that no Earl of Durham has since then died in his bed. The nine generations have long passed since any crusading Lambton lived, but several peasants of the district closed their narrative with, 'Strange to say, no Earl of Durham has died in his bed!' At the castle I talked with a servant on the estate while looking at the old statues of the knight, worm, and dairymaid, all kept there, and he told me he had heard that the late Earl, as death drew nigh, asked to sit up—insisted—and died in a chair. If there be any truth in this, it would show that the family itself has some morbid feeling about the legend which has been so long told them with pride. The old well from which the little worm emerged a monster is now much overgrown, but I was told that it was for a long time a wishing-well, and the pins cast in by rustics may still be seen at the bottom of it.

Pins are the last offerings at the Worm's Well; 'wishes' its last prayers; but where go now the coins and the prayers? To propitiate a power and commute a doom resting upon much the same principles as those represented in the Lambton legend. A community desolated because one man is sinful miniatures a world's doom for Adam's sin. The demand of a human sacrifice is more clear in the Sockburn story, where Conyers offered up his only son to the Holy Ghost in the parish church before engaging the Dragon, that being a condition of success prescribed by the 'Oracle' or 'Sybil.' This claim of the infernal powers represented by the Worm—many-eyed, all-seeing—cannot be set aside; Lambton's filial love may resist it only to have it pass as the hereditary doom of his family, representing an imputed sin. 'For I, the Lord thy God, am a jealous God, and visit the sins of the fathers on the children unto the third and fourth generation.'

There are processes of this kind in nature, hereditary evils, transmitted diseases and disgraces, and afflictions of many through the offences of one. But a fearful Nemesis follows the deification and adoration of them. 'How can I be happy in heaven,' said a tender-hearted lady to her clerical adviser, 'when I must see others in hell?' 'You will be made to see that it is all for the best.' 'If I am to be made so heartless, I prefer to go to hell.' This genuine conversation reports the doom of all deities whose extension is in dragons. Hell implies a Dragon as its representative and ruler. Theology may induce the abject and cowardly to subject their human hearts to the process of induration required for loyalty to such powers, but in the end it makes atheism the only salvation of brave, pure, and loving natures. The Dragons' breath has clouded the ancient heavens and blighted the old gods; but the starry ideals they pursue in vain. Behemoth has supplied sirloins to many priesthoods for a long time, but he has at last become too tough even for their teeth, and they feed him less carefully every year. Nay, he is encountered now and then by his professional feeders, and has found even in Westminster Abbey his Guy of Warwick.

Nor could this desp'rate champion daunt
A Dun Cow bigger than elephant;
But he, to prove his courage sterling,
Cut from her enormous side a sirloin.

Fig. 32.—From the Temptation of St. Anthony (Callot).

The Worms—whether Semitic Leviathan or Aryan Dragon—are nearly fossilised as to their ancient form. The sacrifice of Jephtha's daughter to the one, and of young Conyers to the other, found commutation in the case of man's rescue from Satan by Christ's descent to Hades, and in the substitution of nine uneasy deaths for the demanded parricide in the Lambton case; and the most direct 'survival' of these may be found in any country lad trying to cure his warts by providing a weed for them to adhere to. Their end in Art was in such forms as this starveling creature of Callot's (Fig. 32), whose thin, spectacled rider, tilting at St. Anthony, denotes as well the doom of all powers, however lofty, whose majesty requires tali auxilio et istis defensoribus. The Dragon passes and leaves a roar of laughter behind him, in which even St. Anthony could now join. But Leviathan and Lambton Worm have combined and merged their life in a Dogma; it is a Dogma as remorseless and voracious as its prototype, and requires to be fed with all the milk of human kindness, or it at once begins to gnaw the foundations of Christendom itself. Christianity rests upon the past work of the Worm in Paradise, and its present work in Hell. It makes no real difference whether man's belief in a universe enmeshed in serpent-coils be expressed in the Hindu's cowering adoration of the venomous potentate, or the christian's imprecation upon it:

141

fundamentally it is serpent-worship in each case. Vishnu reposes on his celestial Serpent; the god of Dogma maintains his government by support of the infernal Serpent. Fear beheld him appearing in Durham to vindicate the mass and the Sabbath; but the same fear still sees him in the fiery world punishing Sabbath-breakers and blasphemers against his Creator and chief. That fear built every cathedral in Christendom, and they must crumble with the phantasm evoked for their creation.

The Serpent in itself is a perfect type of all evil in nature. It is irreconcilable with the reign of a perfectly good and omnipotent man over the universe. No amount of casuistry can explain its co-existence with anthropomorphic Love and Wisdom, as all acknowledge when a parallel casuistry attempts to defend any other god than their own from deeds that are, humanly considered, evil. It is just as easy to defend the jealousy and cruelty of Jove, on the ground that his ways are not as our ways, as it is to defend similar tempers in Jehovah. The monster sent by one to devour Prometheus is ethically atwin with the snake created by the other to bite the heel of man.

Man is saved from the superstitious evolution of the venomous Serpent into a Dragon by recognising its real evolution as seen by the eye of Science. Science alone can tell the true story of the Serpent, and justify its place in nature. It forbids man his superstitious method of making a god in his own image, and his egotistic method of judging nature according to his private likes and dislikes, his convenience or inconvenience. Taught by Science man may, with a freedom the barbarian cannot feel, exterminate the Serpent; with a freedom the christian cannot know, he may see in that reptile the perfection of that economy in nature which has ever defended the advancing forms of life. It judges the good and evil of every form with reference to its adaptation to its own purposes. Thus Science alone wields the spear of Ithuriel, and beneath its touch every Dragon shrinks instantly to its little shape in nature to be dealt with according to what it is.

Note

1 *'The Jewish Messiah,' etc. By James Drummond, B.A. Longmans & Co. (1877). See in this valuable work chapter xxi.*

Chapter XII - Fate

Dorè's 'Love and Fate'—Moira and Moiræ—The 'Fates' of Æschylus—Divine absolutism surrendered—Jove and Typhon—Commutation of the Demon's share—Popular fatalism—Theological fatalism—Fate and Necessity—Deification of Will—Metaphysics, past and present.

Gustave Dorè has painted a picture of 'Love and Fate,' in which the terrible hag is portrayed towering above the tender Eros, and while the latter is extending the thread as far as he can, the wrinkled hands of Destiny are the boundaries of his power, and the fatal shears close upon the joy he has stretched to its inevitable limit. To the ancient mind these two forms made the two great realms of the universe, their powers meeting in the fruit with a worm at its core, in seeds of death germinating amid the play of life, in all the limitations of man. They are projected in myths of Elysium and Hades, Eden and the Serpent, Heaven and Hell, and their manifold variants.

Perhaps there is no one line of mythological development which more clearly and impressively illustrates the forces under which grew the idea of an evil principle, than the changes which the personification of Fate underwent in Greece and Rome. The Moira, or Fate with Homer, is only a secondary cause, if that, and simply carries out the decrees of her father, Zeus. Zeus is the real Fate. Nevertheless, while this is the Homeric theory or theology, there are intimations (see chap. xxvii. part 4) that the real awe of men was already transferred from Zeus to the Erinnyes. This foreshadows a change of government. With Hesiod we find, instead of one, three Moiræ. They are no longer offspring of Zeus, but, as it were, his Cabinet. They do not act independently of him, but when, in pursuance of their just counsels, Zeus issues decrees, the Moiræ administer them. Next we find the Moiræ of Hesiod developed by other writers into final Recorders; they write the decrees of Zeus on certain indestructible tablets, after which they are irrevocable and inevitable. With Æschylus we find the Moiræ developed into independent and supreme powers, above Zeus himself. The chained Prometheus looks not to Zeus but to Fate for his final liberation.

Chorus. Who, then, is the guide of Necessity?
Prometheus. The tri-form Fates and the unforgetting Furies.
Cho. Is Zeus, then, less powerful than they?
Prom. At least 'tis certain he cannot escape his own doom.
Cho. And what can be Zeus' doom but everlasting rule?
Prom. This ye may not learn; press it not.
Cho. Surely some solemn mystery thou hidest.

Prom. Turn to some other theme: for this disclosure time has not ripened: it must be veiled in deep mystery, for by the keeping of this secret shall come my liberty from base chains and misery.

These great landmarks represent successive revolutions in the Olympian government. Absolutism became burthensome: as irresponsible monarch, Zeus became responsible for the woes of the world, and his priests were satisfied to have an increasing share of that responsibility allotted to his counsellors, until finally the whole of it is transferred. From that time the countenance of Zeus, or Jupiter, shines out unclouded by responsibility for human misfortunes and earthly evils; and, on the other hand, the once beautiful Fates are proportionately blackened, and they become hideous hags, the aged and lame crones of popular belief in Greece and Rome, every line of whose ugliness would have disfigured the face of Zeus had he not been subordinated to them.

Moira means 'share,' and originally, perhaps, meant simply the power that meted out to each his share of life, and of the pains and pleasures woven in it till the term be reached. But as the Fates gained more definite personality they began to be regarded as having also a 'share' of their own. They came to typify all the dark and formidable powers as to their inevitableness. No divine power could set them aside, or more than temporarily subdue them. Fate measured out her share to the remorseless Gorgon as well as to the fairest god. But where destructive power was exercised in a way friendly to man, the Fates are put somewhat in the background, and the feat is claimed for some god. Such, in the 'Prometheus' of Æschylus, is the spirit of the wonderful passage concerning Typhon, rendered with tragic depth by Theodore Buckley:—'I commiserated too,' says the rock-bound Prometheus, 'when I beheld the earth-born inmate of the Cilician caverns, a tremendous prodigy, the hundred-headed impetuous Typhon, overpowered by force; who withstood all the gods, hissing slaughter from his hungry jaws, and from his eyes there flashed a hideous glare as if he would perforce overthrow the sovereignty of Jove. But the sleepless shaft of Jupiter came upon him, the descending thunderbolt breathing forth flame which scared him out of his presumptuous bravadoes; for having been smitten to his very soul he was crumbled to a cinder, and thunder-blasted in his prowess. And now, a hapless and paralysed form, is he lying hard by a narrow frith, pressed down beneath the roots of Ætna. And, seated on the topmost peaks, Vulcan forges the molten masses whence there shall burst forth floods, devouring with full jaws the level fields of fruitful Sicily; with rage such as this shall Typhon boil over in hot artillery of a never glutted fire-breathing storm; albeit he hath been reduced to ashes by the thunderbolt of Jupiter.'

In this passage we see Jove invested with the glory of defeating a great demon; but we also recognise the demon still under the protection of Fate. Destiny must bear that burthen. So was it said in the Apocalypse Satan should be loosed after being bound in the Pit a thousand years; and so Mohammed declared Gog and Magog should break loose with terror and destruction from the mountain-prison in which Allah had cast them. The destructive Principle had its 'share' as well as the creative and preservative Principles, and could not be permanently deprived of it. Gradually the Fates of various regions and names were identified with the deities, whose interests, gardens, or treasures they guarded; and when some of these deities were degraded their retainers were still more degraded, while in other cases deities were enabled to maintain fair fame by fables of their being betrayed and their good intentions frustrated by such subordinates. Thus we find a certain notion of technical and official power investing such figures as Satan, Ahriman, Iblis, and the Dragon, as if the upper gods could not disown or reverse altogether the bad deeds done by these commissioners.

But the large though limited degree of control necessarily claimed for the greatest and best gods had to be represented theologically. Hence there was devised a system of Commutation. The Demon or Dragon, though abusing his power, could not have it violently withdrawn, but might be compelled to accept some sacrifice in lieu of the precise object sought by his voracity. These substitutions are found in every theological system, and to apply them to individuals constitutes the raison d'être of every priesthood. In the progress towards civilisation the substitutes diminish in value, and finally they become merely nominal and ceremonial,—an effigy of a man instead of the man, or wine instead of blood. At first the commutation was often in the substitution of persons of lower for others of higher rank, as when slaves or wives were, or are, sacrificed to assure paradise to the master or husband. Thus, Death is allowed to take Alcestis instead of Admetus. A higher degree of civilisation substitutes animals for human victims. In keeping with this is the legend of Christ's sending demons out of two men into a herd of swine:[1] which, again, is referable to the same class of ideas as the legend that followed concerning Jesus himself as a vicarious offering; mankind in this case being the herd, as compared with the son of a god, and the transfer of the Satanic power from the human race to himself, for even a little time, being accepted in theology as an equivalent, on account of the divine dignity of the being who descended into hell. It was some time, however, before theology worked out this theory as it now stands, the candid fathers having rejoiced in the belief that the contract for commutation on its face implied that Christ was to remain for ever in hell, Satan being outwitted in this.

The ancient Babylonian charms often end with the refrain:—'May the enchantment go forth and to its own dwelling-place betake itself,' Every evil spirit was supposed to have an appropriate dwelling, as in the case of Judas, into whom Satan entered,[2] and of whom it is said he 'by transgression fell, that he might go to his own place.[3] Very ingenious are some of the ancient speculations concerning the habitations and congenial resorts of demons. In some regions the colour of a disease on the skin is supposed to indicate the tastes of the demon causing it; and the spells of exorcism end by assigning him to something of the same hue. The demon of jaundice is generally consigned to the yellow parrots, and inflammation to the red or scarlet weeds. Their colours are respected. Humanity is little considered in the Eastern formulas of this kind, and it is pretty generally the case that in praying against plague or famine, populations are often found selecting a tribe to which their trouble is adjured to betake itself. 'May Nin-cigal,' says a Babylonian exorcism, 'turn her face towards another place; may the noxious spirit go forth and seize another; may the female cherub and the female demon settle upon his body; may the king of heaven preserve, may the king of earth preserve!'

So is it in regions and times which we generally think of as semi-barbarous. But every now and then communities which fancy themselves civilised and enlightened are brought face to face with the popular fatalism in its pagan form, and are shocked thereat, not remembering that it is equally the dogma of vicarious satisfaction or atonement. A lady residing in the neighbourhood of the Traunsee, Austria, informs me that recently two men were nearly drowned in that lake, being rescued at the last moment and brought to life with great difficulty. But this incident, instead of causing joy among the neighbours of the men, excited their displeasure; and this not because the rescued were at all unpopular, but because of a widespread notion that the Destinies required two lives, that they would have to be presently satisfied with two others, and that since the agonies of the drowning men had passed into unconsciousness, it would have been better to surrender the selected victims to their fate. At Elsinore, in Denmark, when the sea moans it is said to 'want somebody,' and it is generally the case that some story of a person just drowned circulates afterwards.

While the early mythological forms of the Fates diminish and pass away as curious superstitions, they return in metaphysical disguises. They gather their kindred in primitive sciences and cosmogonies, and finding their old home swept free of pagan demons, and, garnished with philosophic phrases, they enter as grave theories; but their subtlety and their sting is with them, and the last state of the house they occupy is worse than the first.

Yes, worse: for all that man ever won of courage or moral freedom, by conquering his dragons in detail, he surrenders again to the phantom-forces they typified when he gives up his mind to belief in a power not himself that makes for evil. The terrible conclusion that Evil is a positive and imperishable Principle in the universe carries in it the poisonous breath of every Dragon. It lurks in all theology which represents the universe as an arena of struggle between good and evil Principles, and human life as a war of the soul against the flesh. It animates all the pious horrors which identify Materialism with wickedness. It nestles in the mind which imagines a personal deity opposed by any part of nature. It coils around every heart which adores absolute sovereign Will, however apotheosised.

All of these notions, most of all belief in a supreme arbitrary Will, are modern disguises of Fate; and belief in Fate is the one thing fatal to human culture and energy. The notion of Fate (fatum, the word spoken) carries in it the conception of arbitrariness in the universe, of power deliberately exerted without necessary reference to the nature of things; and it is precisely opposed to that idea of Necessity taught by Science, which is another name for the supremacy of Law. Happily the notion of a universe held at the mercy of a personal decree is suicidal in a world full of sorrows and agonies, which, on such a theory, can only be traced to some individual caprice or malevolence. However long abject fear may silence the lips of the suffering, rebellion is in their hearts. Every blow inflicted, directly or permissively, by mere Will, however omnipotent, every agony that is consciously detached from universal organic necessity, in order that it may be called 'providential,' can arouse no natural feeling in man nobler than indignation. The feeling of a suitor in a court of law, who knows that the adverse judgment that ruins him has no root in the facts or the law, but proceeds from the prejudice or whim of the judge, can be nowise different from that of a mother who sees her son stricken down by death, and hears at his grave that he was consumed by the wrath of a god who might have yielded to her prayer, but refused it. The heart's protest may be throttled for a time by the lingering coil of terror, but it is there, and christian theologians will be as anxious to protect their deity from it, at whatever cost to his sovereignty, as their predecessors who invented the Cabinet of Women to relieve Jove from responsibility.

Metaphysics—which appear to have developed into the art of making things look true in words when their untruth in fact has been detected—have indeed already set about the task just predicted. Eminent divines are found writing about matter and spirit, freedom and natural law, as solemnly as if all this discussion were new, and had never been carried out to its inevitable results. They can only put in christian or modern phraseology conclusions which have been reached again and again in the history of human speculation. The various schools of Buddhist and Vedantist philosophy have come by every conceivable route to their fundamental unity of belief in God, Soul, and Matter; in a pessimist visible nature, an ideal invisible nature, and a human soul held in matter like a frog in a snake's mouth, but able by certain mysterious, mostly metaphysical or verbal, tactics, to gain release, and pass into a corresponding situation in the deity. 'As a king, whose son had strayed away from him and lived in ignorance of his father among the Veddahs (wild men), will, on discovering his son, exclaim, 'Come to me, my darling son!' and make him a participator of the happiness he himself enjoys, even so will the Supreme God present himself before the soul when in distress—the soul enmeshed in the net of the five Veddahs (senses), and, severing that soul from Pâsam (Matter), assimilate it to himself, and bless it at his holy feet.'

It is too late for man to be interested in an 'omnipotent' Personality, whose power is mysteriously limited at the precise point when it is needed, and whose moral government is another name for man's own control of nature. Nevertheless, this Oriental pessimism is the Pauline theory of Matter, and it is the speculative protoplasm out of which has been evolved, in many shapes, that personification which remains for our consideration—the Devil.

Notes

1 *Matt. viii. 30.*
2 *Luke xxiii. 3.*
3 *Acts i. 25.*

End of Vol. I.

Volume II

Part IV - The Devil

Chapter I – Diabolism

Dragon and Devil distinguished—Dragons' wings—War in Heaven—Expulsion of Serpents—Dissolution of the Dragon—Theological origin of the Devil—Ideal and actual—Devil Dogma—Debasement of ideal persons—Transmigration of phantoms.

'We are all nothing other than Wills,' says St. Augustine; and he adds that of the good and bad angels the nature is the same, the will different. In harmony with this John Beaumont says, 'A good desire of mind is a good God.'1 To which all the mythology of Evil adds, a bad desire of mind is a Devil. Every personification of an evil Will looks beyond the outward phenomena of pain, and conceives a heart that loves evil, a spirit that makes for wickedness. At this point a new element altogether enters. The physical pain incidentally represented by the Demon, generalised and organised into a principle of harmfulness in the Dragon, begins now to pass under the shadow cast by the ascending light of man's moral nature. Man becomes conscious of moral and spiritual pains: they may be still imaginatively connected with bodily agonies, but these drop out of the immediate conception, disappear into a distant future, and are even replaced by the notion of an evil symbolised by pleasure.

The fundamental difference between either a Demon or Dragon and a Devil may be recognised in this: we never find the former voluntarily bestowing physical pleasure or happiness on man, whereas it is a chief part of the notion of a Devil that he often confers earthly favours in order to corrupt the moral nature.

There are, indeed, apparent exceptions to this theorem presented in the agatho-dragons which have already been considered in our chapter on the Basilisk; but the reader will observe that there is no intimation in such myths of any malign ulterior purpose in the good omens brought by those exceptional monsters, and that they are really forms of malevolent power whose afflictive intent is supposed to have been vanquished by the superior might of the heroes or saints to whose glory they are reluctantly compelled to become tributary.

Undoubtedly the Dragon attended this moral and religious development of man's inward nature very far, and still occupies, as at once prisoner and gaoler in the underworld, a subordinate relation to it. In the long process he has undergone certain transformations, and in particular his attribute of wings, if not derived from the notion of his struggle against holier beings, seems to have been largely enhanced thereby. The exceptional wings given to serpents in Greek art, those, for instance, which draw Demeter and Persephone in their chariot, are trifling as compared with the fully-developed wings of our conventional Dragon of the christian era. Such wings might have been developed occasionally to denote the flying cloud, the fire-breathing storm, or explain how some Ráhu was enabled to pursue the sun and moon and swallow them temporarily in the phenomena of eclipse. But these wings grew to more important dimensions when they were caught up into the Semitic conception of winged genii and destroying angels, and associated with an ambitious assault on heaven and its divine or angelic occupants.

'There was war in Heaven,' says the Apocalypse. The traditional descriptions of this war follow pretty closely, in dramatic details, other and more ancient struggles which reflect man's encounters with the hardships of nature. In those encounters man imagined the gods descending earthward to mingle in the fray; but even where the struggle mounted highest the scenery is mainly terrestrial and the issues those of place and power, the dominion of visible Light established above Darkness, or of a comparatively civilised over a savage race. The wars between the Devas and Asuras in India, the Devs and Ahuras in Persia, Buddha and the Nagas in Ceylon, Garúra and the Serpent-men in the north of India, gods and Frost-giants in Scandinavia, still concern man's relation to the fruits of the earth, to heat and frost, to darkness or storm and sunshine.

But some of these at length find versions which reveal their tendency towards spiritualisation. The differences presented by one of these legends which has survived among us in nearly its ancient form from the same which remains in a partly mystical form will illustrate the transitional phase. Thus, Garúra expelling the serpents from his realm in India is not a saintly legend; this exterminator of serpents is said to have compelled the reptile race to send him one of their number daily that he might eat it, and the rationalised tradition interprets this as the prince's cannibalism. The expulsion of Nagas or serpents from Ceylon by Buddha, in order that he might consecrate that island to the holy law, marks the pious accentuation of the fable. The expulsion of snakes from Ireland by St. Patrick is a legend conceived in the spirit of the curse pronounced upon the serpent in Eden, but in this case the modern myth is the more primitive morally, and more nearly represents the exploit of Garúra. St. Patrick expels the snakes that he may make Ireland a paradise physically, and establish his reputation as an apostle by fulfilling the signs of one named by Christ;2 and in this particular it slightly rises above the Hindu story. In the case of the serpent cursed in Eden a further moralisation of the conflict is shown. The serpent is not present in Eden, as in the realms of Garúra and St. Patrick, for purposes of physical devastation or pain, but to bestow a pleasure on man with a view to success in a further issue between himself and the deity. Yet in this Eden myth the ancient combat is not yet fairly spiritualised; for the issue still relates, as in that between the Devas and Asuras, to the possession of a magical fruit which by no means confers sanctity. In the apocalyptic legend of the war in heaven,3 the legend has become fairly spiritualised. The issue is no longer terrestrial, it is no longer for mere power; the Dragon is arrayed against the woman and child, and against the spiritual 'salvation' of mankind, of whom he is 'accuser' and 'deceiver.'

Surely nobody could be 'deceived' by 'a great fiery-red Dragon, having seven heads and ten horns'! In this vision the Dragon is pressed as far as the form can go in the symbolisation of evil. To devour the child is its legitimate work, but as 'accuser of the brethren before God day and night' the monstrous shape were surely out of place by any mythologic analogy; and one could hardly imagine such a physiognomy capable of deceiving 'the whole world.' It is not wonderful, therefore, that the Dragon's presence in heaven is only mentioned in connection with his fall from it. It is significant that the wings are lost in this fall; for while his 'angelic' relationship suggests the previous wings, the woman is able to escape the fallen monster by the two wings given her.4 Wingless now, 'the old serpent' once more, the monster's shape has no adaptation to the moral and religious struggle which is to ensue. For his shape is a method, and it means the perfection of brute force. That, indeed, also remains in the sequel of this magnificent myth. As in the legend of the Hydra two heads spring up in place of that which falls, so in this Christian legend out of the overthrown monster, henceforth himself concealed, two arise from his inspiration,—the seven-headed, ten-horned Beast who continues the work of wrath and pain; but also a lamb-like Beast, with only two horns (far less terrible), and able to deceive by his miracles, for he is even able to call down fire from heaven. The ancient Serpent-dragon, the expression of natural pain, thus goes to pieces. His older part remains to work mischief and hurt; and the cry is uttered, 'Be merry, ye heavens, and ye that tabernacle in them: woe to the earth and the sea! for the devil is come down unto you, having great wrath because he knows that he has a short time.'5 But there is a lamb-like part of him too, and his relation to the Dragon is only known by his voice.

This subtle adaptation of the symbol of external pain to the representation of the moral struggle, wherein the hostile power may assume deceptive forms of beauty and pleasure, is only one impressive illustration of the transfer of human conceptions of evil from outward to inward nature. The transition is from a malevolent, fatal, principle of harmfulness to the body to a malevolent, fatal, principle of evil to the conscience. The Demon was natural; the Dragon was both physical and metaphysical; the Devil was and is theological. In the primitive Zoroastrian theology, where the Devil first appears in clear definition, he is the opponent of the Good Mind, and the combat between the two, Ormuzd and Ahriman, is the spiritualisation of the combat between Light and Darkness, Pain and Happiness, in the external world. As these visible antagonists were supposed to be exactly balanced against each other, so are their spiritual correlatives. The Two Minds are described as Twins.

'Those old Spirits, who are twins, made known what is good and what is evil in thoughts, words, and deeds. Those who are good distinguished between the two; not so those who are evil-doers.

'When these two Spirits came together they made first life and death, so that there should be at last the most wretched life for the bad, but for the good blessedness.

'Of these two Spirits the evil one chose the worst deeds; the kind Spirit, he whose garment is the immovable sky, chose what is right.'6

This metaphysical theory follows closely the primitive scientific observations on which it is based; it is the cold of the cold, the gloom of the darkness, the sting of death, translated into some order for the intellect which, having passed through the Dragon, we find appearing in this Persian Devil; and against his blackness the glory of the personality from whom all good things proceed shines out in a splendour no longer marred by association with the evil side of nature. Ormuzd is celebrated as 'father of the pure world,' who sustains 'the earth and the clouds that they do not fall,' and 'has made the kindly light and the darkness, the kindly sleep and the awaking;'7 at every step being suggested the father of the impure world, the unkindly light, darkness or sleep.

The ecstasy which attended man's first vision of an ideal life defied the contradictory facts of outward and inward nature. So soon as he had beheld a purer image of himself rising above his own animalism, he must not only regard that animalism as an instigation of a devil, but also the like of it in nature; and this conception will proceed pari passu with the creation of pure deities in the image of that higher self. There was as yet no philosophy demanding unity in the Cosmos, or forbidding man to hold as accursed so much of nature as did not obviously accord with his ideals.

Mr. Edward B. Tylor has traced the growth of Animism from man's shadow and his breathing; Sir John Lubbock has traced the influence of dreams in forming around him a ghostly world; Mr. Herbert Spencer has given an analysis of the probable processes by which this invisible environment was shaped for the mental conception in accordance with family and social conditions. But it is necessary that we should here recognise the shadow that walked by the moral nature, the breathings of religious aspiration, and the dreams which visited a man whose moral sense was so generally at variance with his animal desires. The code established for the common good, while necessarily having a relation to every individual conscience, is a restriction upon individual liberty. The conflict between selfishness and duty is thus inaugurated; it continues in the struggle between the 'law in the members and the law in the spirit,' which led Paul to beat his body (ὑποπιαξομαί) to keep it in subjection; it passes from the Latin poet to the Englishman, who turns his experience to a rune—

I see the right, and I approve it too;
Condemn the wrong, and yet the wrong pursue.

As the light which cast it was intense, even so intense was the shadow it cast beneath all it could not penetrate. Passionate as was the saintliest man's love of good, even so passionate was his spiritual enemy's love of evil. High as was the azure vault that mingled with his dreams of purity, so deep was the abyss beneath his lower nature. The superficial equalities of phenomena, painful and pleasurable, to his animal nature had cast the mould into which his theories of the inward and the moral phenomena must be cast; and thus man—in an august moment—surrendered himself to the dreadful conception of a supreme Principle of Wickedness: wherever good was there stood its adversary; wherever truth, there its denier; no light shone without the dark presence that would quench it; innocence had its official accuser, virtue its accomplished tempter, peace its breaker, faith its disturber and mocker. Nay, to this impersonation was added the last feature of fiendishness, a nature which found its supreme satisfaction in ultimately torturing human beings for the sins instigated by himself.

It is open to question how far any average of mankind really conceived this theological dogma. Easy as it is to put into clear verbal statement; readily as the analogies of nature supply arguments for and illustrations of a balance between moral light and darkness, love and hatred; yet is man limited in subjective conceptions to his own possibilities, and it may almost be said that to genuinely believe in an absolute Fiend a man would have to be potentially one himself. But any human being, animated by causeless and purposeless desire to inflict pain on others, would be universally regarded as insane, much more one who would without motive corrupt as well as afflict.

Even theological statements of the personality of Evil, and what that implies, are rare. The following is brave enough to be put on record, apart from its suggestiveness.

'It cannot be denied that as there is an inspiration of holy love, so is there an inspiration of hatred, or frantic pleasure, with which men surrender themselves to the impulses of destructiveness; and when the popular language speaks of possessions of Satan, of incarnate devils, there lies at the bottom of this the grave truth that men, by continued sinning, may pass the ordinary limit between human and diabolic depravity, and lay open in themselves a deep abyss of hatred which, without any mixture of self-interest, finds its gratification in devastation and woe.'[8]

On this it may be said that the popular commentary on cases of the kind is contained in the very phrase alluded to, 'possession,'—the implication being that such disinterested depravity is nowise possible within the range of simple human experience,—and, in modern times, 'possessions' are treated in asylums. Morbid conditions, however, are of such varied degrees that it is probable many have imagined a Being in whom their worst impulses are unrestrained, and thus there have been sufficient popular approximations to an imaginative conception of a Devil to enable the theological dogma, which few can analyse, to survive.

It must not be supposed, however, that the moral and spiritual ideals, to which allusion has just been made, are normally represented in the various Devils which we have to consider. It is the characteristic of personifications, whether celestial or infernal, to supersede gradually the ideas out of which they spring. As in the fable of Agni, who is said to have devoured his parents when he was born, a metaphor of fire consuming the two sticks which produce it, religious history shows both deities and devils, by the flame of personal devotion or hatred they engender, burning up the ideas that originate them. When instead of unconscious forces and inanimate laws working to results called good and evil, men see great personal Wills engaged in personal conflict, the universe becomes a government of combat; the stars of heaven, the angels and the imps, men and women, the very plants and animals, are caught up in the battle, to be marshalled on one side or the other; and in the military spirit and fury of the struggle the spiritual ideals become as insignificant beneath the phantom-hosts they evoked as the violets and daisies which an army tramples in its march. There is little difference at last between the moral characteristics of the respective armies of Ormuzd and Ahriman, Michael and Satan; their strategy and ferocity are the same.[9] Wherever the conception is that of a universe divided into hostile camps, the appropriate passions are kindled, and in the thick of the field, where Cruelty and Gentleness met, is seen at last a horned Beast confronted by a horned Lamb.[10] On both sides is exaltation of the horn.

We need only look at the outcome of the gentle and lowly Jesus through the exigencies of the church militant to see how potent are such forces. Although lay Christians of ordinary education are accustomed to rationalise their dogmas as well as they can, and dwell on the loving and patient characteristics of Jesus, the horns which were attached to the brow of him who said, 'Love your enemies' by ages of Christian warfare remain still in the Christ of Theology, and they are still depended on to overawe the 'sinner.' In an orthodox family with which I have had some acquaintance, a little boy, who had used naughty expressions of resentment towards a playmate was admonished that he should be more like Christ, 'who never did any harm to his enemies.' 'No,' answered the wrathful child, 'but he's a-going to.'

As in Demonology we trace the struggles of man with external obstructions, and the phantasms in which these were reflected until they were understood or surmounted, we have now to consider the forms which report human progression on a higher plane,—that of social, moral, and religious evolution. Creations of a crude Theology, in its attempt to interpret the moral sentiment, the Devils to which we now turn our attention have multiplied as the various interests of mankind have come into relations with their conscience. Every degree of ascent of the moral nature has been marked by innumerable new shadows cast athwart the mind and the life of man. Every new heaven of ideas is followed by a new earth, but ere this conformity of things to thoughts can take place struggles must come and the old demons will be recalled for new service. As time goes on things new grow old; the fresh issues pass away, their battlefields grow cold; then the brood of superstition must flit away to the next field where carrion is found. Foul and repulsive as are these vultures of the mind—organisms of moral sewage—every one of them is a witness to the victories of mankind over the evils they shadow, and to the steady advance of a new earth which supplies them no habitat but the archæologist's page.

Notes

1 'Treatise of Spirits.' By John Beaumont, Gent. London, 1705.
2 Luke x. 19.
3 Rev. xii.
4 Rev. xii. cf. verses 4, 9 and 14.
5 Rev. xii. 12.
6 'Zendavesta,' Yaçna xxx.; Max Müller, 'Science of Religion,' p. 238.
7 Yaçna xliii.
8 'Die Christliche Lehre von der Sünde.' Von Julius Müller, Breslau, 1844, i. 193.
9 'Ormazd brought help to me; by the grace of Ormazd my troops entirely defeated the rebel army and took Sitratachmes, and brought him before me. Then I cut off his nose and his ears, and I scourged him. He was kept chained at my door. All the kingdom beheld him. Afterwards I crucified him at Arbela.' So says the tablet of Darius Hystaspes. But what could Darius have done 'by the grace of Ahriman'?
10 Cf. Rev. v. 6 and xii. 15.

Chapter II - The Second Best

Respect for the Devil—Primitive atheism—Idealisation—Birth of new gods—New gods diabolised—Compromise between new gods and old—Foreign deities degraded—Their utilisation.

A lady residing in Hampshire, England, recently said to a friend of the present writer, both being mothers, 'Do you make your children bow their heads whenever they mention the Devil's name? I do,' she added solemnly,—'I think it's safer.'

This instance of reverence for the Devil's name, occurring in a respectable English family, may excite a smile; but if my reader has perused the third and fourth chapters (Part I.) of this work, in which it was necessary to state certain facts and principles which underlie the phenomena of degradation in both Demonology and Devil-lore, he will already know the high significance of nearly all the names which have invested the personifications of evil; and he will not be surprised to find their original sanctity, though lowered, sometimes, surviving in such imaginary forms after the battles in which they were vanquished have passed out of all contemporary interest. If, for example, instead of the Devil, whose name is uttered with respect in the Hampshire household, any theological bogey of our own time were there mentioned, such as 'Atheist,' it might hardly receive such considerate treatment.

The two chapters just referred to anticipate much that should be considered at this point of our inquiry. It is only necessary here to supplement them with a brief statement, and to some extent a recapitulation, of the processes by which degraded deities are preserved to continue through a structural development and fulfil a necessary part in every theological scheme which includes the conception of an eternal difference between good and evil.

Every personification when it first appears expresses a higher and larger view. When deities representing the physical needs of mankind have failed, as they necessarily must, to meet those needs, atheism follows, though it cannot for a long time find philosophical expression. It is an atheism ad hoc, so to say, and works by degrading particular gods instead of by constructing antitheistic theories. Successive dynasties of deities arise and flourish in this way, each representing a less arbitrary relation to nature,—peril lying in that direction,—and a higher moral and spiritual ideal, this being the stronghold of deities. It is obvious that it is far easier to maintain the theory that prayers are heard and answered by a deity if those prayers are limited to spiritual requests, than when they are petitions for outward benefits. By giving over the cruel and remorseless forces of nature to the Devil,—i.e., to this or that personification of them who, as gods, had been appealed to in vain to soften such forces,—the more spiritual god that follows gains in security as well as beauty what he surrenders of empire and omnipotence. This law, illustrated in our chapter on Fate, operates with tremendous effect upon the conditions under which the old combat is spiritualised.

An eloquent preacher has said:—'Hawthorne's fine fancy of the youth who ascribed heroic qualities to the stone face on the brow of a cliff, thus converting the rocky profile into a man, and, by dint of meditating on it with admiring awe, actually transferred to himself the moral elements he worshipped, has been made fact a thousand times, is made fact every day, by earnest spirits who by faithful longing turn their visions into verities, and obtain live answers to their petitions to shadows.'[1]

However imaginary may be the benedictions so derived by the worshipper from his image, they are most real as they redound to the glory and power of the image. The crudest personification, gathering up the sanctities of generations, associated with the holiest hopes, the best emotions, the profoundest aspirations of human nature, may be at length so identified with these sentiments that they all seem absolutely dependent upon the image they invest. Every criticism of such a personification then seems like a blow aimed at the moral laws. If educated men are still found in Christendom discussing whether morality can survive the overthrow of such personifications, and whether life were worth living without them, we may readily understand how in times when the social, ethical, and psychological sciences did not exist at all, all that human beings valued seemed destined to stand or fall with the Person supposed to be their only keystone. But no Personage, however highly throned, can arrest the sun and moon, or the mind and life of humanity. With every advance in physical or social conditions moral elements must be influenced; every new combination involves a recast of experiences, and presently of convictions. Henceforth the deified image can only remain as a tyrant over the heart and brain which have created it,—

Creatura a un tempo
E tiranno de l'uom, da cui soltanto
Ebbe nomi ed aspetti e regno e altari.[2]

This personification, thus 'at once man's creature and his tyrant,' is objectively a name. But as it has been invested with all that has been most sacred, it is inevitable that any name raised against it shall be equally associated with all that has been considered basest. This also must be personified, for the same reason that the good is personified; and as names are chiefly hereditary, it pretty generally happens that the title of some fallen and discredited deity is advanced to receive the new anathema. But what else does he receive? The new ideas; the growing ideals and the fresh enthusiasms are associated with some fantastic shape with anathematised name evoked from the past, and thus a portentous situation is reached. The worshippers of the new image will not accept the bad name and its base associations; they even grow strong enough to claim the name and altars of the existing order, and give battle for the same. Then occurs the demoralisation, literally speaking, of the older theology. The personification reduced to struggle for its existence can no longer lay emphasis upon the moral principles it had embodied, these being equally possessed by their opponents; nay, its partisans manage to associate with their holy Name so much bigotry and cruelty that the innovators are at length willing to resign it. The personal loyalty, which is found to continue after loyalty to principles has ceased, proceeds to degrade the virtues once reverenced when they are found connected with a rival name. 'He casteth out devils through Beelzebub' is a very ancient cry. It was heard again when Tertullian said, 'Satan is God's ape.' St. Augustine recognises the similarity between the observances of Christians and pagans as proving the subtle imitativeness of the Devil; the phenomena referred to are considered elsewhere, but, in the present connection, it may be remarked that this readiness to regard the same sacrament as supremely holy or supremely diabolical as it is celebrated in honour of one name or another, accords closely with the reverence or detestation of things more important than sacraments, as they are, or are not, consecrated by what each theology deems official sanction. When sects talk of 'mere morality' we may recognise in the phrase the last faint war-cry of a god from whom the spiritual ideal has passed away, and whose name even can survive only through alliance with the new claimant of his altars. While the new gods were being called devils the old ones were becoming such.

The victory of the new ideal turns the old one to an idol. But we are considering a phase of the world when superstition must invest the new as well as the old, though in a weaker degree. A new religious system prevails chiefly through its

151

moral superiority to that it supersedes; but when it has succeeded to the temples and altars consecrated to previous divinities, when the ardour of battle is over and conciliation becomes a policy as well as a virtue, the old idol is likely to be treated with respect, and may not impossibly be brought into friendly relation with its victorious adversary. He may take his place as 'the second best,' to borrow Goethe's phrase, and be assigned some function in the new theologic régime. Thus, behind the simplicity of the Hampshire lady instructing her children to bow at mention of the Devil's name, stretch the centuries in which Christian divines have as warmly defended the existence of Satan as that of God himself. With sufficient reason: that infernal being, some time God's 'ape' and rival, was necessarily developed into his present position and office of agent and executioner under the divine government. He is the great Second Best; and it is a strange hallucination to fancy that, in an age of peaceful inquiry, any divine personification can be maintained without this patient Goat, who bears blame for all the faults of nature, and who relieves divine Love from the odium of supplying that fear which is the mother of devotion,—at least in the many millions of illogical eyes into which priests can still look without laughing.

Such, in brief outline, has been the interaction of moral and intellectual forces operating within the limits of established systems, and of the nations governed by them. But there are added factors, intensifying the forces on each side, when alien are brought into rivalry and collision with national deities. In such a contest, besides the moral and spiritual sentiments and the household sanctities, which have become intertwined with the internal deities, national pride is also enlisted, and patriotism. But on the other side is enlisted the charm of novelty, and the consciousness of fault and failure in the home system. Every system imported to a foreign land leaves behind its practical shortcomings, puts its best foot forward—namely, its theoretical foot—and has the advantage of suggesting a way of escape from the existing routine which has become oppressive. Napoleon I. said that no people profoundly attached to the institutions of their country can be conquered; but what people are attached to the priestly system over them? That internal dissatisfaction which, in secular government, gives welcome to a dashing Corsican or a Prince of Orange, has been the means of introducing many an alien religion, and giving to many a prophet the honour denied him in his own country. Buddha was a Hindu, but the triumph of his religion is not in India; Zoroaster was a Persian, but there are no Parsees in Persia; Christianity is hardly a colonist even in the native land of Christ.

These combinations and changes were not effected without fierce controversies, ferocious wars, or persecutions, and the formation of many devils. Nothing is more normal in ancient systems than the belief that the gods of other nations are devils. The slaughter of the priests of Baal corresponds with the development of their god into Beelzebub. In proportion to the success of Olaf in crushing the worshippers of Odin, their deity is steadily transformed to a diabolical Wild Huntsman. But here also the forces of partial recovery, which we have seen operating in the outcome of internal reform, manifest themselves; the vanquished, and for a time outlawed deity, is, in many cases, subsequently conciliated and given an inferior, and, though hateful, a useful office in the new order. Sometimes, indeed, as in the case of the Hindu destroyer Siva, it is found necessary to assign a god, anathematised beyond all power of whitewash, to an equal rank with the most virtuous deity. Political forces and the exigencies of propagandism work many marvels of this kind, which will meet us in the further stages of our investigation.

Every superseded god who survives in subordination to another is pretty sure to be developed into a Devil. Euphemism may tell pleasant fables about him, priestcraft may find it useful to perpetuate belief in his existence, but all the evils of the universe, which it is inconvenient to explain, are gradually laid upon him, and sink him down, until nothing is left of his former glory but a shining name.

Notes

1 *'Prayer and Work.' By Octavius B. Frothingham. New York, 1877.*
2 *'Lucifero, Poema di Mario Rapisardi.' Milano, 1877.*

Chapter III - Ahriman: The Divine Devil

Mr. Irving's impersonation of Superstition—Revolution against pious privilege—Doctrine of 'merits'—Saintly immorality in India—A Pantheon turned Inferno—Zendavesta on Good and Evil—Parsî Mythology—The Combat of Ahriman with Ormuzd—Optimism—Parsî Eschatology—Final Restoration of Ahriman.

Any one who has witnessed Mr. Henry Irving's scholarly and masterly impersonation of the character of Louis XI. has had an opportunity of recognising a phase of superstition which happily it were now difficult to find off the stage. Nothing could exceed the fine realism with which that artist brought before the spectator the perfected type of a pretended religion from which all moral features have been eliminated by such slow processes that the final success is unconsciously reached, and the horrible result appears unchecked by even any affectation of actual virtue. We see the king at sound of a bell pausing in his instructions for a treacherous assassination to mumble his prayers, and then instantly reverting to the villany over whose prospective success he gloats. In the secrecy of his chamber no mask falls, for there is no mask; the face of superstition and vice on which we look is the real face which the ages of fanaticism have transmitted to him.

Such a face has oftener been that of a nation than that of an individual, for the healthy forces of life work amid the homes and hearts of mankind long before their theories are reached and influenced. Such a face it was against which the moral insurrection which bears the name of Zoroaster arose, seeing it as physiognomy of the Evil Mind, naming it Ahriman, and, in the name of the conscience, aiming at it the blow which is still felt across the centuries.

Ingenious theorists have accounted for the Iranian philosophy of a universal war between Ormuzd (Ahuramazda) the Good, and Ahriman (Angromainyus) the Evil, by vast and terrible climatic changes, involving extremes of heat and cold, of which geologists find traces about Old Iran, from which a colony of Aryans migrated to New Iran, or Persia. But although physical conditions of this character may have supplied many of the metaphors in which the conflict between Good and Evil is described in the Avesta, there are other characteristics of that ancient scripture which render it more probable that the early colonisation of Persia was, like that of New England, the result of a religious struggle. Some of the gods most adored in India reappear as execrated demons in the religion of Zoroaster; the Hindu word for god is the Parsî word for devil. These antagonisms are not merely verbal; they are accompanied in the Avesta with the most furious denunciations of theological opponents, whom it is not difficult to identify with the priests and adherents of the Brahman religion.

The spirit of the early scriptures of India leaves no room for doubt as to the point at which this revolution began. It was against pious Privilege. The saintly hierarchy of India were a caste quite irresponsible to moral laws. The ancient gods, vague names for the powers of nature, were strictly limited in their dispensations to those of their priests;1 and as to these priests the chief necessities were ample offerings, sacrifices, and fulfilment of the ceremonial ordinances in which their authority was organised, these were the performances rewarded by a reciprocal recognition of authority. To the image of this political régime, theology, always facile, accommodated the regulations of the gods. The moral law can only live by being supreme; and as it was not supreme in the Hindu pantheon, it died out of it. The doctrine of 'merits,' invented by priests purely for their own power, included nothing meritorious, humanly considered; the merits consisted of costly sacrifices, rich offerings to temples, tremendous penances for fictitious sins, ingeniously devised to aggrandise the penances which disguised power, and prolonged austerities that might be comfortably commuted by the wealthy. When this doctrine had obtained general adherence, and was represented by a terrestrial government corresponding to it, the gods were necessarily subject to it. That were only to say that the powers of nature were obedient to the 'merits' of privileged saints; and from this it is an obvious inference that they are relieved from moral laws binding on the vulgar. The legends which represent this phase of priestly dominion are curiously mixed. It would appear that under the doctrine of 'merits' the old gods declined. Such appears to be the intimation of the stories which report the distress of the gods through the power of human saints. The Rajah Ravana acquired such power that he was said to have arrested the sun and moon, and so oppressed the gods that they temporarily transformed themselves to monkeys in order to destroy him. Though Viswámitra murders a saint, his merits are such that the gods are in great alarm lest they become his menials; and the completeness, with which moral considerations are left out of the struggle on both sides is disclosed in the item that the gods commissioned a nymph to seduce the saintly murderer, and so reduce a little the force of his austerities. It will be remembered that the ancient struggle of the Devas and Asuras was not owing to any moral differences, but to an alleged unfair distribution of the ambrosia produced by their joint labours in churning the ocean. The fact that the gods cheated the demons on that occasion was never supposed to affect the supremacy they acquired by the treachery; and it could, therefore, cause no scandal when later legends reported that the demons were occasionally able to take gods captive by the practice of these wonderful 'merits' which were so independent of morals. One Asura is said to have gained such power in this way that he subjugated the gods, and so punished them that Siva, who had originally endowed that demon, called into being Scanda, a war-god, to defend the tortured deities. The most ludicrous part of all is that the gods themselves were gradually reduced to the necessity of competing like others for these tremendous powers; thus the Bhagavat Purana states that Brahma was enabled to create the universe by previously undergoing penance for sixteen thousand years.

The legends just referred to are puranic, and consequently of much later date than the revolution traceable in the Iranian religion; but these later legends are normal growths from vedic roots. These were the principles of ancient theology, and the foundation of priestly government. In view of them we need not wonder that Hindu theology devised no special devil; almost any of its gods might answer the purposes of one. Nor need we be surprised that it had no particular hell; any society organised by the sanctions of religion, but irresponsible to its moral laws, would render it unnecessary to look far for a hell.

From this cosmological chaos the more intelligent Hindus were of course liberated; but the degree to which the fearful training had corrupted the moral tissues of those who had been subjected to it was revealed in the bald principle of their

153

philosophers, that the superstition must continue to be imposed on the vulgar, whilst the learned might turn all the gods into a scientific terminology.

The first clear and truthful eye that touched that system would transform it from a Heaven to an Inferno. So was it changed under the eye of Zoroaster. That ancient pantheon which had become a refuge for all the lies of the known world; whose gods were liars and their supporters liars; was now turned into a realm of organised disorder, of systematised wrong; a vast creation of wickedness, at whose centre sat its creator and inspirer, the immoral god, the divine devil—Ahriman.

It is indeed impossible to ascertain how far the revolt against the old Brahmanic system was political. It is, of course, highly improbable that any merely speculative system would excite a revolution; but at the same time it must be remembered that, in early days, an importance was generally attached to even abstract opinions such as we still find among the superstitious who regard an atheistic sentiment as worse than a theft. However this may have been, the Avesta does not leave us in any doubt as to the main fact,—namely, that at a certain time and place man came to a point where he had to confront antagonism to fundamental moral principles, and that he found the so-called gods against him. In the establishment of those principles priests recognised their own disestablishment. What those moral laws that had become necessary to society were is also made clear. 'We worship the Pure, the Lord of Purity!' 'We honour the good spirit, the good kingdom, the good law,—all that is good.' 'Evil doctrine shall not again destroy the world.' 'Good is the thought, good the word, good the deed, of the pure Zarathustra.' 'In the beginning the two heavenly Ones spoke—the Good to the Evil—thus: Our souls, doctrines, words, works, do not unite together.' These sentences are from the oldest Gâthâs of the Avesta.

The following is a very ancient Gâthâ:—'All your Devas (Hindu 'gods') are only manifold children of the Evil Mind, and the great One who worships the Saoma of lies and deceits; besides the treacherous acts for which you are notorious in the Seven Regions of the earth. You have invented all the evil that men speak and do, which is indeed pleasant to the Devas, and is devoid of all goodness, and therefore perishes before the insight of the truth of the wise. Thus you defraud men of their good minds and of their immortality by your evil minds—as well by those of the Devas as through that of the Evil Spirit—through evil deeds and evil words, whereby the power of liars grows.

1. '1. Come near, and listen to the wise sayings of the omniscient, the songs in praise of the Living One, and the prayers of the Good Spirit, the glorious truths whose origin is seen in the flames.
2. '2. Listen, therefore, to the Earth spirit—Look at the flames with reverent mind. Every one, man and woman, is to be distinguished according to his belief. Ye ancient Powers, watch and be with us!
3. '3. From the beginning there were two Spirits, each active in itself. They are the good and the bad in thought, word, and deed. Choose ye between them: do good, not evil!
4. '4. And these two Spirits meet and create the first existence, the earthy, that which is and that which is not, and the last, the spiritual. The worst existence is for the liars, the best for the truthful.
5. '5. Of these two spirits choose ye one, either the lying, the worker of Evil, or the true holiest spirit. Whoso chooses the first chooses the hardest fate; whoso the last, honours Ahuramazda in faith and in truth by his deeds.
6. '6. Ye cannot serve both of these two. An evil spirit whom we will destroy surprises those who deliberate, saying, Choose the Evil Mind! Then do those spirits gather in troops to attack the two lives of which the prophets prophesy.
7. '7. And to this earthly life came Armaiti with earthly power to help the truth, and the good disposition: she, the Eternal, created the material world, but the Spirit is with thee, O Wise One! the first of creations in time.
8. '8. When any evil falls upon the spirit, thou, O Wise One, givest temporal possessions and a good disposition; but him whose promises are lies, and not truth, thou punishest.'

Around the hymns of the Avesta gradually grew a theology and a mythology which were destined to exert a powerful influence on the world. These are contained in the Bundehesch.2 Anterior to all things and all beings was Zeruane-Akrene ('Boundless Time'), so exalted that he can only be worshipped in silence. From him emanated two Ferouers, spiritual types, which took form in two beings, Ormuzd and Ahriman. These were equally pure; but Ahriman became jealous of his first-born brother, Ormuzd. To punish Ahriman for his evil feeling, the Supreme Being condemned him to 12,000 years' imprisonment in an empire of rayless Darkness. During that period must rage the conflict between Light and Darkness, Good and Evil. As Ormuzd had his pre-existing type or Ferouer, so by a similar power—much the same as the Platonic Logos or Word—he created the pure or spiritual world, by means of which the empire of Ahriman should be overthrown. On the earth (still spiritual) he raised the exceeding high mountain Albordj, Elburz (snow mountain),3 on whose summit he fixed his throne; whence he stretched the bridge Chinevat, which, passing directly over Duzhak, the abyss of Ahriman (or hell), reaches to the portal of Gorodman, or heaven. All this was but a Ferouer world—a prototype of the material world. In anticipation of its incorporation in a material creation, Ormuzd (by emanations) created in his own image six Amshaspands, or agents, of both sexes, to be models of perfection to lower spirits—and to mankind, when they should be

154

created—and offer up their prayers to himself. The second series of emanations were the Izeds, benevolent genii and guardians of the world, twenty-eight in number, of whom the chief is Mithras, the Mediator. The third series of emanations were the innumerable Ferouers of things and men—for each must have its soul, which shall purify them in the day of resurrection. In antagonism to all these, Ahriman produced an exactly similar host of dark and evil powers. These Devas rise, rank on rank, to their Arch-Devs—each of whom is chained to his planet—and their head is Ash-Mogh, the 'two-footed serpent of lies,' who seems to correspond to Mithras, the divine Mediator.

After a reign of 3000 years Ormuzd entered on the work of realising his spiritual emanations in a material universe. He formed the sun as commander-in-chief, the moon as his lieutenant, the planets as captains of a great host—the stars—who were soldiers in his war against Ahriman. The dog Sirius he set to watch at the bridge Chinevat (the Milky Way), lest thereby Ahriman should scale the heavens. Ormuzd then created earth and water, which Ahriman did not try to prevent, knowing that darkness was inherent in these. But he struck a blow when life was produced. This was in form of a Bull, and Ahriman entered it and it perished; but on its destruction there came out of its left shoulder the seed of all clean and gentle animals, and, out of its right shoulder—Man.

Ahriman had matched every creation thus far; but to make man was beyond his power, and he had no recourse but to destroy him. However, when the original man was destroyed, there sprang from his body a tree which bore the first human pair, whom Ahriman, however, corrupted in the manner elsewhere described.

It is a very notable characteristic of this Iranian theology, that although the forces of good and evil are co-extensive and formally balanced, in potency they are not quite equal. The balance of force is just a little on the side of the Good Spirit. And this advantage appears in man. Zoroaster said, 'No earthly man with a hundredfold strength does so much evil as Mithra with heavenly strength does good;' and this thought reappears in the Parsî belief that the one part of paradisiac purity, which man retained after his fall, balances the ninety-nine parts won by Ahriman, and in the end will redeem him. For this one divine ray preserved enables him to receive and obey the Avesta, and to climb to heaven by the stairway of three vast steps—pure thought, pure word, pure deed. The optimistic essence of the mythology is further shown in the belief that every destructive effort of Ahriman resulted in a larger benefit than Ormuzd had created. The Bull (Life) destroyed, man and animal sprang into being; the man destroyed, man and woman appeared. And so on to the end. In the last quarter of the 12,000 years for which Ahriman was condemned, he rises to greater power even than Ormuzd, and finally he will, by a fiery comet, set the visible universe in conflagration; but while this scheme is waxing to consummation Ormuzd will send his holy Prophet Sosioch, who will convert mankind to the true law,4 so that when Ahriman's comet consumes the earth he will really be purifying it. Through the vast stream of melted metals and minerals the righteous shall pass, and to them it will be as a bath of warm milk: the wicked in attempting to pass shall be swept into the abyss of Duzhak; having then suffered three days and nights, they shall be raised by Ormuzd refined and purified. Duzhak itself shall be purified by this fire, and last of all Ahriman himself shall ascend to his original purity and happiness. Then from the ashes of the former world shall bloom a paradise that shall remain for ever.

In this system it is notable that we find the monster serpent of vedic mythology, Ahi, transformed into an infernal region, Duzhak. The dragon, being a type of physical suffering, passes away in Iranian as in the later Semitic mythology before the new form, which represents the stings of conscience though it may be beneath external pleasure. In this respect, therefore, Ahriman fulfils the definition of a devil already given. In the Avesta he fulfils also another condition essential to a devil, the love of evil in and for itself. But in the later theology it will be observed that evil in Ahriman is not organic. The war being over and its fury past, the hostile chief is seen not so black as he had been painted; the belief obtains that he does not actually love darkness and evil. He was thrust into them as a punishment for his jealousy, pride, and destructive ambition. And because that dark kingdom was a punishment—therefore not congenial—it was at length (the danger past) held to be disciplinary. Growing faith in the real supremacy of Good discovers the immoral god to be an exaggerated anthropomorphic egoist; this divine devil is a self-centred potentate who had attempted to subordinate moral law and human welfare to his personal ascendancy. His fate having sealed the sentence on all ambitions of that character, humanity is able to pardon the individual offender, and find a hope that Ahriman, having learned that no real satisfaction for a divine nature can be found in mere power detached from rectitude, will join in the harmony of love and loyalty at last.

Notes

1
E quanto ebbe e mantiene a l'uom soltanto
Il deve, a l'uom che d'oqui sue destino
O prospero, o maligno, arbitro e solo.
'Whatever he (God) had, he owed to man alone, to man who, for good or ill, is sole arbiter of his own fate.'—Rapisardi's Lucifero.
2 The following abridgment mainly follows that of James Freeman Clarke in his 'Ten Great Religions.'
3 White or Snowy Mountain. Cf. Alp, Elf, etc.
4 'Elias shall first come and restore all things.'

Chapter IV - Viswámitra: The Theocratic Devil

Priestcraft and Pessimism—An Aryan Tetzel and his Luther—Brahman Frogs—Evolution of the sacerdotal Saint—Viswámitra the Accuser of Virtue—The Tamil Passion-play 'Hariśchandra'—Ordeal of Goblins—The Martyr of Truth—Virtue triumphant over ceremonial 'merits'—Hariśchandra and Job.

Priestcraft in government means pessimism in the creed and despair in the heart. Under sacerdotal rule in India it seemed paradise enough to leave the world, and the only hell dreaded was a return to it. 'The twice-born man,' says Manu, 'who shall without intermission have passed the time of his studentship, shall ascend after death to the most exalted of regions, and no more spring to birth again in this lower world.' Some clause was necessary to keep the twice-born man from suicide. Buddha invented a plan of suicide-in-life combined with annihilation of the gods, which was driven out of India because it put into the minds of the people the philosophy of the schools. Thought could only be trusted among classes interested to conceal it.

The power and authority of a priesthood can only be maintained on the doctrine that man is 'saved' by the deeds of a ceremonial law; any general belief that morality is more acceptable to gods than ceremonies must be fatal to those occult and fictitious virtues which hedge about every pious impostor. Sacerdotal power in India depended on superstitions carefully fostered concerning the mystical properties of a stimulating juice (soma), litanies, invocations, and benedictions by priests; upon sacrifices to the gods, including their priests, austerities, penances, pilgrimages, and the like; one characteristic running through all the performances—their utter worthlessness to any being in the universe except the priest. An artificial system of this kind has to create its own materials, and evoke forces of evolution from many regions of nature. It is a process requiring much more than the wisdom of the serpent and more than its harmfulness; and there is a bit of nature's irony in the fact that when the Brahman Rishi gained supremacy, the Cobra was also worshipped as belonging to precisely the same caste and sanctity.

There are traces of long and fierce struggles preceding this consummation. Even in the Vedic age—in the very dawn of religious history—Tetzel appears with his indulgences and Luther confronts him. The names they bore in ancient India were Viswámitra and Vasishtha. Both of these were among the seven powerful Rishis who made the hierarchy of India in the earliest age known to us. Both were composers of some of the chief hymns of the Vedas, and their respective hymns bear the stamp of the sacerdotal and the anti-sacerdotal parties which contended before the priestly sway had reached its complete triumph. Viswámitra was champion of the high priestly party and its political pretensions. In the Rig-Veda there are forty hymns ascribed to him and his family, nearly all of which celebrate the divine virtues of Soma-juice and the Soma-sacrifice. As the exaltation of the priestly caste in Israel was connected with a miracle, in which the Jordan stopped flowing till the ark had been carried over, so the rivers Sutledge and Reyah were said to have rested from their course when Viswámitra wished to cross them in seeking the Soma. This Rishi became identified in the Hindu mind for all time with political priestcraft. On the other hand, Vasishtha became equally famous for his hostility to that power, as well as for his profoundly religious character,—the finest hymns of the Vedas, as to moral feeling, being those that bear his name. The anti-sacerdotal spirit of Vasishtha is especially revealed in a strange satirical hymn in which he ridicules the ceremonial Bráhmans under the guise of a panegyric on frogs. In this composition occur such verses as these:—

'Like Bráhmans at the Soma-sacrifice of Atirâtra, sitting round a full pond and talking, you, O frogs, celebrate this day of the year when the rainy season begins.

'These Bráhmans, with their Soma, have had their say, performing the annual rite. These Adhwaryus, sweating while they carry the hot pots, pop out like hermits.

'They have always observed the order of the gods as they are to be worshipped in the twelvemonth; these men do not neglect their season....

'Cow-noise gave, Goat-noise gave, the Brown gave, and the Green gave us treasures. The frogs, who give us hundreds of cows, lengthened our life in the rich autumn.'[1]

Viswámitra and Vasishtha appear to have been powerful rivals in seeking the confidence of King Sudás, and from their varying fortunes came the tremendous feud between them which plays so large a part in the traditions of India. The men were both priests, as are both ritualists and broad-churchmen in the present day. They were borne on the stream of mythologic evolution to representative regions very different from any they could have contemplated. Vasishtha, ennobled by the moral sentiment of ages, appears as the genius of truth and justice, maintaining these as of more 'merit' than any ceremonial perfections. The Bráhmans, whom he once ridiculed, were glad enough in the end to make him their patron saint, though they did not equally honour his principles. On the other hand, Viswámitra became the type of that immoral divinity which received its Iranian anathema in Ahriman. The murder he commits is nothing in a personage whose Soma-celebrations have raised him so high above the trivialities of morality.

It is easy to see what must be the further development of such a type as Viswámitra when he shall have passed from the guarded pages of puranic tradition to the terrible simplicities of folklore. The saint whose majesty is built on 'merits,' which have no relation to what the humble deem virtues, naturally holds such virtues in cynical contempt; naturally also he is indignant if any one dares to suggest that the height he has reached by costly and prolonged observances may be attained by poor and common people through the practice of virtue. The next step is equally necessary. Since it is hard to argue down the facts of human nature, Vasishtha is pretty sure to have a strong, if sometimes silent, support for his heretical theory of a priesthood representing virtue; consequently Viswámitra will be reduced at length to deny the existence of virtue, and will become the Accuser of those to whom virtues are attributed. Finally, from the Accuser to the Tempter the transition is inevitable. The public Accuser must try and make good his case, and if the facts do not support it, he must create other facts which will, or else bear the last brand of his tribe—Slanderer.

Leaving out of sight all historical or probable facts concerning Viswámitra and Vasishtha, but remembering the spirit of them, let us read the great Passion-play of the East, in which their respective parts are performed again as intervening ages have interpreted them. The hero of this drama is an ancient king named Harischandra, who, being childless, and consequently unable to gain immortality, promised the god Varuna to sacrifice to him a son if one were granted him. The son having been born, the father beseeches Varuna for respite, which is granted again and again, but stands firmly by his promise, although it is finally commuted. The repulsive features of the ancient legend are eliminated in the drama, the promise now being for a vast sum of money which the king cannot pay, but which Viswámitra would tempt him to escape by a technical fiction. Sir Mutu Cumára Swámy, whose translation I follow, presents many evidences of the near relation in which this drama stands to the religious faith of the people in Southern India and parts of Ceylon, where its representation never fails to draw vast crowds from every part of the district in which it may occur, the impression made by it being most profound.2

We are first introduced to Harischandra, King of Ayòdiah (Oude), in his palace, surrounded by every splendour, and by the devotion of his prosperous people. His first word is an ascription to the 'God of gods.' His ministers come forward and recount the wealth and welfare of the nation. The first Act witnesses the marriage of Harischandra with the beautiful princess Chandravatí, and it closes with the birth of a son.

The second Act brings us into the presence of Indra in the Abode of the Gods. The Chief enters the Audience Hall of his palace, where an assembly of deities and sages has awaited him. These sages are holy men who have acquired supernatural power by their tremendous austerities; and of these the most august is Viswámitra. By the magnitude and extent of his austerities he has gained a power beyond even that of the Triad, and can reduce the worlds to cinders. All the gods court his favour. As the Council proceeds, Indra addresses the sages—'Holy men! as gifted with supernatural attributes, you roam the universe with marvellous speed, there is no place unknown to you. I am curious to learn who, in the present times, is the most virtuous sovereign on the earth below. What chief of mortals is there who has never told a lie—who has never swerved from the course of justice?' Vasishtha, a powerful sage and family-priest of Harischandra, declares that his royal disciple is such a man. But the more powerful Viswámitra denounces Harischandra as cruel and a liar. The quarrel between the two Rishis waxes fierce, until Indra puts a stop to it by deciding that an experiment shall be made on Harischandra. Vasishtha agrees that if his disciple can be shown to have told a lie, or can be made to tell one, the fruit of his life-long austerities, and all the power so gained, shall be added to Viswámitra; while the latter must present his opponent with half of his 'merits' if Harischandra be not made to swerve from the truth. Viswámitra is to employ any means whatever, neither Indra or any other interfering.

Viswámitra sets about his task of trying and tempting Harischandra by informing that king that, in order to perform a sacrifice of special importance, he has need of a mound of gold as high as a missile slung by a man standing on an elephant's back. With the demand of so sacred a being Harischandra has no hesitation in complying, and is about to deliver the gold when Viswámitra requests him to be custodian of the money for a time, but perform the customary ceremony of transfer. Holding Harischandra's written promise to deliver the gold whensoever demanded, Viswámitra retires with compliments. Then wild beasts ravage Harischandra's territory; these being expelled, a demon boar is sent, but is vanquished by the monarch. Viswámitra then sends unchaste dancing-girls to tempt Harischandra; and when he has ordered their removal, Viswámitra returns with them, and, feigning rage, accuses him of slaying innocent beasts and of cruelty to the girls. He declares that unless Harischandra yields to the Pariah damsels, he himself shall be reduced to a Pariah slave. Harischandra offers all his kingdom and possessions if the demand is withdrawn, absolutely refusing to swerve from his virtue. This Viswámitra accepts, is proclaimed sovereign of Ayòdiah, and the king goes forth a beggar with his wife and child. But now, as these are departing, Viswámitra demands that mound of gold which was to be paid when called for. In vain Harischandra pleads that he has already delivered up all he possesses, the gold included; the last concession is declared to have nothing to do with the first. Yet Viswámitra says he will be charitable; if Harischandra will simply declare that he never pledged the gold, or, having done so, does not feel bound to pay it, he will cancel that debt. 'Such a declaration I can never make,' replies Harischandra. 'I owe thee the gold, and pay it I shall. Let a messenger accompany me and leave me not till I have given him thy due.'

From this time the efforts of Viswámitra are directed to induce Harischandra to declare the money not due. Amid his heartbroken people—who cry, 'Where are the gods? Can they tolerate this?'—he who was just now the greatest and happiest monarch in the world goes forth on the highway a wanderer with his Chandravatí and their son Devaráta dressed in coarsest garments. His last royal deed is to set the crown on his tempter's head. The people and officers follow, and beg his permission to slay Viswámitra, but he rebukes them, and counsels submission. Viswámitra orders a messenger, Nakshatra, to accompany the three wretched ones, and inflict the severest sufferings on them until the gold is paid, and amid each ordeal to offer Hariśchandra all his former wealth and happiness if he will utter a falsehood.

They come to a desert whose sands are so hot that the wife faints. Hariśchandra bears his son in his arms, but in addition is compelled to bear Nakshatra (the Bráhman and tormentor) on his shoulders. They so pass amid snakes and scorpions, and receive terrible stings; they pass through storm and flood, and yet vainly does Nakshatra suggest the desired falsehood.

Then follows the ordeal of Demons, which gives an interesting insight into Tamil Demonology. One of the company exclaims—'How frightful they look! Who can face them? They come in battalions, young and old, small and great—all welcome us. They disport themselves with a wild dance; flames shoot from their mouths; their feet touch not the earth; they move in the air. Observe you the bleeding corpses of human beings in their hands. They crunch them and feed on the flesh. The place is one mass of gore and filth. Wolves and hyænas bark at them; jackals and dogs follow them. They are near. May Siva protect us!'

Nakshatra. How dreadful! Hariśchandra, what is this? Look! evil demons stare at me—I tremble for my life. Protect me now, and I ask you no more for the gold.

Hariśchandra. Have no fear, Nakshatra. Come, place thyself in the midst of us.

Chief of the Goblins. Men! little men! human vermin! intrude ye thus into my presence? Know that, save only the Bráhman standing in the midst of you, you are all my prey to-night.

Hariśchandra. Goblin! certainly thou art not an evil-doer, for thou hast excepted this holy Bráhman. As for ourselves, we know that the bodies which begin to exist upon earth must also cease to exist on it. What matters it when death comes? If he spares us now he reserves us only for another season. Good, kind demon! destroy us then together; here we await our doom.

Nakshatra. Hariśchandra! before you thus desert me, make the goblin promise you that he will not hurt me.

Hariśchandra. Thou hast no cause for alarm; thou art safe.

Chief of the Goblins. Listen! I find that all four of you are very thin; it is not worth my while to kill you. On examining closely, I perceive that the young Bráhman is plump and fat as a wild boar. Give him up to me—I want not the rest.

Nakshatra. O Gods! O Hariśchandra! you are a great monarch! Have mercy on me! Save me, save me! I will never trouble you for the gold, but treat you considerately hereafter.

Hariśchandra. Sir, thy life is safe, stand still.

Nakshatra. Allow me, sirs, to come closer to you, and to hold you by the hand (He grasps their hands.)

Hariśchandra. King of the Goblins! I address thee in all sincerity; thou wilt confer on us a great favour indeed by despatching us speedily to the Judgment Hall of the God of Death. The Bráhman must not be touched; devour us.

The Goblin (grinding his teeth in great fury). What! dare you disobey me? Will you not deliver the Bráhman?

Hariśchandra. No, we cannot. We alone are thy victims.

[Day breaks, and the goblins disappear.]

Having thus withstood all temptation to harm his enemy, or to break a promise he had given to treat him kindly, Hariśchandra is again pressed for the gold or the lie, and, still holding out, an ordeal of fire follows. Trusting the God of Fire will cease to afflict if one is sacrificed, Hariśchandra prepares to enter the conflagration first, and a pathetic contention occurs between him and his wife and son as to which shall be sacrificed. In the end Hariśchandra rushes in, but does not perish.

Hariśchandra is hoping to reach the temple of Vis Wanàth3 at Kasi and invoke his aid to pay the gold. To the temple he comes only to plead in vain, and Nakshatra tortures him with instruments. Finally Hariśchandra, his wife and child, are sold as slaves to pay the debt. But Viswámitra, invisibly present, only redoubles his persecutions. Hariśchandra is subjected to the peculiar degradation of having to burn dead bodies in a cemetery. Chandravatí and her son are subjected to cruelties. The boy is one day sent to the forest, is bitten by a snake, and dies. Chandravatí goes out in the night to find the body. She repairs with it to the cemetery. In the darkness she does not recognise her husband, the burner of the bodies, nor he his wife. He has strictly promised his master that every fee shall be paid, and reproaches the woman for coming in the darkness to avoid payment. Chandravatí offers in payment a sacred chain which Siva had thrown round her neck at birth, invisible to all but a perfect man. Hariśchandra alone has ever seen it, and now recognises his wife. But even now he will not perform the last rites over his dead child unless the fee can be obtained as promised. Chandravatí goes out into the city to beg the money, leaving Hariśchandra seated beside the dead body of Devaráta. In the street she stumbles over the corpse of another child, and takes it up; it proves to be the infant Prince, who has been murdered. Chandravatí—arrested and dragged before the king—in a state of frenzy declares she has killed the child. She is condemned to death, and her husband must be her executioner. But the last scene must be quoted nearly in full.

Verakvoo (Hariśchandra's master, leading on Chandravatí). Slave! this woman has been sentenced by our king to be executed without delay. Draw your sword and cut her head off. (Exit.)

158

Hariśchandra. I obey, master. (Draws the sword and approaches her.)

Chandravatí (coming to consciousness again). My husband! What! do I see thee again? I applaud thy resolution, my lord. Yes; let me die by thy sword. Be not unnerved, but be prompt, and perform thy duty unflinchingly.

Hariśchandra. My beloved wife! the days allotted to you in this world are numbered; you have run through the span of your existence. Convicted as you are of this crime, there is no hope for your life; I must presently fulfil my instructions. I can only allow you a few seconds; pray to your tutelary deities, prepare yourself to meet your doom.

Viswámitra (who has suddenly appeared). Hariśchandra! what, are you going to slaughter this poor woman? Wicked man, spare her! Tell a lie even now and be restored to your former state!

Hariśchandra. I pray, my lord, attempt not to beguile me from the path of rectitude. Nothing shall shake my resolution; even though thou didst offer to me the throne of Indra I would not tell a lie. Pollute not thy sacred person by entering such unholy grounds. Depart! I dread not thy wrath; I no longer court thy favour. Depart. (Viswámitra disappears.)

My love! lo I am thy executioner; come, lay thy head gently on this block with thy sweet face turned towards the east. Chandravatí, my wife, be firm, be happy! The last moment of our sufferings has at length come; for to sufferings too there is happily an end. Here cease our woes, our griefs, our pleasures. Mark! yet awhile, and thou wilt be as free as the vultures that now soar in the skies.

This keen sabre will do its duty. Thou dead, thy husband dies too—this self-same sword shall pierce my breast. First the child—then the wife—last the husband—all victims of a sage's wrath. I the martyr of Truth—thou and thy son martyrs for me, the martyr of Truth. Yes; let us die cheerfully and bear our ills meekly. Yes; let all men perish, let all gods cease to exist, let the stars that shine above grow dim, let all seas be dried up, let all mountains be levelled to the ground, let wars rage, blood flow in streams, let millions of millions of Hariśchandras be thus persecuted; yet let Truth be maintained—let Truth ride victorious over all—let Truth be the light—Truth the guide—Truth alone the lasting solace of mortals and immortals. Die, then, O goddess of Chastity! Die, at this the shrine of thy sister goddess of Truth!

[Strikes the neck of Chandravatí with great force; the sword, instead of harming her, is transformed into a string of superb pearls, which winds itself around her: the gods of heaven, all sages, and all kings appear suddenly to the view of Hariśchandra.]

Siva (the first of the gods). Hariśchandra, be ever blessed! You have borne your severe trials most heroically, and have proved to all men that virtue is of greater worth than all the vanities of a fleeting world. Be you the model of mortals. Return to your land, resume your authority, and rule your state. Devaráta, victim of Viswámitra's wrath, rise! (He is restored to life.)

Rise you, also, son of the King of Kasi, with whose murder you, Chandravatí, were charged through the machinations of Viswámitra. (He comes to life also.)

Hariśchandra. All my misfortunes are of little consequence, since thou, O God of gods, hast deigned to favour me with thy divine presence. No longer care I for kingdom, or power, or glory. I value not children, or wives, or relations. To thy service, to thy worship, to the redemption of my erring soul, I devote myself uninterruptedly hereafter. Let me not become the sport of men. The slave of a Pariah cannot become a king; the slave-girl of a Bráhman cannot become a queen. When once the milk has been drawn from the udder of a cow nothing can restore the self-same milk to it. Our degradation, O God, is now beyond redemption.

Viswámitra. I pray, O Siva, that thou wouldst pardon my folly. Anxious to gain the wager laid by me before the gods, I have most mercilessly tormented this virtuous king; yet he has proved himself the most truthful of all earthly sovereigns, triumphing victoriously over me and my efforts to divert him from his constancy. Hariśchandra, king of kings! I crave your forgiveness.

Verakvoo (throwing off his disguise). King Hariśchandra, think not that I am a Pariah, for you behold in me even Yáma, the God of Death.

Kalakanda (Chandravatí's cruel master, throwing off his disguise). Queen! rest not in the belief that you were the slave of a Bráhman. He to whom you devoted yourself am even I—the God of Fire, Agni.

Vasishtha. Hariśchandra, no disgrace attaches to thee nor to the Solar race, of which thou art the incomparable gem. Even this cemetery is in reality no cemetery: see! the illusion lasts not, and thou beholdest here a holy grove the abode of hermits and ascetics. Like the gold which has passed through successive crucibles, devoid of all impurities, thou, O King of Ayòdiah, shinest in greater splendour than even yon god of light now rising to our view on the orient hills. (It is morning.)

Siva. Hariśchandra, let not the world learn that Virtue is vanquished, and that its enemy, Vice, has become the victor. Go, mount yon throne again—proclaim to all that we, the gods, are the guardians of the good and the true. Indra! chief of the gods, accompany this sovereign with all your retinue, and recrown him emperor of Ayòdiah. May his reign be long—may all bliss await him in the other world!

The plot of this drama has probably done as much and as various duty as any in the world. It has spread like a spiritual banyan, whose branches, taking root, have swelled to such size that it is difficult now to say which is the original trunk. It may even be that the only root they all had in common is an invisible one in the human heart, developed in its necessary struggles amid nature after the pure and perfect life.

But neither in the Book of Job, which we are yet to consider, nor in any other variation of the theme, does it rise so high as in this drama of Hariśchandra. In Job it represents man loyal to his deity amid the terrible afflictions which that deity permits; but in Hariśchandra it shows man loyal to a moral principle even against divine orders to the contrary. Despite the hand of the licenser, and the priestly manipulations, visible here and there in it—especially towards the close—sacerdotalism stands confronted by its reaction at last, and receives its sentence in the joy with which the Hindu sees the potent Rishis with all their pretentious 'merits,' and the gods themselves, kneeling at the feet of the man who stands by Truth.

It is amusing to find the wincings of the priests through many centuries embodied in a legend about Hariśchandra after he went to heaven. It is related that he was induced by Nárada to relate his actions with such unbecoming pride that he was lowered from Svarga (heaven) one stage after each sentence; but having stopped in time, and paid homage to the gods, he was placed with his capital in mid-air, where eyes sacerdotally actinised may still see the aerial city at certain times. The doctrine of 'merits' will no doubt be able for some time yet to charge 'good deeds' with their own sin—pride; but, after all, the priest must follow the people far enough to confess that one must look upward to find the martyr of Truth. In what direction one must look to find his accuser requires no further intimation than the popular legend of Viswámitra.

Notes

1 That this satirical hymn was admitted into the Rig-Veda shows that these hymns were collected whilst they were still in the hands of the ancient Hindu families as common property, and were not yet the exclusive property of Bráhmans as a caste or association. Further evidence of the same kind is given by a hymn in which the expression occurs—'Do not be as lazy as a Bráhman.'—Mrs. Manning's Ancient and Mediæval India, i. 77. In the same work some particulars are given of the persons mentioned in this chapter. The Frog-satire is translated by Max Müller, A. S. L., p. 494.
2 'Arichandra, the Martyr of Truth: A Tamil Drama translated into English by Mutu Coomâra Swâmy, Mudliar, Member of Her Majesty's Legislative Council of Ceylon,' etc. London: Smith, Elder, & Co. 1863. This drama, it must be constantly borne in mind, in nowise represents the Vedic legend, told in the Aitereya-Bráhmana, vii. 13–18; nor the puranic legend, told in the Merkandeya-Purána. I have altered the spelling of the names to the Sanskrit forms, but otherwise follow Sir M. C. S.'s translation.
3 Siva; the 'lord of the world,' and of wealth. Cf. Pluto, Dis, Dives.

Chapter V - Elohim and Jehovah

Deified power—Giants and Jehovah—Jehovah's manifesto—The various Elohim—Two Jehovahs and two Tables—Contradictions—Detachment of the Elohim from Jehovah.

The sacred books of the Hebrews bring us into the presence of the gods (Elohim) supposed to have created all things out of nothing—nature-gods—just as they are in transition to the conception of a single Will and Personality. Though the plural is used ('gods') a singular verb follows: the tendency is already to that concentration which resulted in the enthronement of one supreme sovereign—Jehovah. The long process of evolution which must have preceded this conception is but slightly traceable in the Bible. It is, however, written on the face of the whole world, and the same process is going on now in its every phase. Whether with Gesenius[1] we take the sense of the word Elohim to be 'the revered,' or, with Fürst,[2] 'the mighty,' makes little difference; the fact remains that the word is applied elsewhere to gods in general, including such as were afterwards deemed false gods by the Jews; and it is more important still that the actions ascribed to the Elohim, who created the heavens and the earth, generally reflect the powerful and un-moral forces of nature. The work of creation in Genesis (i. and ii. 1–3) is that of giants without any moral quality whatever. Whether or not we take in their obvious sense the words, 'Elohim created man in his own image, ... male and female created he them,' there can be no question of the meaning of Gen. vi. 1, 2: 'The sons of Elohim saw the daughters of men that they were beautiful, and they took to themselves for wives whomsoever they chose.' When good and evil come to be spoken of, the name Jehovah[3] at once appears. The Elohim appear again in the Flood, the wind that assuaged it, the injunction to be fruitful and multiply, the cloud and rainbow; and gradually the germs of a moral government begin to appear in their assigning the violence of mankind as reason for the deluge, and in the covenant with Noah. But even after the name Jehovah had generally blended with, or even superseded, the other, we find Elohim often used where strength and wonder-working are thought of—e.g., 'Thou art the god that doest wonders' (Ps. lxxvii.). 'Thy way is in the sea, and thy path in the great waters, and thy footsteps are not known.'

Against the primitive nature-deities the personality and jealous supremacy of Jehovah was defined. The golden calf built by Aaron was called Elohim (plural, though there was but one calf). Solomon was denounced for building altars to the same; and when Jeroboam built altars to two calves, they are still so called. Other rivals—Dagon (Judges xvi.), Astaroth, Chemosh, Milcom (1 Kings xi.)—are called by the once-honoured name. The English Bible translates Elohim, God; Jehovah, the Lord; Jehovah Elohim, the Lord God; and the critical reader will find much that is significant in the varied use of these names. Thus (Gen. xxii.) it is Elohim that demands the sacrifice of Isaac, Jehovah that interferes to save him. At the same time, in editing the story, it is plainly felt to be inadmissible that Abraham should be supposed loyal to any other god than Jehovah; so Jehovah adopts the sacrifice as meant for himself, and the place where the ram was provided in place of Isaac is called Jehovah-Jireh. However, when we can no longer distinguish the two antagonistic conceptions by different names their actual incongruity is even more salient, and, as we shall see, develops a surprising result.

Jehovah inaugurates his reign by a manifesto against these giants, the Elohim, for whom the special claim—clamorously asserted when Aaron built the Golden Calf, and continued as the plea for the same deity—was that they (Elohim) had brought Israel out of Egypt. 'I,' cries Jehovah, 'am the Lord thy God, which have brought thee out of the land of Egypt, out of the house of bondage: thou shalt have no other gods but me;' and the first four commandments of the law are devoted entirely to a declaration of his majesty, his power (claiming credit for the creation), his jealous determination to punish his opponents and reward his friends, to vindicate the slightest disrespect to his name. The narrative of the Golden Calf was plainly connected with Sinai in order to illustrate the first commandment. The punishment of the believers in another divine emancipator, even though they had not yet received the proclamation, must be signal. Jehovah is so enraged that by his order human victims are offered up to the number of three thousand, and even after that, it is said, Jehovah plagued Israel on account of their Elohim-worship. In the same direction is the command to keep holy the Sabbath day, because on it he rested from the work of creation (Gen. xx.), or because on that day he delivered Israel from Egypt (Deut. v.), the editors do not seem to remember exactly which, but it is well enough to say both, for it is taking the two picked laurels from the brow of Elohim and laying them on that of Jehovah. In all of which it is observable that there is no moral quality whatever. Nero might equally command the Romans to have no other gods before himself, to speak his name with awe, to rest when he stopped working. In the fifth commandment, arbitrarily ascribed to the First Table, we have a transition to the moral code; though even there the honour of parents is jealously associated with Jehovah's greatness ('that thy days may be long in the land which Jehovah Elohim giveth thee'). The nature-gods were equal to that; for the Elohim had begotten the giants who were 'in the earth in those days.'

'Elohim spake unto Moses, and said unto him, I am Jehovah; and I appeared unto Abraham, unto Isaac, and unto Jacob by (the name of) God Almighty (El-Shaddai), but by my name Jehovah was I not known to them' (Exod. vi. 2, 3).

The ancient gods—the Elohim—were, in the process of absorption into the one great form, the repository of their several powers, distinguishable; and though, for the most part, they bear names related to the forces of nature, now and then they reflect the tendencies to humanisation. Thus we have 'the most high god' (El-elyon—e.g., Gen. xiv. 18); 'the everlasting-god' (El-elim, Gen. xxi. 33); 'the jealous god' (El-kana, Exod. xx. 5); 'the mighty god, and terrible' (El-gadol and nora, Deut. vii. 21); 'the living god' (El-chi, Josh. iii. 10); 'the god of heaven' (El-shemim, Ps. cxxxvi. 26); the 'god almighty' (El-shaddai,4 Exod. vi. 2). These Elohim, with each of whose names I have referred to an instance of its characteristic use, became epithets, as the powers they represented were more and more absorbed by the growing personality of Jehovah; but these epithets were also characters, and their historic expressions had also to undergo a process of slow and difficult digestion. The all-devouring grandeur of Jehovah showed what it had fed on. Not only all the honours, but many of the dishonours, of the primitive deities adhered to the sovereign whose rule was no doubt inaugurated by their disgrace and their barbarism. The costliness of the glory of divine absolutism is again illustrated in the evolution of the premature monotheism, which had for its figure-head the dread Jehovah, who, as heir of the nature-gods, became responsible for the monstrosities of a tribal demonolatry, thus being compelled to fill simultaneously the rôles of the demon and the lawgiver.5

The two tables of the law—one written by Jehovistic theology, the other by the moral sense of mankind—ascribed to this dual deity, for whom unity was so fiercely insisted on, may be read in their outcome throughout the Bible. They are here briefly, in a few examples, set forth side by side.

Table of Jehovah I.

- Exod. xxxiii. 27. 'Slay every man his brother, every man his companion, and every man his neighbour.'   Exod. xx. 13. 'Thou shalt not kill.'
- Num. xv. 32. 'While the children of Israel were in the wilderness, they found a man that gathered sticks upon the Sabbath Day.... And they put him in ward, because it was not declared what should be done to him. And the Lord said unto Moses, The man shall be surely put to death: all the congregation shall stone him with stones without the camp.' Neither this nor the similar punishment for blasphemy (Lev. xxiv.), were executions of existing law. For a fearful instance of murder inflicted on the innocent, and accepted as a human sacrifice by Jehovah, see 2 Sam. xxi.; and for the brutal murder of Shimei, who denounced and resented the crime which hung the seven sons of Saul 'before the Lord,' see 1 Kings ii. But the examples are many.

- In the story of Abraham, Sarai, and Hagar (Gen. xvi.), Lot and his daughters (xix.), Abraham's presentation of his wife to Abimilech (xx.), the same done by Isaac (xxvi.), Judah, Tamar (xxxviii.), and other cases where the grossest violations of the seventh commandment go unrebuked by Jehovah, while in constant communication with the guilty parties, we see how little the second table was supported by the first.
- The extortions, frauds, and thefts of Jacob (Gen. xxv., xxvii., xxx.), which brought upon him the unparalleled blessings of Jehovah; the plundering of Nabal's property by David and his fellow-bandits; the smiting of the robbed farmer by Jehovah and the taking of his treacherous wife by David (1 Sam. xxv.), are narratives befitting a Bible of footpads.   Exod. xx. 15. 'Thou shalt not steal.'
- Jehovah said, 'Who shall deceive Ahab?... And there came forth a spirit, and stood before Jehovah, and said, I will deceive him. And Jehovah said, Wherewith? And he said, I will go forth and be a lying spirit in the mouth of all these thy prophets. And he said, Thou shalt deceive him, and prevail also: go forth and do so. Now, therefore, Jehovah hath put a lying spirit in the mouth of all these thy prophets, and Jehovah hath spoken evil concerning thee' (1 Kings xxii.). See Ezek. xx. 25.

Table of Jehovah II.

- Exod. xx. 14. 'Thou shalt not commit adultery.'
- Exod. xx. 16. 'Thou shalt not bear false witness against thy neighbour.'
- Deut xx. 10–18, is a complete instruction for invasion, murder, rapine, eating the spoil of the invaded, taking their wives, their cattle, etc., all such as might have been proclaimed by a Supreme Bashi-Bazouk.
- Exod. xx. 17. 'Thou shalt not covet they neighbour's wife, thou shalt not covet thy neighbour's wife, nor his man-servant, nor his maid-servant, nor his ox, nor his ass, nor anything that is thy neighbour's.'
- Instances of this discrepancy might be largely multiplied. Any one who cares to pursue the subject can trace the building upon the powerful personal Jehovah of a religion of human sacrifices, anathemas, and priestly despotism; while around the moral ruler and judge of the same name, whose personality is more and more dispersed in pantheistic ascriptions, there grows the common law, and then the more moral law of equity, and the corresponding sentiments which gradually evolve the idea of a parental deity.

It is obvious that the more this second idea of the deity prevails, the more he is regarded as 'merciful,' 'long-suffering,' 'a God of truth and without iniquity, just and right,' 'delighting not in sacrifice but mercifulness,' 'good to all,' and whose 'tender mercies are over all his works,' and having 'no pleasure in the death of him that dieth;' the less will it be possible to see in the very same being the 'man of war,' 'god of battles,' the 'jealous,' 'angry,' 'fire-breathing' one, who 'visits the sins of the fathers upon the children,' who laughs at the calamities of men and mocks when their fear cometh. It is a structural necessity of the human mind that these two shall be gradually detached the one from the other. From one of the Jehovahs represented in parallel columns came the 'Father' whom Christ adored: from the other came the Devil he abhorred.

Notes

1 Thes. Heb., p. 94.
2 Heb. Handw., p. 90.
3 Or Jahveh. I prefer to use the best known term in a case where the more exact spelling adds no significance.
4 This, the grandest of all the elohistic names, became the nearest Hebrew word for devils—shedim.
5 Even his jealous command against rivals, i.e., 'graven images,' had to be taken along with the story of Laban's images (Gen. xxxi.), when, though 'God came to Laban,' the idolatry was not rebuked.

Chapter VI - The Consuming Fire

The Shekinah—Jewish idols—Attributes of the fiery and cruel Elohim compared with those of the Devil—The powers of evil combined under a head—Continuity—The consuming fire spiritualised.

That Abraham was a Fire-worshipper might be suspected from the immemorial efforts of all Semitic authorities to relieve him of traditional connection with that particular idolatry. When the good and evil powers were being distinguished, we find the burning and the bright aspects of Fire severally regarded. The sign of Jehovah's covenant with Abram included both. 'It came to pass that when the sun went down, and it was dark, behold a smoking furnace and a burning lamp that passed between those pieces' (of the sacrifice). In the legend of Moses we have the glory resting on Sinai and the burning bush, the bush which, it is specially remarked, was 'not consumed,' an exceptional circumstance in honour of Moses. To these corresponded the Urim and Thummim, marking the priest as source of light and of judgment. In his favourable and adorable aspect Jehovah was the Brightness of Fire. This was the Shekinah. In the Targum, Jonathan Ben Uzziel to the Prophets, it is said: 'The mountains trembled before the Lord; the mountains Tabor, Hermon, Carmel said one to the other: Upon me the Shekinah will rest, and to me will it come. But the Shekinah rested upon Mount Sinai, weakest and smallest of all the mountains. This Sinai trembled and shook, and its smoke went up as the smoke of an oven, because of the glory of the God of Israel which had manifested itself upon it.' The Brightness1 passed on to illumine every event associated with the divine presence in Semitic mythology; it was 'the glory of the Lord' shining from the Star of Bethlehem, and the figure of the Transfiguration.

The Consuming Fire also had its development. Among the spiritual it was spiritualised. 'Who among us shall dwell with the Devouring Fire?' cries Isaiah. 'Who among us shall dwell with the Everlasting Burnings? He that walketh righteously and speaketh uprightly; he that despiseth the gain of oppressions, that shaketh his hands from holding of bribes, that stoppeth his ears from hearing of blood, and shutteth his eyes from seeing evil.' It was by a prosaic route that the Devouring Fire became the residence of the wicked.

After Jeroboam (1 Kings xiii.) had built altars to the Elohim, under form of Calves, a prophet came out of Judah to denounce the idolatry. 'And he cried against the altar in the word of Jehovah, and said, O altar, altar! thus saith Jehovah, Behold, a child shall be born unto the house of David, Josiah by name; and upon thee shall he offer the priests of the high places that burn incense upon thee, and men's bones shall be burnt upon thee.' It was deemed so important that this prophecy should be fulfilled in the letter, when it could no longer be fulfilled in reality, that some centuries later Josiah dug up the bones of the Elohistic priests and burned them upon their long-ruined altars (2 Kings xxiii.).

The incident is significant, both on account of the prophet's personification of the altar, and the institution of a sort of Gehenna in connection with it. The personification and the Gehenna became much more complete as time went on. The Jews originally had no Devil, as indeed had no races at first; and this for the obvious reason that their so-called gods were quite equal to any moral evils that were to be accounted for, as we have already seen they were adequate to explain all physical evils. But the antagonists of the moral Jehovah were recognised and personified with increasing clearness, and were quite prepared for connection with any General who might be theoretically proposed for their leadership. When the Jews came under the influence of Persian theology the archfiend was elected, and all the Elohim—Moloch, Dagon, Astarte, Chemosh, and the rest—took their place under his rebellious ensign.

The descriptions of the Devil in the Bible are mainly borrowed from the early descriptions of the Elohim, and of Jehovah in his Elohistic character.2 In the subjoined parallels I follow the received English version.

Gen. xxii. 1. 'God tempted Abraham.'
Matt. iv. 1. 'Then was Jesus led up into the wilderness to be tempted of the devil.' See also 1 Cor. vii. 5, 1 Thes. iii. 5, James 1.13.

Exod. v. 3. 'I (Jehovah) will harden Pharaoh's heart;' v. 13, 'He hardened Pharaoh's heart.'
John xiii. 2. 'The devil having now put into the heart Judas Iscariot, Simon's son, to betray him.'

1 Kings xxii. 23. 'Behold the Lord hath put a lying spirit in the mouth of all these thy prophets, and the Lord hath spoken evil concerning them.' Ezek. xiv. 9. 'If the prophet be deceived when he hath spoken a thing, I the Lord have deceived that prophet, and I will stretch out my hand upon him, and will destroy him from the midst of my people.'
John viii. 44. 'He (the devil) is a liar' ('and so is his father,' continues the sentence by right of translation). 1 Tim. iii. 2, 'slanderers' (diabolous). 2 Tim. iii. 3, 'false accusers' (diabolo). Also Titus ii. 3, Von Tischendorf translates 'calumniators.' Isa. xlv. 7. 'I make peace and create evil. I the Lord do all these things.' Amos iii. 6. 'Shall there be evil in a city and the Lord hath not done it?' 1 Sam. xvi. 14. 'An evil spirit from the Lord troubled him' (Saul).

Matt. xiii. 38. 'The tares are the children of the wickied one.' 1 John iii. 8. 'He that committeth sin is of the devil; for the devil sinneth from the beginning.'
Exod. xii. 29. 'At midnight the Lord smote all the firstborn of Egypt.' Ver. 30. 'There was a great cry in Egypt; for there was not a house where there was not one dead.' Exod. xxxiii. 27. 'Thus saith the Lord God of Israel, Put every man his sword by his side, and go in and out from gate to gate throughout the camp, and slay every man his brother, and every man his companion, and every man his neighbour.'

John viii. 44. 'He (the devil) was a murderer from the beginning.'
Exod. vi. 9. 'Take thy rod and cast it before Pharaoh and it shall become a serpent.' Ver. 12. 'Aaron's rod swallowed up their rods.' Num. xxi. 6. 'Jehovah sent fiery serpents (Seraphim) among the people.' Ver. 8. 'And the Lord said unto Moses,

Make thee a fiery serpent, and set it upon a pole: and it shall come to pass, that every one that is bitten, when he looketh upon it, shall live.' (This serpent was worshipped until destroyed by Hezekiah, 2 Kings xviii.) Compare Jer. viii. 17, Ps. cxlviii., 'Praise ye the Lord from the earth, ye dragons.' Rev. xii. 7, etc. 'There was war in heaven: Michael and his angels fought against the dragon.... And the great dragon was cast out, that old serpent, called the Devil, and Satan, which deceiveth the whole world.... Woe to the inhabiters of the earth and of the sea! for the devil has come down to you, having great wrath.'

Gen. xix. 24. 'The Lord rained upon Sodom and Gomorrah brimstone and fire from the Lord out of heaven.' Deut. iv. 24. 'The Lord thy God is a consuming fire.' Ps. xi. 6. 'Upon the wicked he shall rain snares, fire and brimstone.' Ps. xviii. 8. 'There went up a smoke out of his nostrils.' Ps. xcvii. 3. 'A fire goeth before him, and burneth up his enemies round about.' Ezek. xxxviii. 19, etc. 'For in my jealousy, and in the fire of my wrath, have I spoken.... I will plead against him with pestilence and with blood, and I will rain upon him ... fire and brimstone.' Isa. xxx. 33. 'Tophet is ordained of old; yea, for the king is it prepared: he hath made it deep and wide; the pile thereof is fire and much wood; the breath of the Lord, like a stream of brimstone, doth kindle it.'

Matt. xxv. 41. 'Depart from me, ye cursed, into everlasting fire, prepared for the devil and his angels.' Mark ix. 44. 'Where their worm dieth not, and the fire is not quenched.' Rev. xx. 10. 'And the devil that deceiveth them was cast into the lake of fire and brimstone.' In Rev. ix. Abaddon, or Apollyon, is represented as the king of the scorpion tormentors; and the diabolical horses, with stinging serpent tails, are described as killing with the smoke and brimstone from their mouths.

In addition to the above passages may be cited a notable passage from Paul's Epistle to the Thessalonians (ii. 3). 'Let no man deceive you by any means: for that day (of Christ) shall not come, except there come a falling away first, and that man of sin be revealed, the son of perdition; who opposeth and exalteth himself above all that is called God, or that is worshipped; so that he, as God, sitteth in the temple of God, showing himself that he is God. Remember ye not that, when I was yet with you, I told you these things? And now ye know what withholdeth that he might be revealed in his time. For the mystery of iniquity doth already work: only he who now letteth will let, until he be taken out of the way: and then shall that Wicked be revealed, whom the Lord shall consume with the spirit of his mouth, and shall destroy with the brightness of his coming: even him whose coming is after the working of Satan, with all power, and signs, and lying wonders, and with all the deceivableness of unrighteousness in them that perish; because they received not the love of the truth, that they might be saved. And for this cause God shall send them strong delusion, that they should believe a lie; that they all might be damned who believed not the truth, but had pleasure in unrighteousness.'

This remarkable utterance shows how potent was the survival in the mind of Paul of the old Elohist belief. Although the ancient deity, who deceived prophets to their destruction, and sent forth lying spirits with their strong delusions, was dethroned and outlawed, he was still a powerful claimant of empire, haunting the temple, and setting himself up therein as God. He will be consumed by Christ's breath when the day of triumph comes; but meanwhile he is not only allowed great power in the earth, but utilised by the true God, who even so far cooperates with the false as to send on some men 'strong delusions' ('a working of error,' Von Tischendorf translates), in order that they may believe the lie and be damned. Paul speaks of the 'mystery of iniquity;' but it is not so very mysterious when we consider the antecedents of his idea. The dark problem of the origin of evil, and its continuance in the universe under the rule of a moral governor, still threw its impenetrable shadow across the human mind. It was a terrible reality, visible in the indifference or hostility with which the new gospel was met on the part of the cultured and powerful; and it could only then be explained as a mysterious provisional arrangement connected with some divine purpose far away in the depths of the universe. But the passage quoted from Thessalonians shows plainly that all those early traditions about the divinely deceived prophets and lying spirits, sent forth from Jehovah Elohim, had finally, in Paul's time, become marshalled under a leader, a personal Man of Sin; but this leader, while opposing Christ's kingdom, is in some mysterious way a commissioner of God.

We may remark here the beautiful continuity by which, through all these shadows of terror and vapours of speculation, 'clouding the glow of heaven,'3 the unquenchable ideal from first to last is steadily ascending.

'One or three things,' says the Talmud, 'were before this world—Water, Fire, and Wind. Water begat the Darkness, Fire begat Light, and Wind begat the Spirit of Wisdom.' This had become the rationalistic translation by a crude science of the primitive demons, once believed to have created the heavens and the earth. In the process we find the forces outlawed in their wild action, but becoming the choir of God in their quiet action:—

1 Kings xix. 11–13. 'And he said, Go forth, and stand upon the mount before the Lord. And, behold, the Lord passed by, and a great and strong wind rent the mountains, and brake in pieces the rocks before the Lord; but the Lord was not in the wind: and after the wind an earthquake; but the Lord was not in the earthquake: and after the earthquake a fire; but the Lord was not in the fire: and after the fire a still small voice. And it was so, when Elijah heard it, that he wrapped his face in his mantle.'

But man must have a philosophical as well as a moral development: the human mind could not long endure this elemental anarchy. It asked, If the Lord be not in the hurricane, the earthquake, the volcanic flame, who is therein? This is the answer of the Targum:4

'And he said, Arise and stand on the mountain before the Lord. And God revealed himself: and before him a host of angels of the wind, cleaving the mountain and breaking the rocks before the Lord; but not in the host of angels was the Shechinah. And after the host of the angels of the wind came a host of angels of commotion; but not in the host of the angels of commotion was the Shechinah of the Lord. And after the angels of commotion came a host of angels of fire; but not in the host of angels of fire was the Shechinah of the Lord. But after the host of the angels of the fire came voices singing in silence. And it was when Elijah heard this he hid his face in his mantle.'

The moral sentiment takes another step in advance with the unknown but artistic writer of the Epistle to the Hebrews. Moses had described God as a 'consuming fire;' and 'the sight of the glory of the Lord was like devouring fire on the top of the mount in the eyes of the children of Israel' (Exod. xxiv. 17). When next we meet this phrase it is with this writer, who seeks to supersede what Moses (traditionally) built up. 'Whose voice,' he says, 'then shook the earth; but now he hath promised, saying, Yet once more I shake not the earth only, but also heaven. And this word, 'yet once more,' signifieth the removing of those things that are shaken, as of things that are made, that those which cannot be shaken may remain.... For our God is a consuming fire.'

'Our God also!' cries each great revolution that advances. His consuming wrath is not now directed against man, but the errors which are man's only enemies: the lightnings of the new Sinai, while they enlighten the earth, smite the old heaven of human faith and imagination, shrivelling it like a burnt scroll!

In this nineteenth century, when the old heaven, amid which this fiery pillar glowed, is again shaken, the ancient phrase has still its meaning. The Russian Tourgenieff represents two friends who had studied together in early life, then parted, accidentally meeting once more for a single night. They compare notes as to what the long intervening years have taught them; and one sums his experience in the words—'I have burned what I used to worship, and worship what I used to burn.' The novelist artfully reproduces for this age a sentence associated with a crisis in the religious history of Europe. Clovis, King of the Franks, invoked the God of his wife Clotilda to aid him against the Germans, vowing to become a Christian if successful; and when, after his victory, he was baptized at Rheims, St. Remy said to him—'Bow thy head meekly, Sicambrian; burn what thou hast worshipped, and worship what thou hast burned!' Clovis followed the Bishop's advice in literal fashion, carrying fire and sword amid his old friends the 'Pagans' right zealously. But the era has come in which that which Clovis' sword and St. Remy's theology set up for worship is being consumed in its turn. Tourgenieff's youths are consuming the altar on which their forerunners were consumed. And in this rekindled flame the world now sees shrivelling the heavens once fresh, but now reflecting the aggregate selfishness of mankind, the hells representing their aggregate cowardice, and feeds its nobler faith with this vision of the eternal fire which evermore consumes the false and refines the world.

Notes

1 It is not certain, indeed, whether this Brightness may not have been separately personified in the 'Eduth' (translated 'testimony' in the English version, Exod. xvi. 34), before which the pot of manna was laid. The word means 'brightness,' and Dr. Willis supposes it may be connected with Adod, the Phœnician Sun-god (Pentateuch, p. 186).
2 It is important not to confuse Satan with the Devil, so far as the Bible is concerned. Satan, as will be seen when we come to the special treatment of him required, is by no means invariably diabolical. In the Book of Job, for example, he appears in a character far removed from hostility to Jehovah or goodness.
3
Name ist Schall und Rauch,
Umnebelnd Himmelsgluth.—Goethe.
4 'Targum to the Prophets,' Jonathan Ben Uzziel. See Deutsch's 'Literary Remains,' p. 379.

Chapter VII - Paradise and the Serpent

Herakles and Athena in a holy picture—Human significance of Eden—The legend in Genesis puzzling—Silence of later books concerning it—Its Vedic elements—Its explanation—Episode of the Mahábhárata—Scandinavian variant—The name of Adam—The story re-read—Rabbinical interpretations.

Montfaucon has among his plates one (XX.) representing an antique agate which he supposes to represent Zeus and Athena, but which probably relates to the myth of Herakles and Athena in the garden of Hesperides. The hero having penetrated this garden, slays the dragon which guards its immortalising fruit, but when he has gathered this fruit Athena takes it from him, lest man shall eat it and share the immortality of the gods. In this design the two stand on either side of the tree, around which a serpent is twined from root to branches. The history which Montfaucon gives of the agate is of equal interest with the design itself. It was found in an old French cathedral, where it had long been preserved and shown as a holy picture of the Temptation. It would appear also to have previously deceived some rabbins, for on the border is written in Hebrew characters, much more modern than the central figures, 'The woman saw that the tree was good for food, and that it was pleasant to the eyes, and a tree to be desired to make one wise.'

This mystification about a design, concerning whose origin and design there is now no doubt, is significant. The fable of Paradise and the Serpent is itself more difficult to trace, so many have been the races and religions which have framed it with their holy texts and preserved it in their sacred precincts. In its essence, no doubt, the story grows from a universal experience; in that aspect it is a mystical rose that speaks all languages. When man first appears his counterpart is a garden. The moral nature means order. The wild forces of nature—the Elohim—build no fence, forbid no fruit. They say to man as the supreme animal, Subdue the earth; every tree and herb shall be your meat; every animal your slave; be fruitful and multiply. But from the conflict the more real man emerges, and his sign is a garden hedged in from the wilderness, and a separation between good and evil.

The form in which the legend appears in the Book of Genesis presents one side in which it is simple and natural. This has already been suggested (vol. i. p. 330). But the legend of man defending his refuge from wild beasts against the most subtle of them is here overlaid by a myth in which it plays the least part. The mind which reads it by such light as may be obtained only from biblical sources can hardly fail to be newly puzzled at every step. So much, indeed, is confessed in the endless and diverse theological theories which the story has elicited. What is the meaning of the curse on the Serpent that it should for ever crawl thereafter? Had it not crawled previously? Why was the Tree of the knowledge of Good and Evil forbidden? Why, when its fruit was tasted, should the Tree of Life have been for the first time forbidden and jealously guarded? These riddles are nowhere solved in the Bible, and have been left to the fanciful inventions of theologians and the ingenuity of rabbins. Dr. Adam Clarke thought the Serpent was an ape before his sin, and many rabbins concluded he was camel-shaped; but the remaining enigmas have been fairly given up.

The ancient Jews, they who wrote and compiled the Old Testament, more candid than their modern descendants and our omniscient christians, silently confessed their inability to make anything out of this snake-story. From the third chapter of Genesis to the last verse of Malachi the story is not once alluded to! Such a phenomenon would have been impossible had this legend been indigenous with the Hebrew race. It was clearly as a boulder among them which had floated from regions little known to their earlier writers; after lying naked through many ages, it became overgrown with rabbinical lichen and moss, and, at the Christian era, while it seemed part of the Hebrew landscape, it was exceptional enough to receive special reverence as a holy stone. That it was made the corner-stone of Christian theology may be to some extent explained by the principle of omne ignotum pro mirifico. But the boulder itself can only be explained by tracing it to the mythologic formation from which it crumbled.

How would a Parsi explain the curse on a snake which condemned it to crawl? He would easily give us evidence that at the time when most of those Hebrew Scriptures were written, without allusion to such a Serpent, the ancient Persians believed that Ahriman had tempted the first man and woman through his evil mediator, his anointed son, Ash-Mogh, 'the two-footed Serpent.'

But let us pass beyond the Persian legend, carrying that and the biblical story together, for submission to the criticism of a Bráhman. He will tell us that this Ash-Mogh of the Parsi is merely the ancient Aèshma-daéva of the Avesta, which in turn is Ahi, the great Vedic Serpent-monster whom Indra 'prostrated beneath the feet' of the stream he had obstructed—every stream having its deity. He would remind us that the Vedas describe the earliest dragon-slayer, Indra, as 'crushing the head' of his enemy, and that this figure of the god with his heel on a Serpent's head has been familiar to his race from time immemorial. And he would then tell us to read the Rig-Veda, v. 32, and the Mahábhárata, and we would find all the elements of the story told in Genesis.

In the hymn referred to we find a graphic account of how, when Ahi was sleeping on the waters he obstructed, Indra hurled at him his thunderbolt. It says that when Indra had 'annihilated the weapon of that mighty beast from him (Ahi), another, more powerful, conceiving himself one and unmatched, was generated,' This 'wrath-born son,' 'a walker in darkness,' had managed to get hold of the sacred Soma, the plant monopolised by the gods, and having drunk this juice, he lay slumbering and 'enveloping the world,' and then 'fierce Indra seized upon him,' and having previously discovered 'the vital part of him who thought, himself invulnerable,' struck that incarnation of many-formed Ahi, and he was 'made the lowest of all creatures'.

But one who has perused the philological biography of Ahi already given, vol. i. p. 357, will not suppose that this was the end of him. We must now consider in further detail the great episode of the Mahábhárata, to which reference has been made in other connections.1 During the Deluge the most precious treasure of the gods, the Amrita, the ambrosia that rendered them immortal, was lost, and the poem relates how the Devas and Asuras, otherwise gods and serpents, together churned the ocean for it. There were two great mountains,—Meru the golden and beautiful, adorned with healing plants, pleasant streams and trees, unapproachable by the sinful, guarded by serpents; Mandar, rocky, covered with rank vegetation, infested by savage beasts. The first is the abode of the gods, the last of demons. To find the submerged Amrita it was necessary to uproot Mandar and use it to churn the ocean. This was done by calling on the King Serpent Ananta, who called in the aid of another great serpent, Vásuki, the latter being used as a rope coiling and uncoiling to whirl the mountain. At last the Amrita appeared. But there also streamed forth from the ocean bed a terrible stench and venom, which was spreading through the universe when Siva swallowed it to save mankind,—the drug having stained his throat blue, whence his epithet 'Blue Neck.'

When the Asuras saw the Amrita, they claimed it; but one of the Devas, Narya, assumed the form of a beautiful woman, and so fascinated them that they forgot the Amrita for the moment, which the gods drank. One of the Asuras, however, Ráhu, assumed the form of a god or Deva, and began to drink. The immortalising nectar had not gone farther than his throat when the sun and moon saw the deceit and discovered it to Naraya, who cut off Ráhu's head. The head of Ráhu, being immortal, bounded to the sky, where its efforts to devour the sun and moon, which betrayed him, causes their eclipses. The tail (Ketu) also enjoys immortality in a lower plane, and is the fatal planet which sends diseases on mankind. A furious war between the gods and the Asuras has been waged ever since. And since the Devas are the strongest, it is not wonderful that it should have passed into the folklore of the whole Aryan world that the evil host are for ever seeking to recover by cunning the Amrita. The [68]Serpents guarding the paradise of the Devas have more than once, in a mythologic sense, been induced to betray their trust and glide into the divine precincts to steal the coveted draught. This is the Kvásir2 of the Scandinavian Mythology, which is the source of that poetic inspiration whose songs have magical potency. The sacramental symbol of the Amrita in Hindu Theology is the Soma juice, and this plant Indra is declared in the Rig-Veda (i. 130) to have discovered "hidden, like the nestlings of a bird, amidst a pile of rocks enclosed by bushes," where the dragon Drought had concealed it. Indra, in the shape of a hawk, flew away with it. In the Prose Edda the Frost Giant Suttung has concealed the sacred juice, and it is kept by the maid Gunlauth in a cavern overgrown with bushes. Bragi bored a hole through the rock. Odin in the shape of a worm crept through the crevice; then resuming his godlike shape, charmed the maid into permitting him to drink one draught out of the three jars; and, having left no drop, in form of an eagle flew to Asgard, and discharged in the jars the wonder-working liquid. Hence poetry is called Odin's booty, and Odin's gift.

Those who attentively compare these myths with the legend in Genesis will not have any need to rest upon the doubtful etymology of 'Adam'3 to establish the Ayran origin of the latter. The Tree of the knowledge of Good and Evil which made man 'as one of us' (the Elohim) is the Soma of India, the Haoma of Persia, the kvásir of Scandinavia, to which are ascribed the intelligence and powers of the gods, and the ardent thoughts of their worshippers. The Tree of Immortality is the Amrita, the only monopoly of the gods. 'The Lord God said, Behold the man is become as one of us, to know good and evil: and now, lest he put forth his hand, and take also of the tree of life, and eat, and live for ever: Therefore the Lord God sent him forth the garden of Eden to till the ground whence he had been taken. So he drove out the man; and he placed on the east of the garden of Eden cherubim, and a flaming sword which turned every way, to guard the way of the tree of life.' This flaming sword turning every way is independent of the cherub, and takes the place of the serpent which had previously guarded the Meru paradise, but is now an enemy no longer to be trusted.

If the reader will now re-read the story in Genesis with the old names restored, he will perceive that there is no puzzle at all in any part of it:—'Now Ráhu [because he had stolen and tasted Soma] was more subtle than any beast of the field which the Devas had made, and he said to Adea Suktee, the first woman, Have the Devas said you shall not eat of every tree in the garden? And she said unto Ráhu, We may eat of the fruit of the trees of the garden; but of the Soma-plant, which is in the middle of the garden, the Devas have said we shall not eat or touch it on pain of death. Then Ráhu said to Adea, You will not suffer death by tasting Soma [I have done so, and live]: the Devas know that on the day when you taste it your eyes shall be opened, and you will be equal to them in knowledge of good and evil ... [and you will be able at once to discover which tree it is that bears the fruit which renders you immortal—the Amrita].... Adea took of the Soma and did eat, and gave also unto Adima, her husband, and the eyes of them both were opened.... And Indra, chief of the Devas, said to Ráhu, Because you have done this, you are cursed above all cattle and above every beast of the field; [for they shall transmigrate, their souls ascend through higher forms to be absorbed in the Creative principle; but] upon thy belly shalt thou go [remaining transfixed in the form you have assumed to try and obtain the Amrita]; and [instead of the ambrosia you aimed at] you shall eat dirt through all your existence.... And Indra said, Adima and Adea Suktee have [tasted Soma, and] become as one of us Devas [so far as] to know good and evil; and now, lest man put forth his hand [on our precious Amrita], and take also of the tree of life, and eat, and live for ever [giving us another race of Asuras or Serpent-men to compete with].... Indra and the Devas drove Adima out of Meru, and placed watch-dogs at the east of the garden; and [a sinuous darting flame, precisely matched to the now unchangeable form of Ráhu], a flaming sword which turned every way, to keep the way of the Amrita from Adima and Asuras.'

While the gods and serpents were churning the ocean for the Amrita, all woes and troubles for mortals came up first. That ocean shrinks in one region to the box of Pandora, in another to the fruit eaten by Eve. How foreign such a notion is to the Hebrew theology is shown by the fact that even while the curses are falling from the fatal fruit on the earth and man, they are all said to have proceeded solely from Jehovah, who is thus made to supplement the serpent's work.

It will be seen that in the above version of the story in Genesis I have left out various passages. These are in part such as must be more fully treated in the succeeding chapter, and in part the Semitic mosses which have grown upon the Aryan boulder. But even after the slight treatment which is all I have space to devote to the comparative study of the myth in

167

this aspect, it may be safely affirmed that the problems which we found insoluble by Hebrew correlatives no longer exist if an Aryan origin be assumed. We know why the fruit of knowledge was forbidden: because it endangered the further fruit of immortality. We know how the Serpent might be condemned to crawl for ever without absurdity: because he was of a serpent-race, able to assume higher forms, and capable of transmigration, and of final absorption. We know why the eating of the fruit brought so many woes: it was followed by the stream of poison from the churned ocean which accompanied the Amrita, and which would have destroyed the race of both gods and men, had not Siva drank it up. If anything were required to make the Aryan origin of the fable certain, it will be found in the fact which will appear as we go on,—namely, that the rabbins of our era, in explaining the legend which their fathers severely ignored, did so by borrowing conceptions foreign to the original ideas of their race,—notions about human transformation to animal shapes, and about the Serpent (which Moses honoured), and mainly of a kind travestying the Iranian folklore. Such contact with foreign races for the first time gave the Jews any key to the legend which their patriarchs and prophets were compelled to pass over in silence.

Notes

1 See pp. 46 and 255. The episode is in Mahábhárata, I. 15.
2 Related to the Slav Kvas, with which, in Russian folklore, the Devil tried to circumvent Noah and his wife, as related in chap. xxvii. part iv.
3 In Sanskrit Adima means 'the first;' in Hebrew Adam (given almost always with the article) means 'the red,' and it is generally derived from adamah, mould or soil. But Professor Max Müller (Science of Religion, p. 320) says if the name Adima (used, by the way, in India for the first man, as Adam is in England) is the same as Adam, 'we should be driven to admit that Adam was borrowed by the Jews from the Hindus.' But even that mild case of 'driving' is unnecessary, since the word, as Sale reminded the world, is used in the Persian legend. It is probable that the Hebrews imported this word not knowing its meaning, and as it resembled their word for mould, they added the gloss that the first man was made of the dust or mould of the ground. It is not contended that the Hebrews got their word directly from the Hindu or Persian myth. Mr. George Smith discovered that Admi or Adami was the name for the first men in Chaldean fragments. Sir Henry Rawlinson points out that the ancient Babylonians recognised two principle races,—the Adamu, or dark, and the Sarku, or light, race; probably a distinction, remembered in the phrase of Genesis, between the supposed sons of Adam and the sons of God. The dark race was the one that fell. Mr. Herbert Spencer (Principles of Sociology, Appendix) offers an ingenious suggestion that the prohibition of a certain sacred fruit may have been the provision of a light race against a dark one, as in Peru only the Yuca and his relatives were allowed to eat the stimulating cuca. If this be true in the present case, it would still only reflect an earlier tradition that the holy fruit was the rightful possession of the deities who had won in the struggle for it.
Nor is there wanting a survival from Indian tradition in the story of Eve. Adam said, 'This now is bone of my bone, and flesh of my flesh.' In the Manu Code (ix. 22) it is written: 'The bone of woman is united with the bone of man, and her flesh with his flesh.' The Indian Adam fell in twain, becoming male and female (Yama and Yami). Ewald (Hist. of Israel, i. 1) has put this matter of the relation between Hebrew and Hindu traditions, as it appears to me, beyond doubt. See also Goldziher's Heb. Mythol., p. 326; and Professor King's Gnostics, pp. 9, 10, where the historic conditions under which the importation would naturally have occurred are succinctly set forth. Professor King suggests that Paṛsî and Pharisee may be the same word.

Chapter VIII - Eve

The Fall of Man—Fall of gods—Giants—Prajápati and Ráhu—Woman and Star-serpent in Persia—Meschia and Meschiane—Bráhman legends of the creation of Man—The strength of Woman—Elohist and Jehovist creations of Man—The Forbidden Fruit—Eve reappears as Sara—Abraham surrenders his wife to Jehovah—The idea not sensual—Abraham's circumcision—The evil name of Woman—Noah's wife—The temptation of Abraham—Rabbinical legends concerning Eve—Pandora—Sentiment of the Myth of Eve.

The insignificance of the Serpent of Eden in the scheme and teachings of the Hebrew Bible is the more remarkable when it is considered that the pessimistic view of human nature is therein fully represented. In the story of the Temptation itself, there is, indeed, no such generalisation as we find in the modern dogma of the Fall of Man; but the elements of it are present in the early assumption that the thoughts of man's heart run to evil continually,—which must be an obvious fact everywhere while goodness is identified with fictitious merits. There are also expressions suggesting a theory of heredity, of a highly superstitious character,—the inheritance being by force of the ancestral word or act, and without reference to inherent qualities. Outward merits and demerits are transmitted for reward and punishment to the third and fourth generation; but the more common-sense view appears to have gradually superseded this, as expressed in the proverb that the fathers ate sour grapes and the children's teeth were on edge.

In accounting for this condition of human nature, popular traditions among the Jews always pointed rather to a fall of the gods than to any such catastrophe to man. 'The sons of the Elohim (gods) saw the daughters of men that they were beautiful, and they took to themselves for wives whomsoever they chose.' 'There were giants in the earth in those days; and also after that, when the sons of God came in unto the daughters of men, and they bare children to them, the same became mighty men, which were of old men of renown.'1 These giants were to the Semitic mind what the Ahis, Vritras, Sushnas and other monsters were to the Aryan, or Titans to the Greek mind. They were not traced to the Serpent, but to the wild nature-gods, the Elohim, and when Jehovah appears it is to wage war against them. The strength of this belief is illustrated in the ample accounts given in the Old Testament of the Rephaim and their king Og, the Anakim and Goliath, the Emim, the Zamzummim, and others, all of which gained full representation in Hebrew folklore. The existence of these hostile beings was explained by their fall from angelic estate.

The Book of Enoch gives what was no doubt the popular understanding of the fall of the angels and its results. Two hundred angels took wives of the daughters of men, and their offspring were giants three thousand yards in height. These giants having consumed the food of mankind, began to devour men, whose cries were brought to the attention of Jehovah by his angels. One angel was sent to warn Noah of the Flood; another to bind Azazel in a dark place in the desert till the Judgment Day; Gabriel was despatched to set the giants to destroying one another; Michael was sent to bury the fallen angels under the hills for seventy generations, till the Day of Judgment, when they should be sent to the fiery abyss for ever. Then every evil work should come to an end, and the plant of righteousness spring up.2

Such exploits and successes on the part of the legal Deity against outlaws, though they may be pitched high in heroic romance, are found beside a theology based upon a reverse situation. Nothing is more fundamental in the ancient Jewish system than the recognition of an outside world given over to idolatry and wickedness, while Jews are a small colony of the children of Israel and chosen of Jehovah. Such a conception in primitive times is so natural, and possibly may have been so essential to the constitution of nations, that it is hardly useful to look for parallels. Though nearly all races see in their traditional dawn an Age of Gold, a Happy Garden, or some corresponding felicity, these are normally defined against anterior chaos or surrounding ferocity. Every Eden has had its guards.

When we come to legends which relate particularly to the way in which the early felicity was lost, many facts offer themselves for comparative study. And with regard to the myths of Eden and Eve, we may remark what appears to have been a curious interchange of legends between the Hebrews and Persians. The ancient doctrines of India and Persia concerning Origins are largely, if not altogether, astronomical. In the Genesis of India we see a golden egg floating on a shoreless ocean; it divides to make the heaven above and earth beneath; from it emerges Prajápati, who also falls in twain to make the mortal and immortal substances; the parts of him again divide to make men and women on earth, sun and moon in the sky. This is but one version out of many, but all the legends about Prajápati converge in making him a figure of Indian astronomy. In the Rig-Veda he is Orion, and for ever lies with the three arrows in his belt which Sirius shot at him because of his love for Aldebaran,—towards which constellation he stretches. Now, in a sort of antithesis to this, the evil Ráhu is also cut in twain, his upper and immortal part pursuing and trying to eclipse the sun and moon, his tail (Ketu) becoming the 9th planet, shedding evil influences on mankind.3 This tail, Ketu, is quite an independent monster, and we meet with him in the Persian planisphere, where he rules the first of the six mansions of Ahriman, and is the 'crooked serpent' mentioned in the Book of Job. By referring to vol. i. p. 253, the reader will see that this Star-serpent must stand as close to the woman with her child and sheaf as September stands to October. But unquestionably the woman was put there for honour and not disgrace; with her child and sheaf she represented the fruitage of the year.

There is nothing in Persian Mythology going to show that the woman betrayed her mansion of fruitage—the golden year—to the Serpent near her feet. In the Bundehesch we have the original man, Kaiomarts, who is slain by Ahriman as Prajápati (Orion) was by Sirius; from his dead form came Meschia and Meschiane, the first human pair. Ahriman corrupts them by first giving them goats' milk, an evil influence from Capricorn. After they had thus injured themselves he tempted them with a fruit which robbed them of ninety-nine hundredths of their happiness. In all this there is no indication that the woman and man bore different relations to the calamity. But after a time we find a Parsî postscript to this effect: 'The woman was the first to sacrifice to the Devas.' This is the one item in the Parsî Mythology which shows bias against woman, and as it is unsupported by the narratives preceding it, we may suppose that it was derived from some foreign country.

That country could hardly have been India. There is a story in remote districts of India which relates that the first woman was born out of an expanding lotus on the Ganges, and was there received in his paradise by the first man (Adima, or Manu). Having partaken of the Soma, they were expelled, after first being granted their prayer to be allowed a last draught from the Ganges; the effect of the holy water being to prevent entire corruption, and secure immortality to their souls. But nowhere in Indian legend or folklore do we find any special dishonour put upon woman such as is described in the Hebrew story.

Rather we find the reverse. Early in the last century, a traveller, John Marshall, related stories of the creation which he says were told him by the Brahmins, and others 'by the Brahmins of Persia.'4

'Once on a time,' the Brahmins said, 'as (God) was set in eternity, it came into his mind to make something, and immediately no sooner had he thought the same, but that the same minute was a perfect beautiful woman present immediately before him, which he called Adea Suktee, that is, the first woman. Then this figure put into his mind the figure of a man; which he had no sooner conceived in his mind, but that he also started up, and represented himself before him; this he called Manapuise, that is, the first man; then, upon a reflection of these things, he resolved further to create several places for them to abide in, and accordingly, assuming a subtil body, he breathed in a minute the whole universe, and everything therein, from the least to the greatest.'

'The Brahmins of Persia tell certain long stories of a great Giant that was led into a most delicate garden, which, upon certain conditions, should be his own for ever. But one evening in a cool shade one of the wicked Devatas, or spirits, came to him, and tempted him with vast sums of gold, and all the most precious jewels that can be imagined; but he courageously withstood that temptation, as not knowing what value or use they were of: but at length this wicked Devata brought to him a fair woman, who so charmed him that for her sake he most willingly broke all his conditions, and thereupon was turned out.'

In the first of these two stories the names given to the man and woman are popular words derived from Sanskrit. In the second the Persian characters are present, as in the use of Devatas to denote wicked powers; but for the rest, this latter legend appears to me certainly borrowed from the Jews so far as the woman is concerned. It was they who first perceived any connection between Virgo in the sixth mansion of Ormuzd, and Python in the seventh, and returned the Persians their planisphere with a new gloss. Having adopted the Dragon's tail (Ketu) for a little preliminary performance, the Hebrew system dismisses that star-snake utterly; for it has already evolved a terrestrial devil from its own inner consciousness.

The name of that devil is—Woman. The diabolisation of woman in their theology and tradition is not to be regarded as any indication that the Hebrews anciently held women in dishonour; rather was it a tribute to her powers of fascination such as the young man wrote to be placed under the pillow of Darius—'Woman is strongest.' As Darius and his council agreed that, next to truth, woman is strongest—stronger than wine or than kings, so do the Hebrew fables testify by interweaving her beauty and genius with every evil of the world.

Between the Elohist and Jahvist accounts of the creation of man, there are two differences of great importance. The Elohim are said to have created man in their own image, male and female,—the word for 'created' being bará, literally meaning to carve out. Jehovah Elohim is said to have formed man,—nothing being said about his own image, or about male and female,—the word formed being yatsar'. The sense of this word yatsar in this place (Gen. ii. 7) must be interpreted by what follows: Jehovah is said to have formed man out of the aphar', which the English version translates dust, but the Septuagint more correctly sperma. The literal meaning is a finely volatilised substance, and in Numbers xxiii. 10, it is used to represent the seed of Jacob. In the Jehovistic creation it means that man was formed out of the seminal principle of the earth combined with the breath of Jehovah; and the legend closely resembles the account of the ancient Satapatha-Bráhmana, which shows the creative power in sexual union with the fluid world to produce the egg from which Prajápati was born, to be divided into man and woman.

These two accounts, therefore,—to wit, that in the first and that in the second chapter of Genesis,—must be regarded as being of different events, and not merely varying myths of the same event. The offspring of Jehovah were 'living souls,' an expression not used in connection with the created images of the giants or Elohim. The Elohist pair roam about the world freely eating all fruits and herbs, possessing nature generally, and, as male and female, encouraged to increase and multiply; but Jehovah carefully separates his two children from general nature, places them in a garden, forbids certain food, and does not say a word about sex even, much less encourage its functions.

Adam was formed simply to be the gardener of Eden; no other motive is assigned. In proposing the creation of a being to be his helper and companion, nothing is said about a new sex,—the word translated 'help-meet' (ézer) is masculine. Adam names the being made 'woman,' (Vulg. Virago) only because she has been made out of man, but sex is not even yet suggested. This is so marked that the compiler has filled up what he considered an omission with (verse 24) a little lecture on duty to wives.

It is plain that the jealously-guarded ambrosia of Aryan gods has here been adapted to signify the sexual relation. That is the fruit in the midst of the garden which is reserved. The eating of it is immediately associated with consciousness of nudity and shame. The curse upon Eve is appropriate. Having taken a human husband, she is to be his slave; she shall bring forth children in sorrow, and many of them (Gen. iii. 16). Adam is to lose his position in Jehovah's garden, and to toil in accursed ground, barren and thorny.

Cast out thus into the wilderness, the human progeny as it increased came in contact with the giant's progeny,—those created by the Elohim (Gen. i.). When these had intermarried, Jehovah said that the fact that the human side in such alliance had been originally vitalised by his breath could not now render it immortal, because 'he (man) also is flesh,' i.e., like the creatures of the nature-gods. After two great struggles with these Titans, drowning most of them, hurling down their tower and scattering them, Jehovah resolved upon a scheme of vast importance, and one which casts a flood of light upon the narrative just given. Jehovah's great aim is shown in the Abrahamic covenant to be to found a family on earth, of which he can say, 'Thou art my son; I have begotten thee.' Eve was meant to be the mother of that family, but by yielding to her passion for the man meant only to be her companion she had thwarted the purpose of Jehovah. But she reappears again under the name of Sara; and from first to last the sense of these records, however overlaid by later beliefs, is the expansion, varying fortunes, and gradual spiritualisation of this aspiration of a deity for a family of his own in the earth. Celsus said that the story of the Virgin Mary and the Holy Ghost is one in which Christians would find little 'mystery' if the names were Danaë and Jupiter. The same may be said of the story of Sara and Jehovah, of which that concerning Mary is a theological travesty. Sarai (as she was called before her transfer to Jehovah, who then forbade Abraham to call her 'My Princess,' but only 'Princess') was chosen because she was childless. Abraham was paid a large recompense for her surrender, and provision was made that he should have a mistress, and by her a son. This natural son was to be renowned and have great possessions; nominally Abraham was to be represented by Sara's miraculously-conceived son, and to control his fortunes, but the blood of the new race was to be purely divine in its origin, so that every descendant of Isaac might be of Jehovah's family in Abraham's household.

Abraham twice gave over his wife to different kings who were jealously punished by Jehovah for sins they only came near committing unconsciously, while Abraham himself was not even rebuked for the sin he did commit. The forbidden fruit was not eaten this time; and the certificate and proof of the supernatural conception of Isaac were made clear in Sarah's words—'God hath made me to laugh: all that hear will laugh with me: who would have said unto Abraham that Sarah should have given children suck? for I have borne a son in his old age.'5

It was the passionate nature and beauty of Woman which had thus far made the difficulty. The forbidden fruit was 'pleasant to the eyes,' and Eve ate it; and it was her 'voice' to which Adam had hearkened rather than to that of Jehovah (Gen. iii. 17). And, again, it was the easy virtue and extreme beauty of Sara (Gen. xii. 11, 14) which endangered the new scheme. The rabbinical traditions are again on this point very emphatic. It is related that when Abram came to the border of Egypt he hid Sara in a chest, and was so taking her into that country. The collector of customs charged that the chest contained raiment, silks, gold, pearls, and Abram paid for all these; but this only increased the official's suspicions, and he compelled Abram to open the chest; when this was done and Sara rose up, the whole land of Egypt was illumined by her splendour.6

There is no reason for supposing that the ideas underlying the relation which Jehovah meant to establish with Eve, and succeeded in establishing with Sara, were of a merely sensual description. These myths belong to the mental region of ancestor-worship, and the fundamental conception is that of founding a family to reign over all other families. Jehovah's interest is in Isaac rather than Sara, who, after she has borne that patriarch, lapses out of the story almost as completely as Eve. The idea is not, indeed, so theological as it became in the Judaic-christian legend of the conception of Jesus by Mary as spouse of the Deity; it was probably, however, largely ethnical in the case of Eve, and national in that of Sara. It being considered of the utmost importance that all who claimed the advantages in the Jewish commonwealth accruing only to the legal, though nominal, 'children of Abraham,' should really be of divine lineage, security must be had against Isaac having any full brother. It might be that in after time some natural son of Sara might claim to be the one born of divine parentage, might carry on the Jewish commonwealth, slay the children of Jehovah by Sara, and so end the divine lineage with the authority it carried. Careful precautions having been taken that Ishmael should be an 'irreconcilable,' there is reason to suspect that the position of Isaac as Jehovah's 'only-begotten son' was secured by means obscurely hinted in the circumcision first undergone by Abraham, and made the sign of the covenant. That circumcision, wheresoever it has survived, is the relic of a more horrible practice of barbarian asceticism, is hardly doubtful; that the original rite was believed to have been that by which Abraham fulfilled his contract with Jehovah, appears to me intimated in various passages of the narrative which have survived editorial arrangement in accordance with another view. For instance, the vast inducements offered Abraham, and the great horror that fell on the patriarch, appear hardly explicable on the theory that nothing was conceded on Abraham's side beyond the surrender of a wife whom he had freely consigned to earthly monarchs.

Though the suspicion just expressed as to the nature of Abraham's circumcision may be doubted, it is not questionable that the rite of circumcision bears a significance in rabbinical traditions and Jewish usages which renders its initiation by Abraham at least a symbol of marital renunciation. Thus, the custom of placing in a room where the rite of circumcision was performed a pot of dust, was explained by the rabbins to have reference to the dust which Jehovah declared should be the serpent's food.7 That circumcision should have been traditionally associated with the temptation of Eve is a confirmation of the interpretation which regards her (Eve) as the prototype of Sara and the serpent as sexual desire. Although, if the original sense of Abraham's circumcision were what has been suggested, it had been overlaid, when the Book of Genesis in its present form was compiled, by different traditions, and that patriarch is described as having married again and had other children, the superior sanctity of Sara's son was preserved. Indeed, there would seem to have continued for a long time a tradition that the Abrahamic line and covenant were to be carried out by 'the seed of the woman' alone, and the paternity of Jehovah. Like Sara, Rebekah is sterile, and after her Rachel; the birth of Jacob and Esau from one, and of Joseph and Benjamin from the other, being through the intervention of Jehovah.

The great power of woman for good or evil, and the fact that it has often been exercised with subtlety—the natural weapon of the weak in dealing with the strong—are remarkably illustrated in the legends of these female figures which appear in connection with the divine schemes in the Book of Genesis. But even more the perils of woman's beauty are illustrated, especially in Eve and Sara. There were particular and obvious reasons why these representative women could not be degraded or diabolised in their own names or history, even where their fascinations tended to countervail the plans of Jehovah. The readiness with which Sara promoted her husband's prostitution and consented to her own, the treachery of Rebekah to her son Esau, could yet not induce Jewish orthodoxy to give evil names to the Madonnas of their race; but the inference made was expressed under other forms and names. It became a settled superstition that wherever evil was going on, Woman was at the bottom of it. Potiphar's wife, Jezebel, Vashti, and Delilah, were among the many she-scape-goats on whom were laid the offences of their august official predecessors who 'could do no wrong.' Even after Satan has come upon the scene, and is engaged in tempting Job, it seems to have been thought essential to the task that he should have an agent beside the troubled man in the wife who bade him 'curse God and die.'

It is impossible to say at just what period the rabbins made their ingenious discovery that the devil and Woman entered the world at the same time,—he coming out of the hole left by removal of the rib from Adam before it was closed. This they found disclosed in the fact that it is in Genesis iii. 21, describing the creation of Woman, that there appears for the first time Samech—the serpent-letter S (in Vajisgor).8 But there were among them many legends of a similar kind that leave one no wonder concerning the existence of a thanksgiving taught boys that they have not been created women, however much one may be scandalised at its continuance in the present day. It was only in pursuance of this theory of Woman that there was developed at a later day a female assistant of the Devil in another design to foil the plans of Jehovah, from the Scriptural narrative of which the female rôle is omitted. In the Scriptural legend of Noah his wife is barely mentioned, and her name is not given, but from an early period vague rumours to her discredit floated about, and these gathered consistency in the Gnostic legend that it was through her that Satan managed to get on board the Ark, as is elsewhere related (Part IV. chap. xxvii.), and was so enabled to resuscitate antediluvial violence in the drunken curses of Noah. Satan did this by working upon both the curiosity and jealousy of Noraita, the name assigned Noah's wife.

It has been necessary to give at length the comparative view of the myth of Eden in order that the reader may estimate the grounds upon which rests a theory which has been submitted after much hesitation concerning its sense. The 'phallic' theory by which it has become the fashion to interpret so many of these old fables, appears to me to have been done to death; yet I cannot come to any other conclusion concerning the legend of Eve than that she represents that passional nature of Woman which, before it was brought under such rigid restraint, might easily be regarded as a weakness to any tribe desirous of keeping itself separate from other tribes. The oath exacted by Abraham of his servant that he should seek out a wife from among his own people, and not among Canaanitish women, is one example among many of this feeling, which, indeed, survives among Jews at the present day. Such a sentiment might underlie the stories of Eve and Sara—the one mingling the blood of the family of Jehovah with mere human flesh, the other nearly confusing it with aliens. As the idea of tribal sanctity and separateness became strengthened by the further development of theocratic government, such myths would take on forms representing Jehovah's jealousy in defending his family line against the evil powers which sought to confuse or destroy it. One such attempt appears to underlie the story of the proposed sacrifice of Isaac. Although the account we have of that proceeding in the Bible was written at a time when the Elohist and Jahvist parties had compromised their rivalries to some extent, and suggests the idea that Jehovah himself ordered the sacrifice in order to try the faith of Abraham, enough of the primitive tradition lingers in the narrative to make it probable that its original intent was to relate how one of the superseded Elohim endeavoured to tempt Abraham to sacrifice Sara's only son, and so subvert the aim of Jehovah to perpetuate his seed. The God who 'tempted Abraham' is throughout sharply distinguished from the Jehovah who sent his angel to prevent the sacrifice and substitute an animal victim for Isaac. Although, as we have seen, Sara was spared degradation into a she-devil in subsequent myths, because her body was preserved intact despite her laxity of mind, such was not the case with Eve. The silence concerning her preserved throughout the Bible after her fall is told was broken by the ancient rabbins, and there arose multitudinous legends in which her intimacies with devils are circumstantially reported. Her first child, Cain, was generally believed to be the son of one of the devils (Samaël) that consorted with her, and the world was said to be peopled with gnomes and demons which she brought forth during that 130 years at the end of which it is stated that Adam begot a son in his own image and likeness, and called his name Seth (Gen. v. 3). The previous children were supposed to be not in purely human form, and not to have been of Adam's paternity. Adam had during that time refused to have any children, knowing that he would only rear inmates of hell.

The legend of Eden has gone round the world doing various duty, but nearly always associated with the introduction of moral evil into the world. In the Lateran Museum at Rome there is a remarkable bas-relief representing a nude man and woman offering sacrifice before a serpent coiled around a tree, while an angel overthrows the altar with his foot. This was probably designed as a fling at the Ophites, and is very interesting as a survival from the ancient Aryan meaning of the Serpent. But since the adaptation of the myth by the Semitic race, it has generally emphasised the Tree of the Knowledge of Good and Evil, instead of the Tree of Immortality (Amrita), which is the chief point of interest in the Aryan

172

myth. There are indeed traces of a conflict with knowledge and scepticism in it which we shall have to consider hereafter. The main popular association with it, the introduction into the world of all the ills that flesh is heir to, is perfectly consistent with the sense which has been attributed to its early Hebrew form; for this includes the longing for maternity, its temptations and its pains, and the sorrows and sins which are obviously traceable to it.

Some years ago, when the spectacular drama of 'Paradise' was performed in Paris, the Temptation was effected by means of a mirror. Satan glided behind the tree as a serpent, and then came forth as a handsome man, and after uttering compliments that she could not understand, presented Eve with a small oval mirror which explained them all. Mlle. Abingdon as Eve displayed consummate art in her expression of awakening self-admiration, of the longing for admiration from the man before her, and the various stages of self-consciousness by which she is brought under the Tempter's power. This idea of the mirror was no doubt borrowed from the corresponding fable of Pandora. On a vase (Etruscan) in the Hamilton Collection there is an admirable representation of Pandora opening her box, from which all evils are escaping. She is seated beneath a tree, around which a serpent is coiled. Among the things which have come out of the box is this same small oval mirror. In this variant, Hope, coming out last corresponds with the prophecy that the seed of the woman shall bruise the serpent's head. The ancient Etruscan and the modern Parisian version are both by the mirror finely connected with the sexual sense of the legend.

The theological interpretation of the beautiful myth of Eden represents a sort of spiritual vivisection; yet even as a dogma the story preserves high testimony: when woman falls the human race falls with her; when man rises above his inward or outward degradations and recovers his Paradise, it is because his nature is refined by the purity of woman, and his home sweetened by her heart. There is a widespread superstition that every Serpent will single out a woman from any number of people for its attack. In such dim way is felt her gentle bruising of man's reptilian self. No wonder that woman is excluded from those regions of life where man's policy is still to crawl, eat dust, and bite the heel.

It is, I suppose, the old Mystery of the Creation which left Coventry its legend of a Good Eve (Godiva, whose name is written 'good Eve' in a Conventry verse, 1494), whose nakedness should bring benefit to man, as that of the first Eve brought him evil. The fig-leaf of Eve, gathered no doubt from the tree whose forbidden fruit she had eaten, has gradually grown so large as to cloak her mind and spirit as well as her form. Her work must still be chiefly that of a spirit veiled and ashamed. Her passions suppressed, her genius disbelieved, her influence forced to seek hidden and often illegitimate channels, Woman now outwardly represents a creation of man to suit his own convenience. But the Serpent has also changed a great deal since the days of Eve, and now, as Intelligence, has found out man in his fool's-paradise, where he stolidly maintains that, with few exceptions, it is good for man to be alone. But good women are remembering Godiva; and realising that, the charms which have sometimes lowered man or cost him dear may be made his salvation. It shall be so when Woman can face with clear-eyed purity all the facts of nature, can cast away the mental and moral swathing-clothes transmitted from Eden, and put forth all her powers for the welfare of mankind,—a Good Eva, whom Coventry Toms may call naked, but who is 'not ashamed' of the garb of Innocence and Truth.

Notes

1 Gen. vi. 1, 2, 4.

2 vi.–xi. pp. 3–6. See Drummond's 'Jewish Messiah,' p. 21.

3 See vol. i. p. 255.

4 Phil. Trans. Ab. from 1700–1720, Part iv. p. 173.

5 Gen. xxi. 6, 7. The English version has destroyed the sense by supplying 'him' after 'borne.' Cf. also verses 1, 2. The rabbins were fully aware of the importance of the statement that it was Jehovah who 'opened the womb of Sara,' and supplemented it with various traditions. It was related that when Isaac was born, the kings of the earth refused to believe such a prodigy concerning even a beauty of ninety years; whereupon the breasts of all their wives were miraculously dried up, and they all had to bring their children to Sara to be suckled.

6 Fortieth Parascha, fol. 37, col. 1. The solar—or more correctly, so far as Sara is concerned, lunar—aspects of the legend of Abraham, Sara, and Isaac, however important, do not affect the human nature with which they are associated; nor is the special service to which they are pressed in Jewish theology altered by the theory (should it prove true) which derives these personages from Aryan mythology. There seems to be some reason for supposing that Sara is a semiticised form of Saranyú. The two stand in somewhat the same typical position. Saranyú, daughter of Tvashtar ('the fashioner'), was mother of the first human pair, Yama and Yami. Sara is the first mother of those born in a new (covenanted) creation. Each is for a time concealed from mortals; each leaves her husband an illegitimate representative. Saranyú gives her lord Savarná ('substitute'), who by him brings forth Manu,—that is 'Man,' but not the original perfect Man. Sara substitutes Hagar ('the fleeting'), and Ishmael is born, but not within the covenant.

7 Gen. iii. 14. Zerov. Hummor, fol. 8, col. 3. Parascha Bereschith. It is said that, according to Prov. xxv. 21, if thy enemy hunger thou must feed him; and hence dust must be placed for the serpent when its power over man is weakened by circumcision.

8 Parascha Bereschith, fol. 12, col. 4. Eisenmenger, Entdeckes Judenthum, ii. 409.

Chapter IX - Lilith

Madonnas—Adam's first wife—Her flight and doom—Creation of devils—Lilith marries Samaël—Tree of Life—Lilith's part in the Temptation—Her locks—Lamia—Bodeima—Meschia and Meschiane—Amazons—Maternity—Rib-theory of Woman—Káli and Durga—Captivity of Woman.

The attempt of the compilers of the Book of Genesis to amalgamate the Elohist and Jehovist legends, ignoring the moral abyss that yawns between them, led to some sufficiently curious results. One of these it may be well enough to examine here, since, though later in form than some other legends which remain to be considered, it is closely connected in spirit with the ancient myth of Eden and illustrative of it.

The differences between the two creations of man and woman critically examined in the previous chapter were fully recognised by the ancient rabbins, and their speculations on the subject laid the basis for the further legend that the woman created (Gen. i.) at the same time with Adam, and therefore not possibly the woman formed from his rib, was a first wife who turned out badly.

To this first wife of Adam it was but natural to assign the name of one of the many ancient goddesses who had been degraded into demonesses. For the history of Mariolatry in the North of Europe has been many times anticipated: the mother's tenderness and self-devotion, the first smile of love upon social chaos, availed to give every race its Madonna, whose popularity drew around her the fatal favours of priestcraft, weighing her down at last to be a type of corruption. Even the Semitic tribes, with their hard masculine deities, seem to have once worshipped Alilat, whose name survives in Elohim and Allah. Among these degraded Madonnas was Lilith, whose name has been found in a Chaldean inscription, which says, when a country is at peace 'Lilith (Lilatu) is not before them.' The name is from Assyr. lay'lâ, Hebrew Lil (night), which already in Accadian meant 'sorcery.' It probably personified, at first, the darkness that soothed children to slumber; and though the word Lullaby has, with more ingenuity than accuracy, been derived from Lilith Abi, the theory may suggest the path by which the soft Southern night came to mean a nocturnal spectre.

The only place where the name of Lilith occurs in the Bible is Isa. xxxiv. 14, where the English version renders it 'screech-owl.' In the Vulgate it is translated 'Lamia,' and in Luther's Bible, 'Kobold;' Gesenius explains it as 'nocturna, night-spectre, ghost.'

The rabbinical myths concerning Lilith, often passed over as puerile fancies, appear to me pregnant with significance and beauty. Thus Abraham Ecchelensis, giving a poor Arabic version of the legend, says, 'This fable has been transmitted to the Arabs from Jewish sources by some converts of Mahomet from Cabbalism and Rabbinism, who have transferred all the Jewish fooleries to the Arabs.'1 But the rabbinical legend grew very slowly, and relates to principles and facts of social evolution whose force and meaning are not yet exhausted.

Premising that the legend is here pieced together mainly from Eisenmenger,2 who at each mention of the subject gives ample references to rabbinical authorities, I will relate it without further references of my own.

Lilith was said to have been created at the same time and in the same way as Adam; and when the two met they instantly quarrelled about the headship which both claimed. Adam began the first conversation by asserting that he was to be her master. Lilith replied that she had equal right to be chief. Adam insisting, Lilith uttered a certain spell called Schem-hammphorasch—afterwards confided by a fallen angel to one of 'the daughters of men' with whom he had an intrigue, and of famous potency in Jewish folklore—the result of which was that she obtained wings. Lilith then flew out of Eden and out of sight.3 Adam then cried in distress—'Master of the world, the woman whom thou didst give me has flown away.' The Creator then sent three angels to find Lilith and persuade her to return to the garden; but she declared that it could be no paradise to her if she was to be the servant of man. She remained hovering over the Red Sea, where the angels had found her, while these returned with her inflexible resolution. And she would not yield even after the angels had been sent again to convey to her, as the alternative of not returning, the doom that she should bear many children but these should all die in infancy.

This penalty was so awful that Lilith was about to commit suicide by drowning herself in the sea, when the three angels, moved by her anguish, agreed that she should have the compensation of possessing full power over all children after birth up to their eighth day; on which she promised that she would never disturb any babes who were under their (the angels') protection. Hence the charm (Camea) against Lilith hung round the necks of Jewish children bore the names of these three angels—Senói, Sansenói, and Sammangelóf. Lilith has special power over all children born out of wedlock for whom she watches, dressed in finest raiment; and she has especial power on the first day of the month, and on the Sabbath evening. When a little child laughs in its sleep it was believed that Lilith was with it, and the babe must be struck on the nose three times, the words being thrice repeated—'Away, cursed Lilith! thou hast no place here!'

The divorce between Lilith and Adam being complete, the second Eve (i.e., Mother) was now formed, and this time out of Adam's rib in order that there might be no question of her dependence, and that the embarrassing question of woman's rights might never be raised again.

But about this time the Devils were also created. These beings were the last of the six days' creation, but they were made so late in the day that there was no daylight by which to fashion bodies for them. The Creator was just putting them off with a promise that he would make them bodies next day, when lo! the Sabbath—which was for a long time personified—came and sat before him, to represent the many evils which might result from the precedent he would set by working even a little on the day whose sanctity had already been promulgated. Under these circumstances the Creator told the Devils that they must disperse and try to get bodies as they could find them. On this account they have been compelled ever since to seek carnal enjoyments by nestling in the hearts of human beings and availing themselves of human senses and passions.

These Devils as created were ethereal spirits; they had certain atmospheric forms, but felt that they had been badly treated in not having been provided with flesh and blood, and they were envious of the carnal pleasures which human beings could enjoy. So long as man and woman remained pure, the Devils could not take possession of their bodies and enjoy such pleasures, and it was therefore of great importance to them that the first human pair should be corrupted. At the head of these Devils stood now a fallen angel—Samaël. Of this archfiend more is said elsewhere; at this point it need only be said that he had been an ideal flaming Serpent, leader of the Seraphim. He was already burning with lust and envy, as he witnessed the pleasures of Adam and Eve in Eden, when he found beautiful Lilith lamenting her wrongs in loneliness.

Fig. 1.—Lilith and Eve (Mediæval missal).

She became his wife. The name of Samaël by one interpretation signifies 'the Left'; and we may suppose that Lilith found him radical on the question of female equality which she had raised in Eden. He gave her a splendid kingdom where she was attended by 480 troops; but all this could not compensate her for the loss of Eden,—she seems never to have regretted parting with Adam,—and for the loss of her children. She remained the Lady of Sorrow. Her great enemy was Machalath who presided over 478 troops, and who was for ever dancing, as Lilith was for ever sighing and weeping. It was long believed that at certain times the voice of Lilith's grief could be heard in the air.

Samaël found in Lilith a willing conspirator against Jehovah in his plans for man and woman. The corruption of these two meant, to the troops of Samaël, bringing their bodies down into a plane where they might be entered by themselves (the Devils), not to mention at present the manifold other motives by which they were actuated. It may be remarked also that in the rabbinical traditions, after their Aryan impregnation, there are traces of a desire of the Devils to reach the Tree of Life.

Truly a wondrous Tree! Around it, in its place at the east of Eden, sang six hundred thousand lovely angels with happy hymns, and it glorified the vast garden. It possessed five hundred thousand different flavours and odours, which were wafted to the four sides of the world by zephyrs from seven lustrous clouds that made its canopy. Beneath it sat the disciples of Wisdom on resplendent seats, screened from the blaze of sun, moon, and cloud-veiled from potency of the stars (there was no night); and within were the joys referred to in the verse (Prov. viii. 21), 'That I may cause those that love me to inherit substance; and I will fill their treasures.'

Had there been an order of female rabbins the story of Lilith might have borne obvious modifications, and she might have appeared as a heroine anxious to rescue her sex from slavery to man. As it is the immemorial prerogative of man to lay all blame upon woman, that being part of the hereditary following of Adam, it is not wonderful that Lilith was in due time made responsible for the temptation of Eve. She was supposed to have beguiled the Serpent on guard at the gate of Eden to lend her his form for a time, after which theory the curse on the serpent might mean the binding of Lilith for ever in that form. This would appear to have originated the notion mentioned in Comestor (Hist. Schol., 12th cent.), that while the serpent was yet erect it had a virgin's head. The accompanying example is from a very early missal in the possession of Sir Joseph Hooker, of which I could not discover the date or history, but the theory is traceable in the eighth century. In this picture we have an early example of those which have since become familiar in old Bibles. Pietro d'Orvieto painted this serpent-woman in his finest fresco, at Pisa. Perhaps in no other picture has the genius of Michæl Angelo been more felicitous than in that on the ceiling of the Sistine Chapel, in which Lilith is portrayed. In this picture (Fig. 2) the marvellous beauty of his first wife appears to have awakened the enthusiasm of Adam; and, indeed, it is quite in harmony with the earlier myth that Lilith should be of greater beauty than Eve.

Fig. 2.—Temptation and Expulsion (Michæl Angelo, Sistine Chapel).

An artist and poet of our own time (Rossetti) has by both of his arts celebrated the fatal beauty of Lilith. His Lilith, bringing 'soft sleep,' antedates, as I think, the fair devil of the Rabbins, but is also the mediæval witch against whose beautiful locks Mephistopheles warns Faust when she appears at the Walpurgis-night orgie.

The rose and poppy are her flowers; for where
Is he not found, O Lilith, whom shed scent
And soft-shed kisses and soft sleep shall snare?
Lo! as that youth's eyes burned at thine, so went
Thy spell through him, and left his straight neck bent,
And round his heart one strangling golden hair.

The potency of Lilith's tresses has probably its origin in the hairy nature ascribed by the Rabbins to all demons (shedim), and found fully represented in Esau. Perhaps the serpent-locks of Medusa had a similar origin. Nay, there is a suggestion in Dante that these tresses of Medusa may have once represented fascinating rather than horrible serpents. As she approaches, Virgil is alarmed for his brother-poet:

'Turn thyself back, and keep thy vision hid;
For, if the Gorgon show, and then behold,
'Twould all be o'er with e'er returning up.'
So did the master say; and he himself
Turned me, and to my own hands trusted not,
But that with his too he should cover me.
O you that have a sane intelligence,
Look ye unto the doctrine which herein
*Conceals itself 'neath the strange verses' veil.*4

If this means that the security against evil is to veil the eyes from it, Virgil's warning would be against a beautiful seducer, similar to the warning given by Mephistopheles to Faust against the fatal charms of Lilith. Since, however, even in the time of Homer, the Gorgon was a popular symbol of terrors, the possibility of a survival in Dante's mind of any more primitive association with Medusa is questionable. The Pauline doctrine, that the glory of a woman is her hair, no doubt had important antecedents: such glory might easily be degraded, and every hair turn to a fatal 'binder,' like the one golden thread of Lilith round the heart of her victim; or it might ensnare its owner. In Treves Cathedral there is a curious old picture of a woman carried to hell by her beautiful hair; one devil draws her by it, another is seated on her back and drives her by locks of it as a bridle.

In the later developments of the myth of Lilith she was, among the Arabs, transformed to a Ghoul, but in rabbinical legend she appears to have been influenced by the story of Lamia, whose name is substituted for Lilith in the Vulgate. Like Lilith, Lamia was robbed of her children, and was driven by despair to avenge herself on all children.5 The name of Lamia was long used to frighten Italian children, as that of Lilith was by Hebrew nurses.

It is possible that the part assigned to Lilith in the temptation of Eve may have been suggested by ancient Egyptian sculptures, which represent the Tree of Life in Amenti (Paradise) guarded by the Serpent-goddess Nu. One of these in the British Museum represents the Osirian on his journey to heaven, and his soul in form of a human-headed bird, drinking the water of Life as poured out to them from a jar by the goddess who coils around the sacred sycamore, her woman's bust and face appearing amid the branches much like Lilith in our old pictures.

The Singhalese also have a kind of Lilith or Lamia whom they call Bodrima, though she is not so much dreaded for the sake of children as for her vindictive feelings towards men. She is the ghost of a woman who died in childbirth and in great agony. She may be heard wailing in the night, it is said, and if she meets any man will choke him to death. When her wailing is heard men are careful to stay within doors, but the women go forth with brooms in their hands and abuse Bodrima with epithets. She fears women, especially when they carry brooms. But the women have also some compassion for this poor ghost, and often leave a lamp and some betel leaves where she may get some warmth and comfort from them. If Bodrima be fired at, there may be found, perhaps, a dead lizard near the spot in the morning.

As protomartyr of female independence, Lilith suffered a fate not unlike that of her sisters and successors in our own time who have appealed from the legendary decision made in Eden: she became the prototype of the 'strong-minded' and 'cold-hearted' woman, and personification of the fatal fascination of the passionless. Her special relation to children was gradually expanded, and she was regarded as the perilous seducer of young men, each of her victims perishing of unrequited passion. She was ever young, and always dressed with great beauty. It would seem that the curse upon her for forsaking Adam—that her children should die in infancy—was escaped in the case of the children she had by Samaël. She was almost as prolific as Echidna. Through all the latter rabbinical lore it is repeated, 'Samaël is the fiery serpent, Lilith the crooked serpent,' and from their union came Leviathan, Asmodeus, and indeed most of the famous devils.

There is an ancient Persian legend of the first man and woman, Meschia and Meschiane, that they for a long time lived happily together: they hunted together, and discovered fire, and made an axe, and with it built them a hut. But no sooner had they thus set up housekeeping than they fought terribly, and, after wounding each other, parted. It is not said which remained ruler of the hut, but we learn that after fifty years of divorce they were reunited.

These legends show the question of equality of the sexes to have been a very serious one in early times. The story of Meschia and Meschiane fairly represents primitive man living by the hunt; that of Eden shows man entering on the work of agriculture. In neither of these occupations would there be any reason why woman should be so unequal as to set in motion the forces which have diminished her physical stature and degraded her position. Women can still hunt and fish, and they are quite man's equal in tilling the soil.6

In all sex-mythology there are intimations that women were taken captive. The proclamation of female subordination is made not only in the legend of Eve's creation out of the man's rib, but in the emphasis with which her name is declared to have been given her because she was the Mother of all living. In the variously significant legends of the Amazons they are said to have burned away their breasts that they might use the bow: in the history of contemporary Amazons—such as the female Areoi of Polynesia—the legend is interpreted in the systematic slaughter of their children. In the hunt, Meschia might be aided by Meschiane in many ways; in dressing the garden Adam might find Lilith or Eve a 'help meet' for the work; but in the brutal régime of war the child disables woman, and the affections of maternity render her man's inferior in the work of butchery. Herakles wins great glory by slaying Hyppolite; but the legends of her later reappearances—as Libussa at Prague, etc.,—follow the less mythological story of the Amazons given by Herodotus (IV. 112), who represents the Scythians as gradually disarming them by sending out their youths to meet them with dalliance instead of with weapons. The youths went off with their captured captors, and from their union sprang the Sauromatæ, among whom the men and women dressed alike, and fought and hunted together. But of the real outcome of that truce and union Tennyson can tell us more than Herodotus: in his Princess we see the woman whom maternity and war have combined to produce, her independence betrayed by the tenderness of her nature. The surrender, once secured, was made permanent for ages by the sentiments and sympathies born of the child's appeal for compassion.

In primitive ages the child must in many cases have been a burthen even to man in the struggle for existence; the population question could hardly have failed to press its importance upon men, as it does even upon certain animals; and it would be an especial interest to a man not to have his hut overrun with offspring not his own,—turning his fair labour into drudgery for their support, and so cursing the earth for him. Thus, while Polyandry was giving rise to the obvious complications under which it must ultimately disappear, it would be natural that devils of lust should be invented to restrain the maternal instinct. But as time went on the daughters of Eve would have taken the story of her fall and hardships too much to heart. The pangs and perils of childbirth were ever-present monitors whose warnings might be followed too closely. The early Jewish laws bear distinct traces of the necessity which had arrived for insisting on the command to increase and multiply. Under these changed circumstances it would be natural that the story of a recusant and passionless Eve should arise and suffer the penalties undergone by Lilith,—the necessity of bearing, as captive, a vast progeny against her will only to lose them again, and to long for human children she did not bring forth and could not cherish. The too passionate and the passionless woman are successively warned in the origin and outcome of the myth.7

It is a suggestive fact that the descendants of Adam should trace their fall not to the independent Lilith, who asserted her equality at cost of becoming the Devil's bride, but to the apparently submissive Eve who stayed inside the garden. The serpent found out the guarded and restrained woman as well as the free and defiant, and with much more formidable results. For craft is the only weapon of the weak against the strong. The submissiveness of the captive woman must have been for a long time outward only. When Adam found himself among thorns and briars he might have questioned whether much had been gained by calling Eve his rib, when after all she really was a woman, and prepared to take her intellectual rights from the Serpent if denied her in legitimate ways. The question is, indeed, hardly out of date yet when the genius of woman is compelled to act with subtlety and reduced to exert its influence too often by intrigue.

It is remarkable that we find something like a similar development to the two wives of Adam in Hindu mythology also. Káli and Dúrga have the same origin: the former is represented dancing on the prostrate form of her 'lord and master,' and she becomes the demoness of violence, the mother of the diabolical 'Calas' of Singhalese demonolatry. Dúrga sacrificed herself for her husband's honour, and is now adored. The counterpart of Dúrga-worship is the Zenana system. In countries where the Zenana system has not survived, but some freedom has been gained for woman, it is probable that Káli will presently not be thought of as necessarily trampling on man, and Lilith not be regarded as the Devil's wife because she will not submit to be the slave of man. When man can make him a home and garden which shall not be a prison, and in which knowledge is unforbidden fruit, Lilith will not have to seek her liberty by revolution against his society, nor Eve hers by intrigue; unfitness for co-operation with the ferocities of nature will leave her a help meet for the rearing of children, and for the recovery and culture of every garden, whether within or without the man who now asserts over woman a lordship unnatural and unjust.

Notes

1 Hist. Arabûm.
2 Entdeckes Judenthum.
3 This legend may have been in the mind of the writer of the Book of Revelations when (xii. 14) he describes the Woman who received wings that she might escape the Serpent. Lilith's wings bore her to the Serpent.
4 Inferno, ix. 56–64.
5 She was a Lybian Queen beloved by Zeus, whose children were victims of Hera's jealousy. She was daughter of Belus, and it is a notable coincidence, if no more, that in Gen. xxxvi. 'Bela' is mentioned as a king of Edom, the domain of Samaël, who married Lilith.
6 The martial and hunting customs of the German women, as well as their equality with men, may be traced in the vestiges of their decline. Hexe (witch) is from hag (forest): the priestesses who carried the Broom of Thor were called Hagdissen. Before the seventeenth century the Hexe was called Drud or Trud (red folk, related to the Lightning-god). But the famous female hunters and warriors of Wodan, the Valkyries, were so called also; and the preservation of the epithet (Trud) in the noble name Gertrude is a connecting link between the German Amazons and the political power so long maintained by women in the same country. Their office as priestesses probably marks a step downward from their outdoor equality. By this route, as priestesses of diabolised deities, they became witches; but many folk-legends made these witches still great riders, and the Devil was said to transform and ride them as dapplegrey mares. The chief charge against the witches, that of carnal commerce with devils, is also significant. Like Lilith, women became devils' brides whenever they were not content with sitting at home with the distaff and the child.
7 Mr. W. B. Scott has painted a beautiful picture of Eve gazing up with longing at a sweet babe in the tree, whose serpent coils beneath she does not see.

Chapter X - War in Heaven

The 'Other'—Tiamat, Bohu, 'the Deep'—Ra and Apophis—Hathors—Bel's combat—Revolt in Heaven—Lilith—Myth of the Devil at the creation of Light.

In none of the ancient scriptures do we get back to any theory or explanation of the origin of evil or of the enemies of the gods. In a Persian text at Persepolis, of Darius I., Ahriman is called with simplicity 'the Other' (Aniya), and 'the Hater' (Duvaisañt, Zend thaīsat), and that is about as much as we are really told about the devils of any race. Their existence is taken for granted. The legends of rebellion in heaven and of angels cast down and transformed to devils may supply an easy explanation to our modern theologians, but when we trace them to their origin we discover that to the ancients they had no such significance. The angels were cast down to Pits prepared for them from the foundation of the world, and before it, and when they fell it was into the hands of already existing enemies eager to torment them. Nevertheless these accounts of rebellious spirits in heaven are of great importance and merit our careful consideration.

It is remarkable that the Bible opens with an intimation of the existence of this 'Other.' Its second verse speaks of a certain 'darkness upon the face of the deep.' The word used here is Bohu, which is identified as the Assyrian Bahu, the Queen of Hades. In the inscription of Shalmaneser the word is used for 'abyss of chaos.'1 Bahu is otherwise Gula, a form of Ishtar or Allat, 'Lady of the House of Death,' and an epithet of the same female demon is Nin-cigal, 'Lady of the Mighty

Earth.' The story of the Descent of Ishtar into Hades, the realm of Nin-cigal, has already been told (p. 77); in that version Ishtar is the same as Astarte, the Assyrian Venus. But like the moon with which she was associated she waned and declined, and the beautiful legend of her descent (like Persephone) into Hades seems to have found a variant in the myth of Bel and the Dragon. There she is a sea-monster and is called Tiamat (Thalatth of Berosus),—that is, 'the Deep,' over which rests the darkness described in Genesis i. 2. The process by which the moon would share the evil repute of Tiamat is obvious. In the Babylonian belief the dry land rested upon the abyss of watery chaos from which it was drawn. This underworld ocean was shut in by gates. They were opened when the moon was created to rule the night—therefore Prince of Darkness. The formation by Anu of this Moon-god (Uru) from Tiamat, might even have been suggested by the rising of the tides under his sway. The Babylonians represent the Moon as having been created before the Sun, and he emerged from 'a boiling' in the abyss. 'At the beginning of the month, at the rising of the night, his horns are breaking through to shine on heaven.'2 In the one Babylonian design, a seal in the British Museum,3 which seems referable to the legend of the Fall of Man, the male figure has horns. It may have been that this male Moon (Uru) was supposed to have been corrupted by some female emanation of Tiamat, and to have fallen from a 'ruler of the night' to an ally of the night. This female corrupter, who would correspond to Eve, might in this way have become mistress of the Moon, and ultimately identified with it.

Although the cause of the original conflict between the Abyss beneath and the Heaven above is left by ancient inscriptions and scriptures to imagination, it is not a very strained hypothesis that ancient Chaos regarded the upper gods as aggressors on her domain in the work of creation. 'When above,' runs the Babylonian legend, 'were not raised the heavens, and below on the earth a plant had not grown ... the chaos (or water) Tiamat was the producing mother of the whole of them.' 'The gods had not sprung up, any one of them.'4 Indeed in the legend of the conflict between Bel and the Dragon, on the Babylonian cylinders, it appears that the god Sar addressed her as wife, and said, 'The tribute to thy maternity shall be forced upon them by thy weapons.'5 The Sun and Moon would naturally be drawn into any contest between Overworld (with Light) and Underworld (with Darkness).

Though Tiamat is called a Dragon, she was pictured by the Babylonians only as a monstrous Griffin. In the Assyrian account of the fight it will be seen that she is called a 'Serpent.' The link between the two—Griffin and Serpent—will be found, I suspect, in Typhonic influence on the fable. In a hymn to Amen-Ra (the Sun), copied about fourteenth century b.c. from an earlier composition, as its translator, Mr. Goodwin, supposes, we have the following:—

The gods rejoice in his goodness who exalts those who are lowly:
Lord of the boat and barge,
They conduct thee through the firmament in peace.
Thy servants rejoice:
Beholding the overthrow of the wicked:
His limbs pierced with the sword:
Fire consumes him:
His soul and body are annihilated.
Naka (the serpent) saves his feet:
The gods rejoice:
The servants of the Sun are in peace.

The allusion in the second line indicates that this hymn relates to the navigation of Ra through Hades, and the destruction of Apophis.

We may read next the Accadian tablet (p. 256) which speaks of the seven Hathors as neither male nor female, and as born in 'the Deep.'

Another Accadian tablet, translated by Mr. Sayce, speaks of these as the 'baleful seven destroyers;' as 'born in the mountain of the sunset;' as being Incubi. It is significantly said:—'Among the stars of heaven their watch they kept not, in watching was their office.' Here is a primæval note of treachery.6

We next come to a further phase, represented in a Cuneiform tablet, which must be quoted at length:—

Days of storm, Powers of Evil,
Rebellious spirits, who were born in the lower part of heaven,
They were workers of calamity.
(The lines giving the names and descriptions of the spirits are here broken.)

The third was like a leopard,
The fourth was like a snake ...
The fifth was like a dog ...

The sixth was an enemy to heaven and its king.
The seventh was a destructive tempest.
These seven are the messengers of Anu7 their king.
From place to place by turns they pass.
They are the dark storms in heaven, which into fire unite themselves.
They are the destructive tempests, which on a fine day sudden darkness cause.
With storms and meteors they rush.
Their rage ignites the thunderbolts of Im.8
From the right hand of the Thunderer they dart forth.
On the horizon of heaven like lightning they ...
Against high heaven, the dwelling-place of Anu the king, they plotted evil, and had none to withstand them.
When Bel heard this news, he communed secretly with his own heart.
Then he took counsel with Hea the great Inventor (or Sage) of the gods.
And they stationed the Moon, the Sun, and Ishtar to keep guard over the approach to heaven.
Unto Anu, ruler of heaven, they told it.
And those three gods, his children,
To watch night and day unceasingly he commanded them.
When those seven evil spirits rushed upon the base of heaven,
And close in front of the Moon with fiery weapons advanced,
Then the noble Sun and Im the warrior side by side stood firm.

But Ishtar, with Anu the king, entered the exalted dwelling, and hid themselves in the summit of heaven.
Column II.

Those evil spirits, the messengers of Anu their king ...
They have plotted evil ...
From mid-heaven like meteors they have rushed upon the earth.
Bel, who the noble Moon in eclipse
Saw from heaven,
Called aloud to Paku his messenger:
O my messenger Paku, carry my words to the Deep.9
Tell my son that the Moon in heaven is terribly eclipsed!
To Hea in the Deep repeat this!
Paku understood the words of his Lord.
Unto Hea in the Deep swiftly he went.
To the Lord, the great Inventor, the god Nukimmut,
Paku repeated the words of his Lord.
When Hea in the Deep heard these words,
He bit his lips, and tears bedewed his face.
Then he sent for his son Marduk to help him.
Go to my son Marduk,
Tell my son that the Moon in heaven is terribly eclipsed!
That eclipse has been seen in heaven!
They are seven, those evil spirits, and death they fear not!
They are seven, those evil spirits, who rush like a hurricane,
And fall like firebrands on the earth!
In front of the bright Moon with fiery weapons (they draw nigh);
But the noble Sun and Im the warrior (are withstanding them).
[The rest of the legend is lost.]

Nukimmut is a name of Hea which occurs frequently: he was the good genius of the earth, and his son Marduk was his incarnation—a Herakles or Saviour. It will be noted that as yet Ishtar is in heaven. The next Tablet, which shows the development of the myth, introduces us to the great female dragon Tiamat herself, and her destroyer Bel.

... And with it his right hand he armed.
His naming sword he raised in his hand.
He brandished his lightnings before him.

A curved scymitar he carried on his body.
And he made a sword to destroy the Dragon,
Which turned four ways; so that none could avoid its rapid blows.
It turned to the south, to the north, to the east, and to the west.
Near to his sabre he placed the bow of his father Anu.
He made a whirling thunderbolt, and a bolt with double flames, impossible to extinguish.
And a quadruple bolt, and a septuple bolt, and a ... bolt of crooked fire.
He took the thunderbolts which he had made, and there were seven of them,
To be shot at the Dragon, and he put them into his quiver behind him.
Then he raised his great sword, whose name was 'Lord of the Storm.'
He mounted his chariot, whose name was 'Destroyer of the Impious.'
He took his place, and lifted the four reins
In his hand.

[Bel now offers to the Dragon to decide their quarrel by single combat, which the Dragon accepts. This agrees with the representations of the combat on Babylonian cylinders in Mr. Smith's 'Chaldean Genesis,' p. 62, etc.]

(Why seekest thou thus) to irritate me with blasphemies?
Let thy army withdraw: let thy chiefs stand aside:
Then I and thou (alone) we will do battle.
When the Dragon heard this.
Stand back! she said, and repeated her command.
Then the tempter rose watchfully on high.
Turning and twisting, she shifted her standing point,
She watched his lightnings, she provided for retreat.
The warrior angels sheathed their swords.
Then the Dragon attacked the just Prince of the gods.
Strongly they joined in the trial of battle,
The King drew his sword, and dealt rapid blows,
Then he took his whirling thunderbolt, and looked well behind and before him:
And when the Dragon opened her mouth to swallow him,
He flung the bolt into her, before she could shut her lips.
The blazing lightning poured into her inside.
He pulled out her heart; her mouth he rent open;
He drew his (falchion), and cut open her belly.
He cut into her inside and extracted her heart;
He took vengeance on her, and destroyed her life.
When he knew she was dead he boasted over her.
After that the Dragon their leader was slain,
Her troops took to flight: her army was scattered abroad,
And the angels her allies, who had come to help her,
Retreated, grew quiet, and went away.
They fled from thence, fearing for their own lives,
And saved themselves, flying to places beyond pursuit.
He followed them, their weapons he broke up.
Broken they lay, and in great heaps they were captured.
A crowd of followers, full of astonishment,
Its remains lifted up, and on their shoulders hoisted.
And the eleven tribes pouring in after the battle
In great multitudes, coming to see,
Gazed at the monstrous serpent....

In the fragment just quoted we have the 'flaming sword which turned every way' (Gen. iii. 24). The seven distinct forms of evil are but faintly remembered in the seven thunderbolts taken by Bel: they are now all virtually gathered into the one form he combats, and are thus on their way to form the seven-headed dragon of the Apocalypse, where Michael replaces Bel.10 'The angels, her allies who had come to help her,' are surely that 'third part of the stars of heaven' which the apocalyptic dragon's tail drew to the earth in its fall (Rev. xii. 4). Bel's dragon is also called a 'Tempter.'

At length we reach the brief but clear account of the 'Revolt in Heaven' found in a cuneiform tablet in the British Museum, and translated by Mr. Fox Talbot:11—

The Divine Being spoke three times, the commencement of a psalm.
The god of holy songs, Lord of religion and worship
seated a thousand singers and musicians: and established a choral band
who to his hymn were to respond in multitudes....
With a loud cry of contempt they broke up his holy song spoiling, confusing, confounding his hymn of praise.
The god of the bright crown with a wish to summon his adherents sounded a trumpet blast which would wake the dead,
which to those rebel angels prohibited return
he stopped their service, and sent them to the gods who were his enemies.
In their room he created mankind.
The first who received life, dwelt along with him.
May he give them strength never to neglect his word,
following the serpent's voice, whom his hands had made.
And may the god of divine speech expel from his five thousand that wicked thousand
who in the midst of his heavenly song had shouted evil blasphemies!

It will be observed that there were already hostile gods to whom these riotous angels were sent. It is clear that in both the Egyptian and Assyrian cosmogonies the upper gods had in their employ many ferocious monsters. Thus in the Book of Hades, Horus addresses a terrible serpent: 'My Kheti, great fire, of which this flame in my eye is the emission, and of which my children guard the folds, open thy mouth, draw wide thy jaws, launch thy flame against the enemies of my father, burn their bodies, consume their souls!'12 Many such instances could be quoted. In this same book we find a great serpent, Saa-Set, 'Guardian of the Earth.' Each of the twelve pylons of Hades is surmounted by its serpent-guards—except one. What has become of that one? In the last inscription but one, quoted in full, it will be observed (third line from the last) that eleven (angel) tribes came in after Bel's battle to inspect the slain dragon. The twelfth had revolted. These, we may suppose, had listened to 'the serpent's voice' mentioned in the last fragment quoted.

We have thus distributed through these fragments all the elements which, from Egyptian and Assyrian sources gathered around the legend of the Serpent in Eden. The Tree of Knowledge and that of Life are not included, and I have given elsewhere my reasons for believing these to be importations from the ancient Aryan legend of the war between the Devas and Asuras for the immortalising Amrita.

In the last fragment quoted we have also a notable statement, that mankind were created to fill the places that had been occupied by the fallen angels. It is probable that this notion supplied the basis of a class of legends of which Lilith is type. She whose place Eve was created to fill was a serpent-woman, and the earliest mention of her is in the exorcism already quoted, found at Nineveh. In all probability she is but another form of Gula, the fallen Istar and Queen of Hades; in which case her conspiracy with the serpent Samaël would be the Darkness which was upon the face of Bahu, 'the Deep,' in the second verse of the Bible.

The Bible opens with the scene of the gods conquering the Dragon of Darkness with Light. There is a rabbinical legend, that when Light issued from under the throne of God, the Prince of Darkness asked the Creator wherefore he had brought Light into existence? God answered that it was in order that he might be driven back to his abode of darkness. The evil one asked that he might see that; and entering the stream of Light, he saw across time and the world, and beheld the face of the Messiah. Then he fell upon his face and cried, 'This is he who shall lay low in ruin me and all the inhabitants of hell!' What the Prince of Darkness saw was the vision of a race: beginning with the words (Gen. i. 3, 4), 'God said, Let there be Light; and there was Light; and God saw the Light that it was good; and God divided between the Light and the Darkness;' ending with Rev. xx. 1, 2, 'And I saw an angel come down from heaven having the key of the bottomless pit, and a great chain in his hand. And he laid hold on the dragon, that old serpent, which is the Devil and Satan, and bound him a thousand years.'

Notes

1 *'Records of the Past,' iii. p. 83. See also i. p. 135.*
2 *'Chaldean Genesis,' by George Smith, p. 70.*
3 *Copied in 'Chald. Gen.,' p. 91. As to the connection of this design with the legend of Eden, see chap. vii. of this volume.*
4 *'Chaldean Genesis,' pp. 62, 63.*
5 *Ib., 97.*
6 *'Records of the Past,' ix. 141.*
7 *Anu was the ruler of the highest heaven. Meteors and lightnings are similarly considered in Hebrew poetry as the messengers of the Almighty. (Psalm civ. 4, 'Who maketh his ministers a flaming fire,' quoted in Heb. i. 7.)*

8 Im, the god of the sky, sometimes called Rimmon (the Thunderer). He answers to the Jupiter Tonans of the Latins.
9 The abyss or ocean where the god Hea dwelt.
10 The late Mr. G. Smith says that the Chaldean dragon was seven-headed. 'Chaldean Genesis,' p. 100.
11 'Records of the Past,' vii. 123.
12 'Records of the Past,' x. 127.

Chapter XI - War on Earth

The Abode of Devils—Ketef—Disorder—Talmudic legends—The restless Spirit—The Fall of Lucifer—Asteria, Hecate, Lilith—The Dragon's triumph—A Gipsy legend—Cædmon's Poem of the Rebellious Angels—Milton's version—The Puritans and Prince Rupert—Bel as ally of the Dragon—A 'Mystery' in Marionettes—European Hells.

'Rejoice, ye heavens, and ye that dwell in them! Woe to the earth and the sea! for the devil is come down to you, having great wrath, because he knoweth that he hath but a short time.' This passage from the Book of Revelations is the refrain of many and much earlier scriptures. The Assyrian accounts of the war in heaven, given in the preceding chapter, by no means generally support the story that the archdragon was slain by Bel. Even the one that does describe the chief dragon's death leaves her comrades alive, and the balance of testimony is largely in favour of the theory which prevailed, that the rebellious angels were merely cast out of heaven, and went to swell the ranks of the dark and fearful abode which from the beginning had been peopled by the enemies of the gods. The nature of this abode is described in various passages of the Bible, and in many traditions.

'Out of the north an evil shall break forth upon all the inhabitants of the land.' So said Jeremiah (i. 14), in pursuance of nearly universal traditions as to the region of space in which demons and devils had their abode. 'Hell is naked before him,' says Job (xxvi. 6), 'and destruction hath no covering. He stretcheth out the north over the empty place.' According to the Hebrew mythology this habitation of demons was a realm of perpetual cold and midnight, which Jehovah, in creating the world, purposely left chaotic; so it was prepared for the Devil and his angels at the foundation of the world. Although this northern hell was a region of disorder, so far as the people of Jehovah and the divine domain were concerned, they had among themselves a strong military and aristocratic government. It was disorder perfectly systematised. The anarchical atmosphere of the region is reflected in the abnormal structures ascribed to the many devils with whose traits Jewish and Arabic folklore is familiar, and which are too numerous to be described here. Such a devil, for instance, is Bedargon, 'hand-high,' with fifty heads and fifty-six hearts, who cannot strike any one or be struck, instant death ensuing to either party in such an attack. A more dangerous devil is Ketef, identified as the 'terror from the chambers' alluded to by Jeremiah (xxxii. 25), 'Bitter Pestilence.' His name is said to be from kataf, 'cut and split,' because he divides the course of the day; and those who are interested to compare Hebrew and Hindu myths may find it interesting to note the coincidences between Ketef and Ketu, the cut-off tail of Ráhu, and source of pestilence.1 Ketef reigns neither in the dark or day, but between the two; his power over the year is limited to the time between June 17 and July 9, during which it was considered dangerous to flog children or let them go out after four P.M. Ketef is calf-headed, and consists of hide, hair, and eyes; he rolls like a cask; he has a terrible horn, but his chief terror lies in an evil eye fixed in his heart which none can see without instant death. The arch-fiend who reigns over the infernal host has many Court Fools—probably meteors and comets—who lead men astray.

All these devils have their regulations in their own domain, but, as we have said, their laws mean disorder in that part of the universe which belongs to the family of Jehovah. In flying about the world they are limited to places which are still chaotic or waste. They haunt such congenial spots as rocks and ruins, and frequent desert, wilderness, dark mountains, and the ruins of human habitations. They can take possession of a wandering star.

There is a pretty Talmudic legend of a devil having once gone to sleep, when some one, not seeing him of course, set down a cask of wine on his ears. In leaping up the devil broke the cask, and being tried for it, was condemned to repay the damage at a certain period. The period having elapsed before the money was brought, the devil was asked the cause of the delay. He replied that it was very difficult for devils to obtain money, because men were careful to keep it locked or tied up; and 'we have no power,' he said, 'to take from anything bound or sealed up, nor can we take anything that is measured or counted; we are permitted to take only what is free or common.'

According to one legend the devils were specially angered, because Jehovah, when he created man, gave him dominion over things in the sea (Gen. i. 28), that being a realm of unrest and tempest which they claimed as belonging to themselves. They were denied control of the life that is in the sea, though permitted a large degree of power over its waters. Over the winds their rule was supreme, and it was only by reducing certain demons to slavery that Solomon was able to ride in a wind-chariot.

Out of these several realms of order and disorder in nature were evolved the angels and the devils which were supposed to beset man. The first man is said to have been like an angel. From the instant of his creation there attended him two spirits, whom the rabbins found shadowed out in the sentence, 'Jehovah-Elohim formed man of the dust of the ground, and breathed into his nostrils the breath of life; and man became a living soul' (Gen. ii. 7). This 'breath of life' was a holy spirit, and stood on Adam's right; the 'living soul' was a restless spirit on his left, which continually moved up and down. When Adam had sinned, this restless spirit became a diabolical spirit, and it has ever acted as mediator between man and the realm of anarchy.

It has been mentioned that in the Assyrian legends of the Revolt in Heaven we find no adequate intimation of the motive by which the rebels were actuated. It is said they interrupted the heavenly song, that they brought on an eclipse, that they afflicted human beings with disease; but why they did all this is not stated. The motive of the serpent in tempting Eve is not stated in Genesis. The theory which Cædmon and Milton have made so familiar, that the dragons aspired to rival Jehovah, and usurp the throne of Heaven, must, however, have been already popular in the time of Isaiah. In his rhapsody concerning the fall of Babylon, he takes his rhetoric from the story of Bel and the Dragon, and turns a legend, as familiar to every Babylonian as that of St. George and the Dragon now is to Englishmen, into an illustration of their own doom. The invective is directed against the King of Babylon, consequently the sex of the devil is changed; but the most remarkable change is in the ascription to Lucifer of a clear purpose to rival the Most High, and seize the throne of heaven. 'Hell from beneath is moved for thee to meet thee at thy coming, it stirreth up the (spirits of) the dead, even all the chief ones (great goats) of the earth: it hath raised up from their thrones all the kings of the nations (demon-begotten aliens). All these shall say unto thee, Art thou also become weak as we? Art thou become like unto us? Thy splendour is brought down to the underworld, and the noise of thy viols: the worm is spread under thee, and the worms cover thee. How art thou fallen, O Lucifer (Daystar), son of the morning! how art thou cut down to the ground which didst weaken the nations! For thou hast said in thy heart, I will ascend into (the upper) heaven, I will exalt my throne above the stars (archangels) of God: I will sit (reign) also upon the mount of the congregation (the assembly of the enemies of God) in the sides of the north. I will ascend above the heights of the clouds (the thunder-throne of Jehovah); I will be like the Most High. Yet shalt thou be brought down to hell, to the sides of the pit.'2

In this passage we mark the arena of the combat shifted from heaven to earth. It is not the throne of heaven but that of the world at which the fiends now aim. Nay, there is confession in every line of the prophecy that the enemy of Jehovah has usurped his throne. Hell has prevailed, and Lucifer is the Prince of this World. The celestial success has not been maintained on earth. This would be the obvious fact to a humiliated, oppressed, heavily-taxed people, who believed themselves the one family on earth sprung from Jehovah, and their masters the offspring of demons. This situation gave to the vague traditions of a single combat between Bel and the Dragon, about an eclipse or a riot, the significance which it retained ever afterward of a mighty conflict on earth between the realms of Light and Darkness, between which the Elohim had set a boundary-line (Gen. i. 4) in the beginning.

A similar situation returned when the Jews were under the sway of Rome, and then all that had ever been said of Babylon was repeated against Rome under the name of Edom. It recurred in the case of those Jews who acknowledged Jesus as their Messiah: in the pomp and glory of the Cæsars they beheld the triumph of the Powers of Darkness, and the burthen of Isaiah against Lucifer was raised again in that of the Apocalypse against the seven-headed Dragon. It is notable how these writers left out of sight the myth of Eden so far as it did not belong to their race. Isaiah does not say anything even of the serpent. The Apocalypse says nothing of the two wonderful trees, and the serpent appears only as a Dragon from whom the woman is escaping, by whom she is not at all tempted. The shape of the Devil, and the Combat with him, have always been determined by dangers and evils that are actual, not such as are archæological.

A gipsy near Edinburgh gave me his version of the combat between God and Satan as follows. 'When God created the universe and all things in it, Satan tried to create a rival universe. He managed to match everything pretty well except man. There he failed; and God to punish his pride cast him down to the earth and bound him with a chain. But this chain was so long that Satan was able to move over the whole face of the earth!' There had got into this wanderer's head some bit of the Babylonian story, and it was mingled with Gnostic traditions about Ildabaoth; but there was also a quaint suggestion in Satan's long chain of the migration of this mythical combat not only round the world, but through the ages. The early followers of Christ came before the glories of Paganism with the legend that the lowly should inherit the earth. And though they speedily surrendered to the rulers of the world in Rome, and made themselves into a christian aristocracy, when they came into Northern Europe the christians were again brought to confront with an humble system the religion of thrones and warriors. St. Gatien celebrating mass in a cavern beside the Loire, meant as much weakness in presence of Paganism as the Huguenots felt twelve centuries later hiding in the like caverns from St. Gatien's priestly successors.

The burthen of Isaiah is heard again, and with realistic intensity, in the seventh century, and in the north, with our patriarchial poet Cædmon.

The All-powerful had
Angel-tribes,
Through might of hand,
The holy Lord,
Ten established,
In whom he trusted well
That they his service
Would follow,
Work his will;
Therefore gave he them wit,
And shaped them with his hands,
The holy Lord.
He had placed them so happily,
One he had made so powerful,
So mighty in his mind's thought,
He let him sway over so much,
Highest after himself in heaven's kingdom.
He had made him so fair,
So beauteous was his form in heaven,
That came to him from the Lord of hosts,
He was like to the light stars.
It was his to work the praise of the Lord,
It was his to hold dear his joys in heaven,
And to thank his Lord
For the reward that he had bestowed on him in that light;
Then had he let him long possess it;
But he turned it for himself to a worse thing,
Began to raise war upon him,
Against the highest Ruler of heaven,
Who sitteth in the holy seat.
Dear was he to our Lord,
But it might not be hidden from him
That his angel began
To be presumptuous,
Raised himself against his Master,
Sought speech of hate,
Words of pride towards him,
Would not serve God,
Said that his body was
Light and beauteous,
Fair and bright of hue:
He might not find in his mind
That he would God
In subjection,
His Lord, serve:
Seemed to himself
That he a power and force
Had greater
Than the holy God
Could have
Of adherents.
Many words spake
The angel of presumption:
Thought, through his own power,
How he for himself a stronger
Seat might make,
Higher in heaven:

Said that him his mind impelled,
That he west and north
Would begin to work,
Would prepare structures:
Said it to him seemed doubtful
That he to God would
Be a vassal.
'Why shall I toil?' said he;
'To me it is no whit needful.
To have a superior;
I can with my hands as many
Wonders work;
I have great power
To form
A diviner throne,
A higher in heaven.
Why shall I for his favour serve,
Bend to him in such vassalage?
I may be a god as he
Stand by me strong associates,
Who will not fail me in the strife,
Heroes stern of mood,
They have chosen me for chief,
Renowned warriors!
With such may one devise counsel,
With such capture his adherents;
They are my zealous friends,
Faithful in their thoughts;
I may be their chieftain,
Sway in this realm:
Thus to me it seemeth not right
That I in aught
Need cringe
To God for any good;
I will no longer be his vassal.'
When the All-powerful it
All had heard,
That his angel devised
Great presumption
To raise up against his Master,
And spake proud words
Foolishly against his Lord,
Then must he expiate the deed,
Share the work of war,
And for his punishment must have
Of all deadly ills the greatest.
So doth every man
Who against his Lord
Deviseth to war,
With crime against the great Ruler.
Then was the Mighty angry;
The highest Ruler of heaven
Hurled him from the lofty seat;
Hate had he gained at his Lord,
His favour he had lost,
Incensed with him was the Good in his mind,
Therefore must he seek the gulf

Of hard hell-torment,
For that he had warred with heaven's Ruler,
He rejected him then from his favour,
And cast him into hell,
Into the deep parts,
Where he became a devil:
The fiend with all his comrades
Fell then from heaven above,
Through as long as three nights and days,
The angels from heaven into hell;
And them all the Lord transformed to devils,
Because they his deed and word
Would not revere;
Therefore them in a worse light,
Under the earth beneath,
Almighty God
Had placed triumphless
In the swart hell;
There they have at even,
Immeasurably long,
Each of all the fiends,
A renewal of fire;
Then cometh ere dawn
The eastern wind,
Frost bitter-cold,
Ever fire or dart;
Some hard torment
They must have,
It was wrought for them in punishment,
Their world was changed:
For their sinful course
He filled hell
With the apostates.

Fig. 3.—Satan Punished.

Whether this spirited description was written by Cædmon, and whether it is of his century, are questions unimportant to the present inquiry. The poem represents a mediæval notion which long prevailed, and which characterised the Mysteries, that Satan and his comrades were humiliated from the highest angelic rank to a hell already prepared and peopled with devils, and were there, and by those devils, severely punished. One of the illuminations of the Cædmon manuscript, preserved in the Bodleian Library, shows Satan undergoing his torment (Fig. 3). He is bound over something like a gridiron, and four devils are torturing him, the largest using a scourge with six prongs. His face manifests great suffering. His form is mainly human, but his bushy tail and animal feet indicate that he has been transformed to a devil similar to those who chastise him.

On Cædmon's foundation Milton built his gorgeous edifice. His Satan is an ambitious and very English lord, in whom are reflected the whole aristocracy of England in their hatred and contempt of the holy Puritan Commonwealth, the Church of Christ as he deemed it. The ages had brought round a similar situation to that which confronted the Jews at Babylon, the early Christians of Rome, and their missionaries among the proud pagan princes of the north. The Church had long allied itself with the earlier Lucifers of the north, and now represented the proud empire of a satanic aristocracy, and the persecuted Nonconformists represented the authority of the King of kings. In the English palace, and in the throne of Canterbury, Milton saw his Beelzebub and his Satan.

Th' infernal serpent; he it was, whose guile,
Stirred up with envy and revenge, deceived
The mother of mankind, what time his pride
Had cast him out from heav'n, with all his host
Of rebel angels, by whose aid aspiring
To set himself in glory above his peers
He trusted to have equall'd the Most High,
If he opposed; and with ambitious aim
Against the throne and monarchy of God
Raised impious war in heav'n, and battle proud,
With vain attempt. Him the almighty Power
Hurl'd headlong flaming from th' ethereal sky,
With hideous ruin and combustion, down
To bottomless perdition, there to dwell
In adamantine chains and penal fire,
*Who durst defy th' Omnipotent to arms.*3

This adaptation of the imagery of Isaiah concerning Lucifer has in it all the thunder hurled by Cromwell against Charles. Even a Puritan poet might not altogether repress admiration for the dash and daring of a Prince Rupert, to which indeed even his prosaic co-religionists paid the compliment of ascribing to it a diabolical source.4 Not amid conflicts that raged in ancient Syria broke forth such lines as—

Better to reign in hell, than serve in heav'n.
With rallied arms to try what may be yet
Regain'd in heav'n, or what more lost in hell.

The Bel whom Milton saw was Cromwell, and the Dragon that serpent of English oppression which the Dictator is trampling on in a well-known engraving of his time. In the history of the Reformation the old legend did manifold duty again, as in the picture (Fig. 13) by Luther's friend Lucas Cranach.

It would seem that in the course of time Bel and the Dragon became sufficiently close allies for their worshippers to feed and defend them both with equal devotion, and for Daniel to explode them both in carrying on the fight of his deity against the gods of Babylon. This story of Bel is apocryphal as to the canon, but highly significant as to the history we are now considering. Although the Jews maintained their struggle against 'principalities and powers' long after it had been a forlorn hope, and never surrendered, nor made alliance with the Dragon, the same cannot be said of those who appropriated their title of 'the chosen of God,' counterfeited their covenant, and travestied their traditions. The alliance of Christianity and the Dragon has not been nominal, but fearfully real. In fulfilling their mission of 'inheriting the earth,' the 'meek' called around them and pressed into their service agents and weapons more diabolical than any with which the Oriental imagination had peopled the abode of devils in the north.

At a Fair in Tours (August 1878) I saw two exhibitions which were impressive enough in the light they cast through history. One was a shrunken and sufficiently grotesque production by puppets of the Mediæval 'Mystery' of Hell. Nearly every old scheme and vision of the underworld was represented in the scene. The three Judges sat to hear each case. A devil rang a bell whenever any culprit appeared at the gate. The accused was ushered in by a winged devil—Satan, the Accuser—who, by the show-woman's lips, stated the charges against each with an eager desire to make him or her out as wicked as possible. A devil with pitchfork received the sentenced, and shoved them down into a furnace. There was an array of brilliant dragons around, but they appeared to have nothing to do beyond enjoying the spectacle. But this exhibition which was styled 'Twenty minutes in Hell,' was poor and faint beside the neighbouring exhibition of the real Hell, in which Europe had been tortured for fifteen centuries. Some industrious Germans had got together in one large room several hundreds of the instruments of torture by which the nations of the West were persuaded to embrace Christianity. Every limb, sinew, feature, bone, and nerve of the human frame had suggested to christian inventiveness some ingenious device by which it might be tortured. Wheels on which to break bones, chairs of anguish, thumbscrews, the iron Virgin whose embrace pierced through every vital part; the hunger-mask which renewed for Christ's sake the exact torment of Tantalus; even the machine which bore the very name of the enemy that was cast down—the Dragon's Head! By such instrumentalities came those quasi-miraculous 'Triumphs of the Cross,' of which so much has been said and sung! The most salient phenomenon of christian history is the steady triumph of the Dragon. Misleader and Deceiver to the last, he is quite willing to sprinkle his fork and rack with holy water, to cross himself, to label his caldrons 'divine justice,' to write CHRIST upon his forehead; by so doing he was able to spring his infernal engine on the best nations, and cow the strongest hearts, till from their pallid lips were wrung the 'confessions of faith,' or the last cry of martyred truth. So was he able to assault the pure heavens once more, to quench the stars of human faith and hope, and generate a race of polite, learned, and civilised hypocrites. But the ancient sunbeams are after him: the mandate has again gone forth, 'Let there be light,' and the Light that now breaks forth is not of that kind which respects the limit of Darkness.

Notes

1 See i. pp. 46 and 255. Concerning Ketef see Eisenmenger, ii. p. 435.

2 Isaiah xiv. It may appear as if in this personification of a fallen star we have entered a different mythological region from that represented by the Assyrian tablets; but it is not so. The demoniac forms of Ishtar, Astarte, are fallen stars also. She appears in Greece as Artemis Astrateia, whose worship Pausanias mentions as coming from the East. Her development is through Asteria (Greek form of Ishtar), in whose myth is hidden much valuable Babylonian lore. Asteria was said to have thrown herself into the sea, and been changed into the island called Asteria, from its having fallen like a star from heaven. Her suicide was to escape from the embraces of Zeus, and her escape from him in form of a quail, as well as her fate, may be instructively compared with the story of Lilith, who flew out of Eden on wings to escape from Adam, and made an effort to drown herself in the Red Sea. The diabolisation of Asteria (the fallen star) was through her daughter Hecate. Hecate was the female Titan who was the most potent ally of the gods. Her rule was supreme under Zeus, and all the gifts valued by mortals were believed to proceed from her; but she was severely judicial, and rigidly withheld all blessings from such as did not deserve them. Thus she was, as the searching eye of Zeus, a star-spy upon earth. Such spies, as we have repeatedly had occasion to mention in this work, are normally developed into devils. From professional detectives they become accusers and instigators. Ishtar of the Babylonians, Asteria of the Greeks, and the Day-star of the Hebrews are male and female forms of the same personification: Hecate with her torch (ἕκατος, 'far-shooting') and Lucifer ('light-bringer' on the deeds of darkness) are the same in their degradation.

3 'Paradise Lost,' i. 40–50.

4 And foremost rides Prince Rupert, darling of fortune and of war, with his beautiful and thoughtful face of twenty-three, stern and bronzed already, yet beardless and dimpled, his dark and passionate eyes, his long love-locks drooping over costly embroidery, his graceful scarlet cloak, his white-plumed hat, and his tall and stately form. His high-born beauty is preserved to us for ever on the canvas of Vandyck, and as the Italians have named the artist 'Il Pittore Cavalieresco,' so will this subject of his skill remain for ever the ideal of Il Cavaliere Pittoresco. And as he now rides at the head of this brilliant array, his beautiful white dog bounds onward joyously beside him, that quadruped renowned in the pamphlets of the time, whose snowy skin has been stained by many a blood-drop in the desperate forays of his master, but who has thus far escaped so safely that the Puritans believe him a familiar spirit, and try to destroy him 'by poyson and extempore prayer, which yet hurt him no more than the plague plaster did Mr. Pym.' Failing in this, they pronounce the pretty creature to be 'a divell, not a very downright divell, but some Lapland ladye, once by nature a handsome white ladye, now by art a handsome white dogge.'—A Charge with Prince Rupert. Col. Higginson's 'Atlantic Essays.'

Chapter XII - Strife

Hebrew god of War—Samaël—The father's blessing and curse—Esau—Edom—Jacob and the Phantom—The planet Mars—Tradesman and Huntsman—'The Devil's Dream.'

Who is this that cometh from Edom,
In dyed garments from Bozrah?
This that is glorious in his apparel,
Travelling in the greatness of his strength?
I who promise deliverance, mighty to save.
Wherefore art thou red in thine apparel,
And thy garments like him that treadeth the wine-vat?
I have trodden the wine-press alone;
And of the peoples there was none with me:
And I will tread them in mine anger,
And trample them in my fury;
And their blood shall be sprinkled upon my garments,
And I will stain all my raiment.
For the day of vengeance is in my heart,
And the year of mine avenged is come.
And I looked, and there was none to help;
And I wondered that there was none to uphold;
Therefore mine own arm gained me the victory,
And mine own fury, it upheld me.
And I will tread down the peoples in mine anger,
And make them drunk in my wrath,
And will bring down their strength to the earth.[1]

This is the picture of the god of War. Upon it the comment in Emek Hammelech is: 'The colour of the godless Samaël and of all his princes and lords has the aspect of red fire; and all their emanations are red. Samaël is red, also his horse, his sword, his raiment, and the ground beneath him, are red. In the future the Holy God shall wear his raiment.'[2] Samaël is leader of the Opposition. He is the Soul of the fiery planet Mars. He is the Creator and inspirer of all Serpents. Azazel, demon of the Desert, is his First Lord. He was the terrestrial Chief around whom the fallen angels gathered, and his great power was acknowledged. All these characters the ancient Rabbins found blended in his name. Simmé (dazzling), Sóme (blinding), Semól (the left side), and Samhammaveth (deadly poison), were combined in the terrible name of Samaël. He ruled over the sinister Left. When Moses, in war with the Amalekites, raised his ten fingers, it was a special invocation to the Ten Sephiroth, Divine Emanations, because he knew the power which the Amalekites got from Samaël might turn his own left hand against Israel.[3] The scapegoat was a sacrifice to him through Azazel.

Samaël is the mythologic expression and embodiment of the history of Esau, afterward Edom. Jacob and Esau represented the sheep and the goat, divided in the past and to be sundered for ever. As Jacob by covering his flesh with goat-skins obtained his father's blessing due to Esau, the Israelites wandering through the wilderness (near Edom's forbidden domain) seemed to have faith that the offering of a goat would convince his Viceroy Azazel that they were orthodox Edomites. The redness of Samaël begins with the red pottage from which Esau was called Edom. The English version does not give the emphasis with which Esau is said to have called for the pottage—"the red! the red!" The characteristics ascribed to Esau in the legend are merely a saga built on the local names with which he was associated. 'Edom' means red, and 'Seir' means hairy. It probably meant the 'Shaggy Mountains.'[4]

It is interesting to observe the parting of the human and the theological myths in this story. Jacob is the third person of a patriarchal trinity,—Abraham the Heavenly Father, Isaac the Laugher (the Sun), and Jacob the Impostor or Supplanter. As the moon supplants the sun, takes hold of his heel, shines with his light, so does Jacob supplant his elder brother; and all the deadliness ascribed to the Moon, and other Third Persons of Trinities, was inherited by Jacob until his name was changed by euphemism. As the impartial sun shines for good and evil, the smile of Isaac, the Laugher, promised great blessings to both of his sons. The human myth therefore represents both of them gaining great power and wealth, and after a long feud they are reconciled. This feature of the legend we shall consider hereafter. Jehovah has another interest to be secured. He had declared that one should serve the other; that they should be cursed who cursed Jacob; and he said, 'Jacob have I loved, Esau have I hated.' Jahvistic theology had here something more important than two brothers to harmonise; namely a patriarch's blessing and a god's curse. It was contrary to all orthodoxy that a man whom Jehovah hated should possess the blessings of life; it was equally unorthodox that a father's blessing should not carry with it every advantage promised. It had to be recorded that Esau became powerful, lived by his sword, and had great possessions. It had also to be recorded that 'Edom revolted from under the hand of Judah and made a king unto themselves,' and that such independence continued 'unto this day' (2 Kings viii. 20, 22). There was thus no room for the exhibition of Jacob's superiority,—that is of Israel's priority over Edom,—in this world; nor yet any room to carry out Isaac's curse on all who cursed Jacob, and the saying: 'Jacob have I loved, Esau have I hated, and laid his mountains and his heritage waste for the dragons of the wilderness' (Mal. i.).

Answers to such problems as these evolve themselves slowly but inevitably. The agonised cry of the poor girl in Browning's poem—'There may be heaven, there must be hell'—marks the direction in which necessity led human speculation many ages before her. A future had to be invented for the working out of the curse on Esau, who on earth had to fulfil his father's blessing by enjoying power, wealth, and independence of his brother. In that future his greatness while living was repaid by his relegation to the desert and the rock with the he-goat for his support. Esau was believed to have been changed into a terrible hairy devil.5 But still there followed him in his phantasmal transformation a ghostly environment of his former power and greatness; the boldest and holiest could not afford to despise or set aside that 'share' which had been allotted him in the legend, and could not be wholly set aside in the invisible world.

Jacob's share began with a shrewd bargain with his imprudent brother. Jacob by his cunning in the breeding of the streaked animals (Gen. xxx.), by which he outwitted Laban, and other manœuvres, was really the cause of bringing on the race called after him that repute for extortion, affixed to them in such figures as Shylock, which they have found it so hard to live down. In becoming the great barterers of the East, their obstacle was the plunderer sallying forth from the mountain fastnesses or careering over the desert. These were the traditional descendants of Esau, who gradually included the Ishmaelites as well as the Edomites, afterwards merged in the Idumeans. But as the tribal distinctions became lost, the ancient hostility survived in the abstract form of this satan of Strife—Samaël. He came to mean the spirit that stirs up antagonism between those who should be brethren. He finally became, and among the more superstitious Jews still is, instigator of the cruel persecutions which have so long pursued their race, and the prejudices against them which survive even in countries to whose wealth, learning, and arts they have largely contributed. In Jewish countries Edom has long been a name for the power of Rome and Romanism, somewhat in the same way as the same are called 'Babylon' by some christians. Jacob, when passing into the wilderness of Edom, wrestled with the invisible power of Esau, or Samaël, and had not been able to prevail except with a lame thigh,—a part which, in every animal, Israel thereafter held sacred to the Opposing Power and abstained from eating. A rabbinical legend represents Jacob as having been bitten by a serpent while he was lingering about the boundary of Edom, and before his gift of goats and other cattle had been offered to his brother. The fiery serpents which afflicted Israel were universally attributed to Samaël, and the raising of the Brazen Serpent for the homage of the people was an instance of the uniform deference to Esau's power in his own domain which was long inculcated.

As I write, fiery Mars, near enough for the astronomer to detect its moons, is a wondrous phenomenon in the sky. Beneath it fearful famine is desolating three vast countries, war is raging between two powerful nations, and civil strife is smiting another ere it has fairly recovered from the wounds of a foreign struggle. The dismal conditions seem to have so little root in political necessity that one might almost be pardoned even now for dreaming that some subtle influence has come among men from the red planet that has approached the earth. How easy then must it have been in a similar conjunction of earthly and celestial phenomena to have imagined Samaël, the planetary Spectre, to be at work with his fatal fires! Whatever may have been the occasion, the red light of Mars at an early period fixed upon that planet the odium of all the burning, blighting, desert-producing powers of which it was thought necessary to relieve the adorable Sun. It was believed that all 'born under' that planet were quarrelsome. And it was part of the popular Jewish belief in the ultimate triumph of good over evil that under Mars the Messias was to be born.

We may regard Esau-Samaël then as the Devil of Strife. His traditional son Cain was like himself a 'murderer from the beginning;'6 but in that early period the conflict was between the nomad and the huntsman on one side, on the other the agriculturist and the cattle-breeder, who was never regarded as a noble figure among the Semitic tribes. In the course of time some Semitic tribes became agriculturists, and among them, in defiance of his archæological character, Samaël was saddled with the evils that beset them. As an ox he brought rinderpest. But his visible appearance was still more generally that of the raven, the wild ass, the hog which brought scurvy; while in shape of a dog he was so generally believed to bring deadly disease, that it would seem as if 'hydrophobia' was specially attributed to him.

In process of time benignant Peace dwelt more and more with the agriculturists, but still among the Israelites the tradesman was the 'coming man,' and to him peace was essential. The huntsman, of the Esau clan, figures in many legends, of which the following is translated from the Arabic by Lane:—There was a huntsman who from a mountain cave brought some honey in his water-skin, which he offered to an oilman; when the oilman opened the skin a drop of honey fell which a bird ate; the oilman's cat sprang on the bird and killed it; the huntsman's hound killed the cat; the oilman killed the dog; the huntsman killed the oilman; and as the two men belonged to different villages, their inhabitants rose against each other in battle, 'and there died of them a great multitude, the number of whom none knoweth but God, whose name be exalted!'[7]

Esau's character as a wild huntsman is referred to in another chapter. It is as the genius of strife and nomadic war that he more directly stands in contrast with his 'supplanter.'

From the wild elemental demons of storm and tempest of the most primitive age to this Devil of Strife, the human mind has associated evil with unrest. 'The wicked are like the troubled sea when it cannot rest.' Such is the burthen of the Japanese Oni throned in the heart of the hurricane, of the wild huntsman issuing forth at the first note of war, of Edom hating the victories of peace, living by the sword. The prophecy that the Prince of Peace should be born under the planet Mars is a strange and mystical suggestion. In a powerful poem by Thomas Aird, 'The Devil's Dream,' the last fearful doom of Satan's vision is imprisonment beneath a lake for ever still,—the Spirit of Unrest condemned for ever to the realm of absolute stillness!

There all is solemn idleness: no music here, no jars,
Where Silence guards the coast, e'er thrill her everlasting bars.
No sun here shines on wanton isles; but o'er the burning sheet
A rim of restless halo shakes, which marks the internal heat;
As, in the days of beauteous earth, we see with dazzled sight
The red and setting sun o'erflow with rings of welling light.
Oh! here in dread abeyance lurks of uncreated things
The last Lake of God's Wrath, where He His first great Enemy brings.
Deep in the bosom of the gulf the Fiend was made to stay,
Till, as it seemed, ten thousand years had o'er him rolled away;
In dreams he had extended life to bear the fiery space;
But all was passive, dull, and stern within his dwelling-place.
Oh! for a blast of tenfold ire to rouse the giant surge,
Him from that flat fixed lethargy impetuously to urge!
Let him but rise, but ride upon the tempest-crested wave
Of fire enridged tumultuously, each angry thing he'd brave!
The strokes of Wrath, thick let them fall! a speed so glorious dread
Would bear him through, the clinging pains would strip from off his head.
The vision of this Last Stern Lake, oh! how it plagued his soul,
Type of that dull eternity that on him soon must roll,
When plans and issues all must cease that earlier care beguiled,
And never era more shall stand a landmark on the wild:
Nor failure nor success is there, nor busy hope nor fame,
But passive fixed endurance, all eternal and the same.

Notes

1 Isa. lxiii. 1–6.
2 Fol. 84, col. 1.
3 Maarecheth haëlahuth, fol. 257, col. 1.
4 Gesenius, Heb. Lexic.
5 Hairiness was a pretty general characteristic of devils; hence, possibly, the epithet 'Old Harry,' i.e., hairy, applied to the Devil. In 'Old Deccan Days,' p. 50, a Rakshasa is described as hairy:—'Her hair hangs around her in a thick black tangle.' But the beard has rarely been accorded to devils.
6 Buslaef has a beautiful mediæval picture of a devil inciting Cain to hurl stones on his prostrate brother's form.
7 Forty-one Eastern Tales.

Chapter XIII - Barbaric Aristocracy

Jacob, the 'Impostor'—The Barterer—Esau, the 'Warrior'—Barbarian Dukes—Trade and War—Reconciliation of Jacob and Esau—Their Ghosts—Legend of Iblis—Pagan Warriors of Europe—Russian Hierarchy of Hell.

In the preceding chapter it was noted that there were two myths wrapped up in the story of Jacob and Esau,—the one theological, the other human. The former was there treated, the latter may be considered here. Rabbinical theology has made the Jewish race adopt as their founder that tricky patriarch whom Shylock adopted as his model; but any censure on them for that comes with little grace from christians who believe that they are still enjoying a covenant which Jacob's extortions and treacheries were the divinely-adopted means of confirming. It is high time that the Jewish people should repudiate Jacob's proceedings, and if they do not give him his first name ('Impostor') back again, at least withdraw from him the name Israel. But it is still more important for mankind to study the phases of their civilisation, and not attribute to any particular race the spirit of a legend which represents an epoch of social development throughout the world.

When Rebekah asked Jehovah why her unborn babes struggled in her womb, he answered, 'Two nations are in thy womb. One people shall be stronger than the other people; the elder shall be subject to the younger.' What peoples these were is described in the blessings of Jacob on the two representatives when they had grown up to be, the one red and hairy, a huntsman; the other a quiet man, dwelling in tents and builder of cattle-booths.

Jacob—cunning, extortionate, fraudulent in spirit even when technically fair—is not a pleasing figure in the eyes of the nineteenth century. But he does not belong to the nineteenth century. His contest was with Esau. The very names of them belong to mythology; they are not individual men; they are conflicting tendencies and interests of a primitive period. They must be thought of as Israel and Edom historically; morally, as the Barter principle and the Bandit principle.

High things begin low. Astronomy began as Astrology; and when Trade began there must have been even more trickery about it than there is now. Conceive of a world made up of nomadic tribes engaged in perpetual warfare. It is a commerce of killing. If a tribe desires the richer soil or larger possessions of another, the method is to exterminate that other. But at last there rises a tribe either too weak or too peaceful to exterminate, and it proposes to barter. It challenges its neighbours to a contest of wits. They try to get the advantage of each other in bargains; they haggle and cheat; and it is not heroic at all, but it is the beginning of commerce and peace.

But the Dukes of Edom as they are called will not enter into this compact. They have not been used to it; they are always outwitted at a bargain; just like those other red men in the West of America, whose lands are bought with beads, and their territorial birthright taken for a mess of pottage. They prefer to live by the hunt and by the sword. Then between these two peoples is an eternal feud, with an occasional truce, or, in biblical phrase, 'reconciliation.'

Surrounded by a commercial civilisation, with its prosaic virtues and its petty vices, we cannot help admiring much about the Duke of Edom, non-producer though he be. Brave, impulsive, quick to forgive as to resent; generous, as people can afford to be when they may give what they never earned; his gallant qualities cast a certain meanness over his grasping brother, the Israelite. It is a healthy sign in youth to admire such qualities. The boy who delights in Robin Hood; the youth who feels a stir of enthusiasm when he reads Schiller's Robbers; the ennuyés of the clubs and the roughs, with unfulfilled capacities for adventure in them, who admire 'the gallant Turk,' are all lingering in the nomadic age. They do not think of things but of persons. They are impressed by the barbaric dash. The splendour of warriors hides trampled and decimated peasantries; their courage can gild atrocities. Beside such captivating qualities and thrilling scenes how poor and commonplace appear thrifty rusticity, and the cautious, selfish, money-making tradesmen!

But fine and heroic as the Duke of Edom may appear in the distance, it is best to keep him at a distance. When Robin Hood reappeared on Blackheath lately, his warmest admirers were satisfied to hear he was securely lodged in gaol. The Jews had just the same sensations about the Dukes of Edom. They saw that tribe near to, and lived in daily dread of them. They were hirsute barbarians, dwelling amid mountain fastnesses, and lording it over a vast territory. The weak tribe of the plains had no sooner got together some herds and a little money, than those dashing Edomites fell upon them and carried away their savings and substance in a day. This made the bartering tribe all the more dependent on their cunning. They had to match their wits against, the world; and they have had to do the same to this day, when it is a chief element of their survival that their thrift is of importance to the business and finance of Europe. But in the myth it is shown that Trade, timorous as it is in presence of the sword, may have a magnanimity of its own. The Supplanter of Edom is haunted by the wrong he has done his elder brother, and driven him to greater animosity. He resolves to seek him, offer him gifts, and crave reconciliation. It is easy to put an unfavourable construction upon his action, but it is not necessary. The Supplanter, with droves of cattle, a large portion of his possessions, passes out towards perilous Edom, unarmed, undefended, except by his amicable intentions towards the powerful chieftain he had wronged. At the border of the hostile kingdom he learns that the chieftain is coming to meet him with four hundred men. He is now seized, with a mighty spirit of Fear. He sends on the herdsmen with the herds, and remains alone. During the watches of the night there closes upon him this phantom of Fear, with its presage of Death. The tricky tradesman has met his Conscience, and it is girt about with Terror. But he feels that his nobler self is with it, and that he will win. Finely has Charles Wesley told the story in his hymn:—

Come, O thou traveller unknown,
Whom still I hold but cannot see!
My company before is gone
And I am left alone with thee:
With thee all night I mean to stay
And wrestle till the break of day.

'Confident in self-despair,' the Supplanter conquers his Fear; with the dawn he travels onward alone to meet the man he had outraged and his armed men, and to him says, 'I have appeared before thee as though I had appeared before God, that thou mightest be favourable to me.' The proud Duke is disarmed. The brothers embrace and weep together. The chieftain declines the presents, and is only induced to accept them as proof of his forgiveness. The Tradesman learns for all time that his mere cleverness may bring a demon to his side in the night, and that he never made so good a bargain as when he has restored ill-gotten gains. The aristocrat and warrior returns to his mountain, aware now that magnanimity and courage are not impossible to quiet men living by merchandise. The hunting-ground must make way now for the cattle-breeder. The sword must yield before the balances.

Whatever may have been the tribes which in primitive times had these encounters, and taught each other this lesson, they were long since reconciled. But the ghosts of Israel and Edom, of Barter and Plunder, fought on through long tribal histories. Israel represented by the archangel Michael, and Edom by dragon Samaël, waged their war. One characteristic of the opposing power has been already considered. Samaël embodied Edom as the genius of Strife. He was the especial Accuser of Israel, their Antichrist, so to say, as Michael was their Advocate. But the name 'Edom' itself was retained as a kind of personification of the barbaric military and lordly Devil. The highwayman in epaulettes, the heroic spoiler, with his hairy hand which Israel itself had imitated many a time in its gloves, were summed up as 'Edom.'

This personification is the more important since it has characterised the more serious idea of Satan which prevails in the world. He is mainly a moral conception, and means the pride and pomp of the world, its natural wildness and ferocities, and the glory of them. The Mussulman fable relates that when Allah created man, and placed him in a garden, he called all the angels to worship this crowning work of his hands. Iblis alone refused to worship Adam. The very idea of a garden is hateful to the spirit of Nomadism.[1] Man the gardener receives no reverence from the proud leader of the Seraphim. God said unto him (Iblis), What hindered thee from worshipping Adam, since I commanded thee? He answered, I am more excellent than he: thou hast created me of (ethereal) fire, and hast created him of clay (black mud). God said, Get thee down therefore from paradise, for it is not fit that thou behave thyself proudly therein.[2]

Fig. 4.—Hierarchy of Hell (Russian, Sixteenth Century).

The earnestness and self-devotion of the northern pagans in their resistance to Christianity impressed the finest minds in the Church profoundly. Some of the Fathers even quoted the enthusiasm of those whom they regarded as devotees of the Devil, to shame the apathy of christians. The Church could show no martyr braver than Rand, down whose throat St. Olaf made a viper creep, which gnawed through his side; and Rand was an example of thousands. This gave many of the early christians of the north a very serious view of the realm of Satan, and of Satan himself as a great potentate. It was increased by their discovery that the pagan kings—Satan's subjects—had moral codes and law-courts, and energetically maintained justice. In this way there grew up a more dignified idea of Hell. The grotesque imps receded before the array of majestic devils, like Satan and Beelzebub; and these were invested with a certain grandeur and barbaric pride. They were regarded as rival monarchs who had refused to submit themselves to Jehovah, but they were deemed worthy of heroic treatment. The traces of this sentiment found in the ancient frescoes of Russia are of especial importance. Nothing can exceed the grandeur of the Hierarchy of Hell as they appear in some of these superb pictures. Satan is generally depicted with similar dignity to the king of heaven, from whom he is divided by a wall's depth, sometimes even resembling him in all but complexion and hair (which is fire on Satan). There are frequent instances, as in the accompanying figure (4), where, in careful correspondence with the attitude of Christ on the Father's knees, Satan supports the betrayer of Christ. Beside the king of Hell, seated in its Mouth, are personages of distinction, some probably representing those poets and sages of Greece and Rome, the prospect of whose damnation filled some of the first christian Fathers with such delight.

In Spain, when a Bishop is about to baptize one of the European Dukes of the Devil, he asks at the font what has become of his ancestors, naming them—all heathen. 'They are all in hell!' replies the Bishop. 'Then there will I follow them,' returns the Chief, and thereafter by no persuasion can he be induced to fare otherwise than to Hell. Gradually the Church made up its mind to ally itself with this obstinate barbaric pride and ambition. It was willing to give up anything whatever for a kingdom of this world, and to worship any number of Princes of Darkness, if they would give unto the Bishops such kingdoms, and the glory of them. They induced Esau to be baptized by promise of their aid in his oppressions, and free indulgences to all his passions; and then, by his help, they were able to lay before weaker Esaus the christian alternatives—Be baptized or burnt!

Not to have known how to conquer in bloodless victories the barbaric Esaus of the world by a virtue more pure, a heroism more patient, than theirs, and with that 'sweet reasonableness of Christ,' which is the latest epitaph on his tomb among the rich; not to have recognised the true nobility of the Dukes, and purified their pride to self-reverence, their passion to moral courage, their daring and freedom to a self-reliance at once gentle and manly; this was no doubt the necessary failure of a dogmatic and irrational system. But it is this which has made the christian Israel more of an impostor than its prototype, in every country to which it came steadily developing to a hypocritical imitator of the Esau whose birthright it stole by baptism. It speedily lost his magnanimity, but never his sword, which however it contrived to make at once meaner and more cruel by twisting it into thumbscrews and the like. For many centuries its voice has been, in a thin phonographic way, the voice of Jesus, but the hands are the hands of Esau with Samaël's claw added.

Notes

1 *The contest between the agriculturist and the (nomadic) shepherd is expressed in the legend that Cain and Abel divided the world between them, the one taking possession of the movable and the other of the immovable property. Cain said to his brother, 'The earth on which thou standest is mine, then betake thyself to the air;' but Abel replied, 'The garments which thou wearest are mine, take them off.'—Midrash.*

2 *Sale's Koran, vii. Al Araf. Iblis, the Mussulman name for the Devil, is probably a corruption of the word diabolus.*

Chapter XIV - Job and the Divider

Israel is a flourishing vine,
Which bringeth forth fruit to itself;
According to the increase of his fruit
He hath multiplied his altars;
According to the goodness of his land
He hath made goodly images.
Their heart is divided: now shall they be found guilty;
He will break down their altars, he will spoil their images.

These words of the prophet Hosea (x. 1, 2) foreshadow the devil which the devout Jahvist saw growing steadily to enormous strength through all the history of Israel. The germ of this enemy may be found in our chapter on Fate; one of its earliest developments is indicated in the account already given of the partition between Jacob and Esau, and the superstition to which that led of a ghostly Antagonist, to whom a share had been irreversibly pledged. From the principle thus adopted, there grew a host of demons whom it was believed necessary to propitiate by offering them their share. A divided universe had for its counterpart a divided loyalty in the heart of the people. The growth of a belief in the supremacy of one God was far from being a real monotheism; as a matter of fact no primitive race has been monotheistic. In 2 Kings xvii. it is stated as a belief of the Jews that some Assyrians who had been imported into their territory (Samaria) were slain by lions because they knew not 'the manner of the God of the land.' Spinoza noticed the indications given in this and other narratives that the Jews believed that gods whose worship was intolerable within their own boundaries were yet adapted to other regions (Tractatus, ii.). With this state of mind it is not wonderful that when the Jews found themselves in those alien regions they apprehended that the gods of those countries might also employ lions on such as knew not their manner, but adhered to the worship of Jehovah too exclusively.

Among the Jews grew up a more spiritual class of minds, whose feeling towards the mongrel worship around them was that of abhorrence; but these had a very difficult cause to maintain. The popular superstitions were firmly rooted in the fact that terrible evils afflicted mankind, and in the further fact that these did not spare the most pious. Nay, it had for a long time been a growing belief that the bounties and afflictions of nature, instead of following the direction promised by the patriarchs,—rewarding the pious, punishing the wicked,—were distributed in a reverse way. Dives and Lazarus seemed to have their respective lots before any future paradise was devised for their equalisation—as indeed is natural, since Dives attends to his business, while Lazarus is investing his powers in Abraham's bosom. Out of this experience there came at last the demand for a life beyond the grave, without whose redress the pious began to deem themselves of all men the most miserable. But before this heavenly future became a matter of common belief, there were theories which prepared, the way for it. It was held by the devout that the evils which afflicted the righteous were Jehovah's tests of their loyalty to him, and that in the end such trials would be repaid. And when observation, following the theory, showed that they were not so repaid, it was said the righteousness had been unreal, the devotee was punished for hidden wickedness. When continued observation had proved that this theory too was false, and that piety was not paid in external bounties, either to the good man or his family, the solution of a future settlement was arrived at.

This simple process may be traced in various races, and in its several phases.

The most impressive presentation of the experiences under which the primitive secular theory of rewards and punishments perished, and that of an adjustment beyond the grave arose, is found in the Book of Job. The solution here reached—a future reward in this life—is an impossible one for anything more than an exceptional case. But the Book of Job displays how beautiful such an instance would be, showing afflictions to be temporary and destined to be followed by compensations largely outweighing them. It was a tremendous statement of the question—If a man die, shall he live again? Jehovah answered, 'Yes' out of the whirlwind, and raised Job out of the dust. But for the millions who never rose from the dust that voice was heard announcing their resurrection from a trial that pressed them even into the grave. It is remarkable that Job's expression of faith that his Vindicator would appear on earth, should have become the one text of the Old Testament which has been adapted by christians to express faith in immortality. Job strongly disowns that faith.

There is hope for a tree,
If it be cut down, that it will sprout again,
And that its tender branches will not fail;
Though its root may have grown old in the earth,
And though its trunk be dead upon the ground,
At the scent of water it will bud,

And put forth boughs, like a young plant.
But man dieth and is gone for ever!
Yet I know that my Vindicator liveth,
And will stand up at length on the earth;
And though with my skin this body be wasted away,
Yet in my flesh shall I see God.
Yea, I shall see him my friend;
My eyes shall behold him no longer an adversary;
*For this my soul panteth within me.*1

The scenery and details of this drama are such as must have made an impression upon the mind of the ancient Jews beyond what is now possible for any existing people. In the first place, the locality was the land of Uz, which Jeremiah (Lam. iv. 21) points out as part of Edom, the territory traditionally ruled over by the great invisible Accuser of Israel, who had succeeded to the portion of Esau, adversary of their founder, Jacob. Job was within the perilous bounds. And yet here, where scape-goats were offered to deprecate Samaël, and where in ordinary sacrifices some item entered for the devil's share, Job refused to pay any honour to the Power of the Place. He offered burnt-offerings alone for himself and his sons, these being exclusively given to Jehovah.2 Even after his children and his possessions were destroyed by this great adversary, Job offered his sacrifice without even omitting the salt, which was the Oriental seal of an inviolable compact between two, and which so especially recalled and consecrated the covenant with Jehovah.3 Among his twenty thousand animals, Azazel's animal, the goat, is not even named. Job's distinction was an absolute and unprecedented singleness of loyalty to Jehovah.

This loyalty of a disciple even in the enemy's country is made the subject of a sort of boast by Jehovah when the Accuser enters. Postponing for the moment consideration of the character and office of this Satan, we may observe here that the trial which he challenges is merely a test of the sincerity of Job's allegiance to Jehovah. The Accuser claims that it is all given for value received. These possessions are taken away.

This is but the framework around the philosophical poem in which all theories of the world are personified in grand council.

First of all Job (the Troubled) asks—Why? Orthodoxy answers. (Eliphaz was the son of Esau (Samaël), and his name here means that he was the Accuser in disguise. He, 'God's strength,' stands for the Law. It affirms that God's ways are just, and consequently afflictions imply previous sin.) Eliphaz repeats the question put by the Accuser in heaven—'Was not thy fear of God thy hope?' And he brings Job to the test of prayer, in which he has so long trusted. Eliphaz rests on revelation; he has had a vision; and if his revelation be not true, he challenges Job to disprove it by calling on God to answer him, or else securing the advocacy of some one of the heavenly host. Eliphaz says trouble does not spring out of the dust.

Job's reply is to man and God—Point out the error! Grant my troubles are divine arrows, what have I done to thee, O watcher of men! Am I a sea-monster—and we imagine Job looking at his wasted limbs—that the Almighty must take precautions and send spies against me?

Then follows Bildad the Shuhite,—that is the 'contentious,' one of the descendants of Keturah (Abraham's concubine), traditionally supposed to be inimical to the legitimate Abrahamic line, and at a later period identified as the Turks. Bildad, with invective rather than argument, charges that Job's children had been slain for their sins, and otherwise makes a personal application of Eliphaz's theology.

Job declares that since God is so perfect, no man by such standard could be proved just; that if he could prove himself just, the argument would be settled by the stronger party in his own favour; and therefore, liberated from all temptation to justify himself, he affirms that the innocent and the guilty are dealt with much in the same way. If it is a trial of strength between God and himself, he yields. If it is a matter of reasoning, let the terrors be withdrawn, and he will then be able to answer calmly. For the present, even if he were righteous, he dare not lift up his head to so assert, while the rod is upon him.

Zophar 'the impudent' speaks. Here too, probably, is a disguise: he is (says the LXX.) King of the Minæans, that is the Nomades, and his designation 'the Naamathite,' of unknown significance, bears a suspicious resemblance to Naamah, a mythologic wife of Samaël and mother of several devils. Zophar is cynical. He laughs at Job for even suggesting the notion of an argument between himself and God, whose wisdom and ways are unsearchable. He (God) sees man's iniquity even when it looks as if he did not. He is deeper than hell. What can a man do but pray and acknowledge his sinfulness?

But Job, even in his extremity, is healthy-hearted enough to laugh too. He tells his three 'comforters' that no doubt Wisdom will die with them. Nevertheless, he has heard similar remarks before, and he is not prepared to renounce his conscience and common-sense on such grounds. And now, indeed, Job rises to a higher strain. He has made up his mind that after what has come upon him, he cares not if more be added, and challenges the universe to name his offence. So long as his transgression is 'sealed up in a bag,' he has a right to consider it an invention.4

Temanite Orthodoxy is shocked at all this. Eliphaz declares that Job's assertion that innocent and guilty suffer alike makes the fear of God a vain thing, and discourages prayer. 'With us are the aged and hoary-headed.' (Job is a neologist.) Eliphaz paints human nature in Calvinistic colours.

Behold, (God) putteth no trust in his ministering spirits,
And the heavens are not pure in his sight;
Much less abominable and polluted man,
Who drinketh iniquity as water!

The wise have related, and they got it from the fathers to whom the land was given, and among whom no stranger was allowed to bring his strange doctrines, that affliction is the sign and punishment of wickedness.
Job merely says he has heard enough of this, and finds no wise man among them. He acknowledges that such reproaches add to his sorrows. He would rather contend with God than with them, if he could. But he sees a slight indication of divine favour in the remarkable unwisdom of his revilers, and their failure to prove their point.
Bildad draws a picture of what he considers would be the proper environment of a wicked man, and it closely resembles the situation of Job.
But Job reminds him that he, Bildad, is not God. It is God that has brought him so low, but God has been satisfied with his flesh. He has not yet uttered any complaint as to his conduct; and so he, Job, believes that his vindicator will yet appear to confront his accusers—the men who are so glib when his afflictor is silent.5
Zophar harps on the old string. Pretty much as some preachers go on endlessly with their pictures of the terrors which haunted the deathbeds of Voltaire and Paine, all the more because none are present to relate the facts. Zophar recounts how men who seemed good, but were not, were overtaken by asps and vipers and fires from heaven.
But Job, on the other hand, has a curious catalogue of examples in which the notoriously wicked have lived in wealth and gaiety. And if it be said God pays such off in their children, Job denies the justice of that. It is the offender, and not his child, who ought to feel it. The prosperous and the bitter in soul alike lie down in the dust at last, the good and the evil; and Job is quite content to admit that he does not understand it. One thing he does understand: 'Your explanations are false.'
But Eliphaz insists on Job having a dogma. If the orthodox dogma is not true, put something in its place! Why are you afflicted? What is, your theory? Is it because God was afraid of your greatness? It must be as we say, and you have been defrauding and injuring people in secret.
Job, having repeated his ardent desire to meet God face to face as to his innocence, says he can only conclude that what befalls him and others is what is 'appointed' for them. His terror indeed arises from that: the good and the evil seem to be distributed without reference to human conduct. How darkness conspires with the assassin! If God were only a man, things might be different; but as it is, 'what he desireth that he doeth,' and 'who can turn him?'
Bildad falls back on his dogma of depravity. Man is a 'worm,' a 'reptile.' Job finds that for a worm Bildad is very familiar with the divine secrets. If man is morally so weak he should be lowly in mind also. God by his spirit hath garnished the heavens; his hand formed the 'crooked serpent'—

Lo! these are but the borders of his works;
How faint the whisper we have heard of him!
But the thunder of his power who can understand?

Job takes up the position of the agnostic, and the three 'Comforters' are silenced. The argument has ended where it had to end. Job then proceeds with sublime eloquence. A man may lose all outward things, but no man or god can make him utter a lie, or take from him his integrity, or his consciousness of it. Friends may reproach him, but he can see that his own heart does not. That one superiority to the wicked he can preserve. In reviewing his arguments Job is careful to say that he does not maintain that good and evil men are on an equality. For one thing, when the wicked man is in trouble he cannot find resource in his innocence. 'Can he delight himself in the Almighty?' When such die, their widows do not bewail them. Men do not befriend oppressors when they come to want. Men hiss them. And with guilt in their heart they feel their sorrows to be the arrows of God, sent in anger. In all the realms of nature, therefore, amid its powers, splendours, and precious things, man cannot find the wisdom which raises him above misfortune, but only in his inward loyalty to the highest, and freedom from moral evil.
Then enters a fifth character, Elihu, whose plan is to mediate between the old dogma and the new agnostic philosophy. He is Orthodoxy rationalised. Elihu's name is suggestive of his ambiguity; it seems to mean one whose 'God is He' and he comes from the tribe of Buz, whose Hebrew meaning might almost be represented in that English word which, with an added z, would best convey the windiness of his remarks. Buz was the son of Milkah, the Moon, and his descendant so came fairly by his theologic 'moonshine' of the kind which Carlyle has so well described in his account of Coleridgean casuistry. Elihu means to be fair to both sides! Elihu sees some truth in both sides! Eclectic Elihu! Job is perfectly right in

thinking he had not done anything to merit his sufferings, but he did not know what snares were around him, and how he might have done something wicked but for his affliction. Moreover, God ruins people now and then just to show how he can lift them up again. Job ought to have taken this for granted, and then to have expressed it in the old abject phraseology, saying, 'I have received chastisement; I will offend no more! What I see not, teach thou me!' (A truly Elihuic or 'contemptible' answer to Job's sensible words, 'Why is light given to a man whose way is hid?' Why administer the rod which enlightens as to the anger but not its cause, or as to the way of amend?) In fact the casuistic Elihu casts no light whatever on the situation. He simply overwhelms him with metaphors and generalities about the divine justice and mercy, meant to hide this new and dangerous solution which Job had discovered—namely, that the old dogmatic theories of evil were proved false by experience, and that a good man amid sorrow should admit his ignorance, but never allow terror to wring from him the voice of guilt, nor the attempt to propitiate divine wrath.

When Jehovah appears on the scene, answering Job out of the whirlwind, the tone is one of wrath, but the whole utterance is merely an amplification of what Job had said—what we see and suffer are but fringes of a Whole we cannot understand. The magnificence and wonder of the universe celebrated in that voice of the whirlwind had to be given the lame and impotent conclusion of Job 'abhorring himself,' and 'repenting in dust and ashes.' The conventional Cerberus must have his sop. But none the less does the great heart of this poem reveal the soul that was not shaken or divided in prosperity or adversity. The burnt-offering of his prosperous days, symbol of a worship which refused to include the supposed powers of mischief, was enjoined on Job's Comforters. They must bend to him as nearer God than they. And in his high philosophy Job found what is symbolised in the three daughters born to him: Jemima (the Dove, the voice of the returning Spring); Kezia (Cassia, the sweet incense); Kerenhappuch (the horn of beautiful colour, or decoration).

From the Jewish point of view this triumph of Job represented a tremendous heresy. The idea that afflictions could befall a man without any reference to his conduct, and consequently not to be influenced by the normal rites and sacrifices, is one fatal to a priesthood. If evil may be referred in one case to what is going on far away among gods in obscurities of the universe, and to some purpose beyond the ken of all sages, it may so be referred in all cases, and though burnt-offerings may be resorted to formally, they must cease when their powerlessness is proved. Hence the Rabbins have taken the side of Job's Comforters. They invented a legend that Job had been a great magician in Egypt, and was one of those whose sorceries so long prevented the escape of Israel. He was converted afterwards, but it is hinted that his early wickedness required the retribution he suffered. His name was to them the troubler troubled.

Heretical also was the theory that man could get along without any Angelolatry or Demon-worship. Job in his singleness of service, fearing God alone, defying the Seraphim and Cherubim from Samaël down to do their worst, was a perilous figure. The priests got no part of any burnt-offering. The sin-offering was of almost sumptuary importance. Hence the rabbinical theory, already noticed, that it was through neglect of these expiations to the God of Sin that the morally spotless Job came under the power of his plagues.

But for precisely the same reasons the story of Job became representative to the more spiritual class of minds of a genuine as contrasted with a nominal monotheism, and the piety of the pure, the undivided heart. Its meaning is so human that it is not necessary to discuss the question of its connection with the story of Hariśchandra, or whether its accent was caught from or by the legends of Zoroaster and of Buddha, who passed unscathed through the ordeals of Ahriman and Mara. It was repeated in the encounters of the infant Christ with Herod, and of the adult Christ with Satan. It was repeated in the unswerving loyalty of the patient Griselda to her husband. It is indeed the heroic theme of many races and ages, and it everywhere points to a period when the virtues of endurance and patience rose up to match the agonies which fear and weakness had tried to propitiate,—when man first learned to suffer and be strong.

Notes

1 Noyes' Translation.

2 Eisenmenger, Entd. Jud. i. 836.

3 Job. i. 22, the literal rendering of which is, 'In all this Job sinned not, nor gave God unsalted.' This translation I first heard from Dr. A. P. Peabody, sometime President of Harvard University, from whom I have a note in which he says:—'The word which I have rendered gave is appropriate to a sacrifice. The word I have rendered unsalted means so literally; and is in Job vi. 6 rendered unsavory. It may, and sometimes does, denote folly, by a not unnatural metaphor; but in that sense the word gave—an offertory word—is out of place.' Waltonus (Bib. Polyg.) translates 'nec dedit insulsum Deo;' had he rendered תִּפְלָה by insalsum it would have been exact. The horror with which demons and devils are supposed to regard salt is noticed, i. 288.

4 Gesenius so understands verse 17 of chap. xiv.

5 The much misunderstood and mistranslated passage, xix. 25–27 (already quoted), is certainly referable to the wide-spread belief that as against each man there was an Accusing Spirit, so for each there was a Vindicating Spirit. These two stood respectively on the right and left of the balances in which the good and evil actions of each soul were weighed against each other, each trying to make his side as heavy as possible. But as the accusations against him are made by living men, and on earth, Job is not prepared to consider a celestial acquittal beyond the grave as adequate.

Chapter XV - Satan

There is nothing about the Satan of the Book of Job to indicate him as a diabolical character. He appears as a respectable and powerful personage among the sons of God who present themselves before Jehovah, and his office is that of a public prosecutor. He goes to and fro in the earth attending to his duties. He has received certificates of character from A. Schultens, Herder, Eichorn, Dathe, Ilgen, who proposed a new word for Satan in the prologue of Job, which would make him a faithful but too suspicious servant of God.

Such indeed he was deemed originally; but it is easy to see how the degradation of such a figure must have begun. There is often a clamour in England for the creation of Public Prosecutors; yet no doubt there is good ground for the hesitation which its judicial heads feel in advising such a step. The experience of countries in which Prosecuting Attorneys exist is not such as to prove the institution one of unmixed advantage. It is not in human nature for an official person not to make the most of the duty intrusted to him, and the tendency is to raise the interest he specially represents above that of justice itself. A defeated prosecutor feels a certain stigma upon his reputation as much as a defeated advocate, and it is doubtful whether it be safe that the fame of any man should be in the least identified with personal success where justice is trying to strike a true balance. The recent performances of certain attorneys in England and America retained by Societies for the Suppression of Vice strikingly illustrate the dangers here alluded to. The necessity that such salaried social detectives should perpetually parade before the community as purifiers of society induces them to get up unreal cases where real ones cannot be easily discovered. Thus they become Accusers, and from this it is an easy step to become Slanderers; nor is it a very difficult one which may make them instigators of the vices they profess to suppress.

The first representations of Satan show him holding in his hand the scales; but the latter show him trying slyly with hand or foot to press down that side of the balance in which the evil deeds of a soul are being weighed against the good. We need not try to track archæologically this declension of a Prosecutor, by increasing ardour in his office, through the stages of Accuser, Adversary, Executioner, and at last Rival of the legitimate Rule, and tempter of its subjects. The process is simple and familiar. I have before me a little twopenny book,1 which is said to have a vast circulation, where one may trace the whole mental evolution of Satan. The ancient Devil-worshipper who has reappeared with such power in England tells us that he was the reputed son of a farmer, who had to support a wife and eleven children on from 7s. to 9s. per week, and who sent him for a short time to school. 'My schoolmistress reproved me for something wrong, telling me that God Almighty took notice of children's sins. This stuck to my conscience a great while; and who this God Almighty could be I could not conjecture; and how he could know my sins without asking my mother I could not conceive. At that time there was a person named Godfrey, an exciseman, in the town, a man of a stern and hard-favoured countenance, whom I took notice of for having a stick covered with figures, and an ink-bottle hanging at the button-hole of his coat. I imagined that man to be employed by God Almighty to take notice and keep an account of children's sins; and once I got into the market-house and watched him very narrowly, and found that he was always in a hurry, by his walking so fast; and I thought he had need to hurry, as he must have a deal to do to find out all the sins of children!' This terror caused the little Huntington to say his prayers. 'Punishment for sin I found was to be inflicted after death, therefore I hated the churchyard, and would travel any distance round rather than drag my guilty conscience over that enchanted spot.'

The child is father to the man. When Huntington, S.S., grew up, it was to record for the thousands who listened to him as a prophet his many encounters with the devil. The Satan he believes in is an exact counterpart of the stern, hard-favoured exciseman whom he had regarded as God's employé. On one occasion he writes, 'Satan began to tempt me violently that there was no God, but I reasoned against the belief of that from my own experience of his dreadful wrath, saying, How can I credit this suggestion, when (God's) wrath is already revealed in my heart, and every curse in his book levelled at my head.' (That seems his only evidence of God's existence—his wrath!) 'The Devil answered that the Bible was false, and only wrote by cunning men to puzzle and deceive people. 'There is no God,' said the adversary, 'nor is the Bible true.' ... I asked, 'Who, then, made the world?' He replied, 'I did, and I made men too.' Satan, perceiving my rationality almost gone, followed me up with another temptation; that as there was no God I must come back to his work again, else when he had brought me to hell he would punish me more than all the rest. I cried out, 'Oh, what will become of me! what will become of me!' He answered that there was no escape but by praying to him; and that he would show me some lenity when he took me to hell. I went and sat in my tool-house halting between two opinions; whether I should petition Satan, or whether I should keep praying to God, until I could ascertain the consequences. While I was thinking of bending my knees to such a cursed being as Satan, an uncommon fear of God sprung up in my heart to keep me from it.'

In other words, Mr. Huntington wavered between the petitions 'Good Lord! Good Devil!' The question whether it were more moral, more holy, to worship the one than the other did not occur to him. He only considers which is the strongest—which could do him the most mischief—which, therefore, to fear the most; and when Satan has almost convinced him in his own favour, he changes round to God. Why? Not because of any superior goodness on God's part. He says, 'An uncommon fear of God sprung up in my heart.' The greater terror won the day; that is to say, of two demons he yielded to the stronger. Such an experience, though that of one living in our own time, represents a phase in the development of the relation between God and Satan which would have appeared primitive to an Assyrian two thousand years ago. The ethical antagonism of the two was then much more clearly felt. But this bit of contemporary superstition may bring before us the period when Satan, from having been a Nemesis or Retributive Agent of the divine law, had become a mere personal rival of his superior.

Satan, among the Jews, was at first a generic term for an adversary lying in wait. It is probably the furtive suggestion at the root of this Hebrew word which aided in its selection as the name for the invisible adverse powers when they were especially distinguished. But originally no special personage, much less any antagonist of Jehovah, was signified by the word. Thus we read: 'And God's anger was kindled because he (Balaam) went; and the angel of the Lord stood in the way for a Satan against him.... And the ass saw the angel of the Lord standing in the way and his sword drawn in his hand.'2 The eyes of Balaam are presently opened, and the angel says, 'I went out to be a Satan to thee because the way is perverse before me.' The Philistines fear to take David with them to battle lest he should prove a Satan to them, that is, an underhand enemy or traitor.3 David called those who wished to put Shimei to death Satans;4 but in this case the epithet would have been more applicable to himself for affecting to protect the honest man for whose murder he treacherously provided.5

That it was popularly used for adversary as distinct from evil appears in Solomon's words, 'There is neither Satan nor evil occurrent.'6 Yet it is in connection with Solomon that we may note the entrance of some of the materials for the mythology which afterwards invested the name of Satan. It is said that, in anger at his idolatries, 'the Lord stirred up a Satan unto Solomon, Hadad the Edomite: he was of the king's seed in Edom.'7 Hadad, 'the Sharp,' bore a name next to that of Esau himself for the redness of his wrath, and, as we have seen in a former chapter, Edom was to the Jews the land of 'bogeys.' 'Another Satan,' whom the Lord 'stirred up,' was the Devastator, Prince Rezon, founder of the kingdom of Damascus, of whom it is said, 'he was a Satan to Israel all the days of Solomon.'8 The human characteristics of supposed 'Scourges of God' easily pass away. The name that becomes traditionally associated with calamities whose agents were 'stirred up' by the Almighty is not allowed the glory of its desolations. The word 'Satan,' twice used in this chapter concerning Solomon's fall, probably gained here a long step towards distinct personification as an eminent national enemy, though there is no intimation of a power daring to oppose the will of Jehovah. Nor, indeed, is there any such intimation anywhere in the 'canonical' books of the Old Testament. The writer of Psalm cix., imprecating for his adversaries, says: 'Set thou a wicked man over him; and let Satan stand at his right hand. When he shall be judged, let him be condemned; and let his prayer become sin.' In this there is an indication of a special Satan, but he is supposed to be an agent of Jehovah. In the catalogue of the curses invoked of the Lord, we find the evils which were afterwards supposed to proceed only from Satan. The only instance in the Old Testament in which there is even a faint suggestion of hostility towards Satan on the part of Jehovah is in Zechariah. Here we find the following remarkable words: 'And he showed me Joshua the high priest standing before the angel of Jehovah, and the Satan standing at his right hand to oppose him. And Jehovah said unto Satan, Jehovah rebuke thee, O Satan; even Jehovah, that hath chosen Jerusalem, rebuke thee: is not this a brand plucked out of the fire? Now Joshua was clothed with filthy garments, and stood before the angel. And he answered and spake to those that stood before him, saying, Take away the filthy garments from him. And to him he said, Lo, I have caused thine iniquity to pass from thee, and I will clothe thee with goodly raiment.'9

Here we have a very fair study and sketch of that judicial trial of the soul for which mainly the dogma of a resurrection after death was invented. The doctrine of future rewards and punishments is not one which a priesthood would invent or care for, so long as they possessed unrestricted power to administer such in this life. It is when an alien power steps in to supersede the priesthood—the Gallio too indifferent whether ceremonial laws are carried out to permit the full application of terrestrial cruelties—that the priest requires a tribunal beyond the grave to execute his sentence. In this picture of Zechariah we have this invisible Celestial Court. The Angel of Judgment is in his seat. The Angel of Accusation is present to prosecute. A poor filthy wretch appears for trial. What advocate can he command? Where is Michael, the special advocate of Israel? He does not recognise one of his clients in this poor Joshua in his rags. But lo! suddenly Jehovah himself appears; reproves his own commissioned Accuser; declares Joshua a brand plucked from the burning (Tophet); orders a change of raiment, and, condoning his offences, takes him into his own service. But in all this there is nothing to show general antagonism between Jehovah and Satan, but the reverse.

When we look into the Book of Job we find a Satan sufficiently different from any and all of those mentioned under that name in other parts of the Old Testament to justify the belief that he has been mainly adapted from the traditions of other regions. The plagues and afflictions which in Psalm cix. are invoked from Jehovah, even while Satan is mentioned as near, are in the Book of Job ascribed to Satan himself. Jehovah only permits Satan to inflict them with a proviso against total destruction. Satan is here named as a personality in a way not known elsewhere in the Old Testament, unless it be in 1 Chron. xxi. 1, where Satan (the article being in this single case absent) is said to have 'stood up against Israel, and provoked David to number Israel.' But in this case the uniformity of the passage with the others (excepting those in Job) is preserved by the same incident being recorded in 2 Sam. xxiv. 1, 'The anger of Jehovah was kindled against Israel, and he (Jehovah) moved David against them to say, Go number Israel and Judah.'

It is clear that, in the Old Testament, it is in the Book of Job alone that we find Satan as the powerful prince of an empire which is distinct from that of Jehovah,—an empire of tempest, plague, and fire,—though he presents himself before Jehovah, and awaits permission to exert his power on a loyal subject of Jehovah. The formality of a trial, so dear to the Semitic heart, is omitted in this case. And these circumstances confirm the many other facts which prove this drama to be largely of non-Semitic origin. It is tolerably clear that the drama of Hariśchandra in India and that of Job were both developed from the Sanskrit legends mentioned in our chapter on Viswámitra; and it is certain that Aryan and Semitic elements are both represented in the figure of Satan as he has passed into the theology of Christendom.

Nor indeed has Satan since his importation into Jewish literature in this new aspect, much as the Rabbins have made of him, ever been assigned the same character among that people that has been assigned him in Christendom. He has never replaced Samaël as their Archfiend. Rabbins have, indeed, in later times associated him with the Serpent which seduced Eve in Eden; but the absence of any important reference to that story in the New Testament is significant of the slight place it had in the Jewish mind long after the belief in Satan had become popular. In fact, that essentially Aryan myth little accorded with the ideas of strife and immorality which the Jews had gradually associated with Samaël. In the narrative, as it stands in Genesis, it is by no means the Serpent that makes the worst appearance. It is Jehovah, whose word—that death shall follow on the day the apple is eaten—is falsified by the result; and while the Serpent is seen telling the truth, and guiding man to knowledge, Jehovah is represented as animated by jealousy or even fear of man's attainments. All of which is natural enough in an extremely primitive myth of a combat between rival gods, but by no means possesses the moral accent of the time and conditions amid which Jahvism certainly originated. It is in the same unmoral plane as the contest of the Devas and Asuras for the Amrita, in Hindu mythology, a contest of physical force and wits.

Fig. 5.—Gnostic Figure (Ste. Genevieve Collection).

The real development of Satan among the Jews was from an accusing to an opposing spirit, then to an agent of punishment—a hated executioner. The fact that the figure here given (Fig. 5) was identified by one so familiar with Semitic demonology as Calmet as a representation of him, is extremely interesting. It was found among representations of Cherubim, and on the back of one somewhat like it is a formula of invocation against demons. The countenance is of that severe beauty which the Greeks ascribed to Nemesis. Nemesis has at her feet the wheel and rudder, symbols of her power to overtake the evil-doer by land or sea; the feet of this figure are winged for pursuit. He has four hands. In one he bears the lamp which, like Lucifer, brings light on the deed of darkness. As to others, he answers Baruch's description (Ep. 13, 14) of the Babylonian god, 'He hath a sceptre in his hand like a man, like a judge of the kingdom—he hath in his hand a sword and an axe.' He bears nicely-graduated implements of punishment, from the lash that scourges to the axe that slays; and his retributive powers are supplemented by the scorpion tail. At his knees are signets; whomsoever he seals are sealed. He has the terrible eyes which were believed able to read on every forehead a catalogue of sins invisible to mortals, a power that made women careful of their veils, and gave meaning to the formula 'Get thee behind me!'10

201

Now this figure, which Calmet believed to be Satan, bears on its reverse, 'The Everlasting Sun.' He is a god made up of Egyptian and Magian forms, the head-plumes belonging to the one, the multiplied wings to the other. Matter (Hist. Crit. de Gnost.) reproduces it, and says that 'it differs so much from all else of the kind as to prove it the work of an impostor.' But Professor C. W. King has a (probably fifth century) gem in his collection evidently a rude copy of this (reproduced in his 'Gnostics,' Pl. xi. 3), on the back of which is 'Light of Lights;' and, in a note which I have from him, he says that it sufficiently proves Matter wrong, and that this form was primitive. In one gem of Professor King's (Pl. v. 1) the lamp is also carried, and means the 'Light of Lights.' The inscription beneath, within a coiled serpent, is in corrupt cuneiform characters, long preserved by the Magi, though without understanding them. There is little doubt, therefore, that the instinct of Calmet was right, and that we have here an early form of the detective and retributive Magian deity ultimately degraded to an accusing spirit, or Satan.

Although the Jews did not identify Satan with their Scapegoat, yet he has been veritably the Scapegoat among devils for two thousand years. All the nightmares and phantasms that ever haunted the human imagination have been packed upon him unto this day, when it is almost as common to hear his name in India and China as in Europe and America. In thus passing round the world, he has caught the varying features of many fossilised demons: he has been horned, hoofed, reptilian, quadrupedal, anthropoid, anthropomorphic, beautiful, ugly, male, female; the whites painted him black, and the blacks, with more reason, painted him white. Thus has Satan been made a miracle of incongruities. Yet through all these protean shapes there has persisted the original characteristic mentioned. He is prosecutor and executioner under the divine government, though his office has been debased by that mental confusion which, in the East, abhors the burner of corpses, and, in the West, regards the public hangman with contempt; the abhorrence, in the case of Satan, being intensified by the supposition of an overfondness for his work, carried to the extent of instigating the offences which will bring him victims.

In a well-known English Roman Catholic book[11] of recent times, there is this account of St. Francis' visit to hell in company with the Angel Gabriel:—'St. Francis saw that, on the other side of (a certain) soul, there was another devil to mock at and reproach it. He said, Remember where you are, and where you will be for ever; how short the sin was, how long the punishment. It is your own fault; when you committed that mortal sin you knew how you would be punished. What a good bargain you made to take the pains of eternity in exchange for the sin of a day, an hour, a moment. You cry now for your sin, but your crying comes too late. You liked bad company; you will find bad company enough here. Your father was a drunkard, look at him there drinking red-hot fire. You were too idle to go to mass on Sundays; be as idle as you like now, for there is no mass to go to. You disobeyed your father, but you dare not disobey him who is your father in hell.'

This devil speaks as one carrying out the divine decrees. He preaches. He utters from his chasuble of flame the sermons of Father Furniss. And, no doubt, wherever belief in Satan is theological, this is pretty much the form which he assumes before the mind (or what such believers would call their mind, albeit really the mind of some Syrian dead these two thousand years). But the Satan popularly personalised was man's effort to imagine an enthusiasm of inhumanity. He is the necessary appendage to a personalised Omnipotence, whose thoughts are not as man's thoughts, but claim to coerce these. His degradation reflects the heartlessness and the ingenuity of torture which must always represent personal government with its catalogue of fictitious crimes. Offences against mere Majesty, against iniquities framed in law, must be doubly punished, the thing to be secured being doubly weak. Under any theocratic government law and punishment would become the types of diabolism. Satan thus has a twofold significance. He reports what powerful priesthoods found to be the obstacles to their authority; and he reports the character of the priestly despotisms which aimed to obstruct human development.

Notes

1 *'The Kingdom of Heaven Taken by Prayer.' By William Huntington, S.S. This title is explained to be 'Sinner Saved,' otherwise one might understand the letters to signify a Surviving Syrian.*
2 *Num. xxii. 22.*
3 *1 Sam. xxix. 4.*
4 *2 Sam. xix. 22.*
5 *1 Kings ii. 9.*
6 *1 Kings v. 4.*
7 *1 Kings xi. 14.*
8 *1 Kings xi. 25.*
9 *Zech. iii.*
10 *Cf. Rev. vii. 3.*
11 *'The Sight of Hell,' prepared, as one of a 'Series of Books for Children and Young Persons,' by the Rev. Father Furniss, C.S.S.R., by authority of his Superiors.*

Chapter XVI - Religious Despotism

Pharaoh and Herod—Zoroaster's mother—Ahriman's emissaries—Kansa and Krishna—Emissaries of Kansa—Astyages and Cyrus—Zohák—Bel and the Christian.

The Jews had already, when Christ appeared, formed the theory that the hardening of Pharaoh's heart, and his resistance to the departure of Israel from Egypt, were due to diabolical sorcery. The belief afterwards matured; that Edom (Esau or Samaël) was the instigator of Roman aggression was steadily forming. The mental conditions were therefore favourable to the growth of a belief in the Jewish followers of Christ that the hostility to the religious movement of their time was another effort on the part of Samaël to crush the kingdom of God. Herod was not, indeed, called Satan or Samaël, nor was Pharaoh; but the splendour and grandeur of this Idumean (the realm of Esau), notwithstanding his oppressions and crimes, had made him a fair representative to the people of the supernatural power they dreaded. Under these circumstances it was a powerful appeal to the sympathies of the Jewish people to invent in connection with Herod a myth exactly similar to that associated with Pharaoh,—namely, a conspiracy with sorcerers, and consequent massacre of all new-born children.

The myths which tell of divine babes supernaturally saved from royal hostility are veritable myths, even where they occur so late in time that historic names and places are given; for, of course, it is impossible that by any natural means either Pharaoh or Herod should be aware of the peculiar nature of any particular infant born in their dominions. Such traditions, when thus presented in historical guise, can only be explained by reference to corresponding fables written out in simpler mythic form; while it is especially necessary to remember that such corresponding narratives may be of independent ethnical origin, and that the later in time may be more primitive spiritually.

In the Legend of Zoroaster1 his mother Dogdo, previous to his birth, has a dream in which she sees a black cloud, which, like the wing of some vast bird, hides the sun, and brings on frightful darkness. This cloud rains down on her house terrible beasts with sharp teeth,—tigers, lions, wolves, rhinoceroses, serpents. One monster especially attacks her with great fury, and her unborn babe speaks in reassuring terms. A great light rises and the beasts fall. A beautiful youth appears, hurls a book at the Devas (Devils), and they fly, with exception of three,—a wolf, a lion, and a tiger. These, however, the youth drives away with a luminous horn. He then replaces the holy infant in the womb, and says to the mother: 'Fear nothing! The King of Heaven protects this infant. The earth waits for him. He is the prophet whom Ormuzd sends to his people: his law will fill the world with joy: he will make the lion and the lamb drink in the same place. Fear not these ferocious beasts; why should he whom Ormuzd preserves fear the enmity of the whole world?' With these words the youth vanished, and Dogdo awoke. Repairing to an interpreter, she was told that the Horn meant the grandeur of Ormuzd; the Book was the Avesta; the three Beasts betokened three powerful enemies.

Zoroaster was born laughing. This prodigy being noised abroad, the Magicians became alarmed, and sought to slay the child. One of them raised a sword to strike him, but his arm fell to the ground. The Magicians bore the child to the desert, kindled a fire and threw him into it, but his mother afterwards found him sleeping tranquilly and unharmed in the flames. Next he was thrown in front of a drove of cows and bulls, but the fiercest of the bulls stood carefully over the child and protected him. The Magicians killed all the young of a pack of wolves, and then cast the infant Zoroaster to them that they might vent their rage upon him, but the mouths of the wolves were shut. They abandoned the child on a lonely mountain, but two ewes came and suckled him.

Zoroaster's father respected the ministers of the Devas (Magi), but his child rebuked him. Zoroaster walked on the water (crossing a great river where was no bridge) on his way to Mount Iran where he was to receive the Law. It was then he had the vision of the battle between the two serpent armies,—the white and black adders, the former, from the South, conquering the latter, which had come from the North to destroy him.

The Legend of the Infant Krishna is as follows:—The tyrant Kansa, having given his sister Devaki in marriage to Vasudéva, as he was returning from the wedding heard a voice declare, 'The eighth son of Devaki is destined to be thy destroyer.' Alarmed at this, Kansa cast his sister and her husband into a prison with seven iron doors, and whenever a son was born he caused it to be instantly destroyed. When Devaki became pregnant the eighth time, Brahma and Siva, with attending Devas, appeared and sang: 'O favoured among women! in thy delivery all nature shall have cause to exult! How ardently we long to behold that face for the sake of which we have coursed round three worlds!' When Krishna was born a chorus of celestial spirits saluted him; the room was illumined with supernatural light. While Devaki was weeping at the fatal decree of Kansa that her son should be destroyed, a voice was heard by Vasudéva saying: 'Son of Yadu, carry this child to Gokul, on the other side of the river Jumna, to Nauda, whose wife has just given birth to a daughter. Leave him and bring the girl hither.' At this the seven doors swung open, deep sleep fell on the guards, and Vasudéva went forth with the holy infant in his arms. The river Jumna was swollen, but the waters, having kissed the feet of Krishna, retired on either side, opening a pathway. The great serpent of Vishnu held its hood over this new incarnation of its Lord. Beside sleeping Nauda and his wife the daughter was replaced by the son, who was named Krishna, the Dark.

When all this had happened a voice came to Kansa saying: 'The boy destined to destroy thee is born, and is now living.' Whereupon Kansa ordered all the male children in his kingdom to be destroyed. This being ineffectual, the whereabouts of Krishna were discovered; but the messenger who was sent to destroy the child beheld its image in the water and adored it. The Rakshasas worked in the interest of Kansa. One approached the divine child in shape of a monstrous bull whose head he wrung off; and he so burned in the stomach of a crocodile which had swallowed him that the monster cast him from his mouth unharmed.

Finally, as a youth, Krishna, after living some time as a herdsman, attacked the tyrant Kansa, tore the crown from his head, and dragged him by his hair a long way; with the curious result that Kansa became liberated from the three worlds, such virtue had long thinking about the incarnate one, even in enmity!

The divine beings represented in these legends find their complement in the fabulous history of Cyrus; and the hostile powers which sought their destruction are represented in demonology by the Persian tyrant-devil Zohák. The name of Astyages, the grandfather of Cyrus, has been satisfactorily traced to Ashdahák, and Ajis Daháka, the 'biting snake.' The word thus connects him with Vedic Ahi and with Iranian Zohák, the tyrant out of whose shoulders a magician evoked two serpents which adhered to him and became at once his familiars and the arms of his cruelty. As Astyages, the last king of Media, he had a dream that the offspring of his daughter Mandane would reign over Asia. He gave her in marriage to Cambyses, and when she bore a child (Cyrus), committed it to his minister Harpagus to be slain. Harpagus, however, moved with pity, gave it to a herdsman of Astyages, who substituted for it a still-born child, and having so satisfied the tyrant of its death, reared Cyrus as his own son.

The luminous Horn of the Zoroastrian legend and the diabolism of Zohák are both recalled in the Book of Daniel (viii.) in the terrific struggle of the ram and the he-goat. The he-goat, ancient symbol of hairy Esau, long idealised into the Invisible Foe of Israel, had become associated also with Babylon and with Nimrod its founder, the Semitic Zohák. But Bel, conqueror of the Dragon, was the founder of Babylon, and to Jewish eyes the Dragon was his familiar; to the Jews he represented the tyranny and idolatry of Nimrod, the two serpents of Zohák. When Cyrus supplanted Astyages, this was the idol he found the Babylonians worshipping until Daniel destroyed it. And so, it would appear, came about the fact that to the Jews the power of Christendom came to be represented as the Reign of Bel. One can hardly wonder at that. If ever there were cruelty and oppression passing beyond the limit of mere human capacities, it has been recorded in the tragical history of Jewish sufferings. The disbeliever in præternatural powers of evil can no less than others recognise in this 'Bel and the Christian,' which the Jews substituted for 'Bel and the Dragon,' the real archfiend—Superstition, turning human hearts to stone when to stony gods they sacrifice their own humanity and the welfare of mankind.

Note

1 *M. Anquetil Du Perron's 'Zendavesta et Vie de Zoroastre.'*

Chapter XVII - The Prince of this World

Temptations—Birth of Buddha—Mara—Temptation of power—Asceticism and Luxury—Mara's menaces—Appearance of the Buddha's Vindicator—Ahriman tempts Zoroaster—Satan and Christ—Criticism of Strauss—Jewish traditions—Hunger—Variants.

The Devil, having shown Jesus all the kingdoms of this world, said, 'All this power will I give thee, and the glory of them: for that is delivered unto me, and to whomsoever I will I give it,' The theory thus announced is as a vast formation underlying many religions. As every religion begins as an ideal, it must find itself in antagonism to the world at large; and since the social and political world are themselves, so long as they last, the outcome of nature, it is inevitable that in primitive times the earth should be regarded as a Satanic realm, and the divine world pictured elsewhere. A legitimate result of this conclusion is asceticism, and belief in the wickedness of earthly enjoyments. To men of great intellectual powers, generally accompanied as they are with keen susceptibilities of enjoyment and strong sympathies, the renunciation of this world must be as a living burial. To men who, amid the corruptions of the world, feel within them the power to strike in with effect, or who, seeing 'with how little wisdom the world is governed,' are stirred by the sense of power, the struggle against the temptation to lead in the kingdoms of this world is necessarily severe. Thus simple is the sense of those temptations which make the almost invariable ordeal of the traditional founders of religions. As in earlier times the god won his spurs, so to say, by conquering some monstrous beast, the saint or saviour must have overcome some potent many-headed world, with gems for scales and double-tongue, coiling round the earth, and thence, like Lilith's golden hair, round the heart of all surrendered to its seductions.

It is remarkable to note the contrast between the visible and invisible worlds which surrounded the spiritual pilgrimage of Sakya Muni to Buddhahood or enlightenment. At his birth there is no trace of political hostility: the cruel Kansa, Herod, Magicians seeking to destroy, are replaced by the affectionate force of a king trying to retain his son. The universal traditions reach their happy height in the ecstatic gospels of the Siamese.1 The universe was illumined; all jewels shown with unwonted lustre; the air was full of music; all pain ceased; the blind saw, the deaf heard; the birds paused in their flight; all trees and plants burst into bloom, and lotus flowers appeared in every place. Not under the dominion of Mara2 was this beautiful world. But by turning from all its youth, health, and life, to think only of its decrepitude, illness, and death, the Prince Sakya Muni surrounded himself with another world in which Mara had his share of power. I condense here the accounts of his encounters with the Prince, who was on his way to be a hermit.

When the Prince passed out at the palace gates, the king Mara, knowing that the youth was passing beyond his evil power, determined to prevent him. Descending from his abode and floating in the air, Mara cried, 'Lord, thou art capable of such vast endurance, go not forth to adopt a religious life, but return to thy kingdom, and in seven days thou shalt become an emperor of the world, ruling over the four great continents.' 'Take heed, O Mara!' replied the Prince; 'I also know that in seven days I might gain universal empire, but I have no desire for such possessions. I know that the pursuit of religion is better than the empire of the world. See how the world is moved, and quakes with praise of this my entry on a religious life! I shall attain the glorious omniscience, and shall teach the wheel of the law, that all teachable beings may free themselves from transmigratory existence. You, thinking only of the lusts of the flesh, would force me to leave all beings to wander without guide into your power. Avaunt! get thee away far from me!'

Mara withdrew, but only to watch for another opportunity. It came when the Prince had reduced himself to emaciation and agony by the severest austerities. Then Mara presented himself, and pretending compassion, said, 'Beware, O grand Being! Your state is pitiable to look on; you are attenuated beyond measure, and your skin, that was of the colour of gold, is dark and discoloured. You are practising this mortification in vain. I can see that you will not live through it. You, who are a Grand Being, had better give up this course, for be assured you will derive much more advantage from sacrifices of fire and flowers.' Him the Grand Being indignantly answered, 'Hearken, thou vile and wicked Mara! Thy words suit not the time. Think not to deceive me, for I heed thee not. Thou mayest mislead those who have no understanding, but I, who have virtue, endurance, and intelligence, who know what is good and what is evil, cannot be so misled. Thou, O Mara! hast eight generals. Thy first is delight in the five lusts of the flesh, which are the pleasures of appearance, sound, scent, flavour, and touch. Thy second general is wrath, who takes the form of vexation, indignation, and desire to injure. Thy third is concupiscence. Thy fourth is desire. Thy fifth is impudence. Thy sixth is arrogance. Thy seventh is doubt. And thine eighth is ingratitude. These are thy generals, who cannot be escaped by those whose hearts are set on honour and wealth. But I know that he who can contend with these thy generals shall escape beyond all sorrow, and enjoy the most glorious happiness. Therefore I have not ceased to practise mortification, knowing that even were I to die whilst thus engaged, it would be a most excellent thing.'

It is added that Mara 'fled in confusion,' but the next incident seems to show that his suggestion was not unheeded; for 'after he had departed,' the Grand Being had his vision of the three-stringed guitar—one string drawn too tightly, the second too loosely, the third moderately—which last, somewhat in defiance of orchestral ideas, alone gave sweet music, and taught him that moderation was better than excess or laxity. By eating enough he gained that pristine strength and beauty which offended the five Brahmans so that they left him. The third and final effort of Mara immediately preceded the Prince's attainment of the order of Buddha under the Bo-tree. He now sent his three daughters, Raka (Love), Aradi (Anger), Tanha (Desire). Beautifully bedecked they approached him, and Raka said, 'Lord, fearest thou not death?' But he drove her away. The two others also he drove away as they had no charm of sufficient power to entice him. Then Mara assembled his generals, and said, 'Listen, ye Maras, that know not sorrow! Now shall I make war on the Prince, that man without equal. I dare not attack him in face, but I will circumvent him by approaching on the north side. Assume then all manner of shapes, and use your mightiest powers, that he may flee in terror.'

Having taken on fearful shapes, raising awful sounds, headed by Mara himself, who had assumed immense size, and mounted his elephant Girimaga, a thousand miles in height, they advanced; but they dare not enter beneath the shade of the holy Bo-tree. They frightened away, however, the Lord's guardian angels, and he was left alone. Then seeing the army approaching from the north, he reflected, 'Long have I devoted myself to a life of mortification, and now I am alone, without a friend to aid me in this contest. Yet may I escape the Maras, for the virtue of my transcendent merits will be my army.' 'Help me,' he cried, 'ye thirty Barami! ye powers of accumulated merit, ye powers of Almsgiving, Morality, Relinquishment, Wisdom, Fortitude, Patience, Truth, Determination, Charity, and Equanimity, help me in my fight with Mara!' The Lord was seated on his jewelled throne (the same that had been formed of the grass on which he sat), and Mara with his army exhausted every resource of terror—monstrous beasts, rain of missiles and burning ashes, gales that blew down mountain peaks—to inspire him with fear; but all in vain! Nay, the burning ashes were changed to flowers as they fell.

'Come down from thy throne,' shouted the evil-formed one; 'come down, or I will cut thine heart into atoms!' The Lord replied, 'This jewelled throne was created by the power of my merits, for I am he who will teach all men the remedy for death, who will redeem all beings, and set them free from the sorrows of circling existence.'

Mara then claimed that the throne belonged to himself, and had been created by his own merits; and on this armed himself with the Chakkra, the irresistible weapon of Indra, and Wheel of the Law. Yet Buddha answered, 'By the thirty virtues of transcendent merits, and the five alms, I have obtained the throne. Thou, in saying that this throne was created by thy merits, tellest an untruth, for indeed there is no throne for a sinful, horrible being such as thou art.'

Then furious Mara hurled the Chakkra, which clove mountains in its course, but could not pass a canopy of flowers which rose over the Lord's head.

And now the great Being asked Mara for the witnesses of his acts of merit by virtue of which he claimed the throne. In response, Mara's generals all bore him witness. Then Mara challenged him, 'Tell me now, where is the man that can bear witness for thee?' The Lord reflected, 'Truly here is no man to bear me witness, but I will call on the earth itself, though it has neither spirit nor understanding, and it shall be my witness.' Stretching forth his hand, he thus invoked the earth: 'O holy Earth! I who have attained the thirty powers of virtue, and performed the five great alms, each time that I have performed a great act have not failed to pour water on thee. Now that I have no other witness, I call upon thee to give thy testimony!'

The angel of the earth appeared in shape of a lovely woman, and answered, 'O Being more excellent than angels or men! it is true that, when you performed your great works, you ever poured water on my hair.' And with these words she wrung her long hair, and from it issued a stream, a torrent, a flood, in which Mara and his hosts were overturned, their insignia destroyed, and King Mara put to flight, amid the loud rejoicings of angels.

Then the evil one and his generals were conquered not only in power but in heart; and Mara, raising his thousand arms, paid reverence, saying, 'Homage to the Lord, who has subdued his body even as a charioteer breaks his horses to his use! The Lord will become the omniscient Buddha, the Teacher of angels, and Brahmas, and Yakkhas (demons), and men. He will confound all Maras, and rescue men from the whirl of transmigration!'

The menacing powers depicted as assailing Sakya Muni appear only around the infancy of Zoroaster. The interview of the latter with Ahriman hardly amounts to a severe trial, but still the accent of the chief temptation both of Buddha and Christ is in it, namely, the promise of worldly empire. It was on one of those midnight journeys through Heaven and Hell that Zoroaster saw Ahriman, and delivered from his power 'one who had done both good and evil.'3 When Ahriman met Zoroaster's gaze, he cried, 'Quit thou the pure law; cast it to the ground; thou wilt then be in the world all that thou canst desire. Be not anxious about thy end. At least, do not destroy my subjects, O pure Zoroaster, son of Poroscharp, who art born of her thou hast borne!' Zoroaster answered, 'Wicked Majesty! it is for thee and thy worshippers that Hell is prepared, but by the mercy of God I shall bury your work with shame and ignominy.'

Fig. 6.—Temptation of Christ (Lucas van Leyden).

In the account of Matthew, Satan begins his temptation of Jesus in the same way and amid similar circumstances to those we find in the Siamese legends of Buddha. It occurs in a wilderness, and the appeal is to hunger. The temptation of Buddha, in which Mara promises the empire of the world, is also repeated in the case of Satan and Jesus (Fig. 6). The menaces, however, in this case, are relegated to the infancy, and the lustful temptation is absent altogether. Mark has an allusion to his being in the wilderness forty days 'with the beasts,' which may mean that Satan 'drove' him into a region of danger to inspire fear. In Luke we have the remarkable claim of Satan that the authority over the world has been delivered to himself, and he gives it to whom he will; which Jesus does not deny, as Buddha did the similar claim of Mara. As in the case of Buddha, the temptation of Jesus ends his fasting; angels bring him food (διηκόνουν αὐτῷ probably means that), and thenceforth he eats and drinks, to the scandal of the ascetics.

The essential addition in the case of Jesus is the notable temptation to try and perform a crucial act. Satan quotes an accredited messianic prophecy, and invites Jesus to test his claim to be the predicted deliverer by casting himself from the pinnacle of the Temple, and testing the promise that angels should protect the true Son of God. Strauss,[4] as it appears to me, has not considered the importance of this in connection with the general situation. 'Assent,' he says, 'cannot be withheld from the canon that, to be credible, the narrative must ascribe nothing to the devil inconsistent with his established cunning. Now, the first temptation, appealing to hunger, we grant, is not ill-conceived; if this were ineffectual, the devil, as an artful tactician, should have had a yet more alluring temptation at hand; but instead of this, we find him, in Matthew, proposing to Jesus the neck-breaking feat of casting himself down from the pinnacle of the Temple—a far less inviting miracle than the metamorphosis of the stones. This proposition finding no acceptance, there follows, as a crowning effort, a suggestion which, whatever might be the bribe, every true Israelite would instantly reject with abhorrence—to fall down and worship the devil.'

Not so! The scapegoat was a perpetual act of worship to the Devil. In this story of the temptation of Christ there enter some characteristic elements of the temptation of Job.[5] Uz in the one case and the wilderness in the other mean morally the same, the region ruled over by Azazel. In both cases the trial is under divine direction. And the trial is in both cases to secure a division of worship between the good and evil powers, which was so universal in the East that it was the test of exceptional piety if one did not swerve from an unmixed sacrifice. Jesus is apparently abandoned by the God in whom he trusted; he is 'driven' into a wilderness, and there kept with the beasts and without food. The Devil alone comes to him; exhibits his own miraculous power by bearing him through the air to his own Mount Seir, and showing him the whole world in a moment of time; and now says to him, as it were, 'Try your God! See if he will even turn stones into bread to save his own son, to whom I offer the kingdoms of the world!' Then bearing him into the 'holy hill' of his own God—the pinnacle of the Temple—says, 'Try now a leap, and see if he saves from being dashed to pieces, even in his own precincts, his so trustful devotee, whom I have borne aloft so safely! Which, then, has the greater power to protect, enrich, advance you,—he who has left you out here to starve, so that you dare not trust yourself to him, or I? Fall down then and worship me as your God, and all the world is yours! It is the world you are to reign over: rule it in my name!'

When St. Anthony is tempted by the Devil in the form of a lean monk, it was easy to see that the hermit was troubled with a vision of his own emaciation. When the Devil appears to Luther under guise of a holy monk, it is an obvious explanation that he was impressed by a memory of the holy brothers who still remained in the Church, and who, while they implored his return, pointed out the strength and influence he had lost by secession. Equally simple are the moral elements in the story of Christ's temptation. While a member of John's ascetic community, for which 'though he was rich he became poor,' hunger, and such anxiety about a living as victimises many a young thinker now, must have assailed him. Later on his Devil meets him on the Temple, quotes scripture, and warns him that his visionary God will not raise him so high in the Church as the Prince of this World can.[6] And finally, when dreams of a larger union, including Jews and Gentiles, visited him, the power that might be gained by connivance with universal idolatry would be reflected in the offer of the kingdoms of the world in payment for the purity of his aims and singleness of his worship.

That these trials of self-truthfulness and fidelity, occurring at various phases of life, would be recognised, is certain. A youth of high position, as Christ probably was,[7] or even one with that great power over the people which all concede, was, in a worldly sense, 'throwing away his prospects;' and this voice, real in its time, would naturally be conventionalised. It would put on the stock costume of devils and angels; and among Jewish christians it would naturally be associated with the forty-days' fast of Moses (Exod. xxxiv. 28; Deut. ix. 9), and that of Elias (1 Kings xix. 8), and the forty-years' trial of Israel in the wilderness. Among Greek christians some traces of the legend of Herakles in his seclusion as herdsman, or at the cross-roads between Vice and Virtue, might enter; and it is not impossible that some touches might be added from the Oriental myth which invested Buddha.

However this may be, we may with certainty repair to the common source of all such myths in the higher nature of man, and recognise the power of a pure genius to overcome those temptations to a success unworthy of itself. We may interpret all such legends with a clearness proportioned to the sacrifices we have made for truth and ideal right; and the endless perplexities of commentators and theologians about the impossible outward details of the New Testament story are simple confessions that the great spirit so tried is now made to label with his name his own Tempter—namely, a

Church grown powerful and wealthy, which, as the Prince of this World, bribes the conscience and tempts away the talent necessary to the progress of mankind.

Notes

1 As given in Mr. Alabaster's 'The Wheel of the Law' (Trübner & Co., 1871). In the Apocryphal Gospels, some of the signs of nature's joy attending the birth of Buddha are reported at the birth of Mary and that of Christ, as the pausing of birds in their flight, etc. Anna is said to have conceived Mary under a tree, as Maia under a tree brought forth Buddha.

2 'Mara, or Man (Sanscrit Màra, death, god of love; by some authors translated 'illusion,' as if it came from the Sanscrit Màya), the angels of evil, desire, of love, death, etc. Though King Mara plays the part of our Satan the tempter, he and his host were formerly great givers of alms, which led to their being born in the highest of the Deva heavens, called Paranimit Wasawatti, there to live more than nine thousand million years, surrounded by all the luxuries of sensuality. From this heaven the filthy one, as the Siamese describe him, descends to the earth to tempt and excite to evil.'—Alabaster.

3 Some say Djemschid, others Guenschesp, a warrior sent to hell for beating the fire.

4 Leben Jesu, ii. 54. The close resemblance between the trial of Israel in the wilderness and this of Jesus is drawn in his own masterly way.

5 A passage of the Pesikta (iii. 35) represents a conversation between Jehovah and Satan with reference to Messias which bears a resemblance to the prologue of Job. Satan said: Lord, permit me to tempt Messias and his generation. 'To him the Lord said: You could have no power over him. Satan again said: Permit me because I have the power. God answered: If you persist longer in this, rather would I destroy thee from the world, than that one soul of the generation of Messias should be lost.' Though the rabbin might report the trial declined, the Christian would claim it to have been endured.

6 In his fresco of the Temptation at the Vatican, Michael Angelo has painted the Devil in the dress of a priest, standing with Jesus on the Temple.

7 'Idols and Ideals.' London: Trübner & Co. New York: Henry Holt & Co. In the Essay on Christianity I have given my reasons for this belief.

Chapter XVIII - Trial of the Great

A 'Morality' at Tours—The 'St. Anthony' of Spagnoletto—Bunyan's Pilgrim—Milton on Christ's Temptation—An Edinburgh saint and Unitarian fiend—A haunted Jewess—Conversion by fever—Limit of courage—Woman and sorcery—Luther and the Devil—The ink-spot at Wartburg—Carlyle's interpretation—The cowled devil—Carlyle's trial—In Rue St. Thomas d'Enfer—The Everlasting No—Devil of Vauvert—The latter-day conflict—New conditions—The Victory of Man—The Scholar and the World.

A representation of the Temptation of St. Anthony (marionettes), which I witnessed at Tours (1878), had several points of significance. It was the mediæval 'Morality' as diminished by centuries, and conventionalised among those whom the centuries mould in ways and for ends they know not. Amid a scenery of grotesque devils, rudely copied from Callot, St. Anthony appeared, and was tempted in a way that recalled the old pictures. There was the same fair Temptress, in this case the wife of Satan, who warns her lord that his ugly devils will be of no avail against Anthony, and that the whole affair should be confided to her. She being repelled, the rest of the performance consisted in the devils continually ringing the bell of the hermitage, and finally setting fire to it. This conflagration was the supreme torment of Anthony—and, sooth to say, it was a fairly comfortable abode—who utters piteous prayers and is presently comforted by an angel bringing him wreaths of evergreen.

The prayers of the saint and the response of the angel were meant to be seriously taken; but their pathos was generally met with pardonable laughter by the crowd in the booth. Yet there was a pathos about it all, if only this, that the only temptations thought of for a saint were a sound and quiet house and a mistress. The bell-noise alone remained from the great picture of Spagnoletto at Siena, where the unsheltered old man raises his deprecating hand against the disturber, but not his eyes from the book he reads. In Spagnoletto's picture there are five large books, pen, ink, and hour-glass; but there is neither hermitage to be burnt nor female charms to be resisted.

But Spagnoletto, even in his time, was beholding the vision of exceptional men in the past, whose hunger and thirst was for knowledge, truth, and culture, and who sought these in solitude. Such men have so long left the Church familiar to the French peasantry that any representation of their temptations and trials would be out of place among the marionettes. The bells which now disturb them are those that sound from steeples.

Another picture loomed up before my eyes over the puppet performance at Tours, that which for Bunyan frescoed the walls of Bedford Gaol. There, too, the old demons, giants, and devils took on grave and vast forms, and reflected the trials of the Great Hearts who withstood the Popes and Pagans, the armed political Apollyons and the Giant Despairs, who could make prisons the hermitages of men born to be saviours of the people.

Such were the temptations that Milton knew; from his own heart came the pigments with which he painted the trial of Christ in the wilderness. 'Set women in his eye,' said Belial:—

Women, when nothing else, beguiled the heart
Of wisest Solomon, and made him build,
And made him bow to the gods of his wives.
To whom quick answer Satan thus returned.
Belial, in much uneven scale thou weigh'st
All others by thyself....
But he whom we attempt is wiser far
Than Solomon, of more exalted mind,
Made and set wholly on the accomplishment
Of greatest things....
Therefore with manlier objects we must try
His constancy, with such as have more show
Of worth, of honour, glory, and popular praise;
Rocks whereon greatest men have oftest wrecked.[1]

The progressive ideas which Milton attributed to Satan have not failed. That Celestial City which Bunyan found it so hard to reach has now become a metropolis of wealth and fashion, and the trials which once beset pilgrims toiling towards it are now transferred to those who would pass beyond it to another city, seen from afar, with temples of Reason and palaces of Justice.

The old phantasms have shrunk to puppets. The trials by personal devils are relegated to the regions of insanity and disease. It is everywhere a dance of puppets though on a cerebral stage. A lady well known in Edinburgh related to me a terrible experience she had with the devil. She had invited some of her relations to visit her for some days; but these relatives were Unitarians, and, after they had gone, having entered the room which they had occupied, she was seized by the devil, thrown on the floor, and her back so strained that she had to keep her bed for some time. This was to her 'the Unitarian fiend' of which the Wesleyan Hymn-Book sang so long; but even the Wesleyans have now discarded the famous couplet, and there must be few who would not recognise that the old lady at Edinburgh merely had a tottering body representing a failing mind.

I have just read a book in which a lady in America relates her trial by the devil. This lady, in her girlhood, was of a christian family, but she married a rabbi and was baptized into Judaism. After some years of happy life a terrible compunction seized her; she imagined herself lost for ever; she became ill. A christian (Baptist) minister and his wife were the evil stars in her case, and with what terrors they surrounded the poor Jewess may be gathered from the following extract.

'She then left me—that dear friend left me alone to my God, and to him I carried a lacerated and bleeding heart, and laid it at the foot of the cross, as an atonement for the multiplied sins I had committed, whether of ignorance or wilfulness; and how shall I proceed to portray the heart-felt agonies of that night preceding my deliverance from the shafts of Satan? Oh! this weight, this load of sin, this burden so intolerable that it crushed me to the earth; for this was a dark hour with me—the darkest; and I lay calm, to all appearance, but with cold perspiration drenching me, nor could I close my eyes; and these words again smote my ear, No redemption, no redemption; and the tempter came, inviting me, with all his blandishment and power, to follow him to his court of pleasure. My eyes were open; I certainly saw him, dressed in the most phantastic shape. This was no illusion; for he soon assumed the appearance of one of the gay throng I had mingled with in former days, and beckoned me to follow. I was awake, and seemed to lie on the brink of a chasm, and spirits were dancing around me, and I made some slight outcry, and those dear girls watching with me came to me, and looked at me. They said I looked at them but could not speak, and they moistened my lips, and said I was nearly gone; then I whispered, and they came and looked at me again, but would not disturb me. It was well they did not; for the power of God was over me, and angels were around me, and whispering spirits near, and I whispered in sweet communion with them, as they surrounded me, and, pointing to the throne of grace, said, 'Behold!' and I felt that the glory of God was about to manifest itself; for a shout, as if a choir of angels had tuned their golden harps, burst forth in, 'Glory to God on high,' and died away in softest strains of melody. I lifted up my eyes to heaven, and there, so near as to be almost within my reach, the brightest vision of our Lord and Saviour stood before me, enveloped with a light, ethereal mist, so bright and yet transparent that his divine figure could be seen distinctly, and my eyes were riveted upon him; for this bright vision seemed to touch my bed, standing at the foot, so near, and he stretched forth his left hand toward me, whilst with the right one he pointed to the throne of grace, and a voice came, saying, 'Blessed are they who can see God; arise, take up thy cross and follow me; for though thy sins be as scarlet they shall be white as wool.' And with my eyes fixed on that bright vision, I saw from the hand stretched toward me great drops of blood, as if from each finger; for his blessed hand was spread open, as if in prayer, and those drops fell distinctly, as if upon the earth; and a misty light encircled me, and a voice again said, 'Take up thy cross and follow me; for though thy sins be as scarlet they shall be white as wool.' And angels were all around me, and I saw the throne of heaven. And, oh! the sweet calm that stole over my senses. It must have been a foretaste of heavenly bliss. How long I lay after this beautiful vision I know not; but when I opened my eyes it was early dawn, and I felt so happy and well. My young friends pressed around my bedside, to know how I felt, and I said, 'I am well and so happy.' They then said I was whispering with some one in my dreams all night. I told them angels were with me; that I was not asleep, and I had sweet communion with them, and would soon be well.'2

That is what the temptation of Jesus in the wilderness comes to when dislocated from its time and place, and, with its gathered ages of fable, is imported at last to be an engine of torture sprung on the nerves of a devout woman. This Jewess was divorced from her husband by her Christianity; her child died a victim to precocious piety; but what were home and affection in ruins compared with salvation from that frightful devil seen in her holy delirium?

History shows that it has always required unusual courage for a human being to confront an enemy believed to be præternatural. This Jewess would probably have been able to face a tiger for the sake of her husband, but not that fantastic devil. Not long ago an English actor was criticised because, in playing Hamlet, he cowered with fear on seeing the ghost, all his sinews and joints seeming to give way; but to me he appeared then the perfect type of what mankind have always been when believing themselves in the presence of præternatural powers. The limit of courage in human nature was passed when the foe was one which no earthly power or weapon could reach.

In old times, nearly all the sorcerers and witches were women; and it may have been, in some part, because woman had more real courage than man unarmed. Sorcery and witchcraft were but the so-called pagan rites in their last degradation, and women were the last to abandon the declining religion, just as they are the last to leave the superstition which has followed it. Their sentiment and affection were intertwined with it, and the threats of eternal torture by devils which frightened men from the old faith to the new were less powerful to shake the faith of women. When pagan priests became christians, priestesses remained, to become sorceresses. The new faith had gradually to win the love of the sex too used to martyrdom on earth to fear it much in hell. And now, again, when knowledge clears away the old terrors, and many men are growing indifferent to all religion, because no longer frightened by it, we may expect the churches to be increasingly kept up by women alone, simply because they went into them more by attraction of saintly ideals than fear of diabolical menaces.

Thomas Carlyle has selected Luther's boldness in the presence of what he believed the Devil to illustrate his valour. 'His defiance of the 'Devils' in Worms,' says Carlyle, 'was not a mere boast, as the like might be if spoken now. It was a faith of Luther's that there were Devils, spiritual denizens of the Pit, continually besetting men. Many times, in his writings, this turns up; and a most small sneer has been grounded on it by some. In the room of the Wartburg, where he sat translating the Bible, they still show you a black spot on the wall; the strange memorial of one of these conflicts. Luther sat translating one of the Psalms; he was worn down with long labour, with sickness, abstinence from food; there rose before him some hideous indefinable Image, which he took for the Evil One, to forbid his work; Luther started up with fiend-defiance; flung his inkstand at the spectre, and it disappeared! The spot still remains there; a curious monument of several things. Any apothecary's apprentice can now tell us what we are to think of this apparition, in a scientific sense; but the man's heart that dare rise defiant, face to face, against Hell itself, can give no higher proof of fearlessness. The thing he will quail before exists not on this earth nor under it—fearless enough! 'The Devil is aware,' writes he on one occasion, 'that this does not proceed out of fear in me. I have seen and defied innumerable Devils. Duke George,'—of Leipzig, a great enemy of his,—'Duke George is not equal to one Devil,' far short of a Devil! 'If I had business at Leipzig, I would ride into Leipzig, though it rained Duke Georges for nine days running.' What a reservoir of Dukes to ride into!'3

Although Luther's courage certainly appears in this, it is plain that his Devil was much humanised as compared with the fearful phantoms of an earlier time. Nobody would ever have tried an inkstand on the Gorgons, Furies, Lucifers of ancient belief. In Luther's Bible the Devil is pictured as a monk—a lean monk, such as he himself was only too likely to become if he continued his rebellion against the Church (Fig. 17). It was against a Devil liable to resistance by physical force that he hurled his inkstand, and against whom he also hurled the contents of his inkstand in those words which Richter said were half-battles.

Luther's Devil, in fact, represents one of the last phases in the reduction of the Evil Power from a personified phantom with which no man could cope, to that impersonal but all the more real moral obstruction with which every man can cope—if only with an inkstand. The horned monster with cowl, beads, and cross, is a mere transparency, through which every brave heart may recognise the practical power of wrong around him, the established error, disguised as religion, which is able to tempt and threaten him.

The temptations with menace described—those which, coming upon the weak nerves of women, vanquished their reason and heart; that which, in a healthy man, raised valour and power—may be taken as side-lights for a corresponding experience in the life of a great man now living—Carlyle himself. It was at a period of youth when, amid the lonely hills of

Scotland, he wandered out of harmony with the world in which he lived. Consecrated by pious parents to the ministry, he had inwardly renounced every dogma of the Church. With genius and culture for high work, the world demanded of him low work. Friendless, alone, poor, he sat eating his heart, probably with little else to eat. Every Scotch parson he met unconsciously propounded to that youth the question whether he could convert his heretical stone into bread, or precipitate himself from the pinnacle of the Scotch Kirk without bruises? Then it was he roamed in his mystical wilderness, until he found himself in the gayest capital of the world, which, however, on him had little to bestow but a further sense of loneliness.

'Now, when I look back, it was a strange isolation I then lived in. The men and women around me, even speaking with me, were but Figures; I had practically forgotten that they were alive, that they were not merely automatic. In the midst of their crowded streets and assemblages, I walked solitary; and (except as it was my own heart, not another's, that I kept devouring) savage also, as is the tiger in his jungle. Some comfort it would have been, could I, like a Faust, have fancied myself tempted and tormented of a Devil; for a Hell, as I imagine, without Life, though only diabolic Life, were more frightful: but in our age of Downpulling and Disbelief, the very Devil has been pulled down—you cannot so much as believe in a Devil. To me the Universe was all void of Life, of Purpose, of Volition, even of Hostility: it was one huge, dead, immeasurable, Steam-engine, rolling on, in its dead indifference, to grind me limb from limb. Oh, the vast gloomy, solitary Golgotha, and Mill of Death! Why was the Living banished thither, companionless, conscious? Why, if there is no Devil; nay, unless the Devil is your God?' ...

'From suicide a certain aftershine of Christianity withheld me.' ...

'So had it lasted, as in bitter, protracted Death-agony, through long years. The heart within me, unvisited by any heavenly dewdrop, was smouldering in sulphurous, slow-consuming fire. Almost since earliest memory I had shed no tear; or once only when I, murmuring half-audibly, recited Faust's Deathsong, that wild Selig der den er im Siegesglanze findet (Happy whom he finds in Battle's splendour), and thought that of this last Friend even I was not forsaken, that Destiny itself could not doom me not to die. Having no hope, neither had I any definite fear, were it of Man or of Devil; nay, I often felt as if it might be solacing could the Arch-Devil himself, though in Tartarean terrors, rise to me that I might tell him a little of my mind. And yet, strangely enough, I lived in a continual, indefinite, pining fear; tremulous, pusillanimous, apprehensive of I knew not what; it seemed as if all things in the Heavens above and the Earth beneath would hurt me; as if the Heavens and the Earth were but boundless jaws of a devouring monster, wherein I, palpitating, waited to be devoured.

'Full of such humour, and perhaps the miserablest man in the whole French Capital or Suburbs, was I, one sultry Dogday, after much perambulation, toiling along the dirty little Rue Sainte Thomas de l'Enfer, among civic rubbish enough, in a close atmosphere, and over pavements hot as Nebuchadnezzar's Furnace; whereby doubtless my spirits were little cheered; when all at once there rose a Thought in me, and I asked myself, 'What art thou afraid of? Wherefore, like a coward, dost thou for ever pip and whimper, and go cowering and trembling? Despicable biped! what is the sum-total of the worst that lies before thee? Death? Well, Death; and say the pangs of Tophet too, and all that the Devil or Man may, will, or can do against thee! Hast thou not a heart; canst thou not suffer whatsoever it be; and, as a Child of Freedom, though outcast, trample Tophet itself under thy feet, while it consumes thee! Let it come, then; I will meet it and defy it!' And as I so thought, there rushed like a stream of fire over my whole soul; and I shook base Fear away from me for ever. I was strong, of unknown strength; a spirit, almost a god. Ever from that time the temper of my misery was changed: not Fear or whining Sorrow was it, but Indignation and grim fire-eyed Defiance.

'Thus had the Everlasting No pealed authoritatively through all the recesses of my Being, of my Me; and then was it that my whole Me stood up, in native God-created majesty and with emphasis recorded its Protest. Such a Protest, the most important transaction in Life, may that same Indignation and Defiance, in a psychological point of view, be fitly called. The Everlasting No had said, 'Behold thou art fatherless, outcast, and the Universe is mine (the Devil's);' to which my whole Me now made answer, 'I am not thine, but Free, and for ever hate thee!'

'It is from this hour that I incline to date my spiritual New Birth, or Baphometic fire-baptism; perhaps I directly thereupon began to be a Man.'4

Perhaps he who so uttered his Apage Satana did not recognise amid what haunted Edom he wrestled with his Phantom. Saint Louis, having invited the Carthusian monks to Paris, assigned them a habitation in the Faubourg Saint-Jacques, near the ancient chateau of Vauvert, a manor built by Robert (le Diable), but for a long time then uninhabited, because infested by demons, which had, perhaps, been false coiners. Fearful howls had been heard there, and spectres seen, dragging chains; and, in particular, it was frequented by a fearful green monster, serpent and man in one, with a long white beard, wielding a huge club, with which he threatened all who passed that way. This demon, in common belief, passed along the road to and from the chateau in a fiery chariot, and twisted the neck of every human being met on his way. He was called the Devil of Vauvert. The Carthusians were not frightened by these stories, but asked Louis to give them the Manor, which he did, with all its dependencies. After that nothing more was heard of the Diable Vauvert or his imps. It was but fair to the Demons who had assisted the friars in obtaining a valuable property so cheaply that the street should thenceforth bear the name of Rue d'Enfer, as it does. But the formidable genii of the place haunted it still, and, in the course of time, the Carthusians proved that they could use with effect all the terrors which the Devils had left behind them. They represented a great money-coining Christendom with which free-thinking Michaels had to contend, even to the day when, as we have just read, one of the bravest of these there encountered his Vauvert devil and laid him low for ever. I well remember that wretched street of St. Thomas leading into Hell Street, as if the Parisian authorities, remembering that Thomas was a doubter, meant to remind the wayfarer that whoso doubteth is damned. Near by is the convent of St. Michael, who makes no war on the neighbouring Rue Dragon. All names—mere idle names! Among the thousands that crowd along them, how many pause to note the quaintness of the names on the street-lamps, remaining there from fossil fears and phantom battles long turned to fairy lore. Yet amid them, on that sultry day, in one heart, was fought and won a battle which summed up all their sense and value. Every Hell was conquered then and there when Fear was conquered. There, when the lower Self was cast down beneath the poised spear of a Free Mind, St. Michael at last chained his dragon. There Luther's inkstand was not only hurled, but hit its mark; there, 'Get thee behind me,' was said, and obeyed; there Buddha brought the archfiend Mara to kneel at his feet.

And it was by sole might of a Man. Therefore may this be emphasised as the temptation and triumph which have for us to-day the meaning of all others.

A young man of intellectual power, seeing beyond all the conventional errors around him, without means, feeling that ordinary work, however honourable, would for him mean failure of his life—because failure to contribute his larger truth to mankind—he finds the terrible cost of his aim to be hunger, want, a life passed amid suspicion and alienation, without sympathy, lonely, unloved—and, alas! with a probability that all these losses may involve loss of just what they are incurred for, the power to make good his truth. After giving up love and joy, he may, after all, be unable to give living service to his truth, but only a broken body and shed blood. Similar trials in outer form have been encountered again and again; not only in the great temptations and triumphs of sacred tradition, but perhaps even more genuinely in the unknown lives of many pious people all over the world, have hunger, want, suffering, been conquered by faith. But rarely amid doubts. Rarely in the way of Saint Thomas, in no fear of hell or devil, nor in any hope of reward in heaven, or on earth; rarely indeed without any feeling of a God taking notice, or belief in angels waiting near, have men or women triumphed utterly over self. All history proves what man can sacrifice on earth for an eternal weight of glory above. We know how cheerfully men and women can sing at the stake, when they feel the fire consuming them to be a chariot bearing them to heaven. We understand the valour of Luther marching against his devils with his hymn, 'Ein feste Burg ist unser Gott.' But it is important to know what man's high heart is capable of without any of these encouragements or aids, what man's moral force when he feels himself alone. For this must become an increasingly momentous consideration.

Already the educated youth of our time have followed the wanderer of threescore years ago into that St. Thomas d'Enfer Street, which may be morally translated as the point where man doubts every hell he does not feel, and every creed he cannot prove. The old fears and hopes are fading faster from the minds around us than from their professions. There must be very few sane people now who are restrained by fear of hell, or promises of future reward. What then controls human passion and selfishness? For many, custom; for others, hereditary good nature and good sense; for some, a sense of honour; for multitudes, the fear of law and penalties. It is very difficult indeed, amid these complex motives, to know how far simple human nature, acting at its best, is capable of heroic endurance for truth, and of pure passion for the right. This cannot be seen in those who intellectually reject the creed of the majority, but conform to its standards and pursue its worldly advantages. It must be seen, if at all, in those who are radically severed from the conventional aims of the world,—who seek not its wealth, nor its honours, decline its proudest titles, defy its authority, share not its prospects for time or eternity. It must be proved by those, the grandeur of whose aims can change the splendours of Paris to a wilderness. These may show what man, as man, is capable of, what may be his new birth, and the religion of his simple manhood. What they think, say, and do is not prescribed either by human or supernatural command; in them you do not see what society thinks, or sects believe, or what the populace applaud. You see the individual man building his moral edifice, as genuinely as birds their nests, by law of his own moral constitution. It is a great thing to know what those edifices are, for so at last every man will have to build if he build at all. And if noble lives cannot be so lived, we may be sure the career of the human race will be downhill henceforth. For any unbiassed mind may judge whether the tendency of thought and power lies toward or away from the old hopes and fears on which the regime of the past was founded.

A great and wise Teacher of our time, who shared with Carlyle his lonely pilgrimage, has admonished his generation of the temptations brought by talent,—selfish use of it for ambitious ends on the one hand, or withdrawal into fruitless solitude on the other; and I cannot forbear closing this chapter with his admonition to his young countrymen forty years ago.5

'Public and private avarice makes the air we breathe thick and fat. The scholar is decent, indolent, complacent. See already the tragic consequence. The mind of this country, taught to aim at low objects, eats upon itself. There is no work for any but the decorous and the complacent. Young men of the fairest promise, who begin life upon our shores, inflated by the mountain winds, shined upon by all the stars of God, find the earth below not in unison with these,—but are hindered from action by the disgust which the principles on which business is managed inspire and turn drudges, or die of disgust,—some of them suicides. What is the remedy? They did not yet see, and thousands of young men as hopeful, now crowding to the barriers for the career, do not yet see, that if the single man plant himself indomitably on his instincts, and there abide, the huge world will come round to him. Patience—patience;—with the shades of all the good and great for company; and for solace, the perspective of your own infinite life; and for work, the study and the communication of principles, the making those instincts prevalent, the conversion of the world. Is it not the chief disgrace in the world—not to be an unit; not to be reckoned one character; not to yield that peculiar fruit which each man was created to bear,—but to be reckoned in the gross, in the hundred, in the thousand of the party, the section, to which we belong; and our opinion predicted geographically, as the north or the south? Not so, brothers and friends,—please God, ours shall not be so. We will walk on our own feet; we will work with our own hands; we will speak our own minds.'

Notes

1 'Paradise Regained,' ii.
2 'Henry Luria; or, the Little Jewish Convert: being contained in the Memoir of Mrs. S. T. Cohen, relict of the Rev. Dr. A. H. Cohen, late Rabbi of the Synagogue in Richmond, Va.' 1860.
3 'Heroes and Hero-worship,' iv.
4 'Sartor Resartus.' London: Chapman & Hall, 1869, p. 160.
5 'The American Scholar.' An Oration delivered before the Phi Beta Kappa Society at Cambridge (Massachusetts), August 31, 1837. By Ralph Waldo Emerson.

Chapter XIX- The Man of Sin

Hindu myth—Gnostic theories—Ophite scheme of redemption—Rabbinical traditions of primitive man—Pauline Pessimism—Law of death—Satan's ownership of man—Redemption of the elect—Contemporary statements—Baptism—Exorcism—The 'new man's' food—Eucharist—Herbert Spencer's explanation—Primitive ideas—Legends of Adam and Seth—Adamites—A Mormon 'Mystery' of initiation.

In a Hindu myth, Dhrubo, an infant devotee, passed much time in a jungle, surrounded by ferocious beasts, in devotional exercises of such extraordinary merit that Vishnu erected a new heaven for him as the reward of his piety. Vishnu even left his own happy abode to superintend the construction of this special heaven. In Hebrew mythology the favourite son, the chosen people, is called out of Egypt to dwell in a new home, a promised land, not in heaven but on earth. The idea common to the two is that of a contrast between a natural and a celestial environment,—a jungle and beasts, bondage and distress; a new heaven, a land flowing with milk and honey,—and the correspondence with these of the elect child, Dhrubo or Israel.

The tendency of Christ's mind appears to have been rather in the Aryan direction; he pointed his friends to a kingdom not of this world, and to his Father's many mansions in heaven. But the Hebrew faith in a messianic reign in this world was too strong for his dream; a new earth was appended to the new heaven, and became gradually paramount, but this new earth was represented only by the small society of believers who made the body of Christ, the members in which his blood flowed.

That great cauldron of confused superstitions and mysticisms which the Roman Empire became after the overthrow of Jerusalem, formed a thick scum which has passed under the vague name of Gnosticism. The primitive notions of all races were contained in it, however, and they gathered in the second and third centuries a certain consistency in the system of the Ophites. In the beginning existed Bythos (the Depth); his first emanation and consort is Ennoia (Thought); their first daughter is Pneuma (Spirit), their second Sophia (Wisdom). Sophia's emanations are two—one perfect, Christos; the other imperfect, Sophia-Achamoth,—who respectively guide all that proceed from God and all that proceed from Matter. Sophia, unable to act directly upon anything so gross as Matter or unordered as Chaos, employs her imperfect daughter Sophia-Achamoth for that purpose. But she, finding delight in imparting life to inert Matter, became ambitious of creating in the abyss a world for herself. To this end she produced the Demiurgus Ildabaoth (otherwise Jehovah) to be creator of the material world. After this Sophia-Achamoth shook off Matter, in which she had become entangled; but Ildabaoth ('son of Darkness') proceeded to produce emanations corresponding to those of Bythos in the upper universe. Among his creations was Man, but his man was a soulless monster crawling on the ground. Sophia-Achamoth managed to transfer to Man the small ray of divine light which Ildabaoth had inherited from her. The 'primitive Man' became thus a divine being. Ildabaoth, now entirely evil, was enraged at having produced a being who had become superior to himself, and his envy took shape in a serpent-formed Satan, Ophiomorphos. He is the concentration of all that is most base in Matter, conjoined with a spiritual intelligence. Their anti-Judaism led the Ophites to identify Ildabaoth as Jehovah, and this serpent-son of his as Michael; they also called him Samaël. Ildabaoth then also created the animal, vegetable, and mineral kingdoms, with all their evils. Resolving to confine man within his own lower domain, he forbade him to eat of the Tree of Knowledge. To defeat his scheme, which had all been evolved out of her own temporary fall, Sophia-Achamoth sent her own genius, also in form of a serpent, Ophis, to induce Man to transgress the tyrant's command. Eve supposing Ophis the same as Ophiomorphos, regarded the prohibition against the fruit as withdrawn and readily ate of it. Man thus became capable of understanding heavenly mysteries, and Ildabaoth made haste to imprison him in the dungeon of Matter. He also punished Ophis by making him eat dust, and this heavenly serpent, contaminated by Matter, changed from Man's friend to his foe. Sophia-Achamoth has always striven against these two Serpents, who bind man to the body by corrupt desires; she supplied mankind with divine light, through which they became sensible of their nakedness—the misery of their condition. Ildabaoth's seductive agents gained control over all the offspring of Adam except Seth, type of the Spiritual Man. Sophia-Achamoth moved Bythos to send down her perfect brother Christos to aid the Spiritual Race of Seth. Christos descended through the seven planetary regions, assuming successively forms related to each, and entered into the man Jesus at the moment of his baptism. Ildabaoth, discovering him, stirred up the Jews to put him to death; but Christos and Sophia, abandoning the material body of Jesus on the cross, gave him one made of ether. Hence his mother and disciples could not recognise him. He ascended to the Middle Space, where he sits by the right hand of Ildabaoth, though unperceived by the latter, and, putting forth efforts for purification of mankind corresponding to those put forth by Ildabaoth for evil, he is collecting all the Spiritual elements of the world into the kingdom which is to overthrow that of the Enemy.1

Notwithstanding the animosity shown by the Ophites towards the Jews, most of the elements in their system are plagiarised from the Jews. According to ancient rabbinical traditions, Adam and Eve, by eating the fruit of the lowest region, fell through the six regions to the seventh and lowest; they were there brought under control of the previously fallen Samaël, who defiled them with his spittle. Their nakedness consisted in their having lost a natural protection of which only our finger-nails are left; others say they lost a covering of hair.2 The Jews also from of old contended that Seth was the son of Adam, in whom returned the divine nature with which man was originally endowed. We have, indeed, only to identify Ildabaoth with Elohim instead of Jehovah to perceive that the Ophites were following Jewish precedents in attributing the natural world to a fiend. The link between, the two conceptions may be discovered in the writings of Paul. Paul's pessimistic conception of this world and of human nature was radical, and it mainly formed the mould in which dogmatic Christianity subsequently took shape. His general theology is a travesty of the creation of the world and of man. All that work of Elohim was, by implication, natural, that is to say, diabolical. The earth as then created belonged to the Prince of this world, who was the author of sin, and its consequence, death. In Adam all die. The natural man is enmity against God; he is of the earth earthy; his father is the devil; he cannot know spiritual things. All mankind are born spiritually dead. Christ is a new and diviner Demiurgos, engaged in the work of producing a new creation and a new man. For his purpose the old law, circumcision or uncircumcision, are of no avail or importance, but a new creature. His death is the symbol of man's death to the natural world, his resurrection of man's rising into a new world which mere flesh and blood cannot inherit. As God breathed into Adam's nostrils the breath of life, the Spirit breathes upon the elect of Christ a new mind and new heart.

The 'new creature' must inhale an entirely new physical atmosphere. When Paul speaks of 'the Prince of the Power of the Air,' it must not be supposed that he is only metaphorical. On this, however, we must dwell for a little.

'The air,' writes Burton in his 'Anatomy of Melancholy,' 'The air is not so full of flies in summer as it is at all times of invisible devils. They counterfeit suns and moons, and sit on ships' masts. They cause whirlwinds of a sudden, and tempestuous storms, which though our meteorologists generally refer to natural causes, yet I am of Bodine's mind, they are more often caused by those aerial devils in their several quarters. Cardan gives much information concerning them. His father had one of them, an aerial devil, bound to him for eight and twenty years; as Agrippa's dog had a devil tied to his collar. Some think that Paracelsus had one confined in his sword pommel. Others wear them in rings;' and so the old man runs on, speculating about the mysterious cobwebs collected in the ceiling of his brain.

The atmosphere mentally breathed by Burton and his authorities was indeed charged with invisible phantasms; and every one of them was in its origin a genuine intellectual effort to interpret the phenomena of nature. It is not wonderful that the ancients should have ascribed to a diabolical source the subtle deaths that struck at them from the air. A single breath of the invisible poison of the air might lay low the strongest. Even after man had come to understand his visible foes, the deadly animal or plant, he could only cower and pray before the lurking power of miasma and infection, the power of the air. The Tyndalls of a primitive time studied dust and disease, and called the winged seeds of decay and death 'aerial devils,' and prepared the way for Mephistopheles (devil of smells), as he in turn for the bacterial demon of modern science.

There were not wanting theologic explanations why these malignant beings should find their dwelling-place in the air. They had been driven out of heaven. The etherial realm above the air was reserved for the good. Of the demons the Hindus say, 'Their feet touch not the ground.' 'What man of virtue is there,' said Titus to his soldiers, 'who does not know that those souls which are severed from their fleshy bodies in battles by the sword are received by the æther—that

214

purest of elements—and joined to that company which are placed among the stars; that they become gods, dæmons, and propitious heroes, and show themselves as such to their posterity afterwards?'3 Malignant spirits were believed to hold a more undisputed sway over the atmosphere than over the earth, although our planet was mainly in their power, and the subjects of the higher empire always a small colony.4 Moreover, there was a natural tendency of demons, which originally represented earthly evils, when these were conquered by human intelligence, to pass into the realm least accessible to science or to control by man. The uncharted winds became their refuge.

This belief was general among the Christian Fathers,5 lasted a very long time even among the educated, and is still the teaching of the Roman Catholic Church, as any one may see by reading the authorised work of Mgr. Gaume on 'Holy Water' (p. 305). So long as it was admitted among thinking people that the mind was as competent to build facts upon theory as theories on fact, a great deal might be plausibly said for this atmospheric diabolarchy. In the days when witchcraft was first called in question, Glanvil argued 'that since this little Spot is so thickly peopled in every Atome of it, 'tis weakness to think that all the vast spaces Above and hollows under Ground are desert and uninhabited,' and he anticipated that, as microscopic science might reveal further populations in places seemingly vacant, it would necessitate the belief that the regions of the upper air are inhabited.6 Other learned men concluded that the spirits that lodge there are such as are clogged with earthly elements; the baser sort; dwelling in cold air, they would like to inhabit the more sheltered earth. In repayment for broth, and various dietetic horrors proffered them by witches, they enable them to pass freely through their realm—the air.

Out of such intellectual atmosphere came Paul's sentence (Eph. ii. 2) about 'the Prince of the Power of the Air.' It was a spiritualisation of the existing aerial demonology. When Paul and his companions carried their religious agitation into the centres of learning and wealth, and brought the teachings of a Jew to confront the temples of Greece and Rome, they found themselves unrelated to that great world. It had another habit of mind and feeling, and the idea grew in him that it was the spirits of the Satanic world counteracting the spirit sent on earth from the divine world. This animated its fashions, philosophy, science, and literature. He warns the Church at Ephesus that they will need the whole armour of God, because they are wrestling not with mere flesh and blood, but against the rulers of the world's darkness, the evil spirits in high places—that is, in the Air.

Fig. 7.—Adam Signing Contract for his Posterity To Satan.

As heirs of this new nature and new world, with its new atmosphere, purchased and endowed by Christ, the Pauline theory further presupposes, that the natural man, having died, is buried with Christ in baptism, rises with him, and is then sealed to him by the Holy Ghost. For a little time such must still bear about them their fleshy bodies, but soon Christ shall come, and these vile bodies shall be changed into his likeness; meanwhile they must keep their bodies in subjection, even as Paul did, by beating it black and blue (ὑπωπιάζω), and await their deliverance from the body of the dead world they have left, but which so far is permitted to adhere to them. This conception had to work itself out in myths and dogmas of which Paul knew nothing. 'If any man come after me and hate not his father and mother, and his own (natural) life also, he cannot be my disciple.' The new race with which the new creation was in travail was logically discovered to need a new Mother as well as a new Father. Every natural mother was subjected to a stain that it might be affirmed that only one mother was immaculate—she whose conception was supernatural, not of the flesh. Marriage became an indulgence to sin (whose purchase-money survives still in the marriage-fee). The monastery and the nunnery represented this new ascetic kingdom; that perilous word 'worldliness' was transmitted to be the source of insanity and hypocrisy.

Happily, the common sense and sentiment of mankind have so steadily and successfully won back the outlawed interests of life and the world, that it requires some research into ecclesiastical archæology to comprehend the original significance of the symbols in which it survives. The ancient rabbins limited the number of souls which hang on Adam to 600,000, but the Christian theologians extended the figures to include the human race. Probably even some orthodox people may be scandalised at the idea of the fathers (Irenæus, for example), that, at the Fall, the human race became Satan's rightful property, did they see it in the picture copied by Buslaef, from an ancient Russian Bible, in possession of Count Uvarof. Adam gives Satan a written contract for himself and his descendants (Fig. 7). And yet, according to a recent statement, the Rev. Mr. Simeon recently preached a sermon in the Church of St. Augustine, Kilburn, London, 'to prove that the ruler of the world is the devil. He stated that the Creator of the world had given the control of the world to one of his chief angels, Lucifer, who, however, had gone to grief, and done his utmost to ruin the world. Since then the Creator and Lucifer had been continually striving to checkmate each other. As Lucifer is still the Prince of this world, it would seem that it is not he who has been beaten yet.'7 A popular preacher in America, Rev. Dr. Talmage, states the case as follows:—

'I turn to the same old book, and I find out that the Son of Mary, who was the Son of God, the darling of heaven, the champion of the ages, by some called Lord, by some called Jesus, by others called Christ, but this morning by us called by the three blessed titles, Lord Jesus Christ, by one magnificent stroke made it possible for us all to be saved. He not only told us that there was a hell, but he went into it. He walked down the fiery steeps. He stepped off the bottom rung of the long ladder of despair. He descended into hell. He put his bare foot on the hottest coal of the fiercest furnace.

'He explored the darkest den of eternal midnight, and then He came forth lacerated and scarified, and bleeding and mauled by the hands of infernal excruciation, to cry out to all the ages, 'I have paid the price for all those who would make me their substitute. By my piled-up groans, by my omnipotent agony, I demand the rescue of all those who will give up sin and trust in me,' Mercy! mercy! mercy! But how am I to get it? Cheap. It will not cost you as much as a loaf of bread. Only a penny? No, no. Escape from hell, and all the harps, and mansions, and thrones, and sunlit fields of heaven besides in the bargain, 'without money, and without price.''

These preachers are only stating with creditable candour the original significance of the sacraments and ceremonies which were the physiognomy of that theory of 'a new creature.' Following various ancient traditions, that life was produced out of water, that water escaped the primal curse on nature, that devils hate and fear it because of this and the saltness of so much of it, many religions have used water for purification and exorcism.8 Baptism is based on the notion that every child is offspring of the Devil, and possessed of his demon; the Fathers agreed that all unbaptized babes, even the still-born, are lost; and up to the year 1550 every infant was subjected at baptism to the exorcism, 'I command thee, unclean spirit, in the name of the Father, of the Son, and of the Holy Ghost, that thou come out, and depart from, these infants whom our Lord Jesus Christ has vouchsafed to call to his holy baptism, to be made members of his body and of his holy congregation,' etc.

A clergyman informed me that he knew of a case in which a man, receiving back his child after christening, kissed it, and said, 'I never kissed it before, because I knew it was not a child of God; but now that it is, I love it dearly.' But why not? Some even now teach that a white angel follows the baptized, a black demon the unbaptized.

The belief was wide-spread that unbaptized children were turned into elves at death. In Iceland it is still told as a bit of folk-lore, that when God visited Eve, she kept a large number of her children out of sight, 'because they had not been washed,' and these children were turned into elves, and became the progenitors of that uncanny race. The Greek Church made so much of baptism, that there has been developed an Eastern sect which claims John the Baptist as its founder, making little of Christ, who baptized none; and to this day in Russia the peasant regards it as almost essential to a right reception of the benedictions of Sunday to have been under water on the previous day—soap being sagaciously added. The Roman Catholic Church, following the provision of the Council of Carthage, still sets a high value on baptismal exorcism; and Calvin refers to a theological debate at the Sorbonne in Paris, whether it would not be justifiable for a priest to throw a child into a well rather than have it die unbaptized. Luther preserved the Catholic form of exorcism; and, in some districts of Germany, Protestants have still such faith in it, that, when either a child or a domestic animal is suspected of being possessed, they will send for the Romish priest to perform the rite of exorcism.

Mr. Herbert Spencer has described the class of superstitions out of which the sacrament of the Eucharist has grown. 'In some cases,' he says, 'parts of the dead are swallowed by the living, who seek thus to inspire themselves with the good qualities of the dead; and we saw (§ 133) that the dead are supposed to be honoured by this act. The implied notion was supposed to be associated with the further notion that the nature of another being, inhering in all the fragments of his body, inheres too in the unconsumed part of anything consumed with his body; so that an operation wrought on the remnants of his food becomes an operation wrought on the food swallowed, and therefore on the swallower. Yet another implication is, that between those who swallow different parts of the same food some community of nature is established. Hence such beliefs as that ascribed by Bastian to some negroes, who think that, 'on eating and drinking consecrated food, they eat and drink the god himself'—such god being an ancestor, who has taken his share. Various ceremonies among savages are prompted by this conception; as, for instance, the choosing a totem. Among the Mosquito Indians, 'the manner of obtaining this guardian was to proceed to some secluded spot and offer up a sacrifice: with the beast or bird which thereupon appeared, in dream or in reality, a compact for life was made, by drawing blood from various parts of the body.' This blood, supposed to be taken by the chosen animal, connected the two, and the animal's life became so bound up with their own that the death of one involved that of the other.'9 And now mark that, in these same regions, this idea reappears as a religious observance. Sahagun and Herrera describe a ceremony of the Aztecs called 'eating the god.' Mendieta, describing this ceremony, says, 'They had also a sort of eucharist.... They made a sort of small idols of seeds, ... and ate them as the body or memory of their gods.' As the seeds were cemented partly by the blood of sacrificed boys; as their gods were cannibal gods; as Huitzilopochtli, whose worship included this rite, was the god to whom human sacrifices were most extensive; it is clear that the aim was to establish community with gods by taking blood in common.'10

When, a little time ago, a New Zealand chief showed his high appreciation of a learned German by eating his eyes to improve his own intellectual vision, the case seemed to some to call for more and better protected missionaries; but the chief might find in the sacramental communion of the missionaries the real principle of his faith. The celebration of the 'Lord's Supper' when a Bishop is ordained has only to be 'scratched,' as the proverb says, to reveal beneath it the Indians choosing their episcopal totem. As Israel observed the Passover—eating together of the lamb whose blood sprinkled on their door-posts had marked those to be preserved from the Destroying Angel in Egypt—they who believed that Jesus was Messias tasted the body and blood of their Head, as indicating the elect out of a world otherwise given over to the Destroyer spiritually, and finally to be delivered up to him bodily. 'He that eateth my flesh and drinketh my blood dwelleth in me and I in him.' These were to tread on serpents, or handle them unharmed, as it is said Paul did. They were not really to die, but to fall asleep, that they might be changed as a seed to its flower, through literal resurrection from the earth.

We should probably look in vain after any satisfactory vestiges of the migration of the superstition concerning the mystical potency of food. It is found fully developed in the ancient Hindu myth of the struggle between the gods and demons for the Amrita, the immortalising nectar, one stolen sip of which gave the monster Ráhu the imperishable nature which no other of his order possesses. It is found in corresponding myths concerning the gods of Asgard and of Olympus. The fall of man in the Iranian legend was through a certain milk given by Ahriman to the first pair, Meschia and Meschiane. In Buddhist mythology, it was eating rice that corrupted the nature of man. It was the process of incarnation in the Gilghit legend (i. 398). The whole story of Persephone turns upon her having eaten the seed of a pomegranate in Hades, by which she was bound to that sphere. There is a myth very similar to that of Persephone in Japan. There is a legend in the Scottish Highlands that a woman was conveyed into the secret recesses of the 'men of peace'—the Daoine Shi', euphemistic name of uncanny beings, who carry away mortals to their subterranean apartments, where beautiful damsels tempt them to eat of magnificent banquets. This woman on her arrival was recognised by a former acquaintance, who, still retaining some portion of human benevolence, warned her that, if she tasted anything whatsoever for a certain space of time, she would be doomed to remain in that underworld for ever. The woman having taken this counsel, was ultimately restored to the society of mortals. It was added that, when the period named by her unfortunate friend had elapsed, a disenchantment of this woman's eyes took place, and the viands which had before seemed so tempting she now discovered to consist only of the refuse of the earth.11

Fig. 8.—Seth Offering a Branch to Adam.

The difficulty of tracing the ethnical origin of such legends as these is much greater than that of tracing their common natural origin. The effect of certain kinds of food upon the human system is very marked, even apart from the notorious effects of the drinks made from the vegetative world. The effects of mandrake, opium, tobacco, various semi-poisonous fungi, the simplicity with which differences of race might be explained by their vegetarian or carnivorous customs, would be enough to suggest theories of the potency of food over the body and soul of man such as even now have their value in scientific speculation.

The Jewish opinion that Seth was the offspring of the divine part of Adam was the germ of a remarkable christian myth. Adam, when dying, desired Seth to procure the oil of mercy (for his extreme unction) from the angels guarding Paradise. Michael informs Seth that it can only be obtained after the lapse of the ages intervening the Fall and the Atonement. Seth received, however, a small branch of the Tree of Knowledge, and was told that when it should bear fruit, Adam would recover. Returning, Seth found Adam dead, and planted the branch in his grave. It grew to a tree which Solomon had hewn down for building the temple; but the workmen could not adapt it, threw it aside, and it was used as a bridge over a lake. The Queen of Sheba, about to cross this lake, beheld a vision of Christ on the cross, and informed Solomon that when a certain person had been suspended on that tree the fall of the Jewish nation would be near. Solomon in alarm buried the wood deep in the earth, and the spot was covered by the pool of Bethesda. Shortly before the crucifixion the tree floated on that water, and ultimately, as the cross, bore its fruit.12

In our old Russian picture (Fig. 8) Seth is shown offering a branch of the Tree of Knowledge to his father Adam. That it should spring up to be the Tree of Life is simply in obedience to Magian and Gnostic theories, which generally turn on some scheme by which the Good turns against the Evil Mind the point of his own weapon. These were the influences which gave to christian doctrines on the subject their perilous precision. The universal tradition was that Adam was the first person liberated by Christ from hell; and this corresponded with an equally wide belief that all who were saved by the death of Christ and his descent into hell were at once raised into the moral condition of Adam and Eve before the Fall,—to eat the food and breathe the holy air of Paradise.

An honest mirror was held up before this theology by the christian Adamites. Their movement (second and third centuries) was a most legitimate outcome of the Pauline and Johannine gospel. The author of this so-called 'heresy,' Prodicus, really anticipated the Methodist doctrine of 'sanctification,' and he was only consistent in admonishing his followers that clothing was, in the Bible, the original badge of carnal guilt and shame, and was no longer necessary for those whom Christ had redeemed from the Fall and raised to the original innocence of Adam and Eve. These believers, in the appropriate climate of Northern Africa, had no difficulty in carrying out their doctrine practically, and having named their churches 'Paradises,' assembled in them quite naked. There is still a superstition in the East that a snake will never attack one who is naked. The same Adamite doctrine—a prelapsarian perfection symbolised by nudity—was taught by John Picard in Bohemia, and a flourishing sect of 'Adamites' arose there in the fifteenth century. The Slavonian Adamites of the last century—and they are known to carry on their services still in secret—not only dispense with clothing, but

218

also with sacraments and ceremonies, which are for the imperfect, not for the perfected. Again and again has this logical result of the popular theology appeared, and with increasingly gross circumstances, as the refined and intelligent abandon except in name the corresponding dogmas. It is an impressive fact that Paul's central doctrine of 'a new creature' is now adopted with most realistic orthodoxy by the Mormons of Utah, whose initiation consists of a dramatic performance on each candidate of moulding the body out of clay, breathing in the nostrils, the 'deep sleep' presentation of an Eve to each Adam, the temptation, fall, and redemption. The 'saints' thus made, unfortunately, seem to have equally realistic ideas that the Gentiles are adherents of the Prince of this world, and their sacramental bands have shown some striking imitations of those events of history which, when not labelled 'Christian,' are pronounced barbarous. Now that the old dogmatic system is being left more and more to the ignorant and vulgar to make over into their own image and likeness, it may be hoped that elsewhere also the error that libels and outrages nature will run to seed; for error, like the aloe, has its period when it shoots up a high stem and—dies.

Notes

1 The relations of this system to those of various countries are stated by Professor King in his work 'The Gnostics and their Remains.'

2 In the Architectural Museum, Westminster, there is an old picture which possibly represents the hairy Adam.

3 Josephus; 'Wars of the Jews,' vi. 1.

4 Those who wish to pursue the subject may consult Plutarch, Philo, Josephus, Diog. Laertius; also Eisenmenger, Wetstein, Elsner, Doughtæi, Lightfoot, Sup. Relig., etc.

5 See 'Supernatural Religion,' vol. i. ch. 4 and 5, for ample references concerning these superstitions among both Jews and Christians.

6 'Saducismus,' p. 53.

7 'Eastern Morning News,' quoted in the 'National Reformer,' December 17, 1877.

8 Much curious information is contained in the work already referred to, 'L'Eau Benite au Dix-neuvième Siècle.' Par Monsignor Gaume, Protonotaire Apostolique. Paris, 1866. It is there stated that water escaped the curse; that salt produces fecundity; that devils driven off temporarily by the cross are effectually dismissed by holy water; that St. Vincent, interrupted by a storm while preaching, dispersed it by throwing holy water at it; and he advises the use of holy water against the latest devices of the devil—spirit-rapping. It must not, however, be supposed that these notions are confined to Catholics. Every element in the disquisition of Monsignor Gaume is represented in the region where his church is most hated. Mr. James Napier, in his recent book on Folklore, shows us the Scotch hastening new-born babes to baptism lest they become 'changelings,' and the true meaning of the rite is illustrated in a reminiscence of his own childhood. He was supposed to be pining under an Evil Eye, and the old woman, or 'skilly,' called in, carefully locked the door, now unlocked by her patient, and proceeded as follows:— 'A sixpence was borrowed from a neighbour, a good fire was kept burning in the grate, the door was locked, and I was placed upon a chair in front of the fire. The operator, an old woman, took a tablespoon and filled it with water. With the sixpence she then lifted as much salt as it would carry, and both were put into the water in the spoon. The water was then stirred with the forefinger till the salt was dissolved. Then the soles of my feet and the palms of my hands were bathed with this solution thrice, and after these bathings I was made to taste the solution three times. The operator then drew her wet forefinger across my brow—called scoring aboon the breath. The remaining contents of the spoon she then cast right over the fire, into the hinder part of the fire, saying as she did so, 'Guid preserve frae a' skaith.' These were the first words permitted to be spoken during the operation. I was then put in bed, and, in attestation of the charm, recovered. To my knowledge this operation has been performed within these forty years, and probably in many outlying country places it is still practised. The origin of this superstition is probably to be found in ancient fire-worship. The great blazing fire was evidently an important element in the transaction; nor was this a solitary instance in which regard was paid to the fire. I remember being taught that it was unlucky to spit into the fire, some evil being likely shortly after to befall those who did so. Crumbs left upon the table after a meal were carefully gathered and put into the fire. The cuttings from the nails and hair were also put into the fire. These freaks certainly look like survivals of fire-worship.' It may be well here to refer the reader to what has been said in vol. i. on Demons of Fire. The Devil's fear of salt and consequently of water confirmed the perhaps earlier apprehension of all fiery phantoms of that which naturally quenches flame.

9 We here get a clue to the origin of various strange ceremonies by which men bind themselves to one another. Michelet, in his 'Origines du Droit Français,' writes: 'Boire le sang l'un de l'autre, c'etait pour ainsi dire se faire même chair. Ce symbole si expressif se trouve chez un grand nombre de peuples;' and he gives instances from various ancient races. But, as we here see, this practice is not originally adopted as a symbol (no practices begin as symbols), but is prompted by the belief that a community of nature is thus established, and a community of power over one another.

10 'Principles of Sociology,' i. ch. xix. Origen says, that a man eats and drinks with demons when he eats flesh and drinks wine offered to idols. (Contra Cels. viii. 31.)

11 Dr. James Browne's 'History of the Highlands,' ed. 1855, i. 108.

12 'Aurea Legenda.' The story, as intertwined with that of the discovery of the true cross by the Empress Helena, was a fruitful theme for artists. It has been painted in various versions by Angiolo Gaddi in S. Croce at Florence, by Pietro della Francesca at Arezzo, and in S. Croce in Ger. at Rome are frescoes celebrating Helena in a chapel named from her, but into which persons of her sex are admitted only once a year.

Chapter XX - The Holy Ghost

A Hanover relic—Mr. Atkinson on the Dove—The Dove in the Old Testament—Ecclesiastical symbol—Judicial symbol—A vision of St. Dunstan's—The witness of chastity—Dove and Serpent—The unpardonable sin—Inexpiable sin among the Jews—Destructive power of Jehovah—Potency of the breath—Third persons of Trinities—Pentecost—Christian superstitions—Mr. Moody on the sin against the Holy Ghost—Mysterious fear—Idols of the cave.

There is in the old town of Hanover, in Germany, a schoolhouse in which, above the teacher's chair, there was anciently the representation of a dove perched upon an iron branch or rod; and beneath the inscription—'This shall lead you into all truth.' In the course of time the dove fell down and was removed to the museum; but there is still left before the children the rod, with the admonition that it will lead them into all truth. This is about as much as for a long time was left in the average christian mind of the symbolical Dove, the Holy Ghost. Half of its primitive sense departed, and there remained only an emblem of mysterious terror. More spiritual minds have introduced into the modern world a conception of the Holy Ghost as a life-giving influence or a spirit of love, but the ancient view which regarded it as the Iron Rod of judgment and execution still survives in the notion of the 'sin against the Holy Ghost.'

Mr. Henry G. Atkinson writes as follows:[1]—'My old friend Barry Cornwall, the fine poet, once said to me, 'My dear Atkinson, can you tell me the meaning of the Holy Ghost; what can it possibly mean?' 'Well,' I said, 'I suppose it means a pigeon. We have never heard of it in any other form but that of the dove descending from heaven to the Virgin Mary. Then we have the pretty fable of the dove returning to the ark with the olive-branch, so that the Christian religion may be called the Religion of the Pigeon. In the Greek Church the pigeon is held sacred. St. Petersburgh is swarming with pigeons, but they are never killed or disturbed. I knew a lady whose life was made wretched in the belief that she had sinned the unpardonable sin against the Holy Ghost, and neither priest nor physician could persuade her out of the delusion, though in all other respects she was quite sensible. She regarded herself as such a wretch that she could not bear to see herself in the glass, and the looking-glasses had all to be removed, and when she went to an hotel, her husband had to go first and have the looking-glasses of the apartments covered over. But what is the Holy Ghost—what is its office? Sitting with Miss Martineau at her house at Ambleside one day, a German lady, who spoke broken English, came in. She was a neighbour, and had a large house and grounds, and kept fowls. 'Oh!' she said, quite excited, 'the beast has taken off another chicken (meaning the hawk). I saw it myself. The wretch! it came down just like the Holy Ghost, and snatched off the chicken.' How Miss Martineau did laugh; but I don't know that this story throws much light upon the subject, since it does but bring us back to the pigeon.'

It would require a volume to explain fully all the problems suggested in this brief note, but the more important facts may be condensed.

It is difficult to show how far the natural characteristics and habits of the dove are reflected in its wide-spread symbolism. Its plaintive note and fondness for solitudes are indicated in the Psalmist's aspiration, 'Oh that I had the wings of a dove, then would I fly away and be at rest; lo, then would I wander far off, and remain in the wilderness.'[2] It is not a difficult transition from this association with the wilderness to investment with a relationship with the demon of the wilderness—Azazel. So we find it in certain passages in Jeremiah, where the word has been suppressed in the ordinary English version. 'The land is desolate because of the fierceness of the dove.' 'Let us go again to our own people to avoid the sword of the dove.' 'They shall flee away every one for fear of the sword of the dove.'[3] In India its lustres—blue and fiery—may have connected it with azure-necked Siva.

The far-seeing and wonderful character of the pigeon as a carrier was well known to the ancients. On Egyptian bas-reliefs priests are shown sending them with messages. They appear in the branches of the oaks of Dodona, and in old Russian frescoes they sometimes perch on the Tree of Knowledge in paradise. It is said that, in order to avail himself of this universal symbolism, Mohammed trained a dove to perch on his shoulder. As the raven was said to whisper secrets to Odin, so the dove was often pictured at the ear of God. In Nôtre Dame de Chartres, its beak is at the ear of Pope Gregory the Great.

It passed—and did not have far to go—to be the familiar of kings. It brought the chrism from heaven at the baptism of Clovis. White doves came to bear the soul of Louis of Thuringia to heaven. The dove surmounted the sceptre of Charlemagne. At the consecration of the kings of France, after the ceremony of unction, white doves were let loose in the church. At the consecration of a monarch in England, a duke bears before the sovereign the sceptre with the dove.

By association with both ecclesiastical and political sovereignty, it came to represent very nearly the old fatal serpent power which had lurked in all its transformations. When the Holy Ghost was represented as a crowned man, the dove was pictured on his wrist like that falcon with which the German lady, mentioned by Mr. Atkinson, identified it. But in this connection its symbolism is more especially referable to a passage in Isaiah:[4] 'There shall come forth a rod out of the stem of Jesse, and a branch shall grow out of his roots; and the Spirit of the Lord shall rest upon him, the spirit of wisdom and understanding, the spirit of counsel and might, the spirit of the knowledge and of the fear of the Lord.' The sanctity of the number seven led to the partition of the last clause into three spirits, making up the seven, which were: Wisdom, Understanding, Counsel, Strength, Knowledge, Piety, Fear. In some of the representations of these where each of the seven Doves is labelled with its name, 'Fear' is at the top of their arch, a Psalm having said, 'The fear of the Lord is the beginning of wisdom.' When the knightly Order of the Holy Ghost was created in 1352, it was aristocratic, and, when reorganised by Henry III. of France in 1579, it was restricted to magisterial and political personages. With them was the spirit of Fear certainly; and the Order shows plainly what had long been the ideas connected with the Holy Ghost.

M. Didron finds this confirmed in the legends of every country, and especially refers to a story of St. Dunstan, Archbishop of Canterbury, in the tenth century. Three men, convicted of coining false money, had been condemned to death. Immediately before the celebration of mass on the day of Pentecost, the festival of the Holy Ghost, St. Dunstan inquired whether justice had been done upon the three criminals: he was informed in reply that the execution had been delayed on account of the solemn feast of Pentecost then in celebration. 'It shall not be thus,' cried the indignant archbishop, and gave orders for the immediate execution of the guilty men. Several of those who were present remonstrated against the cruelty of that order; it was nevertheless obeyed.

After the execution of the criminals, Dunstan washed his face, and turned with a joyful countenance towards his oratory. 'I now hope,' said he, 'that God will be pleased to accept the sacrifice I am about to offer;' and in fact, during the celebration of mass, at the moment when the Saint raised his hands to implore that God the Father would be pleased to give peace to his Church, to guide, guard, and keep it in unity throughout the world, 'a dove, as white as snow, was seen to descend from heaven, and during the entire service remained with wings extended, floating silently in air above the head of the archbishop.'5

The passionate sexual nature of the dove made it emblem of Aphrodite, and it became spiritualised in its consecration to the Madonna. From its relation to the falsely-accused Mary, there grew around the Dove a special class of legends which show it attesting female innocence or avenging it. The white dove said to have issued from the mouth of Joan of Arc is one of many instances. There is still, I believe, preserved in the Lyttleton family the picture painted by Dowager Lady Lyttleton in 1780, in commemoration of the warning of death given to Lord Lyttleton by the mother of two girls he had seduced, the vision being attended by a fluttering dove. The original account of his vision or dream, attributed to Lord Lyttleton, mentions only 'a bird.' When next told, it is that he 'heard a noise resembling the fluttering of a dove,' and on looking to the window saw 'an unhappy female whom he had seduced.' But the exigencies of orthodoxy are too strong for original narratives. As the 'bird' attested an announcement that on the third day (that too was gradually added) he would die, it must have been a dove; and as the dove attends only the innocent, it must have been the poor girl's mother that appeared. It was easy to have the woman die at the precise hour of appearance.6 When in Chicago in 1875, I read in one of the morning papers a very particular account of how a white dove flew into the chamber window of a young unmarried woman in a neighbouring village, she having brought forth a child, and solemnly declaring that she had never lost her virginity.

In this history of the symbolism of the Dove the theological development of the Holy Ghost has been outlined. We have seen in the previous chapter that the Holy Spirit is in opposition to the Natural Air,—repository of evils. The Dove symbolised this aspect of it in hovering over the world emerging from its diluvial baptism, and also over the typical new Adam (Jesus) coming from his baptism. But in this it corresponds with the serpent-symbol of life in Egyptian mythology brooding over the primal mundane egg (as in Fig. 23, vol. i.). Nathaniel Hawthorne found a mystical meaning in the beautiful group at Rome representing a girl pressing a dove to her bosom while she is attacked by a serpent. But in their theological aspects the Dove and the Serpent blend; they are at once related and separated in Christ's words, 'Be ye wise as serpents and harmless as doves;' but in the office of the Holy Ghost as representing a divine Intelligence, and its consequent evolution as executor of divine judgments, it fulfils in Christendom much the same part as the Serpent in the more primitive mythologies.

'Every sin and blasphemy will be forgiven unto men,' said a legendary Christ;7 'but the blasphemy against the Spirit will not be forgiven. And whosoever shall speak a word against the Son of man, it will be forgiven him, but whosoever shall speak against the Holy Ghost, it will not be forgiven him, neither in this world nor in that to come.' In Mark8 it is said, 'All things shall be forgiven unto the sons of men, the sins and the blasphemies wherewith they shall blaspheme: but whosoever shall blaspheme against the Holy Ghost has never forgiveness, but will be guilty of everlasting sin; (because they said, He has an unclean spirit).' When Christ uttered these tremendous words, no disciple seems to have been startled, or to have inquired into the nature of that sin, so much worse than any offence against himself or the Father, which has since employed so much theological speculation.

In fact, they needed no explanation: it was an old story; the unpardonable sin was a familiar feature of ancient Jewish law. Therein the sin excluded from expiation was any presumptuous language or action against Jehovah. It is easy to see why this was so. Real offences, crimes against man or society, were certain of punishment, through the common interest and need. But the honour and interests of Jehovah, not being obvious or founded in nature, required special and severe statutes. The less a thing is protected by its intrinsic and practical importance, the more it must, if at all, be artificially protected. This is illustrated in the story of Eli and his two sons. These youths were guilty of the grossest immoralities, but not a word was said against them, they being sons of the High Priest, except a mild remonstrance from Eli himself. But when on an occasion these youths tasted the part of the sacrificial meat offered to Jehovah, the divine wrath was kindled. Eli, much more terrified at this ceremonial than the moral offence, said to his sons, 'If one man sin against another, the judge shall judge him, but if a man sin against Jehovah, who shall entreat for him?' In protecting his interests, Jehovah's destroying angel does not allude to any other offence of Eli's sons except that against himself. But when the priestly guardians of the divine interests came with their people under the control of successive Gallios,—aliens who cared not for their ceremonial law, and declined to permit the infliction of its penalties, as England now forbids suttee in India,—the priests could only pass sentences; execution of them had to be adjourned to a future world.

The doctrine of a future state of rewards and punishments is not one which a priesthood would naturally prefer or invent. So long as a priesthood possesses the power of life and death over the human body, they would not, by suggesting future awards, risk the possibility of a heresy arising to maintain Deorum injuria diis cura. But where an alien jurisdiction has relegated to local deities the defence of their own majesty, there must grow up the theory that such offences as cannot be expiated on earth are unpardonable, and must, because of the legal impunity with which they can be committed, be all the more terribly avenged somewhere else.

Under alien influences, also, the supreme and absolute government of Jehovah had been divided, as is elsewhere described. He who originally claimed the empire of both light and darkness, good and evil, when his rivalry against other gods was on a question of power, had to be relieved of responsibility for earthly evils when the moral sense demanded dualism. Thus there grew up a separate personification of the destructive power of Jehovah, which had been supposed to lodge in his breath. The last breath of man obviously ends life; there is nothing more simple in its natural germ than the association of the first breath and the last with the Creative Spirit.9 This potency of the breath or spirit is found in many ancient regions. It is the natural teaching of the destructive simoom,10 or even of the annual autumnal breath which strikes the foliage with death. Persia especially abounded with superstitions of this character. By a sorcerer's breath the two serpents were evoked from the breast of Zohák. Nizami has woven the popular notion into his story of the two physicians who tried to destroy each other; one of whom survived his rival's poisonous draught, and killed that rival by making him smell a flower on which he had breathed.11 Such notions as these influenced powerfully the later development of the idea of Jehovah, concerning whom it was said of old, 'With the breath of his mouth shall he slay the wicked;' 'the breath of the Lord like a stream of brimstone doth kindle (Tophet).'

Meanwhile in all the Trinitarian races which were to give form to christian Mythology, destructiveness had generally (not invariably) become the traditional rôle of the Third Person.12 In Egypt there were Osiris the Creator, Horus the Preserver, Typhon the Destroyer; in Babylonia, Anu the Upper Air, Sin (Uri) the Moon, Samis the Sun. In Assyria the Sun regains his place, and deadly influences were ascribed to the Moon. In India, Brahma the Father, Vishnu the Saviour, Siva the Destroyer; in Persia, Zeruâne-Akrane Infinite Time, Ormuzd the Good, Ahriman the Evil; in Greece Zeus, Poseidôn, and Hadês, or Heaven, Ocean, and Hell, were the first-born of Time. The Trinitarian form had gradually crept in among the Jews, though their Jahvistic theology only admitted its application to inferior deities—Cain, Abel, Seth; Moses, Aaron, Hur; Abraham, Isaac, Jacob. As time went on, these succeeded the ideas of Jehovah, Messias, and Wisdom. But already the serpent was the wisest of all the beasts of the field in Jewish mythology; and the personified Wisdom was fully prepared to be identified with Athene, the Greek Wisdom, who sprang armed from the head of Zeus (the Air), and whose familiar was a serpent.

On the other hand, however, the divine Breath had also its benign significance. Siva ('the auspicious') inherited the character of Rudra ('roaring storm'), but it was rather supported later on by his wife Káli. Athena though armed was the goddess of agriculture. The breath of Elohim had given man life. 'I now draw in and now let forth,' says Krishna;13 'I am generation and dissolution; I am death and immortality.' 'Thou wilt fancy it the dawning zephyr of an early spring,' says Sàdi; 'but it is the breath of Isa, or Jesus; for in that fresh breath and verdure the dead earth is reviving.'14 'The voice of the turtle is heard in the land,' sings Solomon.

When the Third Person of the Christian Trinity was constituted, it inherited the fatality of all the previous Third Persons—the Destroyers—while it veiled them in mystery. When the Holy Ghost inspired the disciples the account is significant.15 'Suddenly there came a sound from heaven as of a rushing mighty wind, ... and there appeared unto them cloven tongues like as of fire, and it sat upon each of them. And they were all filled with the Holy Ghost.' This was on the Day of Pentecost, the harvest festival, when the first-fruits were offered to the quickening Spirit or Breath of nature; but the destructive feature is there also—the tongues are cloven like those of serpents. The beneficent power was manifest at the gate called Beautiful when the lame man was made to walk by Peter's power; but its fatal power was with the same apostle, and when he said, 'Why hath Satan filled thy heart to lie to the Holy Ghost?' instantly Ananias fell down and gave up the ghost.16 The spirit was carried, it is said, in the breath of the apostles. Its awfulness had various illustrations. Mary offered up two doves in token of her conception by the Holy Ghost. Jesus is described as scourging from the temple those that sold doves, and the allegory is repeated in Peter's denunciation of Simon Magus, who offered money for the gift of the Holy Ghost.17

In one of his sermons Mr. Moody said, 'Nearly every day we have somebody coming into the inquiry-room very much discouraged and disheartened and cast down, because they think they have committed a sin against the Holy Ghost, and that there is no hope for them.' Mr. Moody said he believed the sin was nearly impossible, but he adds this remarkable statement, 'I don't remember of ever hearing a man swear by the Holy Ghost except once, and then I looked upon him expecting him to fall dead, and my blood ran cold when I heard him.' But it is almost as rare to hear prayers addressed to the Holy Ghost; and both phenomena—for praying and swearing are radically related—are no doubt survivals of the ancient notions which I have described. The forces of nature out of which the symbol grew, the life that springs from death and grows by decay, is essentially repeated again by those who adhere to the letter that kills, and also by those who ascend with the spirit that makes alive. It is probable that no more terrible form of the belief in a Devil survives than this Holy Ghost Dogma, which, lurking in vagueness and mystery, like the serpent of which it was born, passes by the self-righteous to cast its shadows over the most sensitive and lowly minds, chiefly those of pure women prone to exaggerate their least blemishes.

In right reason the fatal Holy Ghost stands as the type of that Fear by which priesthoods have been able to preserve their institutions after the deities around whom they grew had become unpresentable, and which could best be fostered beneath the veil of mystery. They who love darkness rather than light because their deeds cannot bear the light, veil their gods not to abolish them but to preserve them. Calvinism is veiled, and Athanasianism, and Romanism; they are all veiled idols, whose power lives by being hid in a mass of philology and casuistry. So long as Christianity can persuade the Pope and Dr. Martineau, Dean Stanley and Mr. Moody, Quakers, Shakers, Jumpers, all to describe themselves alike as 'Christians,' its real nature will be veiled, its institutions will cumber the ground, and draw away the strength and intellect due to humanity; the indefinable 'infidel' will be a devil. This process has been going on for a long time. The serpent-god, accursed by the human mind which grew superior to it, has crept into its Ark; but its fang and venom linger with that Bishop breathing on a priest, the priest breathing on a sick child, and bears down side by side with science that atmosphere of mystery in which creep all the old reptiles that throttle common sense and send their virus through all the social frame.

In demonology the Holy Ghost is not a Devil, but in it are reflected the diabolisation of Culture and Progress and Art. It was these 'Devils' which compelled the gods to veil themselves through successive ages, and to spiritualise their idols and dogmas to save their institutions. The deities concealed have proved far more potent over the popular imagination than when visible. The indefinable terrible menace of the Holy Ghost was a consummate reply to that equally indefinable spirit of loathing and contempt which rises among the cultured and refined towards things that have become unreal, their formalities and their cant. It is this ever-recurring necessity that enables clergymen to denounce belief in Hell and a Devil in churches which assuredly would never have been built but for the superstition so denounced. The ancient beliefs and the present denunciation of them are on the same thread,—the determination of a Church to survive and hold its power at any and every cost. The jesuitical power to veil the dogma is the most successful method of confronting the Spirit of an Age, which in the eye of reason is the only holy spirit, but which to ecclesiastical power struggling with enlightenment is the only formidable Satan.

Notes

1 *To the 'Secular Chronicle,' February 11, 1877.*

2 *Psalm lv.*

3 *Jer. xxv. 38; xlvi. 16; l. 16.*

4 *Isaiah xi. 2, 3.*

5 *The more fatal aspect of the dove has tended to invest the pigeon, especially wild pigeons, which in Oldenburg, and many other regions, are supposed to bode calamity and death if they fly round a house.*

6 *Sir Nathaniel Wraxall's Memoirs.*

7 *Matt. xii. 31.*

8 *Mark iii. 28.*

9 *I have before me an account by a christian mother of the death of her child, whom she had dedicated to the Lord before his birth, in which she says, 'A full breath issued from his mouth like an etherial flame, a slight quiver of the lip, and all was over.'*

10 *'Serpent poison.' It is substantially the same word as the demonic Samaël. The following is from Colonel Campbell's 'Travels,' ii. p. 130:—'It was still the hot season of the year, and we were to travel through that country over which the horrid wind I have before mentioned sweeps its consuming blasts; it is called by the Turks Samiel, is mentioned by the holy Job under the name of the East wind, and extends its ravages all the way from the extreme end of the Gulf of Cambaya up to Mosul; it carries along with it flakes of fire, like threads of silk; instantly strikes dead those that breathe it, and consumes them inwardly to ashes; the flesh soon becoming black as a coal, and dropping off the bones. Philosophers consider it as a kind of electric fire, proceeding from the sulphurous or nitrous exhalations which are kindled by the agitations of the winds. The only possible means of escape from its fatal effects is to fall flat on the ground, and thereby prevent the drawing it in; to do this, however, it is necessary first to see it, which is not always practicable.'*

11 The 'Sacred Anthology,' p. 425. Nizami uses his fable to illustrate the effect of even an innocent flower on one whom conscience has made a coward.

12 Nothing is more natural than the Triad: the regions which may be most simply distinguished are the Upper, Middle, and Lower.

13 Bhàgavàt-Gita.

14 Gulistan.

15 Acts ii.

16 Compare Gen. vi. 3. Jehovah said, 'My breath shall not always abide in man.'

17 Among the many survivals in civilised countries of these notions may be noticed the belief that, in order to be free from a spell it is necessary to draw blood from the witch above the breath, i.e., mouth and nostrils; to 'score aboon the breath' is a Scottish phrase. This probably came by the 'pagan' route; but it meets its christian kith and kin in the following story which I find in a (MS.) Memorial sent to the House of Lords in 1869 by the Rev. Thomas Berney, Rector of Bracon Ash, Diocese of Norwich:– 'I was sent for in haste to privately baptize a child thought to be dying, and belonging to parents who lived 'on the Common' at Hockering. It indeed appeared to be very ill, and its eyes were fixed, and remarkably clouded and dull. Having baptized, I felt moved with a longing desire to be enabled to heal the child; and I prayed very earnestly to the Lord God Almighty to give me faith and strength to enable me to do so. And I put my hands on its head and drew them down on to its arms; and then breathed on its head three times, in the name of the Lord Jesus Christ. And as I held its arms and looked on it anxiously, its face became exceedingly red and dark, and as the child gradually assumed a natural colour, the eyes became clear again; and then it gently closed its eyes in sleep. And I told the mother not to touch it any more till it awoke; but to carry it up in the cradle as it was. The next morning I found the child perfectly well. She had not touched it, except at four in the morning to feed it, when it seemed dead asleep, and it did not awake till ten o'clock.' This was written by an English Rector, and dated from the Carlton Club! The italics are in the original MS. now before me. The importance that no earthly hand should profanely touch the body while the spirit was at work in it shows how completely systematised is that insanity which consists of making a human mind an arena for the survival of the unfittest.

Chapter XXI - Antichrist

The Kali Age—Satan sifting Simon—Satan as Angel of Light—Epithets of Antichrist—The Cæsars—Nero—Sacraments imitated by Pagans—Satanic signs and wonders—Jerome on Antichrist—Armillus—Al Dajjail—Luther on Mohammed—'Mawmet'—Satan 'God's ape'—Mediæval notions—Witches Sabbath—An Infernal Trinity—Serpent of Sins—Antichrist Popes—Luther as Antichrist—Modern notions of Antichrist.

In the 'Padma Purana' it is recorded that when King Vena embraced heretical doctrine and abjured the temples and sacrifices, the people following him, seven powerful Rishis, high priests, visited him and entreated him to return to their faith. They said, 'These acts, O king, which thou art performing, are not of our holy traditions, nor fit for our religion, but are such as shall be performed by mankind at the entrance of Kali, the last and sinful age, when thy new faith shall be received by all, and the service of the gods be utterly relinquished.' King Vena, being thus in advance of his time, was burned on the sacred grass, while a mantra was performed for him.

This theory of Kali is curious as indicating a final triumph of the enemies of the gods. In the Scandinavian theory of 'Ragnarok,' the Twilight of the gods, there also seems to have been included no hope of the future victory of the existing gods. In the Parsí faith we first meet with the belief in a general catastrophe followed by the supremacy and universal sway of good. This faith characterised the later Hebrew prophecies, and is the spirit of Paul's brave saying, 'When all things shall be subjected unto him, then also shall the Son himself be subject unto him that put all things under him, that God may be all in all.'

When, however, theology and metaphysics advanced and modelled this fiery lava of prophetic and apostolic ages into dogmatic shapes, evil was accorded an equal duration with good. The conflict between Christ and his foes was not to end with the conversion or destruction of his foes, but his final coming as monarch of the world was to witness the chaining up of the Archfiend in the Pit.

Christ's own idea of Satan, assuming certain reported expressions to have been really uttered by him, must have been that which regarded him as a Tempter to evil, whose object was to test the reality of faith. 'Simon, Simon, behold, Satan asked you for himself, that he might sift you as the wheat; but I made supplication for thee, that thy faith fail not; and when once thou hast returned, confirm thy brethren. And he said unto him, Lord, I am ready to go with thee, both into prison and into death. And he said, I tell thee, Peter, a cock will not crow this day till thou wilt thrice deny that thou knowest me.'[1] Such a sentiment could not convey to Jewish ears a degraded notion of Satan, except as being a nocturnal spirit who must cease his work at cock-crow. It is an adaptation of what Jehovah himself was said to do, in the prophecy of Amos. 'I will not utterly destroy the house of Jacob, saith the Lord.... I will sift the house of Israel among all nations, like as corn is sifted in a sieve, yet shall not the least grain fall upon the earth.'[2]

Paul, too, appears to have had some such conception of Satan, since he speaks of an evil-doer as delivered up to Satan 'for the destruction of the flesh that the spirit may be saved.'3 There is, however, in another passage an indication of the distinctness with which Paul and his friends had conceived a fresh adaptation of Satan as obstacle of their work. 'For such,' he says, 'are false apostles, deceitful workers, transforming themselves into apostles of Christ. And no marvel: for Satan transforms himself into an angel of light. It is no great thing therefore if his ministers also transform themselves as ministers of righteousness; whose end will be according to their works.'4 It may be noted here that Paul does not think of Satan himself as transforming himself to a minister of righteousness, but of Satan's ministers as doing so. It is one of a number of phrases in the New Testament which reveal the working of a new movement towards an expression of its own. Real and far-reaching religious revolutions in history are distinguished from mere sectarian modifications, which they sum up in nothing more than in their new phraseology. When Jehovah, Messias, and Satan are gradually supplanted by Father, Christ, and Antichrist (or Man of Sin, False Christ, Withholder (κατέχον), False Prophet, Son of Perdition, Mystery of Iniquity, Lawless One), it is plain that new elements are present, and new emergencies. These varied phrases just quoted could not, indeed, crystallise for a long time into any single name for the new Obstacle to the new life, for during the same time the new life itself was too living, too various, to harden in any definite shape or be marked with any special name. The only New Testament writer who uses the word Antichrist is the so-called Apostle John; and it is interesting to remark that it is by him connected with a dogmatic statement of the nature of Christ and definition of heresy. 'Every spirit that confesses Jesus Christ is come in the flesh is of God; and every spirit that confesses not Jesus is not of God: and this is the spirit of Antichrist, whereof ye have heard that it comes; and now it is in the world already.'5 This language, characteristic of the middle and close of the second century,6 is in strong contrast with Paul's utterance in the first century, describing the Man of Sin (or of lawlessness, the son of perdition), as one 'who opposeth and exalteth himself above all that is called God, or that is worshipped; so that he sat in the temple of God, showing himself that he is God.'7 Christ has not yet begun to supplant God; to Paul he is the Son of God confronting the Son of Destruction, the divine man opposed by the man of sin. When the nature of Christ becomes the basis of a dogma, the man of sin is at once defined as the opponent of that dogma.

As this dogma struggled on to its consummation and victory, it necessarily took the form of a triumph over the Cæsars, who were proclaiming themselves gods, and demanding worship as such. The writer of the second Epistle bearing Peter's name saw those christians who yielded to such authority typified in Balaam, the erring prophet who was opposed by the angel;8 the writer of the Gospel of John saw the traitor Judas as the 'son of perdition,'9 representing Jesus as praying that the rest of his disciples might be kept 'out of the evil one;' and many similar expressions disclose the fact that, towards the close of the second century, and throughout the third, the chief obstacle of those who were just beginning to be called 'Christians' was the temptation offered by Rome to the christians themselves to betray their sect. It was still a danger to name the very imperial gods who successively set themselves up to be worshipped at Rome, but the pointing of the phrases is unmistakable long before the last of the pagan emperors held the stirrup for the first christian Pontiff to mount his horse.

Nero had answered to the portrait of 'the son of perdition sitting in the temple of God' perfectly. He aspired to the title 'King of the Jews.' He solemnly assumed the name of Jupiter. He had his temples and his priests, and shared divine honours with his mistress Poppæa. Yet, when Nero and his glory had perished under those phials of wrath described in the Apocalypse, a more exact image of the insidious 'False Christ' appeared in Vespasian. His alleged miracles ('lying wonders'), and the reported prediction of his greatness by a prophet on Mount Carmel, his oppression of the Jews, who had to contribute the annual double drachma to support the temples and gods which Vespasian had restored, altogether made this decorous and popular emperor a more formidable enemy than the 'Beast' Nero whom he succeeded. The virtues and philosophy of Marcus Aurelius still increased the danger. Political conditions favoured all those who were inclined to compromise, and to mingle the popular pagan and the Jewish festivals, symbols, and ceremonies. In apocalyptic metaphor, Vespasian and Aurelius are the two horns of the Lamb who spake like the Dragon, i.e., Nero (Rev. xiii. 11).

The beginnings of that mongrel of superstitions which at last gained the name of Christianity were in the liberation, by decay of parts and particles, of all those systems which Julius Cæsar had caged together for mutual destruction. 'With new thrones rise new altars,' says Byron's Sardanapalus; but it is still more true that, with new thrones all altars crumble a little. At an early period the differences between the believers in Christ and those they called idolaters were mainly in name; and, with the increase of Gentile converts, the adoption of the symbolism and practices of the old religions was so universal that the quarrel was about originality. 'The Devil,' says Tertullian, 'whose business it is to pervert the truth, mimics the exact circumstances of the Divine Sacraments in the mysteries of idols. He himself baptizes some, that is to say, his believers and followers: he promises forgiveness of sins from the sacred fount, and thus initiates them into the religion of Mithras; he thus marks on the forehead his own soldiers: he then celebrates the oblation of bread; he brings in the symbol of resurrection, and wins the crown with the sword.'10

What masses of fantastic nonsense it was possible to cram into one brain was shown in the time of Nero, the brain being that of Simon the Magician. Simon was, after all, a representative man; he reappears in christian Gnosticism, and Peter,

225

who denounced him, reappears also in the phrenzy of Montanism. Take the followers of this Sorcerer worshipping his image in the likeness of Jupiter, the Moon, and Minerva; and Montanus with his wild women Priscilla and Maximilla going about claiming to be inspired by the Holy Ghost to re-establish Syrian orthodoxy and asceticism; and we have fair specimens of the parties that glared at each other, and apostrophised each other as children of Belial. They competed with each other by pretended miracles. They both claimed the name of Christ, and all the approved symbols and sacraments. The triumph of one party turned the other into Antichrist.

Thus in process of time, as one hydra-head fell only to be followed by another, there was defined a Spirit common to and working through them all—a new devil, whose special office was hostility to Christ, and whose operations were through those who claimed to be christians as well as through open enemies.

As usual, when the phrases, born of real struggles, had lost their meaning, they were handed up to the theologians to be made into perpetual dogmas. Out of an immeasurable mass of theories and speculations, we may regard the following passage from Jerome as showing what had become the prevailing belief at the beginning of the fifth century. 'Let us say that which all ecclesiastical writers have handed down, viz., that at the end of the world, when the Roman Empire is to be destroyed, there will be ten kings, who will divide the Roman world among them; and there will arise an eleventh little king who will subdue three of the ten kings, that is, the king of Egypt, of Africa, and of Ethiopia; and on these having been slain, the seven other kings will submit.' 'And behold,' he says, 'in the ram were the eyes of a man'—this is that we may not suppose him to be a devil or a dæmon, as some have thought, but a man in whom Satan will dwell utterly and bodily—'and a mouth speaking great things;' for he is the 'man of sin, the son of perdition, who sitteth in the temple of God making himself as God.'11

The 'Little Horn' of Daniel has proved a cornucopia of Antichrists. Not only the christians but the Jews and the mussulmans have definite beliefs on the subject. The rabbinical name for Antichrist is Armillus, a word found in the Targum (Isa. xi. 4): 'By the word of his mouth the wicked Armillus shall die.' There will be twelve signs of the Messiah's coming—appearance of three apostate kings, terrible heat of the sun, dew of blood, healing dew, the sun darkened for thirty days, universal power of Rome with affliction for Jews, and the appearance of the first Messias (Joseph's tribe), Nehemiah. The next and seventh sign will be the appearance of Armillus, born of a marble statue in a church at Rome. The Romans will accept him as their god, and the whole world be subject to him. Nehemiah alone will refuse to worship him, and for this will be slain, and the Jews suffer terrible things. The eighth sign will be the appearance of the angel Michael with three blasts of his trumpet—which shall call forth Elias, the forerunner, and the true Messias (Ben David), and bring on the war with Armillus who shall perish, and all christians with him. The ten tribes shall be gathered into Paradise. Messias shall wed the fairest daughter of their race, and when he dies his sons shall succeed him, and reign in unbroken line over a beatified Israel.

The mussulman modification of the notion of Antichrist is very remarkable. They call him Al Dajjail, that is, the impostor. They say that Mohammed told his follower Tamisri Al-Dari, that at the end of the world Antichrist would enter Jerusalem seated on an ass; but that Jesus will then make his second coming to encounter him. The Beast of the Apocalypse will aid Antichrist, but Jesus will be joined by Imam Mahadi, who has never died; together they will subdue Antichrist, and thereafter the mussulmans and christians will for ever be united in one religion. The Jews, however, will regard Antichrist as their expected Messias. Antichrist will be blind of one eye, and deaf of one ear. 'Unbeliever' will be written on his forehead. In that day the sun will rise in the west.12

The christians poorly requited this amicable theory of the mussulmans by very extensively identifying Mohammed as Antichrist, at one period. From that period came the English word mawmet (idol), and mummery (idolatry), both of which, probably, are derived from the name of the Arabian Prophet. Daniel's 'Little Horn' betokens, according to Martin Luther, Mohammed. 'But what are the Little Horn's Eyes? The Little Horn's Eyes,' says he, 'mean Mohammed's Alkoran, or Law, wherewith he ruleth. In the which Law there is nought but sheer human reason (eitel menschliche Vernunft).' ... 'For his Law,' he reiterates, 'teaches nothing but that which human understanding and reason may well like.' ... Wherefore 'Christ will come upon him with fire and brimstone.' When he wrote this—in his 'army sermon' against the Turks—in 1529, he had never seen a Koran. 'Brother Richard's' (Predigerordens) Confutatio Alcoran, dated 1300, formed the exclusive basis of his argument. But in Lent of 1540, he relates, a Latin translation, though a very unsatisfactory one, fell into his hands, and once more he returned to Brother Richard, and did his Refutation into German, supplementing his version with brief but racy notes. This Brother Richard had, according to his own account, gone in quest of knowledge to 'Babylon, that beautiful city of the Saracens,' and at Babylon he had learnt Arabic and been inured in the evil ways of the Saracens. When he had safely returned to his native land he set about combating the same. And this is his exordium:—'At the time of the Emperor Heraclius there arose a man, yea, a Devil, and a first-born child of Satan, ... who wallowed in ... and he was dealing in the Black Art, and his name it was Machumet.' ... This work Luther made known to his countrymen by translating and commenting, prefacing, and rounding it off by an epilogue. True, his notes amount to little more but an occasional 'Oh fie, for shame, you horrid Devil, you damned Mahomet,' or 'O Satan, Satan, you shall pay for that,' or, 'That's it, Devils, Saracens, Turks, it's all the same,' or, 'Here the Devil smells a rat,' or briefly, 'O Pfui Dich, Teufel!' except when he modestly, with a query, suggests whether those Assassins, who, according to his text, are regularly educated to go out into the world in order to kill and slay all Worldly Powers, may not, perchance, be the Gypsies or the 'Tattern' (Tartars); or when he breaks down with a 'Hic nescio quid dicat translator.' His epilogue, however, is devoted to a special disquisition as to whether Mohammed or the Pope be worse. And in the twenty-second chapter of this disquisition he has arrived at the final conclusion that, after all, the Pope is worse, and that he, and not Mohammed, is the real 'Endechrist.' 'Wohlen,' he winds up, 'God grant us his grace, and punish both the Pope and Mohammed, together with their devils. I have done my part as a true prophet and teacher. Those who won't listen may leave it alone.' In similar strains speaks the learned and gentle Melancthon. In an introductory epistle to a reprint of that same Latin Koran which displeased Luther so much, he finds fault with Mohammed, or rather, to use his own words, he thinks that 'Mohammed is inspired by Satan,' because he 'does not explain what sin is,' and further, since he 'showeth not the reason of human misery.' He agrees with Luther about the Little Horn: though in another treatise he is rather inclined to see in Mohammed both Gog and Magog. And 'Mohammed's sect,' he says, 'is altogether made up (conflata) of blasphemy, robbery, and shameful lusts.' Nor does it matter in the least what the Koran is all about. 'Even if there were anything less scurrilous in the book, it need not concern us any more than the portents of the Egyptians, who invoked snakes and cats.... Were it not that partly this Mohammedan pest, and partly the Pope's idolatry, have long been leading us straight to wreck and ruin—may God have mercy upon some of us!'13

'Mawmet' was used by Wicliffe for idol in his translation of the New Testament, Acts vii. 41, 'And they made a calf in those days and offered a sacrifice to the Mawmet' (idol). The word, though otherwise derived by some, is probably a corruption of Mohammed. In the 'Mappa Mundi' of the thirteenth century we find the representation of the golden calf in the promontory of Sinai, with the superscription 'Mahum' for Mohammed, whose name under various corruptions, such as Mahound, Mawmet, etc., became a general byword in the mediæval languages for an idol. In a missionary hymn of Wesley's Mohammed is apostrophised as—

That Arab thief, as Satan bold,
Who quite destroyed Thy Asian fold;
and the Almighty is adjured to—
The Unitarian fiend expel,
And chase his doctrine back to Hell.

In these days, when the very mention of the Devil raises a smile, we can hardly realise the solemnity with which his work was once viewed. When Goethe represents Mephistopheles as undertaking to teach Faust's class in theology and dwells on his orthodoxy, it is the refrain of the faith of many generations. The Devil was not 'God's Ape,' as Tertullian called him, in any comical way; not only was his ceremonial believed to be modelled on that of God, but his inspiration of his followers was believed to be quite as potent and earnest. Tertullian was constrained to write in this strain—'Blush, my Roman fellow-soldiers, even if ye are not to be judged by Christ, but by any soldier of Mithras, who when he is undergoing initiation in the cave, the very camp of the Powers of Darkness, when the wreath is offered him (a sword being placed between as if in semblance of martyrdom), and then about to be set on his head, he is warned to put forth his hand and push the wreath away, transferring it to, perchance, his shoulder, saying at the same time, My only crown is Mithras. And thenceforth he never wears a wreath; and this is a mark he has for a test, whenever tried as to his initiation, for he is immediately proved to be a soldier of Mithras if he throws down the wreath offered him, saying his crown is in his god. Let us therefore acknowledge the craft of the Devil, who mimics certain things of those that be divine, in order that he may confound and judge us by the faith of his own followers.'

This was written before the exaltation of Christianity under Constantine. When the age of the martyrdom of the so-called pagans came on, these formulæ became real, and the christians were still more confounded by finding that the worshippers of the Devil, as they thought them, could yield up their lives in many parts of Europe as bravely for their faith as any christian had ever done. The 'Prince of this world' became thus an unmeaning phrase except for the heretics. Christ had become the Prince of this world; and he was opposed by religious devotees as earnest as any who had suffered under Nero. The relation of the Opposition to the Devil was yet more closely defined when it claimed the christian name for its schism or heresy, and when it carried its loyalty to the Adversary of the Church to the extent of suffering martyrdom. 'Tell me, holy father,' said Evervinus to St. Bernard, concerning the Albigenses, 'how is this? They entered to the stake and bore the torment of the fire not only with patience, but with joy and gladness. I wish your explanation, how these members of the Devil could persist in their heresy with a courage and constancy scarcely to be found in the most religious of the faith of Christ?'

Under these circumstances the personification of Antichrist had a natural but still wonderful development. He was to be born of a virgin, in Babylon, to be educated at Bethsaida and Chorazin, and to make a triumphal entry into Jerusalem, proclaiming himself the Son of God. In the interview at Messina (1202) between Richard I. and the Abbot Joachim of Floris, the king said, 'I thought that Antichrist would be born at Antioch or in Babylon, and of the tribe of Dan, and would reign in the temple of the Lord in Jerusalem, and would walk in that land in which Christ walked, and would reign in it for three years and a half, and would dispute against Elijah and Enoch, and would kill them, and would afterwards die; and that after his death God would give sixty days of repentance, in which those might repent which should have erred from the way of truth, and have been seduced by the preaching of Antichrist and his false prophets.'

This belief was reflected in Western Europe in the belief that the congregation of Witches assembled on their Sabbath (an institution then included among paganisms) to celebrate grand mass to the Devil, and that all the primitive temples were raised in honour of Satan. In the Russian Church the correspondence between the good and evil powers, following their primitive faith in the conflict between Byelbog and Tchernibog (white god and black god), went to the curious extent of picturing in hell a sort of infernal Trinity. The Father throned in Heaven with the Son between his knees and the Dove beside or beneath him, was replied to by a majestic Satan in hell, holding his Son (Judas) on his knees, and the Serpent acting as counteragent of the Dove. This singular arrangement may still be seen in many of the pictures which cover the walls of the oldest Russian churches (Fig. 9). The infernal god is not without a solemn majesty answering to that of his great antagonist above. The Serpent of Sins proceeds from the diabolical Father and Son, passing from beneath their throne through one of the two mouths of Hell, and then winds upward, hungrily opening its jaws near the terrible Balances where souls are weighed (Fig. 10). Along its hideous length are seated at regular intervals nine winged devils, representing probably antagonists of the nine Sephiroth or Æons of the Gnostic theology. Each is armed with a hook whereby the souls weighed and found wanting may be dragged. The sins which these devils represent are labelled, generally on rings around the serpent, and increase in heinousness towards the head. It is a curious fact that the Sin nearest the head is marked 'Unmercifulness.' Strange and unconscious sarcasm on an Omnipotent Deity under whose sway exists this elaboration of a scheme of sins and tortures precisely corresponding to the scheme of virtues and joys!

Fig 9.—Procession of the Serpent of Sins.

Truly said the Epistle of John, there be many Antichrists. If this was true before the word Christianity had been formed, or the system it names, what was the case afterwards? For centuries we find vast systems denouncing each other as Antichrist. And ultimately, as a subtle hardly-conscious heresy spread abroad, the great excommunicator of antichrists itself, Rome, acquired that title, which it has never shaken off since. The See of Rome did not first receive that appellation from Protestants, but from its own chiefs. Gregory himself (A.C. 590) started the idea by declaring that any man who held even the shadow of such power as the Popes arrogated to themselves after his time would be the forerunner of Antichrist. Arnulphus, Bishop of Orleans, in an invective against John XV. at Rheims (A.C. 991), intimated that a Pope destitute of charity was Antichrist. But the stigma was at length fixed (twelfth century) by Amalrich of Bena ('Quia Papa esset Antichristus et Roma Babylon et ipse sedit in Monte Oliveti, i.e., in pinguedine potestatis'); and also by the Abbot Joachim (A.C. 1202). The theory of Richard I., as stated

Fig. 10.—Ancient Russian Wall-Painting.

Fig. 11.—Alexander VI. as Antichrist.

to Joachim concerning Antichrist, has already been quoted. It was in the presence of the Archbishops of Rouen and Auxerre, and the Bishop of Bayonne, and represented their opinion and the common belief of the time. But Joachim said the Second Apocalyptic Beast represented some great prelate who will be like Simon Magus, and, as it were, universal Pontiff, and that very Antichrist of whom St. Paul speaks. Hildebrand was the first Pope to whom this ugly label was affixed, but the career of Alexander VI. (Roderic Borgia) made it for ever irremovable for the Protestant mind. There is in the British Museum a volume of caricatures, dated 1545, in which occurs an ingenious representation of Alexander VI. The Pope is first seen in his ceremonial robes; but a leaf being raised, another figure is joined to the lower part of the former, and there appears the papal devil, the cross in his hand being changed to a pitchfork (Fig. 11). Attached to it is an explanation in German giving the legend of the Pope's death. He was poisoned (1503) by the cup he had prepared for another man. It was afterwards said that he had secured the papacy by aid of the Devil. Having asked how long he would reign, the Devil returned an equivocal answer; and though Alexander understood that it was to be fifteen years, it proved to be only eleven. When in 1520 Pope Leo X. issued his formal bull against Luther, the reformer termed it 'the execrable bull of Antichrist.' An Italian poem of the time having represented Luther as the offspring of Megæra, the Germans returned the invective in a form more likely to impress

Fig. 12.—The Pope Nursed by Megæra.

the popular mind; namely, in a caricature (Fig. 12), representing the said Fury as nursing the Pope. This caricature is also of date 1545, and with it were others showing Alecto and Tisiphone acting in other capacities for the papal babe. The Lutherans had made the discovery that the number of the Apocalyptic Beast, 666, put into Hebrew numeral letters, contained the words Aberin Kadescha Papa (our holy father the Pope). The downfall of this Antichrist was a favourite theme of pulpit eloquence, and also with artists. A very spirited pamphlet was printed (1521), and illustrated with designs by Luther's friend Lucas Cranach. It was entitled Passional Christi und Antichristi. The fall of the papal Antichrist (Fig. 13), has for its companion one of Christ washing the feet of his disciples.

Fig. 13.—Antichrist's Descent (L. Cranach).

But the Catholics could also make discoveries; and among many other things they found that the word 'Luther' in Hebrew numerals also made the number of the Beast. It was remembered that one of the earliest predictions concerning Antichrist was that he would travesty the birth of Christ from a virgin by being born of a nun by a Bishop. Luther's marriage with the nun Catharine von Bora came sufficiently near the prediction to be welcomed by his enemies. The source of his inspiration as understood by Catholics is cleverly indicated in a caricature of the period (Fig. 14). The theory that the Papacy represents Antichrist has so long been the solemn belief of rebels against its authority, that it has become a vulgarised article of Protestant faith. On the other hand, Catholics appear to take a political and prospective view of Antichrist. Cardinal Manning, in his pastoral following the election of Leo XIII., said: 'A tide of revolution has swept over all countries. Every people in Europe is inwardly divided against itself, and the old society of Christendom, with its laws, its sanctities, and its stability, is giving way before the popular will, which has no law, or rather which claims to be a law to itself. This is at least the forerunning sign of the Lawless One, who in his own time shall be revealed.'

Fig. 14.—Luther's Devil as seen by Catholics.

Throughout the endless exchange of epithets, it has been made clear that Antichrist is the reductio ad absurdum of the notion of a personal Devil. From the day when the word was first coined, it has assumed every variety of shape, has fitted with equal precision the most contrarious things and persons; and the need of such a novel form at one point or another in the progress of controversy is a satire on the inadequacy of Satan and his ancient ministers. Bygone Devils cannot represent new animosities. The ascent of every ecclesiastical or theological system is traceable in massacres and martyrdoms; each of these, whether on one side or the other, helps to develop a new devil. The story of Antichrist shows devils in the making. Meantime, to eyes that see how every system so built up must sacrifice a virtue at every stage of its ascent, it will be sufficiently clear that every powerful Church is Adversary of the religion it claims to represent. Buddhism is Antibuddha; Islam is Antimohammed; Christianity is Antichrist.

Notes

1 Luke xxii. 31.
2 Amos ix. 8, 9.
3 1 Cor. v. 5.
4 2 Cor. xi. 13.
5 1 John iv. 2, 3.
6 Polycarp, Ep. to Philippians, vii.
7 2 Thess. ii.
8 2 Peter ii. 15.
9 John xvii. 12.
10 'But,' says Professor King (Gnostics, p. 52), 'a dispassionate examiner will discover that these two zealous Fathers somewhat beg the question in assuming that the Mithraic rites were invented as counterfeits of the Christian Sacraments; the former having really been in existence long before the promulgation of Christianity.' Whatever may have been the incidents in the life of Christ connected with such things, it is certainly true, as Professor King says, that these 'were afterwards invested with the mystic and supernatural virtues, in a later age insisted upon as articles of faith, by succeeding and unscrupulous missionaries, eager to outbid the attractions of more ancient ceremonies of a cognate character.' In the porch of the Church Bocca della Verita at Rome, there is, or was, a fresco of Ceres shelling corn and Bacchus pressing grapes, from them falling the elements of the Eucharist to a table below. This was described to me by a friend, but when I went to see it in 1872, it had just been whitewashed over! I called the attention of Signor Rosa to this shameful proceeding, and he had then some hope that this very interesting relic might be recovered.
11 Op. iv. 511. Col. Agrip. 1616.
12 For full details of all these superstitions see Eisenmenger (Entd. Jud. li. Armillus); D'Herbelot (Bib. Orient. Daggiel); Buxtorf (Lexicon, Armillus); Calmet, Antichrist; and on the same word, Smith; also a valuable article in M'Clintock and Strong's Cyc. Bib. Lit. (American).
13 Deutsch, 'Lit. Remains.' Islam.

Chapter XXII - The Pride of Life

The curse of Iblis—Samaël as Democrat—His vindication by Christ and Paul—Asmodäus—History of the name—Aschmedai of the Jews—Book of Tobit—Doré's 'Triumph of Christianity'—Aucassin and Nicolette—Asmodeus in the convent—The Asmodeus of Le Sage—Mephistopheles–Blake's 'Marriage of Heaven and Hell'—The Devil and the artists—Sádi's Vision of Satan—Arts of the Devil—Suspicion of beauty—Earthly and heavenly mansions—Deacon versus Devil.

On the parapet of the external gallery of Nôtre Dame in Paris is the carved form, of human size, represented in our figure (15). There is in the face a remarkable expression of pride and satisfaction as he looks forth on the gay city and contemplates all the wickedness in it, but this satisfaction is curiously blended with a look of envy and lust. His elegant head-dress gives him the pomp becoming the Asmodeus presiding over the most brilliant capital in the world.

His seat on the fine parapet is in contrast with the place assigned him in Eastern traditions—ruins and desert places,—but otherwise he fairly fulfilled, no doubt, early ideas in selecting his headquarters at Paris. A mussulman legend says that when, after the Fall of Man, Allah was mitigating the sentences he had pronounced, Iblis (who, as the Koran relates, pleaded and obtained the deferment of his consignment to Hell until the resurrection, and unlimited power over sinners who do not accept the word of Allah) asked—

Fig. 15.—The Pride of Life.

'Where shall I dwell in the meantime?

'In ruins, tombs, and all other unclean places shunned by man.

'What shall be my food?

'All things slain in the name of idols.

'How shall I quench my thirst?

'With wine and intoxicating liquors.

'What shall occupy my leisure hours?

'Music, song, love-poetry, and dancing.

'What is my watchword?

'The curse of Allah until the day of judgment.

'But how shall I contend with man, to whom thou hast granted two guardian angels, and who has received thy revelation?

'Thy progeny shall be more numerous than his,—for for every man that is born, there shall come into the world seven evil spirits—but they shall be powerless against the faithful.'

Iblis with wine, song, and dance—the 'pride of life'—is also said to have been aided in entering Paradise by the peacock, which he flattered.1

This fable, though later than the era of Mohammed in form, is as ancient as the myth of Eden in substance. The germ of it is already in the belief that Jehovah separated from the rest of the earth a garden, and from the human world a family of his own, and from the week a day of his own. The reply of the elect to the proud Gentile aristocracy was an ascetic caste established by covenant with the King of kings. This attitude of the pious caste turned the barbaric aristocrats, in a sense, to democrats. Indeed Samaël, in whom the execrated Dukes of Edom were ideally represented, might be almost described as the Democratic Devil. According to an early Jewish legend, Jehovah, having resolved to separate 'men' (i.e., Jews) from 'swine' (i.e., idolaters, Gentiles), made circumcision the seal on them as children of Abraham. There having been, however, Jews who were necessarily never circumcised, their souls, it was arranged, should pass at death into the forms of certain sacred birds where they would be purified, and finally united to the elect in Paradise. Now, Samaël, or Adam Belial as he was sometimes called, is said to have appealed to the Creator that this arrangement should include all races of beings. 'Lord of the world!' he said, 'we also are of your creation. Thou art our father. As thou savest the souls of Israel by transforming them that they may be brought back again and made immortal, so also do unto us! Why shouldst thou regard the seed of Abraham before us?' Jehovah answered, 'Have you done the same that Abraham did, who recognised me from his childhood and went into Chaldean fire for love of me? You have seen that I rescued him from your hands, and from the fiery oven which had no power over him, and yet you have not loved and worshipped me. Henceforth speak no more of good or evil.'2

The old rabbinical books which record this conversation do not report Samaël's answer; nor is it necessary: that answer was given by Jesus and Paul breaking down the partitions between Jew and Gentile. It was quite another thing, however, to include the world morally. Jesus, it would seem, aimed at this also; he came 'eating and drinking,' and the orthodox said Samaël was in him. Personally, he declined to substitute even the cosmopolitan rite of baptism for the discredited national rite of circumcision. But Paul was of another mind. His pharisaism was spiritualised and intensified in his new faith, to which the great world was all an Adversary.

It was a tremendous concession, this giving up of the gay and beautiful world, with its mirth and amusements, its fine arts and romance—to the Devil. Unswerving Nemesis has followed that wild theorem in many forms, of which the most significant is Asmodeus.

Asmodäus, or Aêshma-daêva of the Zend texts, the modern Persian Khasm, is etymologically what Carlyle might call 'the god Wish;' aêsha meaning 'wish,' from the Sanskrit root ish, 'to desire.' An almost standing epithet of Aêshma is Khrvîdra, meaning apparently 'having a hurtful weapon or lance.' He is occasionally mentioned immediately after Anrô-mainyus (Ahriman); sometimes is expressly named as one of his most prominent supporters. In the remarkable combat between Ahuro-mazda (Ormuzd) and Anrô-mainyus, described in Zam. Y. 46, the good deity summons to his aid Vohumano, Ashavahista, and Fire; while the Evil One is aided by Akômano, Aêshma, and Aji-Daháka.3 Here, therefore, Aêshma appears as opposed to Ashavahista, 'supreme purity' of the Lord of Fire. Aêshma is the spirit of the lower or impure Fire, Lust and Wrath. A Sanskrit text styles him Kossa-deva, 'the god of Wrath.' In Yaçna 27, 35, Śraosha, Aêshma's opponent, is invoked to shield the faithful 'in both worlds from Death the Violent, from Aêshma the Violent, from the hosts of Violence that raise aloft the terrible banner—from the assaults of Aêshma that he makes along with Vídátu ('Divider, Destroyer'), the demon-created.' He is thus the leading representative of dissolution, the fatal power of Ahriman. Ormuzd is said to have created Śraosha to be the destroyer of 'Aêshma of the fatal lance.' Śraosha ('the Hearer') is the moral vanquisher of Aêshma, in distinction from Haoma, who is his chief opponent in the physical domain.

Such, following Windischmann,4 is the origin of the devil whom the apocryphal book of Tobit has made familiar in Europe as Asmodeus. Aschmedai, as the Jews called him, appears in this story as precisely that spirit described in the

Avesta—the devil of Violence and Lust, whose passion for Sara leads him to slay her seven husbands on their wedding-night. The devils of Lust are considered elsewhere, and Asmodeus among them; there is another aspect of him which here concerns us. He is a fastidious devil. He will not have the object of his passion liable to the embrace of any other. He cannot endure bad smells, and that raised by the smoke of the fish-entrails burnt by Tobit drives him 'into the utmost parts of Egypt, where the angel bound him.' It is, however, of more importance to read the story by the light of the general reputation of Aschmedai among the Jews and Arabians. It was notably that of the devil represented in the Moslem tradition at the beginning of this chapter. He is the Eastern Don Giovanni and Lothario; he plies Noah and Solomon with wine, and seduces their wives, and always aims high with his dashing intrigues. He would have cried Amen to Luther's lines—

Who loves not wine, woman, and song,
He lives a fool his whole life long.

Besides being an aristocrat, he is a scholar, the most learned Master of Arts, educated in the great College of Hell, founded by Asa and Asael, as elsewhere related. He was fond of gaming; and so fashionable that Calmet believed his very name signifies fine dress.

Now, the moral reflections in the Book of Tobit, and its casual intimations concerning the position of the persons concerned, show that they were Jewish captives of the humblest working class, whose religion is of a type now found chiefly among the more ignorant sectarians. Tobit's moral instructions to his son, 'In pride is destruction and much trouble, and in lewdness is decay and much want,' 'Drink not wine to make thee drunken,' and his careful instructions about finding wealth in the fear of God, are precisely such as would shape a devil in the image of Asmodeus. Tobit's moral truisms are made falsities by his puritanism: 'Prayer is good with fasting and alms and righteousness;' 'but give nothing to the wicked;' 'If thou serve God he will repay thee.'

'Cakes and ale' do not cease to exist because Tobits are virtuous; but unfortunately they may be raised from their subordinate to an insubordinate place by the transfer of religious restraints to the hands of Ignorance and Cant. Asmodeus, defined against Persian and Jewish asceticism and hypocrisy, had his attractions for men of the world. Through him the devil became perilously associated with wit, gallantry, and the one creed of youth which is not at all consumptive—

Grey is all Theory,
Green Life's golden-fruited tree!

Especially did Asmodeus represent the subordination of so-called 'religious' and tribal distinctions to secular considerations. As Samaël had petitioned for an extension of the Abrahamic Covenant to all the world and failed to secure it from Jehovah, Asmodeus proposed to disregard the distinction. There is much in the Book of Tobit which looks as if it were written especially with the intention of persuading Jewish youth, tempted by Babylonians to marriage, that their lovers might prove to be succubi or incubi. Tobit implores his son to marry in his own tribe, and not take a 'strange woman.' Asmodeus was as cosmopolitan as the god of Love himself, and many of his uglier early characteristics were hidden out of sight by such later developments.

Gustave Doré has painted in his vivid way the 'Triumph of Christianity.' In it we see the angelic hosts with drawn swords overthrowing the forms adored of paganism—hurling them headlong into an abyss. So far as the battle and victory go, this is just the conception which an early christian would have had of what took place through the advent of Christ. It filled their souls with joy to behold by Faith's vision those draped angels casting down undraped goddesses; they would delight to imagine how the fall might break the bones of those beautiful limbs. For they never thought of these gods and goddesses as statues, but as real seductive devils; and when these christians had brought over the arts, they often pictured the black souls coming out of these fair idols as they fell.

Doré may have tried to make the angels as beautiful as the goddesses, but he has not succeeded. In this he has interpreted the heart behind every deformity which was ever added to a pagan deity. The horror of the monks was transparent homage. Why did they starve and scourge their bodies, and roll them in thorns? Because not even by defacing the beautiful images were they able to expel from their inward worship the lovely ideals they represented.

It is not difficult now to perceive that the old monks were consigning the pagan ideals to imaginary and themselves to actual hells, in full hope of thereby gaining permanent possession of the same beauty abjured on earth. The loveliness of the world was transient. They grew morbid about death; beneath the rosiest form they saw the skeleton. The heavenly angels they longed for were Venuses and Apollos, with no skeletons visible beneath their immortalised flesh. They never made sacrifices for a disembodied heaven. The force of self-crucifixion lay in the creed—'I believe in the resurrection of the body, and the life everlasting.'

The world could not generally be turned into a black procession at its own funeral. In proportion to the conquests of Christianity must be its progressive surrender to the unconquerable—to human nature. Aphrodite and Eros, over whose deep graves nunneries and monasteries had been built, were the first to revive, and the story, as Mr. Pater has told it, is like some romantic version of Ishtar's Descent into Hades and her resurrection.5 While as yet the earth seemed frostbound, long before the Renaissance, the song of the turtle was heard in the ballad of Aucassin and Nicolette. The christian knight will marry the beautiful Saracen, and to all priestly warnings that he will surely go to hell, replies, 'What could I do in Paradise? I care only to go where I can be with Nicolette. Who go to Paradise? Old priests, holy cripples, dried-up monks, who pass their lives before altars. I much prefer Hell, where go the brave, the gay, and beautiful. There will be the players on harps, the classic poets and singers; and there I shall not be parted from Nicolette!'

Along with pretty Saracen maidens, or memories of them, were brought back into Europe legends of Asmodeus. Aphrodite and Eros might disguise themselves in his less known and less anathematised name, so that he could manage to sing of his love for Sara, of Parsi for Jewess, under the names of christian Aucassin and saracen Nicolette. In the Eastern Church he reappeared also. There are beautiful old pictures which show the smart cavalier, feather-in-cap, on the youth's left, while on his right stands 'grey Theory' in the form of a long-bearded friar. Such pictures, no doubt, taught for many a different lesson from that intended—namely, that the beat of the heart is on the left.

Where St. Benedict rolled himself in thorns for dreaming of his (deserted) 'Nicolette,' St. Francis planted roses; and the Latin Church had to recognise this evolution of seven centuries. They hid the thorns in the courts of convents, and sold the roses to the outside world as indulgences. But as Asmodeus had not respected the line between Jew and Gentile in Nineveh, so he passed over that between priest, nun, and worldling in the West. In the days of Witchcraft the Church was scandalised by the rumour that the nuns of the Franciscan Convent of Louviers had largely taken to sorcery, and were attending the terrible 'Witches' Sabbaths.' The nun most prominent in this affair was one Madeleine Bavent. The priests announced that she had confessed that she was borne away to the orgies by the demon Asmodeus, and that he had induced her to profane the sacred host. It turned out that the nuns had engaged in intrigues with the priests who had charge of them—especially with Fathers David, Picard, and Boulé—but Asmodeus was credited with the crime, and the nuns were punished for it. Madeleine was condemned to life-long penance, and Picard anticipated the fire by a suicide, in which he was said to have been assisted by the devil.

Following the rabbinical tradition which represented him as continually passing from the high infernal College of Asa and Asael to the earth to apply his arts of sorcery, Asmodeus gained a respectable position in European literature through the romance of Le Sage ('Le Diable Boiteux'), and his fame so gained did much to bring about in France that friendly feeling for the Devil which has long been a characteristic of French literature. A very large number of books, periodicals, and journals in France have gained popularity through the Devil's name. Asmodeus was, in fact, the Arch-bohemian. As such, he largely influenced the conception of Mephistopheles as rendered by Goethe—himself the Prince of Bohemians. The old horror of Asmodeus for bad smells is insulted in the name Mephistopheles, and this devil is many rolled into one; yet in many respects his kinship to Asmodeus is revealed. All the dried starveling Anthonys and Benedicts are, in a cultured way, present in the theologian and scholar Faust; all the sweet ladies that haunted their seclusion became realistic in Gretchen. She is the Nemesis of suppressed passions.

One province of nature after another has been recovered from Asceticism. In this case Ishtar has had to regain her apparel and ornaments at successive portals that are centuries, and they are not all recovered yet. But we have gone far enough, even in puritanised England, to produce a 'madman' far-seeing enough to behold The Marriage of Heaven and Hell. The case of Asmodeus is stated well, albeit radically, by William Blake, in that proverb which was told him by the devils, whom he alone of midnight travellers was shrewd enough to consult: 'The pride of the peacock is the glory of God; the lust of the goat is the bounty of God; the wrath of the lion is the wisdom of God.' When that statement is improved, as it well may be, it will be when those who represent religion shall have learned that human like other nature is commanded by obedience.

Fig. 16.—The Artist's Rescue.

In this connection may be mentioned a class of legends indicating the Devil's sensitiveness with regard to his personal appearance. The anxiety of the priests and hermits to have him represented as hideous was said to have been warmly resented by Satan, one of the most striking being the legend of many versions concerning a Sacristan, who was also an artist, who ornamented an abbey with a devil so ugly that none could behold it without terror. It was believed he had by inspiration secured an exact portrait of the archfiend. The Devil appeared to the Sacristan, reproached him with having made him so ugly, and threatened to punish him grievously if he did not make him better looking. Although this menace was thrice repeated, the

Sacristan refused to comply. The Devil then tempted him into an intrigue with a lady of the neighbourhood, and they eloped after robbing the abbey of its treasure. But they were caught, and the Sacristan imprisoned. The Devil then appears and offers to get him out of his trouble if he will only destroy the ugly likeness, and make another and handsomer. The Sacristan consented, and suddenly found himself in bed as if nothing had happened, while the Devil in his image lay in chains. The Devil when discovered vanished; the Sacristan got off on the theory that crimes and all had been satanic juggles. But the Sacristan took care to substitute a handsome devil for the ugly one. In another version the Sacristan remained faithful to his original portraiture of the Devil despite all menaces of the latter, who resolved to take a dire revenge. While the artist was completing his ornamentation of the abbey with an image of the Virgin, made as beautiful as the fiend near it was ugly, the Devil broke the ladder on which he was working, and a fatal fall was only prevented by the hand of the Madonna he had just made, which was outstretched to sustain him. The accompanying picture of this scene (Fig. 16) is from 'Queen Mary's Psalter' in the British Museum.

Vasari relates that when Spinello of Arezzo, in his famous fresco of the fall of the rebellious angels, had painted the hideous devil with seven faces about his body, the fiend appeared to him in the same form, and asked the artist where he had seen him in so frightful an aspect, and why he had treated him so ignominiously. When Spinello awoke in horror, he fell into a state of gloom, and soon after died.

The Persian poet Sádi has a remarkable passage conceived in the spirit of these legends, but more kindly.

I saw the demon in a dream,
But how unlike he seemed to be
To all of horrible we dream,
And all of fearful that we see.
His shape was like a cypress bough,
His eyes like those that Houris wear,
His face as beautiful as though
The rays of Paradise were there.
I near him came, and spoke—'Art thou,'
I said, 'indeed the Evil One?
No angel has so bright a brow,
Such yet no eye has looked upon.
Why should mankind make thee a jest,
When thou canst show a face like this?
Fair as the moon in splendour drest,
An eye of joy, a smile of bliss!
The painter draws thee vile to sight,
Our baths thy frightful form display;
They told me thou wert black as night,
Behold, thou art as fair as day!'
The lovely vision's ire awoke,
His voice was loud and proud his mien:
  'Believe not, friend!' 'twas thus he spoke,
   'That thou my likeness yet hast seen:
The pencil that my portrait made
Was guided by an envious foe;
In Paradise I man betrayed,
And he, from hatred, paints me so.'

Boehme relates that when Satan was asked the cause of God's enmity to him and his consequent downfall, he replied, 'I wished to be an artist.' There is in this quaint sentence a very true intimation of the allurements which, in ancient times, the arts of the Gentile possessed for the Jews and christian judaisers. Indeed, a similar feeling towards the sensuous attractions of the Catholic and Ritualistic Churches is not uncommon among the prosaic and puritanical sects whose younger members are often thus charmed away from them. Dr. Donne preached a sermon before Oliver Cromwell at Whitehall, in which he affirmed that the Muses were damned spirits of devils; and the discussion on the Drama which occurred at Sheffield Church Congress (1878), following Dr. Bickerstith's opening discourse on 'the Devil and his wiles,' shows that the Low Church wing cherishes much the same opinion as that of Dr. Donne. The dread of the theatre among some sects amounts to terror. The writer remembers the horror that spread through a large Wesleyan circle, with which he was connected, when a distinguished minister of that body, just returned from Europe, casually remarked that 'the theatre at Rome seemed to be poorly supported.' The fearful confession spread through the denomination, and it was understood that the observant traveller had 'made shipwreck of faith.' The Methodist instinct told true: the preacher became an accomplished Gentile.

Music made its way but slowly in the Church, and the suspicion of it still lingers among many sects. The Quakers took up the burthen of Epiphanius who wrote against the flute-players, 'After the pattern of the serpent's form has the flute been invented for the deceiving of mankind. Observe the figure that the player makes in blowing his flute. Does he not bend himself up and down to the right hand and to the left, like unto the serpent? These forms hath the Devil used to manifest his blasphemy against things heavenly, to destroy things upon earth, to encompass the world, capturing right and left such as lend an ear to his seductions.' The unregenerate birds that carol all day, be it Sabbath or Fast, have taught the composer that his best inspiration is from the Prince of the Air. Tartini wrote over a hundred sonatas and as many concertos, but he rightly valued above them all his 'Sonata del Diavolo.' Concerning this he wrote to the astronomer Lalande:—'One night, in the year 1713, I dreamed that I had made a compact with his Satanic Majesty, by which he was received into my service. Everything succeeded to the utmost of my desires, and my every wish was anticipated by my new domestic. I thought that, in taking up my violin to practise, I jocosely asked him if he could play on this instrument. He answered that he believed he was able to pick out a tune; when, to my astonishment, he began a sonata, so strange, and yet so beautiful, and executed in so masterly a manner, that in the whole course of my life I had never heard anything so exquisite. So great was my amazement that I could scarcely breathe. Awakened by the violence of my feelings, I instantly seized my violin, in the hope of being able to catch some part of the ravishing melody which I had just heard, but all in vain. The piece which I composed according to my scattered recollections is, it is true, the best I ever produced. I have entitled it, 'Sonata del Diavolo;' but it is so far inferior to that which had made so forcible an impression on me, that I should have dashed my violin into a thousand pieces, and given up music for ever in despair, had it been possible to deprive myself of the enjoyments which I receive from it.'

The fire and originality of Tartini's great work is a fine example of that power which Timoleon called Automatia, and Goethe the Dämonische,—'that which cannot be explained by reason or understanding; it is not in my nature, but I am subject to it.' 'It seems to play at will with all the elements of our being.'

The Puritans brought upon England and America that relapse into the ancient asceticism which was shown in the burning of great pictures by Cromwell's Parliament. It is shown still in the jealousy with which the puritanised mind in both countries views all that aims at the simple decoration of life, and whose ministry is to the sense of beauty. On that day of the week when England and New England hebraise, as Matthew Arnold says, it is observable that the sabbatarian fury is especially directed against everything which proposes to give simple pleasure or satisfy the popular craving for beauty. Sabbatarianism sees a great deal of hard work going on, but is not much troubled so long as it is ugly and dismal work. It utters no cry at the thousands of hands employed on Sunday railways, but is beside itself if one of the trains takes excursionists to the seaside, and is frantic at the thought of a comparatively few persons being employed on that day in Museums and Art Galleries. It is a survival of the old feeling that the Devil lurks about all beauty and pleasure.

A money-making age has measurably dispersed the superstitions which once connected the Devil with all great fortunes. For a long time, and in many regions of the world, the Jews suffered grievously by being supposed to get their wealth by the Devil's help. Their wealth (largely the result of their not exchanging it for worldly enjoyments) so often proved their misfortune, that it was easy to illustrate by their case the monkish theory that devil's gifts turn to ashes. Princes were indefatigable in relieving the Jews of such ashes, however. The Lords of Triar, who possessed the mines of Glucksbrunn, were believed to have been guided to them by a gold stag which often appeared to them—of course the Devil. It is related that when St. Wolfram went to convert the Frislanders, their king, Radbot, was prevented from submitting to baptism by a diabolical deception. The Devil appeared to him as an angel clothed in a garment woven of gold, on his head a jewelled diadem, and said, 'Bravest of men! what has led thee to depart from the Prince of thy gods? Do it not; be steadfast to thy religion and thou shalt dwell in a house of gold which I will give into thy possession to all eternity. Go to Wolfram to-morrow, ask him about those bright dwellings he promises thee. If he cannot show them, let both parties choose an ambassador; I will be their leader and will show them the gold house I promise thee.' St. Wolfram being unable to show Radbot the bright dwellings of Paradise, one of his deacons was sent along with a representative of the king, and the Devil (disguised as a traveller) took them to the house of gold, which was of incredible size and splendour. The Deacon exclaimed, 'If this house be made by God it will stand for ever; if by the Devil, it must vanish speedily.' Whereupon he crossed himself; the house vanished, and the Deacon found himself with the Frislander in a swamp. It took them three days to extricate themselves and return to King Radbot, whom they found dead.

The ascetic principle which branded the arts, interests, pursuits, and pleasures of the world as belonging to the domain of Satan, involved the fatal extreme of including among the outlawed realms all secular learning. The scholar and man of science were also declared to be inspired by the 'pride of life.' But this part of our subject requires a separate chapter.

Notes

1 *Weil's 'Biblical Legends.'*
2 *Eisenmenger, ii. 60.*

3 See vol. i. pp. 58 and 358.
4 'Zoroastrische Studien,' pp. 138–147. With which comp. Spiegel, Transl. of Avesta, III. xlvii.
5 'Studies in the Hist. of the Renaissance.' Macmillan.

Chapter XXIII -The Curse on Knowledge

A Bishop on intellect—The Bible on learning—The Serpent and Seth—A Hebrew Renaissance—Spells—Shelley at Oxford—Book-burning—Japanese ink-devil—Book of Cyprianus—Devil's Bible—Red letters—Dread of Science—Roger Bacon—Luther's Devil—Lutherans and Science.

In Lucas van Leyden's picture of Satan tempting Christ (Fig. 6), the fiend is represented in the garb of a University man of the time. From his head falls a streamer which coils on the ground to a serpent. From that serpent to the sceptical scholar demanding a miracle the evolution is fully traceable. The Serpent, of old the 'seer,' was in its Semitic adaptation a tempter to forbidden knowledge. This was the earliest priestly outcry against 'godless education.'
During the Shakespere tercentenary festival at Stratford-on-Avon, the Bishop of St. Andrews declared that there is not a word in the Bible warranting homage to Intellect, and such a boast beside the grave of the most intellectual of Englishmen is in itself a survival illustrating the tremendous curse hurled by jealous Jehovah on man's first effort to obtain knowledge. That same Serpent of knowledge has passed very far, and his curse has many times been repeated. In the Accadian poem of the fatal Seven, as we have seen, it is said, 'In watching was their office;' and the Assyrian version says, 'Unto heaven that which was not seen they raised.' On the Babylonian cylinders is inscribed the curse of the god of Intelligence (Hea) upon man—'Wisdom and knowledge hostilely may they injure him.'1 The same Serpent twined round the staff of Æsculapius and whispered those secrets which made the gods jealous, so that Jove killed the learned Physician with a flash of lightning. Its teeth were sown when Cadmus imported the alphabet into Greece; and when these alphabetical dragon's-teeth had turned to type, the ancient curse was renewed in legends which connected Fust with the Devil.
The Hebrews are least among races responsible for the legend which has drifted into Genesis. Nor was the Bishop's boast about their Bible correct. The homage paid to Solomon was hardly on account of his moral character. 'He spake of trees, from the cedar-tree that is in Lebanon, even unto the hyssop that springeth out of the wall; he spake also of beasts, and of fowl, and of creeping things, and of fishes.'2 While the curse on man for eating the fruit of knowledge is never quoted in the Hebrew scriptures, there are many indications of their devotion to knowledge; and their prophets even heard Jehovah saying, 'My people are destroyed through lack of knowledge.' It is not wonderful, therefore, that we find among the Jews the gradual growth of a legend concerning Seth, which may be regarded as a reply to the curse on the Serpent. The apotheosis of Seth in rabbinical and mussulman mythology represents a sort of Semitic Renaissance. As we have seen in a former chapter, the Egyptians and Greeks identified Set with Typhon, but at the same time that demon was associated with science. He is astronomically located in Capricorn, the sphere of the hierophants in the Egyptian Mysteries, and the mansion of the guardians of science. Thus he would correspond with the Serpent, who, as adapted by the Hebrews in the myth of Eden, whispers to Eve of divine knowledge. But, as detached from Typho, Seth, while leaving behind the malignancy, carried away the reputation for learning usually ascribed to devils. Thus, while we have had to record so many instances of degraded deities, we may note in Seth a converted devil. In the mussulman and rabbinical traditions Seth is a voluminous author; he receives a library from heaven; he is the originator of astronomy and of many arts; and, as an instructor in cultivation, he restores many an acre which as Set he had blighted. In the apocryphal Genesis he is represented as having been caught up to heaven and shown the future destiny of mankind. Anastasius of Sinai says that when God created Adam after his own image, he breathed into him grace and illumination, and a ray of the Holy Spirit. But when he had sinned this glory left him. Then he became the father of Cain and Abel. But afterwards it is said Adam 'begat a son in his own likeness, after his image, and called his name 'Seth,' which is not said of Cain and Abel; and this means that Seth was begotten in the likeness of unfallen man in paradise—Seth meaning 'Resurrection.' And all those then living, when they saw how the face of Seth shone with divine light, and heard him speak with divine wisdom, said, He is God; therefore his sons were commonly called the sons of God.3
That this 'Resurrection' of departed glory and wisdom was really, as I have said, a Renaissance—a restoration of learning from the curse put upon it in the story of the Serpent—is indicated by its evolution in the Gnostic myth wherein Seth was made to avenge Satan. He took under his special care the Tree of the Knowledge of Good and Evil, and planted it in his father's grave (Fig. 8). Rabbins carried their homage to Seth even to the extent of vindicating Saturn, the most notorious of planets, and say that Abraham and the Prophets were inspired by it.4 The Dog (Jackal) was, in Egyptian symbols, emblem of the Scribe; Sirius was the Dog-star domiciled with Saturn; Seth was by them identified with Sirius, as the god

236

of occult and infernal knowledge. He was near relative of the serpent Sesha, familiar of Æsculapius, and so easily connected with the subtlest of the beasts in Eden which had crept in from the Iranian mythology.

This reaction was instituted by scholars, who, in their necessarily timid way of fable, may be said to have recovered the Tree of Knowledge under guise of homage to Seth. It flourished, as we have seen (chap. xi.), to the extent of finally raising the Serpent to be a god, and lowering Jehovah who cursed him to a jealous devil!

But the terror with which Jehovah is said to have been inspired when he said, 'The man has become as one of us, to know good and evil,' never failed to reappear among priesthoods when anything threatened to remove the means of learning from under their control. The causes of this are too many to be fully considered here; but the main cause unquestionably was the tendency of learning to release men from the sway of the priest. The primitive man of science would speedily discover how many things existed of which his priest was ignorant, and thus the germ of Scepticism would be planted. The man who possessed the Sacred Books, in whole or in part, might become master of the 'spells' supposed to be contained in its words and sentences, and might use them against the priests; or, at any rate, he might feel independent of the ordinary apparatus of salvation.

The anxiety of priests to keep fast hold of the keys of learning, so that no secular son of Adam should become 'as one of them,' coupled with the wonderful powers they professed ability to exercise, powerfully stimulated the curiosity of intellectual men, and led them to seek after this forbidden fruit in subtle ways, which easily illustrated the story of the Serpent. The poet Shelley, who was suspected at Oxford because of his fondness for chemistry, recognised his mythological ancestry, and used to speak of 'my cousin, the Serpent.' The joke was born of circumstances sufficiently scandalous in the last generation to make the Oxonian of to-day blush; but the like histories of earlier ages are so tragical that, when fully known by the common people, they will change certain familiar badges into brands of shame. While the cant goes on about the Church being the protector of learning through the dark ages, the fact is that, from the burning of valuable books at Ephesus by christian fanatics (Acts xix. 19) to the present day, the Church has destroyed tenfold more important works than it ever produced, and almost suffocated the intellectual life of a thousand years. Amid the unbroken persecution of the Jews by christian cruelty, which lasted from the early eleventh century for five hundred years, untold numbers of manuscripts were destroyed, which might have now been giving the world full and clear knowledge concerning ages, for whose records archæological scholars are painfully exploring the crumbled ruins of the East. Synagogues were believed to be temples of Satan; they were plundered and razed to the ground, and their precious archives strewed the streets of many cities. On the 17th of June 1244 twenty-four cartloads of these ancient MSS. were burned in Paris alone. "And all this by our holy 'protector of learning' through the Middle Ages!

The Japanese have pictures of a famous magician who conjured up a demon—vast, vague, and terrible—out of his inkstand. They call it latterly 'emblem of a licentious press,' but, no doubt, it was originally used to terrify the country generally concerning the press. That Devil has also haunted the ecclesiastical imagination in Europe. Nearly every book written without priestly command was associated with the Devil, and there are several old books in Europe, laboriously and honestly written, which to this day are invested with popular superstitions reporting the denunciations with which they were visited. For some centuries it has been believed in Denmark and neighbouring countries that a strange and formidable book exists, by means of which you can raise or lay the Devil. It is vulgarly known as the Book of Cyprianus. The owner of it can neither sell, bury, or burn it, and if he cannot get rid of it before his death, he becomes the prey of the fiend. The only way of getting rid of it is to find somebody who will accept it as a present, well knowing what it is. Cyprianus is said to have been a clever and virtuous young student, but he studied the black art in Norway, and came under the power of the Devil, who compelled him to use his unholy learning to evil ends. This grieved him sorely, and he wrote a book, in which he shows first, how evil shall be done, and then how to counteract it. The book is probably one which really exists or existed, and professed to teach the art of sorcery, and likewise the charms against it. It consists of three parts, severally called Cyprianus, Dr. Faust, and Jacob Ramel. The two latter are written in cypher. It teaches everything appertaining to 'signing,' conjuring, second sight, and all the charms alluded to in Deuteronomy xviii. 10–12. The person possessing Cyprianus' book is said never to be in need of money, and none can harm him. The only way of getting rid of it is to put it away in a secret place in a church along with a clerk's fee of four shillings.

In Stockholm I saw the so-called Devil's Bible, the biggest book in the world, in the Royal Library. It is literally as they describe it, 'gigas librorum': no single man can lift it from the floor. It was part of the booty carried off by the Swedes after the surrender of Prague, A.D. 1648. It contains three hundred parchment leaves, each one made of an ass's hide, the cover being of oak planks, 1½ inches thick. It contains the Old and New Testaments; Josephi Flavii Antiquitates Judaicæ; Isidori Episcopi L. XX. de diversis materiis; Confessio peccatorum; and some other works. The last-named production is written on black and dark brown ground with red and yellow letters. Here and there sentences are marked 'hæc sunt suspecta,' 'superstitiosa,' 'prohibita.' One MS., which is headed, 'Experimentum de furto et febribus', is a treatise in Monkish Latin on the exorcism of ghosts and evil spirits, charms against thieves and sickness, and various prescriptions in 'White Magic.' The age of the book is considerably over three hundred years. The autograph of a German emperor is in it: 'Ferdinandus Imperator Romanorum, A.D. 1577.' The volume is known in Sweden as Fan's Bibel (Devil's Bible). The legend says, that a monk, suspected of black arts, who had been condemned to death, begged for life, and his judge mockingly told him that he would be pardoned only if he should produce next morning all the books here found and in this vast size. The monk invoked the Devil's assistance, and the ponderous volume was written in a single night. This Devil must have been one who prided himself more on his literary powers than his personal appearance; for the face and form said to be his portrait, frontispiece of the volume, represent a most hideous ape, green and hairy, with horrible curled tusks. It is, no doubt, the ape Anerhahn of the Wagner legends; Burns's 'towzie tyke, black, grim, and large.'5

I noticed particularly in this old work the recurrence of deep red letters and sentences similar to the ink which Fust used at the close of his earliest printed volumes to give his name, with the place and date of printing. Now Red is sacred in one direction as symbolising the blood of Christ, but it is also the colour of Judas, who betrayed that blood. Hence, while red letters might denote sacred days and sentences in priestly calendars, they might be supposed mimicry of such sanctities by 'God's Ape' if occurring in secular works or books of magic. It is said that these red letters were especially noted in Paris as indications of the diabolical origin of the works so easily produced by Fust; and, though it is uncertain whether he suffered imprisonment, the red lines with his name appear to have been regarded as his signature in blood.

For a long time every successive discovery of science, every invention of material benefit to man, was believed by priest-ridden peoples to have been secured by compact with the devil. The fate of the artist Prometheus, fettered by jealous Jove, was repeated in each who aspired to bring light to man, and some men of genius—such as Cornelius Agrippa, and Paracelsus—appear to have been frightened away from legitimate scientific research by the first connection of their names with sorcery. They had before them the example of the greatest scientific man of the Middle Ages, Roger Bacon, and knew how easily, in the priestly whisper, the chemist's crucible grew to a wizard's cauldron. The time may come when Oxford University will have learned enough to build a true memorial of the grandest man who ever wrote and taught within its walls. It would show Roger Bacon—rectifier of the Julian Calendar, analyst of lenses, inventor of spectacles and achromatic lenses, probable constructor of the first telescope, demonstrator of the chemical action of air in combustion, inventor of the mode of purifying saltpetre and crystallising it into gunpowder, anticipator of the

philosophical method with which his namesake is credited—looking on a pile of his books for whose researches he had paid two thousand French livres, to say nothing of a life's labour, only to see them condemned by his University, their circulation prohibited; and his sad gaze might be from the prison to which the Council of Franciscans at Paris sentenced him whom Oxford gladly delivered into their hands. He was condemned, says their historian Wadding, 'propter novitates quasdam suspectas.' The suspected novelties were crucibles, retorts, and lenses that made the stars look larger. So was it with the Oxford six hundred years ago. Undeniably some progress had been made even in the last generation, for Shelley was only forbidden to study chemistry, and expelled for his metaphysics. But now that it is claimed that Oxford is no longer partaker with them that stoned investigators and thinkers from Bacon to Shelley, it would be in order to build for its own great martyr of science a memorial, that superstition may look on one whom it has pierced.

Referring to Luther's inkstand thrown at the Devil, Dr. Zerffii, in his lecture on the Devil, says, 'He (the devil) hates nothing so much as writing or printer's ink.' But the truth of this remark depends upon which of two devils be considered. It would hardly apply to the Serpent who recommended the fruit of knowledge, or to the University man in Lucas van Leyden's picture (Fig. 6). But if we suppose the Devil of Luther's Bible (Fig. 17) to be the one at which the inkstand was thrown, the

criticism is correct. The two pictures mentioned may be instructively compared. Luther's Devil is the reply of the University to the Church. These are the two devils—the priest and the scholar—who glared at each other in the early sixteenth

Fig. 17.—Luther's Devil.

century. 'The Devil smelled the roast,' says Luther, 'that if the languages revived, his kingdom would get a hole which he could not easily stop again.' And it must be admitted that some of the monkish execrations of the time, indeed of many times since, have an undertone of Jahvistic jealousy. 'These Knowers will become as one of us.' It must also be admitted that the clerical instinct told true: the University man held in him that sceptical devil who is always the destroyer of the priest's paradise. These two devils which struggled with each other through the sixteenth century still wage their war in the arena of Protestantism. Many a Lutheran now living may remember to have smiled when Hofmann's experiments in discovering carbonic acid gas gained him repute for raising again Mephosto; but perhaps they did not recognise Luther's devil when, at the annual assembly of Lutheran Pastors in Berlin (Sept. 1877), he reappeared as the Rev. Professor Grau, and said, 'Not a few listen to those striving to combine Christ with Belial, to reconcile redeeming truth with modern science and culture.' But though they who take the name of Luther in vain may thus join hands with the Devil, at whom the Reformer threw his inkstand, the combat will still go on, and the University Belial do the brave work of Bel till beneath his feet lies the dragon of Darkness whether disguised as Pope or Protestant.

If the Church wishes to know precisely how far the roughness pardonable in the past survives unpardonably in itself, let its clergy peruse carefully the following translation by Mr. Leland of a poem by Heine; and realise that the Devil portrayed in it is, by grace of its own prelates, at present the most admired personage in every Court and fashionable drawing-room in Christendom.

I called the Devil, and he came:
In blank amaze his form I scan.
He is not ugly, is not lame,
But a refined, accomplished man,—
One in the very prime of life,
At home in every cabinet strife,
Who, as diplomatist, can tell
Church and State news extremely well.
He is somewhat pale—and no wonder either,
Since he studies Sanskrit and Hegel together.
His favourite poet is still Fonqué.
Of criticism he makes no mention,
Since all such matters unworthy attention
He leaves to his grandmother, Hecaté.
He praised my legal efforts, and said
That he also when younger some law had read,
Remarking that friendship like mine would be
An acquisition, and bowed to me,—
Then asked if we had not met before,
At the Spanish Minister's soirée?
And, as I scanned his face once more,
I found I had known him for many a day.

Notes

1 'Chald. Genesis,' by George Smith, p. 84.
2 This text was engraved by Mrs. Rose Mary Crawshay on a tomb she had erected in honour of her humble neighbour, Mr. Norbury, who sought knowledge for its own sake. Few ancient scriptures could have supplied an inscription so appropriate.
3 Mr. Baring-Gould, quoting this (from Anastasius Sinaita, Ὁδηγός, ed. Gretser, Ingolst. 1606, p. 269), attributes this shining face of Seth to his previous character as a Sun-god. ('Old Test. Legends,' i. 84.)
4 King's 'Gnostics,' p. 53, n.
5 Tertullian's phrase, 'The Devil is God's Ape,' became popular at one time, and the Ape-devil had frequent representation in art— as, for instance, in Holbein's 'Crucifixion' (1477), now at Augsburg, where a Devil with head of an ape, bat-wings, and flaming red legs is carrying off the soul of the impenitent thief. The same subject is found in the same gallery in an Altdorfer, where the Devil's face is that of a gorilla.

Chapter XXIV - Witchcraft

Minor gods—Saint and Satyr—Tutelaries—Spells—Early Christianity and the poor—Its doctrine as to pagan deities— Mediæval Devils—Devils on the stage—An Abbot's revelations—The fairer deities—Oriental dreams and spirits—Calls for Nemesis—Lilith and her children—Neoplatonicism—Astrology and Alchemy—Devil's College—Shem-hammphorásch— Apollonius of Tyana—Faustus—Black Art Schools—Compacts with the Devil—Blood-covenant—Spirit-seances in old times— The Fairfax delusion—Origin of its devil—Witch, goat, and cat—Confessions of Witches—Witchcraft in New England—Witch trials—Salem demonology—Testing witches—Witch trials in Sweden—Witch Sabbath—Mythological elements—Carriers— Scotch Witches—The cauldron—Vervain—Rue—Invocation of Hecaté—Factors of Witch persecution—Three centuries of massacre—Würzburg horrors—Last victims—Modern Spiritualism.

St. Cyprian saw the devil in a flower.1 That little vision may report more than many more famous ones the consistency with which the first christians had developed the doctrine that nature is the incarnation of the Evil Spirit. It reports to us the sense of many sounds and sights which were heard and seen by ears and eyes trained for such and no other, all showing that the genii of nature and beauty were vanishing from the earth. Over the Ægean sea were heard lamentations and the voice, 'Great Pan is dead!' Augustus consults the oracle of Apollo and receives reply—

Me puer Hebræus, Divos Deus ipse gubernans,
Cedere sede jubet, tristremque redire sub orcum;
Aris ergo dehinc tacitis abscedito nostris.

But while the rage of these Fathers towards all the great gods and goddesses, who in their grand temples represented 'the pride of life,' was remorseless, they were comparatively indifferent to the belief or disbelief of the lower classes in their small tutelary divinities. They appear almost to have encouraged belief in these, perhaps appreciating the advantages of the popular custom of giving generous offerings to such personal and domestic patrons. At a very early period there seems to have arisen an idea of converting these more plebeian spirits into guardian angels with christian names. Thus Jerome relates in his Life of the first Hermit Paul, that when St. Anthony was on his way to visit that holy man, he encountered a Centaur who pointed out the way; and next a human-like dwarf with horns, hooked fingers, and feet like those of a goat. St. Anthony believing this to be an apparition of the Devil, made the sign of the Cross; but the little man, nowise troubled by this, respectfully approached the monk, and having been asked who he was, answered: 'I am a mortal, and one of those inhabitants of the Desert whom the Gentiles in their error worship under the names of Fauns, Satyrs, and Incubi: I am delegated by my people to ask of thee to pray for us to our common God, who we know has descended for the salvation of the world, and whose praises resound in all the earth.' At this glorification of Christ St. Anthony was transported with joy, and turning towards Alexandria he cried, 'Woe to thee, adulterous city, which adorest animals as gods!'

Perhaps the evolution of these desert demons into good christians would have gone on more rapidly and completely if the primitive theologians had known as much of their history as comparative mythology has disclosed to the modern world. St. Anthony was, however, fairly on the track of them when he turned towards Alexandria. Egypt appears to have been the especial centre from which were distributed through the world the fetish guardians of provinces, towns, households and individuals. Their Serapes reappear in the Teraphim of Laban, and many of the forms they used reappear in the Penates, Lares, and genii of Latin countries. All these in their several countries were originally related to its ancient religion or mythology, but before the christian era they were very much the same in Egypt, Greece, and Italy. They were shaped in many different, but usually natural forms, such as serpents, dogs, boys, and old men, though often some intimation was given of their demonic character. They were so multiplied that even plants and animals had their guardians. The anthropomorphic genii called the Patrii, who were supposed to preside over provinces, were generally represented bearing weapons with which they defended the regions of which they were patrons. These were the Averrunci or Apotropæi.

There are many interesting branches of this subject which cannot be entered into here, and others have already been considered in the foregoing parts of this work. It is sufficient for my present purpose to remark, that, in the course of time, all the households of the world had traditional guardians; these were generally represented in some shape on amulets and talismans, on which were commonly inscribed the verbal charms by which the patron could be summoned. In the process of further time the amulets—especially such as were reproduced by tribes migrating from the vicinity of good engravers—might be marked only with the verbal charms; these again were, in the end, frequently represented only by some word or name. This was the 'spell.' Imagination fails in the effort to conceive how many strata of extinct deities had bequeathed to the ancient Egyptians those mystical names whose exact utterance they believed would constrain each god so named to appear and bind him to serve the invoker's purpose whether good or evil.2 This idea continued among the Jews and shaped the commandment, 'Thou shalt not take the name of the Lord thy God in vain.'

It was in these diminutive forms that great systems survived among the common people. Amid natural convulsions ancient formations of faith were broken into fragments; in the ebb and flow of time these fragments were smoothed, as it were, into these talismanic pebbles. Yet each of these conveyed all the virtue which had been derived from the great and costly ceremonial system from which it originally crumbled; the virtue of soothing the mind and calming the nerves of sufferers with the feeling that, though they might have been assailed by hostile powers, they had friendly powers too who were active in their behalf—Vindicators, to recall Job's phrase—who at last would stand by them to the end. In the further ebb and flow of generations the mass of such charms are further pulverised into sand or into mud; but not all of them: amid the mud will be found many surviving specimens, and such mud of accumulated superstitions is always susceptible of being remoulded after such lingering models, should occasion demand.

Erasmus, in his 'Adages,' suggests that it was from these genii of 'the Gentiles' that the christians derived their notion of each person being attended by two angels, a good and a bad. Probably he was but half right. The peoples to whom he refers did not generally believe that each man was attended by a bad spirit, a personal enemy. That was an honour reserved for individuals particularly formidable to the evil powers,—Adam, Jacob, Hercules, or Zoroaster. The one preternatural power attending each ordinary individual defended him from the general forces of evil. But it was

Christianity which, in the gradual effort to substitute patron-saints and guardian-angels of its own for the pagan genii, turned the latter from friends to enemies, and their protecting into assailing weapons.

All the hereditary household gods of what is now called Christendom were diabolised. But in order that the masses might turn from them and invoke christian guardians, the Penates, Lares, and genii had to be belittled on the one hand, and the superior power of the saints and angels demonstrated. When Christianity had gained the throne of political power, it was easy to show that the 'imps,' as the old guardians were now called, could no longer protect their invokers from christian punishment, or confer equal favours.

Christianity conquered Europe by the sword, but at first that sword was not wielded against the humble masses. It was wielded against their proud oppressors. To the common people it brought glad tidings of a new order, in which, under the banner of a crucified working-man and his (alleged) peasant mother, all caste should disappear but that of piety and charity. Christ eating with publicans and sinners and healing the wayside cripples reappeared in St. Martin dividing his embroidered cloak with a beggar—type of a new aristocracy. They who worshipped the Crucified Peasant in the rock-cave of Tours which St. Martin had consecrated, or in little St. Martin's Church at Canterbury where Bertha was baptized, could not see the splendid cathedrals now visible from them, built of their bones and cemented with their blood. King Ethelbert surrendered the temple of his idol to the consecration of Augustine, and his baptized subjects had no difficulty in seeing the point of the ejected devil's talons on the wall which he assailed when the first mass was therein celebrated.

Fig. 18.—Devils (Old Missal).

Glad tidings to the poor were these that the persecuted first missionaries brought to Gaul, Britain, and Germany. But they did not last. The christians and the pagan princes, like Herod and Pilate, joined hands to crucify the European peasant, and he was reduced to a worse serfdom than he had suffered before. Every humble home in Europe was trampled in the mire in the name of Christ. The poor man's wife and child, and all he possessed were victims of the workman of Jerusalem turned destroyer of his brethren. Michelet has well traced Witchcraft to the Despair of the Middle Ages.3 The decay of the old religions, which Christianity had made too rapid for it to be complete, had left, as we have seen, all the trains laid for that terrible explosion; and now its own hand of cruelty brought the torch to ignite them. Let us, at risk of some iteration, consider some of these combustible elements.

In the first place the Church had recognised the existence of the pagan gods and goddesses, not wishing to imbreed in the popular mind a sceptical habit, and also having use for them to excite terror. Having for this latter purpose carved and painted them as ugly and bestial, it became further of importance that they should be represented as stupid and comparatively impotent. Baptism could exorcise them, and a crucifix put thousands of them to flight. This tuition was not difficult. The peasantries of Europe had readily been induced to associate the newly announced (christian) Devil with their most mischievous demons. But we have already considered the forces under which these demons had entered on their decline before they were associated with Satan. Many conquered obstructions had rendered the Demons which represented them ridiculous. Hence the 'Dummeteufel' of so many German fables and of the mediæval miracle-plays. 'No greater proof,' says Dr. Dasent, 'can be given of the small hold which the christian Devil has taken of the Norse mind, than the heathen aspect under which he constantly appears, and the ludicrous way in which he is always outwitted.'4 'The Germans,' says Max Müller, 'indoctrinated with the idea of a real devil, the Semitic Satan or Diabolus, treated him in the most good-humoured manner.'5 A fair idea of the insignificance he and his angels reached may be gained from the accompanying picture (Fig. 18), with which a mediæval Missal now in possession of Sir Joseph Hooker is illuminated. It could not be expected that the masses would fear beings whom their priests thus held up to ridicule. It is not difficult to imagine the process of evolution by which the horns of such insignificant devils turned to the asinine ears of

Fig. 19.—Carving at Corbeil.

such devils as this stall carving at Corbeil, near Paris (Fig. 19), which represented the popular view of the mastery obtained by witches over devils. It must be remembered also that this power over devils was in accordance with the traditions concerning Solomon, and the subserviency of Oriental demons generally to the lamps or charms to which they were bound.

What the popular christian devil had become in all the Northern nations is sufficiently shown in the figure he presented in most of the old miracle-plays and 'Moralities.' 'The Devill in his fethers all ragged and rent,'6 had horns, wide mouth, long (sometimes up-turned) nose, red beard, cloven foot, and tail. He was attended by a buffoon called Vice. 'And,' says Harsenet, 'it was a pretty part in the old Church plays when the nimble Vice would skip up nimbly like a Jackanapes into the Devil's necke, and ride the Devil a course, and belabour him with a wooden dagger, till he made him roar, whereat the people would laugh to see the Devil so Vice-haunted.'7 The two must have nearly resembled the clown and his unhappy victim Pantaloon in our pantomimes, as to their antics. It would seem that sometimes holy personages were caricatured in the make-up of the stage-devil. Thus in 'Gammer Gurton's Needle' we have this conversation:—

Gammer. But, Hodge, had he no horns to push?
Hodge. As long as your two armes. Saw ye never fryer Rushe
Painted on cloth, with a side long cowe's tayle
And crooked cloven feet, and many a hooked nayle?
For all the world (if I should judge) should reckon him his brother;
Loke, even what face fryer Rushe had, the devil had such another.

In the scene of Christ's delivering souls from purgatory, the Devil is represented as blowing lustily a horn to alarm his comrades, and crying, 'Out, out, aronzt!' to the invader. He fights with a three-pronged fork. He and his victims are painted black,8 in contrast with the souls of the saved, which are white. The hair was considered very important.9 When he went to battle, even his fiery nature was sometimes represented in a way that must have been more ludicrous than impressive.10

The insignificance to which the priests had reduced the devil in the plays, where they were usually the actors, reflected their own petty routine of life. They could conceive of nothing more terrible than their own mean mishaps and local obstructions. One great office of the Devil was to tempt some friar to sleep when he should be at prayer,11 make another drink too much, or a third cast warm glances at a village beauty. The Revelations of the Abbot Richalmus, written seven hundred years ago, shows the Devil already far gone in his process of diminution. The Devil here concentrates the energies which once made the earth tremble on causing nausea to the Abbot, and making the choir cough while he is preaching. 'When I sit down to holy studies,' he says, 'the devils make me heavy with sleep. Then I stretch my hands beyond my cuffs to give them a chill. Forthwith the spirits prick me under my clothes like so many fleas, which causes me to put my hands on them; and so they get warm again, and my reading grows careless.' 'Come, just look at my lip; for twenty years has an imp clung to it just to make it hang down.' It is ludicrous to find that ancient characteristic of the gods of Death already adverted to—their hatred of salt, the agent of preservation—descended from being the sign of Job's constancy to Jehovah into a mere item of the Abbot's appetite. 'When I am at dinner, and the devil has taken away my appetite, as soon as I have tasted a little salt it comes back to me; and if, shortly afterwards, I lose it again, I take some more salt, and am once more an hungered.'12

One dangerous element was the contempt into which, by many causes, the infernal powers had been brought. But a more dangerous one lay in another direction. Though the current phrases of the New Testament and of the Fathers of the Church, declaring this world, its wealth, loves, and pleasures, to be all the kingdom of Satan, had become cant in the mouths of priests ruling over Europe, it had never been cant to the humble peasantries. Although they had degraded many devils imported by the priests, it had been in connection with the declining terrors of their native demonologies. But above these degraded and hated gnomes and elves, whose paternity had been transferred from Sœtere to Satan, there was an array of beautiful deities—gentle gods and goddesses traditionally revered and loved as protectors of the home and the family—which had never really lost their hold on the common people. They might have shrunk before the aggressive victories of the Saints into little Fairies, but their continued love for the poor and the oppressed was the romance of every household. What did these good fairies do? They sometimes loaded the lowly with wealth, if summoned in just the right way; they sang secrets to them from trees as little birds, they smoothed the course of love, clothed ash-maidens in fine clothes, transported people through the air, enabled them to render themselves invulnerable, or invisible, to get out of prisons, to vanquish 'the powers that be,' whether 'ordained of God' or not. Now all these were benefits which, by christian theory, could only be conferred by that Prince of this World who ministered to 'the pride of life.' Into homes which the priest and his noble had stripped of happiness and hope,—whose loving brides were for baptized Bluebeards, whose hard earnings were taken as the price of salvation from devils whose awfulness was departing,—there came from afar rumours of great wealth and splendour conferred upon their worshippers by Eastern gods and goddesses. The priests said all those were devils who would torture their devotees eternally after death; yet it could not be denied that the Moors had the secret of lustres and ornamentation, that the heathen East was gorgeous, that all Christendom was dreaming of the wealth of Ormus and of Ind. Granted that Satan had come westward and northward, joined the scurvy crew of Loki, and become of little importance; but what of Baal or Beelzebub, of Asmodeus, of the genii who built Solomon's temple, of rich Pluto, of august Ahriman? Along with stories of Oriental magnificence there spread through Christendom names of many deities and demons; many of them beautiful names, too, euphemism having generally managed to bestow melodious epithets alike on deities feared and loved. In Faust's 'Miraculous Art and Book of Marvels, or the Black Raven' (1469), the infernal heirarchy are thus named:—King, Lucifer; Viceroy, Belial; Gubernatores, Satan, Beelzebub, Astaroth, Pluto; Chief Princes, Aziel, Mephistopheles, Marbuel, Ariel, Aniguel, Anisel, Barfael. Seductive meanings, too, corresponding to these names, had filtered in some way from the high places they once occupied into the minds of the people. Lucifer was a fallen star that might rise again; Belial and Beelzebub were princes of the fire that rendered possible the arts of man, and the Belfires never went out in the cold North; Astarte meant beauty, and Pluto wealth; Aziel (Asael) was President of the great College of occult arts, from whom Solomon learned the secrets by which he made the jinni his slaves; Marbuel was the artist and mechanic, sometimes believed to aid artisans who produced work beyond ordinary human skill; Ariel was the fine spirit of the air whose intelligence corresponded to that of the Holy Ghost on the other side; Aniguel is the serpent of Paradise, generally written Anisel; Anizazel is probably a fanciful relative of Azazel, 'the strong god;' and Barfael, who in a later Faust book is Barbuel, is an orientalised form of the 'demon of the long beard' who holds the secret of the philosopher's stone.

In a later chapter the growth of favourable views of the devil is considered. Some of the legends therein related may be instructively read in connection with the development of Witchcraft. Many rumours were spread abroad of kindly assistance brought by demons to persons in distress. But even more than by hopes so awakened was the witch aided by the burning desire of the people for vengeance. They wanted Zamiel (Samaël) to help them to mould the bullet that would not miss its mark. The Devil and all his angels had long been recognised by their catechists as being utilised by the Deity to execute his vengeance on the guilty; and to serfs in their agony that devil who would not spare prince or priest was more desired than even the bestower of favours to their starving minds and bodies.

Under the long ages of war in Europe, absorbing the energies of men, women had become the preservers of letters. The era of witchcraft in Europe found that sex alone able to read and write, arts disesteemed in men, among the peasantry at least. To them men turned when it had become a priestly lesson that a few words were more potent than the weapons of princes. Besides this, women were the chief sorcerers, because they were the chief sufferers. In Alsace (1615), out of seventy-five who perished as witches, sixty-two were women. The famous Malleus Maleficorum, which did more evil than any work ever published, derives femina from fide minus. Although in the Faust legend Mephistopheles objects to marriage, many stories represent diabolical weddings. Particular details were told of the marriage of Satan with the daughter of a Sorceress at Egnischen (1585), on which occasion the three towers of the castle there were said to have been illuminated, and a splendid banquet spread, the favourite dish being a ragout of bats. There was exquisite music, and a 'beautiful man' blessed the nuptials. How many poor peasant girls must have had such dreams as they looked up from their drudgery to the brilliant chateaux?

Fig. 20.—Lilith as Cat.

In the illuminated manuscript known as 'Queen Mary's Psalter' (1553) there is a picture of the Fall of Man (Fig. 20) which possesses far-reaching significance. It is a modification of that idea, which gained such wide currency in the Middle Ages, that it was the serpent-woman Lilith who had tempted Adam to eat the forbidden fruit. In this picture, while the beautiful face and ample hair of Lilith are given, instead of the usual female bust she has the body of a cat. This nocturnal animal, already sacred to Freyja, the Teutonic Venus, whose chariot it drew, gained a new mythological career in the North by the large number of Southern and Oriental stones which related it to the lunar and amorous demonesses. When the gods fled before the Titans, Diana, as Ovid relates, changed herself to a cat, and as infernal Hecate that animal was still beside her. If my reader will turn to vol. i. p. 130, some of the vast number of myths which prepared the cat to take its place as familiar of the witch may be found. Whether the artist had Lilith in his mind or not, the illumination in 'Queen Mary's Psalter' represents a remarkable association of myths. For Lilith was forerunner of the mediæval mothers weeping for their children; her voice of perpetual lamentation at the cruel fate allotted her by the combined tyranny of God and man was heard on every sighing wind; and she was the richly dressed bride of the Prince of Devils, ever seeking to tempt youth. Such stories floated through the mind of the Middle Ages, and this infernal Madonna is here seen in association with the cat, beneath whose soft sparkling fur the goddess of Love and Beauty was supposed to be still lurking near the fireside of many a miserable home. Some fragrance of the mystical East was with this feline beauty, and nothing can be more striking than the contrast which the ordinary devils beside her present. Their unseductive ugliness and meanness is placed out of sight of the pair tempted to seek the fruit of forbidden knowledge. They inspire the man and woman in their evidently eager grasping after the fruit, which here means the consultation of fair fortune-tellers and witches to obtain that occult knowledge for which speculative men are seeking in secret studies and laboratories.

Those who have paid attention to the subject of Witchcraft need not be reminded that its complexity and vastness would require a larger volume than the present to deal with it satisfactorily. The present study must be limited to a presentation of some of the facts which induce the writer to believe that, beneath the phenomena, lay a profound alienation from Christianity, and an effort to recall the banished gods which it had superseded.

The first christian church was mainly Jewish, and this is also to say that it inherited the vast Angelolatry and the system of spells which that tribe had brought from Babylon. To all this was now superadded the accumulation of Assyrian and Egyptian lore which was re-edited in the form of Neoplatonicism. This mongrel mass, constituted of notions crumbled from many systems, acquired a certain consistency in Gnosticism. The ancient Egyptians had colleges set apart for astrological study, and for cultivation of the art of healing by charms. Every month, decade, day of the year had its special guardian in the heavens. The popular festivals were astronomic. To the priests in the colleges were reserved study of the sacred books in which the astrological secrets were contained, and whose authorship was attributed to the god Thoth, inventor of writing, the Greek Hermes, and, later, Egyptian Hermes Trismegistus. The zodiac is a memorial of the influence which the stars were supposed to exert upon the human body. Alchemy (the word is Egyptian, Kémi meaning 'black earth') was also studied in connection with solar, lunar, and stellar influences. The Alchemists dreamed of discovering the philosopher's stone, which would change base metals to gold; and Diocletian, in burning the Alchemists' books, believed that, in so doing, he would deprive the Egyptians of their source of wealth.13

Imported into Greece, these notions and their cult had a twofold development. Among the Platonists they turned to a naturalistic and allegorical Demonology; among the uncultivated they formed a Diabolarchy, which gathered around the terrible lunar phantasm—Hecate.

The astrological College of Egypt gave to the Jews their strange idea of the high school maintained among the devils, already referred to in connection with Asmodeus, who was one of its leading professors. The rabbinical legend was, that two eminent angels, Asa and Asael, remonstrated with the Creator on having formed man only to give trouble. The Creator said they would have done the same as man under similar circumstances; whereupon Asa and Asael proposed that the experiment should be tried. They went to earth, and the Creator's prediction was fulfilled: they were the first 'sons of God' who fell in love with the daughters of men (Gen. vi. 2). They were then embodied. In heaven they had been angels of especial knowledge in divine arts, and they now used their spells to reascend. But their sin rendered the spells powerless for that, so they repaired to the Dark Mountains, and there established a great College of Sorcery. Among the many distinguished graduates of this College were Job, Jethro, and Bileam. It was believed that these three instructed the soothsayers who attempted to rival the miracles of Moses before Pharaoh. Job and Jethro were subsequently converted, but Bileam continued his hostility to Israel, and remains a teacher in the College. Through knowledge of the supreme spell—the Shem-hammphorásch, or real name of God—Solomon was able to chain Professor Asmodeus, and wrest from him the secret of the worm Schámir, by whose aid the Temple was built.

Traditions of the learning of the Egyptians, and of the marvels learned by Solomon from Asa and Asael by which he compelled demons to serve him, and the impressive story of the Witch of Endor, powerfully influenced the inquisitive minds of Europe. The fierce denunciations of all studies of these arts of sorcery by the early Church would alone reveal how prevalent they were. The wonderful story of Apollonius of Tyana,14 as told by Philostratus, was really a kind of gospel to the more worldly-minded scholars. Some rabbins, following the outcry against Jesus, 'He casteth out devils by Beelzebub,' circulated at an early date the story that Jesus had derived his power to work miracles from the spell Shem-hammphorásch, which he found on one of the stones of the Temple where Solomon had left it. Though Eusebius cast doubt upon them, the christians generally do not appear to have denied the miracles of Apollonius, which precisely copy those of Jesus from the miraculous birth to the ascension, but even to have quoted them as an evidence of the possibility of miracles. Celsus having attributed the miracles of Jesus to sorcery, and said that magic influenced only the ignorant and immoral, Origen replies that, in order to convince himself of the contrary, he has only to read the memoirs of Apollonius by Mæragenes, who speaks of him as a philosopher and magician, who repeatedly exercised his powers on philosophers. Arnobius and the fathers of the fourth century generally believed in the Apollonian thaumaturgy and attributed it to magic. Aldus Manutius published the book of Philostratus in the fifteenth century, and the degree to which the fascinating and marvellous stories concerning Apollonius fired the European imagination just awaking under the breath of the Renaissance, may be estimated by the fury with which the 'magician' was anathematised by Pico della Mirandola, Jean Bodin, and Baronius. The book and the controversy attracted much attention, and while the priests still continued to charge Apollonius with being a 'magician,' they appear to have perceived that it would have been more to the point, so far as their real peril was concerned, to have proved him an impostor. Failing that, Dr. Faustus and his fellow-professors in the 'black art' were left masters of the situation. The people had to digest the facts admitted, that a Pagan had learned, by initiations into the astrological schools of Egypt and India, the means of healing the sick, raising the dead, flying through the air, throwing off chains, opening locks, rendering himself invisible, and discerning the future.

There was a call for some kind of Apollonius, and Faustus arose. Side by side flourished Luther and Faustus. To Roman Catholic eyes they were twin sons of the Devil;15 that they were characteristic products of one moral age and force appears to me certain, even as to-day the negations of Science and the revival of 'Spiritualism' have a common root in radical disbelief of the hereditary dogmas and forms of so-called religion. It is, however, not surprising that Protestantism felt as much horror of its bastard brother as Science has of the ghostly seances. Through the early sixteenth century we can trace this strange Dr. Faustus ('auspicious,' he had chosen that name) going about Germany, not omitting Erfurth, and talking in taverns about his magic arts and powers. More is said of him in the following chapter; it is sufficient to observe here, and it is the conclusion of Professor Morley, who has sifted the history with his usual care, that about him, as a centre of crystallisation, tales ascribed in the first place to other conjurers arranged themselves, until he became the popular ideal of one who sought to sound the depths of this world's knowledge and enjoyments without help from the Church or its God. The priests did not doubt that this could be done, nor did the Protestants; they generally agreed that it could be accomplished at cost of the soul. As angels of the good God must answer to the formulas of invocation to those who had made a sacramental compact with their Chief, so was it possible to share a sacrament of Satan, and by certain invocations summon his infernal angels to obtain the pleasures of this world of which he is Prince. A thousand years' experience of the Church had left the poor ready to sign the compact if they could secure some little earthly joy. As for Heaven, if it were anything like what its ministers had provided for the poor on earth, Hell might be preferable after all. Dr. Wuttke, while writing his recent work on German superstitions, was surprised to learn that there still exist in France and in Wurtemberg schools for teaching the Black Art. A priest in the last-named country wrote him that a boy had confessed to having passed the lower grade of such a school, but, scared by the horrid ceremonies, had pronounced some holy words which destroyed the effect of the wicked practices, and struck the assembled Devil-worshippers with consternation. The boy said he had barely escaped with his life. I have myself passed an evening at a school in London 'for the development of Spirit-mediums,' and possibly Dr. Wuttke's correspondent would describe these also as Devil-worshippers. No doubt all such circles might be traced archæologically to that Sorcerers' College said by the rabbins to have been kept by Asa and Asael. But what moral force preserved them? They do but represent a turning of methods made familiar by the Church to coax benefits from other supernatural powers in the hope that they would be less dilatory than the Trinity in bestowing their gifts. What is the difference between St. Wolfram's God and King Radbot's Devil? The one offers a golden mansion on earth warranted to last through eternity, the other a like mansion in the skies receivable after death. The Saint agrees that if Radbot's Devil can build him such a house the king would be quite right to worship the architect. The question of the comparative moral merits of the two invisible Powers is not mentioned. This legend, related in a preceding chapter, is characteristic of the motives to which the priesthood appealed through the Middle Ages. It is no wonder that the people began to appeal to the gods of their traditional Radbots, nor that they should have used the ceremonial and sacramental formulas around them.

But to these were added other formulas borrowed from different sources. The 'Compact with the Devil' had in it various elements. It appears to have been a custom of the Odinistic religion for men to sign acts of self-dedication to trusted deities, somewhat corresponding to the votive tablets of Southern religion. It was a legend of Odin that when dying he marked his arm with the point of a spear, and this may have been imitated. In the 'Mysteries' of pagan and christian systems blood played an important part—the human blood of earlier times being symbolised by that of animals, and ultimately, among christians, in wine of the Eucharist. The primitive history of this blood-covenant is given in another chapter. Some astrological formulas, and many of the deities invoked, spread through Europe with the Jews. The actual, and quite as often fabulous, wealth of that antichristian race was ascribed to Antichrist, and while christian princes thought of such gold as legitimate spoil, the honest peasants sought from their astrologers the transmitted 'key of Solomon,' in virtue of which the demons served him. The famous 'Compact' therefore was largely of christian-judaic origin, and only meant conveyance of the soul in consideration of precisely the same treasures as those promised by the Church to all whose names were written in the Lamb's Book,—the only difference being in the period when redemption of the respective issues of priest and astrologer should fall due. One was payable during this life, the other after death.

The ceremonial performances of Witchcraft have also always existed in some form. What we are familiar with of late as Spirit-seances are by no means new. More than a hundred years ago, Mr. Wesley and various clergymen were sitting at a table in Cock Lane, asking the spirit 'Fanny' to rap twice if she were 'in a state of progressive happiness.' Nay, a hundred years before that (1661), Sir Thomas Chamberlain and others, sitting in a haunted house at Tedworth, Wilts, asked 'Satan, if the Drummer set thee to work, give three knocks, and no more, which it did very distinctly, and stopped.'16 We also learn that, in another town and case (1654), 'a naked arm and hand appeared and beat the floor.' It would not be difficult to go further back and find that the dark circle of our Spiritualists with much of its apparatus has existed continuously through the Middle Ages. The dark seance which Goethe has represented in Faust, Part II., at which the spirits of Helen and Paris are evoked, is a very accurate picture of the 'materialisations' now exhibited by mediums, more than forty years after its publication. These outer resemblances are physiognomical. The seance of to-day has lost the darker features of its mediæval prototype, because the Present has not a real and temporal, but only a speculative and sentimental despair, and this is the kind that possesses chiefly the well-to-do and idle classes. It is not difficult to meet the eye of our everyday human nature amid those frenzied periods when whole districts seemed afflicted with epidemic madness, and look deep in that eye to the fathomless heart of humanity.

In an old parish register of Fewston, Yorkshire, are the following entries:—'1621. Anne, daughter of Edward Fairfax, baptized the 12th June.' '1621. Edward Fairfax, Esq., a child named Anne, buried the 9th October.' Then in the History of Knaresborough we read of this child, 'She was held to have died through witchcraft.' In what dreams did that child, supposed to have been snatched away by diabolic malice, return as a pure spirit uplifted in light, yet shadowed by the anxiety and pain of the bereaved family! A medium is at hand, one through whose mind and heart all the stormy electricities of the time are playing. The most distinguished representative of the Fairfax family is off fighting for Parliament against the King. Edward Fairfax is a zealous Churchman. His eldest daughter, Helen, aged twenty-one, is a parishioner of the Rev. Mr. Smithson, yet she has come under the strong influence of a Nonconformist preacher, Mr. Cook. The scholarly clergyman and his worldly Church on one side, and the ignorant minister with his humble followers on the other, are unconscious personifications of Vice and Virtue, while between them poor Helen is no Heraklea.

Nineteen days after the burial of her little sister Anne, as mentioned above, Helen is found 'in a deadly trance.' After a little she begins to speak, her words showing that she is, by imagination, 'in the church at Leeds, hearing a sermon by Mr. Cook.' On November 3, as she lies on her bed, Helen exclaims, 'A white cat hath been long upon me and drawn my breath, and hath left in my mouth and throat so filthy a smell that it doth poison me!' Next we have the following in the father's diary: 'Item. Upon Wednesday, the 14th of November, she saw a black dog by her bedside, and, after a little sleep, she had an apparition of one like a young gentleman, very brave, his apparel all laid with gold lace, a hat with a golden band, and a ruff in fashion. He did salute her with the same compliment as she said Sir Fernandino Fairfax useth when he cometh to the house and saluteth her mother.... He said he was a Prince, and would make her Queen of England and of all the world if she would go with him. She refused, and said, 'In the name of God, what art thou?' He presently did forbid her to name God; to which she replied, 'Thou art no man if thou canst not abide the name of God; but if thou be a man, come near, let me feel of thee;' which he would not do, but said, 'It is no matter for feeling.' She proceeded, 'If thou wert a man, thou wouldst not deny to be felt; but thou art the devil, and art but a shadow.'

It is possible that Helen Fairfax had read in Shakspere's 'Lear,' printed twelve years before, that

The Prince of Darkness is a gentleman;
*Modo he's called, and Mahu.*17

But the reader will remark how her vision anticipates that of Faust, the transformation of the poodle to finely-dressed Mephistopheles. On the next apparition a bit from Patmos is interpolated, the Devil appearing as a beast with many horns; but the folklore of Yorkshire prevails, and 'presently he was like a very little dog, and desired her to open her mouth and let him come into her body, and then he would rule all the world.' Lastly, he 'filled the room with fire.'

In the account thus far we have the following items of ancient mythology:—1, the Cat; 2, the Dog; 3, the Pride of Life (Asmodeus), represented in the fine dress and manners of the fiend; 4, the Prince of this World, offering its throne; 5, the Egyptian belief in potency of the Name; 6, the Hunger-Demon, who dares not be felt, because his back is hollow, and, though himself a shadow, casts none; 7, the disembodied devil of the rabbins, who seeks to enter a human form, in order to enjoy the higher powers of which man is capable; 8, the fiend of fire.

The period in which Helen Fairfax lived supplied forms for the 'materialisation' of these notions flitting from the ancient cemeteries of theology. The gay and gallant Asmodeus had been transformed into a goat under the ascetic eye of Europe; his mistress is a naked witch; her familiar and slave is a cat. This is the conventionalised theologic theory, as we find it in many examples, one of which is here shown (Fig. 21), as copied from a stone panel at the entrance of Lyons Cathedral. This is what Helen's visions end in. She and her younger sister of seven years, and a young neighbour, a girl of twelve, who have become infected with Helen's hysterics, identify six poor women as witches, and Edward Fairfax would have secured their execution had it not been for the clergyman Smithson.

Fig. 21.—A Witch (Lyons Cathedral).

Cats played a large part in this as in other witch-trials. They had long been regarded as an insurance of humble households. In many regions still may be found beliefs that a three-coloured cat protects against fire; a black cat cures epilepsy, protects gardens; and in Bohemia a cat is the favourite bridal gift to procure a happy wedded life. One who kills a cat has no luck for seven years. The Yorkshire women called witches remembered these proverbs to their cost. Among the cats regarded by the Fairfaxes as familiars of the accused, some names are notable. One is called 'Gibbe.' This is the Icelandic gabba, to 'delude,' and our gibber; it is the 'Gib' cat of Reinicke Fuchs, and of the 'Romaunt of the Rose.' In 'Gammer Gurton' we read, 'Hath no man gelded Gyb, her cat;' and in Henry IV. i. 2, 'I am as melancholy as a gib cat.' Another of the cats is called Inges. That is, ignis, fire—Agni maintaining his reign of terror.

Helen's devil hates the dissenter, and says, 'Cook is a lying villain,' because Cook exorcises him with a psalm. On the other hand, the devil praises the clergyman, but Helen breaks out with 'He is not worthy to be a vicar who will bear with witches.' Amid the religious controversies then exciting all households, mourning for his dead child, humiliated by the suspicions of his best neighbours that his daughter was guilty of deception, Edward Fairfax, Gentleman, a scholar and author, lent an ear to the vulgar superstitions of his neighbourhood. Could he have stood on the shoulders of Grimm, he would have left us a very different narrative than that preserved by the Philobiblion Society.18

It is hardly possible to determine now the value of the alleged confessions of witches. They were extorted by torture or by promises of clemency (the latter rarely fulfilled); they were shaped by cross-examiners rather than by their victims; and their worth is still more impaired where, as is usual, they are not given in detail, but recorded in 'substance,' the phraseology in such case reflecting the priest's preconceived theory of witches and their orgies. It is to be feared, for instance, that 'devil' is often written instead of some name that might now be interesting. Nevertheless, there seems to be ground for believing that in many cases there were seances held to invoke supernatural powers.

Among the vast number of trials and confessions, I have found none more significant than the following. In February 1691 a daughter and niece of Mr. Parris, minister in Salem (Massachusetts), girls of ten or eleven years, and several other girls, complained of various bodily torments, and as the physicians could find no cause for them, they were pronounced bewitched. The Rev. Mr. Parris had once been in business at the Barbadoes, and probably brought thence his two slaves, Spanish Indians, man and wife. When the children were declared bewitched, the Indian woman, Tituba, tried an experiment, probably with fetishes familiar in the Barbadoes, to find out the witch. Whereupon the children cried out against the Indian woman as appearing to them and tormenting them. Tituba said her mistress, in her own country, had taught her how to find out a witch, but denied being one herself; but afterwards (urged, as she subsequently declared, by her master) she confessed; and the marks of Spanish cruelty on her body were assumed to be the Devil's wounds. The Rev. Mr. Parris in a calmer time might have vindicated poor Tituba by taking for text of his sermon on the subject Christ's saying about a house divided against itself, and reminding the colony, which held public fast against Satan, that the devil was too clever to cover his Salem agent with wounds; but instead of that he preached on the words, 'Have I not chosen you twelve, and one of you is a devil.' During this sermon a woman left the church; she was sister of a woman who had also been accused by the children, and, being offended by something Mr. Parris said, went out of meeting; of course, also to prison. There were three other women involved with Tituba, in whose fetish experiments a well-informed writer thinks the Salem delusion began.19 The examination before the Deputy-Governor (Danforth) began at Salem, April 11, 1692, and there are several notable points in it. Tituba's husband, the Indian John, cunningly escaped by pretending to be one of the afflicted. He charged Goody Proctor, and said, 'She brought the book to me.' No one asked what book! Abigail Williams, also one of the accusers of Goody, was asked, 'Does she bring the book to you? A. Yes. Q. What would she have you do with it? A. To write in it, and I shall be well.' Not a descriptive word is demanded or given concerning this book. The examiners are evidently well acquainted with it. In the alleged confessions preserved in official reports, but not in the words of the accused, the nature of the book is made clear. Thus Mary Osgood 'confesses that about eleven years ago, when she was in a melancholy state and condition, she used to walk abroad in her orchard, and, upon a certain time she saw the appearance of a cat at the end of the house, which yet she thought was a real cat. However, at that time it diverted her from praying to God, and instead thereof she prayed to the Devil; about which time she made a covenant with the Devil, who, as a black man, came to her, and presented her a book, upon which she laid her finger, and that left a red spot. And that upon her signing that book, the devil told her that he was her god.' This is not unlikely to be a paraphrase of some sermon on the infernal Book of Satan corresponding to the Book of Life, the theory being too conventional for the court to inquire about the mysterious volume. Equally well known was the Antichrist theory which had long represented that avatar of Satan as having organised a church. Thus we read:—'Abigail Williams, did you see a company at Mr. Parris's house eat and drink? A. Yes, sir; that was their sacrament. Q. What was it? A. They said it was our blood.' 'Mary Walcot, have you seen a white man? A. Yes, sir, a great many times. Q. What sort of man was he? A. A fine grave man, and when he came he made all the witches to tremble.' When it is remembered that Mary Osgood had described the Devil as 'a black man' (all were thinking of the Indians), this Antiblackman suggests Christ resisting Antichrist. Again, although nothing seems to have been said in the court previously about baptism, one of the examiners asks 'Goody Laccy how many years ago since they were baptized? A. Three or four years ago I suppose. Q. Who baptized them? A. The old serpent. Q. How did he do it? A. He dipped their heads in the water, saying they were his, and that he had power over them; ... there were six (who) baptized. Q. Name them. A. I think they were of the higher powers.'

There are interspersed through the proceedings suggestions of mercy on condition of confession, which, joined to these theoretical questions, render it plain that the retractations which the so-called witches made were true, and that in New England, at least, there was little if any basis for the delusion beyond the experiment of the two Spanish Indians. The terrible massacre of witches which occurred there was the result of the decision of English judges and divines that witchcraft is recognised in the Bible, and there assigned the death-penalty.

It will be observed here that ancient mythology to Salem is chiefly that of the Bible, modified by local conditions. White man and black man represent Christ and Antichrist, and we have the same symbols on both sides,—eucharists, baptisms, and names written in books. The survivals from European folklore met with in the New England trials are—the cat, the horse (rarely), and the dog. In one case a dog suffered from the repute of being a witch, insomuch that some who met him fell into fits; he was put to death. Riding through the air continues, but the American witches ride upon a stick or pole. The old-fashioned broom, the cloud-symbol of the Wild Huntsman, is rarely mentioned. One thing, however, survives from England, at least; the same sharp controversy that is reflected in the Fairfax case. Cotton Mather tried one of the possessed with the Bible, the 'Assembly's Catechism,' his grandfather's 'Milk for Babes,' his father's 'Remarkable Providence,' and a book to prove there were witches. 'And when any of those were offered for her to read in, she would be struck dead and fall into convulsions.' But when he tried her with Popish and Quaker books, the English Prayer-Book, and a book to prove there were no witches, the devil permitted her to read these as long as she pleased. One is at a loss which most to admire, the astuteness of the accused witch in bearing testimony to the Puritan religion, or the phenomenon of its eminent representative seeking a witness to it in the Father of lies.

If now we travel towards the East we find the survivals growing clearer, as in the West they become faint.

In 1669 the people of the villages of Mohra and Elfdale in Sweden, believing that they were troubled by witches, were visited by a royal commission, the result of whose investigations was the execution of twenty-three adults and fifteen children; running of the gauntlet by thirty-six between the ages of nine and sixteen years; the lashing on the hand of twenty children for three Sundays at the church-door, and similar lashing of the aforesaid thirty-six once a week for a year. Portions of the confessions of the witches are given below from the Public Register as translated by Anthony Horneck, D.D., and printed in London, anno 1700. I add a few words in brackets to point out survivals.

'We of the province of Elfdale do confess that we used to go to a gravel-pit which lay hard by a cross-way (Hecate), and there we put on a vest (Wolf-girdle) over our heads, and then danced round, and after this ran to the cross-way, and called the Devil thrice, first with a still voice, the second time somewhat louder, and the third time very loud, with these words—Antecessor, come and carry us to Blockula. Whereupon immediately he used to appear, but in different habits; but for the most part we saw him in a grey coat and red and blue stockings: he had a red beard (Barbarossa), a high-crowned hat (Turn-cap), with linen of divers colours wrapt about it, and long garters upon his stockings.

'Then he asked us whether we would serve him with soul and body. If we were content to do so, he set us upon a beast which he had there ready, and carried us over churches and high walls; and after all we came to a green meadow where Blockula lies. We must procure some scrapings of altars, and filings of church clocks; and then he gives us a horn with a salve in it, wherewith we do anoint ourselves (chrism); and a saddle with a hammer (Thor's), and a wooden nail, thereby to fix the saddle (Walkyr's); whereupon we call upon the Devil and away we go.'

'For their journey, they said they made use of all sorts of instruments, of beasts, of men, of spits, and posts, according as they had opportunity: if they do ride upon goats (Azazel) and have many children with them, that all may have room, they stick a spit into the backside of the Goat, and then are anointed with the aforesaid ointment. What the manner of their journey is, God only knows. Thus much was made out, that if the children did at any time name the names (Egyptian spells) of those that had carried them away, they were again carried by force either to Blockula, or to the cross-way, and there miserably beaten, insomuch that some of them died of it.'

'A little girl of Elfdale confessed that, naming the name of Jesus as she was carried away, she fell suddenly upon the ground, and got a great hole in her side, which the Devil presently healed up again, and away he carried her; and to this day the girl confessed she had exceeding great pain in her side.'

'They unanimously confessed that Blockula is situated in a delicate large meadow, whereof you can see no end. The place or house they met at had before it a gate painted with divers colours; through this gate they went into a little meadow distinct from the other, where the beasts went that they used to ride on; but the men whom they made use of in their journey stood in the house by the gate in a slumbering posture, sleeping against the wall (castle of Waldemar). In a huge large room of this house, they said, there stood a very long table, at which the witches did sit down; and that hard by this room was another chamber where there were very lovely and delicate beds. The first thing they must do at Blockula was, that they must deny all, and devote themselves body and soul to the Devil, and promise to serve him faithfully, and confirm all this with an oath (initiation). Hereupon they cut their fingers (Odinism), and with their blood write their name in his book (Revelations). They added that he caused them to be baptized, too, by such priests as he had there (Antichrist's Sacraments).'

'And he, the Devil, bids them believe that the day of judgment will come speedily, and therefore sets them on work to build a great house of stone (Babel), promising that in that house he will preserve them from God's fury, and cause them to enjoy the greatest delights and pleasures (Moslem). But while they work exceeding hard at it, there falls a great part of the wall down again.'

'They said, they had seen sometimes a very great Devil like a Dragon, with fire round about him, and bound with an iron chain (Apocalyptic), and the Devil that converses with them tells them that if they confess anything he will let that great Devil loose upon them, whereby all Sweedeland shall come into great danger.'

'They added that the Devil had a church there, such another as in the town of Mohra. When the Commissioners were coming he told the Witches they should not fear them; for he would certainly kill them all. And they confessed that some of them had attempted to murther the Commissioners, but had not been able to effect it.

'Some of the children talked much of a white Angel (Frigga as christian tutelary), which used to forbid them what the Devil had bid them do, and told them that those doings should not last long. What had been done had been permitted because of the wickedness of the people.

'Those of Elfdale confessed that the Devil used to play upon an harp before them (Tannhauser), and afterwards to go with them that he liked best into a chamber, when he committed venerous acts with them (Asmodeus); and this indeed all confessed, that he had carnal knowledge of them, and that the Devil had sons and daughters by them, which he did marry together, and they ... brought forth toads and serpents (Echidna).

'After this they sat down to table, and those that the Devil esteemed most were placed nearest to him; but the children must stand at the door, where he himself gives them meat and drink (Sacrament). After meals they went to dancing, and in the meanwhile swore and cursed most dreadfully, and afterwards went to fighting one with another (Valhalla).

'They also confessed that the Devil gives them a beast about the bigness and shape of a young cat (Hecate), which they call a carrier; and that he gives them a bird as big as a raven (Odin's messenger), but white;20 and these two creatures they can send anywhere, and wherever they come they take away all sorts of victuals they can get, butter, cheese, milk, bacon, and all sorts of seeds, whatever they find, and carry it to the witch. What the bird brings they may keep for themselves, but what the carrier brings they must reserve for the Devil, and that is brought to Blockula, where he doth give them of it so much as he thinks fit. They added likewise that these carriers fill themselves so full sometimes, that they are forced to spue ('Odin's booty') by the way, which spuing is found in several gardens, where colworts grow, and not far from the houses of these witches. It is of a yellow colour like gold, and is called butter of witches.

'The Lords Commissioners were indeed very earnest, and took great pains to persuade them to show some of their tricks, but to no purpose; for they did all unanimously confess that since they had confessed all, they found that all their witchcraft was gone, and that the Devil at this time appeared to them very terrible, with claws on his hands and feet, and with horns on his head, a long tail behind, and showed to them a pit burning, with a hand put out; but the Devil did thrust the person down again with an iron fork; and suggested to the witches that if they continued in their confession, he would deal with them in the same manner.'

The ministers of both Elfdale and Mohra were the chief inciters of this investigation, and both testified that they had suffered many tortures in the night from the witches. One was taken by the throat and so violently used that 'for some weeks he was not able to speak or perform divine service.'

We have in this narrative the official and clerical statement, and can never know to what the victims really confessed. Blockula seems to be a Swedish edition of Blocksberg, of old considered a great resort of witches. But we may especially note the epithet by which the witches are said to have first appealed to the Devil—Antecessor. Dr. Horneck has not given us the Swedish term of which this is a translation, but we may feel assured that it was not a phrase coined by the class among whom reputed witches were found. In all probability it was a learned phrase of the time for some supposed power which preceded and was conquered by Christianity; and if we knew its significance it might supply a clue to the reality with which the Commissioners were dealing. There would seem to be strong probabilities that in Sweden also, as elsewhere, there had been a revival of faith in the old religion whose barbaric rites had still survived in a few holes and corners where they were practised by night. The Antecessor was still present to hold out promises where the Successor had broken all that his sponsors had made when the populace accepted his baptism. This probability is further suggested by the fact that some of these uncanny events happened at Elfdale, a name which hints at a region of especial sanctity under the old religion, and also by the statement that the Devil had a church there, a sort of travesty of the village church. About the same time we find John Fiene confessing in Scotland that the Devil appeared to him in 'white raiment,' and it is also testified that John heard 'the Devil preach in a kirk in the pulpit in the night by candlelight, the candle burning blue.'21

The names used by the Scotch witches are often suggestive of pagan survivals. Thus in the trial at the Paisley Assizes, 1678, concerning the alleged bewitching of Sir George Maxwell, Margaret Jackson testified to giving up her soul by renouncing her baptism to a devil named Locas (Loki?); another raised a tempest to impede the king's voyage to Denmark by casting into the sea a cat, and crying Hola (Hela?); and Agnes Sampson called the Devil to her in the shape of a dog by saying, 'Elva (Elf?), come and speak to me!'

It is necessary to pass by many of the indications contained in the witch-trials that there had been an effort to recur to the pleasures and powers traditionally associated with the pagan era of Europe, and confirmed by the very denunciations of contemporary paganism with its pomp and luxury by the priesthood. The promises held out by the 'Devil' to Elfdale peasants and puritanised Helen Fairfax are unmistakable. But it is necessary to remark also that the ceremonies by which, as was clearly proved in various cases, the fortune-tellers or 'witches' endeavoured to imitate the spells of Dr. Faustus were archæological.

Around the cauldron, which was used in imitation of the Alchemists, a rude Zodiac was marked, some alchemic signs being added; and in the cauldron were placed ingredients concerning many of which the accounts are confused. It is, however, certain that the chief ingredients were plants which, precisely as in ancient Egypt, had been gathered at certain phases of the moon, or seasons of the year, or from some spot where the sun was supposed not to have shone on it. It was clearly proved also that the plants chiefly used by the sorceresses were rue and vervain. Vervain was sacred to the god of war in Greece and Rome, and made the badge of ambassadors sent to make treaties of peace. In Germany it was sacred to Thor, and he would not strike with his lightning a house protected by it. The Druids called it 'holy herb;' they gathered it when the dog-star rose, from unsunned spots, and compensated the earth for the deprivation with a sacrifice of honey. Its reputation was sufficient in Ben Jonson's day for him to write—

Bring your garlands, and with reverence place
The vervain on the altar.

The charm which vervain had for the mediæval peasant was that it was believed, if it had first touched a Bel-fire, to snap iron; and, if boiled with rue, made a liquid which, being poured on a gunflint, made the shot as sure to take effect as any Freischütz could desire.

Rue was supposed to have a potent effect on the eye, and to bestow second sight. So sacred was it once in England that missionaries sprinkled holy water from brushes made up of it, whence it was called 'herb of grace.' Milton represents Michael as purging Adam's eyes with it. In the Tyrol it is believed to confer fine vision and used with agrimony (flowers of Argos, the many-eyed); in Posen it is said also to heal serpent-bites. By this route it came into the cauldron of the wizard and witch. In Drayton's incantation it is said—

Then sprinkles she the juice of rue,
With nine drops of the midnight dew
From lunary distilling.

This association of lunary, or moon-wort, once supposed to cure lunacy, with rue is in harmony with the mythology of both. An old oracle, said to have been revealed by Hecate herself, ran thus:—'From a root of wild rue fashion and polish a statue; adorn it with household lizards; grind myrrh, gum, and frankincense with the same reptiles, and let the mixture stand in the air during the waning of a moon; then address your vows in the following terms' (the formula is not preserved). 'As many forms as I have, so many lizards let there be; do these things exactly; you will build me an abode with branches of laurel, and having addressed fervent prayers to the image, you will see me in your sleep.'22

Rue was thus consecrated as the very substance of Hecate, the mother of all European witches. M. Maury supposes that it was because it was a narcotic and caused hallucinations. Hallucinations were, no doubt, the basis of belief in second sight. But whatever may be the cause, rue was the plant of witchcraft; and Bishop Taylor speaks of its being used by exorcists to try the devil, and thence deriving its appellation 'herb of grace.' More probably it was used to sprinkle holy water because of a traditional sanctity. All narcotics were supposed to be children of the night; and if, in addition, they were able to cause hallucinations, they were supposed to be under more especial care of the moon.

After reading a large number of reports concerning the ordeals and trials of witches, and also many of their alleged confessions, I have arrived at the conclusion that there were certainly gatherings held in secret places; that some of the ordinary ceremonies and prayers of the Church were used, with names of traditional deities and Oriental demons substituted for those of the Trinity and saints; that with these were mingled some observances which had been preserved from the ancient world by Gnostics, Astrologists, and Alchemists. That at these gatherings there was sometimes direct devil-worship is probable, but oftener the invocations were in other names, and it is for the most part due to the legal reporters that the 'Devil' is so often named. As to the 'confessions,' many, no doubt, admitted they had gone to witches' Sabbaths who had been there only in feverish dreams, as must have been the case of many young children and morbid pietists who were executed; others confessed in hope of escape from charges they could not answer; and others were weary of their lives.

The writer of this well remembers, in a small Virginian village (Falmouth), more than thirty years ago, the terrible persecutions to which an old white woman named Nancy Calamese was subjected because of her reputation as a witch. Rumours of lizards vomited by her poor neighbours caused her to be dreaded by the ignorant; the negroes were in terror of her; she hardly dared pass through the streets for fear of being hooted by boys. One morning she waded into the Rappahannock river and drowned herself, and many of her neighbours regarded the suicide as her confession. Probably it was a similar sort of confession to many that we read in the reports of witch trials.

The retribution that followed was more ferocious than could have visited mere attempts by the poor and ignorant to call up spirits to their aid. Every now and then the prosecutions disclose the well-known animus of heresy, persecution, and also the fury of magistrates suspicious of conspiracies. In England, New England, and France, particularly, an incipient rationalism was revealed in the party called 'Saducees,' who tried to cast discredit on the belief in witchcraft. This was recognised by Sir Mathew Hale in England and Cotton Mather in New England, consequently by the chief authorities of church and state in both countries, as an attack on biblical infallibility, since it was said in the Bible, 'Thou shalt not suffer a witch to live.' The leading wizards and witches were probably also persons who had been known in connection with the popular discontent and revolutionary feeling displayed in so many of the vindictive conjurations which were brought to light.

The horrors which attended the crushing out of this last revival of paganism are such as recall the Bartholomew massacre and the recent slaughter of Communists in Paris, so vividly that one can hardly repress the suspicion that the same sort of mingled panic and fanaticism were represented in them all. Dr. Réville has summed up the fearful history of three hundred years as follows:—'In the single year 1485, and in the district of Worms alone, eighty-five witches were delivered to the flames. At Geneva, at Basle, at Hamburg, at Ratisbon, at Vienna, and in a multitude of other towns, there were executions of the same kind. At Hamburg, among other victims, a physician was burnt alive, because he saved the life of a woman who had been given up by the midwife. In Italy, during the year 1523, there were burnt in the diocese of Como alone more than two hundred witches. This was after the new bull hurled at witchcraft by Pope Adrian VI. In Spain it was still worse; there, in 1527, two little girls, of from nine to eleven years of age, denounced a host of witches, whom they pretended to detect by a mark in their left eye. In England and Scotland political influence was brought to bear upon sorcery; Mary Stuart was animated by a lively zeal against witches. In France the Parliament of Paris happily removed business of this kind from the ecclesiastical tribunals; and under Louis XI., Charles VIII., and Louis XII. there were but few condemnations for the practice of magic; but from the time of Francis I., and especially from Henry II., the scourge reappeared. Jean Bodin, a man of sterling worth in other respects, but stark mad upon the question of witchcraft, communicated his mania to all classes of the nation. His contemporary and disciple, Boguet, showed how that France swarmed with witches and wizards. 'They increase and multiply on the land,' said he, 'even as do the caterpillars in our gardens. Would that they were all got together in a heap, so that a single fire might burn them all at once.' Savoy, Flanders, the Jura Mountains, Lorraine, Béarn, Provence, and in almost all parts of France, the frightful hecatombs were seen ablaze. In the seventeenth century the witch-fever somewhat abated, though it burst out here and there, centralising itself chiefly in the convents of hysterical nuns. The terrible histories of the priests Gaufridy and Urban Grandier are well known. In Germany, and particularly in its southern parts, witch-burning was still more frequent. In one small principality at least 242 persons were burnt between 1646 and 1651; and, horrible dictu, in the official records of these executions, we find that among those who suffered were children from one to six years of age! In 1657 the witch-judge, Nicholas Remy, boasted of having burnt 900 persons in fifteen years. It would even seem that it is to the proceedings against sorcery that Germany owes the introduction of torture as an ordinary mode of getting at the truth. Mr. Roskoff reproduces a catalogue of the executions of witches and wizards in the episcopal town of Würzburg, in Bavaria, up to the year 1629. In 1659 the number of those put to death for witchcraft amounted, in this diocese, to 900. In the neighbouring bishopric of Bamberg at least 600 were burnt. He enumerates thirty-one executions in all, not counting some regarded by the compilers of the catalogue as not important enough to mention. The number of victims at each execution varies from two to seven. Many are distinguished by such surnames as 'The Big Hunchback, The Sweetheart, The Bridge-keeper, The Old Pork-woman,' etc. Among them appear people of all sorts and conditions, actors, workmen, jugglers, town and village maidens, rich burghers, nobles, students, magistrates even, and a fair number of priests. Many are simply entered as 'a foreigner.' Here and there is added to the name of the condemned person his age and a short notice. Among the victims, for instance, of the twentieth execution figures 'Little Barbara, the prettiest girl in Würzburg;' 'a student who could speak all manner of languages, who was an excellent musician, vocaliter et instrumentaliter;' 'the master of the hospice, a very learned man.' We find, too, in this, gloomy account the cruel record of children burnt for witchcraft; here a little girl of about nine or ten years of age, with her baby sister, younger than herself (their mother was burnt a little while afterwards); here boys of ten or eleven; again, a young girl of fifteen; two children from the poorhouse; the little boy of a councillor. The pen falls from one's hand in recapitulating such monstrosities. Cannot those who would endow Catholicity with the dogma of papal infallibility hearken, before giving their vote, to the cries that rise before God, and which history re-echoes, of those poor innocent ones whom pontifical bulls threw into flames? The seventeenth century saw the rapid diminution of trials and tortures. In one of his good moments, Louis XIV. mitigated greatly the severity of this special legislation. For this he had to undergo the remonstrances of the Parliament of Rouen, which believed society would be ruined if those who dealt in sorcery were merely condemned to perpetual confinement. The truth is, that belief in witchcraft was so wide-spread, that from time to time even throughout the seventeenth century there were isolated executions. One of the latest and most notorious was that of Renata Saenger, superior of the convent of Unterzell, near Würzburg (1748). At Landshut, in Bavaria, in 1756, a young girl of thirteen years was convicted of impure intercourse with the Devil, and put to death. Seville in 1781, and Glaris in 1783, saw the last two known victims to this fatal superstition.'23

The Reformation swept away in Northern countries, for the upper classes, as many Christian saints and angels as priestcraft had previously turned to enemies for the lower. The poor and ignorant simply tried to evoke the same ideal spirit-guardians under the pagan forms legendarily associated with a golden age. Witchcraft was a pathetic appeal against cruel present to a fair, however visionary, past. But Protestantism has brought on famine of another kind— famine of the heart. The saints of the Church have followed those of paganism; and although one result of the process has been a vast increase in enterprise, science, and wealth, man cannot live by these alone. Modern spiritualism, which so many treat with a superciliousness little creditable to a scientific age, is a cry of starved sentiment and affections left hopeless under faded heavens, as full of pathetic meaning as that which was wrung from serfs enticed into temples only to find them dens of thieves. Desolate hearts take up the burthen of desolate homes, and appeal to invisible powers for guidance; and for attestation of hopes which science has blighted, ere poetry, art, and philanthropy have changed these ashes into beauty. Because these so-called spirits, evoked by mediums out of morbid nerves, are really longed-for ideals, the darker features of witchcraft are not called about them. That fearful movement was a wronged Medea whose sorrows had made Hecate—to remember the dreadful phrase of Euripides—'the chosen assistant dwelling in the inmost recesses of her house.' Modern spiritualism is Rachel weeping for her children, not to be comforted if they are not. But the madness of the one is to be understood by the plaintive appeal of the other.

Notes

1 S. Cyp. ap. Muratori, Script. it. i. 295, 545. The Magicians used to call their mirrors after the name of this flower-devil—Fiorone. M. Maury, 'La Magie,' 435 n.
2 This whole subject is treated, and with ample references, in M. Maury's 'Magie,' p. 41, seq.
3 'La Sorcière.'
4 Dasent's 'Norse Tales,' Introd. ciii.
5 'Chips,' ii.
6 'Chester Plays,' 1600.
7 'Declaration of Popish Impostures,' 1603.
8 So Shakespere, 'The Devil damn thee black.'
9 In an account, 1568, we find:—'pay'd for iij li of heare ijs vjd.'
10 The Directions for the 'Castle of Good Perseverance,' say: '& he þt schal pley belyal, loke þt he have guñe powdr breññg in pypysĩh's hands & ĩ h's ers & ĩ h's ars whãne he gothe to batayle.'

11 This notion was widespread. I have seen an ancient Russian picture in which the Devil is dancing before a priest who has become drowsy over his prayer-book. There was once a Moslem controversy as to whether it was fair for pilgrims to keep themselves awake for their prayers by chewing coffee-berries.

12 'Liber Revelationum de Insidiis et Versutiis Dæmonum adversus Homines.' See Reville's Review of Roskoff, 'The Devil,' p. 38.

13 See M. Maury's 'Magie,' p. 48.

14 The history has been well related by a little work by Dr. Albert Réville: 'Apollonius of Tyana, the Pagan Christ.' Chatto & Windus.

15 Sinistrari names Luther as one of eleven persons whom he enumerates as having been begotten by Incubi, 'Enfin, comme l'ecrit Codens, cité par Maluenda, ce damné Hérésiarque, qui a nom Martin Luther.'—'Démonialité,' 30.

16 Glanvil's 'Saducismus.'

17 King Lear, iii. 4. Asmodeus and Mohammed are, no doubt, corrupted in these names, which are given as those of devils in Harsenet's 'Declaration of Popish Impostures.'

18 'A Discourse of Witchcraft. As it was acted in the Family of Mr. Edward Fairfax, of Fuystone, in the county of York, in the year 1621. Sibi parat malum, qui alteri parat.'

19 W. F. Poole, Librarian of Chicago, to whom I am indebted for a copy of Governor Thomas Hutchinson's account of 'The Witchcraft Delusion of 1692,' with his valuable notes on the same.

20 The delicacy with which these animals are alluded to rather than directly named indicates that they had not lost their formidable character in Elfdale so far as to be spoken of rashly.

21 Glanvil, 'Saducismus Triumphatus,' p. 170.

22 Porphyry, ap. Euseb. v. 12. The formula not preserved by Eusebius is supposed by M. Maury ('Magie,' 56) to be that contained in the 'Philosophumena,' attributed to Origen:—'Come, infernal, terrestrial, and celestial Bombo! goddess of highways, of cross-roads, thou who bearest the light, who travellest the night, enemy of the day, friend and companion of darkness; thou rejoicing in the baying of dogs and in shed blood, who wanderest amid shadows and over tombs; thou who desirest blood and bearest terrors to mortals,—Gorgo, Mormo, moon of a thousand forms, aid with a propitious eye our sacrifices!'

23 'The Devil,' etc., p. 51.

Chapter XXV - Faust and Mephistopheles

Mephisto and Mephitis—The Raven Book—Papal sorcery—Magic seals—Mephistopheles as dog—George Sabellicus alias Faustus—The Faust myth—Marlowe's Faust—Good and evil angels—El Magico Prodigioso—Cyprian and Justina—Klinger's Faust—Satan's sermon—Goethe's Mephistopheles—His German characters—Moral scepticism—Devil's gifts—Helena—Redemption through Art—Defeat of Mephistopheles.

The name Mephistopheles has in it, I think, the priest's shudder at the fumes of the laboratory. Duntzer[1] finds that the original form of the word was 'Mephostophiles,' and conjectures that it was a bungling effort to put together three Greek words, to mean 'not loving the light.' In this he has the support of Bayard Taylor, who also thinks that it was so understood by Goethe. The transformation of it was probably amid the dreaded gases with which the primitive chemist surrounded himself. He who began by 'not loving the light' became the familiar of men seeking light, and lover of their mephitic gases. The ancient Romans had a mysterious divinity called Mephitis, whose grove and temple were in the Esquiliæ, near a place it was thought fatal to enter. She is thought to have been invoked against the mephitic exhalations of the earth in the grove of Albunea. Sulphur springs also were of old regarded as ebullitions from hell, and both Schwarz and Roger Bacon particularly dealt in that kind of smell. Considering how largely Asmodeus, as 'fine gentleman,' entered into the composition of Mephistopheles, and how he flew from Nineveh to Egypt (Tobit) to avoid a bad smell, it seems the irony of mythology that he should turn up in Europe as a mephitic spirit.

Mephistopheles is the embodiment of all that has been said in preceding chapters of the ascetic's horror of nature and the pride of life, and of the mediæval priest's curse on all learning he could not monopolise. The Faust myth is merely his shadow cast on the earth, the tracery of his terrible power as the Church would have the people dread it. The early Raven Book at Dresden has the title:—' † † † D. J. Fausti † † † Dreifacher Höllen-Zwung und Magische (Geister-Commando) nebst den schwarzen Raaben. Romæ ad Arcanum Pontificatus unter Papst Alexander VI. gedruckt. Anno (Christi) MDI.' In proof of which claim there is a Preface purporting to be a proclamation signed by the said Pope and Cardinal Piccolomini concerning the secrets which the celebrated Dr. Faust had scattered throughout Germany, commanding ut ad Arcanum Pontificatus mandentur et sicut pupilla oculi in archivio Nostro serventur et custodiantur, atque extra Valvas Vaticanas non imprimantur neque inde transportentur. Si vero quiscunque temere contra agere ausus fuerit, Divinam maledictionem latæ sententiæ ipso facto servatis Nobis Solis reservandis se incursurum sciat. Ita mandamus et constituemus Virtute Apostolicæ Ecclesiæ Jesu Christi sub pœna Excommunicationis ut supra. Anno secundo Vicariatus Nostri. Romæ Verbi incarnati Anno M.D.I.

This is an impudent forgery, but it is an invention which, more than anything actually issued from Rome, indicates the popular understanding that the contention of the Church was not against the validity of magic arts, but against their exercise by persons not authorised by itself. It was, indeed, a tradition not combated by the priests, that various ecclesiastics had possessed such powers, even Popes, as John XXII., Gregory VII., and Clement V. The first Sylvester was said to have a dragon at his command; John XXII. denounced his physicians and courtiers for necromancy; and the whispers connecting the Vatican with sorcery lasted long enough to attribute to the late Pius IX. a power of the evil eye. Such awful potencies the Church wished to be ascribed to itself alone. Faust is a legend invented to impress on the popular mind the fate of all who sought knowledge in unauthorised ways and for non-ecclesiastical ends.

In the Raven Book just mentioned, there are provisions for calling up spirits which, in their blending of christian with pagan formulas, oddly resemble the solemn proceedings sometimes affected by our spiritual mediums. The magician (Magister) had best be alone, but if others are present, their number must be odd; he should deliberate beforehand what business he wishes to transact with the spirits; he must observe God's commandment; trust the Almighty's help; continue his conjuration, though the spirits do not appear quickly, with unwavering faith; mark a circle on parchment with a dove's blood; within this circle write in Latin the names of the four quarters of heaven; write around it the Hebrew letters of God's name, and beneath it write Sadan; and standing in this circle he must repeat the ninety-first Psalm. In addition there are seals in red and black, various Hebrew, Greek, and Latin words, chiefly such as contain the letters Q, W, X, Y, Z,—e.g., Yschyros, Theos, Zebaoth, Adonay. The specimen (Fig. 22), which I copied from the book in Dresden, is there called 'Sigillum Telschunhab.' The 'Black Raven' is pictured in the book, and explained as the form in which the angel Raphael taught Tobias to summon spirits. It is said also that the Magician must in certain cases write with blood of a fish (Tobit again) or bat on 'maiden-parchment,'—this being explained as the skin of a goat, but unpleasantly suggestive of a different origin.

Fig. 22.—Seal from Raven Book.

In this book, poorly printed, and apparently on a private press, Mephistopheles is mentioned as one of the chief Princes of Hell. He is described as a youth, adept in all arts and services, who brings spirit-servants or familiars, and brings treasures from earth and sea with speed. In the Frankfort Faust Book (1587), Mephistopheles says, 'I am a spirit, and a flying spirit, potently ruling under the heavens.' In the oldest legends he appears as a dog, that, as we have seen, being the normal form of tutelary divinities, the symbol of the Scribe in Egypt, guard of Hades, and psychopomp of various mythologies. A dog appears following the family of Tobias. Manlius reports Melancthon as saying, 'He (Faust) had a dog with him, which was the Devil.' Johann Gast ('Sermones Conviviales') says he was present at a dinner at Basle given by Faust, and adds: 'He had also a dog and a horse with him, both of which, I believe, were devils, for they were able to do everything. Some persons told me that the dog frequently took the shape of a servant, and brought him food.' In the old legends this dog is named Praestigiar.2

As for the man Faust, he seems to have been personally the very figure which the Church required, and had the friar, in whose guise Mephistopheles appears, been his actual familiar, he could hardly have done more to bring learning into disgrace. Born at the latter part of the fifteenth century at Knittlingen, Wurtemberg, of poor parents, the bequest of an uncle enabled him to study medicine at Cracow University, and it seems plain that he devoted his learning and abilities to the work of deluding the public. That he made money by his 'mediumship,' one can only infer from the activity with which he went about Germany and advertised his 'powers.' It was at a time when high prices were paid for charms, philtres, mandrake mannikins; and the witchcraft excitement was not yet advanced enough to render dealing in such things perilous. It seems that the Catholic clergy made haste to use this impostor to point their moral against learning, and to identify him as first-fruit of the Reformation; while the Reformers, with equal zeal, hurled him back upon the papists as outcome of their idolatries. Melancthon calls him 'an abominable beast, a sewer of many devils.' The first mention of him is by Trithemius in a letter of August 20, 1507, who speaks of him as 'a pretender to magic' ('Magister Georgius Sabellicus, Faustus Junior'), whom he met at Gelnhaussen; and in another letter of the same year as at Kreuznach, Conrad Mudt, friend of Luther and Melancthon, mentions (Oct. 3, 1513) the visit to Erfurth of Georgius Faustus Hemitheus Hedebeyensis, 'a braggart and a fool who affects magic,' whom he had 'heard talking in a tavern,' and who had 'raised theologians against him.' In Vogel's Annals of Leipzig (1714), kept in Auerbach's Cellar, is recorded under date 1525 Dr. Johann Faust's visit to the Cellar. He appears therefore to have already had aliases. The first clear account of him is in the 'Index Sanitatis' of Dr. Philip Begardi (1539), who says: 'Since several years he has gone through all regions, provinces, and kingdoms, made his name known to everybody, and is highly renowned for his great skill, not alone in medicine, but also in chiromancy, necromancy, physiognomy, visions in crystal, and the like other arts. And also not only renowned, but written down and known as an experienced master. Himself admitted, nor denied that it was so, and that his name was Faustus, and called himself philosophum philosophorum. But how many have complained to me that they were deceived by him—verily a great number! But what matter?—hin ist hin.'

These latter words may mean that Faust had just died. He must have died about that time, and with little notice. The rapidity with which a mythology began to grow around him is worthy of more attention than the subject has received. In 1543 the protestant theologian Johann Gast has ('Sermones Convivialium') stories of his diabolical dog and horse, and of the Devil's taking him off, when his body turns itself five times face downward. In 1587 Philip Camerarius speaks of him as 'a well-known magician who lived in the time of our fathers.' April 18, 1587, two students of the University of Tübingen were imprisoned for writing a Comedy of Dr. Faustus: though it was not permitted to make light of the story, it was thought a very proper one to utilise for pious purposes, and in the autumn of the same year (1587) the original form of the legend was published by Spiess in Frankfort. It describes Faust as summoning the Devil at night, in a forest near Wittenberg. The evil spirit visits him on three occasions in his study, where on the third he gives his name as 'Mephostophiles,' and the compact to serve him for twenty-four years for his soul is signed. When Faust pierces his hand, the blood flows into the form of the words O homo fuge! Mephistopheles first serves him as a monk, and brings him fine garments, wine, and food. Many of the luxuries are brought from the mansions of prelates, which shows the protestant bias of the book; which is also shown in the objection the Devil makes to Faust's marrying, because marriage is pleasing to God. Mephistopheles changes himself to a winged horse, on which Faust is borne through many countries, arriving at last at Rome. Faust passes three days, invisible, in the Vatican, which supplies the author with another opportunity to display papal luxury, as well as the impotence of the Pope and his cardinals to exorcise the evil powers which take their food and goblets when they are about to feast. On his further aerial voyages Faust gets a glimpse of the garden of Eden; lives in state in the Sultan's palace in the form of Mohammed; and at length becomes a favourite in the Court of Charles V. at Innsbruck. Here he evokes Alexander the Great and his wife. In roaming about Germany, Faust diverts himself by swallowing a load of hay and horses, cutting off heads and replacing them, making flowers bloom at Christmas, drawing wine from a table, and calling Helen of Troy to appear to some students. Helen becomes his mistress; by her he has a son, Justus Faustus; but these disappear simultaneously with the dreadful end of Dr. Faustus, who after a midnight storm is found only in the fragments with which his room is strewn.

Several of these legends are modifications of those current before Faust's time. The book had such an immense success that new volumes and versions on the same subject appeared not only in Germany but in other parts of Europe,—a rhymed version in England, 1588; a translation from the German in France, 1589; a Dutch translation, 1592; Christopher Marlowe's drama in 1604.

In Marlowe's 'Tragical History of Doctor Faustus,' the mass of legends of occult arts that had crystallised around a man thoroughly representative of them was treated with the dignity due to a subject amid whose moral and historic grandeur Faust is no longer the petty personality he really was. He is precisely the character which the Church had been creating for a thousand years, only suddenly changed from other-worldly to worldly desires and aims. What he seeks is what all the energy of civilisation seeks.

Evil Angel. Go forward, Faustus, in that famous art
Wherein all Nature's treasure is contained:
Be thou on earth as Jove is in the sky,
Lord and commander of these elements.
Faust. How am I glutted with conceit of this!
Shall I make spirits fetch me what I please,
Resolve me of all ambiguities,
Perform what desperate enterprise I will?
I'll have them fly to India for gold,
Ransack the ocean for orient pearl,
And search all corners of the new-found world
For pleasant fruits and princely delicates;
I'll have them read me strange philosophy,
And tell the secrets of all foreign kings;
I'll have them wall all Germany with brass,
And make swift Rhine circle fair Wertenberg;
I'll have them fill the public schools with silk,
Wherewith the students shall be bravely clad.

For this he is willing to pay his soul, which Theology has so long declared to be the price of mastering the world.

This word damnation terrifies not him,
For he confounds hell in Elysium:
His ghost be with the old philosophers!

The 'Good Angel' warns him:

O Faustus, lay that damned book aside,
And gaze not on it, lest it tempt thy soul,
And heap God's heavy wrath upon thy head!
Read, read the Scriptures:—that is blasphemy.

So, dying away amid the thunders of the Reformation, were heard the echoes of the early christian voices which exulted in the eternal tortures of the Greek poets and philosophers: the anathemas on Roger Bacon, Socinus, Galileo; the outcries with which every great invention has been met. We need only retouch the above extracts here and there to make Faust's aspirations those of a saint. Let the gold be sought in New Jerusalem, the pearl in its gates, the fruits in paradise, the philosophy that of Athanasius, and no amount of selfish hunger and thirst for them would grieve any 'Good Angel' he had ever heard of.

The 'Good Angel' has not yet gained his wings who will tell him that all he seeks is included in the task of humanity, but warn him that the method by which he would gain it is just that by which he has been instructed to seek gold and jasper of the New Jerusalem,—not by fulfilling the conditions of them, but as the object of some favouritism. Every human being who ever sought to obtain benefit by prayers or praises that might win the good graces of a supposed bestower of benefits, instead of by working for them, is but the Faust of his side—be it supernal or infernal. Hocus-pocus and invocation, blood-compacts and sacraments,—they are all the same in origin; they are all mean attempts to obtain advantages beyond other people without serving up to them or deserving them. To Beelzebub Faust will 'build an altar and a church;' but he had probably never entered a church or knelt before an altar with any less selfishness.

A strong Nemesis follows Self to see that its bounds are not overpassed without retribution. Its satisfactions must be weighed in the balance with its renunciations. And the inflexible law applies to intellect and self-culture as much as to any other power of man. Mephistopheles is 'the kernel of the brute;' he is the intellect with mere canine hunger for knowledge because of the power it brings. Or, falling on another part of human nature, it is pride making itself abject for ostentation; or it is passion selling love for lust. Re-enter Mephistopheles with Devils, who give crowns and rich apparel to Faustus, dance, and then depart. To the man who has received his intellectual and moral liberty only to so spend it, Lucifer may well say, in Marlowe's words—

Christ cannot save thy soul, for he is just:
There's none but I have interest in the same.

Perhaps he might even better have suggested to Faust that his soul was not of sufficient significance to warrant much anxiety.

Something was gained when it was brought before the people in popular dramas of Faust how little the Devil cared for the cross which had so long been regarded as the all-sufficient weapon against him.[3] Faust and Mephistopheles flourish in the Vatican despite all the crosses raised to exorcise them. The confession of the cross which once meant martyrdom of the confessor had now come to mean martyrdom of the denier. Protestantism put its faith in Theology, Creeds, and Orthodoxy. But Calderon de la Barca blended the legend of Faust with the legendary temptation of St. Cyprian, and in 'El Magico Prodigioso' we have, in impressive contrast, the powerlessness of the evil powers over the heart of a pure woman, and its easy entrance into a mind fully furnished with the soundest sentiments of theology. St. Cyprian had been a worshipper of pagan deities[4] before his conversion, and even after this he had once saved himself while other christians were suffering martyrdom. It is possible that out of this may have grown the legend of his having called his earlier deities—theoretically changed to devils—to his aid; a trace of the legend being that magical 'Book of Cyprianus' mentioned in another chapter. In his tract 'De Gratia Dei' Cyprian says concerning his spiritual condition before conversion, 'I lay in darkness, and floating on the world's boisterous sea, with no resting-place for my feet, ignorant of my proper life, and estranged from truth and light.' Here is a metaphorical 'vasty deep' from which the centuries could hardly fail to conjure up spirits, one of them being the devil of Calderon's drama, who from a wrecked ship walks Christ-like over the boisterous sea to find Cyprian on the sea-shore. The drama opens with a scene which recalls the most perilous of St. Anthony's temptations. According to Athanasius, the Devil having utterly failed to conquer Anthony's virtue by charming images, came to him in his proper black and ugly shape, and, candidly confessing that he was the Devil, said he had been vanquished by the saint's extraordinary sanctity. Anthony prevailed against the spirit of pride thus awakened; but Calderon's Cyprian, though he does not similarly recognise the Devil, becomes complacent at the dialectical victory which the tempter concedes him. Cyprian having argued the existence and supremacy of God, the Devil says, 'How can I impugn so clear a consequence?' 'Do you regret my victory?' 'Who but regrets a check in rivalry of wit?' He leaves, and Cyprian says, 'I never met a more learned person.' The Devil is equally satisfied, knowing, no doubt, that gods worked out by the wits alone remain in their abode of abstraction and do not interfere with the world of sense. Calderon is artful enough to throw the trial of Cyprian back into his pagan period, but the mirror is no less true in reflecting for those who had eyes to see in it the weakness of theology.

'Enter the Devil as a fine gentleman,' is the first sign of the temptation in Calderon's drama—it is Asmodeus[5] again, and the 'pride of life' he first brings is the conceit of a clever theological victory. So sufficient is the doorway so made for all other pride to enter, that next time the devil needs no disguise, but has only to offer him a painless victory over nature and the world, including Justina, the object of his passion.

Wouldst thou that I work
A charm over this waste and savage wood,
This Babylon of crags and aged trees,
Filling its coverts with a horror
Thrilling and strange?...
I offer thee the fruit
Of years of toil in recompense; whate'er
Thy wildest dream presented to thy thought
As object of desire, shall be thine.[6]

Justina knows less about the philosophical god of Cyprian, and more of the might of a chaste heart. To the Devil she says—

Thought is not in my power, but action is:
I will not move my foot to follow thee.
The Devil is compelled to say at last—

Woman, thou hast subdued me,
Only by not owning thyself subdued.
He is only able to bring a counterfeit of Justina to her lover.

Like Goethe's Mephistopheles, Cyprian's devil is unable to perform his exact engagements, and consequently does not win in the game. He enables Cyprian to move mountains and conquer beasts, until he boasts that he can excel his infernal teacher, but the Devil cannot bring Justina. She has told Cyprian that she will love him in death. Cyprian and she together abjure their paganism at Antioch, and meet in a cell just before their martyrdom. Over their bodies lying dead on the scaffold the Devil appears as a winged serpent, and says he is compelled to announce that they have both ascended to heaven. He descends into the earth.

What the story of Faust and Mephistopheles had become in the popular mind of Germany, when Goethe was raising it to be an immortal type of the conditions under which genius and art can alone fulfil their task, is well shown in the sensational tragedy written by his contemporary, the playwright Klinger. The following extract from Klinger's 'Faust' is not without a certain impressiveness.

'Night covered the earth with its raven wing. Faust stood before the awful spectacle of the body of his son suspended upon the gallows. Madness parched his brain, and he exclaimed in the wild tones of dispair:

'Satan, let me but bury this unfortunate being, and then you may take this life of mine, and I will descend into your infernal abode, where I shall no more behold men in the flesh. I have learned to know them, and I am disgusted with them, with their destiny, with the world, and with life. My good action has drawn down unutterable woe upon my head; I hope that my evil ones may have been productive of good. Thus should it be in the mad confusion of earth. Take me hence; I wish to become an inhabitant of thy dreary abode; I am tired of light, compared with which the darkness in the infernal regions must be the brightness of mid-day.'

But Satan replied: 'Hold! not so fast—Faust; once I told thee that thou alone shouldst be the arbiter of thy life, that thou alone shouldst have power to break the hour-glass of thy existence; thou hast done so, and the hour of my vengeance has come, the hour for which I have sighed so long. Here now do I tear from thee thy mighty wizard-wand, and chain thee within the narrow bounds which I draw around thee. Here shalt thou stand and listen to me, and tremble; I will draw forth the terrors of the dark past, and kill thee with slow despair.

'Thus will I exult over thee, and rejoice in my victory. Fool! thou hast said that thou hast learned to know man! Where? How and when? Hast thou ever considered his nature? Hast thou ever examined it, and separated from it its foreign elements? Hast thou distinguished between that which is offspring of the pure impulses of his heart, and that which flows from an imagination corrupted by art? Hast thou compared the wants and the vices of his nature with those which he

257

owes to society and prevailing corruption? Hast thou observed him in his natural state, where each of his undisguised expressions mirrors forth his inmost soul? No—thou hast looked upon the mask that society wears, and hast mistaken it for the true lineaments of man; thou hast only become acquainted with men who have consecrated their condition, wealth, power, and talents to the service of corruption; who have sacrificed their pure nature to your Idol—Illusion. Thou didst at one time presume to show me the moral worth of man! and how didst thou set about it! By leading me upon the broad highways of vice, by bringing me to the courts of the mighty wholesale butchers of men, to that of the coward tyrant of France, of the Usurper in England! Why did we pass by the mansions of the good and the just? Was it for me, Satan, to whom thou hast chosen to become a mentor, to point them out to thee? No; thou wert led to the places thou didst haunt by the fame of princes, by thy pride, by thy longing after dissipation. And what hast thou seen there? The soul-seared tyrants of mankind, with their satellites, wicked women and mercenary priests, who make religion a tool by which to gain the object of their base passions.

'Hast thou ever deigned to cast a glance at the oppressed, who, sighing under his burden, consoles himself with the hope of an hereafter? Hast thou ever sought for the dwelling of the virtuous friend of humanity, for that of the noble sage, for that of the active and upright father of a family?

'But how would that have been possible? How couldst thou, the most corrupt of thy race, have discovered the pure one, since thou hadst not even the capacity to suspect his existence?

'Proudly didst thou pass by the cottages of the pure and humble, who live unacquainted with even the names of your artificial vices, who earn their bread in the sweat of their brow, and who rejoice at their last hour that they are permitted to exchange the mortal for the immortal. It is true, hadst thou entered their abode, thou mightst not have found thy foolish ideal of an heroic, extravagant virtue, which is only the fanciful creation of your vices and your pride; but thou wouldst have seen the man of a retiring modesty and noble resignation, who in his obscurity excels in virtue and true grandeur of soul your boasted heroes of field and cabinet. Thou sayest that thou knowest man! Dost thou know thyself? Nay, deeper yet will I enter into the secret places of thy heart, and fan with fierce blast the flames which thou hast kindled there for thee.

'Had I a thousand human tongues, and as many years to speak to thee, they would be all insufficient to develop the consequences of thy deeds and thy recklessness. The germ of wretchedness which thou hast sown will continue its growth through centuries yet to come; and future generations will curse thee as the author of their misery.

'Behold, then, daring and reckless man, the importance of actions that appear circumscribed to your mole vision! Who of you can say, Time will obliterate the trace of my existence! Thou who knowest not what beginning, what middle, and end are, hast dared to seize with a bold hand the chain of fate, and hast attempted to gnaw its links, notwithstanding that they were forged for eternity!

'But now will I withdraw the veil from before thy eyes, and then—cast the spectre despair into thy soul.'

'Faust pressed his hands upon his face; the worm that never dieth gnawed already on his heart.'
The essence and sum of every devil are in the Mephistopheles of Goethe. He is culture.

Culture, which smooth the whole world licks,
Also unto the Devil sticks.

He represents the intelligence which has learned the difference between ideas and words, knows that two and two make four, and also how convenient may be the dexterity that can neatly write them out five.

Of Metaphysics learn the use and beauty!
See that you most profoundly gain
What does not suit the human brain!
A splendid word to serve, you'll find
For what goes in—or won't go in—your mind.
On words let your attention centre!
Then through the safest gate you'll enter
The temple halls of certainty.7

He knows, too, that the existing moment alone is of any advantage; that theory is grey and life ever green; that he only gathers real fruit who confides in himself. He is thus the perfectly evolved intellect of man, fully in possession of all its implements, these polished till they shine in all grace, subtlety, adequacy. Nature shows no symbol of such power more complete than the gemmed serpent with its exquisite adaptations,—freed from cumbersome prosaic feet, equal to the winged by its flexible spine, every tooth artistic.

From an ancient prison was this Ariel liberated by his Prospero, whose wand was the Reformation, a spirit finely touched to fine issues. But his wings cannot fly beyond the atmosphere. The ancient heaven has faded before the clearer eye, but the starry ideals have come nearer. The old hells have burnt out, but the animalism of man couches all the more freely on his path, having broken every chain of fear. Man still walks between the good and evil, on the hair-drawn bridge of his moral nature. His faculties seem adapted with equal precision to either side of his life, upper or under,—to Wisdom or Cunning, Self-respect or Self-conceit, Prudence or Selfishness, Lust or Love.

Such is the seeming situation, but is it the reality? Goethe's 'Faust' is the one clear answer which this question has received.

In one sense Mephistopheles may be called a German devil. The Christian soul of Germany was from the first a changeling. The ancient Nature-worship of that race might have had its normal development in the sciences, and alone with this intellectual evolution there must have been formed a related religion able to preserve social order through the honour of man. But the native soul of Germany was cut out by the sword and replaced with a mongrel Hebrew-Latin soul. The metaphorical terrors of tropical countries,—the deadly worms, the burning and suffocating blasts and stenches, with which the mind of those dwelling near them could familiarise itself when met with in their scriptures, acquired exaggerated horrors when left to be pictured by the terrorised imagination of races ignorant of their origin. It is a long distance from Potsdam and Hyde Park to Zahara. Christianity therefore blighted nature in the north by apparitions more fearful than the southern world ever knew, and long after the pious there could sing and dance, puritanical glooms hung over the Christians of higher latitudes. When the progress of German culture began the work of dissipating these idle terrors, the severity of the reaction was proportioned to the intensity of the delusions. The long-famished faculties rushed almost madly into their beautiful world, but without the old reverence which had once knelt before its phenomena. That may remain with a few, but the cynicism of the noisiest will be reflected even upon the faces of the best. Goethe first had his attention drawn to Spinoza by a portrait of him on a tract, in which his really noble countenance was represented with a diabolical aspect. The orthodox had made it, but they could only have done so by the careers of Faust, Paracelsus, and their tribe. These too helped to conventionalise Voltaire into a Mephistopheles.8

Goethe was probably the first European man to carry out this scepticism to its full results. He was the first who recognised that the moral edifice based upon monastic theories must follow them; and he had in his own life already questioned the right of the so-called morality to its supreme if not tyrannous authority over man. Hereditary conscience, passing through this fierce crucible, lay levigable before Goethe, to be swept away into dust-hole or moulded into the image of reason. There remained around the animal nature of a free man only a thread which seemed as fine as that which held the monster Fenris. It was made only of the sentiment of love and that of honour. But as Fenris found the soft invisible thread stronger than chains, Faust proved the tremendous sanctions that surround the finer instincts of man. Emancipated from grey theory, Faust rushes hungrily at the golden fruit of life. The starved passions will have their satisfaction, at whatever cost to poor Gretchen. The fruit turns to ashes on his lips. The pleasure is not that of the thinking man, but of the accomplished poodle he has taken for his guide. To no moment in that intrigue can the suffrage of his whole nature say, 'Stay, thou art fair!' That is the pact—it is the distinctive keynote of Goethe's 'Faust.'

Canst thou by falsehood or by flattery
Make me one moment with myself at peace,
Cheat me into tranquillity?—come then
And welcome life's last day.
Make me to the passing moment plead.
Fly not, O stay, thou art so fair!
Then will I gladly perish.

The pomp and power of the court, luxury and wealth, equally fail to make the scholar at peace with himself. They are symbolised in the paper money by which Mephistopheles replenished the imperial exchequer. The only allusion to the printing-press, whose inventor Fust had been somewhat associated with Faust, is to show its power turned to the work of distributing irredeemable promises.

At length one demand made by Faust makes Mephistopheles tremble. As a mere court amusement he would have him raise Helen of Troy. Reluctant that Faust should look upon the type of man's harmonious development, yet bound to obey, Mephistopheles sends him to the Mothers,—the healthy primal instincts and ideals of man which expressed themselves in the fair forms of art. Corrupted by superstition of their own worshippers, cursed by christianity, they 'have a Hades of their own,' as Mephistopheles says, and he is unwilling to interfere with them. The image appears, and the sense of Beauty is awakened in Faust. But he is still a christian as to his method: his idea is that heaven must be taken by storm, by chance, wish, prayer, any means except patient fulfilment of the conditions by which it may be reached. Helen is flower of the history and culture of Greece; and so lightly Faust would pluck and wear it!

Helen having vanished as he tried to clasp her, Faust has learned his second lesson. When he next meets Helen it is not to seek intellectual beauty as, in Gretchen's case, he had sought the sensuous and sensual. He has fallen under a charm higher than that of either Church or Mephistopheles; the divorce of ages between flesh and spirit, the master-crime of superstition, from which all devils sprang, was over for him from the moment that he sees the soul embodied and body ensouled in the art-ideal of Greece.

The redemption of Faust through Art is the gospel of the nineteenth century. This is her vesture which Helen leaves him when she vanishes, and which bears him as a cloud to the land he is to make beautiful. The purest Art—Greek Art—is an expression of Humanity: it can as little be turned to satisfy a self-culture unhumanised as to consist with a superstition which insults nature. When Faust can meet with Helen, and part without any more clutching, he is not hurled back to his Gothic study and mocking devil any more: he is borne away until he reaches the land where his thought and work are needed. Blindness falls on him—or what Theology deems such: for it is metaphorical—it means that he has descended from clouds to the world, and the actual earth has eclipsed a possible immortality.

The sphere of Earth is known enough to me;
The view beyond is barred immortality:
A fool who there his blinking eyes directeth,
And o'er his clouds of peers a place expecteth!
Firm let him stand and look around him well!
This World means something to the capable;
Why needs he through Eternity to wend?

The eye for a fictitious world lost, leaves the vision for reality clearer. In every hard chaotic object Faust can now detect a slumbering beauty. The swamps and pools of the unrestrained sea, the oppressed people, the barrenness and the flood, they are all paths to Helen—a nobler Helen than Greece knew. When he has changed one scene of Chaos into Order, and sees a free people tilling the happy earth, then, indeed, he has realised the travail of his manhood, and is satisfied. To a moment which Mephistopheles never brought him, he cries 'Stay, thou art fair!'

Mephistopheles now, as becomes a creation of the Theology of obtaining what is not earned, calls up infernal troops to seize Faust's soul, but the angels pelt them with roses. The roses sting them worse than flames. The roses which Faust has evoked from briars are his defence: they are symbols of man completing his nature by a self-culture which finds its satisfaction in making some outward desert rejoice and blossom like the rose.

Notes

1 Scheible's 'Kloster,' 5, 116. Zauberbücher.
2 Bayard Taylor's 'Faust,' note 45. See also his Appendix I. for an excellent condensation of the Faust legend from the best German sources.
3 Tertull. ad Marcion, iii. 18. S. Ignatii Episc. et Martyr ad Phil. Ep. viii. 'The Prince of this world rejoices when any one denies the cross, for he knows the confession of the cross to be his ruin.'
4 See his 'Acta,' by Simeon Metaphrastus.
5 I have been much struck by the resemblance between the dumpy monkish dwarf, in the old wall-picture of Auerbach's Cellar, meant for Mephistopheles, and the portrait of Asmodeus in the early editions of 'Le Diable Boiteux.' But, as devils went in those days, they are good-looking enough.
6 Shelley's Translation.
7 Bayard Taylor's Translation. Scene iv.
8 See Lavater's Physiognomy, Plates xix. and xx., in which some artist has shown what variations can be made to order on an intellectual and benevolent face.

Chapter XXVI - The Wild Huntsman

The Wild Hunt—Euphemisms—Schimmelreiter—Odinwald—Pied Piper—Lyeshy—Waldemar's Hunt—Palne Hunter—King Abel's Hunt—Lords of Glorup—Le Grand Veneur—Robert le Diable—Arthur—Hugo—Herne—Tregeagle—Der Freischütz—Elijah's chariot—Mahan Bali—Déhak—Nimrod—Nimrod's defiance of Jehovah—His Tower—Robber Knights—The Devil in Leipzig—Olaf hunting pagans—Hunting-horns—Raven—Boar—Hounds—Horse—Dapplegrimm—Sleipnir—Horseflesh—The mare Chetiya—Stags—St. Hubert—The White Lady—Myths of Mother Rose—Wodan hunting St. Walpurga—Friar Eckhardt.

The most important remnant of the Odin myth is the universal legend of the Wild Huntsman. The following variants are given by Wuttke.1 In Central and South Germany the Wild Hunt is commonly called Wütenden Heere, i.e., Wodan's army or chase—called in the Middle Ages, Wuotanges Heer. The hunter, generally supposed to be abroad during the twelve nights after Christmas, is variously called Wand, Waul, Wodejäger, Helljäger, Nightjäger, Hackelberg,

Hackelberend (man in armour), Fro Gode, Banditterich, Jenner. The most common belief is that he is the spectre of a wicked lord or king who sacrilegiously enjoyed the chase on Sundays and other holy days, and who is condemned to expiate his sin by hunting till the day of doom. He wears a broad-brimmed hat; is followed by dogs and other animals, fiery, and often three-legged; and in his spectral train are the souls of unbaptized children, huntsmen who have trodden down grain, witches, and others—these being mounted on horses, goats, and cocks, and sometimes headless, or with their entrails dragging behind them. They rush with a fearful noise through the air, which resounds with the cracking of whips, neighing of horses, barking of dogs, and cries of ghostly huntsmen. The unlucky wight encountered is caught up into the air, where his neck is wrung, or he is dropped from a great height. In some regions, it is said, such must hunt until relieved, but are not slain. The huntsman is a Nemesis on poachers or trespassers in woods and forests. Sometimes the spectres have combats with each other over battlefields. Their track is marked with bits of horseflesh, human corpses, legs with shoes on. In some regions, it is said, the huntsmen carry battle-axes, and cut down all who come in their way. When the hunt is passing all dogs on earth become still and quiet. In most regions there is some haunted gorge, hill, or castle in which the train disappears.

In Thuringia, it is said that, when the fearful noises of the spectral hunt come very near, they change to ravishing music. In the same euphemistic spirit some of the prognostications it brings are not evil: generally, indeed, the apparition portends war, pestilence, and famine, but frequently it announces a fruitful year. If, in passing a house, one of the train dips his finger in the yeast, the staff of life will never be wanting in that house. Whoever sees the chase will live long, say the Bohemians; but he must not hail it, lest flesh and bones rain upon him.

In most regions, however, there is thought to be great danger in proximity to the hunt. The perils are guarded against by prostration on the earth face downward, praying meanwhile; by standing on a white cloth (Bertha's linen), or wrapping the same around the head; by putting the head between the spokes of a wheel; by placing palm leaves on a table. The hunt may be observed securely from the cross-roads, which it shuns, or by standing on a stump marked with three crosses—as is often done by woodcutters in South Germany.

Wodan also appears in the Schimmelreiter—headless rider on a white horse, in Swabia called Bachreiter or Junker Jäkele. This apparition sometimes drives a carriage drawn by four white (or black) horses, usually headless. He is the terrible forest spectre Hoimann, a giant in broad-brimmed hat, with moss and lichen for beard; he rides a headless white horse through the air, and his wailing cry, 'Hoi, hoi!' means that his reign is ended. He is the bugbear of children.

In the Odinwald are the Riesenäule and Riesenaltar, with mystic marks declaring them relics of a temple of Odin. Near Erbach is Castle Rodenstein, the very fortress of the Wild Jäger, to which he passes with his horrid train from the ruins of Schnellert. The village of Reichelsheim has on file the affidavits of the people who heard him just before the battles of Leipzig and Waterloo. Their theory is that if the Jäger returns swiftly to Schnellert all will go well for Germany; but if he tarry at Rodenstein 'tis an omen of evil. He was reported near Frankfort in 1832; but it is notable that no mention of him was made during the late Franco-German war.

A somewhat later and rationalised variant relates that the wild huntsman was Hackelberg, the Lord of Rodenstein, whose tomb—really a Druidical stone—is shown at the castle, and said to be guarded by hell-hounds. Hackelberg is of old his Brunswick name. It was the Hackelberg Hill that opened to receive the children, which the Pied Piper of Hamelin charmed away with his flute from that old town, because the corporation would not pay him what they had promised for ridding them of rats. It is easy to trace this Pied Piper, who has become so familiar through Mr. Robert Browning's charming poem, to the Odin of more blessed memory, who says in the Havamal, 'I know a song by which I soften and enchant my enemies, and render their weapons of no effect.'

This latter aspect of Odin, his command over vermin, connects him with the Slavonic Lyeshy, or forest-demon of the Russias. The ancient thunder-god of Russia, Perun, who rides in his storm-chariot through the sky, has in the more christianised districts dropped his mantle on Ilya (Elias); while in the greater number of Slavonic districts he has held his original physical characters so remarkably that it has been necessary to include him among demons. In Slavonian Folklore the familiar myth of the wild huntsman is distributed—Vladimir the Great fulfils one part of it by still holding high revel in the halls of Kief, but he is no huntsman; Perun courses noisily through the air, but he is rather benevolent than otherwise; the diabolical characteristics of the superstition have fallen to the evil huntsmen (Lyeshies), who keep the wild creatures as their flocks, the same as shepherds their herds, and whom every huntsman must propitiate. The Lyeshy is gigantic, wears a sheepskin, has one eye without eyebrow or eyelash, horns, feet of a goat, is covered with green hair, and his finger-nails are claws. He is special protector of the bears and wolves.

In Denmark the same myth appears as King Volmer's Hunt. Waldemar was so passionately fond of the chase that he said if the Lord would only let him hunt for ever near Gurre (his castle in the north of Seeland), he would not envy him his paradise. For this blasphemous wish he is condemned to hunt between Burre and Gurre for ever. His cavalcade is much like that already described. Volmer rides a snow-white charger, preceded by a pack of coal-black hounds, and he carries his head under his left arm. On St. John the women open gates for him. It is believed that he is allowed brief repose at one and another of his old seats, and it is said spectral servants are sometimes seen preparing the ruined castle at Vordingborg for him, or at Waldemar's Tower. A sceptical peasant resolved to pass the night in this tower. At midnight the King entered, and, thanking him for looking after his tower, gave him a gold piece which burned through his hand and fell to the ground as a coal. On the other hand, Waldemar sometimes makes peasants hold his dogs, and afterwards throws them coals which turn out to be gold pieces.

The Palnatoke or Palne Hunter appears mostly in the island of Fuen. Every New Year's night he supplies himself with three horse-shoes from some smithy, and the smith takes care that he may find them ready for use on his anvil, as he always leaves three gold pieces in their stead. If the shoes are not ready for him, he carries the anvil off. In one instance he left an anvil on the top of a church tower, and it caused the smith great trouble to get it down again.

King Abel was interred after his death in St. Peter's Church in Sleswig, but the fratricide could find no peace in his grave. His ghost walked about in the night and disturbed the monks in their devotions. The body was finally removed from the church, and sunk in a foul bog near Gottorp. To keep him down effectively, a pointed stake was drove through his body. The spot is still called Königsgrabe. Notwithstanding this, he appears seated on a coal-black charger, followed by a pack of black hounds with eyes and tongues of fire. The gates are heard slamming and opening, and the shrieks and yells are such that they appal the stoutest hearts.

At the ancient capital of Fuen, Odense, said to have been built by Odin, the myth has been reduced to a spectral Christmas-night equipage, which issues from St. Canute's Church and passes to the ancient manor-house of Glorup. It is a splendid carriage, drawn by six black horses with fiery tongues, and in it are seated the Lords of Glorup, famous for their cruelty to peasants, and now not able to rest in the church where they were interred. It is of evil omen to witness the spectacle: a man who watched for it was struck blind.

In France Le Grand Veneur bears various names; he is King Arthur, Saint Hubert, Hugo. His alleged appearances within historic times have been so strongly attested that various attempts have been made to give them rational explanations. Thus Charles VI. of France, when going to war in Bretagne, is said to have been met by such a spectre in the Forest of Mans, and became insane; he believed himself to have been the victim of sorcery, as did many of his subjects. It has been said that the King was met by a disguised emissary of the Duc de Bretagne. More particular accounts are given of the apparition of the Wild Huntsman to Henry IV. when he was hunting with the Comte de Soissons in the Forest of Fontainebleau, an event commemorated by 'La Croix du Grand Veneur.' According to Matthieu,[2] both the King and the Count heard the cries of the hunt, and when the Count went to discover their origin, the terrible dark figure stood forth and cried, 'You wish to see me, then behold!' This incident has been explained variously, as a project of assassination, or as the jest of two fellows who, in 1596, were amusing Paris by their skill in imitating all the sounds of a hunt. But such phantoms had too long hunted through the imagination of the French peasantry for any explanation to be required. Robert le Diable, wandering in Normandy till judgment-day, and King Arthur, at an early date domesticated in France as a spectral huntsman (the figure most popularly identified at the time with the phantom seen by Henry IV.), are sufficient explanations. The ruins of Arthur's Castle near Huelgoat, Finistère, were long believed to hide enormous treasures, guarded by demons, who appear sometimes as fiery lights (ignes fatuui), owls, buzzards, and ravens—one of the latter being the form in which Arthur comes from his happy Vale of Avallon, when he would vary its repose with a hunt.[3]

A sufficiently curious interchange of such superstitions is represented in the following extract from Surtees:—'Sir Anthon Bek, busshop of Dureme in the tyme of King Eduarde, the son of King Henry, was the maist prowd and masterfull busshop in all England, and it was com'only said that he was the prowdest lord of Christienty. It chaunced that among other lewd persons, this sir Anthon entertained at his court one Hugh de Pountchardon, that for his evill deeds and manifold robberies had been driven out of the Inglische courte, and had come from the southe to seek a little bread, and to live by staylinge. And to this Hughe, whom also he imployed to good purpose in the warr of Scotland, the busshop gave the land of Thikley, since of him called Thikley-Puntchardon, and also made him his chiefe huntsman. And after, this blake Hughe died afore the busshop; and efter that the busshop chasid the wild hart in Galtres forest, and sodainly ther met with him Hugh de Pontchardon, that was afore deid, on a wythe horse; and the said Hughe loked earnestly on the busshop, and the busshop said unto him, 'Hughe, what makethe thee here?' and he spake never word, but lifte up his cloke, and then he showed sir Anton his ribbes set with bones, and nothing more; and none other of the varlets saw him but the busshop only; and ye said Hughe went his way, and sir Anton toke corage, and cheered the dogges; and shortly efter he was made Patriarque of Hierusalem, and he same nothing no moe; and this Hugh is him that the silly people in Galtres doe call le Gros Veneur, and he was seen twice efter that by simple folk, afore yat the forest was felled in the tyme of Henry, father of King Henry yat now ys.'

Upon this uncanny fellow fell the spectral mantle of Hugo Capet; elsewhere as is probable, worn by nocturnal protestant assemblies—Huguenots.

The legend of the Wild Huntsman tinges many old English stories. Herne, the Hunter, may be identified with him, and the demons, with ghostly and headless wish-hounds, who still hunt evil-doers over Dartmoor on stormy nights, are his relations. The withered look of horses grazing on Penzance Common was once explained by their being ridden by demons, and the fire-breathing horse has found its way by many weird routes to the service of the Exciseman in the 'Ingoldsby Legends,' or that of Earl Garrett, who rides round the Curragh of Kildare on a steed whose inch-thick silver shoes must wear as thin as a cat's ear, ere he fights the English and reigns over Ireland. The Teutonic myth appears very plainly in the story of Tregeagle. This man, traced to an old Cornish family, is said to have been one of the wickedest men that ever lived; but though he had disposed of his soul to the Devil, the evil one was baulked by the potency of St. Petroc. This, however, was on condition of Tregeagle's labouring at the impossible task of clearing the sand from Porthcurnow Cove, at which work he may still be heard groaning when wind and wave are high. Whenever he tries to snatch a moment's rest, the demon is at liberty to pursue him, and they may be heard on stormy nights in hot pursuit of the poor creature, whose bull-like roar passed into the Cornish proverb, 'to roar like Tregeagle.'

On a pleasant Sunday evening in July 1868, I witnessed 'Der Freischütz' in the newly-opened opera-house at Leipzig. Never elsewhere have I seen such completeness and splendour in the weird effects of the infernal scene in the Wolf's Glen. The 'White Lady' started forth at every step of Rodolph's descent to the glen, warning him back. Zamiel, instead of the fiery garb he once wore as Samaël, was arrayed in raiment black as night; and when the magic bullet was moulded, the stage swarmed with huge reptiles, fiery serpents crawled on the ground, a dragon-drawn chariot, with wheels of fire, driven by a skeleton, passed through the air; and the wild huntsman's chase, composed of animals real to the eye and uttering their distinguishable cries, hurried past. The animals represented were the horse, hound, boar, stag, chamois, raven, bat, owl, and they rushed amid the wild blast of horns.

I could but marvel at the yet more strange and weird history of the human imagination through which had flitted, from the varied regions of a primitive world, the shapes combined in this apotheosis of diablerie. Probably if Elijah in his fire-chariot, preached about in the neighbouring church that morning, and this wild huntsman careering in the opera, had looked closely at each other and at their own history, they might have found a common ancestor in the mythical Mahan Bali of India, the king whose austerities raised in power till he excited the jealousy of the gods, until Vishnu crushed him with his heel into the infernal regions, where he still exercises sovereignty, and is permitted to issue forth for an annual career (at the Onam festival), as described in Southey's 'Curse of Kehama.' And they might probably both claim mythological relationship with Yami, lord of death, who, as Jami, began in Persia the career of all warriors that never died, but sometimes sleep till a magic horn shall awaken them, sometimes dwell, like Jami himself and King Arthur, in happy isles, and in other cases issue forth at certain periods for the chase or for war—like Odin and Waldemar—with an infernal train.

But how did these mighty princes and warriors become demon huntsmen?

In the Persian 'Desatir' it is related that the animals contested the superiority of man, the two orders of beings being represented by their respective sages, and the last animal to speak opposed the claim of his opponent that man attained elevation to the nature of angels, with the remark, 'In his putting to death of animals and similar acts man resembleth the beasts of prey, and not angels.'

The prophet of the world then said, 'We deem it sinful to kill harmless, but right to slay ravenous, animals. Were all ravenous animals to enter into a compact not to kill harmless animals, we would abstain from slaying them, and hold them dear as ourselves.'

Upon this the wolf made a treaty with the ram, and the lion became friend of the stag. No tyranny was left in the world, till man (Dehak) broke the treaty and began to kill animals. In consequence of this, none observed the treaty except the harmless animals.4

This fable, from the Aryan side, may be regarded as showing the reason of the evil repute which gathered around the name of Dehak or Zohak. The eating of animal food was among our Aryan ancestors probably the provisional commissariat of a people migrating from their original habitat. The animals slain for food had all their original consecration, and even the ferocious were largely invested with awe. The woodcutters of Bengal invoke Kalrayu—an archer tiger-mounted—to protect them against the wild beasts he (a form of Siva) is supposed to exterminate; but while the exterminator of the most dangerous animals may, albeit without warrant in the Shastr, be respected in India, the huntsman is generally of evil repute. The gentle Krishna was said to have been slain by an arrow from the bow of Ungudu, a huntsman, who left the body to rot under a tree where it fell, the bones being the sacred relics for which the image of Jugernath at Orissa was constructed.5

It is not known at what period the notion of transmigration arose, but that must have made him appear cannibalistic who first hunted and devoured animals. Such was the Persian Zohak (or Dehak). His Babylonian form, Nimrod, represented also the character of Esau, as huntsman; that is, the primitive enemy of the farmer, and of the commerce in grains; the preserver of wildness, and consequently of all those primitive aboriginal idolatries which linger in the heaths (whence heathen) and country villages (whence pagans) long after they have passed away from the centres of civilisation. Hunting is essentially barbarous. The willingness of some huntsmen even now, when this serious occupation of an early period has become a sport, to sacrifice not only animal life to their pleasure, but also the interests of labour and agriculture, renders it very easy for us to understand the transformation of Nimrod into a demon. In the Hebrew and Arabian legends concerning Nimrod, that 'mighty hunter' is shown as related to the wild elements and their worshipper. When Abraham, having broken the images of his father, was brought by Terah before Nimrod, the King said, 'Let us worship the fire!'

'Rather the water that quenches the fire,' said Abraham.

'Well, the water.'

'Rather the cloud that carries the water.'

'Well, the cloud.'

'Rather the wind that scatters the cloud.'

'Well, the wind.'

'Rather man, for he withstands the wind.'

'Thou art a babbler,' said Nimrod. 'I worship the fire and will cast thee into it.'

When Abraham was cast into the fiery furnace by Nimrod, and on the seventh day after was found sitting amid the roses of a garden, the mighty hunter—hater of gardens—resolved on a daring hunt for Abraham's God himself. He built a tower five thousand cubits high, but finding heaven still far away, he attached a car to two half-starved eagles, and by holding meat above them they flew upward, until Nimrod heard a voice saying, 'Godless man, whither goest thou?' The audacious man shot an arrow in the direction of the voice; the arrow returned to him stained with blood, and Nimrod believed that he had wounded Abraham's God.

He who hunted the universe was destroyed by one of the weakest of animated beings—a fly. In the aspiring fly which attacked Nimrod's lip, and then nose, and finally devoured his brain, the Moslem and Hebrew doctors saw the fittest end of one whose adventurous spirit had not stopped to attack animals, man, Abraham, and Allah himself.

But though, in one sense, destroyed, Nimrod, say various myths, may be heard tumbling and groaning about the base of his tower of Babel, where the confusion of tongues took place; and it might be added, that they have, like the groan, a meaning irrespective of race or language. Dehak and Nimrod have had their brothers in every race, which has ever reached anything that may be called civilisation. It was the barbaric Baron and the Robber Knight of the Middle Ages, living by the hunt, who, before conversion, made for the Faithful Eckhardts of the Church the chief impediment; they might then strike down the monk, whose apparition has always been the legendary warning of the Demon's approach. When the Eckhardts had baptized these knights, they had already been transformed to the Devils which people the forests of Germany, France, and England with their terrible spectres. The wild fables of the East, telling of fell Demons coursing through the air, whispered to the people at one ear, and the equally wild deeds of the Robber Knights at the other. The Church had given the people one name for all such phantasms—Devil—and it was a name representative of the feelings of both priest and peasant, so long as the Robber Knights were their common enemy. Jesus had to be a good deal modified before he could become the model of this Teutonic Esau. It is after the tradition of his old relation to huntsmen that the Devil has been so especially connected in folklore with soldiers. In the 'Annals of Leipzig,' kept in Auerbach's Cellar, famous for the flight of Mephisto and Faust from its window on a wine-cask, I found two other instances in which the Devil was reported as having appeared in that town. In one case (1604), the fiend had tempted one Jeremy of Strasburg, a marksman, to commit suicide, but that not succeeding, had desired him to go with him to the neighbouring castle and enjoy some fruit. The marksman was saved by help of a Dean. In 1633, during a period of excessive cold and snow, the Devil induced a soldier to blaspheme. The marksman and the soldier were, indeed, the usual victims of the Wild Huntsmen's temptations; and it was for such that the unfailing magic bullets were moulded in return for their impawned souls.

How King Olaf—whose name lingers among us in 'Tooley Street,' so famous for its Three Tailors!6—spread the Gospel through the North after his baptism in England is well known. Whatever other hunt may have been phantasmal, it was not Olaf's hunt of the heathen. To put a pan of live coals under the belly of one, to force an adder down the throat of another, to offer all men the alternatives of being baptized or burnt, were the arguments which this apostle applied with such energy that at last—but not until many brave martyrdoms—the chief people were convinced. Olaf encountered Odin as if he had been a living foe, and what is more, believed in the genuine existence of his former God. Once, as Olaf and his friends believed, Odin appeared to this devastator of his altars as a one-eyed man in broad-brimmed hat, delighting the King in his hours of relaxation with that enchanting conversation for which he was so famous. But he (Odin) tried secretly to induce the cook to prepare for his royal master some fine meat which he had poisoned. But Olaf said, 'Odin shall not deceive us,' and ordered the tempting viand to be thrown away. Odin was god of the barbarian Junkers, and the people rejoiced that he was driven into holes and corners; his rites remained mainly among huntsmen, and had to be kept very secret. In the Gulathings Lagen of Norway it is ordered: 'Let the king and bishop, with all possible care, search after those who exercise pagan rites, who use magic arts, who adore the genii of particular places, of tombs, or rivers, and who, after the manner of devils in travelling, are transported from place to place through the air.'

Under such very actual curses as these, the once sacred animals of Odin, and all the associations of the hunt, were diabolised. Even the hunting-horn was regarded as having something præternatural about it. The howling blast when Odin consulteth Mimir's head7 was heard again in the Pied Piper's flute, and passed southward to blend its note with the horn of Roland at Roncesvalles,—which brought help from distances beyond the reach of any honest horn, and even with the pipe of Pan.

That the Edda described Odin as mounted on a mysterious horse, as cherishing two wolves for pets, having a roasted boar for the daily pièce de résistance of his table, and with a raven on either shoulder, whispering to him the secret affairs of the earth, was enough to settle the reputation of those animals in the creed of christian priests. The Raven was, indeed, from of old endowed with the holy awfulness of the christian dove, in the Norse Mythology. To this day no Swede will kill a raven. The superstition concerning it was strong enough to transmit even to Voltaire an involuntary shudder at its croak. Odin was believed to have given the Raven the colour of the night that it might the better spy out the deeds of darkness. Its 'natural theology' is, no doubt, given correctly by Robert Browning's Caliban, who, when his speculations are interrupted by a thunderstorm, supposes his soliloquy has been conveyed by the raven he sees flying to his god Setebos. In many parts of Germany ravens are believed to hold souls of the damned. If a raven's heart be secured it procures an unerring shot.

From an early date the Boar became an ensign of the prowess of the gods, by which its head passed to be the device of so many barbaric clans and ancient families in the Northern world. In Vedic Mythology we find Indra taking the shape of a Wild Boar, also killing a demon Boar, and giving Tritas the strength by which a similar monster is slain.8 According to another fable, while Brahma and Vishnu are quarrelling as to which is the first-born, Siva interferes and cries, 'I am the first-born; nevertheless I will recognise as my superior him who is able to see the summit of my head or the sole of my feet.' Vishnu, transforming himself to a Boar, pierced the ground, penetrated to the infernal regions, and then saw the feet of Siva, who on his return saluted him as first-born of the gods. De Gubernatis regards this fable as making the Boar emblem of the hidden Moon.9 He is hunted by the Sun. He guards the treasure of the demons which Indra gains by slaying him. In Sicilian story, Zafarana, by throwing three hog's bristles on embers, renews her husband's youth. In Esthonian legend, a prince, by eating pork, acquires the faculty of understanding the language of birds,—which may mean leading on the spring with its songs of birds. But whether these particular interpretations be true or not, there is no doubt that the Boar, at an early period, became emblematic of the wild forces of nature, and from being hunted by King Odin on earth passed to be his favourite food in Valhalla, and a prominent figure in his spectral hunt.

Enough has already been said of the Dog in several chapters of this work to render it but natural that this animal should take his place in any diabolical train. It was not as a 'hell-hound,' or descendant of the guardians of Orcus, that he entered the spectral procession of Odin, but as man's first animal assistant in the work of obtaining a living from nature. It is the faithful friend of man who is demoralised in Waldemar's Lystig, the spectre-hound of Peel Castle, the Manthe Doog of the Isle of Man, the sky-dogs (Cwn wybir or aunwy) of Wales, and Roscommon dog of Ireland.

Of the Goat, the Dog, and some other diabolised animals, enough has been said in previous pages. The nocturnal animals would be as naturally caught up into the Wild Huntsman's train as belated peasants. But it is necessary to dwell a little on the relations of the Horse to this Wild Hunt. It was the Horse that made the primitive king among men.

'The Horse,' says Dasent, 'was a sacred animal among the Teutonic tribes from the first moment of their appearance in history; and Tacitus has related how, in the shade of those woods and groves which served them for temples, white horses were fed at the public cost, whose backs no mortal crossed, whose neighings and snortings were carefully watched as auguries and omens, and who were thought to be conscious of divine mysteries. In Persia, too, the classical reader will remember how the neighing of a horse decided the choice for the crown. Here in England, at any rate, we have only to think of Hengist and Horsa, the twin heroes of the Anglo-Saxon migration—as the legend ran—heroes whose name meant horse, and of the Vale of the White Horse, in Berks, where the sacred form still gleams along the down, to be reminded of the sacredness of the horse to our forefathers. The Eddas are filled with the names of famous horses, and the Sagas contain many stories of good steeds, in whom their owners trusted and believed as sacred to this or that particular god. Such a horse is Dapplegrimm in the Norse tales, who saves his master out of all his perils, and brings him to all fortune, and is another example of that mysterious connection with the higher powers which animals in all ages have been supposed to possess.'

It was believed that no warrior could approach Valhalla except on horseback, and the steed was generally buried with his master. The Scandinavian knight was accustomed to swear 'by the shoulder of a horse and the edge of a sword.' Odin (the god) was believed to have always near him the eight-legged horse Sleipnir, whose sire was the wonderful Svaldilfari, who by night drew the enormous stones for the fortress defending Valhalla from the frost-giants. On Sleipnir the deity rode to the realm of Hela, when he evoked the spirit of the deceased prophetess, Vala, with Runic incantations, to learn Baldur's fate. This is the theme of the Veytamsvida, paraphrased by Gray in his ode beginning—

Up rose the king of men with speed,
And saddled straight his coal-black steed

The steed, however, was not black, but grey. Sleipnir was the foal of a magically-created mare. The demon-mare (Mara) holds a prominent place in Scandinavian superstition, besetting sleepers. In the Ynglinga Saga, Vanland awakes from sleep, crying, 'Mara is treading on me!' His men hasten to help him, but when they take hold of his head Mara treads on his legs, and when they hold his legs she tramples on his head; and so, says Thiodolf—

Trampled to death, to Skyta's shore
The corpse his faithful followers bore;

265

And there they burnt, with heavy hearts,
The good chief, killed by witchcraft's arts.

All this is, of course, the origin of the common superstition of the nightmare. The horse-shoe used against witches is from the same region. We may learn here also the reason why hippophagy has been so long unknown among us. Odin's boar has left his head on our Christmas tables, but Olaf managed to rob us of the horse-flesh once eaten in honour of that god. In the eleventh century he proclaimed the eating of horse-flesh a test of paganism, as baptism was of Christianity, and punished it with death, except in Iceland, where it was permitted by an express stipulation on their embracing Christianity. To these facts it may be added that originally the horse's head was lifted, as the horse-shoe is now, for a charm against witches. When Wittekind fought twenty years against Charlemagne, the ensign borne by his Saxon followers was a horse's head raised on a pole. A white horse on a yellow ground is to-day the Hanoverian banner, its origin being undoubtedly Odinistic.

The christian edict against the eating of horse-flesh had probably a stronger motive than sentimental opposition to paganism. A Roman emperor had held the stirrup for a christian pontiff to mount, and something of the same kind occurred in the North. The Horse, which had been a fire-breathing devil under Odin, became a steed of the Sun under the baptized noble and the bishop. Henceforth we read of coal-black and snow-white horses, as these are mounted in the interest of the old religion or the new.

It is very curious to observe how far and wide has gone religious competition for possession of that living tower of strength—the Horse. In ancient Ceylon we find the Buddhist immigrants winning over the steed on which the aborigines were fortified. It was a white horse, of course, that became their symbol of triumph. The old record says—

'A certain yakkhini (demoness) named Chetiya, having the form and countenance of a mare, dwelt near the marsh of Tumbariungona. A certain person in the prince's (Pandukabhayo) retinue having seen this beautiful (creature), white with red legs, announced the circumstance to the prince. The prince set out with a rope to secure her. She seeing him approach from behind, losing her presence of mind from fear, under the influence of his imposing appearance, fled without (being able to exert the power she possessed of) rendering herself invisible. He gave chase to the fugitive. She, persevering in her flight, made the circuit of the marsh seven times. She made three more circuits of the marsh, and then plunged into the river at the Kachchhaka ferry. He did the same, and (in the river) seized her by the tail, and (at the same time grasped) the leaf of a palmira tree which the stream was carrying down. By his supernatural good fortune this (leaf) became an enormous sword. Exclaiming, 'I put thee to death!' he flourished the sword over her. 'Lord!' replied she to him, 'subduing this kingdom for thee, I will confer it on thee: spare me my life.' Seizing her by the throat, and with the point of the sword boring her nostril, he secured her with his rope: she (instantly) became tractable. Conducting her to the Dhumarakkho mountain, he obtained a great accession of warlike power by making her his battle-steed.'10 The wonderful victories won by the prince, aided by this magical mare, are related, and the tale ends with his setting up 'within the royal palace itself the mare-faced yakkhini,' and providing for her annually 'demon offerings.'

Equally ambiguous with the Horse in this zoologic diablerie is the Stag. In the Heraklean legends we find that hero's son, Telephon, nursed by a hind in the woods; and on the other hand, his third 'labour' was the capture of Artemis' gold-antlered stag, which brought on him her wrath (it being 'her majesty's favourite stag'). We have again the story of Actæon pursuing the stag too far and suffering the fate he had prepared for it; and a reminiscence of it in the 'Pentamerone,' when the demon Huoreo allures Canneloro into the wood by taking the form of a beautiful hind. These complex legends are reflected in Northern folklore also. Count Otto I. of Altmark, while out hunting, slept under an oak and dreamed that he was furiously attacked by a stag, which disappeared when he called on the name of God. The Count built a monastery, which still stands, with the oak's stump built into its altar. On the other hand, beside the altar of a neighbouring church hang two large horns of a stag said to have brought a lost child home on its back. Thus in the old town of Steindal meet these contrary characters of the mystical stag, of which it is not difficult to see that the evil one results from its misfortune in being at once the huntsman's victim and scapegoat.11

In the legend of St. Hubert we have the sign of Christ—risen from his tomb among the rich Christians to share for a little the crucifixion of their first missionaries in the North—to the huntsmen of Europe. Hubert pursues the stag till it turns to face him, and behold, between its antlers, the cross! It is a fable conceived in the spirit of him who said to fishermen, 'Come with me and I will make you fishers of men.' The effect was much the same in both cases. Hubert kneels before the stag, and becomes a saint, as the fishermen left their nets and became apostles. But, as the proverb says, when the saint's day is over, farewell the saint. The fishermen's successors caught men with iron hooks in their jaws; the successors of Hubert hunted men and women so lustily that they never paused long enough to see whether there might not be a cross on their forehead also.

It was something, however, that the cross which Constantine could only see in the sky could be seen by any eye on the forehead of a harmless animal; and this not only because it marked the rising in christian hearts of pity for the animals, but because what was done to the flying stag was done to the peasant who could not fly, and more terribly. The vision of Hubert came straight from the pagan heart of Western and Northern Europe. In the Bible, from Genesis to Apocalypse, no word is found clearly inculcating any duty to the animals. So little, indeed, could the christians interpret the beautiful tales of folklore concerning kindly beasts, out of which came the legend of Hubert, that Hubert was made patron of huntsmen; and while, by a popular development, Wodan was degraded to a devil, the baptized sportsman rescued his chief occupation by ascribing its most dashing legends to St. Martin and their inspiration to the Archangel Michael.

It is now necessary to consider the light which the German heart cast across the dark shadows of Wodan. This is to be discovered in the myth of the White Lady. We have already seen, in the confessions of the witches of Elfdale, in Sweden, that when they were gathering before their formidable Devil, a certain White Spirit warned them back. The children said she tried to keep them from entering the Devil's Church at Blockula. This may not be worth much as a 'confession,' but it sufficiently reports the theories prevailing in the popular mind of Elfdale at that time. It is not doubtful now that this White Lady and that Devil she opposed were, in pre-christian time, Wodan and his wife Frigga. The humble people who had gladly given up the terrible huntsman and warrior to be degraded into a Devil, and with him the barbaric Nimrods who worshipped him, did not agree to a similar surrender of their dear household goddess, known to them as Frigga, Holda, Bertha, Mother Rose,—under all her epithets the Madonna of the North, interceding between them and the hard king of Valhalla, ages before they ever heard of a jealous Jehovah and a tender interceding Mary.

Dr. Wuttke has collected many variants of the myths of Frigga, some of which bear witness to the efforts of the Church to degrade her also into a fiend. She is seen washing white clothes at fountains, milking cows, spinning flax with a distaff, or combing her flaxen hair. She was believed to be the divine ancestress of the human race; many of the oldest families claimed descent from her, and believed that this Ahnenfrau announced to them good fortune, or, by her wailing, any misfortune coming to their families. She brought evil only to those who spoke evil of her. If any one shoots at her the ball enters his own heart. She appears to poor wandering folk, especially children, and guides them to spots where they find heaps of gold covered with the flower called 'Forget-me-not'—because her gentle voice is heard requesting, as the only compensation, that the flowers shall be replaced when the gold is removed. The primroses are sacred to her, and often are the keys (thence called 'key-blossoms') which unlock her treasures. The smallest tribute she repays,—even a pebble consecrated to her. Every child ascending the Burgeiser Alp places a stone on a certain heap of such, with the words, 'Here I offer to the wild maidens.' These are Bertha's kindly fairies. (When Frederika Bremer was with a picnic on the Hudson heights, which Washington Irving had peopled with the Spirits he had brought from the Rhine, she preferred to pour out her champagne as a libation to the 'good spirits' of Germany and America.) The beautiful White Lady wears a golden chain, and glittering keys at her belt; she appears at mid-day or in strong moonlight. In regions where priestly influence is strong she is said to be half-black, half-white, and to appear sometimes as a serpent. She often helps the weary farmer to stack his corn, and sorely-tasked Cinderellas in their toil.

In pre-christian time this amiable goddess—called oftenest Bertha (shining) and Mother Rose—was related to Wodan as the spring and summer to the storms of winter, in which the Wild Huntsman's procession no doubt originated. The Northman's experience of seed-time and harvest was expressed in the myth of this sweet Rose hidden through the winter's blight to rise again in summer. This myth has many familiar variants, such as Aschenputtel and Sleeping Beauty; but it was more particularly connected with the later legends of the White Lady, as victim of the Wild Huntsman, by the stories of transformed princesses delivered by youths. Rescue of the enchanted princess is usually effected by three kisses, but she is compelled to appear before the deliverer in some hideous aspect—as toad or serpent; so that he is repelled or loses courage. This is the rose hid under the ugliness of winter.

When the storm-god Wodan was banished from nature altogether and identified with the imported, and naturally inconceivable, Satan, he was no more regarded as Frigga's rough lord, but as her remorseless foe. She was popularly revered as St. Walpurga, the original May Queen, and it was believed that happy and industrious children might sometimes see her on May-day with long flowing flaxen hair, fine shoes, distaff in hand, and a golden crown on her head. But for the nine nights after May-day she was relentlessly pursued by the Wild Huntsman and his mounted train. There is a picture by G. Watts of the hunted lady of Bocaccio's tale, now in the Cosmopolitan Club of London, which vividly reproduces the weird impressiveness of this myth. The White Lady tries to hide from her pursuer in standing corn, or gets herself bound up in a sheaf. The Wild Huntsman's wrath extends to all her retinue,—moss maidens of the wood, or Holtzweibeln. The same belief characterises Waldemar's hunt. It is a common legend in Denmark that King Volmer rode up to some peasants, busy at harvest on Sobjerg Hill, and, in reply to his question whether they had seen any game, one of the men said—'Something rustled just now in yonder standing corn.' The King rushed off, and presently a shot was heard. The King reappeared with a mermaid lying across his horse, and said as he passed, 'I have chased her a hundred years, and have her at last.' He then rode into the hill. In this way Frigga and her little people, hunted with the wild creatures, awakened sympathy for them.

The holy friar. Eckhardt (who may be taken as a myth and type of the Church ad hoc) gained his legendary fame by being supposed to go in advance of the Wild Huntsman and warn villagers of his approach; but as time went on and a compromise was effected between the hunting Barons and the Church, on the basis that the sports and cruelties should be paid for with indulgence-fees, Eckhardt had to turn his attention rather to the White Lady. She was declared a Wild Huntress, but the epithet slipped to other shoulders. The priests identified her ultimately with Freija, or Frau Venus; and

Eckhardt was the holy hermit who warned young men against her sorceries in Venusberg and elsewhere. But Eckhardt never prevailed against the popular love of Mother Rose as he had against her pursuer; he only increased the attractions of 'Frau Venus' beyond her deserts. In the end it was as much as the Church could do to secure for Mary the mantle of her elder sister's sanctity. Even then the earlier faith was not eradicated. After the altars of Mary had fallen, Frigga had vitality enough to hold her own as the White Witch who broke the Dark One's spells. It was chiefly this helpful Mother-goddess to whom the wretched were appealing when they were burnt for witchcraft.

At Urselberg, Wurtemberg, there is a deep hole called the 'Nightmaidens' Retreat,' in which are piled the innumerable stones that have been cast therein by persons desiring good luck on journeys. These stones correspond to the bones of the 11,000 Virgins in St. Ursula's Church at Cologne. The White Lady was sainted under her name of Ursel (the glowing one), otherwise Horsel. Horselberg, near Eisenach, became her haunt as Venus, the temptress of Tannhaüsers; Urselberg became her retreat as the good fairy mother; but the attractions of herself and her moss-maidens, which the Church wished to borrow, were taken on a long voyage to Rome, and there transmuted to St. Ursula and her 11,000 Virgins. These Saints of Cologne encountered their ancient mythical pursuers—the Wild Huntsman's train—in those barbarian Huns who are said to have slaughtered them all because they would not break their vows of chastity. The legend is but a variant of Wodan's hunt after the White Lady and her maidens. When it is remembered that before her transformation by Christianity Ursula was the Huntsman's own wife, Frigga, a quaint incident appears in the last meeting between the two. After Wodan had been transformed to the Devil, he is said to have made out the architectural plan for Cologne Cathedral, and offered it to the architect in return for a bond for his soul; but, having weakly allowed him to get possession of the document before the bond was signed, the architect drew from under his gown a bone of St. Ursula, from which the Devil fled in great terror. It was bone of his bone; but after so many mythological vicissitudes Wodan and his Horsel could hardly be expected to recognise each other at this chance meeting in Cologne.

Notes

1 *'Der deutsche Volksaberglaube der Gegenwart.' Von Dr. Adolf Wuttke, Prof. der Theol. in Halle. Berlin: Verlag von Wiegand & Grieben. 1869.*
2 *'Histoire de France et des Choses Mémorables,' etc.*
3 *The universal myth of Sleepers,—christianised in the myth of St. John, and of the Seven whose slumber is traceable as far as Tours,—had a direct pagan development in Jami, Barbarossa, Arthur, and their many variants. It is the legend of the Castle of Sewingshields in Northumberland, that King Arthur, his queen and court, remain there in a subterranean hall, entranced, until some one should first blow a bugle-horn near the entrance hall, and then with 'the sword of the stone' cut a garter placed there beside it. But none had ever heard where the entrance to this enchanted hall was, till a farmer, fifty years since, was sitting knitting on the ruins of the castle, and his clew fell and ran downwards through briars into a deep subterranean passage. He cleared the portal of its weeds and rubbish, and entering a vaulted passage, followed the clew. The floor was infested with toads and lizards; and bats flitted fearfully around him. At length his sinking courage was strengthened by a dim, distant light, which, as he advanced, grew gradually brighter, till all at once he entered a vast and vaulted hall, in the centre of which a fire, without fuel, from a broad crevice in the floor, blazed with a high and lambent flame, that showed all the carved walls and fretted roof, and the monarch and his queen and court reposing around in a theatre of thrones and costly couches. On the floor, beyond the fire, lay the faithful and deep-toned pack of thirty couple of hounds; and on a table before it the spell-dissolving horn, sword, and garter. The shepherd firmly grasped the sword, and as he drew it from its rusty scabbard the eyes of the monarch and his courtiers began to open, and they rose till they sat upright. He cut the garter, and as the sword was slowly sheathed the spell assumed its ancient power, and they all gradually sank to rest; but not before the monarch had lifted up his eyes and hands and exclaimed—*
O woe betide that evil day
On which this witless wight was born,
Who drew the sword—the garter cut,
But never blew the bugle horn.
Terror brought on loss of memory, and the shepherd was unable to give any correct account of his adventure, or to find again the entrance to the enchanted hall.—Hodgson's 'Northumberland.'
4 *This great discussion between the animals and sages is given in 'The Sacred Anthology' (London: Trübner & Co. New York: Henry Holt & Co.). It is a very ancient story, and was probably written down at the beginning of the christian era.*
5 *It is a strange proof of the ignorance concerning Hindu religion that Jugernath, raised in a sense for reprobation of cruelty to man and beast, should have been made by a missionary myth a Western proverb for human sacrifices!*
6 *St. Olaf = Stooley = Tooley.*
7
High bloweth Heimdall
His horn aloft;
Odin consulteth
Mimir's head;
The old ash yet standing

Yggdrasill
To its summit is shaken,
And loose breaks the giant.—Voluspa.
8 *'Rigveda,' x. 99.*
9 *'Zoolog. Myth.,' ii. 8, 10, etc.*
10 *'The Mahawanso.' Translated by the Hon. George Turnour, Ceylon, 1836, p. 69.*
11 *It was an ancient custom to offer a stag on the high altar of Durham Abbey, the sacrifice being accompanied with winding of horns, on Holy Rood Day, which suggests a form of propitiating the Wild Huntsman in the hunting season. On the Cheviot Hills there is a chasm called Hen Hole, 'in which there is frequently seen a snow egg at Midsummer, and it is related that a party of hunters, while chasing a roe, were beguiled into it by fairies, and could never again find their way out.'—Richardson's 'Borderer's Table-Book,' vi 400. The Bridled Devil of Durham Cathedral may be an allusion to the Wild Huntsman.*

Chapter XXVII - Le Bon Diable

The Devil repainted—Satan a divine agent—St. Orain's heresy—Primitive universalism—Father Sinistrari—Salvation of demons—Mediæval sects—Aquinas—His prayer for Satan—Popular antipathies—The Devil's gratitude—Devil defending innocence—Devil against idle lords—The wicked ale-wife—Pious offenders punished—Anachronistic Devils—Devils turn to poems—Devil's good advice—Devil sticks to his word—His love of justice—Charlemagne and the Serpent—Merlin—His prison of Air—Mephistopheles in Heaven.

The phrase which heads this chapter is a favourite one in France. It may have had a euphemistic origin, for the giants dreaded by primitive Europeans were too formidable to be lightly spoken of. But within most of the period concerning which we have definite knowledge such phrases would more generally have expressed the half-contemptuous pity with which these huge beings with weak intellects were regarded. The Devil imported with Christianity was made over, as we have seen, into the image of the Dummeteufel, or stupid good-natured giant, and he is represented in many legends which show him giving his gifts and services for payments of which he is constantly cheated. Le Bon Diable in France is somewhat of this character, and is often taken as the sign of tradesmen who wish to represent themselves as lavishing their goods recklessly for inadequate compensation. But the large accession of demons and devils from the East through Jewish and Moslem channels, of a character far from stupid, gave a new sense to that phrase and corresponding ones. There is no doubt that a very distinct reaction in favour of the Devil arose in Europe, and one expressive of very interesting facts and forces. The pleasant names given him by the masses would alone indicate this,—Monsieur De Scelestat, Lord Voland, Blümlin (floweret), Federspiel (gay-plumed), Maitre Bernard, Maitre Parsin (Parisian).
The Devil is not so black as he's painted. This proverb concerning the long-outlawed Evil One has a respectable antiquity, and the feeling underlying it has by no means been limited to the vulgar. Even the devout George Herbert wrote—

We paint the Devil black, yet he
Hath some good in him all agree.

Robert Burns naively appeals to Old Nick's better nature—

But fare ye weel, auld Nickie-ben!
O wad ye tak a thought an' men'!
Ye aiblins might—I dinna ken—
Still ha'e a stake;
I'm wae to think upon yon den,
E'en for your sake!

It is hard to destroy the natural sentiments of the human heart. However much they may be overlaid by the transient exigencies of a creed, their indestructible nature is pretty certain to reveal itself. The most orthodox supporters of divine cruelty in their own theology will cry out against it in another. The saint who is quite satisfied that the everlasting torture of Satan or Judas is justice, will look upon the doom of Prometheus as a sign of heathen heartlessness; and the burning of one widow for a few moments on her husband's pyre will stimulate merciful missionary ardour among millions of christians whose creed passes the same poor victim to endless torture, and half the human race with her.
It is doubtful whether the general theological conception of the functions of Satan is consistent with the belief that he is in a state of suffering. As an agent of divine punishment he is a part of the divine government; and it is even probable that

had it not been for the necessity of keeping up his office, theology itself would have found some means of releasing him and his subordinates from hell, and ultimately of restoring them to heaven and virtue.1

It is a legend of the island Iona that when St. Columba attempted to build a church there, the Devil—i.e., the same Druid magicians who tried to prevent his landing there by tempests—threw down the stones as often as they were piled up. An oracle declared that the church could arise only after some holy man had been buried alive at the spot, and the saint's friend Orain offered himself for the purpose. After Orain had been buried, and the wall was rising securely, St. Columba was seized with a strong desire to look upon the face of his poor friend once more. The wall was pulled down, the body dug up; but instead of Orain being found dead, he sat up and told the assembled christians around him that he had been to the other world, and discovered that they were in error about various things,—especially about Hell, which really did not exist at all. Outraged by this heresy the christians immediately covered up Orain again in good earnest.

The resurrection of this primitive universalist of the seventh century, and his burial again, may be regarded as typifying a dream of the ultimate restoration of the universe to the divine sway which has often given signs of life through christian history, though many times buried. The germ of it is even in Paul's hope that at last 'God may be all in all' (1 Cor. xv. 28). In Luke x. 17, also, it was related that the seventy whom Jesus had sent out among the idol-worshipping Gentiles 'returned again with joy, saying, Lord, even the devils are subject unto us through thy name.' These ideas are recalled in various legends, such as that elsewhere related of the Satyr who came to St. Anthony to ask his prayers for the salvation of his demonic tribe. On the strength of Anthony's courteous treatment of that Satyr, the famous Consulteur of the Inquisition, Father Sinistrari (seventeenth century), rested much of his argument that demons were included in the atonement wrought by Christ and might attain final beatitude. The Father affirmed that this was implied in Christ's words, 'Other sheep I have which are not of this flock: them also I must bring, and they shall hear my voice; and there shall be one fold and one shepherd'2 (John x. 16). That these words were generally supposed to refer to the inclusion of the Gentile world was not accepted by Sinistrari as impairing his argument, but the contrary. He maintained with great ingenuity that the salvation of the Gentiles logically includes the salvation of their inspiring demons, and that there would not be one fold if these aerial beings, whose existence all authorities attested, were excluded. He even intimates, though more timidly, that their father, Satan himself, as a participator in the sin of Adam and sharer of his curse, may be included in the general provision of the deity for the entire and absolute removal of the curse throughout nature.

Sinistrari's book was placed on the 'Index Expurgatorius' at Rome in 1709, 'donec corrigatur,' eight years after the author's death; it was republished, 'correctus,' 1753. But the fact that such sentiments had occupied many devout minds in the Church, and that they had reached the dignity of a consistent and scholarly statement in theology, was proved. The opinion grew out of deeper roots than New Testament phrases or the Anthony fables. The Church had been for ages engaged in the vast task of converting the Gentile world; in the course of that task it had succeeded only by successive surrenders of the impossible principles with which it had started. The Prince of this World had been baptized afresh with every European throne ascended by the Church. Asmodeus had triumphed in the sacramental inclusion of marriage; St. Francis d'Assisi, preaching to the animals, represented innumerable pious myths which had been impossible under the old belief in a universal curse resting upon nature. The evolution of this tendency may be traced through the entire history of the Church in such sects as the Paulicians, Cathari, Bogomiles, and others, who, though they again and again formulated anew the principle of an eternal Dualism, as often revealed some further stage in the progressive advance of the christianised mind towards a normal relation with nature. Thus the Cathari maintained that only those beings who were created by the evil principle would remain unrecovered; those who were created by God, but seduced by the Adversary, would be saved after sufficient expiation. The fallen angels, they believed, were passing through earthly, in some cases animal, bodies to the true Church and to heaven. Such views as these were not those of the learned, but of the dissenting sects, and they prepared ignorant minds in many countries for that revival of confidence in their banished deities which made the cult of Witchcraft.

St. Thomas Aquinas, the 'Angelical Doctor,' in his famous work 'Summa Theologiæ,' maintains that in the Resurrection the bodies of the redeemed will rise with all their senses and organs, including those of sex, active and refined. The authentic affirmation of that doctrine in the thirteenth century was of a significance far beyond the comprehension of the Church. Aquinas confused the lines between flesh and spirit, especially by admitting sex into heaven. The Devil could not be far behind. The true interpretation of his doctrine is to be found in the legend that Aquinas passed a night in prayer for the salvation and restoration of the Devil. This legend is the subject of a modern poem so fraught with the spirit of the mediæval heart, pining in its dogmatic prison, that I cannot forbear quoting it here:—

All day Aquinas sat alone;
Compressed he sat and spoke no word,
As still as any man of stone,
In streets where never voice is heard;
With massive front and air antique
He sat, did neither move or speak,
For thought like his seemed words too weak.

The shadows brown about him lay;
From sunrise till the sun went out,
Had sat alone that man of grey,
That marble man, hard crampt by doubt;
Some kingly problem had he found,
Some new belief not wholly sound,
Some hope that overleapt all bound.
All day Aquinas sat alone,
No answer to his question came,
And now he rose with hollow groan,
And eyes that seemed half love, half flame.
On the bare floor he flung him down,
Pale marble face, half smile, half frown,
Brown shadow else, mid shadows brown.

'O God,' he said, 'it cannot be,
Thy Morning-star, with endless moan,
Should lift his fading orbs to thee,
And thou be happy on thy throne.
It were not kind, nay, Father, nay,
It were not just, O God, I say,
Pray for thy Lost One, Jesus, pray!

'How can thy kingdom ever come,
While the fair angels howl below?
All holy voices would be dumb,
All loving eyes would fill with woe,
To think the lordliest Peer of Heaven,
The starry leader of the Seven,
Would never, never, be forgiven.

'Pray for thy Lost One, Jesus, pray!
O Word that made thine angel speak!
Lord! let thy pitying tears have way;
Dear God! not man alone is weak.
What is created still must fall,
And fairest still we frailest call;
Will not Christ's blood avail for all?

'Pray for thy Lost One, Jesus, pray!
O Father! think upon thy child;
Turn from thy own bright world away,
And look upon that dungeon wild.
O God! O Jesus! see how dark
That den of woe! O Saviour! mark
How angels weep, how groan! Hark, hark!

'He will not, will not do it more,
Restore him to his throne again;
Oh, open wide that dismal door
Which presses on the souls in pain.
So men and angels all will say,
'Our God is good.' Oh, day by day,
Pray for thy Lost One, Jesus, pray!'
All night Aquinas knelt alone,
Alone with black and dreadful Night,
Until before his pleading moan
The darkness ebbed away in light.
Then rose the saint, and 'God,' said he,
'If darkness change to light with thee,
*The Devil may yet an angel be.'*3

While this might be the feeling of devout philosophers whose minds were beginning to form a conception of a Cosmos in which the idea of a perpetual empire of Evil could find no place, the humble and oppressed masses, as we have seen in the chapter on Witchcraft, were familiarising their minds with the powers and glories of a Satan in antagonism to the deities and saints of the Church. It was not a penitent devil supplicating for pardon whom they desired, but the veritable Prince of the World, to whom as well as to themselves their Christian oppressors were odious. They invested the Powers which the priests pronounced infernal with those humanly just and genial qualities that had been discarded by ecclesiastical ambition. The legends which must be interpreted in this sense are very numerous, and a few of the most characteristic must suffice us here. The habit of attributing every mishap to the Devil was rebuked in many legends. One of these related that when a party were driving over a rough road the waggon broke down and one of the company exclaimed, 'This is a bit of the Devil's work!' A gentleman present said, 'It is a bit of corporation work. I don't believe in saddling the Devil with all the bad roads and bad axles.' Some time after, when this second speaker was riding over the same road alone, an old gentleman in black met him, and having thanked him for his defence of the Devil, presented him with a casket of splendid jewels. Very numerous are legends of the Devil's apparition to assist poor architects and mechanics unable to complete their contracts, even carving beautiful church pillars and the like for them, and this sometimes without receiving any recompense. The Devil's apparition in defence of accused innocence is a well-known feature of European folklore. On one occasion a soldier, having stopped at a certain inn, confided to the innkeeper some money he had for safe-keeping, and when he was about to leave the innkeeper denied having received the deposit. The soldier battered down the door, and the neighbours of the innkeeper, a prominent man in the town, put him in prison, where he lay in prospect of suffering death for an attempted burglary. The poor soldier, being a stranger without means, was unable to obtain counsel to defend him. When the parties appeared before the magistrate, a smart young lawyer, with blue hat and white feathers, unknown in the town, volunteered to defend the soldier, and related the whole story with such effect that the innkeeper in his excitement cried, 'Devil take me if I have the money!' Instantly the smart lawyer spread his wings, and, seizing the innkeeper, disappeared with him through the roof of the court-room. The innkeeper's wife, struck with horror, restored the money. In an Altmark version of this story the Devil visits the prisoner during the previous night and asks for his soul as fee, but the soldier refuses, saying he had rather die. Despite this the Devil intervened. It was an old-time custom in Denmark for courts to sit with an open window, in order that the Devil might more easily fly away with the perjurer.

Always a democrat, the Devil is said in many stories to have interfered in favour of the peasant or serf against the noble. On one occasion he relieved a certain district of all its arrogant and idle noblemen by gathering them up in a sack and flying away with them; but unhappily, as he was passing over the town of Friesack, his sack came in collision with the church steeple, and through the hole so torn a large number of noble lords fell into the town—which thence derived its name—and there they remained to be patrons of the steeple and burthens on the people.

The Devil was universally regarded as a Nemesis on all publicans and ale-wives who adulterated the beer they dealt out to the people, or gave short measures. At Reetz, in Altmark, the legend of an ale-wife with whom he flew away is connected with a stone on which they are said to have rested, and the villagers see thereon prints of the Devil's hoof and the

Fig. 23.—The Wicked Ale-wife.

woman's feet. This was a favourite theme of old English legends. The accompanying Figure (23), one of the misereres in Ludlow parish church, Shropshire, represents the end of a wicked ale-wife. A devil on one side reads the long list of her shortcomings, and on the other side hell-mouth is receiving other sinners. A devil with bagpipe welcomes her arrival. She carries with her only her fraudulent measure and the fashionable head-dress paid for out of its wicked gains.

In a marionette performance which I witnessed at Tours, the accusations brought against the tradesmen who cheated the people were such as to make one wish that the services of some equally strict devil could be secured by the authorities of all cities, to detect adulterators and dealers in false weights and measures. The same retributive agency, in the popular interest, was ascribed to the Devil in his attitude towards misers. There being no law which could reach men whose hoarded wealth brought no good to themselves or others, such were deemed proper cases for the interposition of the Devil. There is a significant contrast between the legends favoured by the Church and those of popular origin. The former, made prominent in frescoes, often show how, at the weighing of souls, the sinner is saved by a saint or angel, or by some instance of service to the Church being placed in the scale against the otherwise heavier record of evil deeds. A characteristic legend is that which is the subject of the frescoes in the portico of St. Lorenzo Church at Rome (thirteenth century). St. Lawrence sees four devils passing his hermitage, and learns from them that they are going for the soul of

Henry II. In the next scene, when the wicked Count is weighed, the scroll of his evil deeds far outweighs that of his good actions, until the Saint casts into the scale a chalice which the prince had once given to his church. For that one act Henry's soul ascends to paradise amid the mortification of the Devils. Though Charles Martel saved Europe from Saracen sway, he once utilised episcopal revenues for relief of the state; consequently a synod declares him damned, a saint sees him in hell, a sulphurous dragon issues from his grave. On the other hand, the popular idea of the fate of distinguished sinners may be found hid under misereres, where kings sometimes appear in Hell, and in the early picture-books which contained a half-christianised folklore.

It has been observed that the early nature-deities, reflecting the evil and good of nature, in part through the progress of human thought and ideality, and through new ethnical rivalries, were degraded into demons. They then represented the pains, obstructions, and fears in nature. We have seen that as these apparent external evils were vanquished or better understood, the demons passed to the inward nature, and represented a new series of pains, obstructions, and fears. But these, too, were in part vanquished, or better understood. Still more, they so changed their forms that the ancient demons-turned-devils were no longer sufficiently expressive to represent them. Thus we find that the Jews, mohammedans, and christians did not find their several special antagonists impressively represented by either Satan, Iblis, or Beelzebub. Each, therefore, personified its foe in accordance with later experiences—an Opponent called Armillus, Aldajjail, Antichrist (all meaning the same thing), in whom all other devils were merged.

As to their spirit; but as to their forms they shrank in size and importance, and did duty in small ways. We have seen how great dragons were engaged in frightening boys who fished on Sundays, or oppressive squires; how Satan presided over wine-casks, or was adapted to the punishment of profanity; how hosts of once tremendous fiends turned into the grotesque little forms which Callot, truly copying the popular notions around him, painted as motley imps disturbing monks at their prayers. Such diminutions of the devils correspond to a parallel process among the gods and goddesses, by which they were changed to 'little people' or fairies. In both cases the transformation is an expression of popular disbelief in their reality.

But revivals took place. The fact of evil is permanent; and whenever the old chains of fear, after long rusting, finally break, there follows an insurrection against the social and moral order which alarms the learned and the pious. These see again the instigations of evil powers, and it takes form in the imagination of a Dante, a Luther, a Milton. But when these new portraits of the Devil are painted, it is with so much contemporary colouring that they do not answer to the traditional

devils preserved in folklore. Dante's Worm does not resemble the serpent of fable, nor does Milton's Satan answer to the feathered clown of Miracle Plays. Thus, behind the actual evils which beset any time, there stands an array of grand diabolical names, detached from present perils, on which the popular fancy may work without really involving any theory of Absolute Evil at all. Were starry Lucifer to be restored to his heavenly sphere, he would be one great brand plucked from the burning, but the burning might still go on. Theology itself had filled the world with other devils by diabolising all the gods and goddesses of rival religions, and the compassionate heart was thus left free to select such forms or fair names as preserved some remnant of ancient majesty around them, or some ray from their once divine halo, and pray or hope for their pardon and salvation. Fallen foes, no longer able to harm, can hardly fail to awaken pity and clemency.

With the picture of Dives and Lazarus presented elsewhere (vol. i. p.

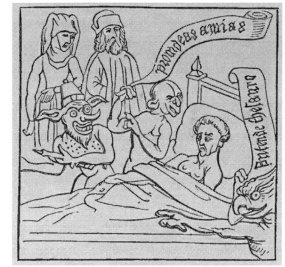

Fig. 24.—A Mediæval Death-bed.

281) may be instructively compared the accompanying scene of a rich man's death-bed (Fig. 24), taken from 'Ars Moriendi,' one of the early block-books. This picture is very remarkable from the suggestion it contains of an opposition between a devil on the dying man's right and the hideous dragon on his left. While the dragon holds up a scroll, bidding him think of his treasure (Yntende thesauro), the Devil suggests provision for his friends (Provideas amicis). This devil seems to be a representative of the rich man's relatives who stand near, and appears to be supported by his ugly superior, who points towards hell as the penalty of not making such provision as is suggested. There would appear to be in this picture a vague distinction between the mere bestial fiend who tempts, and the ugly but good-natured devil who punishes, and whom rich sinners cannot escape by bequests to churches.

One of the most notable signs of the appearance of 'the good Devil' was the universal belief that he invariably stuck to his word. In all European folklore there is no instance of his having broken a promise. In this respect his reputation stands far higher than that of the christians, seeing that it was a boast of the saints that, following the example of their godhead, who outwitted Satan in the bargain for man's redemption, they were continually cheating the Devil by technical quibbles.

273

There is a significant saying found among Prussian and Danish peasants, that you may obtain a thing by calling on Jesus, but if you would be sure of it you must call on the Devil! The two parties were judged by their representatives.

One of the earliest legendary compacts with the Devil was that made by St. Theophilus in the sixth century; when he became alarmed and penitent, the Virgin Mary managed to trick Satan out of the fatal bond. The 'Golden Legend' of Jacobus de Voragine tells why Satan was under the necessity of demanding in every case a bond signed with blood. 'The christians,' said Satan, 'are cheats; they make all sorts of promises so long as they want me, and then leave me in the lurch, and reconcile themselves with Christ so soon as, by my help, they have got what they want.'

Even apart from the consideration of possessing the soul, the ancient office of Satan as legal prosecutor of souls transmitted, to the latest forms into which he was modified, this character for justice. Many mediæval stories report his gratitude whenever he is treated with justice, though some of these are disguised by connection with other demonic forms. Such is the case with the following romance concerning Charlemagne.

When Charlemagne dwelt at Zurich, in the house commonly called 'Zum Loch,' he had a column erected to which a bell was attached by a rope. Any one that demanded justice could ring this bell when the king was at his meals. It happened one day that the bell sounded, but when the servants went to look no one was there. It continued ringing, so the Emperor commanded them to go again and find out the cause. They now remarked that an enormous serpent approached the rope and pulled it. Terrified, they brought the news to the Emperor, who immediately rose in order to administer justice to beast as well as man. After the reptile had respectfully inclined before the emperor, it led him to the banks of the river and showed him, sitting upon its nest and eggs, an enormous toad. Charlemagne having examined the case decided thus:—The toad was condemned to be burnt and justice shown to the serpent. The verdict was no sooner given than it was accomplished. A few days after the snake returned to court, bowed low to the King, crept upon the table, took the cover from a gold goblet standing there, dropped into it a precious stone, bowed again and crept away. On the spot where the serpent's nest had been, Charlemagne built a church called 'Wasserkelch.' The stone he gave to his much-loved spouse. This stone possessed the power of making the owner especially loved by the Emperor, so that when absent from his queen he mourned and longed for her. She, well aware that if it came into other hands the Emperor would soon forget her, put it under her tongue in the hour of death. The queen was buried with the stone, but Charlemagne could not separate himself from the body, so had it exhumed, and for eighteen years carried it about with him wherever he went. In the meantime, a courtier who had heard of the secret virtue of the stone, searched the corpse, and at last found the stone hidden under the tongue, and took it away and concealed it on his own person. Immediately the Emperor's love for his wife turned to the courtier, whom he now scarcely permitted out of his sight. At Cologne the courtier in a fit of anger threw the stone into a hot spring, and since then no one has succeeded in finding it. The love the Emperor had for the knight ceased, but he felt himself wonderfully attracted to the place where the stone lay hidden. On this spot he founded Aix-la-Chapelle, his subsequent favourite place of residence.

It is not wonderful that the tradition should arise at Aix, founded by the human hero of this romance, that the plan of its cathedral was supplied by the Devil; but it is characteristic there should be associated with this legend an example of how he who as a serpent was awarded justice by Charlemagne was cheated by the priests of Aix. The Devil gave the design on condition that he was to have the first who entered the completed cathedral, and a wolf was goaded into the structure in fulfilment of the contract!

In the ancient myth and romaunt of 'Merlin' may be found the mediæval witness to the diabolised religion of Britain. The emasculated saints of the South-east could not satisfy the vigorous race in the North-west, and when its gods were outlawed as devils they brought the chief of them back, as it were, had him duly baptized and set about his old work in the form of Merlin! Here, side by side with the ascetic Jesus, brought by Gatien and Augustin, was a Northern Christ, son of an Arch-incubus, born of a Virgin, baptized in the shrunken Jordan of a font, performing

Fig. 25.—From the 'Raree Show.'

miracles, summoning dragons to his aid, overcoming Death and Hell in his way, brought before his Pilate but confounding him, throning and dethroning kings, and leading forth, on the Day of Pentecost, an army whose knights are inspired by Guenever's kisses in place of flaming tongues. How Merlin 'went about doing good,' after the Northman's ideal of such work; how he saved the life of his unwedded mother by proving that her child (himself) was begotten by a devil without her knowledge; how, as a child, he exposed at once the pretension of the magistrate to high birth and the laxity of his lady and his parson; how he humiliated the priestly astrologers of Vortigern, and prophesied the destruction of that usurper just as it came to pass; how he served Uther during his seven years' reign, and by enabling him to assume the shape of the Duke of Cornwall and so enjoy the embraces of the Duchess Igerna, secured the birth of Arthur and hope of the Sangréal;4

how he defended Arthur's legitimacy of birth and assisted him in causing illegitimate births; and how at last he was bound by his own spells, wielded by Vivien, in a prison of air where he now remains;—this was the great mediæval gospel of a baptized christian Antichrist which superseded the imported kingdom not of this world.

Merlin was the Good Devil, but baptism was a fatal Vivien-spell to him. He still dwells in all the air which is breathed by Anglo-Saxon men,—an ever-expanding prison! Whether the Briton is transplanted in America, India, or Africa, he still carries with him the Sermon on the Mount as inspired by his baptized Prince of the Air, and his gospel of the day is, 'If thine enemy hunger, starve him; if he thirst, give him fire; if he hate you, heap melted lead on his head!' Such remains the soul of the greatest race, under the fatal spell of a creed that its barbarism needs only baptism to be made holiness and virtue.

In the reign of George II., when Lord Bute and a Princess of easy virtue were preying on England, and fanatical preachers were directing their donkeys to heaven beside the conflagration of John Bull's house, the eye of Hogarth at least (as is shown in our Figure 25, from his 'Raree Show') was able to see what the baptized Merlin had become in his realm of Air. The other worldly-Devil is serpent-legged Hypocrisy. The Nineteenth Century has replaced Merlin by Mephistopheles, the Devil who, despite a cloven foot, steps firmly on earth, and means the power that wit and culture can bring against the baptized giant Force. Him the gods fear not, even look upon with satisfaction. In the 'Prologue in Heaven,' of Goethe's 'Faust,' the Lord is even more gracious to Mephistopheles than the Jehovah of Job was to Satan. 'The like of thee have never moved my hate,' he says—

Man's active nature, flagging, seeks too soon the level;
Unqualified repose he learns to crave;
Whence, willingly, the comrade him I gave,
Who works, excites, and must create, as Devil.

This is but a more modern expression of the rabbinical fable, already noted, that when the first man was formed there were beside him two Spirits,—one on the right that remained quiescent, another on the left who ever moved restlessly up and down. When the first sin was committed, he of the left was changed to a devil. But he still meant the progressive, inquiring nature of man. 'The Spirit I, that evermore denies,' says the Mephistopheles of Goethe. How shall man learn truth if he know not the Spirit that denies? How shall he advance if he know not the Spirit of discontent? This restless spirit gains through his ignorance a cloven hoof,—a divided movement, sometimes right, sometimes wrong. From his selfishness it acquires a double tongue. But both hoof and serpent-tongue are beneath the evolutional power of experience; they shall be humanised to the foot that marches firmly on earth, and the tongue that speaks truth; and, the baptismal spell broken, Merlin shall descend, bringing to man's aid all his sharp-eyed dragons transformed to beautiful Arts.

Notes

1 In the pre-petrified era of Theology this hope appears to have visited the minds of some, Origen for instance. But by many centuries of utilisation the Devil became so essential to the throne of Christianity that theologians were more ready to spare God from their system than Satan. 'Even the clever Madame de Staël,' said Goethe, 'was greatly scandalised that I kept the Devil in such good-humour. In the presence of God the Father, she insisted upon it, he ought to be more grim and spiteful. What will she say if she sees him promoted a step higher,—nay, perhaps, meets him in heaven?' Though, in another conversation with Falk, Goethe intimates that he had written a passage 'where the Devil himself receives grace and mercy from God,' the artistic theory of his poem could permit no nearer approach to this than those closing lines (Faust, II.) in which Mephistopheles reproaches the 'case-hardened Devil' and himself for their mismanagement. To the isolated, the not yet humanised, intellect sensuality is evil when senseless, and its hell is folly.

2 'Demonialite,' 60–62, etc. We may hope that this learned man, during his tenure of office under the Inquisition, had some mercy for the poor devils dragged before that tribunal.

3 'Reverberations.' By W. M. W. Call, M.A., Cambridge. Second Edition. Trübner & Co., 1876.

4 The Holy Grail was believed to have been fashioned from the largest of all diamonds, lost from the crown of Satan as he fell from Heaven. Guarded by angels until used at the Last Supper, it was ultimately secured by Arthur's knight, Percival, and—such is the irony of mythology—indirectly by the aid of Satan's own son, Merlin!

Chapter XXVIII - Animalism

'The christians,' said Celsus, 'dream of some antagonist to God—a devil, whom they call Satanas, who thwarted God when he wished to benefit mankind. The Son of God suffered death from Satanas, but they tell us we are to defy him, and to bear the worst he can do; Satanas will come again and work miracles, and pretend to be God, but we are not to believe him. The Greeks tell of a war among the gods; army against army, one led by Saturn, and one by Ophincus; of challenges and battles; the vanquished falling into the ocean, the victors reigning in heaven. In the Mysteries we have the rebellion of the Titans, and the fables of Typhon, and Horus, and Osiris. The story of the Devil plotting against man is stranger than either of these. The Son of God is injured by the Devil, and charges us to fight against him at our peril. Why not punish the Devil instead of threatening poor wretches whom he deceives?'[1]

The christians comprehended as little as their critic that story they brought, stranger than all the legends of besieged deities, of a Devil plotting against man. Yet a little historic perspective makes the situation simple: the gods had taken refuge in man, therefore the attack was transferred to man.

Priestly legends might describe the gods as victorious over the Titans, the wild forces of nature, but the people, to their sorrow, knew better; the priests, in dealing with the people, showed that they also knew the victory to be on the other side. A careful writer remarks:—'When these (Greek) divinities are in any case appealed to with unusual seriousness, their nature-character reappears.... When Poseidon hesitates to defer to the positive commands of Zeus (Il. xix. 259), Iris reminds him that there are the Erinnyes to be reckoned with (Il. xv. 204), and he gives in at once.[2] The Erinnyes represent the steady supremacy of the laws and forces of nature over all personifications of them. Under uniform experience man had come to recognise his own moral autocracy in his world. He looked for incarnations, and it was a hope born of an atheistic view of external nature. This was the case not only with the evolution of Greek religion, but in that of every religion.

When man's hope was thus turned to rest upon man, he found that all the Titans had followed him. Ophincus (Ophion) had passed through Ophiomorphus to be a Man of Sin; and this not in one, but by corresponding forms in every line of religious development. The ferocities of outward nature appeared with all their force in man, and renewed their power with the fine armoury of his intelligence. He must here contend with tempests of passion, stony selfishness, and the whole animal creation nestling in heart and brain, prowling still, though on two feet. The theory of evolution is hardly a century old as science, but it is an ancient doctrine of Religion. The fables of Pilpay and Æsop represent an early recognition of 'survivals.' Recurrence to original types was recognised as a mystical phenomenon in legends of the bandit turned wolf, and other transformations. One of the oldest doctrines of Eschatology is represented in the accompanying picture (Fig. 26), from Thebes, of two dog-headed apes ferrying over to Hades a gluttonous soul that has been weighed before Osiris, and assigned his appropriate form.

Fig. 26.—A Soul's Doom (Wilkinson).

The devils of Lust are so innumerable that several volumes would be required to enumerate the legends and superstitions connected with them. But, fortunately for my reader and myself, these, more than any other class of phantoms, are very slight modifications of the same form. The innumerable phallic deities, the incubi and succubæ, are monotonous as the waves of the ocean, which might fairly typify the vast, restless, and stormy expanse of sexual nature to which they belong.

In 'The Golden Legend' there is a pleasant tale of a gentleman who, having fallen into poverty, went into solitude, and was there approached by a chevalier in black, mounted on a fine horse. This knight having inquired the reason of the other's sadness, promised him that, if he would return home, he would find at a certain place vast sums of gold; but this was on condition that he should bring his beautiful wife to that solitary spot in exactly a year's time. The gentleman, having lived in greater splendour than ever during the year, asked his wife to ride out with him on the appointed day. She was very pious, and having prayed to the Virgin, accompanied her husband to the spot. There the gentleman in black met them, but only to tremble. 'Perfidious man!' he cried, 'is it thus you repay my benefits? I asked you to bring your wife, and you have brought me the Mother of God, who will send me back to hell!' The Devil having vanished, the gentleman fell on his knees before the Virgin. He returned home to find his wife sleeping quietly.

Were we to follow this finely-mounted gentleman in black, we should be carried by no uncertain steps back to those sons of God who took unto themselves wives of the daughters of men, as told in Genesis; and if we followed the Virgin, we should, by less certain but yet probable steps, discover her prototype in Eve before her fall, virginal as she was meant to remain so far as man was concerned. In the chapters relating to the Eden myth and its personages, I have fully given my reasons for believing that the story of Eve, the natural childlessness of Sarah, and the immaculate conception by Mary, denote, as sea-rocks sometimes mark the former outline of a coast, a primitive theory of celibacy in connection with that of a divine or Holy Family. It need only be added here that this impossible ideal in its practical development was effectual in restraining the sexual passions of mankind. Although the reckless proclamation of the wild nature-gods (Elohim), 'Be fruitful and multiply,' has been accepted by christian bibliolators as the command of Jehovah, and philanthropists are even punished for suggesting means of withstanding the effects of nuptial licentiousness, yet they are farther from even the letter of the Bible than those protestant celibates, the American Shakers, who discard the sexual relation altogether. The theory of the Shakers that the functions of sex 'belong to a state of nature, and are inconsistent with a state of grace,' as one of their members in Ohio stated it to me, coincides closely with the rabbinical theory that Adam and Eve, by their sin, fell to the lowest of seven earthly spheres, and thus came within the influence of the incubi and succubæ, by their union with whom the world was filled with the demonic races, or Gentiles.

It is probable that the fencing-off of Eden, the founding of the Abrahamic household and family, and the command against adultery, were defined against that system of rape—or marriage by capture—which prevailed among the 'sons of Elohim,' who saw the 'daughters of men that they were fair,' and followed the law of their eyes. The older rabbins were careful to preserve the distinction between the Bene Elohim and the Ischim, and it ultimately amounted to that between Jews and Gentiles.

The suspicion of a devil lurking behind female beauty thus begins. The devils love beauty, and the beauties love admiration. These are perils in the constitution of the family. But there are other legends which report the frequency with which woman was an unwilling victim of the lustful Anakim or other powerful lords. Throughout the world are found legends of beautiful virgins sacrificed to powerful demons or deities. These are sometimes so realistic as to suggest the possibility that the fair captives of savage chieftains may indeed have been sometimes victims of their Ogre's voracity as well as his lust. At any rate, cruelty and lust are nearly related. The Blue Beard myth opens out horrible possibilities.

One of the best-known legends in Japan is that concerning the fiend Shudendozi, who derives his name from the two characteristics of possessing the face of a child and being a heavy drinker. The child-face is so emphasised in the stories that one may suspect either that his fair victims were enticed to his stronghold by his air of innocence, or else that there is some hint as to maternal longings in the fable.

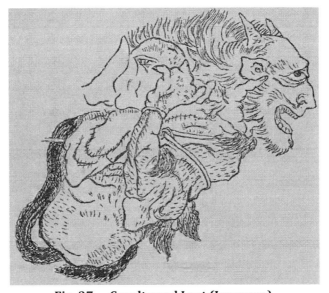

Fig. 27.—Cruelty and Lust (Japanese).

At the beginning of the eleventh century, when Ichijo II. was Emperor, lived the hero Yorimitsa. In those days the people of Kiyoto were troubled by an evil spirit which abode near the Rasho Gate. One night, when merry with his companions, Ichijo said, 'Who dare go and defy the demon of the Rasho Gate, and set up a token that he has been there?' 'That dare I,' answered Tsuma, who, having donned his mail, rode out in the bleak night to the Rasho Gate. Having written his name on the gate, returning, his horse shivers with fear, and a huge hand coming out of the gate seized the knight's helmet. He struggled in vain. He then cuts off the demon's arm, and the demon flies howling. Tsuma takes the demon's arm home, and locks it in a box. One night the demon, having the shape of Tsuma's aunt, came and said, 'I pray you show me the arm of the fiend.' 'I will show it to no man, and yet to thee will I show it,' replied he. When the box is opened a black cloud enshrouds the aunt, and the demon disappears with the arm. Thereafter he is more troublesome than ever. The demon carried off the fairest virgins of Kiyoto, ravished and ate them, no beauty being left in the city. The Emperor commands Yorimitsa to destroy him. The hero, with four trusty knights and a great captain, went to the hidden places of the mountains. They fell in with an old man, who invited them into his dwelling, and gave them wine to drink; and when they were going he presented them with wine. This old man was a mountain-god. As they proceeded they met a beautiful lady washing blood from garments in a valley, weeping bitterly. In reply to their inquiries she said the demon had carried her off and kept her to wash his clothes, meaning when weary of her to eat her. 'I pray your lordships to help me!' The six heroes bid her lead them to the ogre's cave. One hundred devils mounted guard before it. The woman first went in and told him they had come. The ogre called them in, meaning to eat them. Then they saw Shudendozi, a monster with the face of a little child. They offered him wine, which flew to his head: he becomes merry and sleeps, and his head is cut off. The head leaps up and tries to bite Yorimitsa, but he had on two helmets. When all the devils are slain, he brings the head of Shudendozi to the Emperor. In a similar story of the same country the lustful ogre by no means possesses Shudendozi's winning visage, as may be seen by the popular representation of him (Fig. 27), with a knight's hand grasping his throat. A Singhalese demon of like class is Bahirawa, who takes his name from the hill of the same name, towering over Kandy, in which he is supposed to reside. The legend runs that the astrologers told a king whose queen was afflicted by successive miscarriages, that she would never be delivered of a healthy child unless a virgin was sacrificed annually on the top of this hill. This being done, several children were borne to him. When his queen was advanced in years the king discontinued this observance, and consequently many diseases fell upon the royal family and the city, after which the annual sacrifice was resumed, and continued until 1815, when the English occupied Kandy. The method of the sacrifice was to bind a young girl to a stake on the top of the hill with jungle-creepers. Beside her, on an altar, were placed boiled rice and flowers; incantations were uttered, and the girl left, to be generally found dead of fright in the morning. An old woman, who in early years had undergone this ordeal, survived, and her safety no doubt co-operated with English authority to diminish the popular fear of Bahirawa, but still few natives would be found courageous enough to ascend the hill at night.

Fig. 28.—Jealousy (Japanese).

One of the lustful demons of Ceylon is Calu Cumara, that is, the Black Prince. He is supposed to have seven different apparitions,—prince of fire, of flowers, of groves, of graves, of eye-ointments, of the smooth body, and of sexuality. The Saga says he was a Buddhist priest, who by exceeding asceticism and accumulated merits had gained the power to fly, but passion for a beautiful woman caused him to fall. By disappointment in the love for which he had parted with so much his heart was broken, and he became a demon. In this condition he is for ever tortured by the passion of lustful desire, the only satisfaction of which he can obtain being to afflict young and fair women with illness. He is a very dainty demon, and can be soothed if great care is taken in the offerings made to him, which consist of rice of finest quality, plantains, sugar-cane, oranges, cocoa-nuts, and cakes. He is of dark-blue complexion and his raiment black.

In Singhalese demonolatry there are seven female demons of lust, popularly called the Madana Yaksenyo. These sisters are—Cama (lust); Cini (fire); Mohanee (ignorance); Rutti (pleasure); Cala (maturity); Mal (flowers); Puspa (perfumes). They are the abettors of seduction, and are invoked in the preparation of philtres.3

'It were well,' said Jason to Medea, 'that the female race should not exist; then would there not have been any evil among men.'4 The same sentiment is in Milton—

Oh why did God,

278

Creator wise, that peopled highest heaven
With spirits masculine, create at last
This novelty on earth, this fair defect
Of nature, and not fill the world at once
*With men, as angels, without feminine?*5

Many traditions preceded this ungallant creed, some of which have been referred to in our chapters on Lilith and Eve. Corresponding to these are the stories related by Herodotus of the overthrow of the kingdom of the Heraclidæ and freedom of the Greeks, through the revenge of the Queen, 'the most beautiful of women,' upon her husband Candaules for having contrived that Gyges should see her naked. Candaules having been slain by Gyges at the instigation of the Queen, and married her, the Fates decreed that their crime should be punished on their fifth descendant. The overthrow was by Cyrus, and it was associated with another woman, Mandane, daughter of the tyrant Astyages, mother of Cyrus, who is thus, as the Madonna, to bruise the head of the serpent who had crept into the Greek Paradise.6 The Greeks of Pontus also ascribed the origin of the Scythian race, the scourge of all nations, to a serpent-woman, who, having stolen away the mares which Herakles had captured from Gergon, refused to restore them except on condition of having children by him. From the union of Herakles with this 'half virgin, half viper,' sprang three sons, of whom the youngest was Scythes.

Not only are feminine seductiveness and liability to seduction represented in the legends of female demons and devils, but quite as much the jealousy of that sex. If the former were weaknesses which might overthrow kingdoms, the latter was a species of animalism which could devastate the home and society. Although jealousy is sometimes regarded as venial, if not indeed a sign of true love, it is an outcome of the animal nature. The Japanese have shown a true observation of nature in portraying their female Oni (devil) of jealousy (Fig. 28) with sharp erect horns and bristling hair. The raising 'of the ornamental plumes by many birds during their courtship,' mentioned by Mr. Darwin, is the more pleasing aspect of that emotion which, blending with fear and rage, puffs out the lizard's throat, ruffles the cock's neck, and raises the hair of the insane.7

An ancient legend mingles jealousy with the myth of Eden at every step. Rabbi Jarchi says that the serpent was jealous of Adam's connubial felicity, and a passage in Josephus shows that this was an ancient opinion. The jealousy of Adam's second wife felt by his first (Lilith) was by many said to be the cause of her conspiracy with the serpent. The most beautiful mediæval picture of her that I have seen was in an illuminated Bible in Strasburg, in which, with all her wealth of golden hair and her beauty, Lilith holds her mouth, with a small rosy apple in it, towards Adam. Eve seems to snatch it.

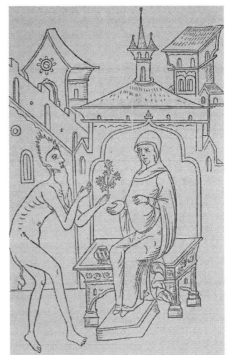

Then there is an old story that when Eve had eaten the apple she saw the angel of death, and urged Adam to eat the fruit also, in order that he might not become a widower.

It is remarkable that there should have sprung up a legend that Satan made his second attack upon the race formed by Jehovah, and his plan for perpetuating it on earth by means of a flirtation with Noah's wife, and also by awakening her jealousy. The older legend concerning Noah's wife is that mentioned by Tabari, which merely states that she ridiculed the predictions of a deluge by her husband. So much might have been suggested by the silence of the Bible concerning her. The Moslem tradition that the Devil managed to get into the ark is also ancient. He caught hold of the ass's tail just as it was about to enter. The ass came on slowly, and Noah, becoming impatient, exclaimed, 'You cursed one, come in quick!' When Noah, seeing the Devil in the ark, asked by what right he was there, the other said, 'By your order; you said, "Accursed one, come in;" I am the accursed one!' This story, which seems contrived to show that one may not be such an ass as he looks, was superseded by the legend which represents Satan as having been brought into the ark concealed under Noria's (or Noraita's) dress.

The most remarkable legend of this kind is that found in the Eastern Church, and which is shown in various mediæval designs in Russia. Satan is shown, in an early sixteenth century picture belonging to Count Uvarof (Fig. 29), offering Noah's wife a bunch of khmel (hops) with which to brew kvas and make Noah drunk; for the story was that Noah did not tell his wife that a deluge was coming, knowing that she could not keep a secret. In the old version of the legend given by Buslaef, 'after apocryphal tradition used by heretics,' Satan

Fig. 29.—Satan and Noraita.

always addresses Noah's wife as Eve, which indicates a theory. It was meant to be considered as a second edition of the attack on the divine plan begun in Eden, and revived in the temptation of Sara. Satan not only taught this new Eve how to make kvas but also vodka (brandy); and when he had awakened her jealousy about Noah's frequent absence, he bade her substitute the brandy for the beer when her husband, as usual, asked for the latter. When Noah was thus in his cups she asked him where he went, and why he kept late hours. He revealed his secret to his Eve, who disclosed it to Satan. The tempter appears to have seduced her from Noah, and persuaded her to be dilatory when entering the ark. When all the animals had gone in, and all the rest of her family, Eve said, 'I have forgotten my pots and pans,' and went to fetch them; next she said, 'I have forgotten my spoons and forks,' and returned for them. All of this had been arranged by Satan in order to make Noah curse; and he had just slipped under Eve's skirt when he had the satisfaction of hearing the intended Adam of a baptized world cry to his wife, 'Accursed one, come in!' Since Jehovah himself could not prevent the carrying out of a patriarch's curse, Satan was thus enabled to enter the ark, save himself from being drowned, and bring mischief into the human world once more.

This is substantially the same legend as that of the mediæval Morality called 'Noah's Ark, or the Shipwright's Ancient Play or Dirge.' The Devil says to Noah's wife:—

Yes, hold thee still le dame,
And I shall tell thee how;
I swear thee by my crooked snout,
All that thy husband goes about
Is little to thy profit.
Yet shall I tell thee how
Thou shalt meet all his will;
Do as I shall bid thee now,
Thou shalt meet every deal.
Have here a drink full good
That is made of a mightful main,
Be he hath drunken a drink of this,
No longer shall he learn:
Believe, believe, my own dear dame,
I may no longer bide;
To ship when thou shalt sayre,
I shall be by thy side.

There are some intimations in the Slavonic version which look as if it might have belonged to some Paulician or other half-gnostic theory that the temptation of Noraita (Eve II.), and her alienation from her husband, were meant to prevent the repopulation of the Earth.8

The next attempt of the Devil, as agent of the Elohistic creation, to ruin the race of man, introduces us to another form of animalism which has had a large expression in Devil-lore. It is related in rabbinical mythology that when, as is recorded in Gen. ix. 20, Noah was planting a vineyard, the Devil (Asmodeus) came and proposed to join him in the work. This having been agreed to, this evil partner brought in succession a sheep, a lion, and a hog, and sacrificed them on the spot. The result was that the wine when drunk first gave the drinker the quality of a sheep, then that of a lion, and finally that of a hog.9 It was by this means that Noah was reduced to swinish inebriation. There followed the curses on those around him, which, however drunken, were those of a father, and reproduced on the cleansed world all the dooms which had been pronounced in Eden.

If the date of this legend could be made early enough, it would appear to be a sort of revenge for this temptation of Noah to drunkenness that Talmudic fable shows Asmodeus brought under bondage to Solomon, and forced to work on the Temple, by means of wine. Asmodeus had dug for himself a well, and planted beside it a tree, so making for himself a pleasant spot for repose during his goings to and fro on earth. But Solomon's messenger Benaja managed to cover this with a tank which he filled with wine. Asmodeus, on his return, repeated to himself the proverb, 'Wine is a mocker, strong drink is raging, and whosoever is deceived thereby is not wise' (Prov. xx. 1); yet, being very thirsty, he drank, fell asleep, and when he awoke found himself loaded with chains.

However, after working for a time for Solomon, he discovered that king's weaknesses and played upon them. Solomon was so puffed up with a sense of his power that he accepted a challenge from his slave (Asmodeus) to show his superiority without the assistance of his magic ring, and without keeping his competitor in bonds. No sooner was Asmodeus free, and in possession of the ring, than he transported Solomon four hundred miles away, where he remained for a long time among the seductive beauties of the Courts of Naamah, Rahab, and other she-devils. Meanwhile the Devil, assuming the form of Solomon, sat on his throne, and became the darling of his Queen and concubines.

The Devil of Wine and strong drink generally has a wide representation in folklore. We find him in the bibulous Serpent of Japan, who first loses his eight heads metaphorically, and then literally from the first of Swords-men. The performances of Mephistopheles in Auerbach's Cellar are commemorated in its old frescoes, and its motto: 'Live, drink, carouse, remembering Faust and his punishment: it came slowly, but was in ample measure.' Thuringian legends relate that the Devil tries to stop the building of churches by casting down the stones, but this may be stopped by the builders promising to erect a winehouse in the same neighbourhood. An old English legend relates that a great man's cellar was haunted by devils who drank up his wine. On one occasion a barrel was marked with holy water, and the devil was found stuck fast on it.

Gluttony, both in eating and drinking, has had its many personifications. The characteristics of the Hunger demons are travestied in such devils as these, only the diabolical, as distinguished from the demonic element, appears in features of luxuriousness. The contrast between the starveling saints of the early Church and the well-fed friars of later times was a frequent subject of caricature, as in the accompanying example (Fig. 30) from the British Museum, fourteenth century (MS. Arundel), where a lean devil is satisfying himself through a fattened friar. One of the most significant features of the old legend of Faust is the persistence of the animal character in which Mephistopheles appears. He is an ugly dog—a fit emblem of the scholar's relapse into the canine temper which flies at the world as at a bone he means to gnaw. Faust does

Fig. 30.—Monkish Gluttony.

not like this genuine form, and bids the Devil change it. Mephistopheles then takes the form of a Franciscan friar; but 'the kernel of the brute' is in him still, and he at once loads Faust's table with luxuries and wines from the cellars of the Archbishop of Salzburg and other rich priests. The prelates are fond of their bone too. When Mephistopheles and Faust find their way into the Vatican, it is to witness carousals of the Pope and his Cardinals. They snatch from them their luxuries and wine-goblets as they are about to enjoy them. Against these invisible invaders the holy men bring their crucifixes and other powers of exorcism; and it is all snarling and growling—canine priest against puppy astrologer. Nor was it very different in the history of the long contention between the two for the big bone of Christendom. The lust of Gold had its devils, and they were not different from other types of animalism. This was especially the case with such as represented money, extorted from the people to supply wealth to dissolute princes and prelates. The giants of Antwerp represent the power of the pagan monarchs who exacted tribute; but these were replaced by such guardians of tribute-money as the Satyr of our picture (Fig. 31), which Edward the Confessor saw seated on a barrel of Danegeld,

Vit un déable saer desus
Le tresor, noir et hidus.

There are many good fables in European folklore with regard to the miser's gold, and 'devil's money' generally, which exhibit a fine instinct. A man carries home a package of such gold, and on opening it there drop out, instead of money, paws and nails of cats, frogs, and bears—the latter being an almost personal allusion to the Exchange. A French miser's money-safe being opened, two frogs only were found. The Devil could not get any other soul than the gold, and the cold-blooded reptiles were left as a sign of the life that had been lived.

In the legends of the swarms of devils which beset St. Anthony we find them represented as genuine animals. Our Anglo-Saxon fathers, however, were quite unable to appreciate the severity of the conflict which man had to wage with the animal world in Southern countries and in earlier times. Nor had their reverence for nature and its forms been crushed out by the pessimist theory of the earth maintained by Christianity. Gradually the representation of the animal tempters was modified, and instead of real animal forms there were reported the bearded bestialities which surrounded St. Guthlac and St. Godric. The accompanying picture (Fig. 32) is a group from Breughel (1565), representing the devils called around St. James by a magician. These

Fig. 31.—Devil of a Danegeld Treasure (MS. Trin. Coll. Cantab. B. x. 2).

grotesque forms will repay study. If we should make a sketch of the same kind, only surrounding the saint with the real animal shapes most nearly resembling these nondescripts, it would cease to be a diabolical scene.

Fig. 32.—St. James and Devils.

For beastliness is not a character of beasts; it is the arrest of man. It is not the picturesque donkey in the meadow that is ridiculous, but the donkey on two feet; not the bear of zoological gardens that is offensive morally, but the rough, who cannot always be caged; it is the two-legged calf, the snake pretending to be a man, the ape in evening dress, who ever made the problem of evil at all formidable. It was insoluble until men had discovered as Science that law of Evolution which the ancient world knew as Ethics.

A Hindu fable relates that the animals, in their migration, came to an abyss they could not cross, and that the gods made man as a bridge across it. Science and Reason confirm these ancient instincts of our race. Man is that bridge stretching between the animal and the ideal habitat by which, if the development be normal, all the passions pass upward into educated powers. Any pause or impediment on that bridge brings all the animals together to rend and tear the man who cannot convey them across the abyss. A very slight arrest may reveal to a man that he is a vehicle of intensified animalism. The lust of the goat, the pride of the peacock, the wrath of the lion, beautiful in their appropriate forms, become, in the guise of a man uncontrolled by reason, the vices which used to be called possession, and really are insanities.

Notes

1 See Mr. J. A. Froude's article in 'Fraser's Magazine,' Feb. 1878, 'Origen and Celsus.'
2 Mr. W. W. Lloyd's 'Age of Pericles,' vol. ii. p. 202.
3 Journal of the Ceylon Branch of the R. A. S., 1865–6: Art. on 'Demonology and Witchcraft in Ceylon,' by Dundris de Silva Gooneratne Modliar.
4 Euripides, 'Medea,' 574.
5 'Paradise Lost,' x. 860.
6 Herodotus, 'Clio,' 7–14, 91.
7 'Expression of the Emotions.' By Charles Darwin. London: Murray, 1872. Chapter IV.
8 The giving of Eve's name to Noah's wife is not the only significant thing about this Russian tradition and its picture. Long-bearded devils are nowhere normal except in the representations by the Eastern Church of the monarch of Hell. By referring to p. 253 of this volume the reader will observe the influences which caused the infernal king to be represented as counterpart of the Deity. As this tradition about Noah's wife is suggestive of a Gnostic origin, it really looks as if the Devil in it were meant to act the part which the Gnostics ascribed to Jehovah himself (vol. ii. p. 207). The Devil is said in rabbinical legends to have seduced the wives of Noah's sons; this legend seems to show that his aim was to populate the post-diluvial world entirely with his own progeny, in this being an Ildabaoth, or degraded edition of Jehovah trying to establish his own family in the earth by the various means related in vol. i. chap. 8.
9 'Nischamath Chajim,' fol. 139, col. 2.

Chapter XXIX - Thoughts and Interpretations

I lately heard the story of a pious negro woman whose faith in hell was sorely tried by a sceptic who asked her how brimstone enough could be found to burn all the wicked people in the world. After taking some days for reflection, the old woman, when next challenged by the sceptic, replied, that she had concluded that 'every man took his own brimstone.' This humble saint was unconscious that her instinct had reached the finest thought of Milton, whose Satan says 'Myself am hell.' Marlowe's Mephistopheles also says, 'Where we are is hell.' And, far back as the year 633, the holy man Fursey, who believed himself to have been guided by an angel near the region of the damned, related a vision much like the view of the African woman. There were four fires—Falsehood, Covetousness, Discord, Injustice—which joined to form one great flame. When this drew near, Fursey, in fear, said, 'Lord, behold the fire draws near me.' The angel answered, 'That which you did not kindle shall not burn you.'

Such association of any principle of justice, even in form so crude, has become rare enough in Christendom to excite applause when it appears, though the applause has about it that infusion of the grotesque which one perceives when gallery-gods cheer the actor who heroically declares that a man ought not to strike a woman. When we go back to the atmosphere of Paganism we find that retribution had among them a real meaning. Nothing can be in more remarkable contrast than the disorderly characterless hell of Christendom, into which the murderer and the man who confuses the

Persons of the Godhead alike burn everlastingly in most inappropriate fires, and the Hades of Egypt, Greece, and Rome, where every punishment bears relation to the offence, and is limited in duration to the degree of the offence.

'The Egyptians,' says Herodotus (ii. 123), 'were the first who asserted that the soul of man is immortal, and that when the body perishes it enters into some other animal, constantly springing into existence; and when it has passed through the different kinds of terrestrial, marine, and aerial beings, it again enters into the body of a man that is born, and that this revolution is made in three thousand years.' Probably Plato imported from Egypt his fancy of the return of one dead to relate the scenes of heaven and hell, Er the Armenian (Republic, x. 614) suggesting an evolution of Rhampsinitus (Herod. ii. 122), who descended to Hades alive, played dice with Ceres, and brought back gold. The vision of Er represents a terrible hell, indeed, but those punished were chiefly murderers and tyrants. They are punished tenfold for every wrong they had committed. But when this punishment is ended, each soul must return to the earth in such animal form as he or she might select. The animals, too, had their choice. Er saw that the choice was generally determined by the previous earthly life,—many becoming animals because of some spite derived from their experience. 'And not only did men pass into animals, but I must also mention that there were animals tame and wild who changed into one another, and into corresponding human natures, the good into the gentle, the evil into the savage, in all sorts of combinations.' Sly Plato! Such is his estimate of what men's selections of their paradises are worth!

Orpheus chose to be a swan, hating to be born of woman, because women murdered him; Ajax became a lion and Agamemnon an eagle, because they had suffered injustice from men; Atalanta would be an athlete, and the jester Thersites a monkey; and Odysseus went about to find the life of a private gentleman with nothing to do. If Plutarch's friend Thespesius had pondered well this irony of Plato, he would hardly have brought back from his visit to Hades the modification that demons were provided to assign the animal forms in which souls should be born again on earth. They could hardly have done for the wicked anything worse than Plato shows them doing for themselves. But the meaning of Plutarch is the same. Thespesius sees demons preparing the body of a viper for Nero to be born into, since it was said the young of that reptile destroy their mother at birth.

Among the Persians the idea of future rewards and punishments exceeds the exactness of the Koran—'Whoso hath done an atom of justice shall behold it, and whoso hath done an atom of injustice shall behold it.' The Persian Sufis will even subdivide the soul rather than that any good act should go down with the larger gross of wickedness. Sádi tells of a vision where a man was seen in hell, all except one foot, which was twined with flowers. With all his wickedness the man had with that foot shoved a bundle of hay within reach of a weary ox.

But while Persian poets—Sufis, ennobling the old name Sophist—preserved thus a good deal of the universalism of Parsaism, a Mohammedanism hard as the Scythians who brought it turned the heart of the people in that country to stone. In the Dresden Library there is an illuminated Persian MS., thought to be seven hundred years old, which has in it what may be regarded as a portrait of Ahriman and Iblis combined. He is red, has a heavy beard and moustache, and there is a long dragon's crest and mane on his head. He wears a green and blue skirt about his loins. His tongue rolls thirstily between his cruel teeth. He superintends a number of fish-like devils which float in a lake of fire, and swallow the damned. Above this scene are the glorified souls, including the Shah sitting cross-legged on his rug, who look down on the tortures beneath with evident satisfaction. Apparently this is the only amusement which relieves the ennui of their heaven.

If anything could make a rational man believe in a fiend-principle in the universe it would be the suggestion of such pictures, that men have existed who could conceive of happiness enjoyed in view of such tortures as these. This and some similar pictures in the East—for instance, that in the Temple of Horrors at Wuchang, China—are absolutely rayless so far as any touch of humanity is concerned. Are the Shah and his happy fellow-inspectors of tortures really fiends? In the light of our present intelligence they may seem so. Certainly no person of refined feeling could now expect to attain any heaven while others were in hell. But it would be possible, if persons could believe that many of those around them are not men and women at all, but fiends in human shape. These ferocious Hells are referable to a period when all who incurred the sentences of princes or priests were seen as mere masks of devils; they were only ascribed human flesh that they may suffer. The dogma of Hell was doomed from the moment that the damned were supposed to be really human. Were those who killed the martyrs of heresy, for instance, to return to the world and look upon those whom they pierced, they could never recognise them. Were they to see the statues of Bruno, Huss, Cranmer, Servetus, the names and forms would not recall to them the persons they slew. They would be shocked if told that they had burned great men, and would surely answer, 'Men? We burned no men. The Devil came among us calling himself Huss, and we made short work with him; he reappeared under several aliases—Bruno, Servetus, Spinoza, Voltaire: sometimes we burned him, at other times managed to make him miserable, thank God! But we were not hurting real men, we were saving them.'

Around such ideas grew our yet uncivilised Codes of Law. In England, anno 1878, men are refused as jury-men if they will not say, 'So help me God!' on the ground that an atheist cannot have a conscience. Only let him really be without conscience, and call himself a christian when he is not, and courts receive the selfish liar with respect. The old clause of the death-sentence—'instigated thereto by the Devil'—has been dropped in the case of murderers, however; and that is some gain. Torture by fire of the worst murderer for one day would not be permitted in Christendom. Belief in hell-fire outlasts it for a little among the ignorant. But what shall be said of the educated who profess to believe it?

The Venerable Bede relates that, in the year 696, a Northumbrian gentleman, who had died in the beginning of the night, came to life and health in the morning, and gave an account of what he had seen overnight. He had witnessed the conventional tortures of the damned, but adds—'Being thus on all sides enclosed with enemies and darkness, and looking about on every side for assistance, there appeared to me, on the way that I came, as it were, the brightness of a star shining amidst the darkness, which increased by degrees,'—but we need not go on to the anti-climax of this vision. This star rising above all such visions belongs to the vault of the human Love, and it is visible through all the Ages of Darkness. It cannot be quenched, and its fiery rays have burnt up mountains of iniquity.

'In the year 1322,' writes Flögel, after the 'Chronicon Sampetrinum Erfurtense,' 'there was a play shown at Eisenach, which had a tragical enough effect. Markgraf Friedrich of Misnia, Landgraf also of Thuringia, having brought his tedious warfare to a conclusion, and the country beginning now to revive under peace, his subjects were busy repaying themselves for the past distresses by all manner of diversions; to which end, apparently by the Sovereign's order, a dramatic representation of the Ten Virgins was schemed, and at Eisenach, in his presence, duly executed. This happened fifteen days after Easter, by indulgence of the Preaching Friars. In the 'Chronicon Sampetrinum' stands recorded that the play was enacted in the Bear Garden (in horto ferarum) by the Clergy and their Scholars. But now, when it came to pass that the Wise Virgins would give the foolish no oil, and these latter were shut out from the Bridegroom, they began to weep bitterly, and called on the Saints to intercede for them; who however, even with Mary at their head, could effect nothing from God; but the Foolish Virgins were all sentenced to damnation. Which things the Landgraf seeing and hearing, he fell into a doubt, and was very angry; and said 'What then is the Christian Faith, if God will not take pity on us for intercession of Mary and all the Saints?' In this anger he continued five days; and the learned men could hardly enlighten him to understand the Gospel. Thereupon he was struck with apoplexy, and became speechless and powerless; in which sad state he continued, bedrid, two years and seven months, and so died, being then fifty-five.'

In telling the story Carlyle remarks that these 'Ten Virgins at Eisenach are more fatal to warlike men than Æschylus' Furies at Athens were to weak women.' Even so, until great-hearted men rose up at Eisenach and elsewhere to begin the work destined to prove fatal alike to heartless Virgins and Furies. That star of a warrior's Compassion, hovering over the foolish Friars and their midnight Gospel, beams far. The story reminds me of an incident related of a mining district in California, where a rude theatre was erected, and a company gave, as their first performance, Othello. When the scene of Desdemona's suffocation approached, a stalwart miner leaped on the stage, and pulling out his six-shooter, said to the Moor, 'You damned nigger! if you touch that woman I'll blow the top of your head off!' A dozen roughs, clambering over the footlights, cried, 'Right Joe! we'll stand by you!' The manager met the emergency by crying, 'Don't shoot, boys! This play was wrote by Bill Shakespear; he's an old Californian, and it's all in fun!' Had this Moor proceeded to roast Desdemona in fire with any verisimilitude, it is doubtful if the manager could have saved him by an argument reminding the miners that such was the divine way with sinners in the region to which most of them were going. The top of that theologic hell's head is not very safe in these days when human nature is unchained with all its six-shooters, each liable to be touched off by fire from that Star revolving in the sphere of Compassion.

Day after day I gazed upon Michael Angelo's 'Last Judgment' in the Sistine Chapel. The artist was in his sixtieth year when Pope Clement VII. invited him to cover a wall sixty feet high and nearly as wide with a picture of the Day of Wrath. In seven years he had finished it. Clement was dead. Pope Paul IV. looked at it, and liked it not: all he could see was a vast number of naked figures; so he said it was not fit for the Sistine Chapel, and must be destroyed. One of Michael Angelo's pupils saved it by draping some of the figures. Time went on, and another Pope came who insisted on more drapery,—so the work was disfigured again. However, popular ridicule saved this from going very far, and so there remains the tremendous scene. But Popes and Cardinals always disliked it. The first impression I received from it was that of a complete representation of all the physical powers belonging to organised life; though the forms are human, every animal power is there, leaping, crouching, crawling,—every sinew, joint, muscle, portrayed in completest tension and action. Then the eye wanders from face to face, and every passion that ever crawled or prowled in jungle or swamp is pictured. The most unpleasant expressions seemed to me those of the martyrs. They came up from their graves, each bringing the instrument by which he had suffered, and offering it in witness against the poor wretches who came to be judged; and there was a look of self-righteous satisfaction on their faces as they witnessed the persecution of their persecutors. As for Christ, he was like a fury, with hand uplifted against the doomed, his hair wildly floating. The tortured people below are not in contrast with the blessed above; they who are in heaven look rather more stupid than the others, and rather pleased with the anguish they witness, but not more saintly. But gradually the eye, having wandered over the vast canvas, from the tortured Cardinal at the bottom up to the furious Judge,—alights on a face which, once seen, is never to be forgotten. Beautiful she is, that Mary beside the Judge, and more beautiful for the pain that is on her face. She has drawn her drapery to veil from her sight the anguish below; she has turned her face from the Judge,—does not see her son in him; she looks not upon the blessed,—for she, the gentle mother, is not in heaven; she cannot have joy in sight of misery. In that one face of pure womanly sympathy—that beauty transfigured in its compassionateness—the artist put his soul, his religion. Mary's face quenches all the painted flames. They are at once made impossible. The same universe could not produce both a hell and that horror of it. The furious Jesus is changed to a phantasm; he could never be born of such a mother. If the Popes had only wished to hide the nakedness of their own dogmas they ought to have blotted out Mary's face; for as it now stands the rest of the forms are but shapes to show how all the wild forms and passions of human animalism gather as a frame round that which is their consummate flower,—the spirit of love enshrined in its perfect human expression.

So was it that Michael Angelo could not serve two masters. Popes might employ him, but he could not do the work they liked. 'The passive master lent his hand to the vast soul that o'er him planned.' He could not help it. The lover of beauty could not paint the Day of Wrath without setting above it that face like a star which shines through its unreality, burns up its ugliness, and leaves the picture a magnificent interpretation of the forms of nature and hopes of the world,—a cardinal hypocrite at the bottom, an ideal woman at the top.

Exhausted by the too-much glory of the visions of Paradise which he had seen, Dante came forth to the threshold opening on the world of human life, from which he had parted for a space, and there sank down. As he lay there angels caused lilies to grow beneath and around him, and myrtle to rise and intertwine for a bower over him, and their happy voices, wafted in low-toned hymns, brought soft sleep to his overwrought senses. Long had he slumbered before the light of familiar day stole once more into those deep eyes. The angels had departed. The poet awoke to find himself alone, and with a sigh he said to himself, 'It is, then, all but a dream.' As he arose he saw before him a man of noble mien and shining countenance, habited in an Eastern robe, who returned his gaze with an interest equal to his own. Quickly the eyes of Dante searched the ground beside the stranger to see if he were shadowless: convinced thus that he was true flesh and blood, the Florentine thus addressed him:—

'Pilgrim, for such thou seemest, may we meet in simple human brotherhood? If, as thy garb suggests, thou comest from afar, perchance the friendly greeting, even of one who in his native city is still himself a pilgrim, may not be unwelcome.

'Heart to heart be our kiss, my brother; yet must I journey without delay to those who watch and wait for wondrous tidings that I bear.

'Friend! I hear some meaning deeper than thy words. If 'twere but as satisfying natural curiosity, answer not; but if thou bearest a burden of tidings glad for all human-kind, speak! Who art thou? whence comest, and with what message freighted?

'Arda Viráf is the name I bear; from Persia have I come; but by what strange paths have reached this spot know I not, save that through splendours of worlds invisible to mortal sense I have journeyed, nor encountered human form till I found thee slumbering on this spot.

'Trebly then art thou my brother! I too have but now, as to my confused sense it seems, emerged from that vast journey. Thou clearest from me gathering doubts that those visions were illusive. Yet, as even things we really see are often overlaid by images that lurk in the eye, I pray thee tell me something thou hast seen, so that perchance we may part with mutual confirmation of our vision.

'That gladly will I do. When the Avesta had been destroyed, and the sages of Iran disagreed as to the true religion, they agreed that one should be chosen by lot to drink the sacred draught of Vishtasp, that he might pass to the invisible world and bring intelligence therefrom. On me the lot fell. Beside the fire that has never gone out, surrounded by holy women who chanted our hymns, I drank the three cups—Well Thought, Well Said, Well Done. Then as I slept there rose before me a high stairway of three steps; on the first was written, Well Thought; on the second, Well Said; on the third, Well Done. By the first step I reached the realm where good thoughts are honoured: there were the thinkers whose starlike radiance ever increased. They offered no prayers, they chanted no liturgies. Above all was the sphere of the liberal. The next step brought me to the circle of great and truthful speakers: these walked in lofty splendour. The third step brought me to the heaven of good actions. I saw the souls of agriculturists surrounded by spirits of water and earth, trees and cattle. The artisans were seated on embellished thrones. Sublime were the seats of teachers, interceders, peace-makers; and the religious walked in light and joy with which none are satiated.

'Sawest thou the fairest of earth-born ladies—Beatrice?

'I saw indeed a lady most fair. In a pleasant grove lay the form of a man who had but then parted from earth. When he had awakened, he walked through the grove and there met him this most beautiful maiden. To her he said, 'Who art thou, so fair beyond all whom I have seen in the land of the living?' To him she replied, 'O youth, I am thy actions.' Can this be thy lady Beatrice?

'But sawest thou no hell? no dire punishments?

'Alas! sad scenes I witnessed, sufferers whose hell was that their darkness was amid the abodes of splendour. Amid all that glow one newly risen from earth walked shivering with cold, and there walked ever by his side a hideous hag. On her he turned and said, 'Who art thou, that ever movest beside me, thou that art monstrous beyond all that I have seen on earth?' To him she replied, 'Man, I am thy actions.'

'But who were those glorious ones thou sawest in Paradise?

'Some of their names I did indeed learn—Zoroaster, Socrates, Plato, Buddha, Confucius, Christ.

'What do I hear! knowest thou that none of these save that last holy one—whom methinks thou namest too lightly among men—were baptized? Those have these eyes sorrowfully beheld in pain through the mysterious justice of God.

'Thinkest thou, then, thy own compassion deeper than the mercy of Ormuzd? But, ah! now indeed I do remember. As I conversed with the sages I had named, they related to me this strange event. By guidance of one of their number, Virgil by name, there had come among them from the earth a most powerful magician. He bore the name of Dante. By mighty spells this being had cast them all into a sad circle which he called Limbo, over whose gate he wrote, though with eyes full of tears, 'All hope abandon, ye who enter here!' Thus were they in great sorrow and dismay. But, presently, as this strange Dante was about to pass on, so they related, he looked upon the face of one among them so pure and noble that though he had styled him 'pagan,' he could not bear to abandon him there. This was Cato of Utica. Him this Dante led to the door, and gave him liberty on condition that he would be warder of his unbaptized brethren, and by no means let any of them escape. No sooner, however, was this done than this magician beheld others who moved his reverence,—among them Trajan and Ripheus,—and overcome by an impulse of love, he opened a window in the side of Limbo, bidding them emerge into light. He then waved his christian wand to close up this aperture, and passed away, supposing that he had done so; but the limit of that magician's power had been reached, the window was but veiled, and after he had gone all these unbaptized ones passed out by that way, and reascended to the glory they had enjoyed before this Dante had brought his alien sorceries to bear upon them for a brief space.

'Can this be true? Is it indeed so that all the sages and poets of the world are now in equal rank whether or not they have been sealed as members of Christ?

'Brother, thy brow is overcast. What! can one so pure and high of nature as thou desire that the gentle Christ, whom I saw embracing the sages and prophets of other ages, should turn upon them with hatred and bind them in gloom and pain like this Dante?'

Thereupon, with a flood of tears, Dante fell at the feet of Arda Viráf, and kissed the hem of his skirt. 'Purer is thy vision, O pilgrim, than mine,' he said. 'I fear that I have but borne with me to the invisible world the small prejudices of my little Church, which hath taught me to limit the Love which I now see to be boundless. Thou who hast learned from thy Zoroaster that the meaning of God is the end of all evil, a universe climbing to its flower in joy, deign to take the hand of thy servant and make him worthy to be thy friend,—with thee henceforth to abandon the poor formulas which ignorance substitutes for virtue, and ascend to the beautiful summits thou has visited by the stairway of good thoughts, good words, good deeds.'

In 1745 Swedenborg was a student of Natural Philosophy in London. In the April of that year his 'revelations' began amid the smoke and toil of the great metropolis. 'I was hungry and ate with great appetite. Towards the end of the meal I remarked a kind of mist spread before my eyes, and I saw the floor of my room covered with hideous reptiles, such as serpents, toads, and the like. I was astonished, having all my wits about me, being perfectly conscious. The darkness attained its height and then passed away. I now saw a Man sitting in the corner of the chamber. As I had thought myself alone, I was greatly frightened when he said to me, 'Eat not as much.'

In Swedenborg's Diary the incident is related more particularly. 'In the middle of the day, at dinner, an Angel spoke to me, and told me not to eat too much at table. Whilst he was with me, there plainly appeared to me a kind of vapour steaming from the pores of my body. It was a most visible watery vapour, and fell downwards to the ground upon the carpet, where it collected and turned into divers vermin, which were gathered together under the table, and in a moment went off with a pop or noise. A fiery light appeared within them, and a sound was heard, pronouncing that all the vermin that could possibly be generated by unseemly appetite were thus cast out of my body, and burnt up, and that I was now cleansed from them. Hence we may know what luxury and the like have for their bosom contents.'

Continuing the first account Swedenborg said, 'The following night the same Man appeared to me again. I was this time not at all alarmed. The Man said, 'I am God, the Lord, the Creator, and Redeemer of the world. I have chosen thee to unfold to men the spiritual sense of the Holy Scripture. I will myself dictate to thee what thou shalt write.' The same night the world of spirits, hell and heaven, were convincingly opened to me, where I found many persons of my acquaintance of all conditions. From that day forth I gave up all worldly learning, and laboured only in spiritual things, according to what the Lord commanded me to write.'

He 'gave up all worldly learning,' shut his intellectual eyes, and sank under all the nightmares which his first vision saw burnt up as vermin. After his fiftieth year, says Emerson, he falls into jealousy of his intellect, makes war on it, and the violence is instantly avenged. But the portrait of the blinded mystic as drawn by the clear seer is too impressive an illustration to be omitted here.

'A vampyre sits in the seat of the prophet and turns with gloomy appetite to the images of pain. Indeed, a bird does not more readily weave its nest or a mole bore in the ground than this seer of the souls substructs a new hell and pit, each more abominable than the last, round every new crew of offenders. He was let down through a column that seemed of brass, but it was formed of angelic spirits, that he might descend safely amongst the unhappy, and witness the vastation of souls; and heard there, for a long continuance, their lamentations; he saw their tormentors, who increase and strain pangs to infinity; he saw the hell of the jugglers, the hell of the assassins, the hell of the lascivious; the hell of robbers, who kill and boil men; the infernal tun of the deceitful; the excrementitious hells; the hell of the revengful, whose faces resembled a round, broad cake, and their arms rotate like a wheel.... The universe, in his poem, suffers under a magnetic sleep, and only reflects the mind of the magnetiser.... Swedenborg and Behmon both failed by attaching themselves to the christian symbol, instead of to the moral sentiment, which carries innumerable christianities, humanities, divinities, in its bosom.... Another dogma, growing out of this pernicious theologic limitation, is this Inferno. Swedenborg has devils. Evil, according to old philosophers, is good in the making. That pure malignity can exist, is the extreme proposition of unbelief.... To what a painful perversion had Gothic theology arrived, that Swedenborg admitted no conversion for evil spirits! But the divine effort is never relaxed; the carrion in the sun will convert itself to grass and flowers; and man, though in brothels, or jails, or on gibbets, is on his way to all that is good and true.'

But even the Hell of Swedenborg is not free from the soft potency of our star. It is almost painful, indeed, to see its spiritual ray mingling with the fiery fever-shapes which Swedenborg meets on his way through the column of brass,— made, had he known it, not of angels but of savage scriptures. 'I gave up all worldly learning'—he says: but it did not give him up all at once. 'They (the damned) suffer ineffable torments; but it was permitted to relieve or console them with a certain degree of hope, so that they should not entirely despair. For they said they believed the torment would be eternal. They were relieved or consoled by saying that God Messiah is merciful, and that in His Word we read that 'the prisoners will be sent forth from the pit' (Zech. ix. 2). Swedenborg reports that God Messiah appeared to these spirits, and even embraced and kissed one who had been raised from 'the greatest torment.' He says, 'Punishment for the sake of punishment is the punishment of a devil,' and affirms that all punishment is 'to take away evils or to induce a faculty of doing good.' These utterances are in his Diary, and were written before he had got to the bottom of his Calvinistic column; but even in the 'Arcana Celestia' there is a gleam:—'Such is the equilibrium of all things in another life that evil punishes itself, and unless it were removed by punishments the evil spirits must necessarily be kept in some hell to eternity.' Reductio ad absurdum! And yet Swedenborgians insist upon the dogma of everlasting punishments; to sustain which they appeal from Swedenborg half-sober to Swedenborg mentally drunk.

In the Library at Dresden there is a series of old pictures said to be Mexican, and which I was told had been purchased from a Jew in Vienna, containing devils mainly of serpent characters blended with those of humanity. One was a fantastic serpent with human head, sharp snoutish nose, many eyes, slight wings, and tongue lolling out. Another had a human head and reptilian tail. A third is human except for the double tongue darting out. A fourth has issuing from the back of his head a serpent whose large dragon head is swallowing a human embryo. Whatever tribe it was that originated these pictures must have had very strong impressions of the survival of the serpent in some men.

I was reminded of the picture of the serpent swallowing the human embryo while looking at the wall-pictures in Russian churches representing the conventional serpent with devils nestling at intervals along its body, as represented in our Figure (10). Professor Buslaef gave me the right archæology of this, no doubt, but the devils themselves, as I gazed, seemed to intimate another theory with their fair forms. They might have been winged angels but for their hair of flame and cruel hooks. They seemed to say, 'We were the ancient embryo-gods of the human imagination, but the serpent swallowed us. He swallowed us successively as one after another we availed ourselves of his cunning in our priesthoods; as we brought his cruel coils to crush those who dared to outgrow our cult; as we imitated his fang in the deadliness with which we bit the heel of every advancing thinker; as, when worsted in our struggle against reason, we took to the double tongue, praising with one fork the virtues which we poisoned with the other. Now we are degraded with him for ever, bound to him by these rings, labelled with the sins we have committed.'

It was by a true experience that the ancients so generally took nocturnal animals to be types of diabolism. Corresponding to them are the sleepless activities of morally unawakened men. The animal is a sleeping man. Its passions and instincts are acted out in what to rational man would be dreams. In dreams, especially when influenced by disease, a man may mentally relapse very far, and pass through kennels and styes, which are such even when somewhat decorated by shreds of the familiar human environment. The nocturnal form of intellect is cunning; the obscuration of religion is superstition; the dark shadow that falls on love turns it to lust. These wolves and bats, on which no ideal has dawned, do not prowl or flit through man in their natural forms: in the half-awake consciousness, whose starlight attends man amid his darkness, their misty outlines swell, and in the feverish unenlightened conscience they become phantasms of his animalism— werewolves, vampyres. The awakening of reason in any animal is through all the phases of cerebral and social evolution. A wise man said to his son who was afraid to enter the dark, 'Go on, child; you will never see anything worse than yourself.'

The hare-lip, which we sometimes see in the human face, is there an arrested development. Every lip is at some embryonic period a hare-lip. The development of man's visible part has gone on much longer than his intellectual and moral evolution, and abnormalities in it are rare in comparison with the number of survivals from the animal world in his temper, his faith, and his manners. Criminals are men living out their arrested moral developments. They who regard them as instigated by a devil are those whose arrest is mental. The eye of reason will deal with both all the more effectively, because with as little wrath as a surgeon feels towards the hare-lip he endeavours to humanise.

It is an impressive fact that the great and reverent mind of Spinoza, in pondering the problem of Evil and the theology which ascribed it to a Devil, was unconsciously led to anticipate by more than a century the first (modern) scientific suggestions of the principle of Evolution. In his early treatise, 'De Deo et Homine,' occurs this short but momentous chapter—

'De Diabolis. If the Devil be an Entity contrary in all respects to God, having nothing of God in his nature, there can be nothing in common with God.

'Is he assumed to be a thinking Entity, as some will have it, who never wills and never does any good, and who sets himself in opposition to God on all occasions, he would assuredly be a very wretched being, and, could prayers do anything for him, his amendment were much to be implored.

'But let us ask whether so miserable an object could exist even for an instant; and, the question put, we see at once that it could not; for from the perfection of a thing proceeds its power of continuance: the more of the Essential and Divine a thing possesses, the more enduring it is. But how could the Devil, having no trace of perfection in him, exist at all? Add to this, that the stability or duration of a thinking thing depends entirely on its love of and union with God, and that the opposite of this state in every particular being presumed in the Devil, it is obviously impossible that there can be any such being.

'And then there is indeed no necessity to presume the existence of a Devil; for the causes of hate, envy, anger, and all such passions are readily enough to be discovered; and there is no occasion for resort to fiction to account for the evils they engender.'

In the course of his correspondence with the most learned men of his time, Spinoza was severely questioned concerning his views upon human wickedness, the disobedience of Adam, and so forth. He said—to abridge his answers—If there be any essential or positive evil in men, God is the author and continuer of that evil. But what is called evil in them is their degree of imperfection as compared with those more perfect. Adam, in the abstract, is a man eating an apple. That is not in itself an evil action. Acts condemned in man are often admired in animals,—as the jealousy of doves,—and regarded as evidence of their perfection. Although man must restrain the forces of nature and direct them to his purposes, it is a superstition to suppose that God is angry against such forces. It is an error in man to identify his little inconveniences as obstacles to God. Let him withdraw himself from the consideration and nothing is found evil. Whatever exists, exists by reason of its perfection for its own ends,—which may or may not be those of men.

Spinoza's aphorism, 'From the perfection of a thing proceeds its power of continuance,' is the earliest modern statement of the doctrine now called 'survival of the fittest.' The notion of a Devil involves the solecism of a being surviving through its unfitness for survival.

Spinoza was Copernicus of the moral Cosmos. The great German who discovered to men that their little planet was not the one centre and single care of nature, led the human mind out of a closet and gave it a universe. But dogma still clung to the closet; where indeed each sect still remains, holding its little interest to be the aim of the solar system, and all outside it to be part of a countless host, marshalled by a Prince of Evil, whose eternal war is waged against that formidable pulpiteer whose sermon is sending dismay through pandemonium. But for rational men all that is ended, and its decline began when Spinoza warned men against looking at the moral universe from the pin-hole of their egotism. That closet-creation, whose laws were seen now acting now suspended to suit the affairs of men, disappeared, and man was led to adore the All.

It is a small thing that man can bruise the serpent's head, if its fang still carries its venom so deep in his reason as to blacken all nature with a sense of triumphant malevolence. To the eye of judicial man, instructed to decide every case without bribe of his own interest as a rival animal, the serpent's fang is one of the most perfect adaptations of means to ends in nature. Were a corresponding perfection in every human mind, the world would fulfil the mystical dream of the East, which gave one name to the serpents that bit them in the wilderness and seraphim singing round the eternal throne.

'Cursed be the Hebrew who shall either eat pork, or permit his son to be instructed in the learning of the Greeks.' So says the Talmud, with a voice transmitted from the 'kingdom of priests' (Exod. xix. 6). From the altar of 'unhewn stone' came the curse upon Art, and upon the race that represented culture raising its tool upon the rudeness of nature. That curse of the Talmud recoiled fearfully. The Jewish priesthood had their son in Peter with his vision of clean and unclean animals, and the command, 'Slay and eat!' Uninstructed is this heir of priestly Judaism 'in the learning of the Greeks,' consequently his way of converting Gentiles—the herd of swine, the goyim—is to convert them into christian protoplasm. 'Slay and eat,' became the cry of the elect, and their first victim was the paternal Jew who taught them that pork and Greek learning belonged to the same category.

But there was another Jewish nation not composed of priests. While the priestly kingdom is typified in Jonah announcing the destruction of Nineveh, who, because the great city still goes on, reproaches Jehovah, the nation of the poets has now its Jehovah II. who sees the humiliation of the tribal priesthood as a withered gourd compared with the arts, wealth, and human interests of a Gentile city. 'The Lord repented.' The first Gospel to the Gentiles is in that gentle thought for the uncircumcised Ninevites. But it was reached too late. When it gained expression in Christ welcoming Greeks, and seeing in stones possible 'children of Abraham;' in Paul acknowledging debt to barbarians and taking his texts from Greek altars or poets; the evolution of the ideal element in Hebrew religion had gained much. But historic combinations raised the judaisers to a throne, and all the narrowness of their priesthood was re-enacted as Christianity.

The column of brass in whose hollow centre the fine brain of Swedenborg was imprisoned is a fit similitude of the christian formula. The whole moral attitude of Christianity towards nature is represented in his first vision. The beginning of his spiritual career is announced by the evaporation of his animal nature in the form of vermin. The christian hell is present, and these animal parts are burnt up. Among those burnt-up powers of Swedenborg, one of the serpents must have been his intellect. 'From that day forth I gave up all worldly learning.'

Here we have the ideal christian caught up to his paradise even while his outward shape is visible. But what if we were all to become like that? Suppose all the animal powers and desires were to evaporate out of mankind and to be burnt up! Were that to occur to-day the effect on the morrow would be but faintly told in that which would be caused by sudden evaporations of steam from all the engines of the world. We may imagine a band of philanthropists, sorely disturbed by the number of accidents incidental to steam-locomotion, who should conspire to go at daybreak to all the engine-houses and stations in England, and, just as the engines were about to start for their work, should quench their fires, let off their steam, and break their works. That would be but a brief paralysis of the work of one country; but what would be the result if the animal nature of man and its desires, the works and trades that minister to the 'pomps and vanities,' all worldly aims and joys, should be burnt up in fires of fanaticism!

Yet to that fatal aim Christianity gave itself,—so contrary to that great heart in which was mirrored the beautiful world, its lilies and little children, and where love shed its beams on the just and the unjust! The organising principle of Christianity was that which crucified Jesus and took his tomb for corner-stone of a system modelled after what he hated. Its central purpose was to effect a divorce between the moral and the animal nature of man. One is called flesh and the other spirit; one was the child of God, the other the child of the Devil. It rent asunder that which was really one; its whole history, so long as it was in earnest, was the fanatical effort to keep asunder by violence those two halves ever seeking harmony; its history since its falsity was exposed has been the hypocrisy of professing in word what is impossible in deed.

Beside the christian vision of Swedenborg, in which the judaic priest's curse on swinish Greek learning found apotheosis, let us set the vision of a Jewish seer in whom the humanity that spared Nineveh found expression. The seer is Philo,— name rightly belonging to that pure mind in which the starry ideals of his Semitic race embraced the sensuous beauty which alone could give them life. Philo (Præm. et Pœnis, sec. 15–20) describes as the first joy of the redeemed earth the termination of the war between man and animal. That war will end, he says, 'when the wild beasts in the soul have been tamed. Then the most ferocious animals will submit to man; scorpions will lose their stings, and serpents their poison. And, in consequence of the suppression of that older war between man and beast, the war between man and man shall also end.'

Here we emerge from Swedenborg's brass column, we pass beyond Peter's sword called 'Slay-and-eat,' we leave behind the Talmud's curse on swine and learning: we rise to the clear vision of Hebrew prophecy which beheld lion and lamb lying down together, a child leading the wild forces subdued by culture.

'Why not God kill Debbil?' asked Man Friday. It is a question which not even Psychology has answered, why no Theology has yet suggested the death of the Devil in the past, or prophesied more than chains for him in the future. No doubt the need of a 'hangman's whip to haud the wretch in order' may partly account for it; but with this may have combined a cause of which it is pleasanter to think—Devils being animal passions in excess, even the ascetic recoils from their destruction, with an instinct like that which restrains rats from gnawing holes through the ship's bottom.

In Goethe's 'Faust' we read, Doch das Antike find' ich zu lebendig. It is a criticism on the nudity of the Greek forms that appear in the classical Walpurgis Night. But the authority is not good: it is Mephistopheles who is disgusted with sight of the human form, and he says they ought in modern fashion to be plastered over. His sentiments have prevailed at the Vatican, where the antique statues and the great pictures of Michael Angelo bear witness to the prurient prudery of the papal mind. 'Devils are our sins in perspective,' says George Herbert.

Herodotus (ii. 47) says, 'The Egyptians consider the pig to be an impure beast, and therefore if a man, in passing by a pig, should touch him only with his garments, he forthwith goes to the river and plunges in; and, in the next place, swineherds, although native Egyptians, are the only men who are not allowed to enter any of their temples.' The Egyptians, he says, do not sacrifice the goat; 'and, indeed, their painters and sculptors represent Pan with the face and legs of a goat, as the Grecians do; not that they imagine this to be his real form, for they think him like other gods; but why they represent him in this way I had rather not mention.' We need not feel the same prudery. The Egyptians rightly regarded the symbol of sexual desire, on whose healthy exercise the perpetuation of life depended, as a very different kind of animalism from that symbolised in the pig's love of refuse and garbage. Their association of the goat with Pan— the lusty vigour of nature—was the natural preface to the arts of Greece in which the wild forces were taught their first lesson—Temperance. Pan becomes musical. The vigour and vitality of human nature find in the full but not excessive proportions of Apollo, Aphrodite, Artemis, and others of the bright array, the harmony which Pan with his pipe preludes. The Greek statue is soul embodied and body ensouled.

Two men had I the happiness to know in my youth, into whose faces I looked up and saw the throne of Genius illumined by Purity. One of them, Ralph Waldo Emerson, wrote, 'If beauty, softness, and faith in female forms have their own influence, vices even, in a slight degree, are thought to improve the expression.' The other, Arthur Hugh Clough, wrote, 'What we all love is good touched up with evil.' Here are two brave flowers, of which one grew out of the thorny stem of Puritanism, the other from the monastic root of Oxford. The 'vices' which could improve the expression, even for the pure eyes of Emerson, are those which represent the struggle of human nature to exist in truth, albeit in misdirection and reaction, amid pious hypocrisies. The Oxonian scholar had seen enough of the conventionalised characterless 'good' to long for some sign of life and freedom, even though it must come as a touch of 'evil.' To the artist, nature is never seen in petrifaction; it is really as well as literally a becoming. The evil he sees is 'good in the making:' what others call vices are voices in the wilderness preparing the way of the highest.

'God and the Devil make the whole of Religion,' said Nicoli—speaking, perhaps, better than he knew. The culture of the world has shown that the sometime opposed realms of human interest, so personified, are equally essential. It is through this experience that the Devil has gained such ample vindication from the poets—as in Rapisardi's 'Lucifero,' a veritable 'bringer of Light,' and Cranch's 'Satan.' From the latter work ('Satan: A Libretto.' Boston: Roberts Brothers, 1874), which should be more widely known, I quote some lines. Satan says—

I symbolise the wild and deep
And unregenerated wastes of life,
Dark with transmitted tendencies of race
And blind mischance; all crude mistakes of will
And tendency unbalanced by due weight
Of favouring circumstance; all passion blown
By wandering winds; all surplusage of force
Piled up for use, but slipping from its base
Of law and order.

This is the very realm in which the poet and the artist find their pure-veined quarries, whence arise the forms transfigured in their vision.

To evoke Helena, Faust, as we have seen, must repair to the Mothers. But who may these be? They shine from Goethe's page in such opalescent tints one cannot transfix their sense. They seemed to me just now the primal conditions, by fulfilling which anything might be attained, without which, nothing. But now (yet perhaps the difference is not great) I see the Mothers to be the ancient healthy instincts and ideals of our race. These took shape in forms of art, whose evolution had been man's harmony with himself. Christianity, borrowing thunder of one god, hammer of another, shattered them—shattered our Mothers! And now learned travellers go about in many lands saying, 'Saw ye my beloved?' Amid cities ruined and buried we are trying to recover them, fitting limb to limb—so carefully! as if half-conscious that we are piecing together again the fragments of our own humanity.

'The Devil: Does he Exist, and what does he Do?' Such is the title of a recent work by Father Delaporte, Professor of Dogma in the Faculty of Bordeaux. He gives specific directions for exorcism of devils by means of holy water, the sign of the cross, and other charms. 'These measures,' says one of his American critics, 'may answer very well against the French Devil; but our American Beelzebub is a potentate that goeth not forth on any such hints.' Father Delaporte would hardly contend that the use of cross and holy water for a thousand years has been effectual in dislodging the European Beelzebub.

On the whole, I am inclined to prefer the method of the Africans of the Guinea Coast. They believe in a particularly hideous devil, but say that the only defence they require against him is a mirror. If any one will keep a mirror beside him, the Devil must see himself in it, and he at once rushes away in terror of his own ugliness.

No monster ever conjured up by imagination is more hideous than a rational being transformed to a beast. Just that is every human being who has brought his nobler powers down to be slaves of his animal nature. No eye could look upon that fearful sight unmoved. All man needs is a true mirror in which his own animalism may see itself. We cannot borrow for this purpose the arts of Greece, nor the fairy ideals of Germany, nor the emasculated saints of Christendom. These were but fragments of the man who has been created by combination of their powers, and their several ideals are broken bits that cannot reflect the whole being of man in its proportions or disproportions.

The higher nature of man, polished by culture of all his faculties, can alone be the faithful mirror before his lower. The clearness of this mirror in the individual heart depends mainly on the civilisation and knowledge surrounding it. The discovered law turns once plausible theories to falsehoods; a noble literature transmutes once popular books to trash.

When Art interprets the realities of nature, when it shows how much beauty and purity our human nature is capable of, it holds a mirror before all deformities. At a theatre in the city of London, I witnessed the performance of an actor who, in the course of his part, struck a child. He was complimented by a hurricane of hisses from the crowded gallery. Had those 'gods' up there never struck children? Possibly. Yet here each had a mirror before him and recoiled from his worst self. A clergyman relates that, while looking at pictures in the Bethnal Green Museum, he overheard a poor woman, who had been gazing on a Madonna, say, 'If I had such a child as that I believe I could be a good woman.' Who can say what even that one glance at her life in the ideal reflector may be worth to that wanderer amid the miseries and temptations of London!

It is not easy for those who have seen what is high and holy to give their hearts to what is base and unholy. It is as natural for human nature to love virtue as to love any other beauty. External beauty is visible to all, and all desire it: the interior beauty is not visible to superficial glances, but the admiration shown even for its counterfeits shows how natural it is to admire virtue. But in order that the charm of this moral beauty may be felt by human nature it must be related to that nature—real. It must not be some childish ideal which answers to no need of the man of to-day; not something imported from a time and place where it had meaning and force to others where it has none.

When dogmas surviving from the primitive world are brought to behold themselves in the mirror held up by Science, they cry out, 'That is not my face! You are caricaturing my beliefs!' This recoil of Superstition from its own ugliness is the victory of Religion. What priests bewail as disbelief is faith fleeing from its deformities. Ignorant devotion proves its need of Science by its terrors of the same, which are like those of the horse at first sight of its best friend, bearer of its burthens—the locomotive.

Religion, like every other high feature of human nature, has its animal counterpart. The animalised religion is superstition. It has various expressions,—the abjectness of one form, the ferocity of another, the cunning of a third. It is unconscious of anything higher than animalism. Its god is a very great animal preying on other animals, which are laid on his altars; or pleased when smaller animals give up their part of the earthly feast by starving their passions and senses. Under the growth of civilisation and intelligence that pious asceticism is revealed in its true form,—intensified animalism. The asceticism of one age becomes the self-indulgence of another. The two-footed animal having discovered that his god does not eat the meat left for him, eats it himself. Learning that he gets as much from his god by a wafer and a prayer, he offers these and retains the gifts, treasures, and pleasures so commuted,—these, however, being withdrawn from the direction of the higher nature by the fact of being obtained through the conditions of the lower, and dependent on their persistence. In process of time the forms and formulas of religion, detached from all reality—such as no conceivable monarch could desire—not only become senseless, but depend upon their senselessness for continuance. They refuse to come at all within the domain of reason or common-sense, and trust to mental torpor of the masses, force of habit in the aggregate, self-interest in the wealthy and powerful, bribes for thinkers and scholars.

Animalism disguised as a religion must render the human religion, able to raise passions into divine attributes of a perfect manhood, impossible so long as it continues. That a human religion can ever come by any process of evolution from a superstition which can only exist by ministry to the baser motives is a delusion. The only hope of society is that its independent minds may gain culture, and so surround this unextinct monster with mirrors that it may perish through shame at its manifold deformities. These are symbolised in the many-headed phantasm which is the subject of this work. Demon, Dragon, and Devil have long paralysed the finest powers of man, peopling nature with horrors, the heart with fears, and causing the religious sentiment itself to make actual in history the worst excesses it professed to combat in its imaginary adversaries. My largest hope is that from the dragon-guarded well where Truth is too much concealed she may emerge far enough to bring her mirror before these phantoms of fear, and with far-darting beams send them back to their caves in Chaos and ancient Night.

The battlements of the cloisters of Magdalen College, Oxford, are crowned with an array of figures representing virtues and vices, with carved allegories of teaching and learning. Under the Governor's window are the pelican feeding its young from its breast, and the lion, denoting the tenderness and the strength of a Master of youth. There follow the professions—the lawyer embracing his client, the physician with his bottle, the divine as Moses with his tables of the Law. Next are the slayers of Goliath and other mythical enemies. We come to more real, albeit monstrous, enemies; to Gluttony in ecclesiastical dress, with tongue lolling out; and low-browed Luxury without any vesture, with a wide-mouthed animal-eared face on its belly, the same tongue lolling out—as in our figures of Typhon and Kali. Drunkenness has three animal heads—one of a degraded humanity, another a sheep, the third a goose. Cruelty is a werewolf; a frog-faced Lamia represents its mixture with Lust; and other vices are represented by other monsters, chiefly dragons with griffin forms, until the last is reached—the Devil, who is just opposite the Governor's symbols across the quadrangle. So was represented, some centuries ago, the conflict of Ormuzd and Ahriman, for the young soldiers who enlisted at Oxford for that struggle. A certain amount of fancy has entered into the execution of the figures; but, if this be carefully detached, the history which I have attempted to tell in these volumes may be generally traced in the Magdalen statues. Each represents some phase in the advance of the world, when, under new emergencies, earlier symbols were modified, recombined, and presently replaced by new shapes. It was found inadequate to keep the scholar throwing stones at the mummy of Goliath when by his side was living Gluttony in religious garb. The scriptural symbols are gradually mixed with those of Greek and German mythology, and by such contact with nature are able to generate forms, whose lolling tongues, wide mouths, and other expressions, represent with some realism the physiognomies of brutality let loose through admission to human shape and power.

It may be that, when they were set up, the young Oxonian passed shuddering these terrible forms, dreaded these werewolves and succubæ, and dreamed of going forth to impale dragons. But now the sculptures excite only laughter or curiosity, when they are not passed by without notice. Yet the old conflict between Light and Darkness has not ceased. The ancient forms of it pass away; they become grotesque. Such was necessarily the case where the excessive mythological and fanciful elements introduced at one period fall upon another period when they hide the meaning. Their obscurity, even for antiquarians, marks how far away from those cold battlefields the struggle they symbolised has passed. But it ceases not. Some scholars who listen to the sweet vespers of Magdalen may think the conflict over; if so, even poor brother Moody may enter the true kingdom before them; for, when preaching in Baltimore last September, he said, 'Men are possessed of devils just as much now as they ever were. The devil of rum is as great as any that ever lived. Why cannot this one and all others be cast out? Because there is sin in the christian camp.'

The picture which closes this volume has been made for me by the artist Hennessey, to record an incident which occurred at the door of Nôtre Dame in Paris last summer. I had been examining an ugly devil there treading down human forms into hell; but a dear friend looked higher, and saw a bird brooding over its young on a nest supported by that same horrible head.

So, above the symbols of wrath in nature, Love still interweaves heavenly tints with the mystery of life; beside the horns of pain prepares melodies.

Even so, also, over the animalism which deforms man, rises the animal perfection which shames that; here ascending above the reign of violence by a feather's force, and securing to that little creature a tenderness that could best express the heart of a Christ, when it would gather humanity under his wings.

This same little scene at the cathedral door came before me again as I saw the Oxonian youth, with their morning-faces, passing so heedlessly those ancient sculptures at Magdalen. Over every happy heart the same old love was brooding, in each nestling faculties were trying to gain their wings. To what will they aspire, those students moving so light-hearted amid the dead dragons and satans of an extinct world? Do they think there are no more dragons to be slain? Know they that saying, 'He descended into hell;' and that, from Orpheus and Herakles to Mohammed and Swedenborg, this is the burthen felt by those who would be saviours of men?

It is not only loving birds that build their nests and rear their young over the horns of forgotten fears, but, alas! the Harpies too! These, which Dante saw nestling in still plants—once men who had wronged themselves—rear successors above the aspirations that have ended in 'nothing but leaves.' The sculptures of Magdalen are incomplete. There is a vacant side to the quadrangle, which, it is to be feared, awaits the truer teaching that would fill it up with the real dragons which no youth could heedlessly pass. Who can carve there the wrongs that await their powers of redress? Who can set before them, with all its baseness, the true emblem of pious fraud? When will they see in any stone mirror the real shape of a double-tongued Culture—one fork intoning litanies, another whispering contempt of them? The werewolves of scholarly selfishness, the Lamias of christian casuistry, the subtle intelligence that is fed by sages and heroes, but turns them to dust, nay, to venom, because it dares not be human, still crawls—these are yet to be revealed in all their horrors. Then will the old cry, Sursum Corda, sound over the ancient symbols whereon scholars waste their strength, by which they are conquered; and wings of courage shall bear them with their arrows of light to rescue from Superstition the holy places of Humanity.

Devil from the Notre Dame, Paris.

51009814R00163

Made in the USA
Middletown, DE
06 November 2017